THE COMPLETE FARMHOUSE KITCHEN COOK BOOK

Over 1,000 recipes
based on the Yorkshire Television series

**YORKSHIRE
TELEVISION**

Edited by
MARY WATTS

GUILD PUBLISHING
LONDON

First published in this hardback edition 1984
in association with Yorkshire Television Enterprises Ltd
by Book Club Associates
By arrangement with
William Collins Sons & Co Ltd
Reprinted 1985 (five times), 1986

Most of the material in this book first appeared in
Farmhouse Kitchen I, *II* and *III*, published by Yorkshire
Television Enterprises Limited.

Typeset in Ehrhardt
Printed and bound in Great Britain by
William Collins Sons & Co Ltd

Front cover: by courtesy of Fine Art Photographs, London.
Back cover: by courtesy of Phillips, The International Fine Art Auctioneers
(photo: Bridgeman Art Library).

ACKNOWLEDGEMENTS

p. 5: Topham
pp. 22, 144, 145, 223, 257, 314, 389, 424: Mary Evans Picture Library
pp. 49, 60, 105, 138, 197, 432: The Mansell Collection
pp. 62, 202: BBC Hulton Picture Library
pp. 70, 282, 331: Peter Newark's Historical Pictures

CONTENTS

FOREWORD

WHOLEFOOD is not new: good, plain, home cooking from fresh ingredients is wholefood at its best. Traditional recipes, which form a large part of this book, are ones which have survived the years and changed only slightly, and these days more and more people are concerned with the quality of the food they eat and are rejecting packaged and prepared dishes.

I welcome the new surge of interest and emphasis on good, healthy eating, of course, yet I smile smugly to myself when I remember the 'meal shop' of my Scottish youth. It looked and smelt for all the world like the health food shops of today. All around were hessian sacks of coarse oatmeal for porridge and bannocks, and fine oatmeal for coating fresh herrings and making thin oatcakes. There too were the pulses and grains now being rediscovered and enjoyed. My 'message' (shopping) list was for flour, rice, semolina, split peas, green peas, butter beans and haricot beans – all weighed out on big brass scales and poured into brown paper bags whose tops had to be very carefully folded and pleated to keep the contents in. A ha'penny bought me a couple of ounces of dark 'pieces' sugar, which was poured into a small, hand-rolled paper 'poke' and eaten with the help of a wet finger. I even remember a skipping song about 'oats and beans and barley-o''.

Throughout this book there are recipes from every corner of the land, with delightful names like Huffed Chicken, Love in Disguise, Haslett, and Sussex Churdles. Spices and aromatic ingredients from the East combine with European foods to tempt even the most jaded palate. There is a strong bakery section with a wonderful array, ranging from hearty fruit loaves and deep egg custards to delicate meringue japs, buttery shortbread and, since the television programme is made by Yorkshire Television, the delectable Yorkshire Curd Tart.

Vegetable and non-meat dishes feature in recipes of enormous character both from this country and abroad – Cauliflower Bhaji, Spicy Cabbage with Coconut, and Red Bean Hot Pot, to name but a few. Raw food, in the form of uncooked vegetables and fruit, is indispensable in a well-balanced and varied diet.

The section on preserving covers jams, jellies, pickles and wines in many different forms. White Currant Wine, Rosemary Jelly, Pear and Ginger Jam, and Sweet Pickled Prunes, for example, are easy to make, economical, and better flavoured than many mass-produced articles full of chemical preservatives, food colouring and additives of one kind or another.

Potted Beef may sound like something out of Dickens, but it is easy to make at home and is spectacularly rewarding. Hot Boiled Salt Beef, immortalized in the

old song 'Boiled Beef and Carrots', is also superb and bursting with flavour. It is almost as good when pressed and eaten cold with English mustard and a crispy salad. More economical dishes like Cheshire Fidget Pie, Oxtail Mould, and Stuffed Marrow Rings are great value for those working within a tight budget.

For delicious British puddings, try Fig Dumpling, Apple Dappy, and Ginger Marmalade Pudding, all filling and tasty. At the other end of the scale there is delicate Chocolate Suprême and Lemon Solid which, despite its name, is a jellied concoction with a zinging flavour that only fresh lemons can produce.

Bread and yeast cookery is well represented here too, ranging from nutty wholemeal bread and Kentish Huffkins to pizzas and pitta bread. The simplest bread of all is Irish Soda Bread, but if you want a more exotic, rich taste, try the Swedish Tea Ring with its layer of almond paste hidden inside and a thick layer of icing, nuts and cherries outside.

We hope that you will enjoy our book on good, plain cooking and perhaps add one or two of our recipes to your firm family favourites.

Grace Mulligan

Grace Mulligan is the Presenter of Yorkshire Television's 'Farmhouse Kitchen' series.

INTRODUCTION

COLLECTING recipes must be a universal pastime. How many dog-eared, spattered notebooks have you seen, with their covers half off and their pages loose, interleaved with old bills, bank statements, or any other scrap of paper that was to hand when the hostess generously agreed to disclose her recipe to an appreciative guest? The whole unsavoury bundle is usually held together by a series of rubber bands, if not an old garter; but what reading they contain, what stories they tell. Each recipe has its own history: Mrs Robin's Fruit Cake, Grace's Chocolate Fancy, Dorothy Sleightholme's Salt and Pepper Mix, Mary Berry's Savoury Tart, Aunt Nellie's Mustard Sauce, Mother's Excellent Recipe for Christmas Pudding. These are a few of the recipes to be found in this book. My own notebook, containing the collections of three generations, includes from 1860 Mrs Glennie's Jelly, a sweet, sherry-flavoured concoction made with cow-heel and cleared with egg-shell. My grandmother had this recipe from her mother-in-law, and I now possess the same old, crazed, white pottery mould in which it was always made.

These old collections always include household hints – To Keep Bananas from Going Brown, To Make a Bouquet Garni, To Keep Tomato Purée Fresh – and you will also find these tips in this book. My old notebook, for example, includes Mother Jowett's Furniture Polish and Auntie Elf's Silver Polishing Cloths. Some of the old, old recipes and hints may not be relevant to the present time, but it is to be hoped that they are never lost or destroyed, for if times become more frugal they may, under the eye of the practised cook, come into their own once again, just as the classic older collections of Eliza Acton and Elizabeth Raffald are so prized now.

The 'Farmhouse Kitchen' television programme began thirteen years ago with just such a nostalgic feeling. Graham Watts and I were given this evocative title for an adult education series by Yorkshire Television's then Director of Programmes, Donald Baverstock. He had recently moved into a very old stone-built Yorkshire farmhouse near Ilkley and probably would have been glad if the programmes had also included quite precise information about coping with mice and cockroaches! However, he readily agreed to our plans for baking bread, making preserves, cheese and butter, brewing beer and country wines, and dealing with rabbit, poultry and all the cheaper cuts of meat.

Thirteen years ago only one television cookery programme had ever shown how to bake bread. It was still Fanny Craddock's heyday: television cooks were pouring wine into casseroles and cream into soups and sauces, and it was all delightfully rich, exotic and extravagant. Baking bread at home was almost unheard of in the south of England; home brewing and wine making was a rediscovered pastime for a very few; and such time-consuming joys as making marmalade, jam, pickles and chutney, bottling fruit and drying herbs were considered only suitable for the Women's Institute.

It was, however, to the WI in Yorkshire that I turned for guidance. Our cookery programme was to cover everyday meals with economical, wholesome and nourishing dishes. It was to revive interest in homebaking and preservation, for nothing can rival the satisfactions of real home cooking – the smell of baking bread, tins full of your own biscuits and cakes, a cupboard full of bright jars of jam, pickles, vinegars, syrups, all nicely labelled and stored – all your own work!

Naturally the old ways could not be taught without regard to more modern conditions of today; few people have time to spend all day making enough marmalade to last a year, and not many can be expected to spend a whole day baking. Nevertheless, it was with the guidance and authority of the Women's Institute, who provide not only trained expertise and very high standards in all household art and craft, but also experienced and confident demonstrators, that 'Farmhouse Kitchen' began.

Launched by Mary Berry, a highly qualified home economist and Cordon Bleu cook, and the late Paul Kaye, each programme had a WI guest cook. Amongst these was Dorothy Sleightholme, who presented the programmes for twelve years. The subjects in that first series included making cheese and butter, bee-keeping and honey, and country crafts such as dried flower arrangements, rag rugs and willow baskets. The programmes were set, as they have been ever since, in what can only be described as evolved kitchens – old farm kitchens still showing vestiges of earlier, labour-intensive times, but realistically up to date – and certainly with no cockroaches!

It was when Graham Watts and I walked down the long corridor to our office at Yorkshire Television and counted not one or two, but ten, twelve, twenty sacks of mail every day that we realized just how much our audience wanted this kind of programme, these everyday recipes, this matter-of-fact advice, homeliness and a reminder of how things used to be. The stamped addressed envelopes sent in for duplicated recipe sheets created, for a short time, a cottage industry for certain retired or child-bound ex-secretaries, until the sheets were replaced by colourful recipe cards and, in turn, by Book 1. Book 2 was assembled in 1978 to provide enough recipes for a further four years of programmes, and Book 3 followed in 1982 with the same intention. By then, however, our attentive and critical viewers – and how grateful I am for their complaints as well as their appreciation – began to say, 'You never demonstrate recipes from Book 1 now', or 'I've just bought the second book and you've brought out a third.' I realized recently that 'Farmhouse Kitchen' is the longest-running television cookery programme, and when I counted precisely and discovered that 1984 would see the 200th programme, it did seem worth celebrating. So here you have it: over 1,000 recipes collected from all over England, Scotland, Wales and Ireland, plus a few from further afield still, assembled in one volume.

To return to my opening remarks about collecting recipes, I must add that each recipe in this complete collection has a story of its own. Once, when she was dealing with those most difficult of cheap cuts of meat – bellypork and breast of lamb – Dorothy Sleightholme casually asked viewers, 'Let me know how *you* prepare these cuts.' Literally dozens of recipes were sent in and only a selection of them can be included here.

You will discover many traditional county recipes which I began to collect on extensive and most enjoyable, if waist-expanding, tours of Women's Institutes about ten years ago. Recipes like Sussex Bacon Roly Poly have been skilfully updated: gone is the old pudding cloth, from the days when many people had only a boiling pot and very few an oven, and in its place is a crisp, golden, appetizing roll of bacon, onion and sage in a light suet pastry crust. If you find the quantities of ingredients for Yorkshire Parkin very odd, this is because Mrs Nan Moran of Addingham in Yorkshire always put together the recipe with the aid of an Edward VIII coronation mug and a very old, half burnt away, wooden spoon. The result, nevertheless, was an excellent parkin (or 'moggy' as it is described in the West Riding).

Considerable space is given to recipes using wholefoods, to vegetables and to salads, and the programmes also reflect the very welcome move in this country towards a general awareness of what we eat, and the knowledge that in the end it is the freshly grown, freshly prepared foods that really nourish us.

All the recipes in this book have been tried and tested before reaching the printed page, and many contributors have also had to endure interminable cross-examination from me about their recipe instructions. As a simple-minded, would-be cook myself, I hope the results prove clean and unambiguous. There should be no moments when you have to roll in flour or stand under the cold tap, but please do not hesitate to let us know our mistakes should you discover any. One of the advantages of collecting other people's recipes is that you know they work. I hope and believe you will find this so.

This book and the television programmes are designed to increase your repertoire, give you a few hints and tips, teach you a little perhaps, but most of all to boost your confidence in your own creative cooking, so that your guests will ask for *your* recipes for *their* notebook collections.

Mary Watts
1984

Yorkshire Television's 'Farmhouse Kitchen' series is produced and directed by Mary and Graham Watts.

1

SOUPS AND STARTERS

TO MAKE STOCK

CHICKEN–BONE STOCK

The carcass of chickens, or game birds, makes good stock. Put it in a large saucepan with plenty of water, an onion, a piece of carrot, leek, celery, parsley stalks or any vegetable stock or peelings that might otherwise get thrown out. Add 2 or 3 peppercorns, or a bay leaf. Simmer gently for at least an hour. Strain off liquid, let it cool and then refrigerate or freeze it. *Giblet stock* is made in the same way.

BEEF BONES

Put bones in a large saucepan with plenty of water and bring to boil. Add pieces of onion, carrot, leek, celery tops, parsley stalks, vegetable peelings and hard outer leaves. Add peppercorns, bay leaf, herbs. Any of these will enrich the stock. Simmer for at least an hour.

HAM BONE

Simmer it with peppercorns and 1 or 2 cloves. The flavour is rich so use this stock with caution or add plenty of water.

VEGETABLE STOCK

Save the water in which vegetables are cooked. It will keep 24 hours in refrigerator.

Stock from a piece of meat or a whole chicken has the most flavour. The following recipe uses an excellent broth derived from cooking a piece of lamb or beef which is removed after about 2 hours and served as a main course with vegetables. Remember to start the night before.

DUNDEE BROTH

Soup serves 6

50 g/2 oz dried green peas
50 g/2 oz barley
2.8 litres/5 pints cold water
675 g/1½ lb piece of beef or lamb, tied with
     string
225 g/8 oz diced carrots
125 g/4 oz diced turnip
125 g/4 oz chopped cabbage
2 whole leeks, chopped
Extra carrot and turnip cut in chunks to serve
     with the boiled meat
1 tablespoon chopped parsley
Salt and pepper

1. Wash and soak the dried peas overnight.
2. Put peas and barley on to cook in a large pan with the water.
3. Tie meat with string so that it can be carved as a joint. Put it into pan when water is hot.
4. Add diced and chopped vegetables. Put lid on pan.
5. Cook steadily for about 2 hours.
6. 30 minutes before the soup is to be served add the extra vegetables.
7. When the time is up and the meat and vegetables cooked, lift out meat and remove string. Lift out vegetables. Keep hot.
8. Add salt and pepper to soup as required. Add parsley and serve.

Mrs Grace McGlinn
Dundee, Scotland

CLEAR BEEF SOUP

Freezes well.

Serves 4 to 6

25 g/1 oz dripping or more
1 large onion, chopped
A clove of garlic, chopped
1 teaspoon sugar
225 to 350 g/8 to 12 oz shin of beef, cut small
225 g/8 oz ox liver, cut small
1 pig's trotter or calf's foot
1 small carrot, scrubbed and chopped
1 large tomato, halved and grilled
A bouquet garni (a sprig of thyme, parsley and
     1 bay leaf tied together)
1.75 litres/3 pints water
Salt and pepper
1 large egg-white
2 to 3 tablespoons sherry or Madeira (optional)

1. Melt dripping in a frying pan. Fry onion and garlic until soft. Sprinkle with sugar and stir. Leave to cook without stirring until sugar caramelises (i.e., browns) but do not allow onion to burn.
2. Lift onion and garlic out of frying pan into a large saucepan or flame-proof casserole.
3. Now brown beef and liver in frying pan, adding a little more fat if necessary.
4. Put beef, liver, trotter, carrot, tomato and herbs into the saucepan with onion and garlic. Pour in water.
5. Bring to the boil, season with salt and pepper, put on lid and simmer for about 2 hours either on top of

stove or in a moderate oven, Gas 3, 325°F, 160°C.
6. Strain off liquid and leave overnight so that fat can rise.
7. Next day scrape off the fat and put jellied stock into a large saucepan over gentle heat.
8. When it is liquid and warm but *not* hot, add egg-white. Start to whisk with a hand rotary egg-beater or an electric whisk so that surface of soup is covered in a white froth. Allow to boil for 2 or 3 minutes.
9. Turn off heat and leave for 10 minutes. A brownish scum will cling to the egg-white, thus clearing the soup underneath.
10. Now pour contents of pan very gently through a sieve lined with muslin or thin cloth.
11. Re-heat soup and adjust seasoning. Taste it and if flavour is not strong enough boil it uncovered, reducing water content and so increasing flavour.
12. Take pan from heat and add wine just before serving. Although it is given as optional there is no doubt that this traditional ingredient adds to the flavour.

Serve with Sippets (*see page 21*) or some cooked pasta, or parsley.
Also delicious served chilled as a jelly. It will set in a jelly if the pig's trotter or calf's foot has been well cooked.

HAM SHANK

There are many ways to use an inexpensive shank. A smoked bacon or ham shank can also be used. From 1 shank you should get 2.25 litres/4 pints of rich stock, 225 g/8 oz ham pieces and some ham fat.

TO COOK SHANK AND MAKE STOCK
1. Put shank in a large saucepan with 2.7 to 3 litres/ 4½ to 5½ pints of water. Cover pan, bring to boil and simmer 1½ hours until meat and fat is falling off bones. Or, pressure cook for ¾ hour adding only the maximum quantity of water indicated in your pressure cooker manual.
2. Strain liquid into jugs. Allow to cool. Then put in refrigerator or wait until fat has risen and stock is set to a firm jelly.
3. When shank has cooled remove meat and separate fatty bits, skin and bones.
4. Lift fat off jellied stock to use for frying, etc.
   Skin and fatty bits from meat can be rendered down to produce more dripping. Put them into a

small pan, cover with water and put on lid. Simmer for 1 hour, then pour into a small bowl. As it cools fat will rise and when set can be lifted off liquid beneath.
Stock freezes well.

Ham may be chopped into white sauce and used on toast or in Vol-au-vents (*see page 206*) or pancakes (*see page 182*).

Try these dishes too: Ham Soup (*see below*), Ham, Egg and Onion Flan (*page 212*), Ham Rissoles (*page 69*).

HAM SOUP

Using stock from ham shank take care to taste before using. It may be very salty and require diluting with water.

Serves 6 or more

175 to 225 g/6 to 8 oz yellow split peas
2 medium-sized carrots
2 medium-sized onions
1.75 litres/3 pints ham stock

Other vegetables can be used e.g., cabbage, leek, parsnips, turnips—400 to 450 g/14 to 16 oz vegetables is about right.

TO SERVE
A little finely-chopped ham
2 tablespoons chopped, fresh parsley

1. Soak split peas in water for 3 hours. Then drain. If pressure cooking it is not necessary to soak first.
2. Scrub and chop carrots. Peel and chop onions.
3. Put split peas, vegetables and stock in a saucepan with a lid and simmer for 1 hour. Or pressure cook for 30 minutes taking care not to exceed maximum quantity of liquid indicated in your pressure cooker manual.
4. Add ham, parsley, and seasoning if necessary, and cook for 5 minutes.

This soup can be liquidised before parsley is added. It is then particularly delicious served with Sippets fried in ham fat (*see page 21*).

Serve very hot.

BACON AND SPLIT PEA SOUP

Serves 4 to 6

1 sheet of bacon ribs, plain or smoked
Water
1 large onion
1 carrot
1 potato
2 sticks celery
A little seasoning
225 g/8 oz split peas, yellow or green, or both

1. Put bacon ribs in a large saucepan, cover with water, bring to the boil and boil for a few minutes, then pour water away. This removes excess salt.
2. Meanwhile, peel and chop onion, scrub and grate carrot and potato. Finely slice celery.
3. Pour 1.75 litres/3 pints fresh, cold water over the ribs and add rest of ingredients.
4. Bring to the boil, stirring occasionally. Put lid on pan, lower heat and cook gently for 1 to 1½ hours. This can be done in pressure cooker, in which case cook under maximum pressure for 30 minutes.
5. Remove bacon ribs and strip off any meat.
6. Sieve or liquidise the soup.
7. Serve the soup either with the meat chopped and added or save the meat for another meal.

> Margaret Heywood
> Todmorden, Yorkshire

See also Cawl Cennin, page 15

BARLEY BROTH OR MUTTON BROTH

To do this in the traditional way buy 450 g/1 lb scrag end of neck of lamb or mutton, cut it up small (discarding fat) and cook slowly, with the bones, in 1.2 litres/2 pints water for 2 hours. Use the stock and meat in the broth as below.

Serves 4

75 g/3 oz barley kernels or pearl or pot barley
600 ml/1 pint water
2 onions
1 large carrot
1 small parsnip or turnip
1 or 2 sticks celery
25 g/1 oz butter or margarine
1 litre/1½ pints mutton, vegetable or chicken stock

A bouquet garni or bunch of fresh herbs such as parsley, thyme and rosemary
Salt
Black pepper

1. Put barley in water to soak overnight.
2. Peel onions and chop finely.
3. Scrub and finely chop or grate the carrot and parsnip or turnip.
4. Cut up the celery very fine.
5. Melt butter or margarine in a large saucepan with a well-fitting lid, put in the vegetables, cover pan tightly and let vegetables 'sweat' over a very low heat for 10 minutes.
6. Add soaked barley with its water, the stock and bouquet garni or bunch of fresh herbs (or a pinch of dried mixed herbs) and a little salt. Bring back to the boil.
7. Simmer for 20 to 30 minutes until barley is soft. Remove bouquet garni.
8. Add a little black pepper just before serving.

CULLEN SKINK

A delicious fish soup from the Moray Firth.

Serves 4

1 smoked haddock (Finnan is best)
Water
1 chopped onion
600 ml/1 pint milk
Hot mashed potato, quantity depends on desired consistency of soup
25 to 50g/1 to 2 oz butter
Salt and pepper

1. Skin haddock and place in pan with just enough water to cover.
2. Bring to boil and add chopped onion. Cook till ready, about 5 to 10 minutes.
3. Lift fish from pan and remove the bones.
4. Return bones to pan and boil for three quarters to one hour.
5. Meanwhile prepare the potatoes, mash them well while hot adding a little butter.
6. Flake the fish and lay aside.
7. Strain the bone stock, add the slightly warmed milk, the fish and enough hot mashed potato to give a creamy consistency. Stir in the butter and season to taste.

Serve very hot.

> Mrs Muriel Hume
> Carmyllie, Scotland

ARTICHOKE SOUP

Serves 4

450 g/1 lb Jerusalem artichokes
1 stalk celery
1 onion
1 tablespoon oil
25 g/1 oz wholewheat or plain flour
600 ml/1 pint water
Salt
450 ml/¾ pint milk
Black pepper
1 tablespoon chopped parsley

1. Wash and slice artichokes.
2. String and slice celery.
3. Peel onion and chop finely.
4. Put oil in a pan, add vegetables and sauté them for a few minutes—i.e., turn them over in the fat over moderate heat.
5. Stir in flour and let it cook for a minute.
6. Add water and a little salt. Bring to the boil, reduce heat, cover pan and let vegetables simmer until tender but not mushy.
7. If you like a creamy soup, sieve or liquidise, then return to pan.
8. Add milk and reheat the soup, but do not boil.
9. Add freshly-ground black pepper and chopped parsley and serve.

Isabel James
McCarrison Society

See also Uncooked Soups, page 20

HOT BEETROOT SOUP

This soup freezes well, but do so before yoghurt or soured cream is added.
A liquidiser is needed.

Serves 6

450 g/1 lb raw beetroot
450 g/1 lb potatoes
2 onions
50 g/2 oz butter or margarine
1.5 to 1.75 litres/2½ to 3 pints strong chicken stock
Salt
Freshly ground pepper
To garnish: yoghurt or soured cream

1. Peel and dice beetroot and potatoes. Peel and chop onions.
2. Melt butter in a large saucepan and cook vegetables gently with lid on pan for about 5 minutes.
3. Stir in the stock, bring to the boil and simmer until beetroot is cooked.
4. Cool the soup and reduce it to a purée in liquidiser. Return to pan. Adjust seasoning.
5. Just before serving, bring soup to boiling point and serve with a swirl of yoghurt or soured cream in each bowl.

See also Uncooked Soups, page 20

CARROT SOUP

Serves 4

25 g/1 oz butter, bacon fat or pork fat
450 g/1 lb carrots, cleaned and grated
1 grated onion
1 chopped stick of celery
½ teaspoon sugar
1 litre/1½ pints stock
2 tablespoons top of milk or single cream
Chopped parsley to decorate

1. Melt butter in large saucepan, add carrot, onion and celery. Cover and cook gently for 10 minutes to soften vegetables.
2. Add sugar, 600 ml/1 pint of the stock and simmer gently for 15 minutes.
3. Sieve or liquidise.
4. Add rest of stock, test for seasoning (if stock is well flavoured, extra seasoning may not be necessary).
5. Bring to the boil. Stir in cream. Heat, but do not boil again.

Serve, sprinkled with chopped parsley.

CREAM OF CARROT SOUP

Serves 4

450 g/1 lb carrots
2 medium-sized potatoes
1 onion
25 g/1 oz butter
1 litre/1½ pints chicken stock
1 small orange
1 bay leaf
¼ teaspoon salt
Pepper
Pinch of nutmeg
2 tablespoons double cream
Chopped parsley or chives, to garnish

1. Scrub carrots, peel potato and onion. Slice them all thinly.
2. Melt butter in a pan, add vegetables, cook gently for 3 or 4 minutes.
3. Add stock.
4. Add grated orange rind and juice, bay leaf, salt, pepper and nutmeg.
5. Simmer soup for about 20 minutes until vegetables are tender.
6. Allow to cool slightly and remove bay leaf.
7. Sieve or liquidise.
8. Return soup to pan, check seasoning and reheat.
9. Remove pan from heat, stir in cream and serve with a sprinkling of parsley or chives.

CARROT AND CORIANDER SOUP

Serves 4 to 6

2 onions
40 g/1½ oz butter
1 clove of garlic
A pinch of salt
450 g/1 lb carrots
Pepper
1 dessertspoon coriander seeds
1 glass of sherry
600 ml/1 pint chicken stock
600 ml/1 pint milk
To garnish: chopped parsley

1. Peel and slice onions and cook carefully in butter in a large pan until transparent.

2. Crush garlic with salt and add to onions.
3. Scrub carrots, slice thinly and add to pan.
4. Season with salt and pepper. Add coriander seeds and sherry. Cover and cook gently until vegetables are soft, about 10 to 15 minutes.
5. Add stock and cook a further 15 to 20 minutes. Allow to cool.
6. Liquidise or sieve the soup, then strain into a clean pan.
7. Add milk when ready to serve. Reheat carefully. Adjust seasoning.
8. Sprinkle parsley in each bowl of soup.

CARROT AND LEEK SOUP

Serves 4

2 carrots
2 large leeks
25 g/1 oz butter
1 teaspoon horseradish sauce
25 g/1 oz medium oatmeal
Salt and pepper
Mace (or bay leaf)
600 ml/1 pint chicken stock
150 ml/¼ pint milk

1. Slice carrots and leeks.
2. Sauté in butter for seven minutes. Add horseradish sauce, oatmeal, salt, pepper and mace (or bay leaf).
3. Pour on stock and milk.
4. Bring to the boil, simmer for 25 minutes.

CELERY SOUP

Serves 4

1 medium-sized head of celery
1 small onion
40 g/1½ oz butter or margarine
40 g/1½ oz wholewheat or plain white flour
1 litre/1½ pints vegetable or chicken stock
A bouquet garni, or sprig of parsley, thyme
  and marjoram or bay leaf tied together
300 ml/½ pint milk
Salt and pepper
2 tablespoons single cream

1. Chop up celery, including inner leaves. Save a few chopped leaves for garnish. Chop up the onion.

2. Melt butter or margarine in a saucepan with a well-fitting lid. Add vegetables.

3. Stir vegetables for 1 minute then put lid on the saucepan. Turn heat down very low and let the vegetables 'sweat', without browning, for 10 minutes.

4. Stir in the flour and let it cook for 1 minute.

5. Add stock and bouquet garni. Bring to the boil and simmer until vegetables are tender but not mushy. Remove bouquet garni.

6. If you prefer a creamy soup, put it through liquidiser or through a sieve. Return it to pan.

7. Add milk, a little salt and pepper. Reheat.

8. Just before serving stir in finely-chopped celery leaves and cream.

Isabel James
McCarrison Society

CAWL CENNIN

Leek Broth. Traditionally in Wales, this cawl or soup would be made when a piece of bacon was being boiled and would either be served as a first course or kept for another meal. It was made with whatever vegetables were available and the quantities also just depended upon what there was. So the following may be regarded simply as a guide and altered to suit what vegetables you have.

1 litre/1½ pints stock from boiling a joint of
  bacon
250 g/8 oz potatoes, peeled and diced
250 g/8 oz carrots, diced
2 leeks, sliced
½ small cabbage, shredded
2 tablespoons oatmeal
Salt and pepper
Chopped parsley

The addition of oatmeal is optional and may be omitted if a thinner broth is preferred.

1. Put potatoes and carrots in the stock, bring to the boil and cook for 10 minutes.

2. Add the leeks and cabbage.

3. Mix oatmeal with a little cold water and add.

4. Bring to boil again and simmer 10 to 15 minutes until the vegetables are cooked. Check for seasoning.

5. Serve sprinkled with chopped parsley.

Mrs Wesley Evans
Denbighshire

CREAM OF LEEK AND POTATO SOUP

Serves 4

4 medium-sized leeks
50 g/2 oz butter
4 small potatoes
150 ml/¼ pint water
600 ml/1 pint chicken stock
Salt and pepper
150 ml/¼ pint double cream

1. Wash and trim leeks and chop into small pieces, using both white and green parts.

2. Melt butter in a saucepan and add leeks. Cover pan and reduce heat so that leeks cook slowly without browning, for about 5 minutes. Shake pan occasionally.

3. Meanwhile, peel potatoes and cut into small cubes.

4. Add potatoes to leeks with water and stock. Season to taste.

5. Bring to boil, cover pan and simmer soup for 25 minutes.

6. Sieve or liquidise soup and return it to the pan.

7. Add cream. Heat, but do not boil.

Mrs Eileen Trumper
Llanvair Kilgeddin, Gwent

GOLDEN VEGETABLE SOUP

Serves 4 to 6

675 g/1½ lb diced vegetables—onion, carrot,
  swede, celery
50 g/2 oz butter
25 g/1 oz flour
1.2 litres/2 pints well-seasoned stock, preferably a light one, like chicken or bacon
125g/4 oz fresh or frozen peas

1. Fry vegetables in butter until lightly golden, but do not brown.

2. Stir in flour, sizzle 1 minute.

3. Gradually add stock, bring to boil and simmer with lid on pan until vegetables are tender. Test for seasoning.

4. Add peas and boil up. If frozen peas are used add and cook for time advised on packet.

GAME SOUP

Serves 4 to 6

1 onion
1 carrot
1 stick celery
50 g/2 oz butter
1.2 litres/2 pints game stock, from carcasses of 2 game birds (*see page 10*)
1 bay leaf
Salt and pepper
25 g/1 oz margarine or butter
25 g/1 oz plain flour
2 teaspoons redcurrant jelly
2 teaspoons lemon juice
2 tablespoons sherry or red wine

1. Peel and chop onion. Scrub and chop carrot. Wash and slice celery.
2. Melt butter in a large pan and sauté—i.e., lightly fry—the vegetables, turning them over in the hot fat for 2 or 3 minutes until lightly browned.
3. Add stock, bay leaf, salt and pepper and simmer for 1 hour.
4. Finely chop any meat picked from the carcasses.
5. Make a brown roux with the margarine and flour: i.e., melt margarine, stir in flour and fry till light brown.
6. Strain the soup and gradually stir it into the roux. Bring to the boil and cook for 2 or 3 minutes.
7. Add the meat and reheat. The soup may now be liquidised if a smooth texture is preferred.
8. Add the redcurrant jelly and lemon juice and sherry or wine.

Reheat and serve at once.

Anne Wallace
Dunlop, Scotland

MINESTRONE

Serves 6

15 g/½ oz butter
bacon dripping
50 g/2 oz streaky bacon, diced
1 large onion
1 stalk celery
50 g/2 oz swede
50 g/2 oz carrot
125 g/4 oz potato

1.5 litres/2½ pints light stock
2 tablespoons tomato purée
25 g/1 oz macaroni or spaghetti
1 teaspoon sugar
125 to 175 g/4 to 6 oz cabbage
Pepper and salt, seasoned salt gives more piquancy

TO SERVE
Parmesan cheese

1. Melt fat in large pan, add bacon and diced onion, cook 1 minute.
2. Add celery, swede, carrot and potato, all finely-diced, and fry gently for 3 to 4 minutes.
3. Heat stock, mix in tomato purée and stir into pan of bacon and vegetables.
4. Add macaroni or spaghetti broken into small pieces. Cover and simmer for 30 minutes. Add sugar.
5. Shred cabbage finely, cut into 2.5 cm/1 inch lengths, add to pan and simmer 12 to 15 minutes until tender. Add salt and pepper to taste.

Serve with grated Parmesan cheese on top.

MUSHROOM SOUP

Serves 4

25 g/1 oz butter
1 large onion, finely-chopped
25 g/1 oz green pepper, finely-chopped
1 small clove of garlic, crushed
125 g/4 oz mushrooms, chopped small
Salt and black pepper
2 dessertspoons flour
450 ml/¾ pint chicken stock
450 ml/¾ pint milk
Chopped parsley

1. Melt butter in a heavy-based pan which has a lid. Fry onion, green pepper and garlic until beginning to soften but not going brown.
2. Add mushrooms and toss together over low heat. Add salt and pepper taking care not to over-salt if stock is well-seasoned.
3. Put lid on pan and leave on very low heat for 5 to 10 minutes so that vegetables 'sweat'. If using old mushrooms 5 minutes is enough. Do not let them catch. An asbestos mat under the pan will help.
4. Stir in flour, add stock and bring to boil. Simmer 2 or 3 minutes.
5. Add milk and reheat. Sprinkle on chopped parsley, stir and serve.

ONION SOUP

Serves 4 to 6

50 g/2 oz margarine or butter
675 g/1½ lb finely-chopped onion
1 level tablespoon flour
1 teaspoon Salt and Pepper Mix (*see below*)
1.2 litres/2 pints stock, chicken is excellent but
   a light bone stock is adequate (*see page 10*)

TO SERVE
Thick slices of French bread, one for each
   serving of soup
Grated cheese

1. Melt fat in large pan, add onions, cook gently until soft.
2. Add flour and seasonings and cook for 2 minutes, stirring.
3. Stir in the stock, bring to boil and simmer for 30 minutes. Check for seasoning.
4. Toast the slices of French bread on one side only.
5. Cover untoasted side of bread thickly with cheese. Place under grill just to melt.
6. Place a slice in each soup bowl, ladle soup over and serve at once.

DOROTHY SLEIGHTHOLME'S SALT AND PEPPER MIX
For seasoning: 3 teaspoons of salt to 1 teaspoon of pepper. Mix well together. Keep in screw-top or sprinkler top jar.

SIMPLE ONION SOUP

Serves 4

4 large onions, about 675 g/1½ lb
40 g/1½ oz butter or margarine
1 litre/1½ pints well-flavoured chicken stock
Salt and Pepper Mix (*see above*)

1. Cut up onions very fine.
2. Melt butter or margarine in a saucepan. Add onion, stir well and put on lid.
3. Turn heat down very low and allow onion to sweat for 10 minutes. Shake pan from time to time but avoid taking off lid.
4. Add stock, season to taste, bring to the boil and simmer for 3 minutes or until onion is tender. Serve the soup piping hot.

POTATO AND CELERY SOUP

Serves 4

50 g/2 oz butter
450 g/1 lb potatoes, peeled and cut into pieces
2 onions, peeled and quartered
5 stalks celery, washed and cut into pieces
1 litre/1½ pints chicken or bacon stock
Salt and pepper
150 ml/¼ pint milk
Nutmeg

1. Melt butter and fry vegetables gently for 4 minutes.
2. Add stock, salt and pepper, bring to boil, cover and simmer for 40 minutes.
3. Sieve or liquidise.
4. Add milk, reheat, adjust seasoning and grate in a little nutmeg.

Garnish with a few chopped celery leaves.

DOROTHY SOUP

Serves 4 to 6

900 g/2 lb onions
50 g /2 oz butter
450 g/1 lb tomatoes or a 400 g/14 oz tin of
   tomatoes
1 litre/1½ pints water
1 good tablespoon medium oatmeal
Salt and pepper
1 level teaspoon sugar

1. Chop onions finely.
2. Melt butter in saucepan, add onion and cook about 5 minutes until soft but not brown.
3. Wash and slice tomatoes and add to pan. Cook until both tomatoes and onions are very soft, stirring occasionally.
4. Pour on half of the water, bring to boil and put through a sieve. Or you can liquidise it and then sieve.
5. Meanwhile, rinse pan and boil oatmeal with remaining water for 10 minutes.
6. Add vegetable purée to oatmeal, season with salt, pepper and sugar. Simmer 20 minutes. Add more water if it is too thick. Taste and season again if necessary. Also good with a tablespoon of cream added, but do not let it boil again or it may curdle.

TOMATO SOUP

Serves 4

450 g/1 lb fresh ripe tomatoes, or a 400 g/14 oz tin
1 large onion
25 g/1 oz green pepper
25 g/1 oz butter, margarine or good bacon dripping
0.5 to 1 litre/1 to 1½ pints chicken stock
Pinch of basil (optional)
1 bay leaf
Salt
Black pepper
½ teaspoon sugar (Barbados preferred)
1 tablespoon chopped parsley
1 dessertspoon chopped mint

1. If fresh tomatoes are used, peel them. To do this, put them in a bowl and cover with boiling water. Wait 15 seconds then pour off hot water and cover with cold. Wait half a minute and skins will be easy to remove. Chop up tomatoes finely.
2. Peel onion and chop finely.
3. Chop green pepper very small.
4. Melt fat in a large saucepan. Fry onion and green pepper for 2 to 3 minutes until softening but not brown.
5. Add tomatoes, stock, basil and bay leaf. Bring to the boil and simmer for 10 to 15 minutes.
6. Test seasoning, adding a very little salt if necessary, plenty of freshly-ground black pepper and the sugar.
7. Just before serving add chopped parsley and mint.

To make a meal of this soup add a handful of brown rice, brown macaroni or fancy pasta when soup comes to the boil. Make sure rice or pasta is cooked before serving.

CREAM OF TOMATO SOUP

Freezes well, but do so before milk or cream is added.

Serves 4

1 medium-sized carrot, scrubbed
1 onion, peeled
2 sticks of celery, washed
75 g/3 oz butter or margarine

A 400 g/14 oz tin of tomatoes
1 teaspoon sugar
600 ml/1 pint light stock
Salt and Pepper Mix (*see page 17*)
25 g/1 oz plain flour
1 tablespoon tomato paste or purée*
150 ml/¼ pint top of milk or single cream

TO GARNISH:
Chopped parsley

(**To keep tomato purée fresh, see page 84*)

1. Slice carrot, onion and celery finely.
2. Soften 40 g/1½ oz of butter or margarine in a large saucepan. Add vegetables, put on lid and cook gently until soft, shaking pan occasionally.
3. Add tomatoes with their juice, sugar, 300 ml/½ pint of the stock, salt and pepper to taste. Simmer for 5 minutes.
4. Sieve contents of pan into a bowl. Rinse out pan.
5. Melt remaining 40 g/1½ oz butter or margarine in pan. Stir in flour and cook for 1 minute. Stir in rest of stock and tomato paste. Cook for 1 minute. Stir until boiling and simmer for 1 minute.
6. Add tomato mixture from bowl, and the milk or cream. Check seasoning. Heat to nearly boiling point, but do not actually boil or the soup may curdle.

Serve sprinkled with chopped parsley.

SPICED RED LENTIL SOUP

This soup is a flaming orange colour.

4 large or 6 good helpings. Easy to make less.

1 medium-sized onion
1 red pepper
2 sticks of celery
225 g/8 oz marrow or courgettes
125 g/4 oz red lentils
1 tablespoon oil
1 teaspoon paprika
1 teaspoon turmeric
A pinch of cinnamon
A pinch of cayenne pepper
A 400 g/14 oz can of tomatoes
About 750 ml/1¼ pints water or vegetable stock
1 teaspoon basil
1 bay leaf
Salt and pepper
1 tablespoon shoyu (*see page 162*)

1. Chop vegetables finely.
2. Wash lentils and pick them over for stones.
3. Heat oil and fry spices—i.e., paprika, turmeric, cinnamon and cayenne.
4. Add vegetables and lentils. Stir well so that oil and spices coat the vegetables. Cook about 5 minutes, stirring occasionally.
5. Cut up tomatoes, put them in a measuring jug and add enough water or stock to make 1.2 litres/2 pints.
6. Add this with basil and bay leaf to pan of vegetables. Bring to boil and simmer for 40 minutes or until lentils are cooked.
7. Add salt and pepper to taste. Add the shoyu. Add more water or stock if necessary.

Sarah Brown
Scarborough, Yorkshire

WHITE FOAM SOUP

Serves 6 but easy to make half quantity

1 onion
1 stick of celery
A clove of garlic
40 g/1½ oz butter
25 g/1 oz flour
1.2 litres/2 pints of milk
A blade of mace
2 eggs, separated
Salt and pepper
50 g/2 oz finely-grated cheese
1 tablespoon chopped parsley

1. Chop onion and celery very fine. Crush garlic.
2. Melt butter in a 2 litre/3½ pint saucepan. Stir in flour, then add milk slowly, stirring thoroughly till smooth. Bring to the boil and cook for 2 minutes.
3. Add onion, celery, garlic and mace. Let the soup barely simmer for 20 to 30 minutes until it is well flavoured.
4. Cool slightly, then add beaten yolks of the eggs.
5. Reheat without boiling. Then add salt and pepper to taste, and grated cheese. Do not allow to boil.
6. Beat egg-whites to a stiff froth. Fold half into the soup. Pour the rest into a hot tureen and pour soup over. Sprinkle with chopped parsley.

Serve with tiny cubes of bread fried in butter or margarine. (*See Sippets, page 21*)

Mrs Irene Mills
For Leckhampton W.I., Glos.

MINTY GREEN SOUP

For this you need a liquidiser.

Serves at least 6 but freezes well

176 g/6 oz green split peas
1 medium-sized onion
225 g/8 oz carrots
2 small potatoes
2 sticks celery
1 small parsnip
1 tablespoon oil
1.2 litres/2 pints light stock or water
½ to 1 tablespoon dried mint or chopped fresh mint to taste
Salt and pepper
1 tablespoon shoyu (*see page 162*)
Milk (optional)

TO GARNISH:
2 tablespoons cream, sprigs of fresh mint

1. Wash the split peas.
2. Peel and finely chop onion.
3. Scrub and finely chop carrots, potatoes, celery and parsnip.
4. Gently fry onion in oil until translucent.
5. Add other vegetables and fry gently for 5 minutes, mixing well so that oil coats vegetables and seals in flavour.
6. Add green split peas and stock or water. Bring to boil and simmer for about 40 minutes until peas are cooked.
7. Put soup through liquidiser, adding mint, seasoning and shoyu as it blends. Return to pan.
8. If soup is too thick either stock, water or milk may be added. Heat gently, check seasoning.

Serve with a swirl of cream and sprigs of mint floating on surface.

Sarah Brown
Scarborough, Yorkshire

CHILLED AVOCADO SOUP

Delicious and nutritious. You need an electric blender or liquidiser.

Serves 4 to 6

600 ml/1 pint chicken stock
2 ripe avocado pears
About a 10 cm/4 inch length of cucumber
1 teaspoon lemon juice
275 ml/10 fl oz natural yoghurt
Salt and pepper

1. Prepare stock and allow to cool.
2. Halve the avocado pears, peel off skins and remove stones. Dice the flesh.
3. Dice the cucumber leaving skin on.
4. Put avocado, cucumber and a little stock in electric blender and liquidise. Pour out into a bowl.
5. Add remaining stock and stir in lemon juice and yoghurt. Season to taste with salt and pepper.
6. Chill well. Serve with hot toast.

UNCOOKED SOUPS

Many vegetables make delicious hot or cold soup even though they have not been cooked. If you can get organically grown vegetables, so much the better. You need an electric liquidiser.

ARTICHOKE

Serves 4 to 6

450 g/1 lb Jerusalem artichokes
450 g/1 lb potatoes
1 stick celery
600 ml/1 pint milk, preferably goat's milk
Seasoning, try herb salt or kelp powder and paprika
1 tablespoon chopped parsley
A little butter

1. Scrub the artichokes and potatoes and grate them.
2. String the celery and grate or slice it.
3. Put vegetables in the liquidiser with milk and seasoning and blend till smooth. Eat it as soon as possible, either hot or cold.
4. *To eat cold.* Chill the soup and garnish with parsley.
5. *To eat hot.* Heat a little butter in a pan. Pour in the soup and heat but do not cook. Stir in the parsley just before serving.

WATERCRESS

Serves 4

450 g/1 lb potatoes
1 small onion
1 bunch watercress
1 pint milk, preferably goat's milk
Seasoning, try herb salt or kelp powder and paprika

1. Peel onion and grate with potatoes.
2. Wash watercress thoroughly and cut it up small.
3. Put vegetables, milk and seasoning into liquidiser and blend till smooth.

BEETROOT

Serves 4

6 raw beetroot
2 tablespoons chopped chives
2 cartons soured cream
Seasoning, try herb salt or kelp powder and paprika

1. Wash and shred beetroot.
2. Chop the chives.
3. Put beetroot, chives and seasoning in liquidiser with 1½ cartons of soured cream. Blend until smooth.
4. Pour into soup bowls and chill.
5. Serve with remaining soured cream swirled on top and a sprinkling of chopped chives.

Elizabeth Shears
author of 'Why Do We Eat'

SOUP NUTS

To accompany soup, 12 to 15 portions

Using half the quantity of choux pastry given on *page 207* bake tiny raisin-sized pieces of the paste on a greased baking tray in a moderately hot oven, Gas 6, 400°F, 200°C, for 10 to 12 minutes until pale golden brown and dry.

Store in an airtight container, or freeze.

Anne Wallace
Stewarton, Ayrshire

SIPPETS OR CROÛTONS

Fry cubes or small triangles of bread in hot bacon, ham fat, or butter until brown and crisp, turning often.

Delicious if a clove of garlic, chopped into 2 or 3 pieces, is first fried in the fat. Try these also cold surrounding salads with soft ingredients.

MELBA TOAST

1. Cut slices of bread for toast—not too thick.
2. Toast lightly brown on both sides.
3. Cut in half diagonally to make triangles. Then slice the bread through the centre between the toasted sides to make two pieces from one.
4. Place in a large roasting tin and dry off at the bottom of the oven until crisp.
5. Store in an airtight tin.

Goes well with hot or cold soup.

FRESH HERB AND GARLIC BREAD

Use any of these herbs and then try your own ideas.

HERB BREAD

Parsley or chives or thyme
50 g/2 oz butter
A fresh crusty loaf, French bread or wholemeal
or even crusty bread rolls

1. Chop the herb finely—2 tablespoons is enough.
2. Soften the butter but do not melt it. Mix in the herb.
3. Slice load into thick pieces without quite cutting through the bottom crust.
4. Spread one side of each slice with herb butter.
5. Wrap loaf in greaseproof paper and foil and put it in a moderate oven, Gas 3, 325°F, 160°C, for 15 to 20 minutes until butter has melted and soaked into the bread. Eat hot with soups or cold meat and salad, or omelettes.

GARLIC BREAD

½ to 1 clove garlic
A little salt
1 tablespoon chopped parsley
50 g/2 oz butter

1. If you do not have a crusher put garlic on a small plate with a sprinkle of salt. Use a palette knife or an old-fashioned table knife with a flexible rounded blade and crush garlic to a cream.
2. Mix garlic and parsley into butter.
3. Now use it as described above.

APRICOT AND ORANGE

A simple and refreshing starter to a meal, or a sweet, or even for breakfast.

Serves 2 to 3

125 g/4 oz dried apricots
Boiling water
3 oranges
A sprig of mint, for decoration

1. Cut apricots into small pieces. Easy with kitchen scissors. Put them in a bowl or jar and cover with boiling water.
2. Squeeze oranges. Add juice and pulp to apricots.
3. Leave in a cool place or refrigerator overnight or longer so that flavours blend and apricots are really plump.

Serve in separate glasses or little bowls with a mint leaf to decorate.

Anne Wallace
Stewarton, Ayrshire

HONEY COCKTAIL

Serves 2

Juice of 1 large or 2 small oranges
Juice of 2 lemons
2 tablespoons honey
2 eggs, separated
Glacé cherries on cocktail sticks, to decorate

1. Put orange and lemon juice in a bowl, add honey and egg-yolks. Whisk until light and creamy in colour.
2. Whisk egg-whites in another basin until very stiff. Fold carefully with a metal spoon into egg and honey mixture.
3. Divide into glasses.
4. Decorate with glacé cherries on cocktail sticks.

Serve at once.

Mrs Emily Williams
Moggerhanger, Bedfordshire

GRILLED GRAPEFRUIT

Serves 4

25 g/1 oz demerara sugar
15 g/½ oz butter
2 grapefruit
4 teaspoons sherry
2 glacé cherries

1. Mix sugar and butter together.
2. Cut grapefruit in half and prepare in the usual way removing core with scissors.
3. Put a teaspoonful of sherry in each grapefruit.
4. Spread sugar mixture over each grapefruit.
5. Put them under moderately hot grill for 3 to 5 minutes.

Serve at once with half a cherry on top.

CUCUMBER AND GRAPEFRUIT SALAD

Nice as a starter or a salad.

Serves 4

2 grapefruit
¼ cucumber
50 g/2 oz diced Cheddar cheese
150 ml/5 fl oz natural yoghurt

1. Cut grapefruit in half and remove segments. Discard all pith and chop up the fruit.
2. Dice the cucumber.
3. Mix all ingredients together with the yoghurt and fill the halved grapefruit shells.
4. Serve chilled.

Judith Adshead
Mottram St. Andrew, Cheshire

PASTA COCKTAIL

Serves 6

40 g/1½ oz small pasta shapes
2 sticks celery
1 crisp eating apple

SAUCE
4 tablespoons mayonnaise (*see page 134*)
1 tablespoon tomato sauce
1 tablespoon cream
2 teaspoons lemon juice
A dash of Tabasco sauce

TO SERVE AND GARNISH
Lettuce leaves
Lemon twists or paprika

1. First cook the pasta in boiling salted water until tender. Strain in colander and pour cold water through it to rinse away excess starch. This prevents pasta sticking together.
2. Now prepare the sauce by mixing together all the ingredients.
3. Slice the celery.
4. Core, quarter and chop the apple.
5. Mix cold pasta, celery and apple into the sauce.
6. Line small dishes or sundae glasses with lettuce leaves and fill with the cocktail.
7. Garnish with twists of lemon or sprinkle with paprika—or both.

Anne Wallace
Dunlop, Scotland

HUMUS

A dish from the eastern Mediterranean and the Middle East.

Will keep 4 or 5 days in refrigerator.

Enough for 8 people—easy to make in small quantities

225 g/8 oz dry chick peas
150 ml/¼ pint stock (use cooking water from chick peas)
4 to 5 tablespoons tahini*, white if possible
Juice of 1½ lemons
A teaspoon shoyu (*see page 162*) or soya sauce
A clove of garlic, crushed, or 1 teaspoon garlic powder
½ teaspoon salt
¼ teaspoon paprika
Black pepper

*Tahini is a paste made from crushed sesame seeds, similar in texture to creamy peanut butter. Its purpose is to thicken the chick pea paste as well as to add flavour. White tahini is made from hulled sesame seeds, brown tahini is from whole seed. Both have a nutty flavour, but the brown type has a much stronger flavour. It is available from most Greek foodstores and good delicatessens.

TO SERVE
Slices of lemon
Parsley
Wholemeal bread or pitta (*see page 293*)

1. Soak chick peas in water overnight.
2. Next day drain them, discarding water. Rinse, re-cover with about 1.5 litres/3 pints water, put on lid and boil hard for 25 minutes. Then reduce heat and simmer until soft but not mushy.
3. Meanwhile prepare other ingredients.
4. Drain chick peas, reserving liquid for stock and grind them to a fine powder. This can be done in a food processor or through a mincer or mouli-grater. If chick peas are cooked for about 2 hours until really soft they can be mashed by hand.
5. Add enough of the reserved liquid to make a stiff paste. Mix in all other ingredients.
6. Put humus in a shallow dish garnished with lemon slices and parsley.

Serve with bread. Traditionally served with Pitta bread (*see page 293*)

Sarah Brown
Scarborough, Yorkshire

MUSHROOM SALAD

Serves 4

225 g/8 oz small cultivated mushrooms
1 small, red pepper
1 small, green pepper
1 to 2 tablespoons French dressing (*see page 133*)
Leaves of crisp lettuce

1. Wash mushrooms in tepid, lightly-salted water. Drain and pat very dry. Slice.
2. Remove core and seeds from peppers. Cut flesh into strips, or dice. Blanch as follows: drop the strips or dice into a pan of boiling water and bring back to the boil. Drain, refresh in cold water, drain again and pat dry. If you like the full flavour of peppers blanching is not necessary.
3. Place dressing in bowl, add mushrooms and peppers, toss together lightly. Spoon on to lettuce leaves just before serving. Serve with brown bread and butter, rye bread or crispbreads.

STUFFED RINGS OF RED AND GREEN PEPPERS

A very pretty and delicious dish. For this you need a liquidiser or food processor.

Serves 6 or more

2 small red peppers
2 small green peppers
STUFFING
This is a pâté of chicken livers which can be made in larger quantities to serve on its own. Can be frozen, but only for 1 or 2 weeks.

125 g/4 oz chicken livers
25 g/1 oz butter
1 tablespoon oil
1 onion, finely-chopped
A clove of garlic, finely-chopped
½ level teaspoon chopped fresh thyme, or ¼ level teaspoon dried
2 tablespoons medium-sweet sherry
125 g/4 oz cream cheese
Salt and pepper

TO SERVE
Hot buttered toast

1. Cut a lid off each pepper with its stalk and hollow out by removing core, seeds and white membrane.

2. Prepare chicken livers by scraping out core and cutting away any part tinged with green. Chop, but not small.

3. Melt butter with oil and fry liver, onion, garlic and thyme, gently turning all the time, about 5 minutes. Cool.

4. Add sherry to the pan. Then blend in a liquidiser or food processor.

5. Add cream cheese, salt and pepper. Continue processing until well combined.

6. Fill this mixture into the hollowed-out peppers. Chill.

7. Just before serving, cut in 1 cm/½ inch rings.

Serve with hot buttered toast.

CHEESE AND WALNUT PÂTÉ

Keeps for several days in refrigerator and freezes well.

Enough for 8 to 10

225 g/8 oz cottage cheese
75 g/3 oz ground walnuts
3 tablespoons butter
75 g/3 oz Cheddar cheese, finely grated
1 teaspoon caraway seeds, nice but not essential
1 to 2 teaspoons wholegrain mustard
Salt and black pepper
5 to 6 tablespoons fresh wholewheat breadcrumbs (*see page 52*)

TO GARNISH
Lettuce leaves, cress, tomato slices, walnut halves

1. If you like a fine-textured pâté, first sieve the cottage cheese.

2. Walnuts may be ground in an electric coffee grinder.

3. Cream butter and cottage cheese.

4. Add grated cheese, walnuts, caraway seeds and seasonings. Mix well.

5. Mix in breadcrumbs.

6. Press pâté into a nice dish or into ramekins. Or serve with an ice cream scoop on individual plates garnished with lettuce, cress, tomato slices and extra walnut halves.

Sarah Brown
Scarborough, Yorkshire

CHEESE STRUDEL SLICES

Serves 6

A 225 g/8 oz packet of frozen puff pastry or use home-made rough puff pastry (*see page 206*)

FILLING
1 large beaten egg
125 g/4 oz Cheddar cheese, finely-grated
225 g/8 oz curd or single cream cheese
1 level tablespoon chopped parsley or chives, or a mixture
A pinch of garlic salt
Pepper and salt

TO DECORATE
Sesame seeds

1. Roll out pastry on a floured board to a rectangle about 30 by 23 cm/12 by 9 inches.

2. Prepare filling. Keep aside 1 tablespoon of the egg and mix all other ingredients together.

3. Spread filling over pastry to within 2.5 cm/1 inch of edges.

4. Turn edges in to hold filling in place and then fold three times to make a flattened Swiss-roll shape about 8 cm/3 inches deep.

5. Lift roll on to a baking sheet, brush with remaining egg and scatter sesame seeds over top. Cut six shallow slits through pastry top.

6. Bake near top of a hot oven, Gas 7, 425°F, 220°C, for 10 minutes. Then reduce heat to moderately hot, Gas 5, 375°F, 190°C, for a further 15 minutes.

7. Cut into slices and serve hot.

Judith Adshead
Mottram St Andrew, Cheshire

SMOKED COD'S ROE PÂTÉ

Serves 4

225 g/8 oz smoked cod's roe
Juice of 1 lemon
150 ml/¼ pint double cream, or 75 g/3 oz soft
  butter mixed with milk made up to 150 ml/
  ¼ pint
A pinch each of ground ginger, cayenne pepper
  and paprika

Do not use an electric mixer or blender for this as it
would break up the tiny eggs.
1. Remove skin from the cod's roe and empty into
a bowl.
2. Put in half of the lemon juice and mash well with
a fork. Add rest of lemon juice and beat again.
3. Gradually beat in cream, or the butter and milk.
4. Season to taste with the ginger and cayenne pepper.
5. Transfer to serving dish. Sprinkle with paprika
and refrigerate.

Serve with hot buttered toast.

AVOCADO AND SALMON MOUSSE

A liquidiser or food processor is useful.

Serves 4 to 6

225 g/8 oz tinned salmon
15 g/½ oz gelatine
3 tablespoons water
2 avocado pears
½ teaspoon salt
A dash of pepper
2 teaspoons anchovy essence
3 tablespoons single cream
2 or 3 drops of green food-colouring
2 egg-whites

TO GARNISH
1 stuffed green olive, chopped fresh parsley

1. Drain salmon. Reserve juice. Remove bones, skin
and flake the flesh finely.
2. Put gelatine in 3 tablespoons water in a cup or
small bowl. Set the cup in a pan of hot water and
heat gently until the gelatine is completely dissolved.
Stir well.
3. Split, stone, skin and cut up the avocados. Scrape
as much pulp as possible from skin as this will give
the mousse a deep green colour.
4. Liquidise the avocados, salt, pepper, anchovy
essence and salmon juice. Or, if you do not have a
liquidiser or food processor, mash thoroughly and
beat until smooth.
5. Place in a large bowl, strain in the dissolved
gelatine. Stir in cream and flaked salmon adding
green colouring if needed.
6. Whisk egg-whites until they will stand up in
peaks. Then fold into salmon mixture.
7. Turn into a fish or ring mould which has been
rinsed in cold water and leave to set.
8. Turn out into a serving dish. Garnish with the
stuffed olive, for eyes, and parsley.

This recipe would make excellent individual ramekins too.

SMOKED MACKEREL PÂTÉ

For this you need a liquidiser or food processor.

Serves 6

350 g/12 oz smoked mackerel
2 thick slices wholemeal or brown bread
45 ml/3 tablespoons wine or cider vinegar
Half a tart eating apple, about 125 g/4 oz peeled
  and cored
Black pepper to taste

1. If using home-smoked mackerel proceed straight
to step 2. Otherwise proceed as follows. Soak fish in
water for an hour or two to relieve strong smoky
taste. Wash thoroughly and cook in water just to
cover, simmering for 5 minutes. Drain.
2. Remove bones and skin from fish.
3. Soak bread with vinegar.
4. Place all ingredients in liquidiser or food processor
and switch on until all is blended and smooth.
5. Press into a ½ kg/1 lb loaf tin or a 13 cm/5 inch
round tin or a soufflé dish. Chill.
6. Turn out on an attractive plate to serve.

Serve with Melba Toast (*see page 21*) and butter, a
nice salad or plain watercress.

Anne Wallace
Stewarton, Ayrshire

MARINATED SMOKED MACKEREL

Serves 4

Buy two 125 g/4 oz fillets of smoked mackerel, cooked

MARINADE
1 small onion, finely-chopped
2 tablespoons salad oil
1 tablespoon wine vinegar or lemon juice
$\frac{1}{4}$ teaspoon dry mustard

TO SERVE
Chopped fresh parsley

1. Skin mackerel and divide into portions in a shallow dish.
2. Mix marinade ingredients and pour over mackerel.
3. Cover with a lid or greaseproof paper and foil and put in refrigerator or a cool place for about 3 hours.
4. Lift mackerel on to separate plates. Sprinkle with parsley.

Delicious with crusty French bread.

FRESH MUSSELS WITH PARSLEY

Serves 2

450 g/1 lb fresh mussels in the shells*
15 g/$\frac{1}{2}$ oz butter
$\frac{1}{2}$ a large clove of garlic, crushed
1 dessertspoon parsley

* Try to buy the mussels on the day you mean to use them. If it is necessary to keep them overnight put them in a flat dish or basin in a cool place with a sprinkling of water, or cover with a wet cloth.

1. Wash and scrub mussels, pull off the beards. Using the back of an old knife knock off any barnacles. Discard any open mussels.
2. Put mussels in a large pan with the other ingredients. Cover and cook over a high heat. Shake pan from time to time. Cook for only enough time to open the mussel shells. Shake again so that the liquor gets into the mussels. Not more than five minutes in all.
3. Serve immediately with crusty French bread to mop up the delicious soup.

LIVER PÂTÉ

For this you need a liquidiser or a food processor.

Can be kept in refrigerator for a week or in freezer for 6 weeks, but long freezing is not suitable because garlic flavour tends to get a bit strong.

As a lunch or supper dish, enough for 5 people. As a starter, 10 portions.

150 ml/$\frac{1}{4}$ pint thick white sauce made with 20 g/$\frac{3}{4}$ oz butter, 20 g/$\frac{3}{4}$ oz flour, 150 ml/$\frac{1}{4}$ pint milk, salt and pepper
225 g/8 oz chicken, calves or lamb's liver
15 g/$\frac{1}{2}$ oz butter
A clove of garlic, crushed
125 g/4 oz fat bacon pieces
Half a sour apple, peeled, cored and sliced
4 anchovy fillets
1 egg
125 g/4 oz streaky bacon rashers
1 bay leaf

1. Make white sauce. Melt butter, stir in flour and cook 1 minute. Add milk gradually, stirring till it is thick, and boil gently for 2 minutes. Season with salt and pepper.
2. Trim skin and gristle from liver if necessary and cut into 2.5 cm/1 inch pieces.
3. Fry it quickly in butter, just to seal it. Put into liquidiser.
4. Add garlic, bacon pieces, apple, anchovy, egg and sauce to liver in liquidiser, with salt and pepper to taste. Switch on and blend till mixture is smooth.
5. Line a $\frac{1}{2}$ kg/1 lb loaf tin or oven dish with streaky bacon.
6. Pour in liver mixture and arrange bay leaf on top.
7. Cover closely (greaseproof paper and foil will do) and put it in a roasting tin half filled with water.
8. Cook in middle of a moderate oven, Gas 4, 350°F, 180°C, for 2 hours.
9. Remove from oven and roasting tin. Press the pâté with a weight on top until it is cold.
10. Turn out on a plate and serve in slices with salad, Melba Toast (*see page 21*) or hot toast and butter.

Anne Wallace
Stewarton, Ayrshire

MARY BERRY'S FARMHOUSE PÂTÉ

For this you need a liquidiser or food processor.

Serves 6 to 8

A sprig of parsley
6 rashers streaky bacon, de-rinded
1 egg
4 thin slices of yesterday's bread broken into pieces (without crusts)
4 tablespoons port or madeira, or if unavailable, sherry
225 g/8 oz chicken livers
1 clove garlic, peeled
225 g/8 oz pig's liver
$\frac{1}{8}$ level teaspoon freshly-ground black pepper
$\frac{1}{2}$ level teaspoon ground nutmeg
$\frac{1}{4}$ level teaspoon dried mixed herbs
$\frac{1}{2}$ level teaspoon dried marjoram
125 g/4 oz bacon trimmings, or streaky bacon, cut in small pieces
125 g/4 oz lard or bacon fat, melted
2 level teaspoons salt.

1. Well grease a 1.2 litre/2 pint ovenproof dish and put a sprig of parsley in the centre.
2. Stretch the 6 rashers of streaky bacon with the back of a knife on a board, then use them to line the base and sides of dish.
3. Put all the other ingredients into the liquidiser and reduce to pulp.
4. Pour pâté into prepared dish, cover tightly with a lid or foil. Place dish in a meat tin containing 1 cm/$\frac{1}{2}$ inch warm water and bake in a moderate oven, Gas 3, 325°F, 160°C, for 2$\frac{1}{2}$ hours.
5. Remove from oven and turn out of dish when cold.

SUSSEX FARMHOUSE PÂTÉ

Freezes well.

Serves 6 to 8

450 g/1 lb belly pork
225 g/8 oz bacon pieces
225 g/8 oz pig's liver
1 medium-sized onion

2 teaspoons chopped fresh herbs, such as parsley, thyme, sage, marjoram, etc., or 1 teaspoon mixed dried herbs
Salt and black pepper
125 g/4 oz wholewheat breadcrumbs

1. Remove all skin, white bones, etc., from pork and bacon and any pipes from liver.
2. Put meat through mincer twice with onion, herbs, seasoning and breadcrumbs.
3. Put the mixture into a greased $\frac{1}{2}$ kg/1 lb loaf tin. Cover with greaseproof paper and foil and place in a baking tin with enough water to come halfway up sides.
4. Bake in the centre of a slow oven, Gas 2, 300°F, 150°C, for 1$\frac{1}{2}$ to 1$\frac{3}{4}$ hours.
5. Do not strain fat or juices off but leave to get cold in tin with a weight on top.

Mrs Janice Langley
Shoreham-by-Sea, West Sussex

PÂTÉ OF GAMMON, PIG'S LIVER AND SAUSAGE

This pâté freezes well, but do not keep longer than a week or two: garlic does not freeze well and may give it an 'off' flavour.

Serves 6

225 g/8 oz raw gammon
225 g/8 oz sausage meat
1 clove garlic
$\frac{1}{2}$ teaspoon mixed herbs
1 teaspoon dried parsley
1 small onion
Black pepper
Salt
225 g/8 oz pig's liver
1 tablespoon brandy
125 g/4 oz streaky bacon rashers
3 bay leaves

1. Mince gammon coarsely and put in a large bowl.
2. Add sausage meat, crushed garlic and herbs. Stir together.
3. Add peeled and grated onion, with pepper and salt.
4. Mix together well.
5. Liquidise the liver with the brandy and add to mixture.

6. Mix it all up again really well.

7. Remove rinds from bacon and cut rashers into suitable strips to line a $\frac{1}{2}$ kg/1 lb loaf tin.

8. Spoon the mixture into the tin and lay the bay leaves on top.

9. Cover with greased, greaseproof paper and a piece of foil to hold it in place.

10. Stand loaf tin in a small roasting tin and pour in enough cold water to come half-way up sides.

11. Cook in the centre of a moderate oven, Gas 4, 350°F, 180°C, for 1$\frac{1}{2}$ hours.

Mrs Hylda Rodwell
Keighley, W. Yorkshire

COUNTRY LOAF

Serves 4 to 6

125 g/4 oz pig's liver
1 onion
2 sticks celery
75 g/3 oz wholemeal breadcrumbs
325 g/12 oz pork sausage meat
Salt
Pepper
1 clove garlic
1 egg-yolk

1. Cut liver into strips, place in a pan and pour boiling water over them. Simmer for 2 or 3 minutes. Then drain off water.

2. Peel onion and chop coarsely.

3. Cut up celery.

4. Mince liver, onion and celery.

5. Add breadcrumbs and combine with the sausage meat.

6. Add salt, pepper and crushed garlic. (To crush garlic, *see page 139*).

7. Bind with beaten egg-yolk and make sure it is thoroughly mixed.

8. Pack into a greased $\frac{1}{2}$ kg/1 lb loaf tin. Cover with greaseproof paper and foil.

9. Stand loaf tin in a small roasting tin and pour in cold water to come half-way up sides of tin. This is known as a water bath.

10. Cook in a moderate oven, Gas 4, 350°F, 180°C, for 1$\frac{1}{2}$ hours.

Serve cold, like pâté.

Mrs Edith Griffiths

PORK SPARE RIBS IN A BARBECUE SAUCE

This recipe makes a good first course with, say, 3 ribs per person. There is enough sauce for 4 people.

About 1 dozen meaty spare ribs of pork, split into singles.

SAUCE
300 ml/$\frac{1}{2}$ pint dry cider or dry home-made white wine
1 dessertspoon cornflour
2 tablespoons cold water
1 large teaspoon dry mustard
1 tablespoon soya sauce
1 level tablespoon brown sugar
125 g/4 oz tinned pineapple pieces, drained and cut in half

1. Cook the spare ribs. Either roast in a moderately hot oven, Gas 6, 400°F, 200°C, for 30 minutes until brown and crisp, or put them in a saucepan, cover with water and boil until meat is tender. Drain well and put ribs into a roasting tin or oven dish.

2. Heat cider. Slake cornflour with the water and add to pan. Stir as it thickens and cook for 2 minutes.

3. Mix mustard into soya sauce and add to pan with sugar and pineapple.

4. Pour sauce over spare ribs and put in oven to heat through, reducing temperature to moderate, Gas 4, 350°F, 180°C, for 15 minutes.

Best eaten with your fingers.

2
FISH

COCKLE CAKES

A recipe from Gwent where they are called Teisen Gocos.

Serves 4

4 dozen cockles in their shells, or 325g/12 oz
    shelled cockles, fresh or frozen
Salt
A little oatmeal
Deep oil for cooking

FOR THE BATTER
225 g/8 oz flour
A pinch of salt
2 tablespoons oil
1 egg, separated
300 ml/½ pint tepid water

TO SERVE
Brown bread and butter, lemon wedges

1. If the cockles are in shells stand them overnight in salted water sprinkled with oatmeal.
2. Next day, drain, scrub well, put in a saucepan with 1 teaspoon salt. Pour boiling water over to cover and boil cockles for 3 minutes. Then drain and leave to cool. If using shelled cockles, wash very well to remove grit and soak for 1 hour.
3. Meanwhile, start the batter. Put flour and salt in a basin, add oil, beaten egg-yolk and water. Beat well and leave in a cool place.
4. Remove cockles from shells.
5. Beat egg-white stiffly and fold it into batter.
6. Take 3 or 4 cockles at a time on a dessertspoon. Fill spoon with batter and drop into hot oil. Fry until golden.
7. Drain on kitchen paper.

Serve with brown bread and butter and lemon wedges.

Mrs Eileen Trumper
Llanvair Kilgeddin, Gwent

COD COOKED IN WINE WITH TOMATOES

Coley can also be used for this dish

Serves 4

450 g/1 lb ripe tomatoes, or 400 g/14 oz tin
1 clove garlic
½ level teaspoon salt
1 medium-sized onion
1 tablespoon oil
15 g/½ oz margarine
1 level tablespoon plain flour
4 tablespoons dry white wine or dry cider
1 tablespoon chopped parsley
4 cod steaks
Salt and Pepper Mix (*see page 17*)

1. If using fresh tomatoes, skin and slice them. (To skin *see page 139*.)
2. Peel garlic and crush it. (*See page 139.*)
3. Peel onion and slice thinly.
4. Heat 1 tablespoon oil with the margarine in a frying pan. Add onion and garlic and fry until onion is soft but not brown.
5. Stir in flour and let it sizzle a minute without browning.
6. Stir in wine or cider, tomatoes and 1 level tablespoon of parsley. Bring to the boil stirring, and transfer to a shallow, ovenproof dish.
7. Wash the cod steaks and pat dry. Arrange them on the tomato mixture.
8. Brush with oil and sprinkle on Salt and Pepper Mix.
9. Cover dish. A piece of greased, greaseproof paper will do.
10. Bake in centre of a moderately hot oven, Gas 5, 375°F, 190°C, for 25 to 30 minutes. Remove cover, sprinkle with remaining parsley and serve hot.

BAKED COD STEAKS

Serves 2

2 cod steaks, approx. 150 to 175 g/5 to 6 oz each
Salt and pepper
15 g/½ oz margarine
1 small, finely-chopped onion
25 g/1 oz fresh breadcrumbs
1 level teaspoon finely-chopped parsley
2 teaspoons lemon juice

TO ACCOMPANY
2 tomatoes
A little melted fat

1. Prepare 2 pieces of foil, each large enough to enclose a fish steak and to wrap securely. Grease them lightly.
2. Place one piece of cod on each square of foil, dust with salt and pepper.
3. Melt margarine, fry onion until softening—it can be lightly golden. Stir in crumbs, parsley and lemon juice. Divide into 2, place a portion in cavity of cod steak.
4. Wrap foil loosely round fish and secure edges. Place on ovenproof plate.
5. Bake in a moderate oven, Gas 4, 350°F, 180°C, for about 20 minutes.
6. Meanwhile prepare tomatoes. Make an incision around each tomato just below the middle. Brush with a little melted fat. Stand them upside down on the plate beside the fish and return to oven for 10 more minutes.

Serve with new or boiled potatoes.

HEREFORDSHIRE COD

Serves 4

450 g/1 lb cod fillet
8 medium-sized mushrooms
2 large tomatoes, halved
300 ml/½ pint strong cider
Salt and pepper
25 g/1 oz butter
25 g/1 oz flour
Creamed potato, optional
50 to 75 g/2 to 3 oz grated cheese

1. Cut the cod into four serving pieces and arrange in a greased ovenproof dish with the mushrooms and tomatoes.
2. Pour the cider slowly over the ingredients in the dish, and then season them with salt and pepper.
3. Bake for 15 minutes in a fairly hot oven, Gas 5, 375°F, 190°C.
4. Meanwhile, melt the butter, add the flour and cook for a few minutes.
5. Add the liquid from the fish, bring to the boil and cook gently for a few minutes.
6. Pour this sauce over the fish, and, if liked, pipe creamed potatoes round the edge of the dish.
7. Sprinkle with the grated cheese and brown under a hot grill.

Mrs A. Searle
Holme Lacy

SPANISH COD

A delicious dish for a special occasion.

Serves 4

4 cod steaks, allow 150 to 175 g/5 to 6 oz per
person

SAUCE
25 g/1 oz butter or good margarine
25 g/1 oz plain flour
150 ml/¼ pint white wine
150 ml/¼ pint water
Pepper and salt

TOPPING
50 g/2 oz chopped onion
1 tablespoon olive oil
50 g/2 oz sliced mushrooms
1 tablespoon chopped green pepper
2 tomatoes, peeled (*see page 139*), sliced and
seeds removed
50 g/2 oz prawns
1 tablespoon chopped parsley
Pepper and salt

1. Prepare a moderately hot oven—Gas 6, 400°F,
200°C.
2. Start with sauce. Melt butter or margarine over
low heat, stir in flour and let it sizzle for a minute.
Pour in wine and water gradually, stirring as it
thickens and let it boil gently for 3 minutes. Season
with pepper and salt.
3. Pour sauce into an oven dish. Use a dish in which
cod steaks will fit side by side.
4. Wash and dry fish and place on top of sauce.
5. Fry onion in oil till soft but not brown.
6. Add mushrooms and green pepper and continue
cooking for a moment longer until pepper starts to
soften.
7. Stir in tomato, prawns, parsley, pepper and salt.
Spread this topping over fish steaks.
8. Cover with a piece of greased paper and bake for
about 30 minutes. Test fish by using the point of a
knife in the centre of steaks. Fish loses its translucent
appearance when cooked.

Anne Wallace
Stewarton, Ayrshire

A TURBAN OF COD

Or Baked Cod and Egg Sauce but this dish looks so
good it needs a better name!

Serves 4

1 large cod fillet, about 675 g/1½ lb
Salt and pepper
Juice of 1 lemon
50 g/2 oz butter
50 g/2 oz flour
450 ml/¾ pint milk
2 hard-boiled eggs

GARNISH
Lemon slices
Parsley

1. Wash and dry the fillet of cod, sprinkle with salt
and pepper.
2. Coil the fish round into a turban shape with the
skin inside and place in a shallow ovenproof dish
just large enough to hold it, securing the 'turban' in
space with a wooden cocktail stick or skewer if necessary.
3. Brush the outside of the fish with a little of the
lemon juice.
4. Put into moderate oven Gas 4, 350°F, 180°C, and
cook for 20 to 25 minutes or until fish is tender.
5. Meanwhile make the sauce. Melt the butter, stir
in flour and allow it to sizzle a little. Add the milk,
season to taste with salt and pepper and continue
stirring until the mixture forms a thick smooth
sauce, cook for 2 minutes. Add strained lemon juice.
6. Remove the cooked fish from the oven, pour off
most of the liquor which will have formed in cooking.
7. Strain the liquor into the sauce. Stir until smooth
then add the roughly-chopped, hard-boiled eggs.
8. Pour a little of the egg sauce into the centre of the
'turban'. Serve the rest in a sauce boat.
9. Make a slit in each lemon slice, form into a cone
and place on top of the turban. Sprinkle with
chopped parsley and decorate with parsley sprigs.

FISH PUFFS AND A PIQUANT SAUCE

Serves 2

225 g/8 oz fresh or smoked cod or haddock
Milk and water

FOR THE FRITTER BATTER
125 g/4 oz plain flour, wholewheat or white
Pinch salt
1 tablespoon cooking oil
150 ml/¼ pint tepid water
1 tablespoon lemon juice
1 egg-white

1. Poach the fish in even quantities of milk and water sufficient almost to cover. Drain, then flake the fish.
2. Make the batter. Beat together flour, salt, oil, water and lemon juice. Leave 15 minutes, beat again, then fold in firmly whisked egg-white.
3. Stir in the fish.
4. Deep-fry in hot fat, dropping mixture in a dessertspoon at a time. Fry for about 3 minutes until golden. Drain on kitchen paper.

PIQUANT SAUCE
25 g/1 oz margarine
25 g/1 oz plain flour
¼ teaspoon Salt and Pepper Mix (*see page 17*)
300 ml/½ pint milk
2 teaspoons lemon juice
1 egg-yolk
Chopped parsley or capers (optional)

1. Melt margarine, add flour and seasonings, sizzle one minute.
2. Stir in milk, boil one minute.
3. Add lemon juice
4. Mix 2 tablespoons sauce into egg-yolk, return this to pan, hold over heat—do not boil.
5. Add chopped parsley or capers if desired.

Serve the sauce separately.

CRISP FISH BALLS

Serves 2

225 g/8 oz cooked and flaked fish
175 g/6 oz mashed potato
25 g/1 oz melted margarine
1 teaspoon lemon juice
½ teaspoon Salt and Pepper Mix (*see page 17*)
2 beaten eggs
1 tablespoon chopped parsley

1. Combine all ingredients.
2. Drop spoonfuls into deep hot fat. Cook until golden.

Serve with a piquant parsley sauce (*see below*).

A PIQUANT PARSLEY SAUCE

25 g/1 oz butter
25 g/1 oz flour
½ teaspoon Salt and Pepper Mix (*see page 17*)
300 ml/½ pint milk
1 teaspoon lemon juice
A nut of butter
2 tablespoons freshly-chopped parsley

1. Melt butter in saucepan, stir in flour and cook 1 minute.
2. Add salt and pepper and milk. Stir until boiling and cook 1 to 2 minutes.
3. Remove from heat, beat in lemon juice and a nut of butter. Stir in lots of parsley.

HADDOCK PUFFS

A Devonshire recipe. Very light and especially tasty with smoked fish. An economical alternative to scampi.

Serves 4 as a starter, 3 as a main course

225 g/8 oz haddock, fresh or smoked
150 ml/¼ pint milk
50 g/2 oz self-raising flour*
1 tablespoon chopped fresh parsley, 1 teaspoon dried Cayenne pepper
Salt
2 beaten eggs
Deep fat for frying

Wholewheat flour can be used. If you cannot get self-raising wholewheat mix in ¼ level teaspoon baking powder.

1. Poach fish in milk almost to cover. It will take 10 to 15 minutes depending on thickness of fish. Then drain fish, saving the liquid.
2. Flake fish in a basin with 2 tablespoons of the liquid. Mix in flour, parsley, Cayenne pepper and salt to taste. Salt will not be necessary with smoked haddock.
3. Mix in beaten egg and 2 to 3 tablespoons of the cooking liquid to make a soft consistency.
4. Deep-fry in hot fat, dropping mixture in a teaspoon at a time. Fry until golden brown, turning from time to time, about 3 to 4 minutes.

Serve very hot with brown bread and butter and tartare sauce (*see below*).

Mrs Becky Blackmore
Exeter, Devon

TARTARE SAUCE

300 ml/½pint mayonnaise (*see page 134*)
1 tablespoon chopped capers
1 tablespoon chopped cucumber
1 teaspoon chopped parsley
½ teaspoon chopped onion
1 teaspoon vinegar

Prepare mayonnaise then mix into it all the other ingredients.

FISH AND MUSHROOM PIE

Makes about 6 portions

275 g/10 oz rich pie pastry (*see page 204*)
125 g/4 oz mushrooms
150 ml/¼ pint water
450 g/1 lb white fish—e.g., cod, coley, haddock, whiting, etc.

BASIC WHITE SAUCE
50 g/2 oz butter or good margarine
50 g/2 oz flour
About 300 ml/½ pint milk
1 teaspoon chopped fresh tarragon, or ¼ teaspoon dried
Salt and pepper

1. Roll out two thirds of pastry to fit an 18 cm/7 inch pie plate and roll out the rest to fit top.
2. Stew mushrooms gently in the water in a covered pan for 5 minutes.
3. Drain liquid into a measuring jug. Slice mushrooms.
4. Meanwhile remove and discard skin and any bones from fish and cut it up into small pieces.
5. Now make the sauce. Melt butter or margarine over low heat, stir in flour and let it sizzle for a minute.
6. Add milk to mushroom liquid to make 450 ml/¾ pint. Add to pan gradually, stirring as it thickens and comes to boil. Let it bubble for 3 minutes.
7. Season sauce well with tarragon, salt and pepper.
8. Add fish and mushrooms to sauce. Allow to cool.
9. Fill the prepared pastry case. Damp edges and fit on lid pressing to seal. Do not make holes in top yet or filling may boil over and spoil top.
10. Bake near top of a moderately hot oven, Gas 6, 400°F, 200°C, for 45 minutes, moving pie to middle as it begins to brown. When it is done remove from oven and cut slits in top in one or two places, to let out steam and keep pastry crisp.

Serve hot or cold. Nice with green peas or beans.

Anne Wallace
Stewarton, Ayrshire

COLEY WITH A HOT CUCUMBER SAUCE

Coley is very like haddock but is dark in appearance when raw. It cooks easily and turns very white.

Serves 4

4 small fillets of fresh coley, skinned
About 300 ml/½ pint milk
A little lemon juice

SAUCE
1 small unskinned cucumber
Salt
A 150 ml/¼ pint carton of single cream
150 ml/¼ pint plain yoghurt
1 teaspoon caster sugar
Pepper

1. Put coley in a shallow pan, barely cover with milk and poach gently either under grill or on top of stove for 15 to 20 minutes until done.
2. Drain off milk and keep fish hot in a serving dish.
3. Meanwhile make sauce. Grate the entire cucumber coarsely. Spread out the pulp in a flat shallow dish. Sprinkle with salt and leave for 20 minutes. Strain.
4. Turn pulp into a small saucepan. Stir in cream and yoghurt. Add sugar and pepper.
5. When mixture starts to bubble turn it into a jug to serve separately with the fish.
6. Sprinkle chopped parsley and a squeeze of lemon over fish.

HADDOCK AND TOMATOES

With a crisp cheese topping

Serves 4

450 g/1 lb haddock fillets
Salt and Pepper Mix (*see page 17*)
2 teaspoons lemon juice
1 small onion, finely-chopped
4 tomatoes, skinned (*see page 139*) and sliced
2 tablespoons finely-grated cheese
4 tablespoons fresh breadcrumbs

1. Wipe and trim fillets, cutting into portions if too large, and arrange them in a shallow oven dish.
2. Sprinkle fish with salt, pepper and lemon juice.

3. Scatter onions on top and then make a layer of sliced tomatoes.
4. Mix together cheese and breadcrumbs. Sprinkle over tomatoes.
5. Cook at top of a moderate oven, Gas 4, 350°F, 180°C, for 30 minutes.

CIDERED HADDOCK CASSEROLE

Good with cod also.

Serves 4 to 5

450 to 675 g/1 to 1½ lb haddock or cod fillet, skinned
225 g/8 oz tomatoes, skinned (*see page 139*) and sliced
50 g/2 oz mushrooms
1 tablespoon chopped parsley
Salt and pepper
150 ml/¼ pint cider
2 tablespoons fresh white breadcrumbs
2 tablespoons grated cheese

1. Wipe the fish, cut into cubes and lay these in an ovenproof dish.
2. Cover with the sliced tomatoes and mushrooms, the parsley and seasonings and pour the cider over.
3. Cover with foil and cook in the centre of a moderate oven, Gas 4, 350°F, 180°C, for 20 to 25 minutes.
4. Remove from the oven, sprinkle with breadcrumbs and cheese, and brown in a hot oven, Gas 7, 425°F, 220°C, or under a hot grill.

Mrs Elspeth Foxton
Kirby Misperton, Yorkshire

HADDOCK AND PRAWN PILAFF

Serves 4

2 eggs
225 to 325 g/8 to 12 oz fresh haddock fillet
1 medium-sized onion
1 small red pepper, or 190 g/7 oz can of red peppers
25 g/1 oz butter or margarine
225 g/8 oz brown or white rice
About 600 ml/1 pint chicken stock (stock cubes will do)
1 level teaspoon ground turmeric
50 g/2 oz peeled prawns
75 g/3 oz sultanas
50 g/2 oz blanched almonds

1. Hard-boil the eggs for 12 minutes. Drain and cool in plenty of cold water.
2. Put haddock in a shallow pan and just cover with water. Poach gently (that is, bring to boil and allow just to simmer) for 5 to 10 minutes.
3. Peel and finely chop onion. Remove core and seeds from the fresh pepper and chop it finely. If using tinned peppers, discard liquid and cut them into neat pieces.
4. Strain liquid from fish into a measuring jug.
5. Melt butter or margarine in a large saucepan. Fry onion and fresh red pepper gently for 5 minutes until just softened, but not brown.
6. Add the rice, stir to prevent sticking and allow to cook for 2 to 3 minutes.
7. Add the fish liquid and most of the chicken stock. Add the turmeric.
8. Bring to the boil, then lower heat. Let it simmer for 12 to 20 minutes until rice is tender and has absorbed nearly all the liquid. Brown rice takes longer to cook than white and more stock may be required.
9. Remove skin and bone from fish and flake the flesh.
10. Shell and chop hard-boiled eggs.
11. Add tinned peppers, haddock, eggs, prawns, sultanas and almonds to rice and mix gently. Cook gently for about 5 minutes until heated through. Stir very carefully to prevent sticking and to avoid breaking up fish.

Serve at once.

CREAMED HADDOCK WITH MUSHROOMS

Serves 4 to 5

900 g/2 lb filleted fresh haddock
4 tablespoons dry white wine or dry cider
325 g/12 oz mushrooms
25 g/1 oz onion, chopped and parboiled
Parsley
65 g/2½ oz butter or margarine
15 g/½ oz flour
150 ml/¼ pint hot milk
Salt and pepper
Juice of ½ lemon
Red pepper
Paprika
50 g/2 oz grated cheese

TO SERVE
Boiled potatoes

1. Skin the fish and divide into 4 or 5 portions. Put into a shallow ovenware dish and pour on the wine or cider.
2. Wash the mushrooms, but do not peel them. Slice one good-sized mushroom and sprinkle it on fish.
3. Cover with a lid, or greased paper, and cook in a hot oven, Gas 8, 450°F, 230°C, for 15 minutes.
4. Fine-chop the rest of mushrooms and mix with the chopped onion and a dessertspoon of chopped parsley.
5. Melt 50 g/2 oz of the butter or margarine in a saucepan, add the mushroom mixture and cook gently for 2 to 3 minutes.
6. When fish is cooked keep it hot but strain off the juices for the sauce.
7. Now make the sauce. Melt remaining butter, add the flour and pour on gradually 150 ml/¼ pint of the fish juices and the hot milk. Simmer for 5 minutes, season to taste, stir in the lemon juice, a pinch of red pepper and a teaspoon of paprika.
8. Add the grated cheese. Reheat but do not boil.
9. Stir about 150 ml/¼ pint of this sauce into the mushroom mixture and cover the bottom of a shallow serving dish with it. Arrange the fish on top and coat with the remaining sauce. Sprinkle with grated cheese.

Serve surrounded with plain boiled potatoes, sprinkled alternately with chopped parsley and paprika. Garnish with sprigs of parsley.

SMOKED HADDOCK IN SCALLOP SHELLS

Or in a fish pie.

Serves 4

900 g/2 lb boiled and creamed potatoes
675 g/1½ lb smoked haddock
700 ml/1¼ pints milk
50 g/2 oz butter or margarine
50 g/2 oz flour
75 g/3 oz grated cheese, Parmesan and Cheddar mixed
Pepper and salt
125 g/4 oz lightly-cooked green peas

1. Prepare potatoes.
2. Cook haddock gently in the milk. Strain, saving milk for the thick white sauce.
3. Melt 40 g/1½ oz of the butter, stir in flour and sizzle for 1 minute.
4. Gradually add milk, stirring as sauce thickens. Cook 3 minutes.
5. Stir in 50 g/2 oz of the grated cheese. Remove from heat.
6. Meanwhile flake the haddock, removing skin and any bones.
7. Fold the haddock and peas into the thick white sauce and adjust the seasoning.

TO MAKE A FISH PIE
Pour the fish mixture into a greased pie dish and top with the creamed potato. Smooth the potato then score across in a rough pattern. Dot with remaining 15 g/½ oz butter. Sprinkle on remaining cheese and brown under the grill.

Reheat when required in a moderate oven, Gas 4, 350°F, 180°C, for about 30 minutes.

TO SERVE IN SCALLOP SHELLS
Using a piping bag with a large star nozzle, put in the potato and decorate the border of each shell generously with stars. Fill centre of shells with haddock mixture. Sprinkle on remaining cheese and dot potato with last 15 g/½ oz of butter.

Reheat near top of a moderate oven, Gas 4, 350°F, 180°C, for about 20 minutes.

FISH PIE

450 g/1 lb filleted haddock or cod, skinned and cut into serving pieces
1 tablespoon lemon juice or dry white wine
Salt and pepper
40 g/1½ oz margarine or butter
450 g/1 lb potatoes, weighed after peeling

FOR THE SAUCE
25 g/1 oz margarine
25 g/1 oz flour
½ teaspoon Salt and Pepper Mix (*see page 17*)
300 ml/½ pint liquid, the fish liquor made up with milk
75 g/3 oz grated cheese

TO GARNISH
2 or 3 tomatoes, skinned, sliced
A little melted margarine, about 15 g/½ oz

1. Lay fish in a greased, shallow dish just to fit in a single layer. Sprinkle on juice or wine, salt and pepper and dot with 15 g/½ oz of the margarine or butter.
2. Cover, foil will do, and cook in a moderately hot oven, Gas 5, 375°F, 190°C, for 15 minutes, or until cooked.
3. Meanwhile, boil the potatoes and mash them with ½ teaspoon salt and 25 g/1 oz margarine
4. When fish is cooked spoon off liquor into a measure and add milk to make up quantity to 300 ml/½ pint.
5. *Now make the sauce*. Melt margarine, add flour and cook for 1 minute.
6. Add salt and pepper. Stir in liquid. Bring to boil, stirring, and simmer for 2 minutes.
7. Beat in cheese. Do not let sauce boil again. Pour it over the fish.
8. Pipe potato round edge of fish.
9. Arrange tomato down centre. Brush potato and tomato with melted margarine.
10. Place dish under grill to tinge potato golden.

SMOKED HADDOCK PANCAKES

This dish could be made with other fish.

Serves 4

4 thin pancakes (*see page 182*)
225 g/8 oz smoked haddock
A little water

SAUCE
25 g/1 oz butter
25 g/1 oz wholewheat flour
300 ml/½ pint warm milk
2 tablespoons cream or top of the milk
Pepper
1 tablespoon finely grated cheese

1. Prepare pancakes and keep them warm.
2. Wash the fish well and poach it gently in a little water. Then remove skin and break fish into small flakes. Keep it warm.
3. *For the sauce:* melt butter in a pan, add flour and let it sizzle a minute. Add warm milk gradually and bring to the boil.
4. Let it simmer for 2 or 3 minutes then stir in cream and pepper to taste.
5. Pour half of this sauce into a jug to use later.
6. Mix fish into rest of sauce and fill the 4 pancakes.
7. Roll up the pancakes and lay them in a warmed ovenproof dish.
8. Pour remaining sauce over the pancakes, sprinkle on the cheese and put dish under a hot grill for 2 or 3 minutes to colour the top.

PILAFF OF SMOKED HADDOCK

Serves 4

325 g/12 oz smoked haddock
25 g/1 oz butter
1 tablespoon oil
1 onion, chopped
175 g/6 oz brown rice
1 green pepper, chopped
2 tomatoes, skinned (*see page 139*) **and chopped**
600 ml/1 pint chicken stock
1 teaspoon turmeric
Pepper
Chopped parsley

1. Trim fish, removing any skin and bone. Cut it into bite-sized pieces.
2. Melt butter in oil and fry onion lightly. When soft but not brown stir in rice and fry for a minute.
3. Add fish, green pepper, tomatoes, stock, turmeric and pepper.
4. Bring to boil, cover pan, lower heat and cook gently until rice is almost tender—about 20 minutes.
5. Sprinkle liberally with chopped parsley just before serving.

Anne Wallace
Stewarton, Ayrshire

SMOKED FISH AND EGG ON TOAST

A snack for 4 people but a smaller quantity could easily be made

325 g/12 oz smoked fish fillet
150 ml/¼ pint milk
150 ml/¼ pint water
2 eggs
25 g/1 oz butter or margarine
25 g/1 oz wholemeal or white flour
Black pepper
2 tablespoons chopped parsley
Pieces of freshly-toasted crisp wholemeal bread
Mustard and cress

1. Put fish in a saucepan, pour over it the milk and water. Bring to the boil, cover pan and simmer for 10 minutes.
2. Put eggs in water to boil for 10 minutes.
3. When fish is done, remove from liquid and flake into largish pieces. Save the liquid.
4. When eggs are done, plunge them into cold water and remove the shells. (Held under running cold tap the eggs will not burn your fingers while you shell them.)
5. Roughly chop eggs and put them with flaked fish.
6. Melt butter or margarine in a pan, add flour and let it sizzle for a minute without browning.
7. Stir in 150 to 300 ml/¼ to ½ pint of the fish liquid. Stir over low heat until sauce is thick and let it simmer 2 or 3 minutes.
8. Add fish, egg, a grating of black pepper and the parsley and heat gently.

Serve on or with crisply-toasted wholemeal bread and have mustard and cress with it.

KEDGEREE

Freezes well.

Serves 4

325 g/12 oz smoked haddock
300 ml/½ pint milk and water mixed
125 g/4 oz long grain brown or white rice
50 g/2 oz butter or margarine
A good shake of pepper
2 tablespoons cream or top of milk
2 hard-boiled eggs
Chopped parsley

1. Poach the haddock in milk and water until just beginning to flake. Drain.
2. Remove skin, and flake the fish roughly.
3. Cook rice in plenty of boiling, salted water until a grain will crush between the fingers. Do not overcook—12 minutes is usually enough.
4. Drain well in sieve, pour boiling water over rice to separate grains.
5. Mix into fish, with butter, pepper, cream, and 1 chopped egg. Heat through carefully, stirring. If a little firm add more cream or top of milk.
6. Pile into hot serving dish. Garnish with sliced egg and chopped parsley.

SAVOURY PUFFS

These are light and crisp with a moist centre. Good as a supper dish for 4 or 5 people or on cocktail sticks as hot savouries for a party.

Can be frozen

Makes 40 bite-sized puffs

Choux pastry, quantity given on *page 207*
About 175 g/6 oz flaked smoked fish or any
  canned fish
Deep fat to fry
Chopped parsley
Paprika pepper

1. Prepare choux pastry paste and mix fish into it.
2. When the fat is hot drop small teaspoons of mixture into it, turning if necessary, so that they brown evenly. They puff up as they cook.
3. When golden brown, remove with a draining spoon on to kitchen paper. Keep hot while cooking rest of puffs.

4. Pile on a hot dish, sprinkle with parsley and paprika pepper.

Anne Wallace
Stewarton, Ayrshire

HERRINGS IN OATMEAL

Serves 4

4 herrings
50 g/2 oz medium oatmeal
½ teaspoon of salt
25 to 50 g/1 to 2 oz butter
Juice of ½ lemon
Parsley

1. Clean and bone herrings. Dry.
2. Dip in oatmeal and salt.
3. Melt 25 g/1 oz of the butter in a pan, fry herrings about 3 minutes each side, adding the extra butter as necessary. Place on hot dish.
4. Add a little more butter to pan, heat until frothy, add the lemon juice, pour over fish and sprinkle with chopped parsley.

SOUSED HERRINGS

Serves 6

6 herrings
Salt and pepper
300 ml/½ pint mixed distilled malt vinegar and
  water
1 tablespoon mixed pickling spice
4 bay leaves
2 small onions cut into rings

1. Scale, clean and bone herrings.
2. Season well with salt and pepper.
3. Roll up fillets, skin inwards, from tail end.
4. Place neatly and fairly close together in an oven-proof dish.
5. Cover with vinegar and water mixture.
6. Sprinkle with pickling spice.
7. Garnish with bay leaves and onion rings.
8. Cover with baking foil or lid and bake slowly in a warm oven, Gas 2, 300°F, 150°C, for about 1½ hours.

WATERCRESS AND ORANGE SALAD WITH SOUSED HERRINGS

Watercress
Oranges
Soused herrings
French dressing (*see page 133*)

1. Wash watercress thoroughly, pat dry.
2. Remove peel and pith from 1 to 2 small oranges, cut them into thin slices and remove pips.
3. Arrange herrings down centre of dish, sliced oranges overlapping down each side.
4. Just before serving, dip sprigs of watercress in French dressing and arrange attractively at ends of dish and on orange slices.

JUGGED KIPPERS—A TIP

Place kippers head down in a heated deep jug and cover with boiling water. Cover with lid and stand in warm place for about 8 minutes. Drain well and serve with pat of butter.

KIPPER PASTE OR PÂTÉ

Makes a good pâté to start a meal, or a paste for sandwiches.

225 g/8 oz boneless kippers
Boiling water
125 g/4 oz butter or margarine, softened
1 tablespoon lemon juice
1 tablespoon grated onion
A good grating of black pepper

1. Place kippers in a large basin, cover with boiling water, leave 5 to 8 minutes.
2. Drain kippers, discard liquid. Remove skin and fin bones, if any, and flake the fish.
3. Add remaining ingredients, beat to a smooth consistency, tasting for seasoning. No salt is required, but use lots of pepper.
4. Place in small dish, fork over the top.

As a pâté, serve with toast or brown bread or small savoury biscuits and garnish with small pieces of tomato, lettuce or watercress.

See also Kipper Savoury, page 214.

MUSTARD HERRINGS

Serves 4

4 fresh herrings
Salt and freshly-ground black pepper
40 g/1½ oz butter
50 g/2 oz onion, finely-chopped

MUSTARD SAUCE
15 g/½ oz butter
15 g/½ oz flour
1 large teaspoon made English mustard
A pinch of sugar
300 ml/½ pint water
4 tablespoons milk
25 g/1 oz grated cheese

1. Scale, gut, wash and trim heads, tails and fins from herrings. Cut each one open from belly to tail. Press out flat, skin side uppermost, and press along backbone. Turn fish over and lift out backbone from tail to head.
2. Lay fish in a large flat oven dish, season with salt and pepper. Cover with foil or a lid.
3. Bake in a moderately hot oven Gas 6, 400°F, 200°C, for 15 to 20 minutes.
4. Meanwhile melt butter in a small pan and cook onions until tender. Set aside.
5. Take another pan to make the sauce. Melt butter, remove from the heat and beat in the flour and mustard.
6. Add sugar and blend in water gradually.
7. Return to heat and bring to boiling point. Simmer for 4 to 5 minutes, stirring often. Remove from the heat.
8. Add milk and half of the cheese.
9. Take dish out of oven, scatter cooked onion over herrings. Pour sauce over. Sprinkle with rest of cheese and brown under a hot grill.

MACKEREL BAKED WITH APPLES AND CIDER

Serves 3

3 small or medium-sized mackerel
150 ml/¼ pint dry cider
Salt and pepper
225 g/8 oz cooking apples
1 level tablespoon chopped parsley

1. Clean the mackerel thoroughly and wipe them.
2. Make 3 diagonal cuts in the flesh on each side of each fish.
3. Arrange fish in a shallow ovenproof dish. Pour over the cider and add a shake of salt and pepper.
4. Leave to soak for 3 hours in the cider marinade. Turn the fish over once.
5. Preheat oven to moderate, Gas 4, 350°F, 180°C.
6. Peel, quarter and core apples. Cut the quarters into small pieces.
7. Sprinkle apple pieces round the fish, pushing them down into the cider. Cover dish.
8. Put dish on centre shelf of oven and cook for 15 minutes.
9. Spoon the juices over fish and apple and return to oven for a further 10 to 15 minutes.
10. Sprinkle with parsley.

COLD SPICED MACKEREL

Serves 6

6 small mackerel
Salt and pepper
150 ml/¼ pint malt vinegar
150 ml/¼ pint water
½ level teaspoon pickling spice
2 bay leaves
1 medium-sized onion

The fishmonger might clean and fillet the mackerel for you. If not, follow instructions in Portland-style Mackerel, *see page 42*.

1. Sprinkle fish with a little salt and pepper.
2. Roll up fish from tail to head and place them close together in a fairly deep, ovenproof fish.
3. Pour over malt vinegar and water, then sprinkle with pickling spice and add bay leaves. Peel and slice onion and spread over fish.

4. Cover dish with a lid or greaseproof paper and foil and put in a cool oven, Gas 1, 275°F, 140°C, **for 1½ hours.**
5. Remove from oven and allow to cool in the liquid.

Serve with boiled potatoes or brown bread and butter.

FRESH MACKEREL SPICED IN CIDER

Serves 6

6 small mackerel
Wholewheat flour seasoned with salt and pepper
300 ml/½ pint apple juice, sparkling or still, or cider
½ level teaspoon pickling spice
2 bay leaves
1 medium-sized onion

1. To fillet the fish, follow instructions in Portland-style Mackerel (*see page 42*).
2. Sprinkle inside fish with a little seasoned flour.
3. Roll up fish loosely from tail to head and place them close together in a fairly deep oven dish.
4. Pour over apple juice or cider. Then sprinkle with pickling spice and add bay leaves. Peel and slice onion and spread over fish.
5. Cover dish with a lid or greaseproof paper and foil and put in a cool oven, Gas 1, 275°F, 140°C, for 1½ hours.
6. Remove from oven and allow to cool in the liquid.

Serve with boiled potatoes or brown bread and butter.

Sybil Norcott
Irlam, Nr Manchester

AUNT NELLIE'S MUSTARD SAUCE

May be kept in a covered jar in the fridge.

1 egg
1 level tablespoon dry mustard, or more if you like more 'bite'
1 level tablespoon sugar
4 tablespoons milk
4 tablespoons malt vinegar

1. Beat egg well in a basin.
2. Add mustard and sugar and mix well.
3. Add milk and vinegar. Mix all together.
4. Stand basin over a saucepan of simmering water. Do not let water touch basin. A double saucepan can be used instead.
5. Stir sauce until it thickens.

Serve with cold meats or with oily fish such as mackerel.

Miss Joan Parkinson,
Ovenden, Nr Halifax

PORTLAND-STYLE MACKEREL

Serves 4

4 fresh mackerel
Wholewheat flour, seasoned with salt and pepper

GOOSEBERRY SAUCE
225 g/8 oz gooseberries, fresh or frozen
30 ml/2 tablespoons water
50 g/2 oz sugar
25 g/1 oz butter
A pinch of nutmeg

1. If you have to bone mackerel yourself this is the way to do it. Gut and clean, removing head and tail. Cut open to backbone from belly to tail. Open out slightly and place on a board, cut side down. Bang with a rolling pin along the backbone until mackerel is flat. Turn fish over and backbone just pulls out, bringing most of the other bones as well. Pull out any long rib bones remaining. Trim off fins and tiny spines. Wash fish and pat dry.
2. Simmer gooseberries in the water until tender.

3. Put gooseberries through a sieve and then return purée to the pan.
4. Add sugar and stir well over gentle heat till it is dissolved.
5. Add butter and nutmeg and simmer for 5 minutes.
6. Dust mackerel with seasoned wholewheat flour.
7. Grill until golden brown, 4 to 5 minutes each side. Time varies according to size of fish.

Serve sauce separately.

John Firrell
Piddletrenthide, Dorset

PILCHARD CURRY

You can adapt this dish to include what you have available. Try 2 or 3 sticks celery instead of green pepper. Or add 2 tablespoons sultanas with the green pepper, or 2 tablespoons desiccated coconut or a little finely chopped crystallised ginger. Alternatively, sultanas, coconut and crystallised ginger may be served separately in little dishes.

Serves 2 or 3, but easy to make in smaller quantities.

2 medium-sized onions
1 tablespoon oil or 15 g/$\frac{1}{2}$ oz butter
1 tablespoon curry powder
1 green pepper
1 teaspoon curry sauce (optional)
Pinch of salt
A 400 g/15 oz can of pilchards in tomato sauce
1 tablespoon water, or wine if you have it

1. Peel and chop onions.
2. Heat oil or butter in a frying pan and fry onions for a minute or two.
3. Sprinkle curry powder over the onion and continue frying gently till onion is soft.
4. Remove core and seeds from the green pepper, chop up the flesh and add it to the pan.
5. Stir in the curry sauce and a small pinch of salt.
6. Tip the pilchards out of the can on top of the onion mixture.
7. Rinse out the can with a tablespoon of water or wine and pour over the fish. Cover pan and let the curry simmer until it is heated right through.

Serve with brown rice or white rice boiled with a pinch of turmeric.

Ann Bridger
Wallingford, Berkshire

PILCHARD CRUMBLE

Serves 2

A 155 g/5½ oz can of pilchards in tomato sauce
1 beaten egg
3 tablespoons milk
½ level teaspoon Salt and Pepper Mix (*see page 17*)

TOP
75 g/3 oz plain wholewheat or white flour
Shake of salt and pepper
40 g/1½ oz margarine
25 g/1 oz grated cheese

1. Remove bones and then place the pilchards in a pie dish and break them up lightly.
2. Mix egg, milk and Salt and Pepper Mix and pour over.
3. *For the top:* shake salt and pepper into flour and lightly rub in margarine. Mix in cheese. Sprinkle over fish.
4. Bake in a moderate oven, Gas 4, 350°F, 180°C for 20 minutes.

PILCHARD PIZZA

Serves 2

SCONE BASE
125 g/4 oz self-raising flour
Pinch of salt
40 g/1½ oz margarine
50 g/2 oz grated cheese
2 to 3 tablespoons milk

FILLING
1 small onion
50 g/2 oz mushrooms
15 g/½ oz butter or margarine
A 210 g/7½ oz can of pilchards in tomato sauce
50 g/2 oz grated cheese
1 skinned tomato (*see page 139*)

1. Sift flour and salt together.
2. Rub in margarine.
3. Mix in 50 g/2 oz of the grated cheese.
4. Add sufficient milk to make a soft but not sticky dough.
5. Roll out lightly, on a floured board, to fit a pie-plate.
6. *For the filling:* peel and finely chop the onion.
7. Chop mushrooms.
8. Melt 15 g/½ oz butter or margarine and fry onions for 2 or 3 minutes.
9. Add mushrooms and fry 2 or 3 minutes more.
10. Spread this mixture lightly over the scone base.
11. Then arrange pilchards nicely on top and pour sauce from tin over them.
12. Sprinkle with grated cheese.
13. Cut tomato into slices and place on top.
14. Bake in a moderately hot oven, Gas 5, 375°F, 190°C, for 20 to 25 minutes.

Mrs A.E. Phillips
Selsey, W. Sussex

PILCHARD SNACK

Serves 4

4 standard eggs
225 g/8 oz tomatoes
A 225 g/8 oz can pilchards in tomato sauce
Salt and pepper
75 g/3 oz Cheddar cheese, grated
Sprigs of watercress, to garnish

1. Hard boil eggs for 10 minutes; crack and leave to cool in cold water. Shell and cut in halves, lengthwise.
2. Meanwhile, skin tomatoes and cut into thin slices. (To skin *see page 139*).
3. Carefully lift egg-yolks out of whites with a teaspoon. Put them in a basin and mash with a fork.
4. Add contents of can of pilchards and mix well. Taste and season with salt and pepper.
5. Pile mixture into egg-whites and arrange on an oven-proof plate.
6. Place tomato slices, overlapping, around edge of plate. Sprinkle eggs and tomatoes with grated cheese.
7. Put under a moderately hot grill until cheese is bubbling and eggs are hot.

Garnish with sprigs of watercress.

PRAWN PILAFF

If you have a shallow pan suitable for frying and for the table, use it for this dish. Easy to make in an electric frying pan.

Serves 2 to 3

1 onion
1 green pepper
325 g/12 oz fresh tomatoes
300 ml/½ pint water
Pinch of salt
150 to 175 g/5 to 6 oz long grain brown or white rice
50 g/2 oz butter
125 g/4 oz peeled prawns
A little sugar
Black pepper

1. Peel and cut up onion.
2. Remove core and seeds from pepper and cut up flesh.
3. Skin tomatoes (to skin *see page 139*).
4. Chop half the tomatoes roughly. Cut the rest into thick slices.
5. Bring ½ pint water to boil in a saucepan, add salt and shower in the rice. Bring to the boil. Turn heat very low and cover pan. Allow to cook very gently: brown rice for about 25 minutes, white for about 12 minutes.
6. Meanwhile, using the oven-to-table pan, melt butter, add onion and green pepper and fry gently for 2 to 3 minutes until softening but not brown.
7. Add roughly chopped tomatoes and prawns. Season lightly with salt and black pepper. Cover and cook gently for 2 to 3 minutes.
8. Drain any liquid from the rice. Tip rice into the prawn mixture, forking it over gently to mix.
9. Arrange tomato slices in a circle on top and sprinkle them with a few grains of sugar and a little more black pepper. Cover and reheat gently (4 to 5 minutes should be enough).

Serve at once with green peas. Frozen peas may be added, for decoration, at same time as prawns or later with tomatoes.

SALMON MOUSSE

It is nice to use a fish-shaped mould for this.

Serves 4

A 212 g/7½ oz tin of salmon
1 dessertspoon tomato purée*
15 g/½ oz gelatine
2 tablespoons water
1 tablespoon vinegar
1 egg-white
A 175 g/6 oz tin of evaporated milk, refrigerated for 1 hour before using
1 teaspoon lemon juice

DECORATION
A little paprika pepper
1 stuffed olive
2 gherkins

*To keep tomato purée fresh, see page 84.

1. Lightly oil a suitable 1 litre/1½ pint mould.
2. Flake salmon, removing bones and dark skin. Mash it with tomato purée.
3. Using a small basin which will fit over a pan of very hot but not boiling water, put gelatine to dissolve in the water and vinegar. Stir once and leave until it becomes clear.
4. Whisk egg-white until firm.
5. In another bowl whisk cold evaporated milk until thick, adding lemon juice to help it thicken.
6. Stir gelatine into salmon. Fold in whisked milk, and then egg-white. Mix all together gently.
7. Pour into mould and leave 3 to 4 hours to set in a cool place. Goes a bit tough if it sets too quickly.
8. Turn out on to a flat dish. Sprinkle a little paprika pepper down the centre, place half a stuffed olive for the eye, and gherkins, sliced part-way and fanned out for fins.

See also Avocado and Salmon Mousse, page 25. Salmon and Cucumber Flan, page 213.

A GOOD IMITATION ASPIC JELLY

Gives a shining finish to pieces of cold chicken set out for a salad. Can also be used to top a savoury mousse by decorating with slices of cucumber and tomato and then covering with jelly to a depth of 7 mm/¼ inch. Spectacular used to coat a large salmon or ham for a special meal. Try it for Avocado and Salmon Mousse (*see page 25*), or Salmon Mousse (*see opposite*), Fresh Trout with Herb Mayonnaise (*see page 47*), Poached Chicken (*see page 57*).

For this you need 1 or 2 refrigerator trays of ice-cubes.

25 ml/1 fl oz water
25 g/1 oz gelatine
A 300 g/11 oz tin of consommé
3 tablespoons sherry
Juice of half a lemon
425 ml/¾ pint water

1. Put the 25 ml/1 fl oz of water in a cup or small bowl, sprinkle the gelatine over the surface.
2. Set the cup or bowl in a pan of warm water. Heat gently, stirring all the time until the gelatine dissolves.
3. In a pan mix consommé, sherry, lemon juice and 425 ml/¾ pint water. Stir over low heat until it is liquid.
4. Strain in the gelatine and stir.
5. Now stand pan on a baking tin full of ice. Stir until the aspic is syrupy. It is now ready to use.

SARDINE POTATO PIE

Serves 4

225 g/8 oz mashed potatoes
225 g/8 oz fresh tomatoes, or 1 small can
2 small onions
Large can of sardines
15 g/½ oz margarine
2 tablespoons chopped parsley
50 g/2 oz grated cheese
Pepper and salt

1. Prepare the mashed potatoes.
2. Skin and slice the tomatoes. (To skin *see page*

139.) If using tinned tomatoes, drain off excess liquid into a cup and chop them roughly.
3. Peel and grate onions.
4. Break up sardines into smaller pieces.
5. Grease a small pie dish with a little of the margarine.
6. Put a layer of tomato in bottom of dish, then a layer of sardine, a little onion, parsley, grated cheese and a sprinkling of salt and pepper.
7. Continue with similar layers till ingredients are used.
8. Spread mashed potatoes on top, mark with a fork and dot with margarine.
9. Bake in a moderately hot oven, Gas 6, 400°F, 200°C, for 30 minutes.

Mrs Reenie Lynn
Skegness, Lincolnshire

SAVOURY SARDINES

Serves 4

A 400 g/14 oz can of tomatoes
4 tablespoons oil
1 finely-chopped onion
1 level teaspoon mixed herbs
Salt and pepper
¼ teaspoon baking powder
175 g/6 oz self-raising wholewheat or white flour
Pinch of salt
40 g/1½ oz butter or margarine
About 5 tablespoons milk
1 tin sardines in oil
50 g/2 oz grated cheese

1. Heat the tomatoes gently in a pan. Drain through a sieve (save the juices to drink or for soup). Rinse the pan.
2. Place 1 tablespoon oil in the rinsed pan, add onion, cook until fairly soft but not brown (about 5 minutes). Add the tomatoes, herbs, salt and pepper. Keep warm.
3. Sieve baking powder into flour, add salt, rub in margarine, mix with milk to make a soft but not sticky dough.
4. Pat or roll into a circle to fit a large frying pan.
5. Heat remaining oil in frying pan, place in circle of dough, cook over medium heat to brown underside, about 5 minutes. Turn and cook a further 5 minutes.
6. Meanwhile prepare grill to medium heat.

7. Spread tomato mixture over cooked dough, arrange sardines like spokes of a wheel on top, sprinkling cheese between.

8. Place under grill to heat sardines and melt cheese.

9. Slide on to a warmed plate if you can or serve straight from pan.

Serve with green salad.

See also Kipper Savoury, page 214.

SOLE ON A BED OF PASTA SHELLS WITH PRAWNS AND CREAM SAUCE

Serves 4

125 g/4 oz butter
Salt and pepper
8 small fillets of sole
450 ml/¾ pint milk
175 g/6 oz pasta shells
50 g/2 oz flour
4 tablespoons dry sherry
150 ml/¼ pint single cream
1 teaspoon anchovy essence or sauce
50 to 125 g/2 to 4 oz frozen prawns

TO GARNISH
2 tomatoes, lemon slices

1. Use 50 g/2 oz of the butter and divide it into 8 little pieces.

2. Shake a little salt and pepper on each fish fillet and roll it up around a piece of butter.

3. Place fish in an oven dish. Pour round 150 ml/¼ pint of the milk. Cover dish with greased paper or foil.

4. Cook in middle of a moderate oven, Gas 4, 350°F, 180°C, for about 20 minutes until fish is cooked.

5. Meanwhile, put pasta on to cook in slightly salted boiling water, allowing for it to be done when fish comes out of oven.

6. Then make a roux of remaining butter and flour. This means melting butter in a pan, stirring in flour and allowing it to sizzle for 1 minute without browning.

7. Stir in remaining milk and then liquid from fish. Stir over low heat until thick, and boil for 2 minutes.

8. When fish is done lift it carefully out of dish on to a plate for a moment.

9. Drain pasta and put it in fish dish. Set fish on top and keep it warm.

10. Return to the sauce. Add sherry, cream, anchovy essence and prawns. Bring it back to boiling point so that prawns are well heated.

11. Pour sauce over fish and garnish with slices of tomato and lemon.

Anne Wallace
Stewarton, Ayrshire

TROUT STUFFED WITH MUSHROOMS

Serves 4

4 fresh river trout
225 g/8 oz mushrooms
1 medium-sized onion
40 g/1½ oz butter
2 tablespoons chopped parsley
Salt and pepper
2 lemons
Extra parsley, to garnish

1. Heat the oven to moderate Gas 4, 350°F, 180°C.

2. Cut along the belly of the fish and remove intestines (or ask the fishmonger to do this for you). Wash fish thoroughly.

3. Clean mushrooms and chop finely.

4. Peel onion and chop finely.

5. Melt butter in a frying pan, add onion. Fry until soft but not brown, about 3 minutes.

6. Add mushrooms and cook for 2 minutes longer.

7. Stir in chopped parsley and seasoning.

8. Strain contents of pan through a sieve and save liquid for later.

9. Divide mushroom mixture into 4 and stuff fish.

10. Place fish on individual pieces of foil lined with greased, greaseproof paper.

11. Mix mushroom liquid and juice of 1 lemon and pour it over the fish. Add seasoning to taste.

12. Close the foil securely round the fish and put the packages into a shallow roasting tin.

13. Bake in a moderate oven Gas 4, 350°F, 180°C, for 25 to 30 minutes.

14. When cooked, unwrap and serve on a large dish, garnished with lemon wedges and parsley sprigs.

FRESH TROUT WITH HERB MAYONNAISE

A liquidiser is needed.

Serves 4

4 fresh trout, about 275 g/10 oz each
Wine vinegar
Salt

MAYONNAISE
A bundle of fresh herbs, parsley, chervil (or fennel), chives, tarragon, spinach and water-cress (or sorrel), about 50 g/2 oz herbs altogether
1 very small onion or small shallot, very finely chopped
2 anchovy fillets
1 dessertspoon capers
1 small pickled gherkin
1 hard-boiled egg-yolk
1 fresh egg-yolk
1 teaspoon lemon juice
25 ml to 50 ml/1 to 2 fl oz sunflower oil
Salt and freshly-ground pepper

TO GARNISH
Lettuce, cucumber slices

1. Leave heads and tails on trout, gut them, wash and wipe out with salt and kitchen paper.
2. Take a large pan, big enough to lay trout out flat. Try them for size and cover with water.
3. To each pint of water add 1 tablespoon vinegar and $\frac{1}{2}$ teaspoon salt. Now remove trout.
4. Bring water to the boil, then slip in each trout. Bring back to the boil and at once remove pan from heat. Allow the trout to get quite cold in the pan of stock.
5. *Now for the mayonnaise.* Wash herbs.
6. Chop the onion or shallot very finely and put it in a pan of boiling water. Boil for 1 minute. Drain into a sieve and run under tap.
7. Put herbs, onion, anchovy fillets, capers, gherkin, both egg-yolks and lemon juice into a liquidiser.
8. Liquidise for 10 seconds at high speed. Then start to dribble in the oil, a little at a time until the mixture thickens and emulsifies.
9. Season with salt and pepper and more lemon juice if necessary.
10. Lift cold trout out of stock. Pat dry and lay it on a nice dish with lettuce and cucumber.
11. Serve mayonnaise separately, giving each person a little pot.

COLD TROUT WITH CUCUMBER SAUCE

Serves 4

4 Rainbow trout
1 lemon
1 bay leaf
Sprig of parsley, sprig of fresh thyme and a few peppercorns
Slice of onion and of carrot

SAUCE
$\frac{1}{2}$ small cucumber
Salt and pepper
150 ml/$\frac{1}{4}$ pint natural yoghurt

1. Clean out the trout, trim the tails but leave the heads on. Wash well.
2. Cut a wedge from the lemon and place it with the bay leaf, parsley, thyme, peppercorns, onion and carrot in a shallow pan. Add water to a depth of 4 cm/$1\frac{1}{2}$ inches.
3. Bring to the boil, cover and simmer for 2 to 3 minutes.
4. Add trout, cover and poach gently for 5 minutes. Remove pan from heat and leave trout to cool in the stock.

TO MAKE THE SAUCE
5. Peel and finely dice the cucumber.
6. Cover with a plate and leave to stand for 15 to 20 minutes.
7. Drain off excess water.
8. Stir cucumber into the yoghurt and add seasoning to taste.

TO SERVE THE DISH
9. When trout is quite cold, remove it from liquor, drain and arrange on a serving dish.
10. Cut rest of lemon into wedges and use to garnish the fish.
11. Serve sauce separately.

TUNA FISH CASSEROLE

For 2 people, or can be served in ramekins as a starter for 6.

1.2 litres/2 pints water
Salt
125 g/4 oz wholewheat pasta
A 100 g/3½ oz can of tuna fish
1 tin of condensed cream of mushroom soup
50 g/2 oz butter
Pepper
A squeeze of lemon juice (optional)
1 tablespoon chopped parsley

1. Bring the water to the boil. Add a little salt, then the pasta, and bring back to simmering point. Stir to make sure pasta is not sticking together (a little oil added to the water will help), then partly cover the pan and simmer for 7 minutes or more. Cooking time will depend on the type of pasta you use. It should be not quite done when you drain it.
2. Meanwhile, remove bones from the fish and flake the meat.
3. Drain the pasta and add to it the fish with the soup, butter, pepper and lemon juice. Mix well. Taste for seasoning and return pan to heat.
4. As soon as it is hot stir in most of the chopped parsley. Turn the mixture into a warmed oven dish and brown it under the grill.

Sprinkle the rest of the parsley on top just before serving.

Anne Wallace
Stewarton, Ayrshire

TUNA TART

Serves 4

225 g/8 oz self-raising flour
½ level teaspoon salt
40 g/1½ oz butter or margarine
150 ml/¼ pint milk
190 g/7 oz can of tuna fish
2 teaspoons vinegar
225 g/8 oz tomatoes, fresh or tinned
75 g/3 oz grated Lancashire cheese
Stuffed olives (optional)

1. Sift the flour and salt into a bowl.
2. Rub in the butter or margarine until mixture is like fine breadcrumbs.

3. Mix to a soft dough with the milk.
4. Roll out on a floured board to 25 cm/10 inch round and lay this on a lightly-greased baking sheet, or use a loose-based flan tin of the same size. However, as this is like a pizza, roll dough to fit bottom only, not sides.
5. Drain oil from tuna, break it up and mix in vinegar.
6. Skin tomatoes (*see page 139*) and slice. If using tinned tomatoes, drain well before slicing.
7. Arrange the tomato slices on top of dough. Then cover with tuna.
8. Sprinkle on the cheese and decorate the top with sliced, stuffed olives.
9. Bake in a moderately hot over, Gas 6, 400°F, 200°C, for 30 minutes.

Eat hot.

Sybil Norcott
Irlam, Nr Manchester

See also Tuna Plait, page 215.

WHITING WITH MUSHROOMS

Quick to make.

Serves 2 or 3, but can be made in any quantity

40 g/1½ oz butter
3 or 4 fillets of whiting
50 g/2 oz mushrooms, sliced
1 tablespoon chopped fresh parsley
25 to 50 g/1 to 2 oz fresh breadcrumbs

WHITE SAUCE
15 g/½ oz butter or margarine
15 g/½ oz flour
150 ml/¼ pint milk
Salt and pepper

1. Start with sauce. Melt the 15 g/½ oz butter or margarine, stir in the flour and let it sizzle for 1 minute.
2. Gradually add milk, stirring as it thickens. Then cook for 2 minutes. Season to taste with salt and pepper.
3. Use some of the 40 g/1½ oz butter to grease an oven dish. Melt rest of butter in a pan.
4. Spread white sauce in dish.

5. Lay whiting fillets on sauce. Cover with mushrooms, and pour over melted butter.

6. Sprinkle parsley over mushrooms and finish with a layer of breadcrumbs.

7. Bake in a moderately hot oven, Gas 5, 375°F, 190°C, for 15 to 18 minutes.

MERLAN PUDDING

Merlan or merling is another name for whiting.

Serves 2

You need a 600 ml/1 pint pudding basin or plain mould.

125 g/4 oz cooked whiting
50 g/2 oz fresh white breadcrumbs
Salt and pepper
1 teaspoon grated lemon rind
150 ml/¼ pint milk
50 g/2 oz butter
1 beaten egg
1 teaspoon chopped parsley
Parsley sauce (*see below*)

1. Flake the fish and put it in a bowl.

2. Mix in the breadcrumbs, salt, pepper and lemon rind.

3. Heat milk in a small pan with 40 g/1½ oz of the butter, but do not let it boil. Pour over fish mixture.

4. Add beaten egg and mix well.

5. Grease the pudding basin or mould with the last 10 g/½ oz butter. Sprinkle parsley in bottom of basin.

6. Spoon mixture into the basin. Cover with a piece of greased, greaseproof paper pleated across middle. Put over this, loosely, a sheet of foil and press it firmly under rim of basin.

7. Steam pudding for 45 minutes to 1 hour. If you do not have a steamer, stand basin on a trivet or upturned saucer in a saucepan. Pour in enough boiling water to come halfway up sides of basin. Keep water on the boil and replenish with more boiling water if necessary.

8. Turn pudding out on to a warmed dish and serve with parsley sauce.

PARSLEY SAUCE
25 g/1 oz butter
25 g/1 oz flour
½ teaspoon Salt and Pepper Mix (*see page 17*)
300 ml/½ pint milk
1 teaspoon lemon juice
A nut of butter
2 tablespoons chopped fresh parsley

1. Melt butter in saucepan, stir in flour and cook 1 minute.

2. Add salt and pepper and milk. Stir until boiling and cook 1 to 2 minutes.

3. Remove from heat, beat in lemon juice and a nut of butter. Stir in the parsley.

See also Chapter 7 for Smoked Haddock and Cottage Cheese Flan, Salmon and Cucumber Flan, Tuna Plait.

3

POULTRY
GAME
AND
RABBIT

TO PLUCK POULTRY AND GAME

POULTRY

This is best done as soon after killing as possible, because the feathers are more easy to pull before the flesh stiffens. There is no quick way: the feathers must be pulled out a few at a time until the job is done. You can plunge the bird into hot (not boiling) water for about one minute and then pluck it at once. But do not leave it long in the water as the skin becomes tender and may be torn as the feathers are pulled. Sometimes fine hairs remain and these can be removed by singeing. A lighted taper does the job efficiently. Move it quickly over the body so as not to scorch the bird.

GAME

Game, such as pheasant and grouse, has tender skin that is easily torn. Be particularly careful over the breast.

TO CLEAN AND TRUSS POULTRY OR GAME BIRDS

1. To remove leg sinews, make a circular incision about 2.5 cm/1 inch below the hock joint, taking care not to cut into the sinews. Break the legs and pull off the feet (a loop of strong twine may help here).
2. Trim the extreme portions of the wings.
3. Place the bird on the table breast down and head away from you. With the finger and thumb take up the skin between the shoulders, cut a strip of skin about 12 mm/½ inch wide from that point to half-way up the neck. Sever the neck-bone at the shoulder and the skin half-way up the neck.
4. Remove the crop and wind-pipe.
5. Put your finger in the opening and by circular movement loosen the lungs and other organs.
6. Place the bird neck down, grasp the tail in one hand. Then take the knife and make an incision mid-way between the tail and the vent. Cut around the vent. Place the bird back down and tail towards you, feel inside and remove the fat around the abdomen. Then feel for the gizzard—it will be something firm to grasp—and draw gently. All the internal organs will come out.
7. Save the neck, gizzard, liver and heart for stock. These should be wrapped in greaseproof paper. The gizzard should be split, emptied and the inner tough skin peeled off. Take care not to break the gall bladder, a tiny greenish bag, in removing the liver.
8. Clean the bird thoroughly with a damp cloth or kitchen paper.
9. *To tie up.* Fold the flap of skin over the back and fold the wings back over this.
10. Take a trussing needle threaded with strong white string about 45 cm/18 inches long. With back downwards pull the legs back towards the head and press down firmly. Pass the needle through the body where the legs join the body.
11. Then turn the bird over and pass the needle through the joint of one wing, across the back of the bird and through the other wing. Now tie the two strings and cut off.
12. With the back downwards again, and keeping the tail towards you, pass the needle and thread through the loose skin underneath and near the tip of the breast bone. Leave the string above the legs. Turn the bird on its breast. The two ends of string are then brought round the legs, crossed and tied tightly round the tail. The trussing complete, strings should not be cut to stuff the bird. All stuffings can be put in at the neck end.

TO JOINT A CHICKEN

Utensils if you don't have secateurs: a sharp knife, a 450 g/1 lb weight or similar hard object to help knock the knife through.

1. Cut the chicken in half lengthways through breast bone and then the backbone.
2. To obtain four joints, cut each half diagonally, between the leg and the wing, (upwards from the leg).
3. If six joints required divide drumstick from thigh.
4. With a large chicken the wing joint can be removed with a little breast meat.

TO BONE POULTRY

A sharp knife is essential.

1. Cut down the centre of the back of the bird from neck to tail.
2. Taking first one side of the bird, cut and work the flesh off the bones. Take care not to puncture the skin.

3. Work down the leg. To facilitate pulling the drumstick bone through, cut off at the joint any remaining lower limb.

4. Work down the shoulder in the same way as the leg.

5. Continue working flesh off until the centre breast bone is reached.

6. Now repeat the process on the other side of the bird from back bone round to breast bone.

7. When all the flesh is loose and ready to be lifted right off the carcass, take care not to cut through the skin at the edge of the breast bone where it is thin. Use the carcass to make stock.

BASIC STUFFING FOR POULTRY AND MEAT

This can be made in bulk and frozen without its main seasoning or flavouring ingredients.

675 g/1½ lb onions
325 g/12 oz fresh breadcrumbs, wholewheat or white
50 g/2 oz butter or margarine
50 g/2 oz shredded suet
2 lemons
1 beaten egg
Salt and pepper

A variety of flavourings, some of which combine well with each other:

Chopped prunes, soaked in water overnight
Chopped apricots, soaked overnight
Chopped apples
Chopped celery
Chopped herbs like sage, parsley, marjoram, thyme, etc.
Chopped nuts

1. Peel and finely chop onions, fry in butter until soft.

2. Cool, mix with the rest of the ingredients. Season well.

3. Divide into four: freeze in separate bags.

4. To use, defrost and add the selected flavouring ingredients. The stuffing is then ready to use.

TO MAKE BREADCRUMBS

1. Lay slices of stale bread in a dry roasting tin and place in the bottom of the oven while something else is cooking. Remove when dry and brittle.

2. Now crush, using a rolling pin.

If really well dried they should keep in airtight jars for months.

Use for coating fish, chicken, rissoles, etc., before either shallow or deep frying.

Fresh breadcrumbs are made from semi-fresh bread using an electric coffee grinder, blender or food processor. Or by hand with a grater. Most sliced bread is unsuitable because of its foam plastic nature.

Keep in a fridge for a few days.
Freeze well.

For stuffings, treacle tart, etc.

CHICKEN, BONED, STUFFED AND ROAST

A 1.3 kg/3 lb chicken, boned (*see page 51*)

Serves 4 to 6

THE STUFFING
450 g/1 lb pork sausage meat
1 tablespoon finely chopped parsley
2 chopped shallots (or 1 small onion, finely chopped)
2 tablespoons stock, or wine

Mix all together.

GARNISH
4 hard-boiled eggs
Trim a little off the ends so that they will lie close.

TO STUFF THE BONED BIRD
1. Spread the bird out on a board, skin side down.

2. Stuff the legs and shoulders with a little of the stuffing mixture.

3. Spread half the stuffing down the centre of the bird. Place the eggs down the centre end to end. Cover with remaining stuffing.

4. Shape the bird again and stitch with fine string.

5. Wrap in tin foil with a little stock and cook in a moderately hot oven, Gas 5, 375°F, 190°C, allowing 20 minutes to the ½ kg/1 lb stuffed weight, plus a further 20 minutes.

May be eaten hot, in which case open foil 30 minutes before end of cooking time to allow to brown.

FOR EATING COLD
COATING SAUCE
50 g/2 oz butter
50 g/2 oz flour
450 ml/¾ pint milk
Salt and pepper
2 tablespoons top of the milk, or cream
150 ml/¼ pint water
25 g/1 oz gelatine

1. Melt the butter, add flour and allow to sizzle without browning 1 to 2 minutes to cook the flour.
2. Pour on milk. Stir until boiling. Simmer 1 to 2 minutes stirring continuously.
3. Dissolve gelatine in the water. Reserve one tablespoon of it in a cup and add the rest to the sauce with cream and seasoning.
4. Put through a fine sieve, or even a clean, damp tea cloth, to be sure sauce is smooth. Stir frequently whilst cooling to keep the sauce smooth and velvety. When the consistency of thick cream, it is ready for coating.

DECORATION
Any colourful vegetables, peels, etc. (Carrot, cucumber skin, lemon/orange peel, gherkin, olives.)
1. When the bird is cold, remove strings and skin.
2. Place on a wire tray over a dish. Pour over the coating sauce. Allow to set. Give another coating if necessary, (sauce may need rewarming for this.)
3. Decorate with small cuttings of colourful vegetables, peels, etc., first dipping the pieces in a little dissolved gelatine which will stop them slipping off.

PARSLEY AND LEMON STUFFING

Very good with chicken.

50 g/2 oz butter
Finely-grated rind and juice of one lemon
75 g/3 oz fresh brown or white breadcrumbs
4 tablespoons finely-chopped parsley
Pinch of thyme or marjoram
Salt and freshly milled pepper

1. Melt butter in a saucepan over a low heat and add lemon juice.
2. Put all the other ingredients into a basin and mix well.

3. Stir in lemon juice and melted butter until it is well incorporated and the stuffing is moist.
4. Spoon into breast or body of bird.

CHICKEN AND ALMONDS

Serves 4 to 6

1 boiling fowl, or roasting chicken, jointed
600 ml/1 pint water
4 tablespoons oil
2 small onions
2 small carrots
2 bay leaves
2 sprigs of thyme
3 or 4 peppercorns
Pinch of salt
Slice of lemon including peel
125 g/4 oz blanched almonds
3 sticks celery
125 g/4 oz mushrooms
1 good clove of garlic
Small piece of fresh ginger
1 dessertspoon soya sauce
1 dessertspoon dry sherry
1 dessertspoon cornflour
Salt
Black pepper
Spring onions and finely chopped parsley or fresh coriander, to garnish

1. Put giblets, neck and wing tips in a pan with water. Cover and simmer gently to make stock.
2. Heat 2 tablespoons oil in a heavy pan and brown the chicken joints all over.
3. Add 1 peeled onion, 1 scrubbed carrot cut into quarters, a bay leaf, a sprig of thyme, peppercorns, salt and slice of lemon and pour in a cupful of the stock. Put on a well-fitting lid.
4. Bring slowly to the boil and let the chicken steam in the stock till tender. If it is a boiling fowl it may take an hour, depending on its age. If it is a young roasting chicken, 30 to 40 minutes may be enough.
5. Take joints out of pan and remove the flesh.
6. Return the bones to the pan of stock, add fresh onion and carrot and herbs. Continue cooking until stock is rich.
7. Meanwhile, prepare the other ingredients. Cut almonds in slices. Slice the celery. Cut mushrooms in half or quarters. Crush the garlic. Chop the ginger finely.

8. Heat 2 tablespoons oil in pan and fry almonds until golden brown. Lift them out of the fat on to a paper bag to drain.

9. Toss celery and mushrooms, garlic and ginger in the fat for a minute or two.

10. Add soy sauce and sherry. Then add chicken flesh and one strained cupful of the chicken stock. Cook over moderate heat for 5 minutes.

11. Put cornflour in a cup and blend it with a little chicken stock. Add this to the chicken and stir as it thickens. Add almonds. Season with a little more salt if necessary, and some freshly-milled black pepper.

12. Serve at once. Do not overcook at this stage. Garnish with spring onions and finely-chopped parsley or fresh coriander.

Serve with Indian Fried Rice (*see page 173*).

Betty Yeatman
Adelaide, South Australia

SIMPLE BARBECUED CHICKEN

This dish freezes well.

Serves 4

4 chicken joints
1 tablespoon oil
40 g/1½ oz butter
1 onion, chopped
2 dessertspoons tomato purée
2 level teaspoons Barbados sugar
1 teaspoon prepared mustard
1 teaspoon Worcestershire sauce
1 level teaspoon salt
Black pepper
Juice of half a lemon
150 ml/¼ pint water

1. Dry the chicken joints and fry in oil and 25 g/1 oz of the butter until nicely browned. Lift out into a casserole.

2. Add remaining butter to pan and lightly fry onion until soft and golden.

3. Add all remaining ingredients and simmer for 5 minutes. Pour over chicken.

4. Cover casserole and cook in a moderate oven, Gas 4, 350°F, 180°C, for 1 hour.

Judith Adshead
Mottram St Andrew, Cheshire

DOROTHY SLEIGHTHOLME'S CHICKEN WITH APPLE

For this you need a large sauté or frying pan with a good lid.

An electric frying pan is ideal.

The dish can be cooked in a covered casserole in the oven, transferring contents of frying pan after each stage. The cooking time for this method is 35 to 40 minutes in a moderately hot oven, Gas 5, 375°F, 190°C.

Serves 4 to 6

2 level tablespoons plain flour
1 level teaspoon salt
⅓ level teaspoon pepper
1 jointed chicken
50 g/2 oz bacon fat, butter or lard
1 large sliced onion
1 large carrot, cut in rings
2 sharp eating apples, peeled, cored and cut into quarters
225 g/8 oz peas
300 ml/½ pint cider (or sharp apple wine)
150 ml/¼ pint chicken stock (from giblets, *see page 10*)

1. Mix flour, salt and pepper on a plate and coat joints well in it.

2. Heat fat in large sauté or frying pan until quite hot; brown joints all over, turning once or twice (about four minutes).

3. Add onion and carrot coated in rest of flour, turn over in pan for one minute. Push aside.

4. Place apple quarters, and peas if fresh, in the pan. Pour over the cider or apple wine. This will sizzle. Add stock, allow to boil and reduce heat until simmering.

5. Cook 30 minutes with lid on. Frozen or tinned peas (well drained) can be added now. Cook another 10 minutes.

Arrange on a hot dish, sprinkle chicken with chopped parsley and arrange triangles of toast round edge. Or serve with new potatoes tossed in butter.

CHICKEN CASSEROLE

Freezes well.

Serves 4

65 g/2½ oz butter or margarine
4 chicken joints
1 onion, finely-chopped
2 sticks celery, finely-chopped
225 g/8 oz long grain brown or white rice
A 400 g/14 oz tin of tomatoes
600 ml/1 pint stock
1 teaspoon mixed herbs
1 level teaspoon sugar
125 g/4 oz mushrooms, sliced

1. Heat 50 g/2 oz of the butter or margarine and brown the chicken joints. Lift them out of fat into a casserole.
2. Fry onion, celery and rice gently for 3 to 4 minutes.
3. Stir in tomatoes, stock, herbs and sugar. Bring to the boil, stirring.
4. Pour rice mixture over chicken. Cover the casserole and cook in a moderately hot oven, Gas 6, 400°F, 200°C, for 1 hour.
5. Heat remaining butter and fry mushrooms quite briskly for 2 minutes. Add to casserole.

COUNTRY CHICKEN CASSEROLE

Serves 4

50 g/2 oz bacon dripping, lard or butter
4 rashers streaky bacon
1 medium-sized, sliced onion
1 level tablespoon flour
1 level teaspoon Salt and Pepper Mix (*see page 17*)
4 chicken joints
125 g/4 oz pork sausage meat
225 g/8 oz tinned tomatoes
½ teaspoon oregano, marjoram or mixed herbs
150 ml/¼ pint stock (if necessary)
Chopped parsley

1. Melt 25 g/1 oz of the fat and fry chopped bacon and onion for a few minutes. Drain into a casserole, leaving fat in pan.

2. Mix flour and Salt and Pepper Mix, dust chicken joints well. Put them into the frying pan skin side down, using extra dripping only if necessary. Fry joints turning them over in pan until they are golden. Put them into casserole.
3. Divide sausage meat into 8 small balls, roll in the seasoned flour and fry briskly to seal and brown. Place in between joints in casserole.
4. Measure fat in frying pan. Remove some or add a little so that there is just 1 tablespoon. Add remaining flour.
5. Stir to cook flour 1 minute, then add tin of tomatoes, herbs and as much stock as necessary to make a thick sauce. Stir until boiling.
6. Pour over chicken, cover and cook in a moderate oven, Gas 4, 350°F, 180°C, for about 1 hour until chicken is cooked. Sprinkle with parsley and serve from casserole with plain boiled or new potatoes.

CHICKEN FAVOURITE

Serves 4

A 1.5 kg/3½ lb chicken with giblets

STUFFING
25 g/1 oz butter
50 g/2 oz chopped onion
50 g/2 oz mushroom stalks
Chicken liver and heart
3 tablespoons wholemeal or white breadcrumbs
Pinch of tarragon
Salt and pepper
1 beaten egg

TO FINISH
25 g/1 oz butter
1 tablespoon oil
½ teaspoon salt
50 g/2 oz breadcrumbs, soft not dried
Pinch of tarragon

1. Chicken is divided into 4 even-sized pieces as follows. Cut legs from body including body-flesh behind breast. Cut breast away from carcass, with the wing.
2. Remove outer, bony wing joint.
3. With a pointed, sharp knife remove bones from legs.
4. Wipe the four pieces of chicken and cut a pocket in each of the breasts.

5. *To make the stuffing:* melt butter in a frying pan.
6. Add onion and let it fry gently.
7. Chop mushroom stalks and toss them in with onion.
8. Finely chop the chicken liver and heart. Add these to pan and toss all together over moderate heat for 3 or 4 minutes.
9. Put breadcrumbs in a bowl with tarragon, salt and pepper.
10. Add contents of pan and half of the beaten egg.
11. Mix well. Then stuff the cavities in the chicken pieces and secure with poultry pins or small skewers.
12. *To finish and cook the chicken:* melt 25 g/ 1 oz butter and beat it into the remaining egg with the oil and salt.
13. Mix breadcrumbs and tarragon together on a sheet of paper.
14. Dip stuffed chicken pieces into egg-mixture, and pat them into the crumbs to coat well.
15. Lay crumbed chicken pieces on a baking tray.
16. Bake in a moderately hot oven, Gas 5, 375°F, 190°C, for about 1 hour.
Very good served with sweetcorn and broccoli. (Try the next recipe to use up the chicken.)

CHICKEN RICE

A recipe to use chicken remaining from previous recipe.

1. First cook the chicken carcass, wing bones and remaining giblets in a large pan with 1.5 litres/2½ pints water, salt, bay leaf, and a few peppercorns. Cover pan, bring slowly to the boil and simmer for 1 hour or more.
2. Remove meat from bones.
3. Strain the stock.
4. Now proceed with the dish.

1 tablespoon oil
25 g/1 oz butter
1 chopped onion
175 g/6 oz brown rice
1 chopped green pepper
2 skinned and chopped tomatoes (to skin *see page 139*)
1 pint chicken stock
1 teaspoon turmeric
Salt and pepper
Chicken pieces
Chopped parsley

1. Heat oil and butter in a frying pan with lid.
2. Fry onion lightly. When soft, but not brown, add rice and fry for a minute.
3. Add green pepper, tomatoes, stock, turmeric, salt and pepper.
4. Cover pan and cook gently till rice is almost tender—about 20 minutes.
5. Fork in chicken and cook till rice is done and chicken is hot.
6. Sprinkle liberally with chopped parsley just before serving.

Anne Wallace
Dunlop, Scotland

CHICKEN AND HONEY

Delicious with cold Yoghurt and Tahini Dip (*see page 135*).

Serves 3

6 chicken wings, thighs or legs
50 g/2 oz melted butter
2 tablespoons oil
2 teaspoons soya sauce
A little clear honey
Salt

1. Preheat grill to high.
2. Trim chicken, but leave skin on.
3. Mix butter, oil and soya sauce and brush this all over chicken. Put under grill.
4. Turn grill down to moderate heat and cook chicken for 15 minutes, turning several times.
5. Brush with any remaining oil mixture. Smear each wing with honey and sprinkle with salt.
6. Return to grill for another 10 minutes until cooked and the skin is dark brown and crisp.

Elizabeth Mickery
Pudsey, West Yorkshire

HUFFED CHICKEN

In this old Sussex recipe a chicken was stuffed, then wrapped in suet pastry and probably a pudding cloth, and boiled for several hours. This is an up-dated and delicious adaptation.

Serves 4

4 chicken breasts

STUFFING
125 g/4 oz prunes, stoned and chopped
125 g/4 oz cooking apples, peeled, cored and chopped fine
1 large onion, finely-chopped
25 g/1 oz fresh wholewheat or white bread-crumbs
Rind of half a lemon
Pepper and salt
1 small beaten egg

SUET PASTRY
450 g/1 lb plain flour
½ level teaspoon salt
225 g/8 oz shredded suet
225 to 275 ml/8 to 10 fl oz cold water
Beaten egg, to glaze

1. Remove skin from chicken and bone it if necessary. Cut a pocket in each breast.
2. Mix stuffing ingredients and fill the pockets.
3. Prepare suet pastry. Mix flour, salt and suet, then mix with water to make a firm dough.
4. Using a floured board, roll out about 7 mm/¼ inch thick.
5. Cut pastry to wrap around each piece of chicken. Damp edges and press together. Put on a greased baking tray with pastry join underneath.
6. Make pastry leaves to decorate and stick them on with water. Brush with beaten egg.
7. Bake in a moderately hot oven, Gas 6, 400°F, 200°C, for 30 minutes, when the pastry will be golden brown and crisp.

Mrs Janice Langley
Shoreham-by-Sea, West Sussex

POACHED CHICKEN

A way to prepare chicken when really moist cooked chicken is required. Provides also a delicious jellied stock. (*See Chicken and Ham Pie, page 58.*)

1 chicken
1 litre/1½ pints water
1 onion, sliced
1 teaspoon mixed dried herbs
Salt and pepper

1. Put whole chicken into a pan which just contains it. *Or*, cut chicken into joints and put in a pan.
2. Add water, onion, herbs and seasoning. Cover pan.
3. Bring to the boil over gentle heat and cook until tender, 1½ to 2 hours.
4. Remove chicken from pan.
5. Boil stock to reduce quantity and so strengthen flavour and jelly properties.

Sybil Norcott
Irlam, Nr Manchester

FRIED TARRAGON CHICKEN

Serves 2 or 3

225 g/8 oz chicken pieces, breast, wings or legs
1 beaten egg
1 to 2 tablespoons dried breadcrumbs (*see page 52*)
20 g/¾ oz butter
20 g/¾ oz lard

MARINADE (*see page 106*)
2 tablespoons oil
2 tablespoons white wine, or cider vinegar, or lemon juice
1 large teaspoon finely-chopped fresh tarragon or ½ teaspoon dried
A clove of garlic, crushed
½ teaspoon dry mustard

SAUCE
150 ml/¼ pint chicken stock
1 teaspoon cornflour
1 tablespoon water
Salt and pepper

1. Remove skin from chicken.

2. Mix marinade ingredients.

3. Lay chicken pieces in a flat dish. Pour marinade over the chicken and leave for 2 or 3 hours. If you like tarragon flavour leave overnight.

4. Remove chicken and pat dry. Save marinade for the sauce.

5. Dip chicken pieces in beaten egg and then in breadcrumbs.

6. Heat butter and lard and fry chicken until crisp, brown and cooked.

7. Meanwhile, make sauce. Put marinade in a pan with chicken stock.

8. Slake cornflour in water and add to pan. Bring to the boil, stirring as sauce thickens. Simmer 2 or 3 minutes. Season to taste.

9. Put chicken on a warm dish. Serve sauce separately.

BERKSWELL LEMON CHICKEN

Serves 4

50 g/2 oz butter or margarine
Juice of 1 large or 2 small lemons
Salt and pepper
A young 1 to 1.3 kg/2½ to 3 lb chicken jointed, (*see page 51*)
300 ml/½ pint chicken stock
1 to 2 tablespoons chopped parsley, chives and mint mixed
1 tablespoon flour

1. Melt butter in a flameproof casserole with lemon juice, salt and pepper until very hot.

2. Put in chicken joints and 150 ml/¼ pint of the stock; slowly turn chicken in the mixture so that every part is covered and the liquid boils.

3. Cover at once and put in a slow oven, Gas 3, 325°F, 160°C, for 1 hour, or simmer it very gently on top of the stove.

4. Put chicken on hot dish.

5. Add flour to liquid in casserole and stir until smooth.

6. Add other 150 ml/¼ pint of stock and herbs and bring to boil.

7. Pour over chicken and serve.

Mrs Redgrave
Warwickshire

CHICKEN AND HAM PIE

A delicious pie to eat hot or cold. Can be made with left-over chicken but it needs to be moist, preferably poached, so that stock sets in a jelly when pie is cold.

Serves 4

175 g/6 oz shortcrust pastry (*see page 203*)
325 g/12 oz cooked chicken, preferably poached
1 small onion, finely-chopped
15 g/½ oz butter
75 g/3 oz fresh breadcrumbs
75 to 125 g/3 to 4 oz cooked ham, minced or finely-chopped
1 teaspoon mixed herbs
Salt and pepper
A little beaten egg
300 ml/½ pint stock from poaching chicken or chicken bone stock

1. Make pastry and chill.

2. Remove skin and bones from chicken and cut meat into pieces. Put them in a 1.2 litre/2 pint pie dish. A pie funnel may be useful.

3. Fry onion gently in butter for 3 minutes. Add to breadcrumbs with ham, herbs, seasoning and a little beaten egg to bind if needed.

4. Form into balls and place in dish with chicken. Pour in stock.

5. Roll out pastry to 1.5 cm/½ inch wider than needed to cover pie. Cut off a strip of this width.

6. Moisten edge of pie dish with water. Lay strip in place, moisten it, then cover pie with pastry, pressing to seal. Flute or fork the edge.

7. Brush with beaten egg or milk and decorate pie with the trimmings.

8. Bake near top of a moderately hot oven, Gas 6, 400°F, 200°C, for 20 minutes.

Mrs Aileen Houghton
Kemsing, Nr Sevenoaks, Kent

SPICY CHICKEN JOINTS

Serves 4
4 chicken joints
25 g/1 oz butter
1 tablespoon oil
2 large onions, finely-chopped
1 green pepper, de-seeded and chopped
A clove of garlic, finely-chopped
2 teaspoons dry mustard
2 tablespoons tomato purée*
300 ml/½ pint chicken stock
25 g/1 oz soft brown sugar
3 tablespoons vinegar
1 teaspoon Worcestershire sauce
½ teaspoon salt
1 large sprig fresh tarragon, or ½ teaspoon dried

*To keep tomato purée fresh, see page 84.

1. Skin the chicken joints.
2. In a pan, combine butter and oil and fry chicken joints on all sides until brown.
3. Remove joints to a large casserole.
4. Now lightly fry onion, green pepper and garlic for 3 to 4 minutes. Add to casserole.
5. Mix mustard into tomato purée and add stock, sugar, vinegar, Worcestershire sauce and salt. Lastly add the tarragon. Stir until sugar is dissolved. Pour over the chicken.
6. Cover casserole and put it in a moderate oven, Gas 3, 325°F, 160°C, for about 2 hours or until chicken is tender.

CHICKEN WITH TOMATO RICE

Serves 4

2 medium-sized onions
25 g/1 oz butter
225 g/8 oz long-grain rice
A 400 g/14 oz can of tomatoes
600 ml/1 pint chicken stock (a stock cube will do)
2 teaspoons Worcestershire sauce
1½ level teaspoons Salt and Pepper Mix (*see page 17*)
4 chicken joints
2 teaspoons oil
225 g/8 oz packet of frozen mixed vegetables
Watercress, for garnish

1. Peel and slice onions.
2. Melt butter and fry onions to soften but not brown.
3. Add rice, stir it in and cook for 1 or 2 minutes to absorb fat.
4. Add tomatoes, stock, Worcestershire sauce, salt and pepper. Bring to the boil and pour into a large shallow casserole.
5. Place a rack over casserole—rack from grill pan, or a cooling wire will do.
6. Brush chicken joints with oil, place them on rack, sprinkle with salt and pepper.
7. Put into a moderately hot oven, Gas 6, 400°F, 200°C, and cook for 40 minutes.
8. Remove from oven and stir frozen vegetables into the rice. Replace rack on top.
9. Return to oven and cook 15 minutes more.
10. Arrange rice and chicken on a warmed dish and garnish with watercress.

CHICKEN IN WHITE WINE WITH TOMATOES

This is the well-known Poulet Chasseur.

Serves 6

1 chicken, jointed, or 6 chicken pieces
2 tablespoons seasoned flour
50 g/2 oz butter or 2 tablespoons oil
1 large onion, chopped small
A clove of garlic, crushed
450 ml/¾ pint chicken stock
Salt and pepper
A 400 g/14 oz tin of tomatoes
1 tablespoon tomato purée*
1 teaspoon soya sauce
A dash of Worcestershire sauce
A small glass of dry white wine

*To keep tomato purée fresh, see page 84.

1. Roll chicken pieces in seasoned flour and brown in the fat in a frying pan. Remove from the pan.
2. Fry onion and garlic and remove from the pan.
3. Add 1 tablespoon of remaining flour to pan, stir in the chicken stock carefully and allow to thicken on a low heat.
4. Add seasoning, tomatoes, purée, soya sauce, Worcestershire sauce and wine.
5. Lastly, add chicken pieces, put on lid and cook gently on top of the stove for 1 hour. Or, transfer to a covered casserole and cook for 1 hour in a moderate oven, Gas 4, 350°F, 180°C.   Mrs Patricia Chantry
Hook, Goole, N. Humberside

CHICKEN WITH TOMATOES AND YOGHURT

Serves 4

1 large onion
25 g/1 oz plain flour
1 level teaspoon salt
1 level teaspoon paprika
4 chicken joints
25 g/1 oz margarine
A 400 g/14 oz can of peeled tomatoes
150 ml/¼ pint water
1 level teaspoon sugar
150 g/5 fl oz natural yoghurt
1 tablespoon chopped parsley

1. Peel and thinly slice onion.
2. Mix flour, salt and paprika together.
3. Trim chicken joints and coat in seasoned flour.
4. Melt margarine in a large frying pan. Fry chicken joints until lightly browned, then lift out into a 2 litre/3½ pint shallow casserole.
5. Fry onion for 2 minutes in remaining fat.
6. Stir any remaining flour into pan. Add tomatoes, water and sugar. Bring to boil, stirring, and pour over chicken.
7. Cover and cook on centre shelf of moderately hot oven, Gas 5, 375°F, 190°C, for 1 hour until chicken is tender.
8. Just before serving, spoon yoghurt over chicken joints and sprinkle with chopped parsley.

CEYLON CHICKEN CURRY

Serves 4

2 large onions
2 tablespoons ground coriander
2 teaspoons ground cumin
1 teaspoon chilli powder
½ teaspoon turmeric
½ teaspoon cardamom powder
A 5 cm/2 inch piece of cinnamon bark, or ¼ teaspoon ground cinnamon
2 teaspoons salt
4 cloves of garlic, finely-chopped
4 tablespoons vegetable oil
A 1.3 kg/3 lb chicken, jointed
50 g/2 oz creamed coconut
350 ml/12 fl oz hot water
Juice of 1 lemon
2 tablespoons finely-chopped fresh coriander leaves, if you can get them

1. Grate one of the onions and mix with the spices and salt.
2. Finely-slice second onion and fry with garlic in the heated oil until golden brown.
3. Add grated onion and spice mixture and stir for about 5 minutes until heated through.
4. Add chicken joints and fry for another 5 minutes until well-coated in mixture in pan.
5. Dissolve creamed coconut in the hot water and add to chicken.
6. Bring to the boil, lower heat, cover pan and simmer for about 1 hour until chicken is cooked.
7. Before serving, add the lemon juice and garnish with the coriander leaves if available.

Serve with Boiled Rice (*see page 172*) or rice sticks or noodles.

Priya Wickramasinghe
Cardiff

CHICKEN KEBABS

This makes a very nice main course when served with Yoghurt and Tahini Dip (*see page 135*), Stir-fried Vegetables (*see page 170*) and hot Greek Pitta Bread (*see page 293*).

Serves 2

2 chicken portions, breast and wing pieces

It is cheaper to buy the chicken this way, although only the boned breasts are required for this recipe. Cut off the wings and with a sharp-pointed knife cut bones away from breast flesh. The butcher will do this for you. Save the wings for another meal, like Chicken and Honey (*see page 56*).

MARINADE
3 tablespoons corn oil
2 tablespoons soya sauce
2 heaped teaspoons coriander seeds or 2 level teaspoons ground coriander
A clove of garlic, crushed
1 tablespoon lemon juice
1 teaspoon brown sugar
½ teaspoon ground ginger
Salt and pepper

1. Start this the night before it is to be eaten. Prepare the chicken breasts, cutting flesh into bite-sized pieces.
2. Mix all the marinade ingredients, grinding the coriander seeds in a mortar or a mill.
3. Mix chicken into marinade and leave overnight in refrigerator.
4. Next day Yoghurt and Tahini Dip can be made. (It is best made without garlic when accompanying this dish.) Vegetables for stir-frying should be prepared close to the time of the meal.
5. Finally, preheat grill to hot.
6. Thread chicken pieces on to skewers and grill about 5 minutes on each side until browning a little and cooked through. Any remaining marinade can be used to baste chicken as it cooks.
If serving with hot pitta bread cut each piece in half and open it like a pocket. Put in a little of the stir-fried vegetables, then some kebabs and finally the cold dip. Eat it like a sandwich.

Can also be served with well-flavoured brown rice.

Elizabeth Mickery
Pudsey, West Yorkshire

INDONESIAN CHICKEN SATÉ

Serves 4

A 1.8 kg/4 lb fresh chicken

MARINADE
2 tablespoons soya sauce
2 tablespoons cooking oil
2 tablespoons hot water

PEANUT SATÉ SAUCE
175 g/6 oz roasted peanuts
4 dried red chillis
2 tablespoons shallots, chopped
2 tablespoons soya sauce
1 tablespoon brown sugar
1 teaspoon salt
1 tablespoon oil
125 ml/4 fl oz water

TO GARNISH
Lime wedges, if possible, or lemon

1. Skin the chicken, remove flesh from bone and cut it into bite-sized pieces.
2. Take 8 skewers and thread a few pieces of meat on to each skewer.
3. In a shallow dish mix the marinade ingredients.
4. Lay skewered meat in this marinade for at least 3 hours, turning from time to time.
5. While the meat is marinating, prepare the peanut saté sauce.
6. Using an electric blender or a mortar and pestle, grind and blend all sauce ingredients except oil and water to form a smooth paste.
7. In a pan, heat oil and fry these ingredients until the oil separates.
8. Add a half cup of water and bring to the boil.
9. Reduce heat and simmer for 5 minutes.
10. While sauce is simmering, grill or barbecue the skewered chicken on a low flame, taking care to brown evenly on all sides.
11. Just before serving, arrange the skewered chicken pieces on a platter and pour the peanut sauce over them.
12. Garnish with lime wedges when available, or lemon.

This goes well with rice and salads.

Priya Wickramasinghe
Cardiff

See also Mixed Fried Noodles Indonesian Style, page 182, Spicy Risotto, page 175.

TANDOURI CHICKEN

A recipe from the Punjab. Traditionally a brilliant red, but colouring is not necessary.

Serves 4

A fresh 1.5 kg/3½ lb chicken
1 medium-sized onion, minced or finely-chopped
3 cloves of garlic, chopped
1 teaspoon fresh ginger, chopped (*see opposite*)
225 ml/8 fl oz natural yoghurt
Rind and juice of 1 lemon
2 tablespoons vinegar
1 tablespoon paprika powder
2 teaspoons garam masala (*see opposite*)
2 teaspoons coriander powder
1 teaspoon cumin powder
½ teaspoon red food colouring (optional)

TO SERVE AND GARNISH
2 tablespoons ghee (*see opposite*)
Lettuce leaves
Fresh onion rings
Cucumber slices
Lemon wedges

1. Skin the chicken, then cut it into 2 along breast bone and back bone.
2. Using a sharp knife, make slanting incisions 2.5 cm/1 inch long in the chicken on each limb and breast, taking care not to cut through to the bone.
3. In a non-metallic large bowl mix all other ingredients except those listed for serving and garnish. This will make a brilliant red marinade.
4. Marinate the chicken in this spicy yoghurt mixture for between 8 and 24 hours.
5. Turn the chicken occasionally in the marinade to ensure that all sides become uniformly soaked.
6. Heat oven to very hot, Gas 8, 450°F, 230°C.
7. Lift chicken out of marinade and place on a greased wire rack over a baking tray. Cover with foil.
8. Roast on top shelf of oven for 1 hour. Baste chicken with marinade mixture once during the cooking.
9. Just before serving, heat ghee, pour it over the chicken halves and ignite.
10. Serve the chicken on a bed of lettuce garnished with onion rings, cucumber slices and lemon wedges. Serve with Pitta Bread (*see page 293*).

Priya Wickramasinghe
Cardiff

ORIENTAL RECIPES
The oriental recipes to be found in this book have been devised using ingredients readily available in Britain and the West and it is to be hoped you will see Mrs Wickramasinghe making some of the dishes in the television programmes. A few explanatory notes follow.

Curry leaves are used fresh if possible. They are aromatic and slightly pungent and although not like the bay leaf they are used in a similar way. Available from continental and oriental food shops.

Fresh ginger is infinitely preferable to dried ginger powder. Sometimes called green ginger, it can be bought in many supermarkets and greengrocers, besides the oriental food shops. Look for plump, smooth roots. Avoid shrivelled pieces. It freezes well.

Garam Masala, the Indian name for a basic mixture of curry spices. Many people prepare their own, grinding the whole spices specially. It is obtainable ready-prepared from Indian grocery shops and some wholefood shops.

Ghee is much used in Indian cookery. It is simply clarified unsalted butter. It can be bought in oriental food shops. A cheaper way is to make it at home. In a heavy-bottomed pan heat 225 g/8 oz unsalted butter on a very low heat for about 30 minutes. Do not allow it to smoke or burn. Remove the floating scum. Strain through a piece of muslin into a bowl. Allow to cool. Store in refrigerator. Keeps for months.

Poppadoms are made with a special blend of lentil flour. Buy them at oriental food shops. They can either be grilled or deep fried before serving.

CHICKEN AND BACON CROQUETTES

Serves 2 to 3

125 g/4 oz cold, cooked chicken
125 g/4 oz cold, cooked bacon or ham
125 g/4 oz cold, mashed potato
Chopped parsley
Salt and pepper
2 small eggs, beaten
Dried breadcrumbs (*see page 52*)
Deep fat for frying

1. Mince the chicken and bacon.
2. Mix together the minced meat, potato, parsley and seasoning with sufficient beaten egg to bind.
3. Shape into croquettes and leave an hour or two, if possible in the refrigerator, when they will be firmer and easier to handle.
4. Dip in beaten egg then coat with dried breadcrumbs.
5. Fry in deep hot fat until golden. Drain on absorbent kitchen paper.

CREAMED CHICKEN WITH MUSHROOMS AND BUTTER BEANS

Freezes well.

Serves 4

175 g/6 oz butter beans
Water
1 small onion
2 tablespoons cooking oil
125 g/4 oz small white mushrooms
½ small green pepper
½ small red pepper
175 to 225 g/6 to 8 oz cooked chicken flesh
1 glass sherry
2 to 3 tablespoons double cream
Seasoning
Finely-chopped parsley, to garnish

WHITE SAUCE
25 g/1 oz butter
25 g/1 oz flour
300 ml/½ pint milk
Seasoning

1. Soak butter beans overnight in cold water.
2. Next day, put them with their water in a saucepan, adding enough extra water to cover them well. Bring to the boil and boil hard for at least 30 minutes. Reduce heat and cook gently until tender, about 2 hours in all. Add more water if necessary.
3. Peel and finely chop the onion.
4. Heat the oil and sauté the onions—i.e., stand the pan over moderate heat and toss the onions in the hot oil until soft but not brown.
5. Wipe mushrooms with a damp cloth and slice them.
6. Remove core and seeds from green and red peppers and chop flesh finely.
7. Add mushrooms and peppers to onion and cook for 2 minutes.
8. Cut chicken flesh into bite-sized pieces and add these to pan.
9. Add sherry, cream and seasoning. Bring to the boil, stirring. Then simmer gently for 3 minutes.
10. Drain cooked butter beans well and remove any loose outer skins. Add beans to the chicken mixture.
11. *To make the white sauce:* melt butter in a small pan. Add flour and stir over low heat for 1 minute. Remove from heat and gradually stir in the milk. Bring to the boil and cook for 2 or 3 minutes, stirring all the time. Season to taste.
12. Mix white sauce into chicken mixture. Re-heat and adjust seasoning.
13. Turn it out of pan into a warmed serving dish and sprinkle with finely-chopped parsley.

Serve with a green vegetable.

Jean Welshman
Malton, E. Yorkshire

MARROW RINGS STUFFED WITH CHICKEN AND MUSHROOMS

Serves 4

1 marrow
150 ml/¼ pint water
125 g/4 oz cooked chicken
1 small onion
½ green pepper
1 tablespoon cooking oil
125 g/4 oz mushrooms
2 tomatoes
125 g/4 oz sweetcorn (optional)
125 g/4 oz peas (optional)
300 ml/½ pint chicken stock
1 dessertspoon cornflour
Pepper and salt
15 g/½ oz butter or margarine
Small sprigs of parsley

1. Cut marrow into thick rings. Peel and remove seeds.
2. Put rings into a casserole dish, add water, cover dish.
3. Put casserole into a moderate oven, Gas 4, 350°F, 180°C, and cook marrow while you prepare the filling.
4. Cut the chicken into small pieces.
5. Peel onion and chop finely.
6. Slice green pepper, discarding core and seeds.
7. Heat oil in a large pan, fry onion and pepper gently till soft but not brown.
8. Add chicken and chopped mushrooms and toss together over low heat for 3 or 4 minutes.
9. Add chopped tomatoes (but save a few slices for decoration), sweetcorn and peas. Stir together for 3 or 4 minutes.
10. Mix cornflour with a tablespoon of the stock. Add to the rest of the stock and pour this into chicken mixture. Add salt and pepper if necessary.
11. Stir over low heat until it thickens slightly.
12. Take casserole from oven and drain off any liquid (keep it for making soup). Fill each marrow ring with chicken mixture. Lay a slice of tomato on each and dot with butter or margarine.
13. Cover casserole again and return it to the oven to cook for 20 minutes more.
14. Serve with a sprig of parsley on each portion.

Mrs Phyllis E. Roche
Normanton, W. Yorkshire

CHICKEN SALAD

TO COOK THE CHICKEN
1 chicken
1 small onion
A piece of carrot
A piece of celery
1 small bay leaf
4 peppercorns
A little salt

FOR THE SALAD
1 green pepper
3 sticks celery
1 eating apple
Lettuce

THE DRESSING
4 juniper berries
1 large teaspoon curry powder
¼ teaspoon tarragon
¼ teaspoon chervil
2 teaspoons lemon juice
3 large tablespoons mayonnaise (*see page 134*)

1. Put the chicken, with its giblets inside, into a close-fitting pan. Put in the vegetables, bay leaf, peppercorns and salt. Add water just to cover.
2. Bring it to the boil, put on lid and let it poach—i.e., simmer gently—for 45 minutes to 1 hour, until it is cooked.
3. Take out chicken, remove meat and dice it quite small. Let it cool.
4. *To prepare dressing and salad:* crush the juniper berries. Mix them with curry powder, tarragon, chervil and lemon juice. Leave this for 5 minutes.
5. Remove core and seeds from green pepper and cut it up small.
6. Slice celery.
7. Quarter and core the apple, but do not peel it. Cut it up small.
8. Add curry and herbs mixture to the mayonnaise and mix well.
9. Mix together chicken, green pepper, celery, apple and dressing.
10. Lay lettuce leaves on a serving dish and spoon the chicken mixture on to them.

Don't forget to return chicken carcass to pan, with extra water if necessary, and simmer for another hour to make good chicken stock. Strain and refrigerate or freeze.

Mrs M. Lucie-Smith
London S.W.3

CHICKEN SALAD WITH AVOCADO

Serves 2 to 3 as a main course, but served in lettuce leaves on small plates would make a starter for 4 people.

175 g/6 oz small macaroni, pasta shapes or noodles
Boiling water
1 teaspoon corn oil
Salt
2 chicken quarters, cooked*
1 tomato
1 avocado pear

*Chicken can be poached (see page 57)

DRESSING
For this you need a liquidiser.

50 g/2 oz blue cheese
2 tablespoons mayonnaise (*see page 134*)
1 teaspoon lemon juice
A little milk
Salt and pepper

TO SERVE
Lettuce leaves

1. The dressing can be made in advance. Put cheese, mayonnaise and lemon juice in a liquidiser, switch on to blend until smooth.
2. As it blends, add milk a little at a time until a pouring consistency is made. Add salt and pepper to taste.
3. Boil macaroni, pasta or noodles in plenty of water with the oil and salt until it is cooked but firm to the bite. Then drain, run cold water through it and chill.
4. Meanwhile cut chicken and tomato into small pieces.
5. Skin the avocado, remove stone and dice flesh.
6. Toss all ingredients gently together with dressing and serve on lettuce leaves.

Elizabeth Mickery
Pudsey, West Yorkshire

TO ROAST A TURKEY

Note: It is wise to time the cooking so that turkey is removed from oven on to warm dish 10 to 15 minutes before serving the meal. This will allow time to make the gravy and also to 'rest' the bird.
Cooking time: A slow method is recommended unless instructions given with the bird differ.

Stuffed weight		Total cooking
kg	lb	time in hours
2.7 to 3.6	6 to 8	3 to $3\frac{1}{2}$
3.6 to 4.5	8 to 10	$3\frac{1}{2}$ to $3\frac{3}{4}$
4.5 to 5.4	10 to 12	$3\frac{3}{4}$ to 4
5.4 to 6.3	12 to 14	4 to $4\frac{1}{4}$
6.3 to 7.2	14 to 16	$4\frac{1}{4}$ to $4\frac{1}{2}$
7.2 to 8.1	16 to 18	$4\frac{1}{2}$ to $4\frac{3}{4}$

1. Choose and prepare 2 suitable stuffings for neck end and body cavity. (See suggestions this page.)
Note: Body cavity takes more than neck end. Any stuffing left can be put in a pie dish, covered securely and placed in bottom of oven. It will take no harm there for $1\frac{1}{2}$ to 2 hours.
2. Remove giblets from turkey, wash them and place in pan with sufficient water to cover. Add 6 to 8 peppercorns and a small bay leaf. Bring to boil and simmer for at least 2 hours. Strain and keep stock for gravy. The giblets can now be discarded. (Preparation and cooking of giblets can be done the day before.)
3. Wipe inside of turkey and stuff to a plump, even shape.
4. Truss with skewers and fine clean string folding wings under body and tying legs tightly together.
5. Place on rack in a large roasting tin. Cover well with good dripping or pieces of fat pork or bacon. Press foil round legs as they are inclined to dry before being cooked.
6. Place in a moderately hot oven, Gas 6, 400°F, 200°C, for 20 minutes. Then lower heat to moderate, Gas 4, 350°F, 180°C, for remainder of cooking time. Baste frequently turning bird on its side once or twice during cooking time. If breast browns too quickly cover with foil.
7. Remove turkey on to warm dish and make gravy with giblet stock and sediment from roasting tin.

See A Good Gravy, page 71.

Serve with Bread Sauce (*page 66*), Cranberry Sauce, small sausages, bacon rolls, etc.

TWO STUFFINGS FOR TURKEY AND CHICKEN

Adjust quantities for size of bird and cavity to be filled.

CORN AND BACON STUFFING
50 g/2 oz butter
1 large finely-chopped onion
225 g/8 oz bacon pieces
1 can sweetcorn, approx. 300 g/11 oz
4 tablespoons fresh parsley
2 teaspoons Salt and Pepper Mix (*see page 17*)
1 teaspoon mixed herbs
1 small loaf of bread, unsliced but crusts removed
2 small beaten eggs

1. Melt butter in pan. Fry onion and chopped bacon to soften.
2. Place in bowl, add sweetcorn, parsley, salt, pepper and herbs.
3. Cut bread into small cubes.
4. Stir in, mixing eggs in lightly. Do not pack stuffing into bird too tightly.

SAUSAGE MEAT STUFFING
450 to 675 g/1 to 1½ lb pork sausage meat (according to size of bird)
1 teaspoon mixed herbs
1 grated onion
1 grated apple
A little freshly milled black pepper
Fresh breadcrumbs

1. Mix together all ingredients adding 1 to 2 tablespoons breadcrumbs if mixture is too soft.
2. Stuff into bird. Do not pack too tightly.

BREAD SAUCE

1 medium onion
2 cloves
450 ml/¾ pint milk
½ level teaspoon salt
6 peppercorns
A small piece of bay leaf
175 to 225 g/6 to 8 oz fresh wholemeal or white breadcrumbs (*see page 52*)
15 g/½ oz butter

1. Peel onion, stick into it the cloves.
2. Put in saucepan with milk, salt, peppercorns and bay leaf. Cover, place over very low heat and bring to just below boiling point.
3. Remove from heat and set aside for 30 minutes or longer.
4. Strain milk, bring it to boil, pour over the crumbs, add butter and stir.
5. Place in heat-proof dish. Cover and place in oven on low shelf under meat for 20 minutes.

BONED AND STUFFED ROAST TURKEY

The thought of carving a boned and stuffed turkey or chicken is very appealing, especially if you are doing it with a hungry family watching. Boning isn't really as difficult as it sounds. All you need is an extremely sharp, short-bladed knife, a steel to keep it sharp and some nimble finger work.

Serves 5 to 6

A 1.8 to 2.3 kg/4 to 5 lb turkey, with giblets. To bone, *see page 51.*

STUFFING
190 g/7 oz prunes, soaked overnight
75 g/3 oz butter
1 large onion, finely-chopped
125 g/4 oz fresh wholewheat breadcrumbs
50 g /2 oz sultanas
50 g/2 oz chopped walnuts
Grated rind and juice of 1 lemon
2 tablespoons chopped fresh parsley
Salt and pepper
1 beaten egg

TO ROAST
75 g/3 oz bacon fat or good dripping
225 g/8 oz streaky bacon, cut off rinds

GRAVY
Giblets
A piece of onion
A piece of carrot
1 bay leaf and 4 peppercorns
600 ml/1 pint water
25 g/1 oz flour

STUFFING
1. Remove stones from prunes and chop flesh.
2. Melt 25 g/1 oz of the butter and fry onion until soft but not brown.
3. Combine prunes, onions, breadcrumbs, sultanas, walnuts, lemon rind and juice, a little of the parsley, salt and pepper. Mix with beaten egg.
4. Now cream remaining 50 g/2 oz butter with parsley, salt and pepper and use half of it to rub inside of bird.
5. Pack stuffing into all the corners of the bird and make the rest into a large wide sausage for the middle.
6. Using a large needle threaded with fine string, sew up the skin, with large overcasting stitches, reshaping the bird as well as possible. For safety, tie bird up with 2 strings around its middle.
7. Rub remaining parsley-butter over outside of bird.

TO ROAST
1. Melt fat in a roasting tin. Put in the bird and baste it before it goes in oven. Cover with foil.
2. Roast in a moderately hot oven, Gas 6, 400°F, 200°C, for 1¼ to 1½ hours, or until done. 15 minutes before end of cooking time remove foil and spread bacon across bird.
To test if it is cooked, pierce thigh with a skewer. If juice is pink then it needs further cooking. If juice is clear bird is done.
Cooking time is calculated at 15 minutes to the ½ kg/ 1 lb plus 15 minutes. Weigh bird after stuffing.
3. Meanwhile put giblets, onion, carrot, bay leaf, peppercorns and water in a pan. Put on lid and simmer for 40 minutes.
4. Remove bird from oven on to a warm serving dish and keep hot. Make gravy in roasting tin.
5. Pour off as much fat as possible from tin, leaving the residue of turkey juices.
6. Work flour into juices. Put tin on top of stove over low heat.
7. Gradually stir in strained giblet stock and extra water if necessary. Stir until gravy thickens. Let it boil for 1 minute.
8. Pour into a warm jug or serving boat and keep hot.

Try Cranberry and Orange Preserve (*see page 357*) with this.

COLD TURKEY WITH ORANGE AND TOMATO SALAD

Slices of cold, cooked turkey
4 tablespoons mayonnaise (*see page 134*)
2 tablespoons thick cream
2 teaspoons lemon juice
Paprika
Chopped parsley

FOR THE SALAD
2 oranges, peeled and separated into segments
2 to 3 tomatoes, sliced
Cress, and/or lettuce

1. Arrange turkey down centre of a flat serving dish.
2. Mix mayonnaise, cream and lemon juice and spoon over turkey.
3. Garnish with slanting lines of paprika and chopped parsley.
4. Arrange the salad around the turkey or serve separately.

TURKEY OR CHICKEN PÂTÉ

Serves 4

1 large chopped onion
50 g/2 oz butter
325 g/12 oz cold cooked turkey or chicken, in
  pieces
4 tablespoons cream
1 to 2 tablespoons dry sherry
1 teaspoon Salt and Pepper Mix (*see page 17*)
Parsley to garnish

1. Fry onion in butter until soft.
2. Mix in turkey or chicken and mince mixture finely (or put in blender).
3. Add cream and just enough sherry to moisten. Taste and season. Beat till smooth.
4. Place in dish, fork top. Garnish with parsley.

TURKEY, RICE AND CORN SALAD

Serves 6

325 to 450 g/¾ to 1 lb cold turkey, cut into bite-sized pieces
3 tablespoons French dressing (*see page 133*)
150 ml/¼ pint mayonnaise (*page 134*) mixed with 1 tablespoon lemon juice *Or* 150 ml/¼ pint salad cream
A little grated black pepper
¼ teaspoon salt
175 g/6 oz cooked long grain brown or white rice
A 300 g/11 oz can of sweetcorn kernels
1 green pepper* de-seeded and finely diced
2 tomatoes, skinned, de-seeded and roughly chopped (To skin, *see page 139*)
Lettuce

1. Mix turkey into French dressing.
2. In another bowl combine mayonnaise and lemon juice (or salad cream) with seasonings. Fold in turkey, rice, drained corn, green pepper and tomatoes.
3. Line a salad bowl with crisp lettuce leaves and pile mixture in centre.

* Green pepper may be blanched, as the slightly bitter taste does not appeal to everyone. To blanch: prepare pepper, bring to boil in pan of water, boil 1 minute, drain, plunge into cold water to cool.

TURKEY AND HAM LOAF

TO EAT HOT OR COLD

Serves 6

325 g/12 oz cold cooked turkey
225 g/8 oz ham
1 small chopped onion
1 teaspoon mixed herbs
2 teaspoons Salt and Pepper Mix (*see page 17*)
1 large beaten egg
1 teacup fresh breadcrumbs, (*see page 52*)
Stock, if necessary
Browned, dried breadcrumbs for coating (*see page 52*)

1. Mince turkey, ham and onion.
2. Add seasonings, beaten egg and fresh breadcrumbs. Use stock if mixture is very dry.

3. Pack into a greased tin. Cover with foil.
4. Cook in a moderate oven, Gas 4, 350°F, 180°C, for 1 hour.
5. Turn out and coat while hot in browned crumbs.

MRS HART'S TURKEY IN A CHEESE AND SHERRY SAUCE

Serves 4

325 g/12 oz cold cooked turkey or chicken, in bite-sized pieces
40 g/1½ oz butter
50 g/2 oz wholemeal or white flour
300 ml/½ pint milk, warmed
4 tablespoons stock from the bird
2 tablespoons sherry
Nutmeg
Salt
Black pepper, quite a lot
3 tablespoons grated Parmesan and/or Gruyère cheese
2 tablespoons cream
Dried breadcrumbs (*see page 52*)

1. Remove skin and bone from meat.
2. Melt butter in a pan.
3. Add flour and sizzle 1 minute.
4. Add warmed milk and bring to boil, stirring. Add stock, return to boil, and cook 2 minutes.
5. Add sherry and seasonings, bring just to boil.
6. Stir in 2 tablespoons of the cheese and allow to melt. Stir in cream. Reheat, but do not boil.
7. Put layer of meat in shallow oven dish. Pour over a layer of sauce. Fill dish with layers of meat and sauce.
8. Sprinkle with breadcrumbs and remaining cheese.
9. Put in a moderate oven, Gas 4, 350°F, 180°C, for 20 to 25 minutes until turkey is properly heated.
10. Finally put under grill to brown before serving.

TURKEY OR CHICKEN IN SHERRY SAUCE

Serves 4

325 g/12 oz cold cooked turkey or chicken in bite-sized pieces
75 g/3 oz butter
1 small chopped onion
2 lean rashers of bacon, chopped
50 g/2 oz button mushrooms
2 level tablespoons wholemeal or white flour
Salt and pepper
300 ml/½ pint chicken (or turkey) stock (*see page 10*)
3 tablespoons dry sherry
Chopped parsley
Triangles of toast

1. Fry turkey or chicken in hot butter until golden. Drain meat, place it on a hot serving dish and keep warm.
2. Fry onion and bacon in same pan for about 2 minutes, add mushrooms and cook for 2 minutes.
3. Stir in flour and a shake of salt and pepper. Cook 1 minute.
4. Add stock, simmer 2 minutes.
5. Add sherry, bring just to boil. Pour over chicken.
6. Sprinkle on chopped parsley and serve with toast triangles.

RISSOLES

CHICKEN OR TURKEY AND BACON
125 g/4 oz cooked chicken or turkey, finely-minced
1 rasher of bacon
50 g/2 oz fresh brown breadcrumbs (*see page 52*)
Salt and pepper
1 tablespoon basic white sauce (*see page 186*) or 1 egg-yolk
1 beaten egg
Dried breadcrumbs to coat rissoles (*see page 52*)
Deep fat or oil to fry

1. Prepare chicken.
2. De-rind bacon, fry it until really crisp, then crush into small pieces.
3. Mix chicken, bacon and fresh breadcrumbs with enough white sauce or egg-yolk to bind it together.
4. With floured hands, shape mixture into short fat sausages. Leave aside to firm up.
5. Dip rissoles in beaten egg, then in breadcrumbs. Leave aside to firm up.
6. Heat fat or oil until really smoking. Fry rissoles until golden. Drain on kitchen paper.

HAM
125 g/4 oz cooked ham, finely-minced
50 g/2 oz fresh brown breadcrumbs
1 teaspoon chopped fresh parsley
Salt and pepper
1 tablespoon basic white sauce (*see page 186*) or 1 egg-yolk
1 beaten egg
Dried breadcrumbs to coat rissoles
Deep fat or oil to fry

1. Mix ham, fresh breadcrumbs and parsley. Season well with salt and pepper.
2. Bind mixture with sauce or egg-yolk.
3. With floured hands, shape mixture into short fat sausages. Leave in refrigerator to firm up.
4. Dip sausages in beaten egg, then in dried breadcrumbs. Refrigerate for 1 hour.
5. Heat fat or oil until nearly smoking hot. Fry rissoles until golden and crisp. Drain on kitchen paper.

TURKEY RISOTTO

Serves 4

125 g/4 oz mushrooms
50 g/2 oz butter
1 medium-sized onion, chopped
175 to 225 g/6 to 8 oz long grain brown or white rice
450 to 750 ml/$\frac{3}{4}$ to $1\frac{1}{4}$ pints light turkey or chicken stock (*see page 10*)
25 to 50 g/1 to 2 oz sultanas
325 g/12 oz cold cooked turkey, in bite-sized pieces
3 tomatoes, skinned and chopped (to skin, *see page 139*)
125 g/4 oz cooked peas

1. Wipe or wash the mushrooms, but do not peel. If large, cut in half.
2. Melt butter in large saucepan, add onion and soften but do not brown.
3. Add the mushrooms.
4. Add the rice and cook gently until rice absorbs butter and goes transparent.
5. Add 300 to 450 ml/$\frac{1}{2}$ to $\frac{3}{4}$ pint of the stock, bring to boil.
6. Simmer, stirring occasionally, keeping lid on pan when not stirring. (If mixture is becoming too dry before rice is cooked gradually add a little more stock.)
7. After 12 minutes add sultanas and turkey. Allow to cook 2 to 3 minutes more then add tomatoes and peas. Check for seasoning and continue cooking till rice is done. The risotto will take about 20 minutes to cook, depending on type of rice. It should be soft and creamy, but not mushy. 50 to 75 g/2 to 3 oz ham cut in cubes can also be added at same time as turkey pieces. Good also if made with chicken instead of turkey.

AUNT POLLY'S PIE

A way to use left-over turkey, chicken, stuffing and stock.

Serves 4 to 6

225 g/8 oz bacon rashers
225 g/8 oz left-over chicken or turkey
225 g/8 oz pork sausage-meat
50 ml/2 fl oz stock from boiling chicken or turkey carcass
Left-over stuffing

1. De-rind bacon, lay rashers on a board and, using a knife with a wide blade, press out rashers to stretch and widen them.
2. Line a deep pie-dish with bacon rashers, saving 1 or 2 for later.
3. Add chicken or turkey cut up into bite-sized pieces.
4. Cover with a layer of sausage-meat.
5. Pour over the stock.
6. Bake in a warm oven, Gas 3, 325°F, 160°C for 10 to 15 minutes. Then remove pie from oven and press stuffing over top. Cover with remaining bacon. Bake a further 20 minutes.

Can be eaten hot from the dish or cold, turned out and sliced.

Sybil Norcott
Irlam, Nr Manchester

COOKING THE GOOSE

WITH SAGE AND ONION STUFFING

Note: Time the cooking so that goose is removed from oven on to heated dish 10 to 15 minutes before serving the meal. This will allow time to make the gravy and also to 'rest' the bird.

Cooking time: 20 minutes to each 450 g/1 lb weight after stuffing plus 20 to 30 minutes extra depending on age of bird.

1. First make the stuffing (see next recipe).
2. Remove giblets from goose, wash them and place in pan with sufficient water to cover. Add 6 to 8 peppercorns and a small bay leaf. Bring to boil and simmer for at least 2 hours. Strain and keep stock for gravy. The giblets can now be discarded. (Preparation and cooking of giblets can be done the day before.)
3. Wipe inside of goose and fill with sage and onion stuffing, not too tightly packed.
4. Truss goose neatly with skewers and fine clean string. This is simply to keep the stuffing in.
5. Place goose on a roasting rack in oven tin. Rub with salt and sprinkle on a little flour. (The breast can be pricked with a fork to help fat escape, but this is not really necessary.)
6. Place in centre of oven preheated to moderately hot, Gas 6, 400°F, 200°C, for 20 minutes to crisp skin. Then lower heat to moderate, Gas 4, 350°F, 180°C for remainder of cooking time and cover goose with greaseproof paper or foil to prevent excess browning. Remove paper for last 20 minutes if goose is not brown enough.
7. Remove goose on to warm dish and make the gravy, using giblet stock, and onion liquor reserved from preparation of stuffing.

SAGE AND ONION STUFFING

FOR GOOSE AND DUCK

Sufficient for a 3.6 to 4.5 kg/8 to 10 lb goose. Use half quantity for a duck.

900 g/2 lb onions
Water
25 g/1 oz butter
125 to 175 g/4 to 6 oz fresh wholemeal or white breadcrumbs (*see page 52*)
2 teaspoons Salt and Pepper Mix (*see page 17*)
2 to 3 teaspoons dried sage

1. Skin and chop onions, cook in a little water until just softening, about 15 to 20 minutes. Drain well, reserve liquid for gravy.
2. Add butter, crumbs, Salt and Pepper Mix and sage to taste, using sufficient crumbs to make mixture hold together. Do not pack stuffing in bird too tightly.

A GOOD GRAVY

FOR GOOSE AND DUCK

Using giblet stock and onion liquor reserved from preparation of Sage and Onion Stuffing. (*See previous recipe*).

1. Boil together liquor from giblets and onions.
2. Pour off all fat and sediment from roasting tin into cold basin and fat will rise to top at once.
3. Place 2 tablespoons fat in a pan, remove rest with spoon to dripping jar.
4. Place pan on heat, add 2 level tablespoons flour and sizzle for 1 to 2 minutes.
5. Gradually add hot, not boiling, stock and stir well. Add sediment from basin, taste for seasoning, boil up for 2 minutes.

This is the original method of making gravy and can be applied for all meats, using good vegetable and meat stock, with meat juices and/or sediment from roasting tin.

CHOOSING A DUCK

If buying fresh duck the best time of the year is June and early July. Choose a bird with a plump breast. Even a plump duck has a shallow breast and will not feed as many people as a chicken of the same weight. A 1.5 kg/3½ lb bird will feed 4 people adequately. Traditionally, young birds are roasted with sage and onion stuffing, and served with apple sauce, new potatoes and green peas.

Allow 15 minutes for each 450 g/1 lb and 15 minutes over. Remember to weigh the stuffed bird and to calculate cooking time on stuffed weight.

CRISPY DUCKLING—a tip

Prick the duckling all over with a pin or very sharp fork and then roast in a moderately hot oven, Gas 6, 400°F, 200°C, for 15 minutes per ½ kg/1 lb.

APPLE AND PRUNE STUFFING

For goose or duck or, as a change, for pork.

20 prunes, soaked overnight
1 stick celery
Liver of the bird
325 g/12 oz peeled and sliced apple, or left-over
   apple sauce
50 g/2 oz cooked brown rice
1 dessertspoon finely-chopped parsley
Grated rind and juice of ½ lemon
A grating of nutmeg
Salt and pepper
Pinch of brown sugar
1 lightly-beaten egg

1. Stew prunes gently until tender and let them cool.
2. Meanwhile, slice the celery finely.
3. Chop up the liver.
4. Cut prunes in halves and remove stones.
5. Mix prunes, apple and rice.
6. Add celery and liver.
7. Blend in parsley, lemon rind and juice.
8. Season with nutmeg, salt, pepper and brown sugar.
Note: sugar is not necessary if using apple sauce.
9. Bind together with egg.

Sybil Norcott
Irlam, Nr Manchester

APRICOT STUFFING

Excellent with duck but good with other poultry

125 g/4 oz finely-chopped onion
50 g/2 oz butter
175 g/6 oz fresh wholemeal or white breadcrumbs (*see page 52*)
125 g/4 oz finely-chopped dried apricots
50 g/2 oz finely-chopped salted peanuts
1 tablespoon chopped parsley
Grated rind and juice of 1 orange
1 level teaspoon Salt and Pepper Mix (*see page
   17*)
1 small beaten egg

1. Fry onion in butter to soften.
2. In bowl combine crumbs, apricots, peanuts, parsley and finely grated orange rind. Add onion and any butter in pan, orange juice and Salt and Pepper Mix. Mix with sufficient egg to bind.

See also Orange Stuffing, page 117.

ROAST DUCK WITH ORANGE SAUCE

Serves 4

A 1.3 to 1.5 kg/3 to 3½ lb duck
Rind of 1 orange
25 g/1 oz butter
150 ml/¼ pint stock

1. Put the thinly-pared rind of the orange with 15 g/½ oz of the butter inside the duck.
2. Spread remaining butter over the breast.
3. Put into a hot oven, Gas 7, 425°F, 220°C, and immediately reduce heat to moderate, Gas 4, 350°F, 180°C. Roast the duck for 1 hour, basting several times.

ORANGE SAUCE
2 oranges
50 g/2 oz butter
35 g/1¼ oz cornflour
450 ml/¾ pint brown stock (half a beef stock
   cube will do)
Salt and Pepper Mix (*see page 17*)
2 tablespoons sherry

1. Finely grate the zest from one of the oranges. Squeeze the juice from both and add the zest to the juice.
2. Melt butter in a small pan. Blend in cornflour and let it sizzle a little.
3. Remove from heat and stir in the stock. Bring to the boil, stirring, and let it boil for one minute. Season with Salt and Pepper Mix.
4. Stir in orange juice with rind and the sherry.

Heat through but do not boil.

ROAST DUCKLING WITH WALNUT SAUCE

Serves 4

A 2 kg/4½ lb duckling
Salt

SAUCE
2 tablespoons duckling dripping
1 medium-sized onion, chopped
50 g/2 oz walnuts, chopped
1 level tablespoon plain flour
300 ml/½ pint duckling stock
Grated rind and juice of 1 orange
2 tablespoons sherry
2 teaspoons chopped parsley

TO SERVE AND GARNISH
1 tablespoon duckling dripping
25 g/1 oz walnut halves
Watercress
1 orange, cut into slices

1. Wipe duckling dry inside and out. Place on a rack in a shallow roasting tin. Prick the skin all over with a fork. This allows the fat to flow out during cooking and bastes the bird without any attention. Sprinkle well with salt.
2. Place in a hot oven, Gas 7, 425°F, 220°C and immediately reduce heat to a moderate, Gas 4, 350°F, 180°C. Roast for 1½ to 1¾ hours, or until tender and well browned, and the juices run clear when the thickest part of the leg is pierced with a skewer.
3. *To prepare sauce.* Heat duckling dripping in a pan, add chopped onion and walnuts and cook gently until lightly browned.
4. Stir in flour and cook 1 minute.
5. Gradually blend in stock, orange rind and juice and simmer gently for 2 minutes, stirring throughout.
6. Stir in sherry and chopped parsley and season to taste.
7. *To serve.* (a) Gently fry walnut halves in duckling dripping then drain well on kitchen paper.
(b) Put duckling on a hot serving dish and garnish with watercress, fried walnuts and orange slices. Serve walnut sauce in a separate bowl.

FOR A PARTY

ROAST DUCKLING WITH THREE SAUCES

A 2.7 kg/6 lb duck will feed six people

APRICOT
A 425 g/15 oz tin of apricot halves in syrup

APPLE
2 large cooking apples
1 tablespoon lemon juice
2 tablespoons water
15 g/½ oz butter
1 tablespoon sugar

REDCURRANT JELLY SAUCE
3 to 4 tablespoons redcurrant jelly
1 tablespoon water
Finely-grated rind and juice of ½ lemon
A good pinch of nutmeg

TO SERVE AND GARNISH
2 to 3 teaspoons redcurrant jelly
1 rosy dessert apple
A little lemon juice
Watercress

Prepare the duckling as in the previous recipe, but increase cooking time to 2½ hours.

APRICOT SAUCE
1. Reserve 8 apricot halves for decoration and heat through in oven 10 minutes before end of cooking time.
2. Press remaining fruit and syrup through a sieve, or liquidise. Heat through in small pan.

APPLE SAUCE
1. Peel and core apples then slice into a saucepan.
2. Add lemon juice and water and simmer gently until soft and pulpy.
3. Beat in butter and sugar.

REDCURRANT JELLY SAUCE
Place all ingredients in a small saucepan and stir over gentle heat until jelly has dissolved. Simmer 2 minutes.

TO SERVE
Place the duckling on a warmed serving dish. Fill apricot halves with a little redcurrant jelly. Cut fine slices of unpeeled apple and sprinkle with lemon juice. Arrange these around the duckling and decorate with sprigs of watercress.

Serve the three sauces in similar containers so that guests may help themselves.

Any remaining sauces may be mixed together to make a tasty sauce to serve with grilled sausages or cold meats.

Audrey Hundy
Abbots Morton, Worcestershire

DUCK AND ORANGE MAYONNAISE

Quite as good with pork.

Serves 4

Have ready both French dressing and mayonnaise. Try the French dressing suggested for Royal Slaw on *page 146*. A bought mayonnaise will do provided it is a good brand.

450 g/1 lb chopped, cold, cooked duck or pork
½ cup French dressing (*see page 133*)
Celery salt to taste
1 tablespoon chopped cashew nuts
150 ml/¼ pint chopped seedless orange
300 ml/½ pint cooked green peas
4 to 5 tablespoons mayonnaise (*see page 134*)
Salt and pepper

TO GARNISH AND SERVE
4 small sprigs of parsley
Chopped mint
Lettuce heart or curly endive
A little more French dressing
A bowl of mayonnaise

1. Sprinkle meat with the half cup of French dressing. Cover and leave to stand for 2 hours.
2. Drain well. Add celery salt, nuts, orange and green peas.
3. Mix in mayonnaise to coat. Season if necessary with salt and pepper.
4. Divide equally among 4 individual salad plates.
5. Place a sprig of parsley in the centre of each portion. Sprinkle chopped mint around parsley. Fringe with one or two lettuce leaves or sprigs of curly endive, coated with French dressing.

Serve with additional mayonnaise in a bowl.
Note. When required for a party, cut large oranges in half. Carefully scoop out the flesh and all the membrane. Zig-zag round the edges with scissors.

Fill oranges with salad. Place each on an individual plate, and arrange the lettuce or endive round the base. Garnish with parsley and mint as described.

Mrs Sybil Norcott
Irlam, Manchester

CHOOSING A GUINEA FOWL

The average weight of a guinea fowl dressed for the table is 1.3 to 1.5 kg/3 to 3½ lb. It should look firm in texture with a plump breast. One bird is usually enough for 4 people. Its taste is something between pheasant and chicken. However, it is eaten fresh like chicken and not hung to become 'gamey' like pheasant. The meat is slightly darker than chicken.

ROAST GUINEA FOWL

Choose a good-quality roasting fowl. If the bird is frozen, thaw out in refrigerator.
Stuff with veal forcemeat.

Serves 4

VEAL FORCEMEAT
40 g/1½ oz butter
125 g/4 oz wholemeal or white breadcrumbs
2 teaspoons chopped parsley
1 teaspoon mixed herbs, dried or fresh
Grated rind of ½ lemon
Salt, pepper, few grains of cayenne pepper
1 beaten egg
A little milk if necessary
2 to 3 rashers of fat bacon, or 2 good tablespoons lard or dripping, to prepare bird for oven

1. Put butter to soften in a warm place and then cream it.
2. Mix together breadcrumbs, parsley, mixed herbs, lemon rind and seasoning.
3. Mix in the creamed butter, beaten egg and enough milk to make a crumbly mixture that just holds together. Milk may not be required.

TO STUFF AND COOK THE GUINEA FOWL
1. Stuff the forcemeat into the neck or body cavity of the bird and tie it up with skewers and string.
2. Weigh the stuffed bird and calculate cooking time by allowing 20 minutes to the 450 g/1 lb and 20 minutes over.

3. Put it in a roasting tin and cover well with fat bacon, lard or dripping. Cover the breast with greaseproof paper and foil.

4. Roast in a moderate oven, Gas 4, 350°F, 180°C. Remove the paper and foil for the last 15 minutes. Serve with bread sauce (*see page 66*), watercress and pieces of lemon.

Stella Boldy
Sykehouse, N. Humberside

ROAST PHEASANT

Hen birds are more tender and tasty, but cock birds are bigger.

Serves 4 to 5

1 pheasant
125 g/4 oz stewing beef, cheaper cut
3 or 4 rashers streaky bacon

THE TRIMMINGS
Bread sauce (*see page 66*)
Breadcrumbs fried in butter
Brown gravy
Watercress

1. Pluck, draw and truss the bird (*see page 51*).
2. Put piece of stewing beef inside bird. This keeps the bird moist during cooking. It is not served up with the bird but do not throw it away: with the carcass it will make good stock.
2. Spread bacon over bird and put it in a roasting tin.
4. Roast in a moderate oven, Gas 4, 350°F, 180°C, for 45 minutes to 1 hour.
5. Remove on to a warmed serving dish and keep hot.

Serve garnished with bunches of fresh watercress, potato crisps, braised celery or Brussels sprouts.

BREAD SAUCE
(*See page 66*)
This may be cooked in the cooler part of the oven with the meat.

FRIED BREADCRUMBS
25 g/1 oz butter or margarine
50 g/2 oz wholemeal or white breadcrumbs

1. Heat butter or margarine in a frying pan.
2. Tip in breadcrumbs and stir them around in the hot fat until all are nicely browned.

Serve them hot in a small warmed dish.

BROWN GRAVY
Make this in the roasting tin when pheasant is taken out on to warmed serving dish.

1. Sprinkle 25 g/1 oz wholemeal or plain flour into the roasting tin and stir it into the fat and meat juices. Let flour cook for a minute on a low heat.
2. Pour in hot water, or water in which vegetables have been cooked. Stir well until gravy thickens, adding more water if necessary, to make a fairly thin gravy. Boil for 2 or 3 minutes. If too pale it may be darkened with a few drops of gravy browning.
3. Taste and add salt and pepper if necessary. Strain into warmed gravy jug.

PHEASANT CASSEROLE

Pheasant may be cooked whole or in joints.

Serves 4

50 g/2 oz seedless raisins
150 ml/¼ pint cider (or home-made white wine)
1 pheasant, about 1.1 kg/2½ lb
450 ml/¾ pint water
A small piece of carrot
1 medium-sized onion
2 sticks of celery
2 medium-sized cooking apples and 1 dessert apple
15 g/½ oz flour
Salt and pepper
A pinch of mixed spice
65 g/2½ oz butter
300 ml/½ pint stock (from giblets)
150 ml/¼ pint yoghurt or cream

1. Put raisins to soak in cider or wine for 2 hours.
2. Remove giblets from pheasant and make stock by simmering them in the water for ¾ hour with the carrot, a quarter of the onion and a small piece of the celery. Then drain and reserve stock.
3. Chop remaining onion and celery finely. Peel, core and slice cooking apples.
4. Either truss pheasant by tying the legs, or joint it. Dust with flour seasoned with salt, pepper and spice.
5. Melt butter and turn pheasant in it to brown. Then lift it out on to a plate.
6. Fry onion gently until transparent. Then add celery and cooking apple and fry for a further 5 minutes.
7. Stir in any remaining flour and cook for 1 minute.
8. Add cider, raisins and stock and bring to the boil.

9. Put this and the pheasant into a pan which just contains it. Put on a tight-fitting lid and let it just simmer for about 1 to 1½ hours for a whole pheasant, 45 minutes to 1 hour for joints, or until tender. Cooking time will vary according to age of bird.

10. When tender, lift pheasant out into a warmed serving dish and keep it warm.

11. If the sauce is very runny, boil without lid to reduce and thicken. Then add yoghurt or cream, adjust seasoning and reheat but do not boil. Pour into a separate bowl if pheasant is served whole or around the joints in the serving dish.

12. Peel dessert apple, cut out core and slice into fine rings. Fry these lightly in remaining butter and set them on dish around the pheasant.

See also Game Soup, page 16.

CASSEROLED WOOD PIGEON

Serves 4

25 g/1 oz lard
50 g/2 oz belly pork, finely-diced
4 pigeons, or, if plump ones, 2, each split in half
25 g/1 oz wholemeal or white flour
300 ml/½ pint stout (not sweet variety—Guinness is best)
300 ml/½ pint chicken stock or dissolve 1 chicken stock cube in 300 ml/½ pint water
225 g/8 oz onions, cut in wedges
1 clove garlic, crushed
2 sprigs thyme
125 g/4 oz mushrooms, sliced
Salt
Black pepper
Gravy browning

1. Melt lard and fry pork until pale golden and the fat has run out. Lift pieces out into large casserole.

2. Brown pigeons, skin side down, in the fat then add to pork in casserole.

3. Blend in flour to pan, stir in stout and water.

4. Add all remaining ingredients except gravy browning and bring to the boil stirring.

5. Pour over pigeons in casserole.

6. Cover and cook in a moderate oven, Gas 3, 325°F, 160°C for about 3 hours, or until tender.

7. Remove thyme and check seasoning, adding a little gravy browning if necessary.

This can be cooked just as well, and more economically, on top of the stove, using throughout a good-sized, heavy saucepan. Cover and simmer very slowly for about one hour, or until tender (cooking time can vary from half an hour to 3 hours).

CHESHIRE POTTED PIGEON

Will keep in a fridge or cold place for one month. Once open it should be used in a day or two.

3 pigeons
Salt and pepper
A dash of Worcestershire sauce
2 to 3 tablespoons melted butter

Pigeons are plucked and drawn like poultry (*see page 51*).

1. Clean the pigeons.

2. Put them in a pan, cover with water and boil until the meat is leaving the bones.

3. Remove from heat and, when cool enough to handle, carefully remove all bones.

4. Put bones back into saucepan and boil until water has reduced to about 1 cupful.

5. Mince the meat finely.

6. Season with salt, pepper and Worcestershire sauce. Moisten with stock from the bones and a little of the melted butter.

7. Press into pots and run a layer of melted butter over the top to seal each jar.

Sybil Norcott
Irlam, Nr Manchester

See also Thatched House Pie, page 220.

JUGGED HARE

This popular classic British dish is surprisingly cheap and not difficult to make. It is really only a glorified stew enriched with port, and thickened with a liaison—butter kneaded with flour—and the blood of the hare to give a really smooth sauce. Take care not to over cook the hare. Simmer it slowly. A young hare, leveret, will take about 2 hours and serve 6, whereas an older hare will take over 3 hours and be enough for 8 to 10 people.

Serves 6

1 hare cut into neat pieces
50 g/2 oz bacon fat
2 large onions, each stuck with 2 cloves
1 stick celery, cut in 2.5 cm/1 inch pieces
6 peppercorns
Rind of $\frac{1}{2}$ lemon
A pinch of cayenne pepper
1 blade of mace
A bouquet garni (*see page 84*)
Salt and pepper
1.2 litres/2 pints water

FOR THE LIAISON
50 g/2 oz butter
50 g/2 oz wholemeal or white flour
150 ml/$\frac{1}{4}$ pint port wine
1 tablespoon redcurrant jelly
The blood of the hare

FOR THE GARNISH
Salad oil (for frying)
4 slices of bread
Chopped parsley

1. Divide the hare into neat joints, saving as much of the blood as possible. Your butcher will do this for you and, more often than not, will put the blood in a tin for you to carry it home.
2. Melt the bacon fat in a large frying pan and fry the joints briskly until they are a good brown colour; then remove them from the pan.
3. Pack the joints into a heavy ovenproof casserole with the onions, celery, peppercorns, lemon rind, cayenne pepper, mace, bouquet garni, salt and pepper.
4. Pour the water over contents of casserole and cover with a tightly fitting lid. Bake in a moderate oven, Gas 3, 325°F, 160°C for 2 hours or until the hare is tender.
5. Pour the gravy through a sieve into a pan. Remove spices, lemon rind and herbs from the casserole and keep meat and vegetables warm.
6. To make the liaison, work the butter on a plate with a palette knife until it is soft. Then knead in the flour a little at a time to form a smooth paste.
7. Reheat the gravy, but do not allow it to boil, and add the kneaded butter in small pieces, whisking constantly until it has thickened.
8. Add the port and redcurrant jelly to the gravy and simmer gently until the jelly has dissolved.
9. Blend two or three tablespoons of the gravy with the blood and then add the blood to the rest of the gravy. The gravy must not be allowed to boil after this stage. Adjust the seasoning with more salt and pepper.
10. Strain the gravy over the hare. Cover bottom of a frying pan with oil, heat, add the slices of bread and fry until golden. Cut the fried bread into kite shapes and arrange on top of the hare. Sprinkle with parsley.

Serve with redcurrant jelly and savoury forcemeat balls (*see* Rabbit Casserole, *page 79*).

HARE CASSEROLE WITH MUSHROOMS

Serves 6
1 hare, weight about 1.1 kg/2$\frac{1}{2}$ lb, jointed into even-sized pieces

MARINADE (*see page 106*)
1 tablespoon redcurrant jelly
75 ml/3 fl oz port or cream sherry
75 ml/3 fl oz wine vinegar
75 ml/3 fl oz mushroom ketchup
1 dessertspoon chopped mixed fresh thyme and marjoram or 1 level teaspoon of each dried
1 medium-sized onion, chopped

TO COOK HARE
225 g/8 oz streaky bacon rashers
50 g/2 oz butter
2 medium-sized onions
50 g/2 oz plain flour
A clove of garlic, crushed
Salt and pepper
Nutmeg
1.5 to 1.75 litres/2$\frac{1}{2}$ to 3 pints chicken stock
300 ml/$\frac{1}{2}$ pint red wine (home-made would be excellent)
225 g/8 oz button mushrooms

1. Melt redcurrant jelly and pour it into a dish. Mix in the other marinade ingredients.

2. Lay the pieces of hare in the marinade and leave for 3 hours.

3. Remove hare from marinade and pat dry. Strain the marinade, discarding onion, but keep liquid to add to gravy.

4. Cut up bacon, discarding rind.

5. Using a large pan, heat the butter, fry bacon gently for a few minutes, then remove to a dish.

6. Add chopped onion and fry gently until transparent. Remove to dish.

7. Sprinkle the flour into the pan and allow it to colour a rich brown.

8. Now put in pieces of hare, turning and shaking the pan to make sure that they are well browned, and cook for about 10 minutes. Remove hare.

9. To same pan add garlic, salt and pepper, nutmeg, onion, bacon, stock, wine and all the marinade. Stir well. Return the hare.

10. Put on lid, cook steadily for $1\frac{1}{2}$ hours or until tender. This may be done on top of stove or in a warm oven, Gas 3, 325°F, 160°C.

11. Wash mushrooms and chop roughly.

12. When hare is tender, remove it on to a dish and keep warm. Strain the sauce, putting bacon with hare.

13. Add mushrooms to sauce, cover and simmer for 10 minutes. Then return hare and bacon to sauce and reheat for 10 minutes if necessary.

Serve with plain boiled potatoes and a green vegetable.

TO GUT, SKIN, CLEAN AND JOINT A RABBIT

GUTTING

1. A rabbit must be gutted as soon as possible after it is killed. Do this before you tackle the skinning.

2. Start with a very sharp, pointed knife and plenty of newspaper.

3. Lay the rabbit on its back on the newspapers with its head towards you.

4. Feel for the lower edge of the breastbone and make first incision here, just through the skin. Then, without removing knife, cut through the skin from this point straight down to the base of the tail.

5. Pick the rabbit up, forelegs in one hand, hind legs in the other, and turn it over so that the intestines can drop out on to the newspaper.

6. Feel inside the rabbit for any other organs, separating liver and kidneys and keeping them aside.

7. Wrap up the other guts and throw them away.

SKINNING

8. Start with hindquarters. Work the skin off the body up to the backbone and down hind legs. You will be able to pull legs out of the skin.

9. Cut off the feet at heel joint. Cut off the tail.

10. Now work up the backbone and round rib cage.

11. Pull the skin up over head. The forelegs will pull out of the skin.

12. Cut off the front feet at first joint above foot.

13. Where neck joins head cut through backbone. Head and complete skin will then come away.

CLEANING

14. First make a slit between hind legs so that any remaining excrement can be washed out under cold running water.

15. Cut the membrane which encloses heart and lungs inside rib cage. Remove these and wash rabbit out thoroughly under cold running water.

16. A rabbit, particularly a wild rabbit, should be soaked in well-salted water for 1 hour before it is cooked. This may be done before or after jointing.

JOINTING

17. Cut off the hind legs where they join backbone.

18. Make another joint, called the saddle, out of the next section of backbone up to the start of the ribs.

19. Divide the forepart of the animal down the backbone to make 2 joints, each with a foreleg, shoulder and section of rib-cage.

RABBIT CASSEROLE

Serves 4

675 g/1½ lb rabbit joints
175 g/6 oz streaky bacon
25 to 50 g/1 to 2 oz bacon dripping or firm
    margarine
325 g/12 oz chopped onion
325 g/12 oz carrot, cut in chunks
2 good sticks celery
200 ml/⅓ pint light ale
125 g/4 oz button mushrooms
1 level tablespoon cornflour
1 teaspoon Salt and Pepper Mix (*see page 17*)
Chopped parsley

FORCEMEAT BALLS
125 g/4 oz fresh wholemeal or white bread-
    crumbs (*see page 52*)
40 g/1½ oz shredded suet
1 tablespoon grated onion
2 teaspoons chopped fresh thyme, or ½ tea-
    spoon dried thyme
½ teaspoon Salt and Pepper Mix (*see page 17*)
1 beaten egg
A little wholewheat or white flour

1. Soak rabbit in lightly-salted water for half an
hour, drain and dry.
2. Cut bacon into 2.5 cm/1 inch pieces and fry gently
to extract fat.
3. Add 25 g/1 oz dripping or margarine to pan, fry
rabbit joints until golden.
4. Lift out joints and transfer to casserole.
5. Fry onion in fat and transfer to casserole.
6. Add to casserole the carrot and celery cut in 2.5
cm/1 inch pieces. Pour over the light ale.
7. Cover and cook in a moderate oven, Gas 4, 350°F
180°C, for 1 hour.
8. Wash mushrooms and add to casserole. Mix cornflour with Salt and Pepper and mix with a little
water.
9. Cover casserole and return it to oven for half an
hour.
10. Meanwhile, make the forcemeat balls. Mix
breadcrumbs, suet, onion, thyme and seasoning and
bind together with the egg. Make into 12 balls, roll
in flour.
11. Fry lightly in fat to seal.
12. Place in casserole. Cover and cook for half an
hour.

Sprinkle on chopped parsley just before serving.

A TIP WITH FRESH SUET
Buy fresh suet from the butcher. Put it in an oven-
proof basin, cover and when the oven is on put it at
the bottom. As the suet gradually melts pour it off
into another basin. When it has set put it in a
polythene bag, store in the refrigerator and grate off
as needed. Keeps a long time.

Mrs M. Wright
Cleethorpes, Lincolnshire

RABBIT CASSEROLE WITH DUMPLINGS

Can be done in oven or on top of stove.

Serves 4

675 g/1½ lb rabbit, jointed
1 tablespoon vinegar
Water
25 g/1 oz flour, seasoned with salt and pepper
40 g/1½ oz dripping
2 onions, sliced
2 apples, sliced
A 400 g/14 oz can of tomatoes, or 450 g/1 lb
    fresh ripe tomatoes, skinned and sliced (*see
    page 139*)
450 ml/¾ pint stock
1 tablespoon redcurrant jelly
1 slice of dry bread, without crusts
½ teaspoon made mustard
½ teaspoon mixed herbs

DUMPLINGS*
125 g/4 oz self-raising flour
¼ teaspoon salt
50 g/2 oz grated suet
1 tablespoon freshly-chopped parsley or ½ tea-
    spoon dried mixed herbs
3 to 4 tablespoons water

See also Sussex Swimmers, page 107

1. Soak rabbit joints for 1 hour in vinegar and water.
Then drain, pat dry and roll them in seasoned flour.
2. Melt dripping in a pan. Fry rabbit for a few
minutes, turning pieces over in hot fat to brown a
little. Lift joints out into a casserole or large saucepan.
3. Fry onions and apples for just 1 minute. Then put
them with rabbit.
4. Add the tomatoes to rabbit.
5. Stir stock into residue in pan. Add redcurrant
jelly.

6. Spread mustard on dry bread, sprinkle on the herbs and put it into the stock. Allow to soak, then beat in. Pour over rabbit.

7. Cover the casserole and cook in a moderate oven, Gas 4, 350°F, 180°C, for 1½ hours. If using a saucepan, put on the lid, bring gently to the boil and simmer for 1½ hours.

8. Meanwhile, prepare dumplings. Mix flour, salt, suet and herbs. Mix to a softish dough with water.

9. Turn on to a well-floured board, cut into 8 pieces and roll them into balls.

10. 20 to 25 minutes before rabbit is done drop dumplings into casserole or pan and replace lid. Keep rabbit simmering as dumplings cook. In casserole allow 25 minutes. In saucepan allow 20 minutes.

RABBIT WITH MUSTARD

Serves 4 to 5

1 rabbit, jointed*
125 g/4 oz bacon, in one piece or 2 thick slices
6 small onions
25 g/1 oz bacon fat or dripping
2 level tablespoons wholemeal or plain flour
600 ml/1 pint chicken stock (a stock cube will do)
1 level dessertspoon French mustard
Salt
Freshly-ground black pepper
15 g/½ oz soft butter, to thicken sauce
15 g/½ oz plain flour, to thicken sauce
3 tablespoons cream or natural yoghurt
1 level tablespoon chopped parsley

* *To prepare and joint a rabbit, see page 78. Or, when you buy the rabbit, ask for this to be done for you.*

1. Soak rabbit joints in salted water for 2 or 3 hours, then drain and pat dry ready for use.

2. Remove rind and cut bacon into small pieces.

3. Peel onions.

4. Heat fat in a large saucepan, fry bacon and onions for 2 or 3 minutes. Transfer them from pan to a plate.

5. Brown rabbit joints in the fat and lift out on to the plate.

6. Stir 2 tablespoons flour into fat and juices now in pan and cook, stirring, for 1 to 2 minutes.

7. Remove pan from heat and gradually blend in stock and mustard. Return pan to heat and boil stirring constantly. Keep stirring while it simmers for 1 to 2 minutes.

8. Return rabbit, bacon and onions to pan. Season to taste with salt and black pepper.

9. Cover pan and simmer for 1 hour.

10. Remove rabbit joints and arrange them on a warmed dish.

11. If sauce needs thickening, strain it into a small pan, spreading contents of strainer over rabbit. Blend together the 15 g/½ oz of butter and flour and whisk in small bits into the sauce. Bring to the boil and cook for 2 minutes.

12. Stir cream or yoghurt and parsley into sauce and pour over rabbit joints. Serve.

CASSEROLED RABBIT WITH RICE AND TOMATO

Serves 4 to 5

1 rabbit, jointed (*see page 78*)
100 g/4 oz ham or bacon
1 large onion
50 g/2 oz good pork or beef dripping
125 g/4 oz long grain brown or white rice
1 small can tomatoes
300 ml/½ pint stock
1 sprig of thyme
1 bay leaf
Salt and pepper

1. Soak rabbit joints in salted water for 30 minutes. Pat dry.

2. Dice the ham or bacon.

3. Peel and finely chop the onion.

4. Heat dripping in a large frying pan, add rabbit joints and brown on both sides. Transfer them to casserole.

5. Add ham or bacon, onion and rice. Stir gently until onion is beginning to brown and fat is absorbed.

6. Add tomatoes, half the stock, the herbs and salt and pepper if necessary. Bring to the boil.

7. Pour this over the rabbit. Add rest of stock so that rabbit is just covered.

8. Put on the lid and cook in a moderately hot oven, Gas 4, 350°F, 180°C, for 1½ to 1¾ hours until rabbit is tender. Remove stem of thyme and bay leaf before serving.

Serve with Carrots in a Casserole (*see page 152*) or buttered cabbage.

RABBIT AND BACON PUDDING

Serves 4

About 450 g/1 lb rabbit in joints
1 bay leaf
1 small chopped onion
6 to 8 peppercorns
225 g/8 oz bacon pieces
1 level tablespoon plain flour
600 ml/1 pint stock (from cooking rabbit)
Salt and pepper
A little brown gravy colouring

SUET CRUST
225 g/8 oz self-raising flour, wholewheat or white or half and half
½ teaspoon salt
125 g/4 oz shredded suet
7 tablespoons water

1. Put rabbit in pan of water with bay leaf, onion and peppercorns. Bring to boil and simmer until tender.
2. Remove joints on to a plate and pick out the bones. Strain stock.
3. Cut up bacon removing rinds and any bones but do not remove the fat. Fry gently for about 10 minutes. Drain and mix with rabbit.
4. Stir flour into fat in pan (if less than 1 tablespoon add a little more bacon dripping). Stir to form a roux, sizzle one minute.
5. Gradually blend in 600 ml/1 pint of the rabbit stock, bring to boil and boil 1 minute. Taste for seasoning. Add a little colouring to make the gravy light brown.
6. Now make the suet crust mixing flour, salt, suet and water to a soft but not sticky dough.
7. Lightly grease a 1.2 litre/2 pint heat-proof basin. Line with ¾ of pastry.
8. Add the rabbit and bacon mixture and 3 table-spoonfuls of the gravy. The basin should not be full to the top to allow for rising.
9. Roll out remaining pastry, damp edges, fit on top.
10. Cover with a layer of greaseproof paper, lightly greased with 2.5 cm/1 inch pleat in top. Cover loosely with foil and press in round rim of basin to seal.

EITHER PRESSURE COOK
Follow instructions in pressure cooker handbook.

OR STEAM
Place in top of steamer, cook 1¼ hours keeping water boiling. Serve with gravy and green vegetables.

SOMERSET RABBIT

Goes well under a pie crust or cobbler or with dumplings.

Serves 4 but easy to cut down for 1 or 2. Or, as it freezes well, cook quantity given, divide it into portions to suit your household and freeze for future use.

1 rabbit
2 tablespoons flour, seasoned with salt and pepper
50 g/2 oz lard or oil
1 onion, chopped
450 g/1 lb mixed root vegetables, scrubbed and cut into chunks
1 tablespoon tomato purée or ketchup
1 teaspoon yeast extract such as Marmite
½ teaspoon mixed herbs
300 ml/½ pint cider
300 ml/½ pint light chicken stock
Salt and pepper

1. Keep the rabbit whole, or, if it will not fit your pan or casserole, just cut it in two between hind legs and rib cage. Dust it over with seasoned flour.
2. Heat lard in a pan and turn rabbit over in it to brown. Lift out of fat on to a plate.
3. Fry onion gently to soften.
4. Put rabbit in a pan or a casserole. Put vegetables on top and add other ingredients. Cover with a lid or foil. *Either* bring to boil and simmer until tender, about 1½ hours, *or* put casserole into a warm oven, Gas 3, 325°F, 160°C, for about 2 hours or until tender.
5. Lift out rabbit, remove all meat from bones and return it to pan. Be careful to remove the small pieces of bone. Re-heat.

Serve as a stew with potatoes and green vegetables, or with pasta shells.

Or try one of the following:
As a pie, serves 6.
Choose a pastry from pages 203 to 205. Allow meat to cool and put it in a dish which it nearly fills so that it supports pastry.
Bake in a hot oven, Gas 7, 425°F, 220°C, for 30 minutes. Check after 15 minutes, reducing tempera-

ture to moderately hot, Gas 5, 375°F, 190°C, if it is browning too quickly.

As a cobbler, serves 6. Delicious with a wholewheat flour.

225 g/8 oz self-raising wholewheat* or white flour
A pinch of salt
25 g/1 oz margarine
A bare 150 ml/¼ pint milk

*Use 1½ teaspoons baking powder if you cannot buy self-raising flour.

1. Put rabbit and gravy into a casserole which allows 5 cm/2 inches headroom. Let it cool.
2. Mix flour, salt and baking powder, if used. Rub in margarine and mix to a soft dough with milk.
3. Using a floured board, roll out 2 cm/¾ inch thick. Cut 5 cm/2 inch rounds and lay these overlapping on top of meat.
4. Bake above middle of a hot oven, Gas 7, 425°F, 220°C, for 30 minutes. If using wholewheat flour, check after 15 minutes and reduce temperature to Gas 5, 375°F, 190°C, if browning too quickly.

WITH DUMPLINGS, *serves 4*

175 g/6 oz self-raising flour
½ teaspoon salt
75 g/3 oz shredded suet
About 6 tablespoons water

1. Mix ingredients, using enough water to make a firm dough. Form into small balls and drop into bubbling pan or casserole.
2. Cover and simmer for 15 minutes.

Mrs Angela Mottram
Axbridge, Somerset

OLD CHESHIRE RABBIT BRAWN

Serves 4 to 6

2 pig's trotters
Water
1 large rabbit
Salt and pepper
Ground allspice

1. Put pig's trotters in a saucepan, cover with cold water and boil gently for 1½ hours.
2. Meanwhile put rabbit into cold, salted water for ½ hour to whiten the flesh. Then discard water.

3. Put rabbit in pan with pig's trotters, adding more water to cover. Boil, together for 2 hours, or until flesh is tender and leaves bones easily. Add more water from time to time if necessary.
4. Remove from heat and allow to cool until it can be handled.
5. Remove all the bones. Cut the meat in small pieces and season to taste with salt, pepper and allspice.
6. Strain the liquid and return it with meat to the pan. Bring to the boil.
7. Rinse 2 moulds with cold water—pudding basins, casserole or soufflé dishes will do.
8. Put the brawn into the wetted moulds. Leave to set overnight.

Serve turned out on a plate with lettuce and tomatoes.

Sybil Norcott
Irlam, Nr Manchester

RABBIT PASTE

1 jointed rabbit
50 g/2 oz margarine
2 teaspoons sugar
12 allspice
6 peppercorns
3 blades mace
1 onion stuck with 12 cloves
2 tablespoons water
225 g/8 oz butter or margarine
1 dessertspoon Worcestershire sauce
Pinch of cayenne pepper
Melted butter

1. Cut rabbit into small pieces and put in a casserole with the margarine, 1 teaspoon of the sugar, the allspice, peppercorns, mace, onion and water.
2. Cover closely and cook in a moderate oven, Gas 3, 325°F, 160°C until meat will leave bones, about 1 hour.
3. Mince meat finely twice.
4. Put it in a bowl and beat with the 225 g/8 oz butter or margarine, Worcestershire sauce, cayenne and remaining teaspoon of sugar.
5. Put into small dishes. Either cover and freeze or pour melted butter over and store until required in refrigerator where it will keep 3 or 4 days.

Spread on hot toast to serve.

Kate Easlea
Hampshire

4

BEEF LAMB PORK HAM AND BACON

STEAK WITH BLACK PEPPER AND CREAM SAUCE

Serves 4 people for a very special occasion

15 g/½ oz crushed black peppers
4 large steaks, either rump, sirloin or fillet
50 g/2 oz butter
1 tablespoon olive oil
1 small onion, chopped
A 150 ml/¼ pint carton of double cream
Salt to taste

1. Press the crushed black pepper into the steaks.
2. Fry steaks in the butter and oil for no more than 5 minutes each side.
3. Remove steaks to a hot dish. Fry chopped onion in steak pan for 2 minutes.
4. Add cream, heat but do not boil. Add salt to taste.
5. Pour over steaks and serve without delay.

Judith Adshead
Mottram St Andrew, Cheshire

STROGANOFF

Made with either beef or pork.

Serves 6 to 8, but easy to make less

A 900 g/2 lb single piece of fillet of beef or fillet of pork
3 medium-sized onions
225 g/8 oz button mushrooms
About 25 g/1 oz butter
A little chopped fresh parsley

SAUCE
25 g/1 oz butter
25 g/1 oz plain flour
1 level tablespoon tomato purée (*see this page*)
¼ level teaspoon nutmeg, freshly-grated if possible
600 ml/1 pint beef stock
150 ml/¼ pint yoghurt or soured cream
Salt and pepper

1. *Start with the sauce.* In quite a large saucepan melt butter, remove from heat and stir in flour.
2. Stir in tomato purée and nutmeg, then gradually stir in stock.

3. Bring to the boil, stirring as sauce thickens, and simmer for 2 minutes.
4. Stir in yoghurt or soured cream and season with salt and pepper.
5. *Now for the main part of the dish.* Cut meat into strips about 5 cm/2 inches long and 1 cm/½ inch wide.
6. Peel and chop onions. Wipe and finely-slice mushrooms.
7. Heat half of the butter in a large frying pan and quickly brown the meat on all sides. Remove from pan into sauce.
8. Add a little more butter to the pan if necessary and fry onions slowly until tender and light brown. Put these in sauce.
9. In the last of the butter fry mushrooms for just 1 or 2 minutes. Put these with meat and onions.
10. Bring the stroganoff to the boil and simmer it for 15 minutes.

Serve with boiled potatoes or rice (*see page 172*).

TO KEEP TOMATO PURÉE FRESH

To keep tomato purée fresh once a tin has been opened, spoon it into a screw-topped jar. Smooth top and pour in a layer of cooking oil. Keep in a cool place. When it is required, pour off oil, spoon out what you need, then return the oil once again.

TO MAKE A BOUQUET GARNI

Tie the following together firmly with a piece of strong cotton: half a bay leaf, a sprig of thyme and several sprigs of parsley, including stalks.
If dried herbs are used, tie up the following in a small piece of muslin: half bay leaf, 1 teaspoon parsley and ½ teaspoon thyme. Other herbs may be used for particular dishes. Marjoram or basil are often used.
Herbs enhance almost any dish.
For some sauces in particular it is better to use a bouquet garni than to spoil the appearance of the sauce with pieces of dried herbs.

RUMP STEAK WITH RICE

Serves 2

275 g/10 oz rump steak
125 g/4 oz brown or white rice
1 large onion, sliced
2 sticks celery, sliced
1 red pepper (optional) cored and sliced
1 to 2 tablespoons wholewheat or plain flour
1 teaspoon Salt and Pepper Mix (*see page 17*)
150 ml/¼ pint stock
2 teaspoons Worcestershire sauce
Chopped parsley

1. Cut fat from meat. Cut fat up small, put it in frying pan and fry to extract dripping. You will need 1 tablespoon. Discard the scraps of skin. If meat is all lean use 25 g/1 oz beef dripping and heat it in frying pan.
2. Follow instructions for Boiled Rice (*see page 172*).
3. Put onion and celery into frying pan to cook for 5 minutes till softening.
4. Meanwhile, cut steak into strips, 1.2 by 6 cm/½ by 2½ inches. Dust lightly with flour seasoned with Salt and Pepper Mix.
5. Add meat to frying pan and turn it over to seal. Add red pepper. Cook for 7 to 8 minutes.
6. Stir in 3 to 4 tablespoons stock and Worcestershire sauce and let it bubble for 2 minutes, adding a little more stock if it is too thick. Taste and season with more salt and pepper if it is needed.
7. Make a border of rice on a warmed serving dish. Pour meat mixture in centre.
8. Sprinkle on chopped parsley and serve at once.

Serve with green vegetables or green salad.

SWEET AND SOUR BEEF

Serves 4

1 green pepper
450 g/1 lb top rump
50 g/2 oz butter
1 clove garlic
125 g/4 oz mushrooms

SAUCE
50 g/2 oz sugar
300 ml/½ pint stock
3 tablespoons vinegar
2 tablespoons sherry
½ teaspoon soya sauce
1 level tablespoon cornflour
2 tablespoons water

1. Remove seeds from the pepper, cut it into small pieces and boil for 5 minutes. Drain.
2. Cut beef into thin strips and fry in butter for 5 minutes, turning frequently.
3. Meanwhile, make the sauce. Use a small pan and dissolve the sugar in the stock. Add vinegar, sherry and soya sauce.
4. Blend cornflour with the water and add this to the sauce. Bring to the boil and cook gently for 2 minutes.
5. Crush garlic and slice mushrooms. Add these to the beef and cook for 5 minutes more.
6. Add the drained pepper to the beef and mushrooms. Add the sauce and heat thoroughly.

Serve with boiled brown or white rice.

Judith Adshead
Mottram St Andrew, Cheshire

THIN RIB OR FLANK OF BEEF

A good cheap roast

Serves 6–8

1.3 to 1.8 kg/3 to 4 lb thin rib or flank, on the bone

1. Score the top of the meat and sprinkle with salt.
2. Place on rack in roasting tin, with 150 ml/¼ pint of water.
3. Cook in a moderate oven, Gas 3, 325°F, 160°C, allowing 50 minutes to 450 g/1 lb. The meat can be covered loosely with foil, allowing an extra 30 minutes cooking time.
4. Remove bones from meat whilst hot.

Equally good eaten cold.

YORKSHIRE PUDDINGS (1)

Makes 12 small puddings.

125 g/4oz strong plain flour
¼ teaspoon salt
1 large egg
300 ml/½ pint skimmed milk (ie. skim off
    creamy top)

1. Beat all well together until bubbles appear. Can be left to stand until required, but this is not necessary.
2. Heat a little dripping in 12 deep patty tins, half fill with batter. Cook near top of a hot oven, Gas 7, 425°F, 220°C, for about 30 minutes, until puddings are golden and puffy.

YORKSHIRE PUDDINGS (2)

Made with wholewheat flour. Enough for 9 or 10 small, light puddings.

50 g/2 oz plain wholewheat flour
Pinch of salt
1 egg
150 ml/¼ pint milk
2 tablespoons water
Dripping

1. Mix flour and salt.
2. Make a well in the centre. Drop in egg and mix to start drawing in flour.
3. Add milk and water gradually, beating all the time to avoid lumps in the flour.
4. Put a knife-end of dripping in each patty tin and put them in a hot oven, Gas 7, 425°F, 220°C, for 5 minutes to get really hot.
5. Give pudding mixture a final hard whisk with egg beater and pour at once into the tins.
6. Put straight in the oven for 20 to 30 minutes until puffy and golden brown. Can be cooked in a moderately hot oven, Gas 5, 375°F, 190°C, but will take the full 30 minutes. Try not to open oven for first 10 minutes.

TO SAVE TIME

If you are in a hurry you can make Yorkshire Pudding batter in a food processor. It is not necessary to leave it to stand.

POT ROAST BRISKET

Boned and rolled brisket may be used or a piece on the bone.

1. Add to the meat in the pan a stock cube and three quarters of an inch of water.
2. Season well with salt and pepper.
3. Cover with lid or tin foil.
4. Put in a hot oven, Gas 7, 425°F, 220°C. In about half an hour, when you begin to smell the meat cooking, reduce heat to moderate, Gas 3, 325°F, 160°C, and cook for further 2 hours.
5. When you raise the heat and put your Yorkshire puddings in the oven take the lid or covering off the meat to let it brown. The juices make a good gravy which may be thickened if preferred.

PRESSED BRISKET

1.3 to 1.5 kg/3 to 3½ lb brisket
1 pig's trotter

Buy the brisket on the bone. Ask the butcher to loosen the bone but not entirely remove it and to place it in brine for 3 to 4 days.

1 carrot, chopped
1 onion, chopped
A bouquet garni (see page 84)

1. To remove excess salt, soak brisket overnight in cold water, together with trotter if also brined.
2. Next day, place brisket and trotter in large pan, cover with cold water, add carrot, onion and bouquet garni.
3. Cover pan, bring quickly to boil, lower heat and simmer very gently until the meat is tender (about 2 to 2½ hours).
4. Transfer the beef to a dish—the trotter is not used and may have cooked away. Remove bones, gristle and any excess fat from meat.
5. Pack into a mould to fill it and pour over about 150 ml/¼ pint of the strained liquid. Place a board on top and weight down (not too heavily). Leave overnight to set.

STOCK

The liquid from the brisket should be strained into a bowl and left overnight in a cool place. Lift off the fat and use the stock for soups etc. It will freeze well in an airtight container.

TO KEEP AND USE LEFT-OVER FAT

The fat can be removed from stock after boiling beef, bacon or ham, or from the dripping tin after roasting, but do not mix the fats from different meats.

TO CLARIFY

1. Place fat in a saucepan with a little water. Bring slowly to boil.
2. Strain into a basin and allow to set. All sediment will sink into the water.
3. The fat can be removed from the top. Scrape clean, melt and pour into labelled pots.
It is advisable to use beef dripping when cooking beef dishes, pork or bacon dripping for pork, etc. In this way the flavour of the meat is not impaired.
Pork and bacon dripping makes good pastry for using with a savoury filling.
Beef dripping is delicious on toast.
Mutton fat will seal chutneys in the same way as wax.
When fat is clarified it will keep if covered for several weeks. If not covered is inclined to develop an 'off flavour'. Should not be frozen, but will keep in refrigerator.

TO SALT A PIECE OF BEEF

An excellent brine for silverside or brisket. It is worth doing a large piece while you are about it: a 1.8 to 2.7 kg/4 to 6 lb piece is ideal. This will serve 8 to 10 peoplc. A piece of frozen meat can be done straight from the freezer without thawing.

BRINE
4 litres/7 pints water
675 g/1½ lb coarse salt
450 g/1 lb dark brown sugar (Barbados or Muscovado)
50 g/2 oz saltpetre
1 bay leaf
1 sprig of thyme
10 crushed juniper berries
10 crushed peppercorns

1. Put all brine ingredients in a large saucepan, bring to the boil and boil hard for 5 minutes. Then leave to cool.

2. Strain the brine into a crock or a polythene bucket. Put it in a cool place.
3. Immerse the meat and leave it for 7 to 10 days or longer, depending on weight of meat.

The brine may, of course, be used again.

TO COOK THE SALT BEEF
2 onions
2 or 3 cloves
2 or 3 carrots
A bouquet garni (see page 84)
5 or 6 peppercorns

1. Take meat out of brine and rinse in cold water. If it has been in brine over 10 days steep it in plenty of cold water overnight but no longer.
2. Put meat in a pan, cover with cold water and bring to the boil. If water tastes very salty throw it away and start again with fresh water.
3. Add the onions stuck with cloves, sliced carrots, bouquet garni and peppercorns to the pan.
4. Bring slowly to the boil, cover pan and just simmer. Allow 30 minutes to the ½kg/1 lb and 30 minutes over.

Eat either hot or cold. If eaten cold press it lightly in a tight fitting dish. Keep the liquid for stock.

BEEF OLIVES

Serves 8

575 to 675 g/1¼ to 1½ lb topside beef cut into 8 thin slices not less than 8 to 10 cm/3 to 4 inches
8 small slices streaky bacon
25g/1 oz beef dripping
1 level tablespoon flour
300 ml/½ pint stock
1 teaspoon Worcestershire sauce

STUFFING
50g/2 oz fresh wholewheat or white breadcrumbs (see page 52)
25 g/1 oz shredded suet
1 small grated onion
1 teaspoon chopped parsley
1 teaspoon mixed herbs
A good grating of pepper
1 egg-yolk

1. Combine the stuffing ingredients and divide into 8 rolls.

2. Beat slices of beef until thin. A rolling pin is ideal for this.

3. Place a piece of bacon and a roll of stuffing on top of each slice of beef. Roll up and tie with a length of fine string.

4. Melt dripping in large frying pan. When hot put in beef rolls and turn over in fat to seal.

5. Pack neatly into a shallow casserole, if possible just large enough to contain them.

6. Stir flour into fat in pan and cook 1 minute. Add stock gradually, stirring to prevent lumps forming. Add Worcestershire sauce. When boiling, pour over the meat rolls. Cover.

7. Cook in a moderate oven, Gas 4, 350°F, 180°C, until tender, $1\frac{1}{4}$ to $1\frac{1}{2}$ hours.

8. Remove strings and place rolls on hot serving dish. A few drops of gravy browning can be added to the sauce if a little more colour is required. Trickle 1 to 2 tablespoons over Beef Olives. Strain the rest into a sauceboat.

Serve with a border of piped, creamed potatoes or try Jamie Jackson's Bien Pommes de Terre on *page 157*.

BRAISED STEAK WITH VEGETABLES

Serves 4 or 5

A 675 g/1½ lb single piece of lean braising steak cut about 2.5 cm/1 inch thick
675 g/1½ lb mixed vegetables, onions, leeks, carrots, celery, turnip—whatever you prefer
2 teaspoons flour
25 g/1 oz beef dripping
Salt and pepper
150 ml/¼ pint beef stock (*see page 10*)

MARINADE (*see page 106*)
2 tablespoons oil
2 tablespoons vinegar
1 small onion, chopped
A clove of garlic chopped (optional)
6 peppercorns

1. Mix the marinade in a flat dish and soak the meat for 3 to 4 hours, turning occasionally.

2. Meanwhile, prepare vegetables and cut into 5 cm/2 inch pieces.

3. Remove meat from marinade, pat dry and dust well with flour.

4. Heat dripping in frying pan, seal meat quickly on both sides. Lift it out on to a plate.

5. Fry vegetables quickly in the frying pan until just golden.

6. Place them in the bottom of a casserole large enough to hold the steak in one piece. Season with salt and pepper. Place steak on top.

7. Remove peppercorns from marinade and pour it with stock into frying pan. Bring to the boil and pour into casserole.

8. Cover tightly to prevent drying up. If casserole has no lid, cover tightly with greaseproof paper and foil.

9. Cook in a warm oven, Gas 3, 325°F, 160°C for $1\frac{1}{4}$ to $1\frac{1}{2}$ hours.

Can be served with jacket potatoes. Choose small ones, and rub well with butter, bacon dripping or oil. Spear them on skewers and they will cook at the same time as the meat.

STEAK AND KIDNEY PUDDING

Serves 4

FILLING
25 g/1 oz beef dripping
125 g/4 oz chopped onion
450 g/1 lb lean pie beef, cut into cubes
125 g/4 oz ox kidney, trimmed and cut slightly smaller than the beef
1 level tablespoon flour seasoned with 1 teaspoon Salt and Pepper Mix (*see page 17*)
450 ml/¾ pint water
2 teaspoons Worcestershire sauce
125 g/4 oz mushrooms

SUET CRUST
225 g/8 oz self-raising flour
½ teaspoon salt
125 g/4 oz shredded suet
7 tablespoons water

Note: you can use a pressure cooker (trivet removed) for this. It saves 1½ hours' cooking time.

1. Melt dripping in pan, add onion, cook 1 minute.

2. Mix beef and kidney into seasoned flour, coating well. Add to pan and stir over heat to seal—it will change colour.

3. Add water and Worcestershire sauce, stir until boiling.

4. Cover and simmer for about 2 hours until meat is tender. Stir occasionally. Or pressure cook.

5. Pour off all but 3 tablespoons of the gravy and mix the sliced mushrooms with the meat.

6. Make the suet crust mixing flour, salt, suet and water to a soft but not sticky dough.

7. Lightly grease a 1.2 litre/2 pint heat-proof basin.

8. Roll out pastry on a floured board to a round, about 35 cm/14 inches across.

9. Cut away a segment exactly a quarter of the circle. Shape it back into a ball (it will be used for the lid).

10. The large piece of pastry will now fit the basin. Press it in lightly.

11. Tip the meat mixture into the pastry-lined basin.

12. Roll out the lid to fit. Dampen edges and fit it on top.

13. Cover with a layer of greaseproof paper, lightly greased, with a 2.5 cm/1 inch pleat in it.

Cover loosely with a piece of foil and press in round rim of basin to seal.

EITHER PRESSURE COOK:

(a) Place pudding on trivet in pressure cooker with 1¼ pints of water.

(b) With lid on, allow to steam 15 minutes.

(c) Put on control valve at lowest pressure and pressure cook for 25 minutes. Reduce at room temperature (7 to 8 minutes).

OR STEAM

Place on top of steamer. Cook 1¼ hours, keeping water boiling.

OR

If you have neither of these, stand basin on a trivet or upturned saucer in a large saucepan. Pour in boiling water to come halfway up side of basin. Boil for 1¼ hours. Keep pan replenished with boiling water. Do not let it go off the boil or pudding may be heavy.

Serve with gravy and green vegetables.

See also Steak and Kidney Pie, page 223.

BEEF CASSEROLE

Serves 4 to 5

Remember to start the night before.

675 g/1½ lb stewing beef

MARINADE (*see page 106 for a note on marinades*)
3 tablespoons oil
1 tablespoon wine or cider vinegar, or lemon juice
1 wineglass of red wine
1 carrot, sliced in fine rings
1 onion, sliced in rings
1 teaspoon chopped fresh thyme, or ½ teaspoon dried
1 bay leaf

TO COOK
40 g/1½ oz lard
325 g/12 oz carrots, cut in 1 cm/½ inch slices
450 g/1 lb tomatoes, skinned (*see page 139*) and chopped or a 400 g/14 oz tin of tomatoes
Salt and pepper
675 g/1½ lb potatoes, peeled and thinly-sliced
150 ml/¼ pint beef stock

1. Put marinade ingredients in a pan and simmer for 15 minutes. Leave to cool.

2. Trim meat and cut it into 2.5 cm/1 inch cubes. Put in a basin.

3. Pour cold marinade over meat and leave overnight in refrigerator or a cool place.

4. Strain marinade off meat and reserve it.

5. Brown meat in hot lard and place in a very deep casserole.

6. Add carrots, tomatoes and seasoning to casserole.

7. Top with potato slices.

8. Pour over marinade and stock.

9. Cover casserole and cook in a warm oven, Gas 3, 325°F, 160°C, for 2 hours. For the last 15 minutes of cooking time remove lid to let the potatoes brown a little.

BEEF CASSEROLE WITH DUMPLINGS

Serves 4

325 g/12 oz lean stewing beef
225 g/8 oz onions
225 g/8 oz carrots
125 to 175 g/4 to 6 oz swede or turnip
1 level tablespoon plain flour
1 teaspoon Salt and Pepper Mix (*see page 17*)
25 g/1 oz beef dripping
600 ml/1 pint hot stock
2 teaspoons vinegar
Brown colouring if desired

1. Cut stewing beef into 2.5 cm/1 inch cubes.
2. Slice onions thickly and cut the carrots and swede or turnip into 2.5 to 5 cm/1 to 2 inch chunks.
3. Mix flour and salt and pepper and coat beef well.
4. Melt dripping in large saucepan, stir in beef, turning to seal and brown slightly.
5. Add onion and any remaining flour, stir for 1 minute.
6. Add remaining vegetables, stock and vinegar and stir until boiling. Stir in a few drops of colouring.
7. Cover and simmer gently for 1½ hours or until meat is tender. Or, transfer to a large casserole with lid and cook in a moderate oven, Gas 4, 350°F, 180°C, for 1½ hours or until meat is tender.

At this stage the casserole can be frozen. Cool very quickly, place in suitable freezer container, label and place in fridge to become quite cold, then transfer to freezer. When re-heating, the casserole must boil again before dumplings are added.

8. If casserole method is used now turn oven to moderately hot, Gas 6, 400°F, 200°C while mixing dumplings.

DUMPLINGS

125 g/4 oz self-raising flour
¼ teaspoon salt
50 g/2 oz shredded suet
1 tablespoon freshly chopped parsley or ½ teaspoon dried mixed herbs
3 to 4 tablespoons water

1. Mix flour, salt, suet and parsley. Mix to a softish dough with water.

2. Turn on to well-floured board, cut into 8 pieces. Roll into balls using a little flour.
3. Drop dumplings into pan or casserole. Replace lid.
4. Simmer in pan for 20 minutes or in casserole for 25 minutes.

BEEF AND ORANGE STEW

Serves 6

675 g/1½ lb stewing steak
225 g/8 oz onions
25 g/1 oz good dripping
25 g/1 oz flour
2 carrots
2 small turnips
1 clove garlic
Salt
2 oranges
1 litre/1½ pints boiling water
2 or 3 beef stock cubes
150 ml/¼ pint cider

1. Trim meat and cut into cubes.
2. Peel and chop onions.
3. Melt dripping in a large pan and fry beef and onions gently. Add flour and stir.
4. Scrub carrots, peel turnips, dice them and stir into pan.
5. Crush garlic (*see page 139*) and add it to the pan.
6. Thinly peel oranges and blanch the rind in a small pan with ½ pint of the boiling water—that is, simmer for 2 or 3 minutes, then lift it out of the pan. Cut it into thin strips. Squeeze the juice from oranges.
7. Add half of the sliced rind and the orange juice to the stew pan.
8. Dissolve the stock cubes in remaining pint of boiling water and add this stock and the blanching water to the stew pan.
9. Bring stew to the boil and simmer gently for about 2 hours until the meat is tender.
10. Add cider. Check seasoning, adding salt if necessary and some freshly-ground black pepper. Cook for 10 minutes.

Serve the stew garnished with the remaining slices of orange rind.

BEEF AND HARICOT CASSEROLE

This dish freezes well.

Serves 6

175 g/6 oz haricot beans
675 g/1½ lb chuck steak
125 g/4 oz lean bacon
1 large onion
2 carrots
2 medium tomatoes
2 cloves garlic
50 g/2 oz good dripping
Bouquet garni, or a bunch of fresh herbs such as parsley, thyme and marjoram
300 ml/½ pint red wine
Salt and pepper
A little beef stock
Finely-chopped parsley

1. Soak the beans in cold water overnight.
2. Trim beef and cut into 2.5 cm/1 inch squares.
3. Remove rinds and cut bacon into 1.2 cm/½ inch strips.
4. Peel and slice onion. Scrub and slice carrots into ½ inch cubes.
5. Skin tomatoes (*see page 139*). Remove pips and cut flesh into strips.
6. Crush the garlic (*see page 139*).
7. Melt dripping in a heavy flame-proof casserole and fry bacon until golden. Remove from pan.
8. Fry meat until well-browned.
9. Return bacon to the casserole and add onion and carrots, tomatoes, garlic, bouquet garni, wine and seasoning.
10. Bring up to boiling point. Cover with grease-proof paper and the lid and cook very gently for 1½ hours.
11. Meanwhile, boil the soaked beans in water for about 1 hour.
12. Drain the beans, saving the liquid, and add them to the casserole. Stir. Add some beef stock if needed, or some of the haricot liquid. Continue cooking until meat and beans are tender—about 1 hour more. Adjust the seasoning.
13. Remove bouquet garni. Pile meat and vegetables with the sauce on to a hot serving dish.
14. Sprinkle with finely-chopped parsley, and serve.

Jean Welshman
Malton, E. Yorkshire

A PAN STEW

Can be cooked in an electric frying pan.

Serves 2

225 g/8 oz skirt of beef
1½ tablespoons sherry
1½ tablespoons soya sauce
1 large onion
1 clove garlic
2 sticks celery
2 medium-sized carrots
125 g/4 oz mushrooms
2 teaspoons cornflour
300 ml/½ pint stock
2 tablespoons cooking oil
Salt and pepper

1. Cut beef into pencil-thin strips about 3.7 cm/1½ inches long.
2. Mix sherry and soya sauce in a basin. Put in the beef and turn it over in this marinade. Leave it for at least 2 hours, turning meat over from time to time.
3. Peel and slice onion.
4. Crush garlic (*see page 139*).
5. Wash, trim and finely slice the celery.
6. Scrub carrots and cut them into matchstick-sized pieces.
7. Wipe mushrooms and, if large, cut them up.
8. Blend cornflour into a little of the stock then stir in the rest of the stock.
9. Heat oil in a large frying pan or shallow pan. Add meat and cook fairly quickly, turning with a spatula, until almost cooked—about 10 minutes. Push to one side.
10. Fry onion and garlic until soft but not brown. Add celery and carrot and fry for 5 minutes, adding more oil if necessary.
11. Add mushrooms and fry for 2 minutes.
12. Mix contents of pan together, adding stock mixture and any remaining marinade. Simmer for 10 minutes. Taste for seasoning and add salt and pepper if necessary.

Serve with brown rice and green vegetables.

STUFFED SKIRT OF BEEF

A very old Gloucestershire recipe, economical and nourishing.

Serves 6 to 8

900 g/2 lb skirt of beef

STUFFING
125 g/4 oz medium oatmeal
50 g/2 oz shredded suet
1 dessertspoon chopped parsley and other herbs to taste
25 g/ 1 oz finely-chopped onion
Salt and pepper
A little milk

TO COOK
50 g/2 oz dripping
225 g/8 oz chopped onions
1.2 litres/2 pints brown stock (*see page 10*)
Salt and pepper
125 g/4 oz carrots
125 g/4 oz turnips
50 g/2 oz cornflour
2 tablespoons water

1. Buy the skirt in one piece. Remove skin and with a sharp knife slice a deep pocket in the meat.
2. Combine all stuffing ingredients using enough milk just to bind it.
3. Stuff the pocket in meat and sew up the opening.
4. Melt dripping in a heavy saucepan and brown meat and onions.
5. Add stock and salt and pepper if necessary. Bring to the boil and simmer very gently for 2½ to 3 hours.
6. About 45 minutes before end of cooking time add carrots and turnips, scrubbed and sliced into even-sized pieces.
7. Blend cornflour with water and add to pan at last minute to thicken.
8. Lift out meat and remove sewing thread.
9. Put meat on a hot dish surrounded by carrots and turnips.

Gloucester College of Agriculture
Hartpury

SHIN OF BEEF CASSEROLE

Serves 4 to 6

900 g/2 lb shin of beef, in 2.5 cm/1 inch cubes
40 g/1½ oz seasoned flour
40 g/1½ oz beef dripping
1 clove of garlic, crushed
2 sticks of celery, sliced
600 ml/1 pint beef stock
300 ml/½ pint light beer
A 375 g/14 oz can of tomatoes
Salt and pepper
Gravy browning
A small green pepper, diced
50 g/2 oz mushrooms, sliced

1. Toss meat in seasoned flour in plastic or paper bag.
2. Heat dripping, fry meat until golden.
3. Add any remaining flour, cook for 1 minute.
4. Stir in all ingredients except browning, peppers and mushrooms.
5. Add a little gravy browning.
6. Cover and cook for 3½ hours, simmering very slowly.
7. Add peppers and mushrooms, cook for further ½ hour.
8. Check seasoning and serve.

CASSEROLED SHIN OF BEEF

This casserole may be made with varying quantities of meat and vegetables according to what you have and how many are to eat it. It is just as good reheated as when it is freshly made, so it is worth making enough for two meals.

2 large onions
2 large carrots
1 stick of celery
1 small parsnip or turnip
A clove of garlic
900 g/2 lb shin of beef or stewing steak
40 g/1½ oz wholemeal or plain flour
½ teaspoon dried marjoram
½ teaspoon salt
Freshly-grated black pepper
40 g/1½ oz dripping
A wineglass of red wine, or cider or 2 tablespoons vinegar
A 400 g/14 oz tin of tomatoes
Water
Fresh parsley

1. Peel onions and cut them into large pieces. Scrub carrots and cut them into large chunks. Cut up very finely the celery and parsnip or turnip. Crush the garlic.

2. Trim off excess fat and hard gristle from the meat and cut it into easy pieces, about 5 cm/2 inches long, 1.2 cm/½ inch thick. Mix together flour, marjoram, salt and pepper on a plate or in a clean paper or polythene bag. Toss the meat in this seasoned flour to coat it well.

3. Heat half of the dripping in a heavy saucepan or a flameproof casserole. (Flameproof means one which can stand direct heat on top of the stove and can also go into the oven.) Add onion and fry till it begins to brown. Then lift it out with a draining spoon on to a plate.

4. Now add remaining dripping and heat till it begins to smoke. Then add the meat, turning it over quickly to brown.

5. Turn down heat and add wine or cider but not the vinegar. Let it bubble for a minute.

6. Now, if you are using a saucepan which cannot go into the oven, turn the contents into a large casserole.

7. Add the onions, garlic, carrots, celery, parsnip or turnip.

8. Add vinegar, if used instead of wine or cider.

9. Now empty the tin of tomatoes on top, refill the tin with cold water and pour in enough just to cover the meat and vegetables.

10. Tie a bunch of parsley together with cotton or string and lay it on top.

11. Cover the casserole and put it in a moderate oven, Gas 4, 350°F, 180°C, for 2½ to 3 hours. After half an hour, when pot will be bubbling nicely, reduce heat to very cool Gas ½, 250°F, 120°C, and let it go on cooking for another 2 hours. If you are using shin of beef a total of 3½ hours is not too long.

12. Remove the bunch of parsley and add freshly-chopped parsley, if you can spare it, just before serving.

POTTED BEEF (1)

This will freeze successfully for 1 month.

6 servings

450 g/1 lb shin of beef
¼ level teaspoon mixed spice
1 level teaspoon salt
Grating of black pepper
1 teaspoon vinegar
2 teaspoons Worcestershire sauce
4 tablespoons water
125 g/4 oz soft table margarine
A little melted butter

1. Trim excess fat and gristle from meat. Cut meat into 2.5 cm/1 inch cubes.

2. Put in a 1 litre/1½ pint basin with spice, salt, pepper, vinegar, Worcestershire sauce and water. Cover tightly with foil.

3. Stand basin on a trivet or upturned saucer in a large pan. Pour into the pan sufficient boiling water to come halfway up sides of basin.

4. Cover pan and simmer 2½ hours. Check the level of water from time to time, and if necessary top up with boiling water.

5. Cool a little, drain meat, reserving the liquor.

6. Mince meat finely, stir in liquor and beat in margarine. Re-season if necessary.

7. Place in small pots, cover with a little melted butter. Use for sandwiches.

POTTED BEEF (2)

8 servings

1 bacon knuckle
Water
450 g/1 lb shin of beef, cut into large pieces
1 stick of celery, sliced
8 peppercorns
1 bay leaf
A pinch of ground allspice

1. Place bacon knuckle in a large saucepan, cover with cold water. Bring to boil, then discard water.

2. Put beef, celery and rest of ingredients into pan with knuckle and add 1.2 litres/2 pints fresh cold water.

3. Bring to boil, skim off any scum, then lower heat. Cover pan and simmer for 2 to 2½ hours until beef

is very tender. *Or*, pressure cook in 600 ml/1 pint of water for 50 minutes.

4. Strain off stock and reserve. Discard bay leaf and peppercorns. Allow meat to cool.

5. Slice beef finely, removing any fat or gristle.

6. Remove skin from bacon knuckle. Cut bacon into fine cubes.

7. Place meat into a 1 litre/1½ pint mould or bowl. Add stock to almost fill mould. Top up with cold water if necessary. Stir well and cover. Chill and leave to set, overnight if possible.

8. To serve, loosen mould around edges with fingers. Place serving plate on top, invert and shake to release meat.

BEEF CURRY

Made with home-mixed curry powder.

Serves 4 to 6

CURRY SPICES

2 cloves or ¼ teaspoon ground cloves
2 teaspoons coriander seeds, or 1½ teaspoons ground coriander
1 teaspoon ground cumin seed
1 teaspoon turmeric
½ to 1 teaspoon chilli powder
1 teaspoon ground ginger
¼ teaspoon powdered cinnamon

You can crush cloves between 2 spoons. Coriander seeds need a pestle and mortar.
Measure the spices carefully on to a plate and then mix them with a knife.

THE CURRY
Can be made a day in advance. Flavour is better if it is made, left as long as 24 hours and then reheated.

675 g/1½ lb braising steak
225 g/8 oz onions
325 g/12 oz fresh tomatoes, or 400 g/14 oz can
3 to 4 cloves garlic
2 level teaspoons salt
2 to 3 tablespoons cooking oil
Curry spices as above
1 level tablespoon plain flour
300 ml/½ pint beef stock or water, or dissolve 25 g/1 oz creamed coconut in 300 ml/½ pint boiling water

SIDE DISHES
Diced cucumber mixed with plain yoghurt
Sliced bananas sprinkled with lemon juice
Sultanas
Finely-sliced fresh onion rings
Poppadoms (can be bought from oriental shops with a variety of flavours)
Mango chutney, or home-made Sweet Mixed Pickle (*see page 377*)

1. Cut beef into even-sized small pieces.

2. Peel and chop onions.

3. Skin tomatoes (*see page 139*). If using can of tomatoes, drain juice and use it to make up quantity of stock.

4. Crush garlic (*see page 139*).

5. Heat oil in a heavy saucepan and gently fry the spices for 2 minutes.

6. Add meat, fry gently on all sides until brown. Remove from saucepan on to a plate.

7. Add onion and garlic and gently fry to soften the onion.

8. Stir in flour. Let it cook for a minute.

9. Add chopped or canned tomatoes. Cook for about 2 minutes. Return meat to pan.

10. Add stock, bring to the boil, cover pan and simmer for about 1 hour, or until meat is tender and sauce is reduced to a thick gravy.

Serve with a dish of plain boiled brown or white rice and as many side-dishes as you can.

Jill Smith
Cambridge

SRI LANKAN BEEF CURRY

Serves 4

450 g/1 lb braising beef
2 tablespoons oil
1 medium-sized onion, finely-chopped
3 cloves of garlic, crushed
3 whole cardamoms*
3 whole cloves
A 2.5 cm/1 inch piece of cinnamon stick
50 g/2 oz creamed coconut*
125 ml/4 fl oz hot water
1 teaspoon fresh ginger, chopped fine
2 teaspoons malt vinegar
1½ teaspoons ground coriander
1½ teaspoons ground cumin
1 teaspoon chilli powder
1 teaspoon salt
¼ teaspoon ground fenugreek
¼ teaspoon turmeric
¼ teaspoon freshly-milled black pepper

Can be bought at oriental food shops.

1. Cut beef into 2.5 cm/1 inch pieces.
2. Heat oil and fry onions and garlic till just golden.
3. Add the meat and fry over a low heat until quite brown.
4. Grind together in a mortar or electric grinder the cardamom seeds, cloves and cinnamon stick and add to meat.
5. Dissolve the creamed coconut in the hot water and add it with all the other ingredients.
6. Put on the lid and simmer for 1 hour.

Priya Wickramasinghe
Cardiff

MINCED MEAT CURRY

Serves 4

2 tablespoons oil
1 medium onion, chopped
3 cloves garlic, chopped
2 green chillis, finely chopped
½ teaspoon chopped fresh ginger
2 teaspoons ground coriander
2 teaspoons ground cumin
1 teaspoon garam masala*
¼ teaspoon turmeric
450 g/1 lb lean mince
1 teaspoon tomato purée
50 g/2 oz creamed coconut
125 ml/4 fl oz hot water
1 cup fresh or frozen peas

Can be bought at wholefood shops and oriental food shops.

1. Heat oil and fry onions in it until just golden.
2. Add garlic, chillis, fresh ginger and other spices, and fry for a few seconds.
3. Add meat and continue to fry over a low heat.
4. Mix in tomato purée.
5. Dissolve creamed coconut in the water, mix it in, cover pan and allow to simmer for ¾ to 1 hour.
6. Toss in the peas and cook for a further 10 minutes.

Serve with Boiled Rice (*see page 172*), Curried Bhindi (*see page 149*) or Cauliflower Bhaji (*see page 150*) and salad.

Priya Wickramasinghe
Cardiff

A MILD CURRY

Made with a little meat and a lot of vegetables.

Serves 2

CURRY SPICES
1 clove
1 level teaspoon ground coriander
½ teaspoon turmeric
½ teaspoon ginger
¼ teaspoon cinnamon
¼ teaspoon ground mace
¼ teaspoon ground nutmeg
¼ teaspoon paprika

THE CURRY
125 to 175 g/4 to 6 oz cold cooked beef, pork, or
    lamb
1 large onion
1 tablespoon dripping
1 large clove garlic
A 225 g/8 oz can tomatoes
A very little salt
1 small carrot
1 leek
1 tablespoon sultanas
1 tablespoon flaked almonds

TO SERVE
125 g/4 oz long grain brown rice

1. First measure curry spices on to a plate and mix well together. The clove may be crushed between 2 spoons. Grind or grate freshly as many spices as you can: the flavour is better.
2. Cut meat into small cubes, removing fat and gristle.
3. Peel onion and cut it into large chunks.
4. Melt dripping in a heavy, flame-proof casserole. Put in onion and meat and stir in curry spices. Cook gently for 5 minutes, stirring from time to time.
5. Stir in crushed garlic.
6. Break up tomatoes and add half of them. Add a very little salt.
7. Put lid on and cook for 10 minutes on very low heat.
8. Meanwhile, scrub carrot and shred into fine rings. Slice the leek into halves, wash well and cut up.
9. Sprinkle sultanas and nuts over curry. Make a border of carrot slices, pile leek in the middle and pour over the rest of the tomato to moisten. Sprinkle on a few grains of salt. Replace lid and cook very gently for 20 minutes.

10. At the same time, put rice on to cook, following instructions for Boiled Rice on *page 172.*

Serve each helping on a bed of rice. Vegetables are crunchy, full of their own flavour and not swamped by the curry.

A tasty accompaniment to this dish is Cucumber and Yoghurt salad (*see page 143*).

BOBOTIE

From a 19th century cookery book.

Serves 4

1 to 2 thick slices of bread
150 ml/¼ pint milk
1 medium-sized onion
1 tablespoon oil
1 tablespoon butter
50 g/2 oz sultanas or raisins
450 g/1 lb minced beef
25 g/1 oz shredded almonds
2 teaspoons wine or cider vinegar
2 teaspoons sugar
1 tablespoon curry powder
½ teaspoon salt
½ teaspoon mixed herbs
Black pepper
2 teaspoons lemon juice
2 beaten eggs

1. Soak slices of bread in milk and squeeze out. Keep the milk for later.
2. Peel and chop onion. Using a large pan, fry it in oil and butter till softening, but not brown. Remove from heat.
3. Add soaked bread, sultanas, beef, almonds, vinegar, sugar, curry powder, salt, herbs, pepper, lemon juice and 1 tablespoon of the beaten egg. Mix well.
4. Spread mixture in an ovenproof dish.
5. Mix remaining egg and milk. Pour it over the mixture.
6. Bake in a moderate oven, Gas 4, 350°F, 180°C, for 1 to 1½ hours.

Serve hot in portions or cold cut in fingers for a buffet.

Sybil Norcott
Irlam, Nr Manchester

CHILLI CON CARNE

Serves 4

1 onion
1 clove garlic
Pinch of salt
25 g/1 oz good dripping
450 g/1 lb minced beef
1 level tablespoon flour
A 225 g/8 oz can tomatoes
2 level tablespoons tomato pureé*
½ level teaspoon chilli powder
Pinch of dried marjoram or oregano
A 225 g/8 oz can of baked beans

To keep tomato purée fresh, see page 84

1. Peel onion and chop it finely. Crush garlic with a little salt.
2. Melt dripping in large saucepan, add onion and garlic then beef. Fry slowly until beef is browned.
3. Stir in flour and cook for 1 minute.
4. Add can of tomatoes, tomato pureé, chilli powder and marjoram or oregano.
5. Bring to the boil, stirring. Cover pan and simmer for 30 minutes, stirring from time to time. Add a little water if mixture is too thick to stir.
6. Add beans and cook for 5 minutes more.

Serve with green vegetables or a green salad.

SAVOURY BEEF CHARLOTTE

This recipe won first prize in a cooking competition judged by Dorothy Sleightholme and was given to her for this book.

Serves 3 or 4

1 tablespoon oil
1 onion, finely chopped
2 carrots, scrubbed and finely chopped
225 g/8 oz minced beef
15 g/½ oz plain flour, wholewheat or white
2 level tablespoons tomato purée*
125 g/4 oz mushrooms, sliced
2 teaspoons chopped fresh parsley
Salt and Pepper Mix (*see page 17*)
6 large slices bread, wholewheat is best
50 g/2 oz margarine
1 small beaten egg

SAUCE
2 level tablespoons tomato purée
2 tablespoons vinegar
1 level tablespoon golden syrup
A pinch of dry mustard

To keep tomato purée fresh, see page 84.

1. Heat oil in a large pan and put in onions and carrot. Put on lid, turn heat very low and cook for 10 minutes.
2. Stir in meat, flour and tomato purée. Cook, stirring to break up meat, for 5 minutes.
3. Mix in mushrooms, 1 teaspoon of the parsley and salt and pepper. Cook for 5 minutes, then remove from heat to cool a little.
4. Meanwhile, spread margarine on one side of slices of bread. Cut them to fit and line sides and bottom of a greased 1.5 litre/2½ pint oven dish. A 20 cm/8 inch soufflé dish is suitable.
5. Beat egg into cooled meat mixture and turn into prepared dish. Cover with a lid or greaseproof paper and foil.
6. Put dish on a baking tray and into a moderately hot oven, Gas 5, 375°F, 190°C, for 20 minutes.
7. Blend sauce ingredients together. Pour over the charlotte and return dish to oven uncovered for 10 minutes more.
8. Sprinkle on the rest of the parsley just before serving.

Mrs Jean Barnard
Harrogate, Yorkshire

ABERDEEN ROLL

May be eaten hot or cold.

Serves 4

225 g/8 oz streaky bacon
225 g/8 oz minced beef
1 large onion
1 clove of garlic, optional but try it
75 g/3 oz rolled oats
1 tablespoon Worcestershire sauce
1 teaspoon made mustard
1 teaspoon Salt and Pepper Mix (*see page 17*)
1 beaten egg
150 ml/¼ pint stock

FOR EATING COLD
Stock
Dried breadcrumbs (*see page 52*)

1. De-rind bacon and cut into strips. Skin and chop onion, crush garlic to a cream with a little salt. Mix

well with minced beef; mince this mixture using fine cutters.

2. Add oats, sauce, mustard and Salt and Pepper Mix. Mix in beaten egg and a little stock if mixture is dry.

3. Grease a ½ kg/1 lb loaf tin and press mixture in firmly.

4. Cover with foil. Stand in a small roasting tin containing enough hot water to come well up sides.

5. Cook in a moderate oven, Gas 4, 350°F, 180°C, for 2 hours.

TO EAT HOT

Remove from tin, smother with fried onion rings and serve with tomato or brown sauce and jacket potatoes.

TO EAT COLD

1. Do not remove from tin but pour in at once as much boiling stock as it will absorb, pressing mixture gently with back of a spoon.

2. Cover with foil and place a weight on top. Leave overnight in a cool place.

3. Turn out of mould, roll in dried breadcrumbs and serve sliced with potato salad (*see page 145*).

MEAT LOAF

Serves 4 to 6

1 small onion
450 g/1 lb minced beef
225 g/8 oz beef sausage
Pinch of mixed herbs
Salt and pepper
1 beaten egg
2 hard-boiled eggs (optional)

1. Peel and chop or grate onion.

2. Thoroughly mix onion, minced meat, sausage meat, herbs and seasoning.

3. Bind with beaten egg.

4. Grease a ½ kg/1 lb loaf tin and fill it with mixture. If using hard-boiled eggs, put in half the meat mixture then the eggs and pack the rest of the meat on top.

5. Cover with a layer of greaseproof paper and then foil, tucking edges in under rim of tin.

6. Bake in the middle of a moderately hot oven, Gas 4, 350°F, 180°C, for 1 hour. After ½ hour, remove paper and foil.

7. When cooked, pour off the juices and turn loaf out on to a plate.

Serve hot with potatoes in jackets or roast potatoes and vegetables, or cold with salad.

The same meat mixture can be used for beefburgers.

BEEFBURGERS

1. Take tablespoons of raw mixture and, using a floured board, shape into flat cakes, 2 cm/¾ inch thick. Sprinkle with more flour if too sticky to handle.

2. Melt 25 g/1 oz lard or dripping in a frying pan. When hot put in beefburgers. Brown on one side, turn and lower heat to cook slowly. Cook 7 to 8 minutes altogether.

Margaret Heywood
Todmorden, Yorkshire

STUFFED BEEFBURGERS

A good way to use up any kind of stuffing.

Serves 4

325 g/12 oz minced beef
Salt and pepper
1 teaspoon Worcestershire sauce
4 heaped teaspoons stuffing
25 g/1 oz flour
1 to 2 tablespoons dripping
1 sliced onion
Half a cup of stock

1. Season mince with salt, pepper and Worcestershire sauce.

2. Divide mince into 8 portions and flatten each one into a thin round.

3. Place stuffing on four of the rounds and cover with remaining four. Pinch edges well together.

4. Dust beefburgers with flour.

4. Meanwhile fry onions in dripping until golden. Make space for the beefburgers and fry them until brown on both sides.

6. Remove browned beefburgers to a plate.

7. Mix in with fried onions any remaining flour. Stir in stock and let it thicken.

8. Replace beefburgers in pan, put on lid and cook very gently for about 30 minutes.

Serve with creamed potatoes and a green vegetable.

Anne Wallace
Stewarton, Ayrshire

MEAT BALLS IN TOMATO SAUCE

This dish freezes well. Thaw slowly—it is better done in refrigerator overnight—then heat through in a pan, stirring from time to time. If sauce has thickened too much, add a little more stock. Remove meat balls on to dish and whisk sauce a little if it shows signs of curdling.

Serves 4

450 g/1 lb finely-minced beef
50 g/2 oz fresh wholemeal or white bread-crumbs (*see page 52*)
1 large grated onion
1 beaten egg
1 level tablespoon plain flour
1 teaspoon salt
$\frac{1}{2}$ teaspoon pepper
25 g/1 oz beef dripping
A 400 g/14 oz can of tomatoes
300 ml/$\frac{1}{2}$ pint beef or bacon stock

1. Mix together beef, breadcrumbs, half the onion and the beaten egg.
2. Form into 16 even-sized balls. Roll in flour mixed with salt and pepper.
3. Heat dripping in pan and add meat balls. Turn over in hot fat to seal for 1 to 2 minutes and allow to brown a little. Drain on to a plate.
4. Add remaining onion to pan, stir in any seasoned flour left and cook, stirring for 2 minutes.
5. Pour in can of tomatoes, mix well, add stock, and bring to boil.
6. Sieve into a casserole, add meat balls, cover tightly. Cook in a moderate oven, Gas 4, 350°F, 180°C, for 45 minutes.

This dish can also be cooked on top of stove. At paragraph 6 above, use saucepan instead of casserole, cover with lid. Simmer gently for 35 minutes, checking from time to time in case it sticks.

Serve in ring of potatoes or rice, with green vegetables. Pour a little sauce over the meat balls, serve the rest separately.

MEAT BALLS IN A TANGY TOMATO SAUCE

Plenty for 6

Mixture makes about sixteen 50 g/2 oz balls. Smaller balls can be made for a fork-meal.

MEAT BALLS
2 rashers of smoked bacon
450 g/1 lb stewing beef
1 small onion
1 cup fresh wholewheat breadcrumbs
1 egg
225 g/8 oz sausage-meat
1 level teaspoon salt
$\frac{1}{2}$ teaspoon pepper
2 tablespoons flour, seasoned with salt and pepper
50 g/2 oz lard

TOMATO SAUCE
1 large onion
A 400 g/14 oz tin of tomatoes
25 g/1 oz lard
5 tablespoons brown sugar
4 tablespoons malt vinegar and 2 tablespoons water
1 tablespoon Worcestershire sauce
2 teaspoons lemon juice
1 teaspoon dry mustard
Salt and pepper

1. Remove rinds from bacon. Mince rashers together with beef and onion.
2. To this add breadcrumbs, egg, sausage-meat, salt and pepper. Mix thoroughly.
3. Make small balls of the mixture about 4 cm/1$\frac{1}{2}$ inches in diameter and roll them in seasoned flour.
4. Using a heavy frying pan, heat the 50 g/2 oz lard and fry meat-balls until well browned all over. Lift out with a draining spoon on to kitchen paper or brown paper.
5. Cover casserole and put it in oven while you quickly make sauce. Set oven to moderate, Gas 4, 350°F, 180°C.
6. Peel onion and chop finely. Liquidise tomatoes.
7. Fry onion in lard until soft but not brown.
8. Add all other ingredients. Simmer for 3 minutes.
9. Pour sauce over meatballs.

10. Cover casserole and return to the pre-heated oven for a further 30 minutes. *Or*, complete cooking on top of stove instead of oven, simmering for 30 minutes.

Don Oldridge
Goole, N. Humberside

ROAST STUFFED HEART

Remember to start the night before.

Serves 4 or 5

1 calf's heart, about 900 g/2 lb in weight
Water
Salt
Vinegar
300 ml/½ pint beef stock
1 level dessertspoon cornflour
2 tablespoons cold water

STUFFING
50 g/2 oz prunes, soaked overnight
50 g/2 oz cooked brown rice (*see page 172*)
50 g/2 oz walnuts, chopped
1 large cooking apple, peeled, cored and chopped
Grated rind of a lemon
25 g/1 oz melted butter
Pepper and salt

1. To prepare heart, cut away the membranes, gristle and veins. Wash thoroughly in cold running water to remove congealed blood. Soak for 4 hours in cold, salted water with 1 tablespoon of vinegar to each 600 ml/1 pint of water.
2. Meanwhile, prepare stuffing. Drain prunes, remove stones and chop flesh.
3. In a bowl, combine all stuffing ingredients.
4. Using a sharp knife enlarge the cavity of the heart and spoon in the stuffing.
5. Tie up like a parcel and place the heart with its stuffing downwards in a roasting tin.
6. Pour over the stock. Cover and bake for 1½ to 2 hours in a moderate oven, Gas 4, 350°F, 180°C, basting frequently.
7. Put the stuffed heart on to a warm dish and keep hot.
8. Pour juices from the tin into a small pan.
9. Slake cornflour in water and stir into juices. Heat gently, stirring as sauce thickens. Serve sauce separately.

Serve with green vegetables.

LIVER AND BACON CASSEROLE

Serves 6

675 g/1½ lb ox liver
300 ml/½ pint milk or milk and water mixed
6 rashers bacon
1 large onion
2 tablespoons flour
2 teaspoons salt
1 teaspoon pepper
50 g/2 oz butter or margarine
400 g/14 oz tinned tomatoes
2 tablespoons tomato purée*

*To keep tomato purée fresh, see page 84

1. Put slices of liver in a bowl with the milk for one hour to soak and draw out the slightly strong taste.
2. Remove bacon rinds, halve and roll the rashers.
3. Peel and chop onion.
4. Drain milk from liver. Pat each piece dry and toss in flour seasoned with salt and pepper. Discard the milk.
5. Fry onion in the butter or margarine until soft but not brown.
6. Add liver to the frying pan and fry quickly on both sides to seal. This is very important because it keeps the natural juices and flavour in the meat.
7. Put liver and onions into a casserole dish.
8. Chop the tinned tomatoes and mix well with tomato purée. Pour over liver and onions.
9. Place bacon rolls on top.
10. Cook, uncovered, in a moderately hot oven, Gas 5, 375°F, 190°C, for 30 to 40 minutes.

Judith Adshead
Mottram St Andrew, Cheshire

LIVER PATTIES WITH APPLE AND ONION

Nourishing, economical, tender and tasty.

Serves 3 or 4

225 g/8 oz ox liver
1 medium-sized onion
1 medium-sized apple
1 well-rounded tablespoon porridge oats or flake meal
1 level tablespoon bran (optional)
125 ml/4 fl oz beef stock (½ stock cube will do but let it cool before using)
Salt
1 tablespoon oil

1. Wash and skin liver and cut into pieces. Liquidise or put through middle disc of mouli-sieve or medium-coarse cutter of mincer. It is difficult to mince liver but you can blanch it first as follows: put it in a saucepan. Just cover with boiling water and bring to boiling point. Turn down heat, simmer for 2 to 3 minutes. Drain off water.
2. Peel onion and chop finely. Add to liver.
3. Peel and grate apple. Stir into liver and onion.
4. Mix in the porridge oats or flake meal, bran and stock. Season with a little salt.
5. Heat oil in frying pan.
6. Put large spoonfuls of liver mixture into pan and fry 4 to 5 minutes on each side.

Mrs W. Gordon
Glasgow

OXTAIL CASSEROLE WITH PARSLEY DUMPLINGS

Serves 4

1 oxtail, jointed
225g/8 oz carrot
225 g/8 oz turnip
225 g/8 oz onion
25 g/1 oz dripping
600 ml/1 pint boiling water
1 level teaspoon salt
A bouquet garni (*see page 84*)
125 g/4 oz butterbeans, soaked overnight
2 sticks celery
2 level tablespoons cornflour
3 tablespoons water
1 dessertspoon vinegar

1. Wash and dry oxtail, cut away excess fat.
2. Prepare carrot and turnip, cutting coarsely. Peel and slice onion.
3. Melt dripping in large pan or flameproof casserole. Add onion and fry until golden. Add oxtail, fry 1 to 2 minutes, turning over in fat.
4. Add carrot, turnip, boiling water, salt and bouquet garni. Cover and bring to boil. Simmer for 1½ hours.
5. Remove bouquet garni. Add drained beans, also celery cut in pieces. Simmer until oxtail and butterbeans are tender, check seasoning. Remove from heat.
6. Leave overnight if possible. Next day remove fat from top and bring to boil. Mix cornflour, water and vinegar, add to casserole, stirring lightly and bring to boil. (If you wish, the casserole may be left overnight before Stage 5.)

PARSLEY DUMPLINGS
125 g/4 oz self-raising flour
50 g/2 oz shredded suet
A pinch of salt
1 tablespoon chopped parsley

Mix ingredients with sufficient water to make a firm dough. Form into small balls, place on top of casserole. Cover and simmer for 15 minutes.

OXTAIL STEW

It is better to do the first part of the cooking the day before the stew is needed. This ensures that a great deal of the fat can be skimmed off.

Serves 4

1 oxtail
Salt and pepper
225 g/8 oz carrots, diced
225 g/8 oz turnips, diced
225 g/8 oz onions, chopped
2 tablespoons flour
Chopped fresh parsley

1. Trim any surplus fat from the oxtail and cut it into its separate joints. Put into a bowl, cover with water and leave for 1 hour.
2. Drain and put the pieces in a stewpan. Add seasoning and cover with fresh water. Bring to the boil, reduce heat and simmer for 1½ hours.
3. At this point leave overnight.
4. Next day, skim off fat which has risen to the top.

5. Add chopped vegetables. Simmer again for 1½ hours or until tender.

6. Thicken just before serving. Mix flour to a smooth paste with a little cold water. Add to the stew, stir well and simmer again for a further 10 minutes.

Sprinkle generously with chopped freshly parsley if you have it.

Mrs A. Greenwood
Boroughbridge, Yorkshire

OXTAIL MOULD

Serves 4

1 oxtail
225 g/8 oz bacon in a piece or bacon pieces
1 small onion
4 cloves
Water
Pepper and salt to taste

1. Wash and joint the oxtail.

2. Put in a pan, with the bacon cut in chunks and the onion stuck with the cloves. Cover with water. Put on lid and simmer gently for three hours. *Or,* pressure cook for one hour.

3. Strain off liquid. Remove the onion.

4. Take all meat from the bones and cut it up discarding fat. Cut up bacon quite small.

5. Return the strained liquid and meat to the pan. Season with pepper and salt. Bring to the boil.

6. Pour into a mould and leave to set.

Serve cold with hot creamed potatoes.

TO COOK AND PRESS AN OX-TONGUE

Save the stock for soups but use it carefully as it may be salty and strongly flavoured.

1 ox-tongue, salted by the butcher
2 large onions
2 large carrots
1 stick celery
1 bay leaf, sprig of thyme and parsley
5 peppercorns

1. Put tongue to soak in plenty of water for 24 hours. Change water at least twice. This draws out excess salt.

2. Put tongue in a large saucepan and cover with fresh water. Bring slowly to the boil.

3. Peel onion and cut up roughly. Scrub and chop carrot. Slice celery.

4. When tongue reaches boiling point skim off the scum, add vegetables and herbs and peppercorns. Simmer for 3 to 4 hours or until the little bones at root of tongue are easily pulled out.

5. Allow to cool in the liquid.

6. Remove tongue on to a dish, skin it and trim off bone or gristle at the root and some of the excessively fatty bits.

7. Curl tongue round and fit it tightly into a straight-sided dish or cake tin. It needs to be a tight fit to make a neat finished product.

8. Find a plate that will just fit inside the dish or tin. Press it in and put a heavy weight on top.

9. Leave it until the next day to set.

10. Turn it out on to a plate to serve.

FOLDS OF TONGUE

With savoury rice and cheese filling and fresh tomato sauce.
Freezes well.

Serves 4, but easy to make in larger or smaller quantities.

1 small red or green pepper
25 g/1 oz butter
1 teaspoon chopped capers
2 tablespoons cooked brown rice
Salt and pepper
75 g/3 oz grated cheese
4 slices of cooked tongue

SAUCE
675 g/1½ lb ripe tomatoes, or a 400 g/14 oz can of tomatoes
1 onion
1 clove garlic
1 bouquet garni (*see page 84*) **or a bunch of fresh herbs such as thyme, parsley, basil and marjoram**
1 teaspoon sugar
1 teaspoon tomato purée
½ teaspoon salt
Freshly-ground black pepper

1. Blanch the pepper. To do this, cut it in half, remove core and knock out seeds, Cook in boiling salted water for 3 minutes. Drain off hot water and refresh with cold. Drain again. Chop finely.

2. Melt butter in a pan, add chopped capers, rice, peppers, seasoning and 50 g/2 oz of grated cheese.

3. Stir with a fork over a low heat until cheese has just melted. Do not leave it. If it is over-cooked cheese will turn to indigestible strings.

4. Divide mixture roughly into 4. Put a layer on one half of each slice of tongue.

5. Fold over other half on top and lay them slightly overlapping down centre of a fireproof dish.

6. To make sauce, first skin the tomatoes (see page 139) and chop them. Crush garlic.

7. Put all sauce ingredients into a pan, bring to the boil, then simmer gently, stirring occasionally, until thick and mushy. Adjust the seasoning. Remove bouquet garni or bunch of herbs.

8. Pour sauce over folds of tongue.

9. Sprinkle with rest of the cheese and place under a hot grill until cheese is golden brown.

Mrs Jean Welshman
Malton, E. Yorkshire

TRIPE IN BATTER WITH ONION SAUCE

Serves 2 or 3

450 g/1 lb tripe
Salt
Milk
Water
1 tablespoon flour
Pepper

BATTER
125 g/4 oz plain flour
$\frac{1}{4}$ teaspoon salt
1 egg
1 dessertspoon oil
125 ml/$\frac{1}{4}$ pint milk
Deep fat or oil for frying

ONION SAUCE
225 g/8 oz onions
25 g/1 oz butter
25 g/1 oz flour
A bare 300 ml/$\frac{1}{2}$ pint milk
Seasoning

1. Although tripe is blanched, or partially cooked, when bought it may need to be cooked again before being used. If it will cut with a knife it is cooked enough. If not, put it in a pan, add a little salt and cover with mixed milk and water. Put lid on pan and cook until tender.

2. Drain the tripe, pat dry and cut into strips, about 3 × 7 cm/1$\frac{1}{2}$ × 3 inches.

3. Season flour with salt and pepper and toss in it the strips of tripe.

4. *The batter.* Put flour and salt in a bowl. Make a well in centre and drop in egg.

5. Add oil and milk gradually, beating well.

6. Dip tripe strips in batter and deep fry. Drain on kitchen paper.

7. *The onion sauce.* Peel and chop onions finely.

8. Melt butter and fry onions till soft but not brown.

9. Stir in flour and cook 1 minute.

10. Gradually stir in milk, bring to the boil and cook for 2 or 3 minutes.

See also Fried Tripe with Onions, below.

FRIED TRIPE WITH ONIONS

A light meal for 4—enough for 2 or 3 for a main meal

450 g/1 lb tripe
Salt
Milk
Water
2 tablespoons wholewheat flour
Pepper
Deep fat or oil for frying
2 onions, sliced
A small clove of garlic, crushed
25 g/1 oz butter
1 tablespoon cooking oil
A few grains cayenne
1 tablespoon chopped parsley
2 lemons
Slices of wholemeal bread, buttered

1. Although tripe is blanched or partially cooked when bought it may need to be cooked again before being used. If it will cut with a knife it is cooked enough. If not, put it in a pan, add a little salt and cover with mixed milk and water. Put lid on pan and cook until tender.

2. Drain and dry the tripe and cut it into strips.

3. Season the flour and toss in it the strips of tripe. Wholewheat flour gives a nutty flavour and a nice, crisp texture.

4. Deep fry until golden and crisp, 5 to 7 minutes. Drain on kitchen paper and keep hot.

5. Meanwhile, heat butter and oil in a pan. Fry onions and garlic till golden but not brown. Then add parsley and juice of 1 lemon and cook 1 minute more.

6. Turn out on to a warmed dish and put tripe on top.

Serve with quarters of lemon and brown bread and butter. Best just like this, not with extra vegetables.

HONEYED LAMB

Serves 2

½ small onion
15 g/½ oz butter
1 dessertspoon oil
2 teaspoons flour
¼ teaspoon mustard powder
Salt and pepper
A 200 g/7 oz slice of lamb from fillet end of leg
200 ml/7 fl oz apple juice
2 teaspoons honey
½ beef stock cube
1 carrot, cut in spirals
70 g/3 oz pasta
2 slices apple
1 teaspoon oil
Chopped parsley

1. Chop onion finely and fry in butter mixed with oil. Remove to a plate.
2. Sift mustard, salt, pepper and flour together and coat meat with it.
3. Fry meat to seal it all over. Remove to plate with onion.
4. Stir any surplus flour into pan and let it brown.
5. Add apple juice, honey and stock cube. Stir until it boils.
6. Replace onion and lamb in sauce, place carrot round, cover pan and simmer till meat is tender— about 40 to 45 minutes.
7. Meanwhile, put pasta on to cook in boiling salted water, allowing time to be ready with meat.
8. Five minutes before serving, add apple to meat, turning it over in the sauce.
9. Drain pasta and toss it in oil.
10. Arrange meat, carrot and apple on a hot serving dish, strain sauce over, leaving space on dish for pasta.
11. Add pasta to serving dish and sprinkle with chopped parsley.

Anne Wallace,
Dunlop, Scotland

HONEYED WELSH LAMB

OEN CYMREIG MELOG

Good Welsh lamb needs no dressing up and is amongst the best and least adulterated meat that can be bought in Britain. This recipe gives a spicy gloss to the joint and a delicious gravy. It was served to us with medlar jelly (*see page 363*).

Serves 6 to 8

A 1.3 to 1.8 kg/3 to 4 lb joint of lamb, leg or shoulder
Salt and pepper
1 teaspoon ginger
1 dessertspoon dried or 2 sprigs fresh rosemary
2 tablespoons runny honey
About 300 ml/½ pint cider

1. Use a roasting tin in which joint will be a fairly snug fit.
2. Rub salt, pepper and ginger all over joint and put it in tin.
3. Sprinkle rosemary over it and dribble on the honey. Pour cider around it.
4. Allowing 30 minutes per ½ kg/1 lb, roast near top of a moderately hot oven, Gas 6, 400°F, 200°C, for the first half hour. Then baste meat and reduce oven heat to moderate, Gas 4, 350°F, 180°C, for remaining cooking time. Baste every 20 minutes and add a little extra cider if necessary.
5. Lift meat on to a warmed dish and make gravy using residue in roasting tin.

Mrs Joyce Powell
Llanddewi Rhydderch W.I., Gwent

MOSSLANDS SADDLE OF LAMB

For a special occasion.

Serves 10

1 saddle of lamb
1 pork fillet
2 tablespoons chopped fresh parsley or rose-mary jelly
Salt and pepper

1. Bone and skin the saddle, or ask the butcher to do this for you.

2. In place of the bone, lay the pork fillet.

3. Sprinkle inside meat with parsley (or spread on the jelly). Season with salt and pepper.

4. Roll up, tie in place and weigh joint.

5. Roast in a moderate oven, Gas 4, 350°F, 180°C, for 35 minutes per ½ kg/1 lb.

6. Remove from oven and allow to rest for 10 minutes before carving.

Sybil Norcott
Irlam, Nr Manchester

ROAST LAMB WITH APRICOT STUFFING

Remember to start this dish the night before serving.

Serves 4 to 6

50 to 75 g/2 to 3 oz dried apricots
50 g/2 oz butter or margarine
1 medium-sized onion
50 g/2 oz fresh wholemeal or white bread-crumbs
1 tablespoon chopped parsley
Salt and pepper
150 ml/¼ pint stock
1 egg-yolk
900 g/2 lb boned shoulder of lamb
A little dripping

1. Put apricots to soak in water overnight.

2. Next day, drain and cut them up quite small.

3. Melt butter or margarine in a frying pan.

4. Peel and chop onion and lightly fry it until transparent but not brown.

5. Mix in the apricots, breadcrumbs, parsley, salt and pepper. Moisten with 1 to 2 tablespoons stock.

6. Beat egg-yolk and add it to stuffing with a little more stock, if necessary, to make it moist but not sticky.

7. Open out lamb, season with pepper and a very little salt. Spread stuffing over it.

8. Roll it up and secure with string to keep in the filling.

9. Put in roasting tin and dot with dripping.

10. Roast in a hot oven, Gas 8, 450°F, 230°C, for 10 minutes. Reduce to moderate temperature, Gas 4, 350°F, 180°C, for a further 1 to 1¼ hours.

Mrs Emily Williams
Moggerhanger, Bedfordshire

FAST SWEET AND SOUR LAMB CHOPS

Serves 4

4 lamb chops, best end of neck
3 level tablespoons mango chutney or good
    home-made chutney
2 teaspoons made mustard
½ teaspoon mixed herbs
Salt

1. Put chops in a roasting tin with a cover.
2. Mix sauce ingredients, chopping mango pieces if they are large.
3. Pour half of the sauce over chops. Cover.
4. Roast in a moderate oven, Gas 4, 350°F, 180°C, for 15 minutes.
5. Turn chops over and pour rest of sauce over them.
6. Cover and cook 10 to 15 minutes more until chops are done. If chops are very thick allow 5 to 10 minutes longer. If the sauce becomes sticky, moisten with a little water.

MARINATED LAMB CHOPS

Remember to start the night before.

Serves 4

4 loin or chump chops
A little melted lard

MARINADE*
2 tablespoons oil
2 tablespoons lemon juice or wine vinegar
A clove of garlic, crushed
1 bay leaf
½ teaspoon thyme and ½ teaspoon basil, or 1
    teaspoon chopped fresh mint
½ teaspoon dry mustard
Salt and pepper to taste

**For a note on marinades, see below.*

1. Mix marinade ingredients.
2. Put chops in a flat, shallow dish and pour over the marinade. Leave in refrigerator or a cool place overnight. Turn chops in marinade every now and then.
3. Next day, drain chops and pat dry.

4. Brush with lard and cook under a hot grill for about 15 minutes, turning frequently.

A marinade is a highly seasoned liquid in which meat, fish or game may be soaked as a preliminary to cooking. The object is to impregnate the meat with certain flavours. It also helps to tenderise. This is particularly helpful with chops and steaks to be grilled or fried. Lemon juice, oil, vinegar, wine and aromatic flavourings such as bay leaf, parsley, thyme, rosemary, etc., can be used. The marinade itself is often used up by incorporating it in the final sauce. It is not always necessary to cover the meat— sometimes only enough marinade is used to moisten the meat, which can be turned over two or three times during the waiting period. See marinated Fried Tarragon Chicken (*page 57*), Marinated Lamb Chops (*above*), Beef Casserole (*page 89*), Marinated Smoked Mackerel (*page 26*), and others.

LANCASHIRE HOT POT

Serves 3

50 g/2 oz mushrooms
1 small onion
325 g/12 oz potatoes, sliced
1 sheep's kidney
25 g/1 oz lean bacon
3 lamb neck chops
Seasoning
Knob of butter or fat from chops
Parsley, to garnish

1. Wash and halve the mushrooms. Slice the onion and potatoes.
2. Skin, core and quarter the kidney. Dice the bacon.
3. Lay the cleaned chops on the base of a deep ovenproof dish.
4. Place a layer each of onions, kidneys, mushrooms, bacon and potatoes over the chops.
5. Season well. Repeat to use all ingredients, topping off the hot pot with overlapping potato slices and dot with butter or fat.
6. Add water to two thirds fill the casserole dish.
7. Cover and cook in a moderately hot oven, Gas 5, 375°F, 190°C, for 2 hours, removing the lid for the last half hour to brown the top.
8. Serve garnished with parsley.

Mrs M. J. Harkins
Garstang

LAMB HOT-POT WITH PARSLEY DUMPLINGS

Serves 4

1 medium-sized onion
2 carrots
2 sticks of celery
40 g/1½ oz lard or dripping
8 best end or middle neck lamb chops
1 tablespoon plain flour
A 400 g/14 oz tin of tomatoes
150 ml/¼ pint water
1 level teaspoon rosemary or mixed dried
   herbs
1 teaspoon salt
Black pepper

PARSLEY DUMPLINGS (*or try Sussex Swimmers, see page 107*)
125 g/4 oz self-raising flour
½ level teaspoon salt
40 g/1½ oz shredded suet
1 level tablespoon chopped parsley
A little water

1. Peel and slice onion. Scrub and slice carrots. Wash and slice celery.
2. Melt half the lard in a frying pan. Add onion, carrots and celery and fry for 2 to 3 minutes. Lift out into a 1.5 litre/2½ pint shallow casserole.
3. Coat chops in plain flour.
4. Add remaining lard to pan, then brown the chops quickly on both sides.
5. Arrange chops on vegetables in casserole.
6. Pour excess fat out of pan, put in tomatoes, water, rosemary, salt and pepper. Bring to boil, stirring, and pour over lamb.
7. Cover casserole and cook in centre of a moderate oven, Gas 4, 350°F, 180°C, for 1 to 1½ hours until meat is tender.
8. *For the dumplings:* sift flour and salt into a bowl. Mix in suet and parsley. Mix to a soft but not sticky dough with water. Form into 8 small balls.
9. Place dumplings on top of hot-pot and cook, uncovered, for a further 15 to 20 minutes, until dumplings are risen and cooked.

Serve immediately.

SUSSEX SWIMMERS

These dumplings used to be served with a good gravy and, like Yorkshire Puddings in Yorkshire, before the meat course. The rule was that those who ate most puddings could have most meat.
Can also be served as a sweet course with golden syrup.

Serves 6

125 g/4 oz self-raising wholewheat flour*
125 g/4 oz self-raising white flour
125 g/4 oz shredded suet
¼ teaspoon salt
7 to 8 tablespoons milk
Boiling stock or water

*If you cannot buy this use plain wholewheat flour and add 1½ level teaspoons baking powder.

1. Mix dry ingredients and suet.
2. Mix to a stiff dough with milk.
3. Take tablespoons of mixture and form into balls.
4. Have ready a saucepan of boiling stock or water in which the dumplings can be submerged.
5. Slip dumplings into pan and boil for 15 to 20 minutes.
6. Drain well and serve with a very good gravy, or, if for a sweet, golden syrup.

Mrs Ruth Brooke and Mrs Sheila Powell
Hove and Portslade, Sussex

LAMB AND LENTIL HOT-POT

Serves 4

125 g/4 oz lentils
Boiling water
2 medium-sized onions
450 g/1 lb carrots
675 g/1½ lb middle neck of lamb
1 level tablespoon plain flour
40 g/1½ oz lard
2 beef stock cubes
1 tablespoon Salt and Pepper Mix (*see page 17*)
Sprig of fresh rosemary or 1 teaspoon dried rosemary well crushed, or thyme
Chopped parsley

1. Place lentils in a basin, cover with boiling water. Leave for one hour then drain, reserving the water.
2. Peel and chop onions.

3. Scrub and thinly slice carrot.

4. Trim excess fat from meat.

5. Put flour on a plate or in a clean bag and thoroughly coat the meat.

6. Melt half of the lard in a large frying pan. Fry onions and carrots for 3 minutes. Lift them out into a casserole, saving fat in pan.

7. Add remaining lard to pan and put in the floured meat to fry until brown on both sides. Add to casserole.

8. Crumble the beef stock cubes into the casserole.

9. Make the lentil water up to 600 ml/1 pint with fresh cold water and pour this over. Add salt, pepper and rosemary or thyme.

10. Cover casserole and cook in centre of moderate oven, Gas 4, 350°F, 180°C, for 1¼ to 1½ hours until meat is tender.

11. Sprinkle with chopped parsley.

Serve with a lightly-cooked green vegetable.

SUSSEX SHEPHERD'S PIE

A 19th century Sussex pie said to have been a traditional favourite of shepherds tending the Southdown sheep.

Serves 4

1 large onion, chopped
4 tablespoons lentils
1 tablespoon wholewheat flour
½ teaspoon curry powder
Salt and pepper
4 lamb chump chops
About 450 g/1 lb small whole peeled potatoes
1 level tablespoon brown sugar
About 600 ml/1 pint stock

1. Cover the bottom of a 1.2 litre/2 pint casserole with onion and lentils.

2. Season the flour with curry powder, salt and pepper. Coat chops and put them on top of lentils.

3. Pack potatoes around and on top of chops.

4. Sprinkle over remaining seasoned flour and the sugar and pour in the stock. Put lid on casserole.

5. Cook in middle of a warm oven, Gas 3, 325°F, 160°F, for 2½ or even 3 hours, removing lid for last 20 minutes to brown potatoes.

Mrs Ruth Brooke & Mrs Sheila Powell
Hove & Portslade, Sussex

BREAST OF LAMB

A good cheap roast

Serves 2 to 3

A breast of lamb, boned

STUFFING
25 g/1 oz dripping
1 chopped onion
75 g/3 oz fresh breadcrumbs (*see page 52*)
25 g/1 oz grated suet
1 teaspoon each of chopped parsley and mint
1 teaspoon chopped rosemary, optional
1 teaspoon Salt and Pepper Mix (*see page 17*)
A little beaten egg, to bind

1. Melt dripping and fry onion until softening. Mix in dry ingredients and sufficient egg to form a firm consistency.

2. Spread stuffing on lamb and roll up like a Swiss Roll. Tie up or sew loosely with fine string. This will allow for expansion during cooking so that stuffing does not squeeze out at ends.

3. Place on a rack in roasting tin. Cook in a moderate oven, Gas 4, 350°F, 180°C, allowing 35 minutes per ½kg/1 lb—stuffed weight.

SAUSAGE AND MUTTON ROLL

A good cheap dish for small households, nice hot or cold.

Serves 3 to 4

1 finely-chopped onion
1 teaspoon lard
325 g/12 oz pork sausage-meat
Salt and pepper
1 teaspoon dried mixed herbs
1 boned breast of lamb

1. Fry onion in lard until transparent.

2. Mix sausage-meat, onion, salt, pepper and herbs together.

3. Spread this stuffing on inside of breast of lamb, roll it up and tie securely with string. Then weigh it.

4. Place on a rack in a roasting tin and cook in a moderate oven, Gas 3, 325°F, 160°C, at 40 minutes to the ½ kg/1 lb.

Serve hot with vegetables, cold with salad or with chutney or pickles.

Mrs Hilda Whitney
Wellingborough, Northants

FRIED STRIPS OF BREAST OF LAMB

Start this dish the day before you want to eat it. Buy a large breast of lamb—it has more lean meat on it. The stock will make a good soup or even a small stew for another time.

Serves 2

1 large breast of lamb
1 onion
1 small carrot or piece of turnip or parsnip
1 piece celery if you have it
Salt and pepper
Water
1 beaten egg
50 g/2 oz dried breadcrumbs

Try serving this with a sweet and sour sauce (*see below*).

1. Put lamb in a saucepan.
2. Peel onion and chop coarsely. Scrub the other vegetables and cut them up.
3. Add vegetables to pan with salt and pepper and cover with water.
4. Bring to the boil and simmer for about 2 hours until meat is tender. Or pressure cook with 300 ml/ ½ pint of water for 30 minutes.
5. Take meat out of liquor and put both aside to cool.
6. Next day, or when quite cold, cut bones and lumps of fat out of meat and cut lean meat into even-sized strips about 5 cm/2 inches long.
7. Dip slices of meat into beaten egg and coat in breadcrumbs.
8. Lift the dripping off the pan of stock and melt a little in the frying pan.
9. Fry the strips of breast of lamb gently till golden and warmed through.

Mrs V. Greatwood,
Castle Cary, Somerset

PRUNE AND APPLE STUFFING

For breast of lamb.

40 g/1½ oz margarine
50 g/2 oz cooked prunes
1 apple
125 g/4 oz fresh wholemeal or white bread-crumbs
1 teaspoon chopped parsley
A small pinch of mixed herbs
Salt
Pepper

1. Melt the margarine.
2. Chop the prunes, removing stones.
3. Grate or chop the apple.
4. Mix all ingredients, binding with melted margarine.

Mrs M. Clough
Padgate, Cheshire

A SWEET AND SOUR SAUCE

For breast of lamb, but also good with sausages, belly pork, pork chops and spare ribs.

50 g/2 oz chopped pineapple, or 2 tablespoons pineapple jam
50 g/2 oz finely-chopped onion
1 tablespoon vinegar
1 heaped tablespoon sugar
½ tablespoon tomato purée or ketchup
1 dessertspoon cornflour
2 teaspoons soya sauce
300 ml/½ pint water
2 teaspoons oil

1. Prepare pineapple and onion.
2. Blend together in a small pan vinegar, sugar, tomato purée, cornflour, soya sauce, and stir in the water.
3. Cook over low heat until thick.
4. Stir in the oil, pineapple and onion and cook for 5 minutes more.

Mrs Edith Griffiths

BREAST OF LAMB WITH BACON AND LEMON

Serves 2

300 ml/½ pint butterbeans, to serve
450 g/1 lb breast of lamb
Boiling water
125 g/4 oz bacon rashers
1 lemon
1 onion
A bunch of sweet herbs, such as thyme, parsley, marjoram, rosemary, mint
Stock
2 tablespoons dried breadcrumbs
1 tablespoon cornflour
A little gravy browning (optional)
Salt and pepper

1. Cover butterbeans with water and soak overnight.
2. Remove skin from lamb. Put meat in a pan of boiling water and simmer for 5 minutes.
3. Lay meat in cold water.
4. Take rinds off bacon and cut it into smaller pieces.
5. Use half of the bacon to line a small stew pan.
6. Slice lemon thinly and lay slices over bacon.
7. Place lamb on top of bacon and lemon and lay rest of bacon over it.
8. Chop onion coarsely and add with the herbs and enough stock just to cover (use liquid from boiling meat).
9. Bring to the boil and simmer for 1½ hours.
10. Remember to put butterbeans on to cook (in the water they have soaked in) 40 minutes before dish is to be served.
11. Put lamb on to a warmed dish, sprinkle with breadcrumbs and keep hot.
12. Strain stock left in stewpan.
13. Blend cornflour with 2 tablespoons cold water and stir into stock. Put over a low heat and stir as it thickens.
14. Colour the gravy with a little gravy browning and season to taste with salt and pepper.
15. Put butterbeans round the meat and serve the gravy separately.

Mrs Iris Elliott-Potter,
Roborough, Nr. Plymouth

HIGHLAND LAMB STEW

Serves 6

25 g/1 oz pearl or pot barley
3 sticks of celery
225 g/8 oz carrots
1 large onion
25 g/1 oz margarine
575 to 675 g/1¼ to 1½ lb lean lamb cut into 2.5 cm/1 inch cubes
150 ml/¼ pint cider
150 ml/¼ pint light stock
1 teaspoon Salt and Pepper Mix (*see page 17*)
1 sprig fresh thyme or ½ teaspoon dried thyme

SAUCE
25 g/1 oz butter or margarine
25 g/1 oz flour
1 heaped teaspoon parsley

1. Rinse barley in a sieve under running water. Place in small pan, just cover with water and simmer for about 10 minutes.
2. Meanwhile, prepare vegetables, cutting them into chunks.
3. Melt margarine in large pan and soften vegetables without browning for 7 to 8 minutes.
4. Add lamb and turn it over in fat to seal.
5. Pour in cider and stock, add Salt and Pepper Mix and thyme, then drained barley. Cover and cook until meat is tender, about 1 to 1¼ hours.
6. Place meat and vegetables on a serving dish and keep warm. Remove sprig of thyme if used.
7. Now make the sauce. Melt margarine in pan, add flour, cook 1 minute.
8. Strain liquid in pan, pushing any loose vegetables through sieve. Mix into the roux—that is, the cooked flour and margarine in the pan—bring to boil and simmer 2 minutes. Stir in parsley. Taste for seasoning.
9. Spoon a little sauce over meat, serve remainder in a sauce-boat.

SAVOURY LAMB PIE

Serves 4

450 g/1 lb lean lamb cut into 1 cm/½ inch cubes (shoulder will do)
1 dessertspoon plain flour
1 teaspoon Salt and Pepper Mix (*see page 17*)
225 g/8 oz sliced onions
1 large cooking apple, peeled, cored and thickly-sliced
150 ml/¼ pint water, or stock made from bones removed from lamb

1. Toss meat in flour mixed with Salt and Pepper Mix. Place in shallow 1 to 1.2 litre/1½ to 2 pint casserole, sprinkle on remaining flour.
2. Layer onion on top, then apple, add water or stock.
3. Cover tightly (a piece of lightly-greased foil will do).
4. Cook in a moderate oven, Gas 4, 350°F, 180°C, for 1½ to 2 hours until lamb is tender. The time depends on quality of lamb.
5. Increase heat to hot, Gas 7, 425°F, 220°C, ready for scone top.

SCONE TOP
175 g/6 oz self-raising flour
¼ teaspoon salt
1 teaspoon mixed herbs
25 g/1 oz margarine
25 g/1 oz lard
100–125 ml/3 to 4 fl oz milk

1. Place flour in a bowl, add salt and herbs.
2. Rub in fats, mix to a smooth dough with the milk.
3. Roll out just under 1 cm, about ¼ inch thick, cut into approximately 5 cm/2 inch rounds.

TO FINISH THE PIE
Arrange scone rounds on top of casserole, return to oven and bake for 25 to 30 minutes until scone top is crusty and golden.

See also Pilaff of Lamb with Courgettes, page 176.

MOUSSAKA

A delicious Greek dish.

Serves 6

450 g/1 lb aubergines
1 tablespoon salt
Good cooking oil
2 large onions, thinly-sliced
A clove of garlic, crushed
450 g/1 lb lean lamb, from the shoulder or leg, minced
A 400 g/14 oz tin of tomatoes
2 tablespoons tomato purée*
Salt and pepper

TOPPING
2 eggs
A 150 ml/¼ pint carton of single cream
50 g/2 oz grated Cheddar cheese
25 g/1 oz grated Parmesan cheese

*To keep tomato purée fresh, see page 84

1. It is necessary to salt aubergines. (This will help them absorb less oil when fried.) Wipe, top and tail, slice into 7 mm/¼ inch thick slices and lay out in a colander, sprinkling with 1 tablespoon salt. Leave for one hour. Press gently and pat dry on kitchen paper.
2. Fry aubergines lightly in 1 or 2 tablespoons hot oil, adding more oil if needed. Lift aubergines out of pan on to kitchen paper or brown paper.
3. Using 1 tablespoon oil, fry onions and garlic until golden.
4. Add lamb and cook for 10 minutes, stirring every now and then.
5. Add tomatoes and purée and mix well. Bring to the boil and simmer with lid on pan for 20 to 25 minutes. Season with salt and pepper.
6. Arrange alternate layers of aubergine and lamb in a 1.2 litre/2 pint soufflé dish or shallow casserole.
7. Cook in a moderate oven, Gas 4, 350°F, 180°C, for 35 to 40 minutes.
8. Meanwhile, prepare topping. Beat eggs and cream together. Stir in grated cheeses.
9. Pour this on top of the moussaka and return it to the oven for a further 15 to 20 minutes until topping is well-risen and golden brown.

LAMB AND MINT JELLY

Economical

Serves 2

450 g/1 lb scrag end of lamb
1 litre/1½ pints stock, preferably bone-stock (*see page 10*)
1 carrot, scrubbed and cut small
1 onion, chopped
A bunch of mint, about 25 to 50 g/1 to 2 oz
2 tablespoons water
15 g/½ oz powdered gelatine
1 level teaspoon salt

1. Simmer scrag end in stock for about 30 minutes with carrot, onion and bunch of mint (keeping out 2 or 3 mint leaves for later).
2. Strain off liquid and set aside.
3. Scrape all meat from the bones, separating all the fat, and chop up meat into fairly small pieces.
4. Put 2 tablespoons water in a cup and stand it in a saucepan containing about 4 cm/1½ inches hot water. Heat gently. Sprinkle gelatine into cup and stir until dissolved.
5. Strain gelatine mixture into a bare 600 ml/1 pint of strained stock. Stir and leave until on the point of setting.
6. Add the diced lamb, a few small pieces of cooked carrot, the finely-chopped mint leaves and salt to taste.
7. Pour into a wetted mould to set.

Serve cold turned out on to a plate with salad, or with creamy mashed potatoes and a green vegetable.

DURHAM LAMB CUTLETS

Serves 4

225 g/8 oz cold cooked lamb
1 medium-sized onion
1 cooking apple
225 g/8 oz mashed potato
1 teaspoon Salt and Pepper Mix (*see page 17*)
1 tablespoon chopped parsley
2 teaspoons tomato ketchup or 1 teaspoon tomato purée
Flour
1 beaten egg
Dried breadcrumbs (*see page 52*)
Fat for deep frying

1. Mince together lamb, onion and apple.
2. Add potato, Salt and Pepper Mix, parsley and ketchup or tomato purée. Mix well.
3. Shape into 'cutlets', dust with flour, brush with beaten egg, roll in dried crumbs.
4. Deep fry for 3 to 4 minutes. Drain on paper.

BRAISED LAMB HEARTS

Serves 2 or 3

2 lamb's hearts
2 teaspoons salt

STUFFING
1 teaspoon lard or margarine
1 small chopped onion
1 rasher of bacon, de-rind and chop small
4 tablespoons brown breadcrumbs
1 tablespoon finely-chopped suet
1 teaspoon chopped fresh parsley
Grated rind of half a lemon or orange
1 beaten egg, to bind
Salt and pepper

1. Wash hearts well in cold water and cut away veins or gristle.
2. Place hearts in a pan, add salt and cover with water.
3. Bring to the boil and remove any scum. Put on lid and simmer for 1½ hours.
4. Remove hearts and save the liquid.
5. Cut hearts in half or in slices if large. Lay in a casserole or shallow pan.
6. *Meanwhile make the stuffing*. Melt lard or margarine. Fry onion and bacon until cooked. Remove from heat.
7. Add the other ingredients and mix well. Season with salt and pepper to taste.
8. Spread stuffing over the heart slices.
9. Pour 300 ml/½ pint of the reserved liquid around the slices of heart. Cover with lid or foil.
10. Simmer on top of cooker for about 1 hour. *Or* cook for 1 hour in a moderate oven, Gas 4, 350°F, 180°C. Test meat with a skewer.

Serve with creamed potatoes and a green vegetable.
Mrs A. Greenwood
Boroughbridge, N. Yorkshire

STUFFED HEARTS

Serves 2 or 3

2 lamb's or sheep's hearts
50 g/2 oz fresh breadcrumbs
50 g/2 oz shredded suet
1 teaspoon dried sage
1 grated onion
Salt and pepper
1 beaten egg
Stock

TO SERVE
Redcurrant jelly
Creamed potato
Peas

1. Wash hearts, cut away all gristle and membrane and make a single cavity in centre. Soak in salted water for $\frac{1}{2}$ hour.
2. Mix crumbs, suet, sage, 1 tablespoon of the grated onion, salt and pepper with sufficient egg to bind. Stuff the hearts, skewering tops, tying or sewing up with fine string if hearts will not stand up in your casserole.
3. Place in small casserole, add any onion left over, cover with stock.
4. Cover tightly with a lid or foil and cook in a moderate oven, Gas 4, 350°F, 180°C. Contents should simmer gently until hearts are tender—$1\frac{1}{2}$ to 2 hours.
5. Place hearts on hot serving dish, remove string. Strain stock into small pan and thicken. Check seasoning.
6. Pipe potato round dish, garnish with peas. Spoon a little sauce over hearts—these can be cut into 2 portions each. Serve the rest of sauce and redcurrant jelly separately.

LOVE IN DISGUISE

Serves 3

3 sheep's hearts
25 g/1 oz vermicelli
3 bacon rashers
1 small egg yolk
Dried breadcrumbs

STUFFING
50 g/2 oz fresh breadcrumbs (*see page 52*)
2 tablespoons shredded suet
Pinch of mustard
50 g/2 oz minced ham or bacon
2 tablespoons chopped parsley
1 teaspoon marjoram
A grating of lemon rind
Salt and pepper
Water

1. Remove pipes from hearts and discard. Wash hearts well and steep in cold water.
2. Break vermicelli and cook in boiling salted water. Leave to cool.
3. Combine the stuffing ingredients with a little water.
4. Dry the hearts and fill with stuffing. Wrap rashers of bacon around them and fasten with small skewers.
5. Stand in a small baking tin so that they prop each other up. Cover with foil and bake in a moderately hot oven, Gas 5, 375°F, 190°C, for $1\frac{1}{2}$ hours.
6. Remove the foil, carefully lift each heart out of tin, brush with beaten egg-yolk and roll in mixed breadcrumbs and vermicelli.
7. Replace in baking tin without foil. Return to the oven and bake till lightly brown, about 10 minutes.

Serve with freshly-made tomato sauce (*see page 187*).
Mrs A. Searle
Holme Lacy, Herefordshire

LIVER RAGOUT

Serves 4

450 g/1 lb lamb's or calf's liver
15 g/$\frac{1}{2}$ oz seasoned flour
25 g/1 oz dripping
1 finely-chopped onion
Juice of $\frac{1}{2}$ a lemon
5 tablespoons dry red or white wine
125 g/4 oz mushrooms

TO SERVE
675 g/$1\frac{1}{2}$ lb creamed potatoes or 225 g/8 oz Patna rice
Chopped parsley

1. Wash liver, remove skin and any tubes. Cut into 2.5 cm/1 inch cubes.
2. Coat in flour seasoned with a shake of salt and pepper.

3. Melt dripping in pan, add liver and onion turning it over to seal the liver.

4. Cook gently for 8 to 10 minutes with lid on pan but stirring occasionally to prevent catching.

5. Add lemon juice, wine and washed and sliced mushrooms. Cook with lid on about 8 minutes more until liver is tender.

6. Meanwhile, cook potatoes and beat until creamy. Form into a ring on warm dish, pour ragout in centre. Sprinkle with chopped parsley.

If using rice—cook about 12 minutes using bacon stock instead of water if this is available. Form into ring, pour ragout in centre. Sprinkle with chopped parsley.

SMOTHERED LIVER HOT-POT

Serves 4 or 5

3 rashers streaky bacon
450 g/1 lb liver
1 level tablespoon plain flour mixed with 1 level teaspoon Salt and Pepper Mix (*see page 17*)
2 sliced onions
1 sliced apple
1 teaspoon sugar
150 ml/¼ pint light stock
150 ml/¼ pint cider
25 g/1 oz bacon fat, if necessary
125 g/4 oz fresh wholemeal or white breadcrumbs (*see page 52*)

1. De-rind bacon, cut it into 2.5 cm/1 inch pieces and fry lightly to extract a little fat.

2. Wash and slice liver, coat well in seasoned flour and place in a shallow casserole.

3. Drain bacon, scatter on top of liver. Add onions and apple and sprinkle on sugar.

4. Pour over the stock and cider.

5. Add a little fat to pan to make up to a good tablespoon, tip in crumbs and stir to combine.

6. Spread crumbs over casserole. Cover, foil will do.

7. Cook in a moderately hot oven, Gas 5, 375°F, 190°C, for 45 minutes. Test with a skewer to ensure liver is cooked—pig's and ox liver take longer than lamb's.

8. Uncover, cook 10 to 12 minutes to crisp top.

SPICED LIVER

Serves 4, but easy to make in smaller or larger quantities.

450 g/1 lb lamb's liver
1 large onion
3 tablespoons cooking oil
4 tablespoons flour
½ teaspoon salt
¼ teaspoon ground black pepper
¼ teaspoon cinnamon
¼ teaspoon crushed cardamon seeds
¼ teaspoon ground cloves
½ teaspoon ground coriander
300 ml/½ pint stock or water

TO SERVE
225 g/8 oz long grain brown or white rice
4 tomatoes
4 rashers bacon
225 g/8 oz can sweetcorn (optional)

1. Skin liver and cut into small cubes.

2. Peel and chop onion.

3. Heat oil in a frying pan and fry onion gently for 2 minutes.

4. Meanwhile, mix salt, pepper and all the other spices into the flour.

5. Toss liver in the spiced flour. Add it to frying pan and fry quickly, turning it over in the fat until it is brown on all sides.

6. Put rice on to cook in another pan.

7. Add stock to liver, stir until it boils. Reduce heat and simmer for 10 minutes, stirring occasionally.

8. Meanwhile, cut rinds off bacon and cut rashers into smaller pieces.

9. Cut tomatoes in halves or quarters.

10. Grill bacon and tomato.

11. Heat sweetcorn.

12. Arrange rice round edge of large, warmed serving plate with liver in the centre. Arrange bacon, tomatoes and sweetcorn decoratively on the same dish.

Chris Kerton
Heston, Middlesex

See also Liver Pâté, page 26.
Liver Spread, page 200.
Sussex Churdles, page 218.

KIDNEYS WITH RICE

Serves 4

1 large onion
1 green pepper
450 g/1 lb lamb's kidneys
4 tomatoes, or 1 small can
1 clove garlic (optional)
Salt
1 tablespoon corn oil
25 g/1 oz butter
1 teaspoon soft brown sugar
1 teaspoon lemon juice
1 teaspoon vinegar
2 small teaspoons Tabasco sauce
225 g/8 oz long grain brown or white rice

If using brown rice allow 20 to 25 minutes to cook. White rice takes 10 to 12 minutes.

1. Peel and chop onion. Chop up green pepper, discarding core and seeds.
2. Skin, core and slice kidneys.
3. Skin and chop tomatoes (to skin *see page 139*).
4. Crush garlic with a little salt.
5. Heat oil and butter in a pan.
6. Cook onion and green pepper gently for 5 minutes.
7. Add kidneys and cook for 3 minutes, turning them over till they are brown on all sides.
8. Add tomatoes, garlic, sugar, lemon juice, vinegar and Tabasco sauce.
9. Cover pan and simmer gently for 10 minutes.
10. Arrange rice round a warmed dish. Pour kidney mixture into centre.

Mrs Barbara Piper
Balham, London

KIDNEYS IN A SAUCE WITH MUSHROOMS

Serves 2

3 lamb's kidneys
25 g/1 oz plain flour
Salt and pepper
25 g/1 oz lard
1 medium-sized onion, chopped
50 g/2 oz mushrooms, thickly-sliced
300 ml/½ pint beef stock, a stock cube will do

1. Remove skins from kidneys, cut them in half and cut out the core. Then chop up.
2. Season the flour with salt and pepper. Toss chopped kidneys in it.
3. Melt lard in a frying pan and gently fry onion.
4. Add kidneys to pan and fry gently for 2 to 3 minutes, turning them over in the fat.
5. Toss mushrooms in with kidneys for 2 or 3 minutes more.
6. Stir remaining flour into pan and let it sizzle for a minute. Gradually stir in stock and bring to the boil. Taste and season if necessary with more salt and pepper.
7. Cover pan and simmer for 10 minutes.

Serve with plain boiled brown or white rice (*see page 172*) and green vegetables.

KIDNEYS WITH A SHERRY AND CREAM SAUCE

Serves 4

8 lamb's kidneys
25 g/1 oz plain flour
Salt and pepper
A grating or pinch of nutmeg
25 to 50 g/1 to 2 oz butter
150 ml/¼ pint light stock
3 large tablespoons sherry
12 stuffed olives
3 tablespoons soured cream, or natural yoghurt

Note: If you cannot buy soured cream, mix ½ teaspoon lemon juice into fresh cream for a similar effect. Leave it for an hour or more before use.

1. Remove skins and core from kidneys.
2. Season flour with salt, pepper and nutmeg.
3. Toss kidneys in seasoned flour.
4. Warm butter in a pan, add kidneys, turn up the heat. Turn kidneys over in the hot butter until sealed and butter is absorbed.
5. Pour stock and sherry over kidneys and simmer for about 5 minutes, stirring occasionally.
6. Meanwhile, slice the olives.
7. Stir in olives and soured cream.

Serve with rice, green vegetables or a green salad.

Mrs J.M. Clark
Stratford-upon-Avon

KIDNEYS IN RED WINE SAUCE

Serves 4

6 to 8 lamb's kidneys
40 g/1½ oz seasoned flour
50 g/2 oz butter
50 g/2 oz mushrooms
150 ml/¼ pint light stock
150 ml/¼ pint red wine, home-made wine is
  ideal

TO SERVE
Rice and a little chopped parsley

1. Skin kidneys, remove core, and cut into pieces.
2. Toss in seasoned flour, sauté in melted butter until the colour changes, add mushrooms and any left over flour. Cook for 1 minute.
3. Add stock and wine. Simmer for 10 minutes. Check seasoning.
4. Serve in a border of boiled rice. Sprinkle with parsley.

ROAST HAND OF PORK WITH BRAISED ONIONS

It is more economical to buy a hand of pork at the weight given because there is a larger proportion of meat to bone and it is better value than buying a smaller joint. Cooking as suggested ensures that the skin is crisp: this is nicer hot than cold. The pork can be eaten cold and is moist for sandwiches. See Pork Oaties for using up the last of the joint.

Serves 8

1.8 to 2 kg/4 to 4½ lb hand of pork (ask the
  butcher to score skin finely)
15 g/½ oz pork dripping
1 small teaspoon salt
Medium-sized onions, 1 for each person
Water
1 to 2 tablespoons wholewheat or plain flour

1. Preheat oven to moderately hot, Gas 6, 400°F, 200°C.
2. Rub dripping over pork and sprinkle on the salt.
3. Place joint on a small trivet or rack in a large roasting tin and put in the oven.

4. Cook for 30 minutes. Reduce heat to moderate, Gas 4, 350°F, 180°C, and cook for 2 to 2½ hours depending on weight of meat.
5. Peel onions and put them whole into saucepan with water to cover. Boil for 20 minutes. Then drain, saving water for the gravy.
6. Put onions in the fat around the meat for the last ½ hour of cooking time. Turn them over in fat once or twice to brown evenly.
7. When meat and onions are done, set them on a warmed dish and keep hot.
8. *To make the gravy.* Pour nearly all fat off sediment in roasting tin into a basin. Stir flour into remaining fat in tin and let it sizzle for 1 minute. Pour in onion water and any other vegetable water, stir till gravy thickens, boil for 2 to 3 minutes and season to taste. If you like smooth gravy, strain it into a warm jug.

STUFFED BELLY PORK

A good cheap roast.

Serves 4 or 5

1.1 kg/2½ lb belly pork, boned and with rind
  finely-scored
Pork dripping
Salt

STUFFING
75 g/3 oz fresh breadcrumbs (*see page 52*)
1 grated apple
1 grated onion
25 g/1 oz shredded suet
2 teaspoons dried sage
1 egg-yolk
1 teaspoon Salt and Pepper Mix (*see page 17*)

1. Mix stuffing ingredients together to a firm consistency.
2. Spread stuffing on pork.
3. Tie up or sew loosely with fine string. This will allow for expansion during cooking so that stuffing does not squeeze out at ends.
4. Brush rind with softened pork dripping (or lard) and sprinkle with salt.
5. To keep meat out of fat, place on rack in roasting tin. Cook in a moderately hot oven, Gas 5, 375°F, 190°C, allowing 50 minutes per ½ kg/1 lb stuffed weight—about 2 hours.

PORK OATIES

Serves 4

1 medium-sized onion
1 medium-sized apple
225 g/8 oz cold pork
125 g/4 oz wholemeal breadcrumbs
1 level teaspoon dried sage
½ teaspoon salt
A good shake of pepper
1 beaten egg
A little wholewheat flour
50 to 75 g/2 to 3 oz oatmeal
Pork dripping, from joint

1. Peel onion and cut up roughly. Peel, core and quarter apple.
2. Mince together pork, onion and apple.
3. Combine pork mixture with breadcrumbs, sage, salt and pepper.
4. Add half the beaten egg and mix it in well to bind all together.
5. With floured hands, make 8 or 12 balls. Flatten them into round cakes. Chill them for at least 30 minutes.
6. Flour them lightly, brush with beaten egg and coat with oatmeal.
7. Put 2 tablespoons dripping into frying pan and make it hot. Fry the oaties for 6 minutes on each side.

Serve with baked beans, green peas or grilled tomatoes.

ORANGE STUFFING

Try it with roast pork, including roast belly pork, poultry and loin of mutton.

65 g/2½ oz fresh brown or white breadcrumbs
1 level tablespoon chopped fresh mixed herbs, parsley, chives and thyme
1 level tablespoon finely-chopped fresh sage leaves
Salt and black pepper
25 to 40 g/1 to 1½ oz margarine
2 level tablespoons finely-chopped onion
Grated rind and juice of 1 large orange
1 egg

1. Mix the crumbs in a bowl with the herbs and seasoning.
2. Melt margarine and fry onion to soften without browning.
3. Add onion to the crumbs with the grated orange rind and juice.
4. Mix in egg. The mixture should be of moist consistency. Add extra orange juice or a few drops of water to moisten if necessary.

PORK CHOPS WITH ORANGE SAUCE

Serves 4 people, but easy to do for just 1 or 2

4 pork chops
175 g/6 oz brown or white rice (*see Boiled Rice, page 172*)

ORANGE SAUCE
1 level dessertspoon cornflour
1 tablespoon demerara sugar
Finely-grated rind and juice of 2 oranges
1 tablespoon chopped fresh parsley
Salt and Pepper Mix (*see page 17*)

1. Put chops on to grill and rice on to boil.
2. Meanwhile, mix together cornflour, sugar, rind and juice of oranges.
3. When chops are done, put 1 tablespoon of their dripping into a small saucepan. Mix in prepared sauce ingredients and stir over gentle heat until thick. Stir in parsley. Season to taste.
4. Put rice on a hot dish. Put chops on top and pour over the sauce.

PORK CHOPS IN MUSHROOM AND CREAM SAUCE

Serves 4

4 pork loin chops
25 g/1 oz butter
1 onion, finely-chopped
25 g/1 oz plain flour
300 ml/½ pint single cream
225 g/8 oz mushrooms, chopped
Salt and pepper
Chopped parsley (optional)

1. Grill chops for about 8 minutes each side.
2. Meanwhile, fry onion in the butter till golden brown.
3. Mix in mushrooms and fry for 2 minutes.
4. Add flour and stir to a paste.
5. Add cream and cook *very* gently to thicken.
6. Season to taste.
7. Pour sauce over chops and garnish with chopped parsley if desired.

Judith Adshead
Mottram St Andrew, Cheshire

PORK SLICES IN A CAPER SAUCE

Serves 4

4 slices of pork fillet cut about 5 cm/2 inch thick
A little plain flour
1 beaten egg
About 40 g/1½ oz fresh wholewheat or white breadcrumbs
2 tablespoons oil

SAUCE
50 g/2 oz butter or margarine
Half a large onion, chopped
1 anchovy fillet, or 1 teaspoon anchovy essence
2 tablespoons capers, or pickled nasturtium seeds*, or use pickled gherkin
1 tablespoon chopped parsley
1 tablespoon flour
2 tablespoons vinegar
300 ml/½ pint water
Salt and pepper

*French capers, the pickled flower heads of a trailing plant from Southern Europe, are now rather forgotten, although they can still be bought. A good substitute is home-pickled nasturtium seeds (see page 374).

1. Smack the pork slices with a rolling pin to flatten.
2. Flour each slice, dip in beaten egg and then in breadcrumbs.
3. Heat oil and gently fry the slices until cooked. Put on a serving dish and keep hot.
4. *Meanwhile make sauce.* Melt half of the butter or margarine and slightly brown onions.
5. Chop anchovy and mash it down with a wooden spoon. Chop capers. Add these with parsley and flour. Cook gently for 3 or 4 minutes.
6. Add vinegar and water gradually, stirring as sauce thickens. Simmer 2 or 3 minutes.
7. Remove pan from heat, stir in rest of butter and pour sauce over pork slices.

PORK CASSEROLE

You need a shallow casserole dish with a well-fitting lid.

Serves 4

450 g/1 lb pork fillet (tenderloin)
25 g/1 oz lard
4 rashers bacon
1 large onion
1 cooking apple
A little salt
Pepper
6 dried juniper berries
2 large potatoes
300 ml/½ pint cider
50 g/2 oz butter

1. Cut pork into 4 to 6 pieces and fry in lard till brown on each side. Place in casserole dish.
2. Grill bacon lightly and place on top of pork.
3. Peel and chop the onion and the apple and place on top of pork and bacon.
4. Season with a little salt and some pepper.
5. Add crushed juniper berries (crush with the back of a knife).
6. Peel and slice potatoes and place on top.
7. Pour on the cider.
8. Cut a piece of greaseproof paper 12 mm/½ inch larger than casserole dish. Spread this with the butter and put it butter-side down over the potatoes. Cover with tight-fitting lid to ensure it is well sealed.
9. Cook in a slow to moderate oven, Gas 2 to 3, 310°F, 160°C, for 1½ hours.

Judith Adshead
Mottram St Andrew, Cheshire

PORK IN A CASSEROLE WITH TOMATO AND MUSHROOMS

Serves 2 or 3

225 g/8 oz shoulder of pork, or fillet
25 g/1 oz butter
1 large onion
25 g/1 oz flour
300 ml/½ pint stock
2 tablespoons tomato purée*
2 bay leaves
Pepper and salt
75 g/3 oz mushrooms

TO SERVE
125 g/4 oz brown or white rice
125 g/4 oz peas
To keep tomato purée fresh, see page 84

1. Cut meat into even-sized slices.
2. Melt butter in a frying pan, add meat and let it brown on both sides. Lift it out into a casserole dish.
3. Peel and slice onion. Fry it gently in pan until soft but not brown. Lift out of pan with a draining spoon and arrange it over the meat.
4. Add flour to pan, cook for 1 minute.
5. Gradually pour in stock, stirring as it thickens. Bring to boil.
6. Add tomato purée, bay leaves, pepper and salt. Mix well and pour it over the meat.
7. Put lid on casserole and put in a moderate oven, Gas 4, 350°F, 180°C, for ¾ hour.
8. Meanwhile, remember to put rice on to cook, allowing 25 to 35 minutes for brown rice and 10 to 12 minutes for white rice.
9. Wipe mushrooms and cut them up if necessary into even-sized pieces.
10. Add them to casserole and let it cook another 15 to 20 minutes.

Serve each helping on a bed of rice with lightly-cooked green peas.

Mrs Margaret Ferns
Loundsley Green, Derbyshire

CASSEROLE OF PORK

At one time this dish used the pork trimmings after the ribs had been lifted prior to salting the meat for bacon. As this may be hard to get it is suggested that meat from the shoulder is used.
Pork chops are very good this way, but tend to be greasy.

Serves 4

450 to 675 g/1 to 1½ lb lean pork slices about
    1 cm/½ inch thick, from the shoulder
1 heaped tablespoon flour seasoned with salt
    and pepper
Dripping for frying
450 g/1 lb onions, sliced
3 or 4 cooking apples
300 to 450 ml/½ to ¾ pint stock or water
2 tablespoons brown sugar

1. Dip the pork slices in seasoned flour and fry them gently until browned on both sides. Put into a casserole.

2. Fry the sliced onions until softened but not brown and add as a layer on top of the pork.

3. Core the unpeeled apple and slice into thick rings. Fry for a few minutes on each side and put into casserole on top of the onions.

4. Make a gravy with the residue from frying pan and left-over seasoned flour and stock. Strain into casserole—it should just cover the *meat* only.

5. Sprinkle the apples with the brown sugar.

6. Cover the casserole tightly and cook in a moderate oven, Gas 3, 325°F, 160°C, for about 45 to 60 minutes depending on maturity of meat, testing to see if pork is tender.

Serve with vegetables.

Miss G.S. Davies
Flintshire

PORK IN CIDER WITH WALNUT-STUFFED PRUNES

This dish freezes well for about 3 months. Remember to start the night before.

Serves 4 to 6 but easy to cut down for fewer

16 prunes
450-675 g/1 to 1½ lb diced pork, from the shoulder
1 heaped tablespoon cornflour
1 onion, chopped
1 tablespoon oil
300 ml/½ pint dry cider
300 ml/½ pint chicken stock
A clove of garlic, crushed
4 cloves or ¼ teaspoon ground cloves
½ teaspoon marjoram
Salt and pepper
16 walnut halves

1. Start by pouring boiling water over prunes and leaving to soak and plump up for at least 12 hours. If using ready softened prunes, soak in cold water.

2. Toss pork in cornflour.

3. Fry onion gently in oil until softened.

4. Add meat to pan and stir until surfaces are brown.

5. Add cider, stock, garlic, cloves, marjoram, salt and pepper.

6. Bring to boil, cover pan and let it just simmer until meat is tender, about 1½ hours. Or transfer into a covered casserole and cook in a slow oven, Gas 2, 300°F, 150°C, for about 2 hours.

7. Meanwhile, remove stones carefully from prunes and stuff with walnuts.

8. 20 minutes before end of cooking time drop stuffed prunes in with meat.

Serve with rice, pasta or boiled potatoes and freshly-cooked green vegetables.

Mrs Angela Mottram
Axbridge, Somerset

ORIENTAL SWEET AND SOUR PORK

Deep-fried pork in batter with vegetables in a sweet and sour sauce.

Serves 4

450 g/1 lb lean pork
75 g/3 oz cornflour
50 g/2 oz plain flour
1 teaspoon salt
1 egg, separated
3 tablespoons cold water
Oil for deep frying

SWEET AND SOUR VEGETABLES
1 green pepper
2 carrots
1 small onion
2 cloves of garlic
2 tablespoons sugar
1 tablespoon soya sauce
3 tablespoons wine or cider vinegar
1 tablespoon rice wine* or dry sherry
1 tablespoon oil
½ teaspoon grated fresh ginger (*see page 62*)
1 tablespoon cornflour
1 tablespoon water

Can be bought at Chinese supermarkets.

1. Trim any fat from pork, cut it into fairly thin slices and cut these into 2.5 cm/1 inch pieces.

2. In a bowl mix the 75 g/3 oz cornflour, plain flour and salt.

3. Lightly mix egg-yolk and water.

4. Make a well in centre of flour and work in the egg-yolk and water to form a smooth batter.

5. Beat egg-white until stiff. Fold it into batter.

6. Heat the oil until it is nearly smoking hot. To test: drop into it a small piece of dry bread; if it immediately rises bubbling to the surface and goes golden in 1 minute, oil is ready.

7. Cooking just a few pieces of pork at a time, dip them into the batter and deep fry until golden brown and crisp, about 3 to 5 minutes.

8. Drain on kitchen paper and keep warm in a low oven until all the pieces are fried.

9. Meanwhile, wash and dry green pepper and cut into bite-sized squares.

10. Scrub carrots, slice lengthwise into fine strips. Cut these into 2.5 cm/1 inch pieces.

11. Chop onion quite small.

12. Finely chop the garlic.

13. In a small bowl, mix together the sugar, soya sauce, vinegar and wine.

14. In a wok or frying pan heat 1 tablespoon of oil until it is just smoking hot. Add carrots, pepper and onion and stir-fry over a medium heat for 2 minutes.

15. Add garlic, ginger and the vinegar mixture. Allow to boil for 1 minute.

16. Slake the cornflour by mixing it with 1 tablespoon of water and then add it to pan and cook for half a minute, stirring until the sauce has thickened and becomes clear.

17. Arrange the pork pieces in a serving dish and pour the sauce over.

Serve at once with Boiled Rice (*see page 172*) or noodles.

Priya Wickramasinghe
Cardiff

SWEET AND SOUR PORK

Can be cooked in an electric frying pan.

Serves 4, but easy to cut down quantities

450 g/1 lb boneless pork, either from shoulder or belly
2 tablespoons cooking oil
1 small green pepper
4 dessert apples
15 g/½ oz butter
1 tablespoon brown sugar
2 teaspoons soya sauce
2 tablespoons orange or pineapple juice
A dash of wine or cider vinegar or Worcestershire sauce
Salt and pepper

1. Cut pork into 1 cm/½ inch cubes.

2. Heat oil in large, frying pan or shallow pan, or electric frying pan. Fry pork quickly to seal all over. Lower heat and continue frying, turning meat over with spatula from time to time until brown and cooked. This will take about 20 minutes.

3. Meanwhile, remove core and seeds from green pepper and cut up small.

4. Just before they are required, peel and core apples and slice thinly.

5. Push meat to sides of pan. Melt butter in centre of pan. Add apples and fry over medium heat, turning them over until beginning to soften.

6. Sprinkle sugar over apples and push them to sides of pan.

7. Add green pepper and fry for 2 or 3 minutes.

8. Sprinkle with soya sauce, fruit juice and vinegar or Worcestershire sauce. Stir and check seasoning, adding salt and pepper if necessary.

9. Stir over medium heat for 2 to 3 minutes.

Serve with plain boiled brown rice (*see page 172*).

PORK WITH PURÉE OF TOMATOES

Serves 2 to 3

450 g/1 lb fresh tomatoes or a 400 g/14 oz can of tomatoes
2 bay leaves
10 peppercorns or a good shake of black pepper
Nut of butter
Salt
2 or 3 slices belly of pork or spare rib chops
1 teaspoon sugar

FOR THICKENING
About 1 tablespoon rolled oats or 1 to 2 tablespoons fresh wholemeal or white breadcrumbs (*see page 52*)

1. Put tomatoes (skinned, *page 139*, and chopped if fresh are used), bay leaves, peppercorns and butter into a casserole.

2. Add salt and place pork on top.

3. Cover closely (foil will do) and cook in a slow oven, Gas 2, 300°F, 150°C, for 1½ to 2 hours. Turn and baste meat occasionally.

4. When meat is tender remove it from casserole for a moment. Remove bay leaves.

5. Add sugar to the tomato mixture and stir in oats or breadcrumbs.

6. Replace meat on top of tomato mixture, do not cover. Return casserole to oven for 10 to 15 minutes.

Mrs W. A. Sharman
Norton Lindsay, Warwickshire

CRISPY PORK AND POTATO PIE

Serves 4

450 g/1 lb thin slices of belly pork
450 g/1 lb onions
1 carrot, 1 parsnip, 1 stick celery or 50 g/2 oz mixed, dried vegetables may be used
1 tomato (optional)
675 to 900 g/1½ to 2 lb potatoes
1 large cooking apple
Salt and pepper
600 ml/1 pint good stock
50 g/2 oz fresh wholemeal or white bread-crumbs
1 tablespoon mixed herbs
1 egg
1 tablespoon milk

1. Remove rinds from pork slices.
2. Peel onions and slice into rings.
3. Scrub and finely slice carrot, parsnip and celery, if used.
4. Remove skin and seeds from the tomato and chop it small.
5. Peel potatoes and cut into slices.
6. Peel and core apple and cut into rings.
7. Line bottom of a fairly shallow pie-dish with half of the potatoes.
8. Mix onion and apple rings together and lay them evenly on top of potatoes.
9. Mix the carrot and parsnip slices and lay these in dish. Or add mixed, dried vegetables.
10. Add chopped tomato.
11. Cover with rest of potatoes.
12. Season to taste with salt and pepper and sprinkle with a pinch of mixed herbs. Pour over the stock.
13. Mix rest of herbs into breadcrumbs.
14. Beat egg with the milk.
15. Coat each pork slice with egg mixture and then herb and breadcrumb mixture.
16. Lay pork on top of potatoes.
17. Cook in moderately hot oven, Gas 5, 375°F, 190°C, for ½ hour. Reduce temperature to slow, Gas 2, 300°F, 150°C, for 1 hour or until potatoes are cooked.
The pork will be brown and crisp. The herbs and vegetables absorb the fatty taste which so many people dislike in belly pork.

Mrs J. Allison
Nottingham

CASSEROLE OF PORK AND BEANS

Serves 4

125 to 175 g/4 to 6 oz haricot beans, exact quantity depends on personal taste
450 g/1 lb minced shoulder pork
225 g/8 oz diced carrots
1 large chopped onion
¼ teaspoon chilli powder
¼ teaspoon tabasco sauce
Or ¼ teaspoon cayenne pepper
1 teaspoon curry powder
Salt and pepper
450 ml/¾ pint stock

1. Soak beans overnight in plenty of water.
2. Next day, drain beans and put them into a large pan with fresh water. Boil for 15 minutes then drain.
3. Put pork, carrots, onion and beans into a casserole with all the seasonings. Pour over the stock.
4. Cover the casserole and cook in a moderate oven, Gas 3, 325°F, 160°C, for 1½ to 1¾ hours.

See also Pork Spare Ribs in Barbecue Sauce, page 28.

TO MAKE PORK SAUSAGES

Do not start this until you know you can get some sausage-skins. A butcher who makes his own sausages may sell you some. Some electric food mixers have a sausage-filling attachment. If you don't have one, the only alternative will be to use a large piping bag with large nozzle, but it will be difficult (*see paragraph 6 below*). Can be frozen.

Makes about 2.25 kg/5 lb sausages

450 g/1 lb white or wholemeal bread
600 ml/1 pint water
1.3 kg/3 lb lean pork, from the shoulder
450 g/1 lb fat belly pork
25 g/1 oz salt
8 g/½ teaspoon pepper
6 g/¼ teaspoon ground mace
4 g/small pinch of ground ginger
2 g/tiny pinch of ground or rubbed sage

1. Cut bread into cubes and soak in the water for 1 or 2 hours.
2. Mince the meat using coarse blades of mincer.

3. Mix in the seasonings.

4. Squeeze water from bread thoroughly and discard water.

5. Mix all ingredients and put through mincer again, this time using fine blades.

6. Thread skins on to nozzle and fill. Link as desired.

Stella Boldy
Sykehouse, N. Humberside

CUMBERLAND SAUSAGE

If you buy Cumberland Sausage it is usually long and thick. To be truly authentic you must try and get casings—or skins—that will give a thick sausage. Will keep for weeks if hung from hooks in ceiling.

2 kg/4½ lb lean pork, from the shoulder
675 g/1½ lb fat belly pork
6 g/¼ oz powdered sage
Pinch of marjoram
25 g/1 oz white pepper
75 g/3 oz salt
125 g/4 oz soft breadcrumbs

To wash sausage casing attach one end to the cold tap and run fresh water carefully through it. Then leave to soak in salted water overnight. Rinse and use. Some electric mixers have a sausage-filling attachment. Otherwise use a large piping bag and nozzle. Work the casing up over the nozzle, so that as you squeeze the bag sausagemeat is forced into the end of the casing. Casing gradually slides off nozzle as it is filled.

1. Mince the meat but not too finely. Cumberland Sausage is coarser than our usual sausages.

2. Thoroughly mix in all the other ingredients.

3. Test flavour by cooking a little in a greased frying pan.

4. Fill sausage casings and twist into links.

SAUSAGE SAUTÉ

Serves 4

2 tablespoons oil
450 g/1 lb pork sausages
1 medium-sized onion
1 green pepper
225 g/8 oz fresh or tinned tomatoes
1 large cooking apple
Salt and Pepper Mix (*see page 17*)

1. Heat 1 tablespoon of the oil in a large frying pan. Separate the sausages and cook gently for 15 to 20 minutes, turning frequently.

2. Peel and slice onion.

3. Wash and dry green pepper. Cut out core and remove pips. Cut flesh into thin strips.

4. Warm 1 tablespoon oil in another pan. Cook onion and green pepper gently, stirring occasionally, for 5 minutes.

5. Skin the tomatoes (*see page 139*) and chop roughly.

6. Roughly chop the apple.

7. Add tomatoes and apple to onion mixture and continue cooking for 5 minutes, stirring occasionally. Season slightly.

8. Drain sausages and keep hot.

9. Turn out onion mixture into a warmed dish and arrange sausages on top.

Serve with plain boiled potatoes.

SAUSAGES IN SWEET AND SOUR SAUCE

Serves 4

450 g/1 lb sausages
15 g/½ oz margarine

FOR THE SAUCE
25 g/1 oz margarine
1 medium-sized onion, finely-chopped
1 large stick of celery, finely-sliced
1 medium-sized carrot cut into matchstick pieces
1 large, finely-diced apple
300 ml/½ pint light stock
1 heaped teaspoon cornflour
½ teaspoon dry mustard
1 teaspoon Salt and Pepper Mix (*see page 17*)
1 heaped teaspoon Demerara sugar
2 teaspoons Worcestershire sauce
Water

TO SERVE
Rice or mashed potato

1. Start with the sauce. Melt margarine in saucepan, fry onion, celery, carrot and apple gently to soften.

2. Add stock.

3. Mix cornflour, mustard, Salt and Pepper Mix, sugar and Worcestershire sauce with just enough water to blend.

4. Stir this mixture into pan of vegetables and bring to boil. Simmer for 5 minutes.

5. Meanwhile, fry sausages in 15 g/½ oz margarine until nicely brown. Drain away fat.

6. Pour sauce over the sausages. Cover and simmer for 15 minutes. A little water can be added if mixture becomes too thick. Re-season if necessary.

7. Serve on a bed of rice or piped potato.

SAUSAGE AND KIDNEY HOT-POT

Could be made in electric frying pan.

Serves 4

4 sheep's kidneys
4 large sausages
125 g/4 oz bacon
3 small onions or 3 sticks of celery
125 g/4 oz mushrooms
225 g/8 oz carrots
25 g/1 oz butter
15 g/½ oz flour
300 ml/½ pint stock
1 teaspoon tomato purée, or ketchup
1 tablespoon sherry
Salt and pepper
1 small packet frozen peas

1. Remove skins from kidneys, cut them into 4 pieces and cut out core.

2. Skin the sausages and make each into 2 or 3 small balls.

3. De-rind bacon and cut it into strips.

4. Peel and chop onions or celery. Wipe and slice mushrooms. Scrub carrots and cut into short, very thin strips.

5. Melt butter in pan and fry bacon a little. Add kidneys and sausages and fry them quickly till lightly-browned. Lift out of fat on to a plate.

6. Add onions and mushrooms to pan. Reduce heat and cook slowly for 5 minutes, stirring occasionally.

7. Stir flour into pan and let it cook 1 minute.

8. Stir in stock, tomato purée and sherry and bring to simmering point, stirring as it thickens. Season with salt and pepper.

9. Add carrots, bacon, kidney and sausage balls.

10. Cover pan with a well-fitting lid and simmer gently for ½ hour. 10 minutes before end of cooking time add frozen peas.

Ann E. Craib
King's Park, Glasgow

HEREFORD SAUSAGES

Serves 4

450 g/1 lb pork sausages
25 g/1 oz cooking fat or 1 tablespoon oil
2 medium onions, finely chopped
2 rashers back bacon, cut in strips
1 heaped teaspoon plain flour
3 tablespoons cider, made up to 300 ml/½ pint
** with stock**
1 bay leaf
Salt and pepper
125 g/4 oz mushrooms

TO SERVE
675 g/1½ lb creamed potatoes
Finely chopped parsley

1. Fry sausages in fat or oil for about 20 minutes, until golden brown. Remove from pan and pour away some of the fat.

2. Add the onion and bacon and cook gently for 5 minutes.

3. Sprinkle on flour and cook 2 to 3 minutes, stirring well.

4. Pour on stock and cider. Bring to boil, stirring.

5. Add bay leaf, sausages and seasoning. Cover and simmer for 20 minutes, adding mushrooms for the last 10 minutes.

6. Pipe a border of creamed potatoes round a hot serving dish. Fill centre of dish with sausage mixture, removing bay leaf. Sprinkle with chopped parsley and serve.

Mrs A. Searle
Holme Lacy

SAUSAGES AND KIDNEYS IN A WINE AND MUSHROOM SAUCE

Lamb's liver can be used instead of kidneys. Easy to make in smaller or larger quantities.

Serves 2

4 chipolata sausages
Cooking oil
4 lamb's kidneys or 225 g/8 oz lamb's liver
125 g/4 oz mushrooms
1 tablespoon flour
300 ml/$\frac{1}{2}$ pint beef stock (a stock cube will do)
3 tablespoons red wine
1 dessertspoon tomato purée*
25 g/1 oz butter
4 slices bread

*To keep tomato purée fresh, see page 84.

1. Cook sausages gently in a very little oil. Lift them out of pan and keep them warm.
2. Meanwhile, remove skins from kidneys, cut them in halves, trim out the tubes. Or, skin liver and cut it into 4 even-sized slices.
3. Slice mushrooms coarsely.
4. Add mushrooms to sausage pan and fry gently, turning them over in fat for 2 or 3 minutes.
5. Stir in flour and cook for 1 minute.
6. Add stock, wine and tomato purée, bring to boiling point and simmer for 5 minutes. Keep it warm.
7. Cut bread into triangles or fancy shapes.
8. Melt butter and fry bread until brown and crisp. Lift it out on to a paper to drain and keep hot.
9. In same pan, quickly fry kidneys on both sides till brown. Do not overcook or they will be tough and rubbery.
10. Pour sauce into a warmed dish. Arrange sausages and kidneys on top with fried bread standing up in between.

Serve at once, before fried bread goes soggy in sauce.

Mrs Anne Hamblin
Hilton, Derbyshire

See also Sausage and Apple Turnovers, page 222.
Sausage Cartwheel Flan, page 223.
Sausages in a Curry Sauce, page 174.
Savoury Sausage Flan, page 221.
Savoury Sausage Pie, page 221.

Sausage Plait, page 220.
Cheese Sausage Rolls, page 222.
Pâté of Gammon, Pig's Liver and Sausage, page 27.
Sussex Farmhouse Pâté, page 27.
Aunt Polly's Pie, page 70.
Devonshire Pork Pasties, page 218.
Pork Pie, page 216.

LIVER PUFFS

Makes about 12.

125 g/4 oz pig's liver
75 g/3 oz macaroni
15 g/$\frac{1}{2}$ oz butter
1 tablespoon flour
150 ml/$\frac{1}{4}$ pint milk
1 tablespoon chopped parsley
2 eggs
Oil or fat for frying

Note: If flavour of liver is too strong, soak it in some milk and water for 1 hour before cooking. Discard the liquid.

1. Parboil liver.
2. Boil macaroni in salted water till cooked. Drain well.
3. Mince liver and macaroni finely.
4. Melt butter in a pan, stir in flour and cook till golden brown.
5. Add the quarter pint of milk, stir and cook till thick.
6. Add liver, macaroni and parsley and heat through.
7. Add well-beaten eggs.
8. Drop large tablespoons of the mixture into hot fat deep enough to cover. They puff up lightly when cooked.

Kate Easlea
Hampshire

LIVER AND BACON HOT-POT

Serves 4 to 6

450 g/1 lb pig's liver
225 g/8 oz streaky bacon rashers
2 medium-sized onions or 3 sticks of celery
2 medium-sized, sharp, cooking apples
2 tablespoons chopped parsley
1 teaspoon chopped fresh marjoram or ½ teaspoon dried marjoram
75 g/3 oz soft breadcrumbs
Salt and pepper
About 600 ml/1 pint stock or water

1. Cut liver into thin slices.
2. Cut bacon rashers into small pieces.
3. Peel and chop onions. Peel, core and chop apples and mix with onion.
4. Place a layer of liver in a greased casserole, cover it with a layer of bacon and a layer of onion and apple.
5. Mix parsley and marjoram into breadcrumbs and sprinkle over onion and apple. Add a shake of salt and pepper.
6. Repeat these layers until dish is full, saving enough breadcrumbs to cover the final layer of onion and apple.
7. Pour in enough stock or water almost to cover.
8. Put lid on casserole and cook in a warm oven, Gas 3, 325°F, 160°C, for 2 hours.
9. Half an hour before serving, remove lid to let the top brown.

Mrs Becky Blackmore
Exeter, Devon

TOMATO LIVER

Serves 4 to 5

2 medium-sized onions
1 large green pepper
450 g/1 lb fresh tomatoes or a 425 g/15 oz can
25 g/1 oz butter
450 g/1 lb pig's liver
2 tablespoons flour
150 ml/¼ pint white wine or stock
Salt and black pepper
2 tablespoons cream (optional)

1. Peel and chop onions. Chop green pepper, removing core and seeds.

2. Skin and cut up tomatoes. (To skin *see page 139*).
3. Melt butter and gently fry onion and green pepper.
4. Slice liver and dredge in flour.
5. Add to onion mixture, cook for 2 or 3 minutes, turning it over.
6. Add tomatoes, wine, or stock. Cover pan and simmer for 15 minutes.
7. Check seasoning. Add cream if required.

Mrs Alison Seymour
Aston Tirrold, Oxon

FAGGOTS

Ffagod Sir Benfro, which means faggots as made in Pembrokeshire.

Serves 5 or 6, but easy to cut recipe down

675 g/1½ lb pig's liver
2 large onions
125 g/4 oz fresh brown or white breadcrumbs
75 g/3 oz shredded suet
2 level teaspoons sage
1 teaspoon salt
¼ teaspoon pepper

TO SERVE
Green peas and gravy

1. Mince liver and onion into a bowl.
2. Add remaining ingredients and mix thoroughly.
3. Form into balls to fit palm of hand. Traditionally, faggots were wrapped in caul to cook. Nowadays, the best way is to use or make foil cups to hold them in shape. Set these in a small roasting tin and pour boiling water around them.
Or, make a loaf of the mixture. Press into a greased 1 kg/2 lb loaf tin. Set this in a roasting tin and pour boiling water around it to come halfway up sides.
4. Bake in middle of a moderate oven, Gas 4, 350°F, 180°C, for 30 minutes for individual faggots, 1 hour for loaf. Leave loaf in tin for 10 minutes in a warm place. This gives it time to set and it can then be turned out and will slice quite easily.

Serve faggots on a bed of peas with a good gravy in a separate jug.

Mrs Joyce Porvell
Llanddewi Rhydderch W.I., Gwent

LINCOLNSHIRE HASLETT

Serves 4

175 g/6 oz pig's liver
175 g/6 oz lean and fat bits of pork
75 g/3 oz pig's heart
1 small, or half a large, onion
About 40 g/1½ oz fresh wholemeal or white breadcrumbs
2 or 3 leaves of sage, chopped
1 teaspoon salt
Pepper
A piece of pig's veil, optional

1. Mince liver, pork, heart and onion.
2. Add breadcrumbs and sage and season with salt and pepper.
3. Mix all together then wrap in veil or foil and place on small baking tray.
4. Cook in a moderate oven, Gas 4, 350°F, 180°C, for about 1½ hours.

Mrs Bailey
Ruskington

See also Country Loaf, page 28.
Pâté of Gammon, Pig's Liver and Sausage, page 27.
Mary Berry's Farmhouse Pâté, page 27.
Sussex Farmhouse Pâté, page 27.

PIG'S KIDNEY STUFFING

This may be used in roast leg of pork if you get the butcher to remove the bone from the fleshy end. It may also be used to stuff other boned pork joints.
1. Skin, core and chop the pig's kidney.
2. Add chopped fresh herbs; mostly parsley but also thyme and a few chives, even a little garlic.
3. Add salt and pepper and mix well.
4. Stuff into the joint. Use tin foil round the fleshy end to keep the stuffing in place.

PIG'S HEAD BRAWN

Serves 5 to 6

1 pig's head, split in half
Water
Salt
1 tablespoon vinegar
8 black peppercorns
1 large onion, peeled
1 bay leaf
225 g/8 oz shin of beef (optional)
Half a rabbit (optional)
Pepper

1. With a sharp knife, take away ears and eyes. Scoop out brains. Chop off the snout. These bits are not used.
2. Wash the 2 halves in cold running water. Then put in a large bowl of water, adding 1 tablespoon of salt per 600 ml/1 pint of water. Leave to soak for 2 or 3 hours.
3. Drain away water. Put head into a large pan and cover with water.
4. Add vinegar, peppercorns, whole onion, bay leaf and 2 teaspoons salt.
5. If using shin of beef or rabbit, add it now. The addition of either of these helps to counteract the fat-content of the head.
6. Bring to the boil, cover pan and simmer until meat leaves the bones.
7. Turn off heat and leave meat in pan till cool enough to handle.
8. Lift all meat out into a large bowl.
9. Return pan of stock to heat and simmer until it is reduced by about half.
10. Remove all meat from bones. Chop it into small pieces but do not mince.
11. Strain over the meat enough of the reduced stock to 'float' the meat. Season with salt and pepper.
12. Return to a saucepan, bring to boil and simmer for 10 minutes.
13. Pour into a mould and set in a cool place.
14. Turn out on to a plate and serve with pickles and salads.

GAMMON IN CIDER

This Somerset method best suits a large joint such as a half gammon but non-gammon joints such as slipper, forehock and hock can be used. It is boiled then roasted.

If the meat is smoked, soak it first for 12 hours in plenty of cold water. To speed up process, cover pan, bring to boil. Leave until cold. Then discard water, and proceed as follows:

FOR A LARGE JOINT
2.25 litres/4 pints water
600 ml/1 pint dry cider
1 chopped onion
6 allspice berries
4 cloves
2 bay leaves

Place joint in a saucepan with the above ingredients, put lid on, bring slowly to the boil and simmer for 10 minutes to the ½ kg/1 lb.

FOR SMALLER JOINTS
Reduce liquid in same ratio of 1 part cider to 4 parts water using sufficient to cover meat generously. Reduce onion and spices accordingly. Cook as above. Then lift out joint, skin it and score fat in a criss-cross pattern.

FOR BASTING
Dry cider
2 tablespoons
demerara sugar   mixed
1 teaspoon dry   together
mustard
1 teaspoon
mixed spice

1. Put joint in a baking tin, moisten with cider, sprinkle on some of the dry mix, sufficient to cover surface.
2. Bake near top of a hot oven, Gas 6 to 7, 400 to 425°F, 200 to 220°C, for 10 minutes to the ½ kg/1 lb, basting every 10 to 15 minutes with more cider and dry ingredients. When all is used up, baste from liquor around joint.

FOR DECORATING
Sliced oranges
Glacé cherries

Arrange these over joint as it comes out of oven, or if joint is being baked to eat cold, decoration can be done before baking, or part way through for a large joint.

Mrs Angela Mottram
Axbridge, Somerset

GAMMON AND APRICOT PIE

Serves 2

225 g/8 oz dried apricots
1 gammon rasher, 2.5 cm/1 inch thick
1 teaspoon dripping
25 g/1 oz sultanas
Pepper
2 or 3 tablespoons gravy or stock
6 potatoes

1. Soak apricots in water overnight.
2. Lightly brown gammon on both sides in the dripping in a frying pan.
3. Lay rasher in a large oven-proof dish.
4. Arrange apricots and sultanas on top. Sprinkle with pepper and pour the gravy over.
5. Peel and slice potatoes and lay them on top to cover.
6. Cover with a piece of greased, greaseproof paper.
7. Bake in a moderate oven, Gas 4, 350°F, 180°C, for 1 hour.

Sybil Norcott
Irlam, Nr Manchester

See also Pâté of Gammon, Pig's Liver and Sausage, page 27.

FOREHOCK OF BACON

A big joint for a special occasion. Remember to start the night before. Boil up the bones separately for more stock, which makes excellent soup.

Serves 10 to 12

**1 forehock of bacon, weighing about 3.25 kg/
    7 lb before cooking**
3 level tablespoons demerara sugar
2 sprigs of fresh rosemary or 1 teaspoon dried
Whole cloves

The forehock is to be boned and this is what you do:

1. Soak overnight in cold water.
2. Then working on the underside of the joint, take a small sharp knife and cut off rib bones.
3. Slit meat down to the inner bones and work round them to expose completely. Remove them.

TO PREPARE AND COOK

4. Sprinkle inside of meat with 2 tablespoons demerara sugar.
5. Then tie up joint with strings at 5cm/2 inch intervals.
6. Weigh joint and calculate boiling time at 25 minutes per ½ kg/1 lb.
7. Put joint in a pan, cover with water, add rosemary. Bring slowly to the boil. Simmer gently for the calculated time. Leave in the cooking water until cool enough to handle.
8. Skin carefully and score fat in a lattice pattern. Press a clove in each 'box' and sprinkle on the last tablespoon of sugar.
9. Set under a pre-heated grill until brown and bubbly.

Serve cold.

BACON JOINT WITH CIDER SAUCE AND SUET CRUSTIES

This will provide a meal on 2 days for 4 people. On second day: soup for first course and cold bacon (with pickles) to follow.

1.3 kg/3 lb collar bacon
1 bay leaf
12 peppercorns
2 to 3 parsley stalks
450 g/1 lb medium-sized onions
450 g/1 lb carrots
450 g/1 lb parsnips
450 g/1 lb swede

SAUCE
1 level tablespoon cornflour
1 teaspoon dry mustard
300 ml/½ pint cider
150 ml/¼ pint bacon stock, from cooking joint

SUET CRUSTIES
225 g/8 oz self-raising flour
½ teaspoon salt
125g/4 oz shredded suet
Water

1. Soak bacon at least 4 hours or overnight.
2. Place in large pan, cover with fresh water, add herbs tied in muslin.
3. Bring to boil, skim if necessary and simmer 40 minutes.
4. Meanwhile, prepare vegetables, leaving onions whole, cutting rest to similar size.
5. When bacon has simmered 40 minutes add vegetables to pan, bring back to boil, simmer 20 minutes. The vegetables should be slightly undercooked so test at 15 minutes.
6. Take vegetables from pan, drain, then place in a baking dish.
7. Take out bacon, skin, score top into diamonds and place with vegetables. (Save the stock for the excellent soup—see next recipe.)
8. Heat oven to moderately hot, Gas 6, 400°F, 200°C.
9. Meanwhile mix sauce ingredients in small pan, bring to boil and pour over vegetables.
10. Place in oven, middle shelf, for 35 to 40 minutes.
11. *Now make the Suet Crusties:* (a) Lightly mix, with a knife, flour, salt and suet with 7 to 8 tablespoons of water. The dough should be soft, but not too sticky. (b) Turn on to a floured board and roll out about 1 cm/½ inch thick, either round or square. Mark into 8 pieces.
(c) Place on greased tray. Bake on top shelf of oven 25 to 30 minutes until outside is crisp.
12. Set bacon and vegetables on a warm dish. Arrange Crusties around edge. Serve the sauce separately.

BACON AND VEGETABLE SOUP FOR THE NEXT DAY

Freezes well.

1. Strain bacon stock into bowl. Leave overnight and then remove any fat from top.
2. Sieve or liquidise any vegetables left-over (or prepare and cook more in the stock if necessary).
3. Mix 600 ml to 1 litre/1 to 1½ pints bacon stock into vegetable purée, check for seasoning, add any cider sauce left over.
4. Bring to boil. If consistency is a little too thick, add more stock or a little cider according to taste. Or even add a 400 g/14 oz can of tomatoes, sieving them first to remove pips.

SUSSEX BACON ROLY POLY

This is a lovely, crusty, baked version of the traditional Sussex Roly Poly which used to be wrapped in a cloth and boiled for 3 to 3½ hours.

Serves 4 or 5, but easy to make less

225 g/8 oz self-raising flour
A pinch of salt
125 g/4 oz shredded suet
7 to 8 tablespoons water
325 g/12 oz lean bacon rashers, cut small
1 onion, finely-chopped
Finely-chopped fresh or dried sage
Black pepper
Beaten egg or milk, to glaze

1. Sift flour and salt into a bowl. Add suet and mix with water to a soft but not sticky dough.
2. Using a floured board, roll out very thin.
3. Cover generously with bacon and onion and add sage and pepper to taste. Brush edges of pastry with water.
4. Roll up into a long roll, sealing edge and ends. Place on a greased baking tray with join underneath.
5. Decorate with the trimmings made into little leaves. Brush all over with beaten egg or milk.
6. Bake near top of a moderately hot oven, Gas 6, 400°F, 200°C, for 30 to 40 minutes, when it will be crusty and golden.

Mrs Janice Langley
Shoreham-by-Sea, West Sussex

TRADITIONAL SUSSEX BACON PUDDING

Serves 2

125 g/4 oz wholewheat flour
1½ teaspoons baking powder
50 g/2 oz shredded suet
1 onion, finely-chopped
3 to 4 rashers streaky bacon, chopped
1 teaspoon mixed fresh herbs or ½ teaspoon dried
Pepper and a little salt
1 medium to small egg
Milk, if necessary

1. Mix together flour, baking powder, suet, onion, bacon, herbs and seasoning.
2. Mix with egg, adding milk if necessary to make a soft dropping consistency.
3. Grease a 600 ml/1 pint basin and put in a piece of greaseproof paper just to cover bottom.
4. Put pudding mixture into basin. Cover with greaseproof paper and foil, tucked in neatly under the rim.
5. Steam for 1½ hours. If you haven't a steamer, stand basin on a trivet or upturned saucer in a pan of boiling water. Put on lid and boil for 1½ hours, replenishing with boiling water when necessary. Do not let it go off the boil.

Serve with Parsley Sauce (*see page 33*).

Mrs Sheila Powell
Portslade, Sussex

BACON MOULD

Serves 4

2 green bacon shanks or hocks (soaked at least 6 hours)
1 carrot
1 onion
1 small bay leaf
12 black peppercorns

1. Place shanks in pan with fresh water to cover. Add chopped carrot and onion, bay leaf and peppercorns.
2. Cover and simmer gently until meat will leave the bones quite easily but clings a little. (Time taken depends on size and quality of bacon and could be 3 to 4 hours.)
3. Remove shanks from pan and boil stock rapidly to reduce by about a quarter.
4. Meanwhile separate meat and skin from bones and break it up into neat (not too small) pieces.
5. Strain stock and pour over sufficient to cover the meat. Check seasoning, adding salt or pepper if necessary.
6. Spoon into 1 large mould or 3 to 4 small ones and leave overnight in a cool place to set.
7. Turn out and serve with chutney or salad.

QUORN BACON ROLL

This is a dish for a cold day, very popular in the Quorn country.

Serves 4

175 g/6 oz self-raising flour
125 g/4 oz shredded suet
$\frac{1}{4}$ teaspoon salt
Approx. 6 tablespoons water
225 g/8 oz lean bacon rashers, collar is best
1 large onion, chopped
$\frac{1}{2}$ teaspoon dried sage
Pepper

1. Mix suet into flour and salt, adding enough water to make a softish dough which is still firm enough to roll out.
2. Roll out on a floured board to about 30 by 18 cm/ 12 by 7 inches.
3. Lay bacon rashers across pastry leaving 1 cm/ $\frac{1}{2}$ inch around edges. Sprinkle on chopped onion, sage and pepper.
4. Roll up loosely to make roll 18 cm/7 inches wide. Nip the ends firmly to seal.
5. Scald a strong close-woven cotton cloth at least 30 cm/12 inches square and sprinkle it with flour. Lay it on a sheet of foil large enough to enclose the roll.
6. Roll pudding in foil, then in cloth. Tie ends securely with string and pin the join with safety pins.
7. Have a saucepan three quarters full of boiling water. Put pudding in, lid on pan and bring back quickly to boil. Simmer for 2 hours. Don't allow water to go off the boil.
8. Serve on a hot dish, sprinkled with chopped parsley surrounded with vegetables.

Miss Peggy Mills
Leicestershire

HEREFORD HAM

Serves 2 to 3

A 190 g/7 oz can of lean sweet-cure ham
15 g/$\frac{1}{2}$ oz butter or margarine
1 medium-sized onion, chopped coarsely
1 small cooking apple
1 level teaspoon plain flour
2 tablespoons apple juice or cider
A 175 g/6 oz carton of double cream
Salt and pepper
Chopped parsley

1. Prepare a cool oven, Gas 2, 300°F, 150°C. Place a medium-sized serving dish on centre shelf to heat through.
2. Cut the ham into 6 to 8 slices and arrange down the centre of the heated serving dish.
3. Cover, foil will do, and place in the oven until the sauce is ready.
4. Melt the margarine or butter in a frying pan, add the onion, and cook without browning for 5 minutes.
5. Peel, quarter and core the apple. Cut into fairly thin slices.
6. Add the apple to the onion and cook for 5 minutes until the onion is soft but the apple still a little crisp.
7. Sprinkle the flour over the onion and apple mixture.
8. Stir in the apple juice or cider, the cream, salt and pepper. Cook gently, stirring, for 1 minute.
9. Spoon over the ham, sprinkle with the chopped parsley.

Mrs A. Searle
Holme Lacy

5

SALADS
AND
VEGETABLES

FRENCH DRESSING

Enough for one salad for 4 to 6 people

3 tablespoons salad oil
1 tablespoon cider or wine vinegar
A squeeze of lemon juice
1 teaspoon sugar (try Barbados)
$\frac{1}{4}$ teaspoon salt
A knife-end of mustard
Freshly-grated black pepper

Combine all ingredients. Stir well immediately before using.

FRENCH DRESSING

Made in a jar in quite a large quantity, will keep in a cool place for several weeks, to be used a little at a time as required. Saves a lot of time.

1 rounded teaspoon French mustard, try Dijon
1 rounded teaspoon cooking or sea salt
$\frac{1}{2}$ level teaspoon freshly ground black pepper
$\frac{1}{2}$ level teaspoon sugar (optional)
Juice of 1 lemon (optional)
300 ml/$\frac{1}{2}$ pint olive or good salad oil
4 tablespoons wine or cider vinegar

Put all ingredients in a jar with a well-fitting screw top. Shake vigorously to combine.

Try different flavourings but add these to the small amount of dressing required when salad is made. They go stale if kept in the dressing for long:

Crushed garlic or chopped onion; chopped fresh parsley, chives, tarragon, basil, chervil or fennel. Try combinations of one or two. Dried herbs can also be added but take care because most are twice as strong as the fresh ones.

DRESSING WITHOUT OIL

The quantities may seem small but it is plenty for salad for 4 or 5 people if used as described below.

2 tablespoons top of the milk
1 tablespoon wine or cider vinegar
$\frac{1}{2}$ teaspoon sugar (try light cane sugar)
$\frac{1}{4}$ teaspoon salt
Freshly-milled pepper

Mix all ingredients together in a salad bowl and toss salad in it thoroughly just before it is to be eaten.

SIMPLE DRESSING WITHOUT OIL

A mild dressing especially if young children are to eat the salad.

3 tablespoons tarragon vinegar, plain vinegar can be used
2 tablespoons water
$\frac{1}{2}$ teaspoon sugar
Salt and pepper to taste
1 large teaspoon chopped fresh mint, parsley, chives, tarragon, fennel or onion

Mix all ingredients thoroughly in a salad bowl and at last minute toss in the salad ingredients.

DRESSING WITHOUT VINEGAR

4 tablespoons good salad oil, such as olive or sunflower oil
1 tablespoon lemon juice
1 teaspoon dark cane sugar or 1 teaspoon honey
A pinch of salt
Freshly-milled black pepper

Mix all ingredients together in a salad bowl and toss salad in it thoroughly just before it is to be eaten.

MAYONNAISE—BY HAND, WITHOUT A BLENDER

1 egg-yolk
½ level teaspoon dry mustard
½ level teaspoon salt
½ level teaspoon sugar
¼ level teaspoon pepper
150 ml/¼ pint salad oil
1 tablespoon white vinegar or lemon juice

1. Put egg-yolk and seasonings in a basin. Mix really well using a wooden spoon.
2. Add oil, drop by drop at first, stirring briskly with a wooden spoon.
3. When very thick add a teaspoon of vinegar, then remaining oil a little more quickly, then beat in rest of vinegar as required.
It should be thick enough to hold the impression of the spoon.

A MILDER MAYONNAISE
Beat into the finished mayonnaise 2 teaspoons of lemon juice or 2 teaspoons of cream.

BASIC MAYONNAISE

Made in liquidiser. Keeps in refrigerator for 3 to 4 weeks. Can be thinned down when required with milk or single cream, or more lemon or orange juice, or vinegar.

2 to 4 egg-yolks, according to how extravagant you feel
2 dessertspoons lemon or orange juice or wine or cider vinegar
300 ml/½ pint of good salad oil, olive or sunflower is best
1 rounded teaspoon French mustard, try Dijon
½ level teaspoon cooking or sea salt
¼ level teaspoon freshly-ground black pepper
¼ level teaspoon sugar (optional)

1. Put egg-yolks in liquidiser and switch on for 2 minutes or until thick and creamy.
2. With machine running, add juice or vinegar. Then add oil gradually until 150 ml/¼ pint has been absorbed.

3. Now add all the seasonings, switch on again and gradually add the last of the oil.

Try different flavours but always add them to mayonnaise after it is made: tomato purée, anchovy purée, crushed garlic, chopped chives, capers or cucumber.

WHOLE EGG MAYONNAISE

Made in the liquidiser.

Will keep in refrigerator in a screw-topped jar for a week or two.

1 whole egg
½ teaspoon sugar
1 teaspoon salt
½ level teaspoon dry mustard
¼ level teaspoon pepper
2 tablespoons vinegar or lemon juice
300 ml/½ pint salad oil, olive or sunflower oil, if possible

1. Put all ingredients except oil into liquidiser. Switch it on.
2. Pour in 2 tablespoons oil through hole in lid and allow to blend.
3. As it blends, pour in rest of oil in a steady trickle.

If thinner mayonnaise is required mix in a little cream or top of milk when it is needed.

COOKED SALAD DRESSING

A good economical dressing of mayonnaise quality but using no oil, therefore not so rich and fattening.

Keeps for a week in a cool place. Keeps for at least two weeks, covered, in a refrigerator.

2 teaspoons sugar
½ level teaspoon dry mustard
1 level teaspoon salt
25 g/1 oz margarine
2 tablespoons vinegar
1 tablespoon lemon juice
1 egg

A double saucepan is ideal for this but it can also be made as follows:

1. Put sugar, mustard and salt in a bowl.

2. Cut the margarine into small pieces and add it to the bowl.
3. Add vinegar and lemon juice.
4. Beat egg and strain it into bowl.
5. Stand bowl over a pan of simmering water. Do not let bowl touch water. Let the dressing cook, stirring occasionally with a wooden spoon, until it is thick enough to coat the back of the spoon.
6. Then take bowl off pan and let it cool.

Margaret Heywood
Mankinholes, Todmorden, Yorkshire

YOGHURT DRESSING

3 tablespoons yoghurt
1 tablespoon cider vinegar
A squeeze of lemon juice
1 teaspoon honey or dark cane sugar
A little milk

Mix all ingredients together, adding milk if it is too thick. Toss the salad in the dressing.

Kate Watts
London, NW11

A HORSERADISH DRESSING

150 ml/¼ pint yoghurt
2 teaspoons grated horseradish or 3 dessert-spoons horseradish sauce
Grated zest of ½ lemon and
1 teaspoon of juice
1 tablespoon chopped parsley
Salt and black pepper

1. Mix all ingredients together.
2. Allow to stand for a few hours to infuse and mellow.

Serve with red meats, game, smoked mackerel, or as a tangy sauce for hot cauliflower.

Sybil Norcott
Irlam, Nr. Manchester

YOGHURT AND TAHINI DIP

This is a lovely dressing for salads. It may also be used as a dip served with Greek Pitta Bread (*see page 293*). It is used in the recipe for Chicken Kebabs (*see page 61*).

Tahini is made from sesame seed pulp and can be bought at a delicatessen.

3 tablespoons natural yoghurt
1 tablespoon tahini
A clove of garlic, crushed (optional)
Lemon juice
Salt and pepper

Mix yoghurt, tahini and garlic. Beat in lemon juice, salt and pepper to taste.

Serve cold. Will keep in refrigerator for a few days. Stir before serving.

Elizabeth Mickery
Pudsey, West Yorkshire

SOURED CREAM AND CHIVE DRESSING

A 150 ml/¼ pint carton of soured cream
2 level tablespoons chopped fresh chives
1 tablespoon wine vinegar
1 level tablespoon made mustard
Salt and freshly-ground black pepper
A little milk (optional)

Combine all the ingredients, adding milk to thin it down if necessary.

Serve cold. Delicious with crunchy salads—e.g., chopped white cabbage, grated carrots, finely-chopped onion.

COOKING WITH DRIED BEANS, PEAS, LENTILS AND GRAINS

Aduki beans: a small red bean, much prized by the Chinese for its goodness. Very useful substitute for mince when cooked with bouquet garni, onion, carrot, tomato purée.
Barley: moist and chewy. Best in soups or roasted for savoury bakes.
Black-eye beans: earthy flavour. Used often in Mexican cooking. Combines very well with red kidney beans.

Brown rice: nutty flavour. Used for risotto, curry, pilaff and sweet puddings.

Buckwheat: a Russian delicacy. Particularly strong nutty flavour; adds meatiness to dishes.

Bulgar wheat: creamy tasting. Quick to use as it needs no cooking when used for salads. Often confused with white rice.

Butter beans: rather bland taste, versatile.

Chick peas: very popular in Middle Eastern cookery. Nutty in flavour and appearance. Delicious in salads and for making savoury dips.

Field beans: at last something British! Best in soups and stews with root vegetables.

Haricot beans: the traditional baked bean when cooked with treacle and tomatoes.

Lentils: the whole variety: brown, earthy-flavoured; green, more delicate flavour. Hold their shape and make a quick addition to soups and stews. The split red variety purée easily and are excellent for pâtés, rissoles and go well with curry spices.

Lima beans: similar to butter beans but tastier. Good for salads and when combined in creamy dishes and soups.

Millet: a delicate flavoured grain. Easily digested and can be used for sweet and savoury dishes.

Mung beans: best for sprouting.

TO COOK DRIED BEANS, PEAS, LENTILS AND GRAINS

This chart can be followed in conjunction with notes above.

Bean, Pea, Lentil, Grain	Soak overnight in cold water	Cooking time in fresh cold water	Time needed for hard boil at some stage in cooking	A minimum amount of fresh cold water for 1 cup of beans, etc.
		Minutes	*Minutes*	
Aduki beans	Yes	60–80	10	4 cups
Barley—				
pot or pearl	No	45–50	Nil	3 cups
Black-eye beans	Yes	40–45	10	3 cups
Brown rice				
long grain	No	20–25	Nil	2 cups
short grain		20		(*see Boiled Rice* page 172
Buckwheat	No	20–25	Nil	4 cups
Bulgar wheat	Just soak in boiling water for 5 to 10 minutes, then it is ready for salads			
Butter beans	Yes	40	10	4 cups
Chick peas	Yes	2 hours	10	5 cups
Field beans	Yes	60	10	4 cups
Haricot beans	Yes	45–50	10	3 cups
Lentils—brown		40–45		4 cups
green	No	40–45	Nil	4 cups
red		15–20		3 cups
Lima beans	Yes	40–45	10	3 cups
Millet	No	20–25	Nil	3 cups
Mung beans	No	40–45	Nil	3 cups
Oats	No	25–30	Nil	3 cups
Pinto beans	Yes	60	10	6 cups
Red kidney beans	Yes	45–50	10	4 cups
Soya beans	Yes	2½–3 hours	30	6–7 cups
Split peas— green and yellow	No	40–45	Nil	3 cups
Wheat	No	60	Nil	5 cups

Oats: sweet creamy-tasting. Main ingredient for muesli.

Pinto beans: rather like speckled eggs. Can be used instead of black-eye or red kidney beans.

Red kidney beans: beautiful distinctive colour. Brightens stews and salads. Popular with chilli spices.

Soya beans: good source of protein. Excellent for absorbing the flavour of all that is cooked with it. Best in soups and casseroles.

Split peas: best for soups. Green type best cooked with mint or rosemary; yellow type go well with spices.

Wheat: very chewy berries. Adds texture to bean dishes. Also when cooked, a good addition to bread.

NOTES ON COOKING DRIED BEANS, PEAS, LENTILS AND GRAINS

Grains only need bringing to the boil and simmering. But the flavour of some is improved if they are lightly toasted in a little oil in the pan in which they are to be boiled. Use $\frac{1}{4}$ teaspoon oil to the 125 g/$\frac{1}{4}$ lb grain. This applies to buckwheat, millet, rice and barley.

1. Pick over beans, lentils, etc., for sticks and stones then wash before soaking and cooking.
2. Soak beans and peas overnight. This swells them and helps loosen grit and dirt. It also removes excess starch and carbohydrates which cause flatulence. Soak by covering with 8 cm/3 inches of water. Beans, etc., should double in size. This water is then thrown away, the beans washed thoroughly and covered with fresh water.
3. Cook beans, etc., in plenty of water as it is useful stock—125 g/4 oz beans in 1 litre/1½ pints water.
4. All beans and some peas must be fast-boiled for at least 10 minutes. This destroys the anti-nutritional factors on the surface of the beans. Then lightly boil for the remaining time, in a covered pan.
5. Salt is not added during boiling because it tends to harden the outer skin and prevent the bean from becoming soft. The same applies if lemon juice, wine or vinegar is put in at the beginning of cooking. However, adding herbs, spices or vegetables to the cooking water improves the flavour. Adding caraway, aniseed or fennel seed helps counteract flatulence. Fennel is the least dominating. Add ½ teaspoon to 125 g/4 oz beans, etc., during last ½ hour.

6. When cooked, drain liquid and save it for stock. It will keep 3 to 4 days in refrigerator.
7. Cooked beans, etc., drained of ALL liquid to stop fermentation will keep 4 to 5 days in covered containers in refrigerator.
8. Red and brown beans turn the water dark during cooking and will colour any white beans or grains cooked with them. It is best to keep dark beans separate from white during cooking to keep the appearance of each bright and natural.
9. Some people find this type of food indigestible. Dried beans, peas, etc., contain water soluble sugars that the body cannot break down. Some people develop the necessary enzymes to cope with this. Those who have found problems must attack them more thoroughly before cooking. Boil for 3 minutes. Leave to soak in that water for 4 to 5 hours. Drain. Reboil in fresh water for 3 minutes. Leave to soak for 4 to 5 hours. Drain and then cook for use adding 30 minutes on to the recommended times to ensure softness.
10. *Pressure cooking* saves time and fuel and soaking time can be reduced or even eliminated. The anti-nutritional problem (see note 4 above) does not apply because of the higher temperature involved. *Be sure* to follow instructions in your pressure cooker handbook.

MARINADE FOR BEANS

Dried beans are delicious in salads when they have been marinated immediately after cooking.

This is enough for 450 g/1 lb cooked beans. 225 g/8 oz uncooked beans will weigh about 450 g/1 lb when cooked.

175 ml/6 fl oz best salad oil, ideally use a mixture of olive and safflower or sunflower oils
125 ml/4 fl oz cider vinegar
Juice of 1 lemon
A clove of garlic, crushed
1 teaspoon fresh chives, chopped
1 teaspoon marjoram
1 teaspoon oregano
1 teaspoon pepper
½ teaspoon salt

1. Mix everything together.
2. Pour over hot, freshly-cooked, thoroughly-drained beans.
3. Allow beans to remain in marinade until quite cold.

4. Drain marinade into a jar. Beans are ready for use in salads.

Marinade can be used again but will keep only a few days because fresh herbs will go stale. If there is water in it from the beans it will not keep well.

MARINATED BEAN SALAD

Red kidney beans, lima beans and chick peas make a good mixture of contrasting colours, textures and tastes.

1. Cook beans according to directions on page 137.
2. Marinate hot beans as above.
3. Choose favourite salad vegetables, such as radish, celery, green, red or yellow pepper, tomato. Add fresh herbs. No extra dressing is necessary.

Sarah Brown
Scarborough, Yorkshire

TO GROW YOUR OWN MUSTARD AND CRESS

For something green in your salad at any time of year.

A 25 g/1 oz packet of seed will give you several crops—much cheaper than buying the cress itself.

Use plastic trays used for pre-packed foods, saucers or any shallow containers.

1. Make a pad to fit the container from a piece of towelling, folded paper towel or cotton wool. This is the growing pad.
2. Fit it in the container and moisten thoroughly.
3. Grow cress seed first—it takes longer to germinate. Sprinkle cress seed thickly on the growing pad and set the container in a dark place.
4. 2 to 3 days later sow the mustard on a wet growing pad in another container. Put it in a dark place for 2 to 4 days. Keep growing pads moist.
5. Look at seeds daily to see if there is any sign of growth.
6. As soon as seeds start to grow bring them into full light. Keep growing pads moist.
7. Cut crop with sharp scissors when it is 2.5 to 5 cm/1 to 2 inches high.

TO CRUSH GARLIC

If you do not have a garlic crusher, simply peel the clove of garlic and put it on a small plate. Sprinkle with a little salt then crush the garlic with the end of a table knife. The salt helps reduce the garlic to a creamy pulp. The 'bendy' blade of an old-fashioned knife is best.

TO SKIN TOMATOES

Either: Put tomatoes in a bowl, pour boiling water over them and leave for 1 minute. Plunge them into cold water and skin when required.

Or, if only one is needed, spear it on a fork and turn it in the hot air just above a gas flame. Skin will contract and burst and tomato can be easily peeled.

For green tomatoes: prick them in several places with a fork. Then pour on boiling water. Leave for a few minutes. Skins will be easily removed.

APPLE AND CUCUMBER SALAD

Serves 4

1 small cucumber
2 medium-sized dessert apples
Lettuce leaves
Half a box of mustard and cress
2 to 3 radishes

DRESSING
150 ml/¼ pint cream or natural yoghurt
½ teaspoon lemon juice
Salt and black pepper

1. First mix the dressing.
2. Cut cucumber in half lengthways. Remove and discard the centre. Dice up the rest.
3. Quarter, core and dice apple.
4. Mix half of the dressing with the apple and cucumber.
5. Arrange lettuce round the serving dish and pile the apple and cucumber mixture in the centre.
6. Pour remaining dressing evenly over apple and cucumber.
7. Garnish with cress and thinly-sliced radish.

Judith Adshead
Mottram St Andrew, Cheshire

AVOCADO SALAD

A way to make one avocado pear go round at least four people.

French dressing (*see page 133*)
½ clove garlic
1 heaped tablespoon chopped parsley
2 tablespoons finely-chopped green pepper
About 5 cm/2 inches cucumber
½ bunch watercress
1 large avocado pear
1 green-leaved lettuce
50 g/2 oz small fresh mushrooms

1. Put French dressing into salad bowl and mix it up.
2. Crush garlic and mix it with parsley into the dressing.
3. Chop green pepper quite small and mix it into the dressing.

These are the only ingredients that should go into

the dressing at this stage. The rest should be added immediately before salad is to be eaten. However, they may be prepared a little in advance.

4. Cut off 5 cm/2 inches of cucumber, wash and dry. Cut into 4 pieces lengthways then slice. Do not remove skin.
5. Wash and trim watercress.
6. Wash lettuce and shake it dry.
7. Wipe mushrooms and slice, but not too small.
8. Cut avocado pear in half lengthways, remove stone and peel off skin. Turn the halves cut-side down, cut into four or five pieces lengthways. Then cut across these to make large dice. Don't cut it up too small.
9. At the last minute, stir up the dressing again. Tip into it cucumber, watercress, avocado and mushrooms. Toss these about in the dressing.
10. With your fingers, break up lettuce into easy-to-eat pieces. Toss it into bowl and see that all is well-coated with dressing.

It must be eaten at once.

BEANSPROUT AND WALNUT SALAD

Serves 4 to 6 but easy to make less

2 large crisp apples, unpeeled
3 sticks of celery
225 g/8 oz beansprouts
50 g/2 oz walnuts
50 g/2 oz raisins

DRESSING
1 teaspoon lemon juice
200 ml/7 fl oz natural yoghurt
1 tablespoon chopped fresh mint
Pepper and salt

1. Chop apples and celery and mix with beansprouts, walnuts and raisins.
2. Mix dressing ingredients and stir into salad.
3. Chill slightly before serving.

Janet Horsley
Headingley, Yorkshire

BEETROOT AND CELERY SALAD

Equal quantities of cooked beetroot in vinegar and fresh celery, seasoned with a little salt

1. Cut the celery into thin slices and lay it in the dish from which it will be served.
2. Sprinkle with a little salt.
3. Lift the beetroot out of the vinegar, cut it into quarters or neat lumps and lay it on top of the celery.
4. At the last minute pour over a little of the beetroot vinegar.

BUTTER BEAN AND WATERCRESS SALAD

Enough for 4 small side salads—easy to make less or more

(For a more substantial salad, cubes of Cheddar or Gouda cheese may be added.)

SALAD
125 g/4 oz cooked lima or baby butter beans
A quarter of a cucumber
1 firm small pear, Comice or Beurre Hardy are best
Half a bunch of watercress (about 50 g/2 oz)
Salt and pepper

DRESSING
For this you need a liquidiser
2 tablespoons natural yoghurt
25 g/1 oz blue cheese
1 dessertspoon mayonnaise (*see page 134*)
40 g/1½ oz cottage cheese

1. Remember to start the day before by soaking beans overnight and then cooking (*see page 137*).
2. Put dressing ingredients in liquidiser and blend till smooth. This can be done some time ahead.
3. Cut unpeeled cucumber and pear into small cubes.
4. Save a few nice sprigs of watercress to garnish and cut up rest finely.
5. Mix all salad ingredients with dressing. Taste for seasoning.
6. Chill before serving.
7. Garnish with watercress.

Sarah Brown
Scarborough, Yorkshire

ROSY BEETROOT SALAD

1 medium-sized cooked beetroot
2 to 3 stalks celery
2 dessert apples
4 tablespoons French dressing (*see page 133*)

Prepare the French dressing before cutting up the fruit and vegetables.

1. Dice the beetroot.
2. Slice the celery.
3. Core but do not peel the apples, unless skins are tough. Dice them.
4. Mix all the ingredients together in the dressing until a delicate rosy pink.

Judith Adshead
Mottram St Andrew, Cheshire

BEETROOT RELISH

This keeps for about 1 month, preferably in the fridge. Easy to make in smaller quantities.

450 g/1 lb beetroot
225 g/8 oz horseradish
A pinch of salt
125 g/4 oz demerara sugar
300 ml/½ pint wine or cider vinegar

1. Wash beetroot without damaging skin.
2. Boil in plenty of water. Or cook in pressure cooker.
3. Meanwhile, wash horseradish and grate it across the sticks. It is a good idea to do this out of doors or near an open window, as it will make you 'cry'.
4. Peel and shred the cooked beetroot on coarse side of grater.
5. Mix all the ingredients together and pack into jars with vinegar-proof lids.

This relish is ready to eat immediately.

Mrs Doreen Allars
Welbourn, Nr Lincoln

CAULIFLOWER SALAD

Make as much as you need, but make it fresh each time.

Cauliflower
Carrot
Green pepper
Celery

DRESSING
Choose one from *pages 133–5*

1. Wash cauliflower and break into small sprigs.
2. Scrub carrot and grate it coarsely.
3. Wash green pepper, remove core and seeds and slice flesh finely.
4. Wash and finely slice celery.
5. Combine all with the dressing.

COLESLAW

A CABBAGE SALAD
1. Wash, dry and shred finely some firm white cabbage.
2. Chop finely a small onion.
3. Toss cabbage and onion in a dressing of your choice (*see pages 133–5*).

Try also adding chopped celery, grated carrot, a few sultanas, walnuts, chopped parsley.

COTTAGE CHEESE SALAD

Serves 2, but easy to make in smaller or larger quantities

1 hard red apple
1 teaspoon lemon juice
225 g/8 oz cottage cheese
1 tablespoon seedless raisins
25 g/1 oz coarsely-chopped walnuts
Chopped chives
Chopped parsley
Salt
Black pepper
Lettuce leaves

1. Quarter and core apple but do not peel. Cut up into small pieces and toss in lemon juice.

2. Combine apple with the cheese, raisins, walnuts, chopped chives and parsley. Season with a little salt and black pepper.

3. Spread out lettuce leaves and pile cheese mixture on top.

CRUNCHY SALAD

Serves 2

A piece red pepper
2 stalks celery
1½ crisp eating apples
A few sliced nuts
Lettuce leaves

DRESSING
1 dessertspoon wine or cider vinegar
4 dessertspoons salad oil
Pinch of salt, pepper and mustard
1 teaspoon honey

1. Shake all dressing ingredients together in a jar till creamy.

2. Slice red pepper finely and blanch it. To do this, drop into a pan of boiling water, leave for 1 minute, then drain and cover with plenty of cold water. Drain and pat dry.

3. Chop celery and apple. Do not peel apple unless the skin is tough. Toss with nuts in the dressing.

4. Line a salad plate with lettuce leaves and pile the dressed salad on top.

Anne Wallace
Dunlop, Scotland

CUCUMBER AND YOGHURT—I

The European version.

1 cucumber
1 tablespoon salt
Garlic, optional
1 teaspoon vinegar (wine vinegar is best)
1 dessertspoon dried mint
1 teaspoon salad oil (olive oil is best)
300 ml/½ pint yoghurt
A little black pepper

1. Peel the cucumber and chop it finely.

2. Put it in a bowl or colander, sprinkle on the salt and leave it 1 to 2 hours.

3. Take a shallow serving dish and rub around it the raw edge of half a clove of garlic. (Or, crush a quarter of a clove of garlic and put in dish.)

4. Put less than a teaspoon of vinegar into the dish and shake it around.

5. Drain as much liquid as possible from the cucumber.

6. Put the cucumber in the dish, crumble over it the dried mint, shake over the salad oil.

7. Now spoon over the yoghurt and stir very well, adding lastly a little black pepper.

8. Chill for about 1 hour but do not serve it too cold. Keeps in refrigerator for a day or two. If any separation occurs stir before serving.

Particularly good to eat on its own following a rich main course, but also nice with cold meats.

CUCUMBER AND YOGHURT—2

An oriental version of a well-known and exceptionally refreshing salad.

Serves 4

300 ml/½ pint yoghurt
1 cucumber, finely-sliced
1 green chilli, finely-chopped (optional)
½ teaspoon salt
¼ teaspoon dried ginger—freshly-ground if possible

TO GARNISH
Fresh coriander leaves, chopped

Mix all ingredients in a bowl, cover with a well-fitting lid and refrigerate before serving.

Eat this fresh. It does not keep for long. Delicious with Cashew Nut Curry (*see page 174*).

Priya Wickramasinghe
Cardiff

JELLIED HAM RING

For this you need a ring mould.

600 ml/1 pint tomato juice
15 g/½ oz gelatine (1 envelope)
Cucumber
Parsley
Cream cheese
Black pepper
Thin slices cold cooked ham

If you have a ring mould you will be able to work out the quantities of the ingredients needed to fill it.

1. Heat tomato juice nearly to boiling point. Remove pan from heat, sprinkle in gelatine and stir to dissolve.
2. Pour a little into ring mould. Let it set.
3. Dice cucumber, chop parsley and mix them with some black pepper into the cream cheese.
4. Spoon cream cheese mixture on to slices of ham, roll them up and fit them into the ring mould.
5. Pour over rest of the gelatine and tomato juice.
6. Put in a cold place to set.

Turn out on to a plate and serve with a lettuce and tomato salad.

YORKSHIRE SALAD

Lettuce
Onions or spring onions
Mint
Sugar
Vinegar

1. Wash and finely shred some lettuce—the good outer leaves can be used.
2. Finely slice 1 to 2 onions or use spring onions when available.
3. Finely chop a little mint.
4. Add sugar to taste to a cup of vinegar and stir to dissolve. Pour over salad.

Serve with hot roast meats.

LETTUCE WITH PEANUT DRESSING

Serves 4

1 crisp lettuce, washed and dried
Half a cucumber, sliced

DRESSING
2 tablespoons oil
¼ teaspoon mustard seed
½ teaspoon salt
¼ teaspoon cumin seed
A pinch of turmeric
1 tablespoon lemon juice
50 g/2 oz peanuts, coarsely-ground

1. Start with dressing. Heat oil and splutter the mustard seeds in it. To do this put seeds in hot oil, put lid on pan, keep pan over medium heat and listen while seeds leap up against lid for a few seconds until the spluttering sound has stopped. Remove pan from heat before lifting lid.
2. Add salt, cumin and turmeric and fry for 5 seconds.
3. Remove from heat and add lemon juice and peanuts. Leave to cool.
4. Just before serving, break up lettuce into small pieces into a salad bowl. Add cucumber and dressing and toss salad thoroughly.

Priya Wickramasinghe
Cardiff

LAYER SALAD

Serves 4 to 6

Layer the following ingredients in a large glass bowl.

125 g/4 oz shredded cabbage
175 g/6 oz grated carrot
75 g/3 oz chopped peanuts
125 g/4 oz chopped celery
2 chopped red apples, unpeeled
75 g/3 oz chopped dates
125 g/4 oz cooked brown rice (*see page 172*)
25 g/1 oz sesame seeds
1 box mustard and cress, chopped
Garnish with slices of tomato

Janet Horsley
Headingley, Yorkshire

ONION SALAD

Serves 4

225 g/8 oz onions
2 green chillis, finely-chopped
Juice of 1 lemon
½ teaspoon salt
¼ teaspoon freshly-milled black pepper

1. Slice onions into fine rings.
2. Mix all ingredients and leave for at least 1 hour before serving.

Before serving, finely-sliced tomatoes can be added. Delicious served as an accompaniment to rice dishes.

Priya Wickramasinghe
Cardiff

NEW POTATO SALAD

Can be made with left-over potatoes.

Serves 4

450 g/1 lb new potatoes
A little boiling water

1 very small onion
1 tablespoon salad cream or mayonnaise (*see page 134*)
2 tablespoons milk or, if using a bland mayonnaise, 1 tablespoon milk and 1 tablespoon cider vinegar
½ teaspoon sugar, try dark cane sugar
Sea salt
Black pepper
Chopped parsley
Chopped mint

1. Scrub potatoes and put them in a pan with a good lid. Add a very little boiling water. Bring to the boil, turn heat very low. Simmer and steam potatoes for 10 to 12 minutes until done but still firm. Drain and cool.
2. Meanwhile, chop onion very small and put in a serving bowl with the salad cream and milk. If using bland mayonnaise add milk and vinegar.
3. Add sugar. Season with a very little salt and freshly-grated black pepper.
4. Stir in as much chopped mint as you can spare and a little chopped parsley.
5. Cut potatoes into quarters or thick rings and mix them into the dressing until the pieces are nicely coated with dressing.

MORE NEW POTATO SALADS

New potatoes, scrubbed
Chopped chives, onion tops or leek tops
4 tablespoons French dressing (*see page 133*)

1. Steam potatoes or cook them in their jackets over low heat in a very little water. Drain. Skin and slice when they have cooled down a bit.
2. Meanwhile, mix dressing ingredients.
3. Toss potato, while still hot, in the dressing, adding chives, onion or leek tops.

IDEAS FOR MORE SUBSTANTIAL SALADS
Add any of the following:

Cubes of garlic sausage
Strips of green pepper
Tuna fish, drained and chopped

POTATO SALAD

Serves 4

450 g/1 lb large potatoes
French dressing (*see page 133*)
1 or 2 tablespoons mayonnaise (*see page 134*)
Salt and pepper
Parsley or chives

1. Peel and dice potatoes. Put into boiling, salted water. Cook until tender but not broken, 5 to 10 minutes.
2. Drain well and while still hot trickle over a little French dressing.
3. When cool drain away any surplus dressing and then gently mix in the mayonnaise and seasoning to taste.
4. Sprinkle on chopped parsley or chives.

Try also adding cooked peas, diced carrot, sweetcorn.

POTATO SALAD WITH CAPERS

Old potatoes can be used.

Serves 4

450 g/1 lb potatoes cut into 1 cm/$\frac{1}{2}$ inch dice
Water
Salt
1 tablespoon chopped capers
3 tablespoons mayonnaise or salad cream (*see page 134*)

1. Put potatoes in a saucepan with salted water just to cover. Bring to the boil, put on lid and cook for 3 to 5 minutes until almost tender.
2. Drain quickly and thoroughly and toss lightly with capers.
3. When cold coat with mayonnaise, mixing gently.
Anne Wallace
Stewarton, Ayrshire

RED CABBAGE SLAW

Serves 4

2 tablespoons sultanas
Juice of one lemon
50 g/2 oz walnuts
Red cabbage, 3 cups when shredded
2 to 3 tablespoons French dressing (*see page 133*)

1. Place sultanas in a small bowl with the lemon juice and leave for 2 hours to plump up.
2. Chop walnuts.
3. Prepare cabbage. Shred it finely, discarding the very fibrous part of the stalk.
4. Prepare French dressing.
5. Mix sultanas with the cabbage and walnuts.
6. Add dressing and toss all together.
Judith Adshead
Mottram St Andrew, Cheshire

ROYAL SLAW

Keeps in refrigerator for 2 or 3 days.

Serves 4

100 ml/4 fl oz French dressing (*see page 133*)
½ cup of sliced peeled apple
1 banana
2 cups red cabbage, finely-shredded
½ cup diced celery
½ onion, chopped

1. Combine the dressing and apple slices.
2. Slice banana and add. Make sure it is well coated with dressing to prevent discolouration.
3. Gently combine with cabbage, celery and onion.

Mrs Sybil Norcott
Irlam, Manchester

RICE SALAD WITH APPLE DRESSING

A well-balanced meal in itself.

Serves 4

50 g/2 oz cashew nut pieces, toasted
325 g/12 oz cooked brown rice (*see page 172*) or
    150 g/5 oz uncooked
50 g/2 oz raisins
50 g/2 oz beansprouts
Half a red pepper
Lettuce leaves
1 dessert apple

DRESSING
2 tablespoons apple juice
1 tablespoon sunflower oil
1 tablespoon lemon juice
1 teaspoon shoyu (*see page 162*)
¼ teaspoon ground ginger
Salt and pepper

1. Cashew nut pieces are cheaper than whole nuts. Toasting them under a moderately-hot grill until just turning golden makes them crisp and fresh.
2. Mix salad ingredients, except lettuce and apple.
3. Mix dressing ingredients. Beat well. Mix into salad.
4. Serve on a bed of lettuce, garnished at last minute with apple slices.

Sarah Brown
Scarborough, Yorkshire

A SALAD OF RED CABBAGE AND MUSHROOMS WITH BROWN RICE

Keeps for a day or two.

Serves 3 or 4

Juice of 1 small orange
25 g/1 oz sultanas or raisins
4 tablespoons French dressing (*see page 133*)
125 g/4 oz red cabbage
1 small onion
50 g/2 oz mushrooms
125 g/4 oz brown rice
1 tablespoon chopped parsley
2 tablespoons Chinese beansprouts (optional)

1. Put sultanas or raisins to soak in the orange juice.
2. Prepare French dressing and divide it between two small bowls.
3. Finely shred red cabbage and toss it in one bowl of dressing.
4. Peel and finely chop onion and toss it with cabbage.
5. Wipe the mushrooms and slice them thinly. Toss them in the other bowl of dressing.
6. Leave both bowls for at least one hour.
7. Meanwhile, cook the rice (*see Boiled Rice, page 172*).
8. When rice is done, drain off any liquid. Then spread it out thinly to cool. If when it is cool it is not nicely dry, put the dish in a very slow oven, less than Gas ¼, 225°F, 110°C, for 20 minutes or so to draw the moisture out.
9. All these preparations may be done some time in advance, even the day before it is to be served.
10. Stir each bowl of ingredients then combine all together in a serving dish with rice, parsley and beansprouts.

TOMATO AND CUCUMBER SALAD

Tomatoes
Cucumber
French dressing (*see page 133*)
Chives

1. Wash and thinly slice tomatoes and cucumber.
2. Arrange overlapping alternate slices.
3. Pour over a few spoonfuls of French dressing.
4. Sprinkle with chopped chives.

Serve with cold ham or bacon.

TOMATO SALAD

Easy to make in a smaller quantity.

Serves 4

French dressing (*see page 133*)
1 tablespoon finely-chopped green pepper
1 tablespoon freshly-chopped parsley
1 tablespoon chopped fresh mint
1 tablespoon chopped chives
450 g/1 lb tomatoes

1. Prepare dressing in the salad bowl.
2. Prepare green pepper, parsley, mint and chives and mix into dressing. This may all be done in advance.
3. Skin tomatoes (*see page 139*), and slice them thickly.
4. At last minute, stir up dressing and herbs, put in the tomatoes. Toss them gently so that they are covered with the dressing and herbs.

INDONESIAN TOMATO SALAD

Serves 4

4 ripe tomatoes
Salt to taste
2 fresh green chillis
3 tablespoons sugar
Juice of 2 lemons

1. Slice the tomatoes and arrange in a serving platter. Sprinkle with a little salt.

2. Slice the green chillis slantwise into elongated rings and arrange over the tomato slices.
3. Sprinkle with sugar and lemon juice and allow to stand for an hour or two before serving.

Priya Wickramasinghe
Cardiff

COLD STUFFED TOMATOES

Serves 4

4 to 6 firm tomatoes depending on size
1 tin sardines in oil
2 hard-boiled eggs
50 g/2 oz butter, softened
1 teaspoon made mustard
1 teaspoon chopped parsley
Seasoning to taste

1. Stand tomatoes stalk end down, cut a lid from rounded end which is uppermost, remove pulp, sprinkle lightly with salt and invert on a plate to drain.
2. Drain sardines, remove tails and backbones, and mash.
3. Remove yolks from eggs, work into softened butter. Add mustard, parsley, sardines and chopped egg-whites. Season to taste.
4. Fill into tomato shells, replace lids at an angle.

Serve very cold with green salad.

WATERCRESS AND GRAPEFRUIT SALAD

Serves 4

25 g/1 oz lightly-roasted hazelnuts
1 bunch of watercress
1 small lettuce
1 large grapefruit

1. To roast hazelnuts, put them in a shallow tin in a moderate oven, Gas 4, 350°F, 180°C, for 10 minutes. Or put under grill, turning often. Then rub the skins from them and chop coarsely.
2. Wash watercress and lettuce and dry well.
3. Peel grapefruit and remove membrane and pips, working over a bowl so as to retain the juice. Chop flesh into bowl.
4. Break lettuce and watercress into small pieces. Toss it with grapefruit and put it in a salad bowl.
5. Sprinkle hazelnuts over the top.

Janet Horsley
Headingley, Yorkshire

AUBERGINES AND TOMATOES

Serves 4

6 firm ripe tomatoes
2 aubergines, fairly large
1 onion, finely-sliced and chopped small
A clove of garlic
½ level teaspoon fresh basil, or a good pinch of dried
1 tablespoon oil
Salt and pepper

1. Put tomatoes in a bowl, cover with boiling water and leave for 30 seconds. Plunge one at a time into cold water and skin.
2. Slice the tomatoes and arrange half of them in a well-greased, shallow oven dish.
3. Wash the aubergines. Trim off stem ends. Cut in half lengthways.
4. Now, with skin side up make lengthways cuts 1 cm/½ inch apart to within 1 cm/½ inch of stem end.
5. Transfer to dish. Space the aubergine fans out in a single layer. Fill the spaces between the fans with slices of tomato.
6. Arrange the rest of the tomatoes, onion, garlic and basil around the fans. Brush all over with oil. Season with salt and pepper.
7. Cover with lid or foil and bake in a very hot oven, Gas 8, 450°F, 230°C, for 10 minutes. Reduce heat to moderate, Gas 4, 350°F, 180°C for another 25 minutes or until the aubergines are tender.

Serve on its own as a snack or as an accompaniment to grilled lamb.

BROAD BEANS WITH BACON

Can be made in large or small quantities.

Broad beans
Rashers of bacon, or bacon pieces
1 small onion
½ teaspoon oil
2 teaspoons cider or tarragon vinegar
½ teaspoon sugar
Freshly-ground black pepper
Salt

1. Prepare beans. If they are very young and tender do not pod them. String the pods and cut into 5 cm/ 2 inch lengths.
2. Take rinds off rashers and cut bacon into small pieces.
3. Peel and finely chop onion.
4. Put beans on to cook with a very little water in a pan with a good lid. As soon as they reach boiling point turn heat down and simmer and steam for 5 to 8 minutes. Broad beans are unpleasant if over-cooked.
5. As soon as beans are cooking, put bacon on to fry briskly in oil for 1 minute, turning over in pan.
6. Add onion, reduce heat and let it soften for 3 or 4 minutes.
7. Add vinegar, sugar and freshly-ground black pepper and cook slowly for 2 to 3 minutes, stirring.
8. Drain beans, throw them into pan, add a pinch of salt, toss them in the mixture and serve at once.

Betty Yeatman
Adelaide, South Australia

RUNNER BEANS AND ALMONDS

Serves 4

15 g/½ oz flaked almonds
40 g/1½ oz butter
275 g/10 oz frozen runner beans or whole green beans
Salt and pepper

Lightly-cooked, drained, fresh (not frozen) beans can be used.

1. Fry the almonds in butter till both are pale golden brown.
2. Add frozen beans, shake them in amongst butter and almonds. Cover pan and simmer gently for 3 minutes.
3. Uncover pan, turn up heat and stir-fry for 1 minute.
4. Season and serve.

Lightly-cooked non-frozen beans are added to pan when almonds are brown. Stir-fry for 1 minute. Season and serve.

Sybil Norcott
Irlam, Nr Manchester

HOME BAKED BEANS

A delicious home-made version of that ever-popular and nourishing tinned commodity, baked beans in tomato sauce. Remember to start the night before.

Serves 4

225 g/8 oz haricot beans, soaked overnight
50 g/2 oz butter or margarine
1 large onion, chopped
A clove of garlic, crushed
A 400 g/14 oz tin of tomatoes
2 teaspoons brown sugar
1 tablespoon chopped fresh parsley
Salt and pepper

1. Cook beans as directed on page 137.
2. Melt butter and fry onion and garlic until soft but not brown.
3. Break up tomatoes in the tin and pour into pan.
4. Simmer uncovered for about 10 minutes to reduce tomato juice.
5. Add sugar, parsley, salt and pepper.
6. Pour sauce over the hot beans and keep warm for at least 30 minutes so that beans absorb the flavour.

Sue Maddison
Chislehurst, Kent

BEETROOT AS A HOT VEGETABLE

1. Choose small even-sized beetroot.
2. Remove tops and roots, but do not break skin. Wash well.
3. Simmer gently for about $1\frac{1}{2}$ hours until tender.
4. Peel and keep hot.

TO SERVE WITH WHITE SAUCE
25 g/1 oz margarine
25 g/1 oz plain flour
$\frac{1}{2}$ teaspoon Salt and Pepper Mix (*see page 17*)
300 ml/$\frac{1}{2}$ pint milk

1. In pan, melt margarine, add flour and Salt and Pepper Mix, sizzle for one minute.
2. Gradually stir in milk and simmer for 1 minute.
3. Pour over the peeled beetroot.

TO SERVE GLAZED
25 g/1 oz butter
1 teaspoon sugar
Grated rind of 1 lemon
2 teaspoons chopped parsley
Juice of $\frac{1}{2}$ lemon

1. Melt butter in pan, add beetroots, sugar, lemon rind, parsley and lemon juice.
2. Toss over medium heat until hot.

CURRIED BHINDI

This unusual green vegetable is also known as okra and ladies' fingers. Its shape resembles that of a chilli, and it is best bought when small with no discoloration. Bhindi is now quite widely available from supermarkets and greengrocers.

Serves 4

450 g/1 lb bhindi
1 tablespoon oil
1 small onion, finely-chopped
$\frac{1}{2}$ teaspoon ground cumin
$\frac{1}{2}$ teaspoon coriander
$\frac{1}{2}$ teaspoon chilli powder (optional)
$\frac{1}{4}$ teaspoon ground turmeric
$\frac{3}{4}$ teaspoon salt
150 g/5 oz tinned tomatoes

1. Wash and dry the bhindi. Trim the tops and tails and cut into 2.5 cm/1 inch pieces.
2. In a pan, heat oil and fry onion until it is lightly browned.
3. Add spices and salt and cook for 2 minutes on a low heat.
4. Add bhindi and stir until it is well mixed and coated with spices.
5. Lastly, add tomatoes and bring to the boil. Cover and simmer for about 7 minutes or until the bhindi is cooked.

Serve with Boiled Rice (*see page 172*), Chicken Curry (*see page 60*) and Onion Salad (*see page 144*); or with Puris (*see page 308*) and Cauliflower Bhaji (*see page 150*) as part of a vegetarian meal.

Priya Wickramasinghe
Cardiff

BROCCOLI WITH BUTTER SAUCE

Serves 3 to 4

450 g/1 lb broccoli sprigs

SAUCE
65 g/2½ oz butter
25 g/1 oz flour
300 ml/½ pint boiling water
Salt and pepper
1 egg-yolk
2 teaspoons lemon juice

1. Steam the broccoli until it is just tender, or cook in a very little water in a saucepan with a well-fitting lid.
2. Meanwhile, prepare sauce. Melt a third of the butter in a pan.
3. Stir in flour and cook for 1 minute.
4. Pour in boiling water, whisking all the time until sauce thickens, but do not boil it.
5. Remove pan from heat, beat in egg-yolk and remaining butter.
6. Season to taste and add lemon juice.
7. Pour over cooked broccoli or serve in a separate sauce-boat.

If sauce is not served at once it can be reheated in a double saucepan.

Anne Wallace
Stewarton, Ayrshire

CAULIFLOWER WITH ALMOND SAUCE

1 cauliflower
50 g/2 oz butter
50 g/2 oz flour
125 g/4 oz ground almonds
600 ml/1 pint water
½ teaspoon nutmeg
Salt and pepper

1. Steam cauliflower whole or in florets, or simmer it in as little water as possible in a saucepan with well-fitting lid. Do not overcook. The texture should be almost crisp.
2. Meanwhile, melt butter in a pan, stir in flour and cook for 2 minutes.

3. Mix almonds with water in a jug to form a 'milk'.
4. Pour almond milk over roux, bring to the boil, stirring continuously. Simmer for 3 minutes seasoning with nutmeg, salt and pepper.
5. Pour sauce over hot, well-drained cauliflower and serve immediately.

Sarah Brown
Scarborough, Yorkshire

CAULIFLOWER BHAJI

Bhaji is the Indian name for a vegetable dish. This makes a good accompaniment to most curries and rice dishes.

Serves 4

1 medium-sized cauliflower
2 medium-sized potatoes
2 tablespoons oil
¼ teaspoon mustard seed
3 cloves of garlic, chopped
2 green chillis, chopped
½ teaspoon ground cumin
¼ teaspoon ground coriander
¼ teaspoon turmeric
¾ teaspoon garam masala (*see page 62*)
125 ml/4 fl oz warm water

TO GARNISH
Fresh coriander leaves, when available

1. Cut cauliflower into florets and potatoes into matchsticks.
2. Heat oil in a pan and splutter the mustard seeds in it. To do this, put seeds into the hot oil, put lid on pan, keep pan over medium heat and listen while seeds leap up against lid for a few seconds until the spluttering sound has stopped. Remove pan from heat before lifting lid.
3. Add potatoes and fry gently for about 3 minutes.
4. Add the other ingredients, except water, and stir-fry for about 5 minutes.
5. Pour in water and allow to simmer for about 15 minutes until cauliflower and potato are just cooked but not soft.
6. Garnish with freshly-chopped coriander leaves.

To vary the flavour of this dish 1 tablespoon of desiccated coconut may be added during cooking, at paragraph four.

Priya Wickramasinghe
Cardiff

BUTTERED CABBAGE

Cabbage
Salt and pepper
Butter
A little boiling water

1. Cut the cabbage in half. Place it cut side down on a board and slice carefully into thin segments. Do not remove the core because this holds the segments together and stops them falling to pieces during cooking.
2. Stand the segments together on edge in a saucepan small enough to hold them upright.
3. Sprinkle on a little salt and plenty of pepper. Dot with tiny pieces of butter.
4. Pour into the pan only 1 cm/$\frac{1}{2}$ inch of boiling water. Cover pan tightly. Bring to the boil, reduce heat at once and allow to simmer for 5 to 8 minutes.
5. Drain well and using a suitable utensil serve unbroken slices on to the plates.

CABBAGE DELIGHT

Cabbage
Onion and/or green pepper
Butter
Salt
Freshly-ground pepper

Use as much cabbage as you need. Use 1 onion, 1 green pepper to 1 small cabbage.

1. Shred cabbage finely.
2. Peel and slice onion finely. Slice green pepper finely, discarding core and seeds.
3. Melt enough butter in pan to cover the bottom. Fry onion and green pepper gently until it just begins to soften.
4. Add cabbage and let it cook gently until tender but still crunchy. Shake pan frequently to stop it sticking or browning. Do not overcook.
5. Add salt and pepper to taste and serve at once.
Sybil Norcott
Irlam, Nr Manchester

SPICY CABBAGE WITH COCONUT

Serves 4

225 g/8 oz spring greens, cabbage or Chinese leaves, finely-shredded as for coleslaw
$\frac{1}{2}$ medium-sized onion, chopped
2 cloves of garlic
$\frac{1}{2}$ teaspoon ground cumin
$\frac{1}{2}$ teaspoon ground coriander
$\frac{1}{4}$ teaspoon turmeric
1 teaspoon salt
2 tablespoons unsweetened desiccated coconut
2 green chillis, finely-chopped
1 tablespoon water

1. In a bowl mix all the ingredients thoroughly.
2. Using a heavy-bottomed frying pan, stir-fry the cabbage on a low flame for about 5 minutes.
Priya Wickramasinghe
Cardiff

BRAISED RED CABBAGE

This heats very well the following day, losing none of its flavour.

Serves 4

1 small red cabbage, 675 to 900 g/1$\frac{1}{2}$ to 2 lb
50 g/2 oz butter or good bacon dripping
1 medium-sized onion, sliced
1 large cooking apple
150 ml/$\frac{1}{4}$ pint cheap red wine or stock
2 teaspoons salt
1 tablespoon vinegar
$\frac{1}{2}$ level teaspoon powdered cloves
$\frac{1}{2}$ teaspoon grated nutmeg
Plenty of black pepper, to taste
1 level tablespoon soft brown sugar

1. Cut the cabbage into quarters removing outer leaves, white root and any large pieces of white pith. Shred the cabbage finely.
2. Place in a large bowl, pour over sufficient boiling water to cover. Leave 1 minute, drain.
3. Melt butter in a large heavy pan. Add onion and cook gently to soften but not brown, about 5 minutes.
4. Add apple, peeled, cored and thickly sliced, the wine or stock, salt, vinegar, cloves, nutmeg and a

good grating of black pepper. Add cabbage and turn over to mix into liquid. Cover tightly.
5. Cook gently until tender, turning over from time to time, about 1 hour.
6. Stir in sugar and serve.

Serve with a hot joint, especially pork or bacon.

BUTTERED CARROTS AND THYME

Serves 2

225 g/8 oz small carrots
15 g/½ oz butter
1 teaspoon chopped fresh thyme

1. Trim carrots and gently scrub clean, leaving skin on. Cut into matchstick strips (known as julienne).
2. Steam carrots for 10 minutes, or simmer in a very little water in a tightly-covered pan until nearly tender.
3. Toss in butter, sprinkle with thyme and serve at once.

Janet Horsley
Headingley, Yorkshire

CARROTS IN A CASSEROLE

Serves 4

450 g/1 lb carrots
Boiling water or light stock
¼ teaspoon salt
1 teaspoon butter
Pepper

1. Scrub or scrape carrots and cut them into 2.5 cm/ 1 inch pieces.
2. Put them in a small casserole with a well-fitting lid. Pour over boiling water or light stock just to cover.
3. Put in a moderate oven, Gas 3, 325°F, 160°C, for ¾ hour.
4. Just before serving, stir in butter and a shake of pepper.

Delicious served with Casseroled Rabbit (*see page 80*)

BAKED CARROTS WITH HONEY AND MUSTARD

Serves 4

450 g/1 lb carrots
2 tablespoons water
2 tablespoons oil
2 tablespoons honey
1 teaspoon made mustard, try a whole grain one
Pepper and salt
A few sesame seeds for decorating (optional)

1. Scrub carrots and chop into small sticks.
2. Mix water, oil, honey and mustard.
3. Put carrots in a shallow oven dish, pour over the honey mixture. Sprinkle with pepper and a very little salt.
4. Cover dish (greaseproof paper and foil will do) and bake in a moderately hot oven, Gas 5, 375°F, 190°C, for 50 to 60 minutes until tender.

Serve with a sprinkling of sesame seeds.

Sarah Brown
Scarborough, Yorkshire

BRAISED CELERY AND BACON

A nice way to serve celery if the oven is on for something else.

Serves 4

1 head of celery
15 g/½ oz butter or margarine
Salt
Black pepper
½ level teaspoon nutmeg
300 ml/½ pint chicken stock
2 or 3 rashers of streaky bacon, without rinds

1. Wash and trim the celery and cut it into 2.5 to 5 cm/1 to 2 inch lengths.
2. Use the butter or margarine to grease an oven dish with a lid.
3. Lay celery in dish and season with a little salt, freshly-grated black pepper and nutmeg.
4. Pour over the stock.

5. Cut bacon into thin strips and fry them a little, then lay the strips over celery.

6. Put lid on dish and cook in a moderate oven, Gas 4, 350°F, 180°C, for 30 minutes.

7. When celery is tender, drain off excess liquor, toss bacon amongst celery and serve.

COURGETTES

A vegetable with a lovely appearance but so delicate a taste that it needs some other flavour with it. Takes only 5 minutes to prepare.

Serves 4

450 g/1 lb courgettes, do not peel
25 g/1 oz butter
Half a clove of garlic, crushed
Salt and black pepper

1. Wash courgettes, trim off the stalks and cut into even-sized very fine rings. This can be done very quickly on the mandolin cutter of a grater.

2. Melt butter and fry garlic for 1 minute.

3. Add courgettes and stir over moderate heat so that garlic butter is well distributed. Season with a little salt and plenty of freshly-ground black pepper.

4. Put on lid, lower heat and let courgettes just heat through for 3 to 4 minutes. Shake pan every now and then.

Serve at once while the green slices are crisp and still brilliantly green, and not jaded with over-cooking.

LEEKS IN RED WINE

Leeks as required, not too large, preferably all the same size
1 tablespoon oil
25 g/1 oz butter
1 glass (about 150 ml/¼ pint) cheap red wine
150 to 300 ml/¼ to ½ pint well-flavoured stock
Salt and pepper

1. Trim leeks and wash very well in cold, running water to remove any grit.

2. Heat oil and butter in a wide shallow pan and lay leeks in side by side. Gently turn them over until golden all over.

3. Pour on the wine, allow to bubble.

4. Boil stock and pour on just enough to cover leeks. Check seasoning.

5. Cover pan and cook until leeks are tender.

6. Remove leeks to a hot dish, boil liquid rapidly to reduce to about 150 ml/¼ pint. Pour over leeks and serve.

MARROW AND ONION SAVOURY

Serves 4

675 g/1½ lb marrow, peeled, de-seeded, and cut into 2.5 cm/1 inch cubes
450 g/1 lb onions, thinly-sliced
Salt
Pepper
Mixed herbs
Butter

1. Layer marrow and onion in a greased pie-dish, sprinkling seasoning between layers, and ending with marrow. Dot with butter.

2. Cover (foil will do) and cook in a moderate oven, Gas 4, 350°F, 180°C until tender, usually about 1½ hours. This will cook in lower part of oven, under meat.

Serve with lamb or roast pork.

ONIONS BAKED IN CIDER

Serves 4

450 g/1 lb onions
25 g/1 oz butter
1 level teaspoon sugar
½ teaspoon salt
Freshly-ground black pepper
150 ml/¼ pint cider

1. Slice onions thickly, place in a casserole, dot with the butter. Sprinkle on sugar, salt and pepper.

2. Pour the cider over, and cover casserole tightly. Greaseproof paper and foil will do.

3. Cook in a moderate oven, Gas 4, 350°F, 180°C, for 1¼ hours. Then remove lid and cook a further 15 minutes.

Serve with meat dishes, especially pork.

GLAZED PARSNIPS

Quite a sweet dish. Nice with pork or poultry.

Serves 4

675 g/1½ lb parsnips
40 g/1½ oz butter
1 tablespoon brown sugar
¼ teaspoon salt
2 teaspoons lemon juice
Juice of 1 orange (or 4 tablespoons cider)

1. Wash the parsnips and boil them until just tender. Then peel, slice and leave them to drain well.
2. Choose a shallow baking dish, butter it well and arrange half the parsnip slices in a single layer in the dish.
3. Melt 25 g/1 oz of the butter, remove from heat and mix with it the sugar, salt, lemon and orange juice (or cider).
4. Pour half the mixture over the sliced parsnips. Cover with remaining parsnip slices and pour over them the rest of the sugar mixture.
5. Dot with the rest of the butter.
6. Bake in a moderately hot oven, Gas 5, 375°F, 190°C for 20 minutes or until the top is nicely glazed.

Mrs Sybil Norcott
Irlam, Nr Manchester

GLAZED PARSNIPS WITH WALNUTS AND ROSEMARY

Serves 3 to 4

450 g/1 lb parsnips
Salt
50 g/2 oz butter
75 g/3 oz broken walnuts
½ teaspoon dried rosemary
Freshly-ground black pepper
Chopped parsley (optional)

1. Scrub parsnips and slice into rings of even thickness.
2. Steam with a little salt or simmer with a good lid on pan in as little water as possible until just tender. Drain.
3. Melt most of butter in saucepan and toss parsnips and walnuts in it until both are lightly-browned.

4. Mix in rosemary and black pepper.
5. Serve with an extra dot of butter or parsley to garnish.

Sarah Brown
Scarborough, Yorkshire

PEASE PUDDING

The mixture will freeze well but put in freezer before butter and egg are added.

Serves 4

225 g/8 oz yellow split peas
1 chopped onion
25 g/1 oz butter
1 beaten egg
Flavoured stock (bacon stock is best)

1. Soak peas overnight, then drain.
2. Put peas and onion in pan with enough stock to cover.
3. Simmer together with lid on until peas are quite soft, replenishing stock if necessary.
4. Sieve or liquidise.
5. Beat in butter and egg. Test for seasoning.
6. Pour into a greased pie dish, cover and cook in a moderate oven, Gas 3, 325°F, 160°C for half an hour.

Serve hot with roast pork, ham or bacon. When cold, fry in bacon dripping and serve with breakfast bacon.

POTATOES

CHOOSING
Should be reasonably clear of soil, firm and sound, but washed potatoes do not keep. They are better bought from a sack as exposure to daylight causes green patches.

STORING
Keep in brown paper bag in a cool place. Heat causes them to go soft and sprout. Do not let them freeze.

PREPARATION
NEW POTATOES
Should scrub or scrape easily. Do not prepare too long before cooking.

OLD POTATOES
Most nutritious if scrubbed and baked in jackets. If peeling, use a peeler that takes away the minimum of peel. Cut into even sizes. If not cooking at once cover with cold water.

COOKING
NEW POTATOES
Place with a sprig of mint in a saucepan with boiling, lightly salted water to just cover.Bring back to the boil, cover pan, reduce heat and simmer for 12 to 15 minutes according to size. Better still, use a steamer. Drain, place in a hot dish with a good nut of butter.

OLD POTATOES
Place in cold, salted water, almost to cover. Bring to the boil, cover pan and simmer until tender (about 20 minutes). Drain. If keeping warm, cover with a clean folded tea towel to absorb steam.

MASHED OR CREAMED POTATOES

Add 25 g/1 oz butter to each 450 g/1 lb potatoes, with salt and pepper to taste. Mash until creamy. A little top of the milk may also be added to give a softer consistency.

CREAMED POTATO FOR PIPING

DUCHESSE AND POTATO BASKETS
Filled with peas, the potato baskets make a good garnish for a joint of meat.
A large potato basket can be filled with cheese sauce and vegetables.

For each 450 g/1 lb potatoes allow 25 g/1 oz butter, 1 egg-yolk, salt and pepper to taste and a grate of nutmeg and one beaten egg-white.

1. Mash the potatoes entirely free from lumps—a potato ricer is good for this method—and then mix in the butter, egg-yolk, salt, pepper and nutmeg.
2. Use a large forcing bag and a large serrated nozzle. Pipe rosettes of potato or basket shapes on to a greased baking tray.
3. Brush with beaten egg-white and bake in hot oven, Gas 7, 425°F, 220°C, for 10 to 15 minutes.

POTATO CROQUETTES

These freeze well, but this must be done before they are fried, after step 3 below.

For each 450 g/1 lb potatoes:—
25 g/1 oz butter
1 egg, separated
Salt and pepper
1 to 2 teaspoons chopped parsley
A grate of nutmeg
A little flour
Dried breadcrumbs

1. Mash the potatoes free from lumps and mix in the butter, egg-yolk, salt, pepper, parsley and nutmeg. The mixture should be firm, but not dry.
2. Form into cork-shaped pieces about 8 cm/3 inches long and 2.5 cm/1 inch in diameter.
3. Flour, dip in lightly beaten egg-white and roll in dried breadcrumbs.
4. Deep fry for 3 to 4 minutes.

ROAST POTATOES

Peel, cut into even-sized pieces and boil for 10 minutes. Drain well and dry. Place around meat, in the fat, turning them to coat all sides. Allow 30 to 40 minutes cooking time in a moderately hot oven, Gas 6, 400°F, 200°C.

These can also be placed in a separate tin, allowing fat to become hot first, and roasted in a moderately hot oven, Gas 6, 400°F, 200°C, on top shelf of oven. If potatoes are not crisp enough when cooked through, place under medium grill for 5 minutes, turning to ensure even browning.

NEW POTATOES

Served in a sweet glaze.

New potatoes
25 g/1 oz butter
25 g/1 oz sugar

1. Boil new potatoes in their jackets until tender.
2. In a clean pan melt butter and sugar and cook gently until golden.
3. Put in potatoes with or without skins. Turn them over in glaze until they are coated and light brown.

Nice with cold ham and a green crisp salad.

NEW POTATOES IN BUTTERMILK

TATWS LLAETH
New potatoes
Buttermilk

Traditionally, the first new potatoes to be lifted were used for this delicate and nourishing dish.
Nowadays, obtaining buttermilk may be difficult for some people but it is produced for sale by several dairies and sold in many parts of the country.
1. Cook the scraped potatoes in boiling salted water with a sprig of mint.
2. When cooked, drain thoroughly and then put enough for one serving in a basin and just cover with buttermilk. Eat at once.

Miss G.S. Davies
Flintshire

SCALLOPED NEW OR OLD POTATOES

Can be made with old potatoes, but choose really waxy ones like Desirée or Dr Mackintosh.

Serves 4

450 g/1 lb new potatoes, scrubbed
125 g/4 oz mushrooms, chopped
15 g/½ oz butter
125 g/4 oz cooked ham, cut in small pieces

CHEESE SAUCE
50 g/2 oz butter
50 g/2 oz flour
1 teaspoon made mustard
A grating of nutmeg
600 ml/1 pint milk
50 g/2 oz grated cheese

1. Steam potatoes or cook them over low heat in a very little water. Then drain and slice.
2. Meanwhile, chop mushrooms and fry for 1 minute in the 15 g/½ oz butter.
3. Make sauce. Melt butter, stir in flour and cook 1 minute.
4. Stir in mustard and nutmeg. Then add milk gradually, stirring as sauce thickens, and simmer for 3 minutes.
5. Stir in cheese and reheat but do not boil.
6. Arrange slices of potato overlapping in a buttered, shallow oven dish.
7. Cover with mushrooms and ham.
8. Pour over the cheese sauce.
9. Cook at top of a moderately hot oven, Gas 6, 400°F, 200°C, for 15 minutes.

SCALLOPED POTATOES

Serves 4

675 to 900 g/1½ to 2 lb potatoes
150 ml/¼ pint milk
25 g/1 oz butter
½ teaspoon Salt and Pepper Mix (*see page 17*)

1. Peel and thinly slice potatoes. Arrange them in a 1.2 litre/2 pint casserole.
2. Heat milk in a pan with butter, salt and pepper. Do not boil.
3. Pour over the potatoes. Cover dish (greaseproof paper and foil will do).
4. Cook on lower shelf of a moderately hot oven at Gas 5, 375°F, 190°C, for 1 hour. Remove cover for final 15 minutes to crisp top.

BIEN POMMES DE TERRE

Or good spuds French-style!

Serves 4

615 g/1½ lb old potatoes
1 onion
25 g/1 oz butter
Salt and Pepper Mix (*see page 17*)
3 to 4 tablespoons milk

1. Slice potato thickly.
2. Slice onion into thin rings.
3. Use some of the butter to grease a fairly deep ovenproof dish—a 1.5 litre/2½ pint soufflé dish is suitable.
4. Place the potato and onion in the dish in layers, seasoning to taste.
5. Pour over the milk.
6. Dot with small pieces of butter.
7. Cover and put in a moderate oven, Gas 4, 350°F, 180°C, for 1 hour. Remove cover to let contents brown a little for a further 8 to 10 minutes.

Jamie Jackson
London

GOLDEN POTATO BAKE

Serves 4 to 5

900 g/2 lb potatoes, peeled and thinly-sliced
75 g/3 oz grated cheese

ONION SAUCE
25 g/1 oz butter or margarine
1 medium-sized onion, sliced
25 g/1 oz plain flour
450 ml/¾ pint milk
½ teaspoon salt
A shake of pepper

1. Start with the sauce. Melt margarine in saucepan, add onion and soften but do not brown.
2. Stir in flour and sizzle for 1 to 2 minutes. Gradually add milk, salt and pepper, stirring as it thickens, and allow to boil for 2 minutes.
3. Layer potatoes in a large pie dish. Pour sauce over.
4. Cover and cook in a moderate oven, Gas 3, 325°F, 160°C, for 1½ hours.
5. Uncover, sprinkle on cheese, place in oven until cheese melts and begins to bubble.

Serve with any roast joint.

SPINACH WITH CREAM

Serves 4

1 to 1.3 kg/2 to 3 lb fresh spinach
25 g/1 oz butter or margarine
3 to 4 tablespoons fresh breadcrumbs
2 to 3 tablespoons single cream
A good grating of whole nutmeg
Pepper and salt

1. Trim, and wash spinach. Put it in a large saucepan with no extra water. Boil for 4 or 5 minutes.
2. Meanwhile heat butter or margarine and fry breadcrumbs till golden, stirring often.
3. Drain spinach, chop, drain again and squeeze out moisture.
4. Mix in cream, nutmeg, pepper and a little salt. Put in a warmed dish and sprinkle piping hot breadcrumbs on top.

Serve at once.

Mrs Joyce Langley
Shoreham-by-Sea, West Sussex

SCALLOPED TOMATOES

Serves 4

1 onion
15 g/½ oz good dripping or margarine
450 g/1 lb tomatoes
50 g/2 oz grated cheese
50 g/2 oz fresh wholewheat or white breadcrumbs (*see page 52*)
1 teaspoon sugar
1 teaspoon Salt and Pepper Mix (*see page 17*)
A little butter

1. Chop the onion and cook gently in fat for about 5 minutes.
2. Meanwhile, skin the tomatoes (*see page 139*).
3. Thickly slice the tomatoes.
4. Remove onions from heat. Add cheese and crumbs.
5. Place tomatoes in a 1 litre/1½ pint greased pie-dish, sprinkling with sugar, salt and pepper between layers.
6. Spread onion mixture on top, dot with butter.
7. Cook in a moderately hot oven, Gas 5, 375°F, 190°C, for 30 minutes.

TOMATO AND ONION CASSEROLE

Serves 4

450 g/1 lb onions
Salt and pepper
½ level teaspoon marjoram
450 g/1 lb tomatoes, skinned (*see page 139*) and sliced
75 g/3 oz breadcrumbs
75 g/3 oz grated cheese
25 g/1 oz melted butter, margarine or bacon fat

1. Peel and slice onions and boil in salted water for about 20 minutes.
2. Drain well and season with pepper and herbs.
3. Put half onion into a greased casserole.
4. Add a layer of half the sliced tomatoes.
5. Next, add a layer of crumbs and grated cheese.
6. Repeat the layers.
7. Pour over the melted butter, margarine or bacon fat.
8. Bake in a hot oven, Gas 7, 425°F, 220°C, for 20 minutes.

Sybil Norcott
Irlam, Nr Manchester

VEGETABLE HOT POT

Serves 4

RATATOUILLE
3 large onions
1 small green pepper
1 good-sized aubergine
450 g/1 lb ripe tomatoes or a 400 g/14 oz can of tomatoes
1 clove of garlic
4 tablespoons cooking oil
1 teaspoon sugar
Salt
1 bay leaf and/or ½ teaspoon basil
Black pepper

1. Cut the onions into chunks. Cut the green pepper into very small pieces and the aubergine into 1 to 2 cm/½ to 1 inch cubes, skin and roughly chop the tomatoes. Crush the garlic (*see page 139*).
2. Heat oil in a large heavy-based pan. Turn the onions over in the oil for a couple of minutes.

3. Add the pepper and the aubergine and mix well.
4. Add tomatoes, garlic, sugar, salt, bay leaf, basil and a good grating of black pepper. Mix all together.
5. Cover tightly and simmer very gently for at least half an hour. An hour is not too long to cook this dish.

Serve with rice or pasta or even large chunks of crusty bread. Particularly good with an omelette or a cheese soufflé. Reheats well.

TURNIPS WITH ORANGES

Particularly good with duck or pork.

Serves 4 to 6

12 young turnips
2 oranges
Water
Salt
50 g/2 oz butter
Coarsely-ground black pepper

1. Peel turnips.
2. Grate rind finely from one orange and squeeze juice from them both.
3. Put whole turnips with orange juice in a saucepan. Just cover with water and add a little salt. Bring to the boil, cover pan and simmer until tender, about 20 to 25 minutes.
4. Drain turnips, saving liquid for soup or gravy.
5. Put turnips into a warmed, buttered, heatproof dish. Put a dab of butter on each and sprinkle all over with grated orange rind and coarse black pepper.
6. Put under a hot grill for 2 minutes to melt butter and crisp and dry the orange rind and tops of turnips.

Sybil Norcott
Irlam, Nr Manchester

STUFFED AUBERGINES

Allow half a large aubergine or one whole small one per person.

Serves 4

2 large aubergines (about 325 g/12 oz each)
1 medium-sized onion
4 tablespoons oil
125 g/4 oz streaky bacon
1 clove garlic (optional)
75 g/3 oz fresh wholemeal breadcrumbs
½ level teaspoon dried oregano
Pinch of dried thyme
Salt and pepper
2 tomatoes
25 g/1 oz finely-grated, well-flavoured cheese, preferably Parmesan
A little chopped parsley

1. Cut the ends off aubergines and halve lengthways. Cut out some of the flesh to leave 5 to 12 mm/¼ to ½ inch walls.
2. Roughly chop flesh and put aside.
3. Peel and chop onion.
4. Heat oil in a frying pan and quickly fry aubergine cases for ½ minute on the cut side. Lift them out into an oven-proof dish or roasting tin, leaving as much oil as possible behind in the frying pan in which to fry the onion.
5. Add chopped onion to pan and cook gently until beginning to brown.
6. Cut rinds off bacon and chop the rashers. Add to onion.
7. Cook for a minute and add aubergine flesh. Cook for 10 minutes, stirring occasionally.
8. Peel clove of garlic, chop finely and add to frying pan.
9. Mix breadcrumbs and herbs in a bowl and season well.
10. Drain fried mixture and add to the crumbs. Mix well.
11. Pour any remaining oil into aubergine cases.
12. Pile the filling mixture into aubergine cases.
13. Slice tomatoes and arrange on top.
14. Sprinkle with cheese.
15. Cover dish, foil will do, and bake in a moderate oven, Gas 4, 350°F, 180°C, for ¾ to 1 hour until aubergines are tender.
16. Sprinkle a little chopped parsley on to each aubergine and serve with brown rice and a crisp green salad.

BUTTER BEANS AND MUSHROOMS

Under a crisp cheese topping, this is a light but nourishing dish to eat on its own, with lightly-cooked green beans or with some crusty French bread and green salad.

Remember to start the night before.

Serves 2 to 3

175 g/6 oz butter beans, soaked overnight
225 g/8 oz mushrooms
A little butter
Salt and pepper

WHITE SAUCE
25 g/1 oz butter
1 dessertspoon wholewheat flour
150 ml/¼ pint milk
1 tablespoon lemon juice
Salt and pepper

TOPPING
40 g/1½ oz grated cheese
40 g/1½ oz fresh wholewheat breadcrumbs

1. Having soaked beans overnight in water to cover, drain off water. Put beans in saucepan and cover with fresh water. Boil hard for 10 minutes then reduce heat and simmer until tender, about 40 minutes more. Drain (saving liquid for soups, etc.).
2. Put beans into a well-buttered 1.2 litre/2 pint pie dish. Season well with salt and pepper.
3. Meanwhile, cut stalks from mushrooms and chop them finely, leaving mushroom caps whole.
4. Simmer mushroom caps in a very little water for 2 or 3 minutes to soften a little. Then drain, saving the liquid.
5. For the sauce, melt butter and fry mushroom stalks for 2 minutes.
6. Add flour and cook 1 minute.
7. Add milk and lemon juice to pan, stir as sauce thickens and add enough mushroom liquid to make a smooth pouring sauce. Add salt and pepper to taste. Simmer for 3 minutes.
8. Pour sauce over beans.
9. Lay mushroom caps on top with undersides up.
10. Mix grated cheese and breadcrumbs and sprinkle over mushrooms.
11. Bake near top of a moderate oven, Gas 4, 350°F, 180°C, for 15 minutes to brown the top and heat through.

CUMBERLAND HERB PUDDING

Serves 4

1 heaped tablespoon pearl barley
450 g/1 lb spring cabbage
125 g/4 oz young nettles, optional but worth trying
2 medium-sized onions
2 medium-sized leeks
25 g/1 oz butter
1 egg
Salt and pepper to taste

1. Soak barley overnight in 600 ml/1 pint of water.
2. Next day, boil until tender in the same water.
3. Place washed and shredded vegetables in a large heavy saucepan, add cooked barley and the liquid in which it cooked. Add a little more water if necessary.
4. Boil quickly until tender with lid on pan, stirring occasionally to prevent barley sticking to base of pan. This can take from 20 to 30 minutes depending on age and quality of vegetables.
5. Drain through a colander discarding liquid and tip vegetables back into the pan.
6. Add butter and beaten egg, mix in and season to taste with salt and pepper.
7. Turn into a 1.2 litre/2 pint heat-proof basin or pie dish.
8. Cover and re-heat in moderate oven, Gas 4, 350°F, 180°C, for about 10 to 15 minutes.

Serve hot, turned out of basin on to a warmed plate.

Miss H. Holmes
Crosby on Eden

CAULIFLOWER WITH CHEESE AND BACON SAUCE

A cauliflower

FOR THE SAUCE
125 g/4 oz streaky bacon
25 g/1 oz margarine
25 g/1 oz plain flour
$\frac{1}{2}$ teaspoon Salt and Pepper Mix (*see page 17*)
150 ml/$\frac{1}{4}$ pint milk
150 ml/$\frac{1}{4}$ pint of the cauliflower water
75 g/3 oz grated cheese

TO SERVE AU GRATIN
25 to 50 g/1 to 2 oz grated cheese
Crisp breadcrumbs (optional) (*see page 52*)

1. Remove stalk end of the cauliflower and all but the delicate young leaves. Wash well in salted water. Do not leave to soak.
2. Cut a cross at the stalk end to allow both stalk and flower to be evenly cooked.
3. Place in deep pan just big enough to hold the cauliflower with enough boiling, salted water to reach about one inch up the sides. Cover and cook for about 10 to 15 minutes until tender but still firm.
4. Cut the bacon into small pieces and fry till crisp.
5. Melt the margarine in a pan, or if preferred use 1 tablespoon of the bacon dripping. Add flour and Salt and Pepper Mix and sizzle for one minute.
6. Gradually stir in milk and cauliflower water and simmer for one minute.
7. Add cheese, reheat but do not boil. Stir in crisp bacon.
8. Place the well-drained cauliflower in a warm dish and pour over the cheese and bacon sauce.

TO SERVE AU GRATIN
Place cooked cauliflower in a heat-resistant casserole. Pour the cheese sauce over it, sprinkle on cheese and breadcrumbs, place under a medium grill to melt cheese and brown a little.

CAULIFLOWER AND TOMATOES

This dish is good on its own, but don't overcook the cauliflower. If you think flower will be cooked before stalks are tender, split stalks as you do with Brussels sprouts.

Serves 4

1 medium-sized cauliflower
1 onion
1 clove garlic (optional)
Salt
450 g/1 lb tomatoes, or a 400 g/14 oz can
1 tablespoon oil
25 g/1 oz butter
1 tablespoon chopped parsley
Black pepper

SAUCE
40 g/1½ oz margarine
40 g/1½ oz flour
300 ml/½ pint milk
125 g/4 oz grated cheese
25 g/1 oz dry breadcrumbs

1. Divide cauliflower into even-sized florets and put them in a saucepan. Pour in about 300 ml/½ pint of boiling water, bring back to the boil, cover the pan, turn down the heat and let cauliflower cook in this way for 7 minutes.
2. Drain off cauliflower water into a cup for later use and keep cauliflower warm.
3. Peel and chop onion. Crush garlic (*see page 139*).
4. Skin the tomatoes (*see page 139*), and cut into quarters.
5. Heat oil and butter in a frying pan and cook onion and garlic just to soften, not brown.
6. Add tomatoes, parsley, salt and black pepper and cook 1 to 2 minutes.
7. Now make the sauce. Melt margarine in a small saucepan. Stir in flour and allow it to cook for a minute.
8. Stir in 150 ml/¼ pint of cauliflower water and the milk. Bring to the boil, stirring, and cook for 3 minutes.
9. Add 75 g/3 oz of the cheese. Reheat but do not boil.
10. Spread tomato mixture over the base of an oven-proof dish. Lay florets of cauliflower on top, then pour the sauce over.

11. Mix the dry crumbs with rest of the cheese, and sprinkle on top.
13. Put dish under grill until golden-brown and bubbling. Serve hot.

CHESTNUT HOT-POT

Can be cooked on top of stove or as a casserole in oven. Freezes well.
Baked potatoes and spiced red cabbage go well with it, also wholewheat bread rolls.

Serves 4, but this dish improves with keeping and reheating, so 1 or 2 can enjoy it more than once.

50 g/2 oz whole lentils
125 g/4 oz whole dried chestnuts*
1.2 litres/2 pints water
1 medium-sized onion
225 g/8 oz carrots
2 sticks of celery
1 tablespoon oil
2 tablespoons fresh parsley or 1 tablespoon dried
1 teaspoon sage
½ teaspoon thyme
½ to 1 tablespoon shoyu (*see page 162*)
½ teaspoon mustard powder
Salt and pepper

* *Can be bought at good wholefood shops.*

1. Wash lentils and pick them over carefully for any stones.
2. Boil chestnuts and lentils in the water for 40 minutes.
3. Meanwhile, peel onion and scrub carrots and celery and cut into bite-sized pieces.
4. Heat oil and gently fry chopped vegetables for 10 minutes, stirring occasionally so that they do not brown.
5. Combine in one saucepan or casserole the fried vegetables, chestnuts, lentils and their cooking liquid.
6. Add all remaining ingredients and more liquid, either water or stock, if necessary.
7. Cover pan and simmer for 30 minutes. If using casserole, cook in middle of a moderate oven, Gas 4, 350°F, 180°C, for 45 minutes to 1 hour.

Sarah Brown
Scarborough, Yorkshire

CHESTNUT AND MUSHROOM LOAF

A party dish. Delicious cold as a pâté or served hot in the style of a traditional Sunday lunch.

Serves 8 to 10, but easy to reduce quantities

125 g/4 oz dried chestnuts, whole or kibbled*
1.2 litres/2 pints boiling water
50 g/2 oz butter
1 onion, chopped
2 cloves of garlic, crushed
1 tablespoon chopped fresh parsley
2 teaspoons sage
¼ teaspoon winter savory
½ teaspoon paprika
2 tablespoons wholewheat flour
150 ml/¼ pint stock from cooking chestnuts
150 ml/¼ pint red wine
325 g/12 oz walnuts, ground
50 g/2 oz fresh wholewheat breadcrumbs
4 sticks celery, chopped
1 teaspoon salt
1 tablespoon shoyu (*see this page*) or Worcester-
    shire sauce
225 g/8 oz mushrooms, sliced
1 beaten egg

* *Kibbled is the name given to chestnuts which are sold in small broken pieces.*

1. Soak chestnuts in the boiling water for 1 hour.
2. Then cook them in the same water in a covered pan until soft. If whole this will take about 40 minutes; if kibbled, about 20 minutes. Save the cooking water as you drain them. Chop coarsely (not necessary with kibbled chestnuts).
3. Melt butter in a large frying pan and fry onion and garlic gently until transparent.
4. Stir in herbs, paprika and flour and cook 2 minutes.
5. Add the 150 ml/¼ pint stock from chestnuts and wine, stir well. When sauce thickens remove pan from heat.
6. Mix together in a bowl chestnuts, ground walnuts, breadcrumbs, celery, salt, shoyu or Worcestershire sauce and mushrooms.
7. Mix in sauce and beaten egg. Check seasoning.
8. Grease a 1 kg/2 lb loaf tin and line it with greased greaseproof paper. Fill with mixture and press down well.

9. Bake in a moderately hot oven, Gas 5, 375°F, 190°C, for 1 hour until firm to the touch. Remove from oven.

When serving hot, leave loaf in tin for 10 minutes before cutting.

Sarah Brown
Scarborough, Yorkshire

SHOYU OR TAMARI

It is a natural fermentation of soya beans and wheat, not dissimilar to commercial soya sauce. Wholefood and vegetarian cooks use it in preference to that and yeast extracts because they find it is a more versatile condiment. It is also highly concentrated food containing valuable vitamins and minerals. It adds depth of flavour, stimulates the appetite and complements a wide range of foods. It can be used in a number of dishes from seasonings, soups and stews, to dips and dressings.

Although there is no direct substitute, alternatives are yeast extract, soya sauce, tomato purée, mustards and herbs. Also meat extracts or stock cubes if you are not vegetarian.

CIDER WITH ROSEMARY

A well-flavoured casserole of vegetables. The chick peas, wheat grain and cheese provide protein to make this a substantial and nutritionally-balanced main course.

Serves 4

150 g/5 oz cooked chick peas (*see page 136*) or
    50 g/2 oz uncooked
150 g/5 oz cooked wheat grain (*see page 136*) or
    75 g/3 oz uncooked grain
About 900 g/2 lb mixed root vegetables, carrot,
    swede, turnip, parsnip
1 tablespoon oil
175 g/6 oz fennel, cut in chunks
25 g/1 oz butter
50 g/2 oz wholewheat flour
450 ml/¾ pint cider
450 ml/¾ pint water or stock
1 bay leaf
1 dessertspoon chopped fresh parsley
1 teaspoon rosemary
1 teaspoon sage
1 teaspoon thyme
Salt and pepper

1. Don't forget to soak chick peas and wheat grain overnight before cooking, according to instructions on page 136. Save cooking liquid.
2. Cut up root vegetables into even-sized chunky pieces.
3. Heat oil and gently fry fennel for about 5 minutes. This draws out flavour.
4. Add chopped root vegetables and stir well so that all is coated in a very little oil to seal in flavour.
5. Add butter, letting it melt. Stir in flour and let it cook 2 to 3 minutes.
6. Stir in cider and water or stock and bring to the boil.
7. Mix in chick peas, grain and herbs. Bring back to boil, lower heat and simmer for 1 hour. Check seasoning before serving.

Delicious served with baked potatoes and a sprinkling of grated cheese.

Sarah Brown
Scarborough, Yorkshire

CREAMY OAT AND ALMOND CASSEROLE

Serves 4 to 6, but easy to make less

50 g/2 oz whole oats, or barley
50 g/2 oz whole green continental lentils
225 g/8 oz leeks
225 g/8 oz carrots
125 g/4 oz celery
1 parsnip
1 green pepper
25 g/1 oz butter
½ teaspoon thyme
½ teaspoon mustard

SAUCE
50 g/2 oz ground almonds, or grind whole, unblanched almonds yourself if you can
300 ml/½ pint stock from cooking grain and lentils
25 g/1 oz butter
25 g/1 oz wholewheat flour
Salt and pepper

TOPPING
50 g/2 oz porridge oats
50 g/2 oz wholewheat breadcrumbs
1 tablespoon sunflower seeds

1. Pick over lentils for sticks and stones. Then rinse with the grain. Put them together in a pan of fresh water, about 1 litre/1½ pints, and boil for 45 minutes. Then strain off the liquid and keep it for use later.
2. Meanwhile, scrub and chop vegetables finely.
3. Melt 25 g/1 oz butter in a large frying pan and fry vegetables, stirring so that they are coated in butter.
4. Pour in about half a cupful of cooking liquid from grain and lentils. Cook 10 to 15 minutes until vegetables are just about tender but not soft.
5. Mix in thyme, mustard and well-drained grain and lentils. Cook another 5 minutes.
6. Meanwhile, make sauce. Mix ground almonds with the stock to form 'milk'.
7. Melt butter in pan, stir in flour, cook for one minute.
8. Pour in almond milk—stirring continuously. Bring sauce to boil. Season.
9. Pour sauce over cooked vegetables. Turn into a greased oven dish.
10. Mix topping ingredients and sprinkle over.
11. Bake near top of a moderate oven, Gas 4, 350°F, 180°C, for 20 minutes, when it will be nicely browned.

Sarah Brown
Scarborough, Yorkshire

LEEK PUDDING

175 g/6 oz self-raising white or wholewheat flour, or a mixture of both
75 g/3 oz shredded suet
Water to mix, about 6 tablespoons
Pinch of salt

FILLING
Chopped leeks and any cold meat left from another meal

1. Chop or mince the meat and mix with the leeks. There should be enough to spread thickly on the rolled out pastry.
2. Mix suet into flour and salt adding enough water to make a softish dough which is still firm enough to roll out.
3. Roll out on a floured board to about 30 by 18 cm/ 12 by 7 inches.
4. Spread on the filling to within 1 cm/half an inch of edges, sprinkling liberally with salt and pepper. Damp edges with water.
5. Roll up loosely to make a roll 18 cm/7 inches wide. Nip the ends firmly to seal.

6. Wrap the roll loosely in a large piece of greased foil enclosing it completely and sealing ends well.

7. Scald a large, strong, close-woven cotton cloth.

8. Roll pudding in cloth, tie ends securely with string making a strong handle across top also. This helps when removing pudding from water.

9. Have a saucepan two-thirds full of boiling water. Put pudding in, lid on pan and bring back quickly to boil.

10. Boil for 2 hours, keeping water boiling and replenishing if necessary with more boiling water.

Serve with a good gravy.

Mrs M. White
Northumberland

LENTIL PUDDING

Serves 4

175 to 225 g/6 to 8 oz lentils
1 medium-sized onion
175 g/6 oz cheese
1 or 2 tomatoes (optional)

1. Cover lentils in water and soak overnight.

2. Next day, peel and finely chop onion.

3. Put lentils and water in which they were soaking into a large saucepan, add the onion and add more cold water, if necessary, to cover.

4. Bring to the boil, lower heat, cover pan and simmer until lentils are tender and have absorbed most of the water. Stir occasionally, but particularly towards end of cooking time. It will take only about 15 minutes.

5. Meanwhile, grate the cheese.

6. When lentils are done, drain off any excess liquid. Don't throw it away—you can use it in soup.

7. Stir 125 g/4 oz of the cheese into pan of lentils.

8. Turn it all out into a well-greased, 1.2 litre/2 pint pie-dish.

9. Sprinkle rest of cheese on top.

10. Bake in a moderately hot oven, Gas 6, 400°F, 200°C, for 15 to 20 minutes, or until cheese has melted and browned a little.

If using tomatoes, lay them overlapping in a row across the middle, 5 minutes before end of cooking time.

Mrs Grace Dix
Downton, Wiltshire

LENTIL ROAST

Serves 4

225 g/8 oz lentils
2 tablespoons oil
2 onions
1 large cooking apple
2 large tomatoes
50 g/2 oz fresh wholewheat or white bread-crumbs
1 egg
1 teaspoon sage or mixed herbs
Salt and pepper

1. Soak lentils overnight in enough water just to cover.

2. Next day, cook lentils in same water until soft, beat smooth.

3. Heat oil in pan and fry finely-chopped onions gently until soft.

4. Peel, core and finely slice apple. Skin and chop tomatoes. Add both to onion and fry till soft.

5. Add to lentils with breadcrumbs, beaten egg, herbs and seasonings.

6. Press into greased loaf tin and cover.

7. Bake in a moderately hot oven, Gas 5, 375°F, 190°C, for about 50 minutes.

Serve as a main course with green vegetables, gravy or tomato sauce (*see page 187 for a tomato sauce*).

LENTIL SAVOURY

Serves 4 to 6

175 g/6 oz lentils
75 g/3 oz lean bacon
175 g/6 oz carrots
1 onion
1 clove garlic
25 g/1 oz dripping
1 dessertspoon plain flour
150 ml/$\frac{1}{4}$ pint red wine
300 ml/$\frac{1}{2}$ pint hot water, or use 450 ml/$\frac{3}{4}$ pint chicken stock instead of wine and water
A bouquet garni (*see page 84*) or a bunch of fresh herbs such as thyme and parsley
Finely-peeled zest of $\frac{1}{2}$ orange
25 g/1 oz butter

1. Soak lentils in water overnight. Then drain them.

2. Remove rinds and cut bacon into strips.

3. Peel carrots and cut into 7 mm/$\frac{1}{4}$ inch dice.

4. Peel and chop onion finely.

5. Crush the garlic (*see page 139*).

6. Melt dripping in a pan and fry bacon over a low heat.

7. Add carrots and onion and continue cooking until onion is soft.

8. Stir in flour and mix well.

9. Slowly stir in wine and water.

10. Add lentils, crushed garlic, bouquet garni and herbs, and the orange peel cut in strips.

11. Bring to the boil stirring all the time. Lower heat, cover pan and let it just simmer for about 1 hour or until lentils are cooked. Add more boiling water if necessary.

12. Remove bouquet garni and orange peel. Season to taste. Stir in the butter. It should have the consistency of a thick, mushy cream.

13. Pour into a warmed serving dish.

Jean Welshman
Malton, E. Yorkshire

MARROW STUFFED WITH MUSHROOMS

Serves 4

1 marrow, about 900 g/2 lb
2 small onions
190 g/7 oz mushrooms
1 small tomato
25 g/1 oz butter or margarine
2 tablespoons wholemeal breadcrumbs
$\frac{1}{2}$ level teaspoon sage
Salt
Black pepper
A little hot water, if necessary

Use a dish that will be a tight fit for the marrow.

1. Peel marrow and cut off one end. Scoop out the seeds.

2. Peel onions and chop them finely.

3. Wipe mushrooms and chop them finely.

4. Skin and chop up the tomato. (To skin *see page 139.*)

5. Melt butter or margarine in a frying pan. Fry onions gently for 2 or 3 minutes until soft but not brown.

6. Add mushrooms and fry lightly for 2 or 3 minutes.

7. Mix together tomato, breadcrumbs, sage, a little salt and plenty of black pepper, freshly-milled if possible.

8. Add to this the mushroom mixture and combine it all. It may be best to mix it with your hands. It should feel firm. If it is too dry add 2 or 3 tablespoons hot water.

9. Stuff it into the marrow and replace the cut off end. Cover with well-greased, greaseproof paper and foil and put in a tight-fitting dish.

10. Cook in a moderate oven, Gas 3, 325°F, 160°C, for 2 hours or until marrow is soft all over.

Mrs S.J. Collyer
Camborne, Cornwall

STUFFED MARROW RINGS

Vegetable marrow
Cooked meat—any left over meat, even small quantities can be used
Onion
Soft wholemeal or white breadcrumbs (*see page 52*)
Shredded suet (only if meat is lean)
Made mustard
Salt and Pepper Mix (*see page 17*)
Mixed dried herbs
Beaten egg
Gravy

Cut required number of marrow rings about 3.5 cm/ $1\frac{1}{2}$ inches wide, peel and remove seeds. Place in greased oven tin.

MAKE A FILLING

(a) Put meat through mincer.

(b) To 450 g/1 lb meat add
1 grated onion
50 g/2 oz breadcrumbs
25 g/1 oz suet (only if meat is lean)
1 teaspoon of made mustard
1 teaspoon Salt and Pepper Mix
1 teaspoon mixed dried herbs
1 beaten egg

Mix well together.

Fill rings with mixture. Bake in a moderately hot oven, Gas 5, 375°F, 190°C, for 30 to 40 minutes until marrow is soft.

Serve with a good thick gravy.

See also Marrow Rings Stuffed with Chicken and Mushrooms, page 64.

SAVOURY OATMEAL DUMPLING

Serves 2

1 onion
1 carrot
125 g/4 oz chopped or grated suet
125 g/4 oz medium oatmeal
125 g/4 oz white self-raising flour
½ teaspoon mixed dried herbs
Salt and pepper
A little milk

1. Peel and chop onion. Scrub and chop or grate carrot.
2. Mix onion, carrot, suet and oatmeal and season well with salt and pepper.
3. Add enough milk to make mixture soft but not sticky.
4. Turn dumpling into a greased bowl (a 1.75 litre/ 3 pint size is big enough). Tie a layer of greaseproof paper over the top and put on a covering of foil.
5. Steam for 1 hour. If you do not have a steamer, stand basin on a trivet in a saucepan of boiling water and boil it for 1 hour. Water should come half-way up sides of basin. If replenishing, use boiling water.

Serve hot with brown gravy.

Mrs Margaret Hussey
Leeds

SAVOURY PUDDING

Serves 4

450 g/1 lb wholemeal or white bread, without crusts
300 ml/½ pint, hot, light stock
450 g/1 lb finely-chopped onions
75 g/3 oz shredded suet
1 teaspoon mixed herbs
2 beaten eggs
Salt
Black pepper
1 tablespoon chopped parsley

1. Cut the bread into 2.5 cm/1 inch cubes and soak for 1 hour in hot stock.
2. Add rest of ingredients and beat well. Place in a small, greased roasting tin or pie dish.

3. Cook in a moderate to moderately hot oven, Gas 4 to 5, 350° to 375°F, 180° to 190°C, for 30 to 40 minutes.

Serve on its own with thick gravy or serve with pork or poultry.

STUFFED PEPPERS

Allow 1 pepper per person.

TO PREPARE PEPPERS
1. Cut a piece from stalk end, cut out all membrane and seeds.
2. Blanch pepper by dropping into a pan of boiling water, cook 3 minutes. Drain and dry.
3. Brush outside with a little melted oil or fat, and arrange in lightly greased, shallow casserole.

FILLING FOR 4 LARGE PEPPERS
25 g/1 oz butter or good dripping
1 large grated onion
50 g/2 oz finely-sliced mushrooms
225 g/8 oz chopped ham, chicken, turkey or minced cooked beef
50 g/2 oz wholewheat or white breadcrumbs or cooked long-grain rice
2 teaspoons Worcestershire sauce
1 teaspoon Salt and Pepper Mix (*see page 17*)
A little stock to moisten

A sprinkling of grated cheese can be added before cooking for extra flavour.
1. Melt fat in pan, cook onion and mushrooms for 2 to 3 minutes.
2. Add rest of ingredients but use stock only if mixture is a little dry.
3. Stuff the mixture into the peppers. Add 2 table-spoons of water to casserole. Cook in a moderately hot oven, Gas 5, 375°F, 190°C, for about 40 minutes.

STUFFED JACKET POTATOES

A Meal on Its Own.
1. Choose even-sized potatoes. Scrub well.
2. Prick with fine skewer and rub with beef or bacon dripping.
3. Bake in a moderately hot oven, Gas 6, 400°F, 200°C, for 1 to 1¼ hours (according to size).
4. Cut in half, lengthways. Remove most of inside.
5. Mash with a good piece of butter, adding salt and pepper and 50 g/2 oz. grated cheese per potato.
6. Spoon into shells, place in oven 5 to 10 minutes to heat through.

Nice topped with a bacon roll. De-rind rashers of streaky bacon, roll up and place on large skewer on a baking tray. Cook in oven with potatoes. Will take 15 to 20 minutes.

Try also with an egg. After spooning mashed potato and cheese back into potato case, make a hollow with back of spoon, crack in an egg, put on a nut of butter to stop egg going hard on top and return to oven to reheat potato and set the egg.

MASHED SWEET POTATO

With ham, turkey or chicken

Serves 4

450 g/1 lb sweet potatoes
2 tablespoons milk
50 g/2 oz butter or margarine
300 ml/½ pint béchamel sauce (*see page 187*)
Slices of cold meat
2 tablespoons sharp apple purée

1. Cook sweet potatoes with skins on in water just to cover. Then skin and mash with milk and half of the butter or margarine to a creamy consistency.
2. Make up béchamel sauce.
3. Arrange cold meat in a buttered oven dish.
4. Cover with apple purée and béchamel sauce.
5. Top with sweet potatoes.
6. Smooth the surface and score in a pattern. Dot with butter and brown under the grill.
7. Reheat for 30 minutes in a moderate oven, Gas 4, 350°F, 180°C.

CHEESE ONION AND POTATO PIE

Serves 3 to 4

225 g/8 oz potatoes
50 to 75 g/2 to 3 oz cheese
Half an onion
25 g/1 oz margarine
Salt and pepper
75 ml/3 fl oz milk
Chopped parsley

1. Put the potatoes on to boil until they soften.
2. Meanwhile grate cheese and chop onion finely.
3. Fry onion until golden in half of the margarine.
4. Drain the potatoes and add salt, pepper, milk and remaining margarine. Mash well.
5. Add onion, all but 2 tablespoons of the cheese and a little parsley. Mash well, put into a warmed, oven-proof dish and smooth top.
6. Sprinkle on remaining cheese and put under grill to brown a little before serving. Add final touch of parsley.

Miss Jackie Brindley
Biddulph, Stoke-on-Trent

A delicious variation to Miss Brindley's recipe.
1. Before sprinkling the cheese on top (paragraph 6), make 4 hollows in the mixture with the back of a spoon.
2. Drop an egg into each hollow and put a dot of butter on each.
3. Sprinkle the grated cheese between the eggs.
4. Put in a moderately hot oven, Gas 5, 375°F, 190°C, until eggs set, about 15 minutes.

MUSHROOM AND BUCKWHEAT GOULASH

This dish needs slow cooking to bring out the full flavour. The end result is a beautiful dark, rich stew. Goes well with a contrasting vegetable, such as creamed potatoes or leeks. Contains kidney beans, so remember to start the day before.

Serves 6 to 8, but easy to reduce for small households

125 g/4 oz uncooked red kidney beans (or a mixture of these with pinto and black-eye beans)
1 onion
1 green pepper
2 sticks of celery
2 tablespoons oil
2 teaspoons cinnamon
2 teaspoons paprika
50 g/2 oz unroasted buckwheat
2 tablespoons wholewheat flour
1 to 1.2 litres/1½ to 2 pints stock, from cooking beans
50 g/2 oz walnuts
50 g/2 oz currants
225 g/8 oz mushrooms
Salt and pepper

1. Soak beans overnight in plenty of cold water (*see pages 136 and 137*).
2. Next day, drain and rinse beans and cook in 1.2 litres/2 pints fresh water. Boil them hard for 10 minutes then simmer for a further 45 minutes.
3. Meanwhile, chop up onion, green pepper and celery into bite-sized pieces.
4. Heat oil and fry onion gently with cinnamon and paprika for 3 minutes.
5. Add green pepper, celery and buckwheat. Stir well so that all the vegetables get a light coating of hot oil, which will seal in the flavour, and the buckwheat has a chance to toast slightly, which will enhance the flavour.
6. Stir in flour. Cook for 2 or 3 minutes.
7. Save the liquid as you drain the cooked beans and pour 1 litre/1½ pints over vegetables.
8. Add beans, walnuts, currants and mushrooms. Bring to the boil, stirring well. Put into a casserole and put on lid.
9. Cook in a moderate oven, Gas 3, 325°F, 160°C, for 2 or even 3 hours. Check the seasoning before serving.

Sarah Brown
Scarborough, Yorkshire

NEW ENGLAND CASSEROLE

Can be cooked on top of stove or in oven. Very good with Corn Muffins (*see page 307*). If making muffins while casserole is in oven put dish in coolest part.

Serves 6

Remember to start the day before.

50 g/2 oz red kidney beans
50 g/2 oz black-eye beans
1.2 litres/2 pints water
1 medium-sized onion
1 green pepper
225 g/8 oz marrow or courgettes
1 aubergine
50 g/2 oz raisins
1 cooking apple (about 175 g/6 oz)
Salt and pepper

SAUCE
A 400 g/14 oz can of tomatoes
2 tablespoons cider vinegar
1 tablespoon treacle
1 tablespoon apple juice concentrate
½ tablespoon shoyu (*see page 162*)
Juice of ½ lemon

1. Mix beans together and soak in water overnight.
2. Next day, drain beans, rinse and put in saucepan with 1.2 litres/2 pints fresh cold water. Boil hard for 10 minutes then simmer for 45 minutes more.
3. Meanwhile, mix all sauce ingredients together and simmer for about 20 minutes, or until flavours are well-blended.
4. Chop vegetables into bite-sized pieces.
5. Saving the cooking liquid, drain beans and combine them with vegetables, sauce, raisins and apples. Add some of the bean stock or more tomatoes to moisten if necessary, and salt and pepper according to taste.
6. Cover pan, bring to boil and simmer 20 minutes. *Or*, transfer to a casserole and cook in a moderate oven, Gas 4, 350°F, 180°C, for 45 minutes.

Sarah Brown
Scarborough, Yorkshire

RED BEAN HOT-POT

A well-flavoured substantial main course. Remember to start the night before.

Serves 5, but easy to make less

225 g/8 oz red kidney beans
1.2 litres/2 pints water
1 tablespoon oil, olive oil is best
1 onion, sliced
1 green pepper, sliced
225 g/8 oz courgettes
225 g/8 oz mushrooms
225 g/8 oz tomatoes, peeled (*see page 139*) **and chopped**
2 teaspoons soya sauce
2 teaspoons sage
300 ml/½ pint bean stock
Pepper and salt
450 g/1 lb potatoes, peeled and sliced
25 g/1 oz butter

1. Soak beans overnight.
2. Next day, drain beans and put them in a saucepan with 1.2 litres/2 pints of fresh water. Cover pan and boil beans hard for 10 minutes. Then reduce heat and cook until tender, about 1 to 1½ hours. *Or*, pressure cook for 15 minutes.
3. Saving the cooking liquid, drain beans well.
4. Preheat oven to moderately hot, Gas 6, 400°F, 200°C.
5. Heat oil and fry onion, green pepper, courgettes and mushrooms for 5 minutes.
6. Add tomatoes, cooked beans, soya sauce, sage and 300 ml/½ pint of the bean stock. Add pepper and salt to taste.
7. Put mixture into a greased shallow casserole and lay sliced potatoes on top. Cover with a lid or greaseproof paper and foil.
8. Cook for 45 minutes to 1 hour until potatoes are cooked. Then remove cover, dot potatoes with butter, return to top shelf of oven and cook for 10 minutes more until potatoes are brown on top.

Serve with fresh green vegetables.

Janet Horsley
Author of 'The Bean Cuisine'

RED KIDNEY BEAN RISSOLES

Remember to start the night before.

Makes 12 to 14 rissoles

225 g/8 oz red kidney beans
1.2 litres/2 pints water
2 onions, finely-chopped
50 g/2 oz wholewheat flour
1 tablespoon soya sauce
1 teaspoon dried rosemary or sage
Pepper and salt

FOR FRYING
A little oil

1. Soak beans overnight. Drain away the water.
2. Next day, put beans in 1.2 litres/2 pints of fresh cold water. Cover pan and boil hard for 10 minutes, then reduce heat and cook for 1 to 1½ hours until beans are tender. *Or*, pressure cook for 15 minutes.
3. Drain, keep aside half of the beans and mash the rest.
4. Combine all the ingredients, seasoning to taste. Leave aside in a cool place to firm up, about 30 minutes.
5. Shape round rissoles using about 2 tablespoons of mixture for each one. Leave aside in a cool place for 15 minutes to firm up.
6. Heat oil and fry rissoles for 3 to 4 minutes each side until cooked through and lightly-browned and crisp on the outside.

Serve with fried potatoes and a green salad.

Janet Horsley
Headingley, Yorkshire

BAKED STUFFED TOMATOES

Serves 2

4 large firm tomatoes
1 tablespoon grated onion
100 g/4 oz grated cheese
1 thick slice wholemeal or white bread made into crumbs
50 g/2 oz chopped mushrooms (optional)
Salt and pepper
2 rashers bacon

1. Stand tomatoes stalk end down, slice off rounded end and scoop out insides with a teaspoon.

2. Mix tomato pulp with onion, cheese, bread-crumbs, mushrooms and seasoning. This forms a crumbly mixture.

3. Fill tomato shells, replace the tops.

4. Spread remaining mixtures in a small, greased, oven-proof dish. Make 4 hollows in mixture and stand tomatoes in them.

5. Remove rinds from bacon. Cut rashers in halves. Stretch each piece on a board with back of a knife and make it into a roll.

6. Thread bacon rolls on a skewer. Lay these across tomatoes.

7. Bake in middle of a moderately hot oven, Gas 5, 375°F, 190°C, for 20 minutes.

8. To serve, remove skewer and arrange bacon rolls.

Margaret Heywood
Todmorden, Yorkshire

ENGLISH VEGETABLE COBBLER

Can be made without cobbler. Really economical.

Serves 6, but easy to make in quite small quantities

1 tablespoon oil
2 onions, sliced
225 g/8 oz parsnip
225 g/8 oz swede or white turnip
225 g/8 oz carrot
2 sticks of celery, diced
125 g/4 oz cooked field beans or carlins or 50 to 75 g/2 to 3 oz uncooked beans (*see page 136*)
600 ml/1 pint stock, save cooking water from beans
1 tablespoon parsley
2 teaspoons dried sage
Salt and pepper

COBBLER TOPPING
125 g/4 oz self-raising brown* or white flour
A pinch of salt
25 g/1 oz butter or vegetable margarine
25 g/1 oz grated cheese
About 3 tablespoons milk

*81% *extraction rather than pure wholewheat self-raising flour is preferable and often easier to obtain.*

1. Heat oil and fry onions until transparent.

2. Chop root vegetables into bite-sized pieces and toss in the saucepan with onions. Add celery. Allow these vegetables to cook gently for 10 minutes.

3. Add cooked field beans and stock, herbs and seasoning. Bring to the boil, cover pan and simmer gently for 20 minutes. Check seasoning.

4. Meanwhile, make topping, just like a scone. Mix flour and salt.

5. Rub in butter or margarine to form fine bread-crumbs. Mix in cheese.

6. Mix with enough milk to form a soft dough.

7. Knead lightly on floured board. Roll out 7 mm/ ¼ inch thick. Cut into circles.

8. Put vegetable and bean mix in an oven dish.

9. Lay scone circles overlapping on top.

10. Bake near top of a moderately hot oven, Gas 6, 400°F, 200°C, for 20 minutes. Topping will rise slightly and brown. Mixture will bubble underneath.

Nice with baked potatoes.

STIR-FRY VEGETABLES WITH BEANSPROUTS

Serves 4 to 5 as a light meal

2 tablespoons oil, sesame oil is best
1 onion, cut into rings
A clove of garlic, crushed
½ to 1 teaspoon ground ginger
1 green pepper, thinly-sliced
1 large carrot, scrubbed and thinly-sliced
1 leek, sliced
125 g/4 oz small button mushrooms
150 ml/¼ pint water
1 to 2 tablespoons white wine (optional)
1 to 2 teaspoons soya sauce
225 g/8 oz beansprouts

1. Heat oil in a large frying pan with a lid.

2. Fry onion, garlic and ginger until soft but not brown.

3. Add green pepper and fry for 1 minute more.

4. Toss in carrot and fry 3 or 4 minutes more, stirring often.

5. Add leek and mushrooms and stir-fry 3 or 4 minutes more.

6. Stir in water, wine and soya sauce and lay bean-sprouts on top.

7. Cover pan, bring to boil and simmer very gently for 1 minute before serving.

Serve with brown rice (*see page 172*) or wholewheat pasta.

Janet Horsley
Headingley, Yorkshire

6

RICE PASTA PANCAKES SAUCES FRITTERS EGGS CHEESE SAVOURIES SNACKS AND SANDWICH SPREADS

BOILED RICE

This is the best way of making fluffy white rice to serve with curries and other savoury dishes. This method is suitable for all good rice, Basmati, Patna, Chinese, Japanese and Italian. For part-cooked rice follow manufacturers' instructions on packet.

Serves 4

1 cup rice (washed in a sieve under running cold water until the water runs clear)
2 cups water
Salt and pepper

1. Put rice and water in a saucepan and bring to the boil.
2. Stir, cover pan, put on a well-fitting lid, reduce heat and simmer for 15 minutes. At the end of that time the rice will have absorbed all the water and be perfectly cooked, but *it is vital* that the lid be kept on for the full 15 minutes.
3. Fluff with a fork, season to taste and serve.
Brown rice may also be cooked in exactly the same way but 25 minutes is required for it to absorb the water.

Priya Wickramasinghe
Cardiff

SAVOURY RICE

To serve with chops, steak, gammon etc.

Serves 4 to 5

1 tablespoon cooking oil
225 g/8 oz uncooked rice
450 ml/¾ pint hot, well-flavoured stock
Salt and pepper

1. Heat oil in large pan, add rice, and stir gently until oil is absorbed. Do not allow rice to colour.
2. Add stock, test seasoning and bring to boil.
3. Transfer to a 1.5 litre/2½ pint casserole, cover tightly. Cook in a moderately hot oven, Gas 6, 400°F, 200°C, until stock is absorbed and rice is cooked, adding extra water or stock if becoming too dry. Time, approximately 45 minutes.

TO SERVE
Add cooked peas, cooked diced carrot (or a packet of frozen mixed vegetables, cooked), or lightly-fried, sliced mushrooms.

SRI LANKAN YELLOW RICE

This delicately flavoured dish goes well with chicken curries (*see page 60*), Cashew Nut Curry (*see page 174*), Onion Salad (*see page 144*) and poppadoms.

Serves 4

1 cup rice
125 g/4 oz creamed coconut*
2 cups hot water
½ medium-sized onion, finely-chopped
2 tablespoons ghee (*see page 62*), butter or oil
A few curry leaves (*see page 62*)
3 cloves
3 cardamoms
A 2.5 cm/1 inch piece of cinnamon stick
1 teaspoon salt
¼ teaspoon saffron or turmeric
8 peppercorns

Can be bought at wholefood and oriental food shops.

1. Wash rice in a sieve under running water and leave to drain.
2. Dissolve creamed coconut in the hot water.
3. Fry onion in the oil.
4. Add all the other dry ingredients and fry over a low heat, stirring until the grains of rice become yellow.
5. Add coconut liquid and bring to a rapid boil.
6. Cover with a well-fitting lid, reduce heat and simmer for 15 minutes. Simmer 25 minutes if brown rice is used.

Priya Wickramasinghe
Cardiff

TO RE-HEAT RICE

1. Grease a suitable oven dish lightly with butter, tip in cooked rice, put a few shavings of butter on top, cover tightly.
2. Put in a moderate oven, Gas 4, 350°F, 180°C, for about 30 minutes. Stir lightly with fork before serving.

INDIAN FRIED RICE

Goes well with Chicken and Almonds (*see page 53*).

Long grain white or brown rice
1 onion
1 tablespoon butter or oil
1 teaspoon turmeric
1 teaspoon cumin
Salt and pepper
A little curry powder (optional)

1. Cook as much rice as required (*see page 172*).
2. Peel and finely chop onion.
3. Heat butter or oil in a heavy frying pan and fry onion gently until softening but not brown.
4. Add turmeric and cumin and cook a little.
5. Stir in rice and heat gently.
6. Add salt and pepper and a little curry powder to taste.

Betty Yeatman
Adelaide, South Australia

CURRY SAUCE

300 ml/½ pint light stock
1 heaped tablespoon coconut
25 g/1 oz butter or good dripping
1 finely-chopped onion
1 thinly-sliced apple
1 level tablespoon curry powder
1 level tablespoon plain flour
1 tablespoon sultanas
1 tablespoon chutney
1 dessertspoon brown sugar
1 dessertspoon lemon juice

1. Boil stock and pour it over the coconut. Leave to infuse for 10 to 15 minutes. Strain stock, discard coconut.
2. Melt fat in pan, add onion and apple and soften them a little. Stir in curry powder and flour, allow to sizzle and cook, stirring, for 2 minutes.
3. Stir in the stock, bring to boil, simmer 15 minutes.
4. Add remaining ingredients, simmer a further 15 minutes. If becoming too thick, add a little more stock, but the sauce should not be thin.

Serve over hot hard-boiled eggs. Or add cooked meat and vegetables towards end of cooking time, making sure these are thoroughly heated through before serving.

EGG CURRY

Serves 6

6 eggs
2 teaspoons salt
¼ teaspoon turmeric
3 tablespoons oil
Half a medium-sized onion, chopped
25 g/1 oz creamed coconut*
300 ml/½ pint hot water
2 cloves of garlic, chopped
¼ teaspoon fresh ginger (*see page 62*) chopped
A 5 cm/2 inch piece of cinnamon stick
1 dessertspoon ground coriander
1 teaspoon ground cumin
1 teaspoon chilli powder
¼ teaspoon ground fenugreek
A sprig of curry leaves*, if available
Juice of half a lemon

*Can be bought at oriental and some wholefood shops.

1. Boil eggs for 11 minutes and shell them.
2. Mix salt and turmeric and rub it into eggs. Use a pin and prick them in several places so that they do not burst when fried.
3. Heat 3 tablespoons oil and fry eggs until golden brown, about 2 minutes. Lift eggs out of pan.
4. Fry onions until golden brown.
5. Dissolve creamed coconut in the hot water. Add this to pan with all other ingredients, except eggs and lemon juice. Simmer, stirring occasionally, until sauce is thick.
6. Add eggs and lemon juice and allow to simmer for a further 5 minutes.

Serve with Boiled Rice (*see page 187*), or Sri Lankan Yellow Rice (*see page 172*) and vegetables and salads.

Priya Wickramasinghe
Cardiff

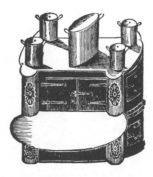

SAUSAGES IN A CURRY SAUCE

No need for oven.

Serves 4, but easy to make less for 1 or 2

675 g/1½ lb sausages
25 g/1 oz dripping
225 g/8 oz brown rice
1 onion, chopped
1 apple, chopped
1 level tablespoon curry powder
1 rounded tablespoon plain flour
A 225 g/8 oz tin of apricot halves
1 green pepper, cut in thin strips
1 dessertspoon mango or good chutney
2 teaspoons lemon juice
Salt and Pepper Mix (*see page 17*)

1. Fry sausages gently in dripping until golden brown. Remove on to a plate, draining all but 1 tablespoon of the fat. (Save this tasty extra fat for something else.)
2. Meanwhile, put rice on to cook, following instructions for Boiled Rice on *page 172*. Keep sausages warm on top of rice pan.
3. Fry onion in sausage pan until softening.
4. Add apple and fry for 2 to 3 minutes.
5. Stir in curry powder, let it sizzle, then stir in flour and cook for 1 minute.
6. Strain juice from apricots into a measure and make up to 300 ml/½ pint with water.
7. Add liquid to pan, stir until boiling.
8. Add green pepper, chutney, lemon juice, salt and pepper. Let sauce simmer for 20 minutes, adding a little more water if it becomes too thick. Add apricots to heat through.
9. Put rice around edge of a serving dish, sausages in the middle, and pour sauce over sausages. Garnish with apricots.

CASHEW NUT CURRY

A favourite Sri Lankan dish.

Serves 4

225 g/8 oz cashew nuts
1 litre/1½ pints cold water
½ teaspoon bicarbonate of soda
1 tablespoon oil
1 medium-sized onion, finely-chopped
2 cloves
2 cardamoms
2 pieces of cinnamon stick, each about 2.5 cm/1 inch long
1½ teaspoons ground coriander
1 teaspoon ground cumin
¼ teaspoon turmeric
1 teaspoon salt
25 g/1 oz creamed coconut
125 ml/4 fl oz hot water

1. Soak the cashew nuts for 8 hours in cold water to which bicarbonate of soda has been added. Drain away water and wash cashew nuts.
2. In a pan, heat oil and fry onions until lightly-browned.
3. Pound or grind the cloves, cardamoms and cinnamon sticks.
4. Add them to pan with rest of spices, salt and cashew nuts and mix thoroughly.
5. Add creamed coconut dissolved in the hot water and bring to the boil.
6. Put lid on pan, lower heat and simmer for 15 minutes.

Serve with Lentil Rice (*see page 174*), or Sri Lankan Yellow Rice (*see page 172*) and a meat dish such as Chicken Curry (*see page 60*), or Egg Curry (*see page 173*). Also Cucumber in Yoghurt (*see page 142*) and Onion Salad (*see page 144*).

Priya Wickramasinghe
Cardiff

LENTIL RICE

Serves 4

½ cup yellow moong dhal*
½ cup long grained rice, white or brown
2 tablespoons oil
1 medium-sized onion, sliced
½ teaspoon salt
½ teaspoon turmeric
2 cups hot water, use same cup as for lentils
    and rice
½ teaspoon ground cumin
¼ teaspoon mustard seed
A few curry leaves (*see page 62*)

*Moong dhal is the lentil most widely used in Asian countries. When used whole it can be sprouted and becomes the familiar Chinese beansprout. Yellow moong dhal is the split version with the green husk removed.

1. Wash the lentils and soak them in plenty of water for 2 hours. If using brown rice, soak it also.
2. Wash and drain lentils and rice in a sieve.
3. Heat oil and fry onion until lightly-browned.
4. Add rice and lentils and fry over low heat for about 5 minutes.
5. Add all the other ingredients and bring to the boil.
6. Cover with a well-fitting lid, reduce heat and simmer for 15 minutes.

It is nice to serve this with pickles such as Date Chutney (*see page 379*), or Tomato Relish (*see page 383*) and with Poppadoms (*see page 62*).

Priya Wickramasinghe
Cardiff

SPICY RISOTTO

This is an ideal way of using meat left over from the Sunday joint. When served with a green salad it provides a balanced meal.

Serves 4

1 cup Basmati* or long-grain brown or white
    rice
2 tablespoons oil
1 medium-sized onion, finely-chopped
2 medium-sized carrots, grated
Half a green pepper, chopped
225 g/8 oz cooked meat cut into small pieces
    (lamb, pork or chicken)
1 teaspoon salt
½ cup frozen peas
⅛ teaspoon ground cardamom
¼ teaspoon ground cinnamon
¼ teaspoon ground cloves
2 cups hot water, use same cup as for rice

*Basmati rice is the best of all the varieties of white rice. It has a distinctive aroma and flavour.

1. Wash the rice in a sieve and allow to drain.
2. Heat oil and fry onion until lightly-browned.
3. Add the rice and fry for about 5 minutes on a low heat, stirring all the time.
4. Add rest of ingredients and bring rapidly to the boil.
5. Reduce heat to a minimum, put on well-fitting lid and cook for 15 minutes. If using brown rice cook 25 minutes.

Priya Wickramasinghe
Cardiff

PILAFF OF LAMB WITH COURGETTES

Enough for 4 but easy to make for 1 or 2 people

50 g/2 oz butter or margarine
225 g/8 oz cold, cooked lamb, cut in 1 cm/ ½ inch cubes
175 g/6 oz uncooked brown or white rice
1 medium-sized onion, chopped
2 tablespoons diced celery
2 tablespoons diced green pepper
1 small clove of garlic, crushed
200 ml/7 fl oz stock
1 tablespoon Worcestershire sauce
½ teaspoon salt
A dash of pepper
125 g/4 oz unpeeled courgettes, sliced in 1 cm/ ½ inch slices
25 g/1 oz grated Parmesan cheese

1. Melt butter in a large heavy saucepan.
2. Add lamb, rice, onion, celery, green pepper and garlic. Cook, stirring, until rice is transparent.
3. Stir in stock, Worcestershire sauce, salt and pepper. Bring to boil.
4. Lower heat, cover pan and cook for 10 minutes. If using brown rice cook 15 to 20 minutes.
5. Stir in courgettes and cook covered for 10 minutes longer.

Serve sprinkled with Parmesan.

See under Rice Dishes in Index for many other curry, pilaff and risotto recipes and a variety of savoury and sweet rice dishes.

MACARONI CHEESE

Serves 4

175 g/6 oz macaroni
40 g/1½ oz margarine
40 g/1½ oz flour
½ level teaspoon made mustard
¼ teaspoon Salt and Pepper Mix (*see page 17*)
450 ml/¾ pint milk
175 g/6 oz grated cheese

1. Cook macaroni in fast-boiling salted water for 15 minutes. Drain well.
2. Melt margarine, stir in the flour and cook 2 minutes. Add mustard and Salt and Pepper Mix. Stir in milk gradually. Bring to boil and stir over heat for 2 minutes as it thickens. Remove from heat and beat in 125 g/4 oz of the grated cheese.
3. Add macaroni, pour into a greased, oven-proof dish, sprinkle on remaining cheese.
4. Bake in the centre of a moderately hot oven, Gas 5, 375°F, 190°C, for 15 to 20 minutes until beginning to bubble and turning golden.

VARIATIONS
Add 2 tablespoons of fresh white breadcrumbs to last 50 g/2 oz cheese before sprinkling on top. Makes it crisp.
Or, as a garnish, for the last 10 minutes of cooking time, put slices of skinned tomato on top brushed with a little oil or melted fat.
Or, add with the macaroni (paragraph 3) 125 g/4 oz cooked, cubed ham or lean bacon, and small tin of sweetcorn with peppers.

LANDER MACCARONEN

A Swiss dish.

Serves 4 to 5

2 medium-sized potatoes
225 g/8 oz brown or white macaroni
2 small onions
50 g/2 oz butter
150 ml/¼ pint milk
125 g/4 oz grated cheese

1. Peel and cut potato into roughly even-sized pieces, about the size of walnuts.
2. Put potato into a pan of boiling, salted water and boil for 3 minutes.
3. Add macaroni and boil for 7 to 10 minutes.
4. While this is boiling, peel and slice onions and fry in butter until golden. Drain onions, leaving butter in frying pan.
5. Drain potatoes and macaroni and place in layers with the cheese in a warm serving dish.
6. Place onions on top.
7. Pour milk into the frying pan and bring to the boil. Pour it over the onions and serve immediately.

Judith Adshead
Mottram St Andrew, Cheshire

CREAMY MACARONI AND VEGETABLES

A nice macaroni cheese which is also pleasant to eat cold as a salad.

Serves 4

150 ml/¼ pint natural yoghurt
50 g/2 oz cottage cheese
50 g/2 oz cream cheese
125 g/4 oz leeks, weighed after preparing
125 g/4 oz macaroni, try wholewheat
2 sticks of celery
Half a green pepper
Half a red pepper
½ teaspoon caraway seeds, or dill weed*
1 dessertspoon shoyu (*see page 162*) or Worces-
**   tershire sauce**
Salt and pepper
50 g/2 oz grated Cheddar cheese

If you are not fond of the flavour of caraway or dill you can use instead a mixture of mustard and paprika.

1. Mix together yoghurt, cottage and cream cheeses.
2. Wash leeks well and slice quite finely.
3. Blanch leeks by immersing them in a pan of boiling water. Bring to the boil and then drain.
4. Cook macaroni in boiling salted water until just tender.
5. Chop celery and peppers finely.
6. Combine vegetables, macaroni and yoghurt mixture, add caraway seeds and shoyu and taste for seasoning.
7. Put in an oven dish and cover with grated cheese.
8. Bake near top of a moderate oven, Gas 4, 350°F, 180°C, for 30 minutes.

Sarah Brown
Scarborough, Yorkshire

MACARONI FRITTERS WITH TOMATO SAUCE

Also a way to use up other left-over cooked pasta.

Serves 2

75 g/3 oz brown or white macaroni
or
125 g/4 oz cooked pasta cut up small
1 level tablespoon plain flour
2 tablespoons milk
2 eggs
50 g/2 oz grated Parmesan cheese
Salt and Pepper Mix (*see page 17*)
Oil for frying

TOMATO SAUCE
A 225 g/8 oz can of tomatoes
1 tablespoon oil
1 small onion, peeled and grated
A good pinch of sugar
Salt and Pepper Mix (*see page 17*)
Pinch of basil or ½ bay leaf (optional)

1. Put macaroni on to cook, following directions on packet.
2. Put into a small pan all the tomato sauce ingredients, bring to the boil and simmer for 20 minutes. Crush tomatoes with a wooden spoon to thicken sauce. While sauce cooks continue with fritters.
3. Drain cooked macaroni and allow to cool a little.
4. Put flour in a bowl and gradually stir in the milk to make a smooth paste.
5. Add eggs, beat lightly with a fork to mix well.
6. Stir in the cheese, season and add macaroni. Stir well to mix.

7. Heat a little oil in a large frying pan. Put the mixture in four, large separate spoonfuls into the pan.

8. Cook gently for 2 to 3 minutes on each side.

Serve at once with the sauce. Sauce may be sieved if you prefer it smooth.

SPAGHETTI IN CREAM SAUCE

Serves 2

1 teaspoon cooking oil
125 g/4 oz spaghetti rings. Try also pasta shells, spirals or shortcut macaroni
125 g/4 oz chopped streaky bacon
50 g/2 oz sliced mushrooms or 2 skinned and chopped tomatoes (*see page 139*)
2 tablespoons cider or dry white wine
A good grating of black pepper
2 beaten eggs
4 tablespoons single cream or good top of milk
50 g/2 oz grated cheese

TO SERVE
Extra grated cheese or grated Parmesan

1. Use a large pan and half fill it with water. Bring water to the boil and add oil. Drop in the spaghetti rings, keep water boiling and cook for 10 to 14 minutes until soft but still firm. Exact cooking time depends on type of pasta. Do not overcook or it may disintegrate when sauce is added. Drain well and return to pan.

2. Meanwhile, fry chopped bacon gently until lightly crisp.

3. Add prepared mushrooms and cook 1 minute.

4. Pour in the cider, turn off heat and grate the pepper over the mixture.

5. Mix eggs and cream or top of milk and add to spaghetti.

6. Place over low heat, stir in cheese. Add tomatoes here if used. Add bacon mixture and stir until sauce thickens but do not let it boil.

7. Pour into hot dish. Serve on hot plates with extra grated cheese, Parmesan if you have it, to sprinkle on top.

SPAGHETTI WITH HAM, BLACK OLIVES AND PARSLEY

Serves 4

Boiling water
Level teaspoon salt
325 g/12 oz brown or white spaghetti
125 g/4 oz cooked ham
50 g/2 oz firm black olives
2 tablespoons chopped parsley
300 ml/½ pint single cream or 225 ml/8 fl oz natural yoghurt
Black pepper

1. Fill a large pan, three quarters full of boiling water. Add the salt.

2. Gently work spaghetti into pan, moving it with a fork so that it does not stick together.

3. Cook spaghetti in the boiling water for 15 to 20 minutes. (10 to 12 minutes for white spaghetti.) It is done when a piece will break apart neatly between finger and thumb. This is called *al dente*. If it is overdone it will be mushy when mixed with other ingredients.

4. Meanwhile, chop up ham finely and remove stones from olives.

5. Drain spaghetti. Return it to pan with ham, olives, 1 tablespoon of parsley, the cream or yoghurt and plenty of freshly-milled black pepper. Toss over a medium heat until piping hot. Sprinkle remaining chopped parsley on top just before serving. Eat at once.

SPAGHETTI WITH MEAT SAUCE

Serves 4 but easy to make less or more.

2 medium-sized onions
2 medium-sized carrots
1 clove garlic
1 tablespoon oil
225 g/8 oz minced beef
2 tablespoons tomato purée*, or 1 small can peeled tomatoes
Pinch basil or mixed herbs
A wine glass of red wine (optional)
300 ml/½ pint beef stock
50 g/2 oz mushrooms
15 g/½ oz butter or margarine
325 g/12 oz brown spaghetti, if available
50 g/2 oz finely-grated cheese, to serve

To keep tomato purée fresh, see page 84.

1. Peel and finely chop onions.
2. Scrub and chop carrots.
3. Peel and crush garlic (*see page 139*).
4. Heat oil in a large pan and fry onions gently for 3 or 4 minutes.
5. Add meat and stir it around over the heat until it separates and colours.
6. Add carrot, garlic, tomato, herbs, wine and enough of the stock just to keep it moist.
7. Put lid on and let sauce simmer gently for 30 minutes, stirring occasionally and adding more stock if necessary.
8. Chop up mushrooms.
9. Put spaghetti on to cook in plenty of boiling, lightly-salted water 15 minutes before it is required.
10. Fry mushrooms lightly in butter or margarine for 2 to 3 minutes and stir them into sauce just before you serve it.
11. Put cheese in a small bowl and serve separately.

A RICH MEAT SAUCE FOR SPAGHETTI

This sauce freezes well.

2 rashers streaky bacon
1 onion
A clove of garlic
1 small pig's kidney
2 tablespoons oil
225 g/8 oz beef mince
1 carrot
1 tablespoon tomato purée*
150 to 300 ml/¼ to ½ pint stock
A pinch of mixed herbs
Black pepper
Salt
2 teaspoons wholewheat flour or cornflour
1 tablespoon water

To keep tomato purée fresh, see page 84.

TO SERVE
Wholewheat spaghetti, if you can get it.
A little grated cheese, preferably Parmesan.

1. Remove rinds from bacon and cut it very small.
2. Peel and finely chop onion. Crush garlic.
3. Dice the kidney very finely.
4. Heat oil and fry bacon gently.
5. Add onion, garlic, mince and kidney. Cook gently for 5 minutes. Stir occasionally.
6. Grate the carrot and add it with tomato purée, 150 ml/¼ pint stock, herbs, pepper and salt. Bring to the boil.
7. Lower heat, cover pan and simmer for 20 minutes. Stir occasionally to prevent sticking, and add more stock if necessary.
8. Meanwhile, cook spaghetti in plenty of boiling salted water.
9. Thicken meat sauce at last minute, if necessary, by mixing flour and water, stirring in and bringing back to the boil.

Serve the grated cheese separately in a small bowl.

CASHEW AND APPLE SAVOURIES

Baked in a tray of 6 Yorkshire pudding tins, allowing one for each person. Served with pasta and a cold creamy piquant sauce.

Enough for 6 generous helpings

225 g/8 oz ground cashew nuts*
1 onion, chopped
A clove of garlic, crushed
50 g/2 oz butter
1 green pepper, chopped
$\frac{1}{4}$ teaspoon each of marjoram, thyme, ground cumin and paprika
50 g/2 oz wholewheat flour
2 tablespoons sweet sherry or madeira
150 ml/$\frac{1}{4}$ pint light vegetable stock (water from cooking chestnuts is ideal) or use apple or grape juice
50 to 75 g/2 to 3 oz fresh breadcrumbs, wholewheat if possible
1 large cooking apple, grated skin and all
Salt and pepper
50 to 75 g/2 to 3 oz fancy pasta, wholewheat if possible

TO GARNISH
Slices of tomato and lemon

*If you cannot buy ground cashew nuts you can grind your own in an electric coffee grinder.

1. Fry onion and garlic gently in butter until transparent.
2. Add green pepper, herbs and spices and fry a further 3 minutes.
3. Stir in flour and cook for 1 minute.
4. Stir in sherry or madeira and stock or fruit juice. Bring to boil and stir over low heat for 2 minutes.
5. Remove pan from heat. Mix in cashews, breadcrumbs and apple. Season with salt and pepper to taste.
6. Spoon mixture into greased tins.
7. Bake in middle of a moderately hot oven, Gas 5, 375°F, 190°C, for about 20 minutes or until cooked thoroughly and browned on top.
8. Meanwhile, cook pasta in boiling, slightly-salted water until tender.
9. Make the sauce.

CREAMY PIQUANT SAUCE
225 g/8 oz cottage cheese
2 tablespoons mayonnaise or cream cheese
2 tablespoons yoghurt
2 tablespoons oil
1 tablespoon cider vinegar
1 tablespoon lemon juice
Herbs to taste—e.g., dillweed, chives or tarragon

Put all ingredients together in a liquidiser and blend until smooth.
Or, if you do not have a liquidiser, press cottage cheese through a sieve, then beat in remaining ingredients.

Sarah Brown
Scarborough, Yorkshire

CANNELLONI

Freezes well, but this should be done before final cooking in oven.

Serves 4

12 cannelloni tubes, the ready-to-bake variety are easiest to use

FILLING
1 medium onion, finely-chopped
A clove of garlic, crushed
2 tablespoons oil
175 g/6 oz minced beef
1 tablespoon tomato ketchup
1 tablespoon Worcestershire sauce
1 teaspoon oregano
Salt and pepper
1 tablespoon grated cheese
A 250 g/9 oz tin of spinach
1 beaten egg

TOMATO SAUCE
1 dessertspoon cornflour
2 tablespoons milk
About 600 g/1 lb 6 oz tomatoes
1 tablespoon tomato ketchup
1 teaspoon sugar
1 level teaspoon oregano
1 level teaspoon sweet basil
Salt and pepper

TO COVER
40 g/1$\frac{1}{2}$ oz grated cheese

1. Fry onion and garlic in oil until soft but not brown.
2. Stir in the mince and cook about 10 minutes. Turn off heat.
3. Stir in remaining filling ingredients, except egg. Allow to cool.
4. Mix in beaten egg.
5. Fill cannelloni tubes with mixture and place them in a buttered, shallow, oven dish.
6. *For the tomato sauce,* slake cornflour by mixing it with milk till smooth.
7. Put all sauce ingredients with cornflour mixture into a pan. Stir over medium heat until boiling.
8. Reduce heat and cook the sauce for 3 minutes, stirring all the time.
9. Pour sauce over cannelloni, sprinkle with grated cheese.
10. Cook at top of a moderate oven, Gas 4, 350°F, 180°C, for 30 minutes.

Elizabeth Mickery
Pudsey, West Yorkshire

LASAGNE

Serves 4. Served with salad, enough for 6.

325 g/12 oz lasagne
1.3 kg/3 lb fresh spinach
175 g/6 oz Mozzarella cheese, thinly-sliced*
125 g/4 oz grated Parmesan cheese

Cheddar cheese can be used.

SAUCE
40 g/1½ oz butter or margarine
1 finely-chopped onion
A crushed clove of garlic
1 chopped green pepper, core and seeds removed
225 g/8 oz minced beef
Two 400 g/14 oz tins of tomatoes
4 tablespoons tomato purée*
1 teaspoon paprika pepper
Pepper and a little salt

To keep tomato purée fresh, see page 84.

1. Put lasagne on to cook in boiling salted water, but put it into water 2 or 3 sheets at a time to prevent it sticking together. Then let it all boil together for about 15 minutes.
2. Wash spinach and simmer it without extra water until just tender. Drain and chop.
3. Meanwhile start sauce. Heat butter or margarine

in a pan. Fry onion, garlic and green pepper for 5 minutes.
4. Stir in beef and fry until it loses its pinkness.
5. Add remaining sauce ingredients, bring to the boil and simmer for 30 minutes.
6. Line the bottom of a well-greased oven dish with about a third of the lasagne.
7. Cover with half of the cooked spinach, then half of the Mozzarella, then half of the sauce.
8. Sprinkle on about a third of the grated Parmesan cheese.
9. Continue making layers, finishing with a thick layer of Parmesan cheese.
10. Put into a moderate oven, Gas 4, 350°F, 180°C, and cook for about 40 minutes.

Judith Adshead
Mottram St Andrew, Cheshire

LASAGNE WITH VEGETABLES

A substantial dish, nutritionally well-balanced. Freezes well for a week or so.

Serves 4 to 6

125 to 175 g/4 to 6 oz aduki beans, soaked overnight
125 to 175 g/4 to 6 oz Brussels sprouts
125 g/4 oz cabbage
125 g/4 oz mushrooms
1 leek
1 carrot
½ green pepper
1 onion
A clove of garlic (optional)
1 tablespoon oil
600 ml/1 pint stock saved from cooking aduki beans
2 tablespoons tomato purée
1 teaspoon oregano
1 teaspoon marjoram
Salt and pepper
175 g/6 oz lasagne, wholewheat if you can get it
75 g/3 oz grated cheese

SAUCE
20 g/¾ oz butter or vegetable margarine
20 g/¾ oz wholewheat flour
450 ml/¾ pint milk
Salt and pepper

1. Remember to start the night before by soaking aduki beans in cold water (*see page 137*).

2. Drain beans, rinse and bring to boil in at least 1.2 litres/2 pints fresh water. Boil for 40 minutes.

3. Cut up all vegetables, except onion and garlic, into even-sized, quite small pieces.

4. Chop onion finely, crush garlic and fry in oil in a large pan until translucent.

5. Mix in prepared vegetables and cook for 5 minutes, stirring occasionally.

6. Drain aduki beans, saving the water, and add them to vegetables.

7. Mix tomato purée into 600 ml/1 pint of the bean stock and pour this over vegetables and beans.

8. Mix well, adding herbs and salt and pepper to taste. Allow to simmer for 30 minutes, stirring occasionally. Adjust seasoning.

9. Meanwhile, make sauce. Melt butter or margarine over low heat, stir in flour and let it sizzle for 1 minute. Gradually add milk, stirring as it thickens and comes to boil. Cook for 3 minutes.

10. Soak lasagne in hot water for 3 to 5 minutes.

11. Grease an oven dish. Make layers of lasagne, vegetables and sauce, ending with a layer of sauce.

12. Put grated cheese on top.

13. Bake near top of a moderate oven, Gas 4, 350°F, 180°C, for 30 minutes until cheese is golden and bubbling and lasagne is cooked.

Serve with green salad, steamed courgettes or broccoli (*see page 150*).

Sarah Brown
Scarborough, Yorkshire

MIXED FRIED NOODLES, INDONESIAN-STYLE

Made with chicken and prawns.

Serves 4

225 g/8 oz egg noodles
1 to 2 tablespoons vegetable oil
Half a medium-sized onion, finely-chopped
2 cloves of garlic, finely-chopped
125 g/4 oz uncooked chicken flesh, cut into very small pieces
125 g/4 oz prawns, shelled
1 stick celery, finely-chopped
50 g/2 oz Chinese cabbage
½ teaspoon salt
1 tablespoon soya sauce
3 spring onions, sliced
Half a cucumber, finely-sliced
1 tablespoon onion flakes

1. Cook the noodles according to the directions on the packet, making sure not to overcook them. Then drain in a colander until needed.

2. In a wok or large frying pan heat the oil.

3. Add onion, garlic, chicken and prawns and stir-fry over a medium to high heat until the chicken and prawns are cooked, about 3 to 5 minutes.

4. Add the celery and cabbage and stir-fry for a few seconds.

5. Add noodles and salt and mix thoroughly.

6. Lastly, add soya sauce and cook for a further minute or so until the dish is heated through.

7. Serve in 4 shallow bowls and garnish with spring onion, cucumber and fried onion flakes.

Priya Wickramasinghe
Cardiff

PANCAKES

This quantity of batter will make about 14 pancakes 15 cm/6 inches in diameter

125 g/4 oz plain flour
½ teaspoon salt
Lard
1 large egg
300 ml/½ pint milk

Use a small frying pan.

1. Place flour and salt in basin. Make a well in centre.

2. Drop in egg and begin to mix gradually adding 150 ml/¼ pint of the milk as the flour is drawn in from the sides.

3. Beat well until bubbles are visible.

4. Gradually beat in remaining milk.

5. Put into a jug for easier pouring into the pan.

6. Heat pan and add a piece of lard (size of hazel nut). Allow to spread over pan and become fairly hot.

7. Pour in a little batter, tilting pan to cover. When nicely golden, toss or turn over to cook the other side. Repeat to use all the batter.

The pancakes can be frozen at this stage. Lay pancakes as they are cooked on a clean cloth placed on a large cooling wire. When cool, pack flat, with greaseproof paper or polythene film in between, into a bag, seal and freeze. To use: allow to thaw and reheat with a stuffing or in a sauce. *See* Chicken and Mushroom Pancakes, *page 184*, Savoury Fillings, *page 186* or Orange Pancakes, *page 256*.

To serve traditionally: sprinkle with lemon juice and sugar and roll up—but there are many other ways.

LAGER PANCAKES

Pancakes made with lager turn out especially light and may be served traditionally with lemon and sugar, or with sweet or savoury fillings. For example, banana or other fruit may be heated through in a little lager, sweetened with syrup and the finished pancake sprinkled with caster or soft brown sugar. Savoury fillings may be fried first if necessary, for example bacon, onions and mushrooms, the fat drained away, then the ingredients cooked over a good heat for about 5 minutes in a little lager. Or cooked meats may be chopped or minced, flavoured with tomato purée or chutney then heated thoroughly over a good heat in a little lager, ready to fill the pancakes.

FOR 6 OR 8 LARGE PANCAKES
125 g/4 oz plain flour
2 eggs
Pinch salt
2 teaspoons oil, olive oil preferably
300 ml/$\frac{1}{2}$ pint lager

1. Beat the eggs into the flour, add salt, oil and lager and beat well or whisk into a smooth batter.
2. Leave for 30 minutes if possible.
3. Heat frying pan, put in a small piece of lard, the size of a hazel nut, or 1 teaspoon oil. Allow to spread over pan and become fairly hot. Pour in batter to make a thin layer in pan. Cook until golden and then flip over to cook other side.

Best served immediately, but may be prepared in advance. Will stay fresh for up to 48 hours if stacked on top of one another, interleaved with greaseproof paper, wrapped in a teacloth and put in refrigerator.

TO REHEAT
1. Spoon filling on pancakes and roll up. Place in fireproof dish.
2. Sprinkle lightly with lager or coat with any remaining filling; roll up loosely and bake in a hot oven, Gas 7, 425°F, 220°C, for 10 minutes or so until heated thoroughly.

WHOLEWHEAT PANCAKES

Makes 6 to 8 pancakes

125 g/4 oz wholewheat flour
$\frac{1}{2}$ level teaspoon sea salt
1 egg
300 ml/$\frac{1}{2}$ pint milk
A little butter, oil or a piece of suet, to cook

1. Mix flour and salt in a bowl and make a well in the centre.
2. Drop in the egg and begin to stir it in, adding the milk slowly until all flour is incorporated.
3. Beat mixture hard or whisk it for 5 minutes. Put it in a jug.
4. Heat a frying pan and grease it lightly with butter, oil or suet.
5. Carefully pour mixture into frying pan to make very thin pancakes. Cook till golden brown underneath and drying on top.
6. Toss or slip them over and cook until golden brown.

BUCKWHEAT PANCAKES

Keep for a day or two in refrigerator. Freeze well.

Makes about 10 pancakes

450 ml/$\frac{3}{4}$ pint milk
1 large egg
A pinch of salt
75 g/3 oz buckwheat flour
75 g/3 oz wholewheat flour
Oil to grease pan

1. *If you do not have a liquidiser:* put flours and salt in a bowl, make a well in centre and drop in egg. Beat in the milk, gradually incorporating flour. Beat thoroughly.
If you have a liquidiser: put in milk, egg and salt and switch on for 15 seconds. Then add flours and switch on again for 30 seconds.
2. Heat a frying pan and lightly grease it. Pour in a little mixture swirling it around to make thin pancakes. Cook till browning a little underneath and drying on top.
3. Toss or flip them over to cook other side.
4. When done, flip on to a cold plate so that they cool quickly. This will prevent them becoming leathery.

5. When cold, stack the pancakes on a plate, layered with greaseproof paper.

Delicious as a sweet with soured cream and maple syrup. In Brittany they are often filled with ham, eggs and onions.

TRY ALSO:

BUCKWHEAT PANCAKES WITH CREAMY LEEK FILLING

The filling is delicious to eat on its own.

Serves 4 for a special occasion

10 buckwheat pancakes
15 g/$\frac{1}{2}$ oz butter

FILLING
450 g/1 lb leeks, finely-chopped
25 g/1 oz butter
125 g/4 oz cottage cheese
2 tablespoons mayonnaise
2 tablespoons yoghurt
1 tablespoon single cream
1 tablespoon lemon juice
1 tablespoon oil
$\frac{1}{4}$ teaspoon tarragon
Pepper and salt

1. Prepare leeks.
2. Heat butter and fry leeks for 5 to 8 minutes until just softening but not brown.
3. Put remaining ingredients together in liquidiser and switch on for 30 seconds. If you do not have a liquidiser, push cottage cheese through a sieve, then mix it with remaining ingredients and beat hard till you have a soft cream.
4. Mix this with leeks.
5. Spoon filling on to each pancake, roll up and place in a greased dish, seam side down.
6. Dot with butter.
7. Bake in middle of a moderate oven, Gas 4, 350°F, 180°C, for 15 to 20 minutes until just heated through.

Sarah Brown
Scarborough, Yorkshire

SUET PANCAKES

Makes about 8 pancakes

175 g/6 oz flour (plain, self-raising or whole-wheat)
Pinch of salt
75 g/3 oz finely-chopped beef suet
6 tablespoons milk
A little extra suet for frying, or a little lard

1. Mix flour, salt, suet and milk to a soft but not sticky dough.
2. Using a floured board, roll out thinly—about as thick as a 50p piece. Cut rounds about 8 cm/3 inches across.
3. Heat a frying pan and grease it lightly with a piece of suet. Fry pancakes until golden brown on both sides.

Serve at once, very hot, with golden syrup. Try also with butter, treacle, marmalade, lemon curd or Marmite.

Mrs Eva Hay
Reigate, Surrey

See also Orange Pancakes, page 256.

CHICKEN AND MUSHROOM PANCAKES

Make pancakes from recipe given on page 182. The pancakes can be kept hot, as they are made, on a plate over a pan of simmering water and covered with foil. They should not then need to be warmed in oven.

To freeze: Allow to become cold after filling, pack into containers, seal. Heat in oven when required.

FILLING
75 g/3 oz butter
50 g/2 oz flour
$\frac{1}{2}$ teaspoon Salt and Pepper Mix (*see page 17*)
300 ml/$\frac{1}{2}$ pint milk
175 g/6 oz cooked and chopped chicken
125 g/4 oz mushrooms, sliced

1. Melt 50 g/2 oz of the butter in a saucepan.
2. Add flour, salt and pepper and cook 1 minute.
3. Gradually stir in the milk and cook 2 minutes.
4. Add chicken.

5. Fry mushrooms in remaining 25 g/1 oz butter for 2 minutes. Add to sauce.

6. Divide filling between pancakes and roll up. To warm in the oven, place in a shallow casserole, and heat through in a moderately hot oven, Gas 5, 375°F, 190°C, for about 10 minutes.

SPINACH AND WHOLEMEAL PANCAKE ROLL

Each part of this dish can be prepared in advance and then completed just in time for the meal. This dish freezes well.

Serves 4 or 5

PANCAKE BATTER
125 g/4 oz wholemeal flour
$\frac{1}{2}$ teaspoon salt
1 egg
150 ml/$\frac{1}{4}$ pint milk
150 ml/$\frac{1}{4}$ pint water
50 g/2 oz lard, for cooking batter

FILLING
450 g/1 lb fresh spinach, or 225 g/8 oz frozen leaf spinach
25g/1 oz butter
1 tablespoon finely-chopped onion
125 g/4 oz cottage cheese
1 egg-yolk
$\frac{1}{4}$ teaspoon grated nutmeg
Seasoning

TOMATO SAUCE
1 onion
1 clove garlic
A 400 g/14 oz can of tomatoes
Pinch mixed herbs
1 level teaspoon Barbados sugar
Seasoning

BASIC WHITE SAUCE
15 g/$\frac{1}{2}$ oz butter
15 g/$\frac{1}{2}$ oz flour
150 ml/$\frac{1}{4}$ pint milk
Seasoning

TO FINISH
50 g/2 oz grated hard cheese

FIRST MIX THE BATTER
1. Mix flour and salt in a bowl and make a well in the centre.
2. Drop in the egg.
3. Mix milk and water together.
4. Beat egg into flour, gradually adding milk and water and beat thoroughly.
5. Leave to stand in a cool place for 20 minutes while you prepare the filling.

NEXT PREPARE THE FILLING
1. Cook spinach in a very little water until it is tender.
2. Melt butter and fry onion until soft but not brown.
3. Sieve cottage cheese.
4. Drain and cut spinach then drain again very thoroughly as it must not be wet.
5. Mix together spinach, onion, cottage cheese, egg-yolk, nutmeg and seasoning.

NOW MAKE TOMATO SAUCE
1. Peel and chop onion finely.
2. Crush garlic (*see page 139*).
3. Mix all ingredients together in a small pan, bring to the boil, cover pan, lower heat and simmer for 20 minutes.

BACK TO THE PANCAKE ROLL
1. Melt the 50 g/2 oz lard in an oblong Swiss-roll type of tin (approx. 23 × 30 cm/9 × 12 inches).
2. Pour in the batter.
3. Bake near top of a moderately hot oven, Gas 6, 400°F, 200°C, for about 10 minutes, or until the mixture is set and cooked, but not crisp.
4. Turn out on to a piece of greased, greaseproof paper.
5. Spread the spinach mixture over the cooked batter and roll up like a Swiss-roll.
6. Cut across the roll into slices 2.5 cm/1 inch thick. Lay these, slightly-overlapping, in an oven-proof serving dish.

THE SAUCES AND FINAL PREPARATION
1. Make the white sauce. Melt butter in a small pan, stir in flour and cook it gently for 1 minute.
2. Add milk gradually, stirring well, and bring to the boil. Let it cook 2 or 3 minutes and season to taste.
3. Mix together white sauce and tomato sauce. Pour over the spinach rolls.
4. Cover with grated cheese.
5. Bake in a hot oven, Gas 7, 425°F, 220°C, for 15 minutes.

Jean Welshman
Malton, E. Yorkshire

SAVOURY FILLINGS FOR PANCAKES OR VOL-AU-VENTS

HAM
For this you need:

300 ml/½ pint thick basic white sauce (*see below*),
    made, if possible, with ham stock—other-
    wise a chicken or ham stock cube will do
125 g/4 oz chopped cooked ham
1 dessertspoon cooked peas
½ teaspoon chopped fresh parsley

MUSHROOM
300 ml/½ pint thick basic white sauce (*see below*),
    using chicken stock
175 g/6 oz chopped, lightly-cooked mushrooms
1 dessertspoon cooked peas

PRAWNS
300 ml/½ pint thick basic white sauce (*see below*),
    using stock made from simmering prawn
    shells in a little water, then making up to 300
    ml/½ pint with milk. Otherwise use all milk.
125 g/4 oz chopped prawns
1 hard-boiled egg, chopped
1 dessertspoon chopped fresh parsley

BASIC WHITE SAUCES

40 g/1½ oz butter or margarine
40 g/1½ oz plain flour
Salt and pepper

THICK SAUCE
300 ml/½ pint milk or stock

MEDIUM THICK
450 ml/¾ pint milk or stock

THIN
600 ml/1 pint milk or stock

SEVERAL METHODS
I. Traditional
1. Melt butter in a heavy pan.
2. Add flour and work it into butter, stirring until it
forms a smooth paste which leaves the sides and
base of the pan clean.
3. Cook gently for a minimum of 2 minutes, stirring
all the time. This is to start flour cooking.
4. Pour in milk or stock a little at a time until all the
liquid is incorporated. Beat vigorously between each
addition of liquid in order to avoid lumps. Season to
taste with salt and pepper.

II. Shortcut
1. Put three tablespoons of milk or stock into a
screw-topped jar or a shaker.
2. Heat rest of milk or stock in a pan until almost at
boiling point. Add butter and melt.
3. Add flour to shaker or jar, put on lid, then pour
contents into the pan and stir well until the sauce
thickens and comes to the boil.

III. All-in
For a thick sauce using 300 ml/½ pint liquid.

1. Put all ingredients together into a pan over gentle
heat and stir continuously while sauce thickens and
comes to the boil.
2. Boil for 5 minutes.

SAVOURY SAUCES

Anchovy: Anchovies pounded to a purée and added
at last minute to medium-thick or thin white sauce,
made with milk or stock as above. Quantity of anchovies to your taste.

Cheese: 50 to 75 g/2 to 3 oz grated hard, well-flavoured cheese added at last minute to medium thick
or thin sauce, made as above with milk. Reheat but
do not boil or cheese may go stringy.

Egg: 1 or 2 hard-boiled eggs, chopped small, added
at last minute to medium thick or thin sauce made
with milk, as above.

Parsley: Medium thick white sauce made with milk
or stock as above, adding plenty of chopped fresh
parsley at the last minute until sauce is nearly green.

Tomato: Using medium thick or thin white sauce
made as above with stock. Remove pan from heat
and stir in tomato purée, thyme or basil to taste and
a pinch of sugar. Reheat.

SWEET SAUCES
Coffee: Make up thin sauce as above with half milk
and half strong coffee. Add sugar to taste—but no
salt and pepper.

Vanilla: Make up thin white sauce as above, using
milk. Add a vanilla pod while sauce is simmering.
Then remove it, wash and dry and store for further
use.

BÉCHAMEL SAUCE

A gently-flavoured classic white sauce.

300 ml/½ pint milk
½ bay leaf
2 peppercorns
1 blade of mace
A piece of carrot, 5 cm/2 inches
¼ of a medium onion
25 g/1 oz butter
25 g/1 oz flour
Salt and pepper

1. Put milk, bay leaf, peppercorns, mace, carrot and onion in a pan. Heat for 10 minutes and strain.
2. Use this milk to make a white sauce. Melt butter, stir in flour and let it sizzle for 1 minute.
3. Gradually add milk, stirring as sauce thickens, and let it cook gently for 3 minutes.

TOMATO SAUCE

A thick sauce which can be thinned as required using water, stock or milk. Will keep in the refrigerator for a week to 10 days.
It is a good sauce or dip for Cotswold Dumplings *(see page 189)*.
Makes an excellent soup if thinned to correct consistency and seasonings adjusted. If adding milk do not actually boil again or it will curdle.

25 g/1 oz butter
1 medium-sized grated onion
1 small grated apple
2 level teaspoons cornflour
2 teaspoons sugar
2 tablespoons tomato purée*
Water
Seasoning—salt, black pepper, garlic salt, seasoned salt—use as desired.

*To keep tomato purée fresh, see page 84.

1. Melt butter in small saucepan, add onion and soften a little. Add apple and cook for about 15 minutes until quite soft.
2. Place cornflour, sugar and purée in a measuring jug. Mix in water to make 300 ml/½ pint.
3. Add to the pan, stir until simmering and cook for 15 to 20 minutes, stirring occasionally.

4. Sieve or preferably liquidise, return to rinsed pan, season to taste (it should be piquant) and bring to the boil.

See Index for other Sauces.

SAVOURY FRITTERS

BASIC FRITTER BATTER
125 g/4 oz wholewheat or white self-raising flour
½ level teaspoon salt
Black pepper
1 large egg
150 ml/¼ pint milk
A little lard, for frying

THE BATTER
1. Mix flour, salt and pepper in a bowl. Make a well in the centre and drop in the egg.
2. Gradually stir in half the milk using a wooden spoon. Mix well and beat until smooth, adding rest of milk. If using wholewheat flour add 1 extra tablespoon milk.

THE FILLINGS
Bacon: Cut 225 g/8 oz streaky bacon into strips and fry until crisp.

Cheese: Grate 175 g/6 oz Cheddar cheese.

Tuna and parsley: Flake 200 g/7 oz tinned tuna and mix into it 2 tablespoons chopped parsley.

Sweetcorn: Drain a 200 g/7 oz can of sweetcorn with peppers.

Salami: Finely chop 125 g/4 oz or more.

Cold cooked chicken with mushrooms: Chop 50 g/2 oz mushrooms, fry for 2 minutes in 15 g/½ oz butter or margarine. Mix with 125 g/4 oz or more finely-chopped chicken.

THE FRITTERS
1. Stir the filling of your choice into the batter or divide the batter and make a variety of fritters.
2. Heat a little lard in a frying pan. Add tablespoonfuls of mixture and fry until golden brown on both sides.

Serve with fresh watercress.

See also Apple or Pineapple Fritters, page 241. Banana Fritters, page 244.

BACON FLODDIES

A way to use up a small amount of cold cooked meat. Turkey or chicken floddies can also be made.

Serves 2

1 large potato peeled
1 medium onion peeled
1 beaten egg
25 g/1 oz self-raising flour
75 g/3 oz bacon, finely-chopped
A pinch of mixed herbs (optional)
Salt and pepper
Oil for frying

1. Grate potato and onion into a basin.
2. Mix in egg.
3. Add flour, chopped bacon, herbs and seasoning and mix well.
4. Heat oil in a heavy-based frying pan.
5. Fry tablespoons of the mixture, turning until golden brown both sides.

Sybil Norcott
Irlam, Nr Manchester

CRISPY BACON BITES

Makes 12 small balls. They are deep-fried and very tasty.

1 medium-sized onion
225 g/8 oz cooked bacon from a joint, or fresh rashers
25 g/1 oz bacon dripping
25 g/1 oz plain wholewheat or white flour
150 ml/$\frac{1}{4}$ pint chicken stock ($\frac{1}{2}$ stock cube will do)
Pepper
75 g/3 oz fresh wholemeal or white breadcrumbs
1 beaten egg
1 tablespoon tomato ketchup (optional)
Deep fat for frying

1. Peel and roughly chop the onion. Cut up bacon.
2. Mince bacon and onion.
3. Melt dripping, stir in flour and cook for 1 minute.
4. Add stock and stir until it comes to the boil. Cook for 1 minute.
5. Remove from heat, add a good shake of pepper, 50 g/2 oz of the crumbs and half the beaten egg. Mix

well. Mix in minced bacon and onion and tomato ketchup.
6. Make 12 small balls of mixture. Leave to become firm—30 minutes in fridge is enough.
7. Brush balls with remaining beaten egg and roll them in rest of breadcrumbs.
8. Deep fry in hot fat for about 7 or 8 minutes. Drain on kitchen paper.

Serve with grilled tomatoes or baked beans.

CHEESE CRISPIES

Serves 2

225 g/8 oz grated potato
25 g/1 oz self-raising flour
50 g/2 oz grated cheese
Pepper and salt
1 egg
About 50 g/2 oz lard for frying

1. Grate potato coarsely into a basin, add self-raising flour, cheese and seasoning.
2. Beat egg and mix in.
3. Heat lard in a frying pan until a light blue smoke rises from it. Then drop in spoonfuls of the mixture.
4. Fry until golden brown on both sides. Then turn down heat until cooked through.
5. Drain on kitchen paper or brown paper.

Serve with grilled sausages, bacon or liver.

Stella Boldy
Sykehouse, N. Humberside

CHEESE CROQUETTES

Makes 12

25 g/1 oz margarine
1 tablespoon grated onion
25 g/1 oz plain wholewheat or white flour
$\frac{1}{2}$ level teaspoon dry mustard
$\frac{1}{2}$ teaspoon Salt and Pepper Mix (*see page 17*)
150 ml/$\frac{1}{4}$ pint milk
175 g/6 oz grated Cheddar cheese
1 large egg, separated
1 teaspoon chopped parsley
1 teaspoon Worcestershire sauce
125 g/4 oz fresh white or wholemeal breadcrumbs (*see page 52*)
Dried crumbs for coating (*see page 52*)
Beef or pork dripping for frying

1. Melt margarine in pan and add onion. Stir in flour, mustard and salt and pepper. Cook together for 1 minute.

2. Add milk, stir until boiling, cook for one minute and remove from heat.

3. Add cheese and beat in. Then drop in egg-yolk, parsley, Worcestershire sauce and fresh crumbs. Mix to a firm paste.

4. Divide into 12, roll out with floured hands into cork-shaped pieces about 6 cm/2½ inches long. Leave 10 to 15 minutes (or overnight) in a cool place for crumbs to swell and croquettes to firm up.

5. Beat egg-white lightly, brush croquettes with this and roll them in dried crumbs.

6. Deep fry for 2 to 3 minutes until golden.

COTSWOLD DUMPLINGS

Makes 36

50 g/2 oz butter
125 g/4 oz grated cheese
Salt and pepper
3 small beaten eggs
150 g/5 oz fresh wholemeal or white breadcrumbs (*see page 52*)
2 to 3 tablespoons dried breadcrumbs (*see page 52*)
Fat for frying

1. Cream together butter and cheese. Add salt and pepper.

2. Beat in all but 2 tablespoons of the beaten eggs and add 1 to 2 tablespoons crumbs.

3. Work in remaining crumbs to make a stiff paste.

4. With floured hands, roll mixture into small balls. It will make about 36. Leave for about 1 hour. This allows the crumbs to absorb the moisture and swell a little—prevents bursting on cooking.

5. Using a skewer, dip each ball in remaining beaten egg, then roll in dried crumbs.

6. Heat fat—it should be 8 to 10 cm/3 to 4 inches deep. A chip basket is an advantage.

To test heat of fat: Drop in a 2.5 cm/1 inch cube of dry bread—it should sizzle at once and gradually go golden in 1 minute.

7. Place dumplings in basket, only 1 layer, and fry for 1½ to 2 minutes until golden. Do not overcook. Drain on kitchen paper.

Eat hot with home-made tomato sauce (*see page 187*). Try also serving the tomato sauce cold as a dip for the hot dumplings.

POTATO CHEESE CAKES

Like tiny soufflés, these can be cooked in oven or frying pan.

To vary the flavour use chives, paprika, chopped tomato, mixed herbs or a dessertspoon of curry powder.

For extremely light cheese cakes replace potato by 50 g/2 oz wholewheat flour and use two more eggs. Otherwise, make as for potato cheese cakes.

Serves 3

225 g/8 oz potatoes
2 eggs, separated
175 g/6 oz grated cheese
1 medium-sized onion, grated
1 tablespoon chopped parsley
Try also 1 teaspoon kelp powder
1 tablespoon sunflower seed oil, for frying

1. If baking these, pre-heat oven to moderately hot, Gas 5, 375°F, 190°C.

2. Cook the potatoes in their skins in a little water, cutting them into reasonable-sized pieces. Peel them while hot and mash.

3. Whisk egg-yolks until fluffy and mix in mashed potato, cheese, onion, parsley and kelp powder.

4. Whisk egg-whites until stiff and fold in.

5. Heat oil in frying pan. Put mixture into pan in small mounds and fry quickly till crisp and brown on both sides. If baking, put small mounds on a greased baking tray and bake for 15 minutes, till they are crisp and brown outside and puffy inside.

Eaten with a green salad, these can make a meal in themselves. Nice with home-made tomato sauce (*see Cannelloni, page 180*).

Elizabeth Shears
Author of 'Why Do We Eat'

OMELETTES

BASIC METHOD
2 large eggs
2 teaspoons water
Salt and pepper
Large nut of butter

1. Beat eggs lightly with water, salt and pepper. Do not whisk.
2. Using a small frying pan (a 15 cm/6-inch is ideal) heat butter until frothy, but not browning, tilting pan so that bottom and sides are well-coated.
3. Pour in eggs. After a few seconds move edges with a fork or spatula to allow uncooked egg to flow underneath.
4. Continue for about 2 minutes until set underneath and turning slightly golden but still a little moist on top.
5. Fold in half, tilt on to a warm plate and eat at once.

VARIATIONS
Add 1 tablespoon finely-chopped fresh parsley or 1 tablespoon grated cheese when beating eggs. Or make a filling of fried mushrooms, or crisp chopped bacon or shredded pieces of poultry, well seasoned and heated in butter, or skinned and sliced fried tomato, or thinly sliced kidney or chicken liver fried lightly in butter. Put the hot fillings on to one half of the omelette, fold the other half over.

POTATO OMELETTE

This is the Spanish Tortilla.

Serves 2 or 3

For this you need a heavy frying pan about 23 cm/9 inches in diameter.

4 small potatoes, 275 g/10 oz total weight
1 small onion
About 200 ml/7 fl oz good quality oil (olive oil would be used in Spain)
1 clove of garlic (optional)
3 large lightly-beaten eggs
Sea salt and freshly-ground black pepper

1. Peel and chop potatoes into 1 cm/½ inch cubes. Rinse and dry.
2. Peel and chop onion finely.

3. Heat the oil and fry the peeled garlic clove for a minute, then remove.
4. Put potato cubes into hot oil and cook gently until soft, turning occasionally.
5. Towards the end of the cooking add onion. Do not let oil get too hot.
6. Remove potatoes and onion and mix gently with eggs.
7. Pour off oil, leaving a light film in pan and heat again. Put in the mixture of eggs, potato and onion and cook gently until the underside is cooked but not too brown and the top is still moist. Season well with sea salt and freshly-ground black pepper.
8. Traditionally the tortilla is turned over at this point. It is inverted on to a large plate, then slid back into the pan, cooked-side uppermost. That is the correct way to do it but a satisfactory method is to put the frying pan and its contents under a hot grill for a couple of minutes. The aim is to serve the tortilla with the centre just a little moist.

Grainne Mulligan
Madrid

VEGETABLE OMELETTE

Serves 1 to 2

2 large eggs
2 teaspoons water
Salt and pepper
25 g/1 oz butter
1 teaspoon oil
1 small onion cut into fine rings
1 small potato, cooked and cut into small dice
1 large tomato, skinned and chopped (*see page 139*)
1 or 2 finely-sliced mushrooms, optional

1. Lightly beat eggs, water and salt and pepper.
2. Melt butter and oil in small frying pan. Fry onions until soft, then add potato, tomato and mushrooms, mix together and cook for 2 to 3 minutes.
3. Pour in eggs and stir lightly. Cook until base is firm.
4. Place under pre-heated medium grill until just set.

Serve flat on a warm dish.

OVEN-BAKED OMELETTE

Serves 4 for a light meal with salad

25 g/1 oz butter
6 eggs
Salt and pepper
50 g/2 oz grated cheese
1 teaspoon chopped fresh parsley or chives
(optional)
2 tomatoes, skinned (*see page 139)* and sliced

1. Preheat oven to moderately hot, Gas 6, 400°F,
200°C.
2. Put butter in an ovenproof dish and place in oven
to melt and get hot.
3. Beat eggs lightly, add grated cheese, seasoning
and parsley, or chives if used.
4. Put tomatoes in oven dish, pour the egg mixture
over and bake in centre of oven for about 15 minutes
until set.
5. Serve immediately.

Margaret Heywood
Todmorden, Yorkshire

*See also Apple Wine Omelette, page 241, Jamaican
Omelette, page 245.*

STUFFED EGGS

Serves 4

4 large eggs
25 g/1 oz butter
25 g/1 oz Parmesan or finely-grated Cheddar
cheese
1 to 2 teaspoons mayonnaise or salad cream
Salt and pepper

TO GARNISH
Paprika pepper or parsley

1. Boil the eggs for 12 minutes and then plunge them
into cold water.
2. Shell when cold and cut in half lengthways. Remove yolks.
3. Sieve the yolks or mash well with a fork.
4. Add softened butter, cheese, enough mayonnaise
or salad cream to soften mixture, and salt and pepper
to taste.
5. Pile or pipe mixture into whites. Sprinkle lightly
with paprika pepper or garnish with tiny sprigs of
parsley, and serve.

HARD-BOILED EGGS IN CUCUMBER SAUCE

Serves 2

$\frac{1}{2}$ a cucumber
300 ml/$\frac{1}{2}$ pint milk
Salt and pepper
3 eggs
15 g/$\frac{1}{2}$ oz butter or margarine
15 g/$\frac{1}{2}$ oz flour

1. Slice cucumber, but not too thinly.
2. Put in a pan with milk and seasoning and simmer
for 20 minutes.
3. When cucumber has cooked for about 10 minutes,
put eggs on to hard-boil for 10 minutes.
4. Melt butter or margarine in a small pan. Stir in
flour and let it sizzle for 1 minute.
5. When cucumber is cooked strain liquid and add
it gradually to butter and flour, stirring over low
heat as it thickens. Bring to the boil and cook for 2
or 3 minutes.
6. Shell hard-boiled eggs, cut in halves lengthways
and lay them in a small, warmed dish.
7. Add cucumber to sauce, reheat and pour over the
eggs.

Serve with thin slices of brown bread-and-butter.

Mrs M. Earl-Spyvee
Cross-in-Hand, Sussex

EGG FINGERS

Particularly good when made with fingers from a
Cheese Loaf (*see page 293).*

1 egg
1 tablespoon milk
Salt and pepper
Fingers of white or brown bread
Bacon fat or a little margarine or butter

1. Beat the egg and milk with a little salt and pepper.
2. Dip bread fingers into the egg mixture.
3. Fry till golden on both sides—best done in the fat
after cooking bacon, but add a little margarine if
necessary.

Serve with bacon. Eat at once or they go like leather.

CHEESE SOUFFLÉ

Serves 2

To start with you need:

A 13 cm/5 inch diameter soufflé dish
Greaseproof paper, 54 by 34 cm/21 by 14 inches
String
Cooking oil
Dried breadcrumbs (*see page 52*)
25 g/1 oz butter
25 g/1 oz white or wholewheat flour
150 ml/¼ pint milk
½ teaspoon salt
½ teaspoon made mustard
¼ teaspoon cayenne pepper
3 eggs
75 g/3 oz grated cheese, either all Cheddar or
**   half Cheddar and half Parmesan**

1. Pre-heat oven to moderately hot, Gas 5, 375°F, 190°C, as it must be up to heat when soufflé is ready to go in.
2. Grease soufflé dish with cooking oil.
3. Prepare a piece of greaseproof paper 54 by 34 cm/ 21 by 14 inches.
(a) Fold it in half so that doubled sheet measures 54 by 18 cm/21 by 7 inches.
(b) Turn up folded edge 5 cm/2 inches (it now measures 54 by 13 cm/21 by 5 inches.
(c) Grease the top 8 cm/3 inches of the paper above the fold.
(d) Wrap the paper folded side inwards and greased section uppermost, around the dish. To contain the risen soufflé there must be 8 cm/3 inches of paper above the top of the dish.
(e) Tie securely with string.
4. Shake in breadcrumbs so that both dish and greased paper are coated. This will stop the soufflé sticking.
5. Now start the soufflé. Make a panada (which is a thick glossy sauce) as follows: Melt butter, add flour, cook gently. Add the milk gradually, stirring as it thickens.
6. Remove from heat, stir in seasonings: salt, cayenne pepper, mustard.
7. Add egg-yolks and stir.
8. Stir in the grated cheese.
9. Beat egg-whites up stiffly so they will stand in a peak. (This could be done a short time in advance but make sure you have them really stiff before folding into soufflé mixture.)
10. Fold egg-whites gently into soufflé mixture.
11. Pour into prepared dish. Make deep cuts in the soufflé mixture, both across and in a circle. This cuts the egg-white and allows the soufflé to rise, if not, the whites would set and not rise very well.
12. Put straight into the pre-heated moderately hot oven, Gas 5, 375°F, 190°C, and cook for exactly half an hour.

Serve immediately.

SPICED HAM AND EGG SALAD

Can be made with a boiled bacon joint or with sliced boiled ham or pork shoulder.

Serves 8, but easy to make less

325 g/12 oz long grain brown or white rice
A small piece of saffron
150 ml/¼ pint mayonnaise (*see page 134*)
12 hard-boiled eggs
450 g/1 lb boiled ham or bacon

DRESSING
3 tablespoons olive oil, or good salad oil
2 tablespoons wine or cider vinegar
2 tablespoons tomato ketchup
2 tablespoons mango chutney
A dash of tabasco
Salt and pepper

TO GARNISH
Watercress

1. Cook rice with saffron following instructions for Boiled Rice on page 172.
2. Mix mayonnaise with rice and spread it on a large serving plate to cool.
3. Cut eggs in half and arrange them on rice.
4. Shred ham finely and place it on top of eggs.
5. Thoroughly mix dressing ingredients, cutting mango chutney pieces very small. *Or*, put all these ingredients into a liquidiser and switch on for 1 minute.
6. Pour dressing over ham and eggs, and garnish with watercress.

Judith Adshead
Mottram St Andrew, Cheshire

HAM AND CHEESE SOUFFLÉ

Serves 2

125 g/4 oz ham
1 small bunch chives
25 g/1 oz butter
25 g/1 oz wholewheat or plain flour
150 ml/¼ pint milk
40 g/1½ oz Parmesan cheese
Salt
Black pepper
3 eggs, separated

1. Preheat oven to moderately hot, Gas 6, 400°F, 200°C, and have ready the centre shelf. Lightly butter a 1.2 litre/2 pint soufflé dish or similar straight-sided dish.
2. Chop up ham finely. Chop chives.
3. Melt butter in a saucepan. Stir in flour to blend smoothly with butter and cook for 2 minutes.
4. Gradually add milk, stirring until thick. Remove from heat.
5. Stir in ham, chives, most of cheese, a very little salt, black pepper and egg-yolks. Beat well together.
6. Whisk egg-whites until stiff enough to stand up in peaks.
7. With a metal spoon, fold in egg-whites.
8. Pour into soufflé dish and sprinkle remaining cheese on top.
9. Put straight away into oven and cook for 30 minutes without opening the door.

Serve immediately. A soufflé sinks almost as soon as it reaches the cold air.

CHEESE AND POTATO SOUFFLÉ

Serves 2 or 3

325 g/12 oz mashed potato
3 eggs, separated
25 g/1 oz margarine, softened
125 g/4 oz grated cheese
2 teaspoons grated onion
2 tablespoons milk
A level teaspoon Salt and Pepper Mix (*see page 17*)

1. Preheat the oven to moderately hot, Gas 5, 375°F, 190°C, and have ready the shelf above the middle.
2. Grease a 1.2 to 1.5 litre/2 to 2½ pint soufflé dish.
3. Have potato well-mashed in a large bowl.
4. Add egg-yolks, margarine, cheese, onion, milk, salt and pepper and mix all well together.
5. Beat up egg-whites till they are stiff and will stand up in peaks.
6. Using a metal spoon, fold egg-whites into the mixture and pour straight into greased dish. Put in the oven without delay.
7. Bake for 50 minutes. Do not be tempted to open oven door while it is cooking.

Serve immediately.

TOMATO AND CHEESE SOUFFLÉ

Serves 2

15 g/½ oz butter
3 large tomatoes skinned (*see page 139*)
Salt and Pepper Mix (*see page 17*)
50 g/2 oz fresh breadcrumbs
150 ml/¼ pint single cream
¼ teaspoon dry mustard
A pinch of cayenne pepper
125 g/4 oz grated cheese
2 large eggs, separated

1. Preheat oven to moderately hot, Gas 5, 375°F, 190°C.
2. Grease a 15 cm/6 inch soufflé dish with the butter.
3. Slice the skinned tomatoes and lay them in dish. Season with a little salt and pepper.

4. Put breadcrumbs in a bowl and pour cream over them. Leave 5 to 6 minutes to soak.

5. Then add mustard and cayenne to bowl. Beat in cheese and egg-yolks.

6. Whisk egg-whites until stiff but not dry. Fold them in.

7. Pour cheese mixture on top of tomatoes and put dish straight into the pre-heated oven. Bake for 40 to 45 minutes.

Serve as soon as it is ready.

CHICKEN SOUFFLÉ

Serves 2 to 3

BASE
1 medium-sized onion
2 rashers back bacon
15 g/½ oz butter or margarine
125 g/4 oz mushrooms

SOUFFLÉ
25 g/1 oz butter
25 g/1 oz plain flour
150 ml/¼ pint milk
225 g/8 oz cooked chicken
3 eggs
Salt and pepper

1. Preheat oven to moderately hot, Gas 5, 375°F, 190°C, and have the centre shelf ready.

2. Peel and slice onion.

3. Remove rind from bacon and cut rashers into pieces.

4. Melt 15 g/½ oz butter in a saucepan and add onion and bacon. Cook gently for 5 minutes until onion is soft.

5. Clean and quarter mushrooms. Add to pan and cook for 3 minutes.

6. Turn mixture into a greased soufflé dish or similar deep ovenproof dish.

7. *For the soufflé:* melt 25 g/1 oz butter in the saucepan and stir in flour. Cook for 2 minutes without browning.

8. Gradually add milk, stirring until thick. Remove from heat.

9. Chop chicken finely.

10. Stir chicken into sauce and remove from heat.

11. Separate egg-yolks from whites. Stir yolks into sauce with a little salt and pepper.

12. Stifily beat whites until they will stand in peaks.

13. With a metal spoon, fold whites lightly into chicken mixture.

14. Pour into the soufflé dish over the mushroom mixture.

15. Put immediately into the oven for 30–35 minutes, until well-risen and golden brown. Try not to open oven during cooking.

Serve at once. A soufflé sinks very soon after it is taken from oven into cooler air.

FLUFFY CHEESE PUDDING

If you add a further ounce of breadcrumbs the pudding will hold together quite well when cool and is good for picnics.

Serves 2 to 3

600 ml/1 pint milk
50 g/2 oz margarine
125 g/4 oz fresh white or wholemeal bread-crumbs (*see page 52*)
1 teaspoon grated onion
1 level teaspoon made mustard
½ teaspoon Salt and Pepper Mix (*see page 17*)
2 eggs, separated
175 g/6 oz grated cheese

1. Heat the milk and margarine, add the onion and crumbs and leave at least half an hour, or overnight.

2. Beat mustard, salt and pepper into egg-yolks and add these and the cheese to crumb mixture.

3. Fold in firmly whisked egg-whites.

4. Pour into a 1.5 litre/2½ pint lightly greased pie dish, and cook in a moderately hot oven, Gas 6, 400°F, 200°C for 40 minutes, lowering heat if necessary as top may brown before centre of pudding is cooked.

Eat hot.

CHEESE AND POTATO BAKE

Serves 1 but easy to make in large quantities.

1 large potato
About 25 g/1 oz cheese
Salt and pepper
A little butter or margarine

1. Boil potato in a little water.
2. Grate cheese.
3. Mash potato and mix in cheese, salt and pepper.
4. Grease a small oven-proof dish with a little butter or margarine. Put in the potato mixture, smooth top and dot with tiny pieces of butter or margarine.
5. Cook in moderate oven, Gas 3, 325°F, 160°C, for 10 to 15 minutes.

Eat hot with bacon, fried egg, green salad, or cold meats. Try also with one small sliced tomato arranged on top of potato and cooked with it (paragraph 5).

Mrs Hilda Whitney
Wellingborough, Northants

CHEESE AND POTATO LUNCH

Serves 2

450 g/1 lb potatoes
75 g/3 oz margarine
2 tablespoons milk
Salt and pepper
125 g/4 oz porridge oats
1 teaspoon dry mustard
125 g/4 oz grated cheese

1. Simmer potatoes in a very little water. Drain and mash with 25 g/1 oz of the margarine, the milk, salt and pepper.
2. Grease a warmed pie-dish with a little of remaining margarine and put in mashed potato.
3. Melt rest of margarine.
4. Mix oats, mustard and cheese and stir in melted margarine.
5. Spread this mixture on top of hot potatoes and grill gently until topping is crisp and brown. Or bake in a hot oven, Gas 6, 400°F, 200°C, for 15 minutes.

TRY THESE VARIATIONS
Add 1 finely-chopped, lightly-fried onion, or chopped chives to potato. Put a layer of skinned and sliced tomatoes under the topping. Enough for 4 people if served with bacon, grilled ham, beefburgers or sausage.

Margaret Heywood
Todmorden, Yorkshire

SAVOURY BREAD AND BUTTER PUDDING

Serves 2

4 large slices wholemeal or white bread
Butter
Yeast extract
125 g/4 oz grated cheese
1 small onion, grated
2 beaten eggs
300 ml/½ pint milk
Salt and pepper
Pinch of dry mustard

1. Butter bread and spread lightly with yeast extract.
2. Cut bread into small cubes.
3. Grease an oven-proof dish.
4. Spread half of bread cubes in bottom of dish.
5. Cover with half of cheese, then onion.
6. Add rest of bread and finally rest of cheese.
7. Add milk and seasoning to beaten eggs and strain this over the pudding.
8. Bake in a moderate oven, Gas 4, 350°F, 180°C, for 35 to 40 minutes.

Margaret Heywood
Todmorden, Yorkshire

CHEESE AND ONION SAVOURY

Serves 2 to 3

450 g/1 lb onions
A little salt
300 ml/$\frac{1}{2}$ pint milk
225 to 275 g/8 to 10 oz Cheshire cheese
2 tablespoons fresh breadcrumbs (*see page 52*)
Pepper
2 tomatoes, to garnish
A little butter
Thick slices of bread

1. Peel and thinly slice the onions.
2. Place them in a pan with half a teaspoon salt and just enough milk to cover. Cook gently until onions are soft.
3. Place in a greased shallow casserole or small oven tin and cover with the thinly-sliced cheese. Sprinkle over the crumbs shaking on a little pepper.
4. Arrange thickly-sliced tomatoes down centre of dish.
5. Dot with butter.
6. Place in oven heated to moderate, Gas 4, 350°F, 180°C, and leave until the cheese melts—about 15 to 20 minutes.

Usually served with a thick slice of bread to mop up the juice.

Miss G. S. Davies
Flintshire

HARVEST PUDDING

Serves 2

1 large onion, chopped
15 g/$\frac{1}{2}$ oz butter
125 g/4 oz fresh wholemeal or white bread-crumbs (*see page 52*)
1 teaspoon dried sage
3 tablespoons milk
Or instead of the above, use 1 packet sage and onion stuffing prepared in a large bowl according to instructions
50 g/2 oz grated cheese
125 g/4 oz cooked ham, chopped
2 large eggs, separated
Black pepper
Pinch of mustard powder

1. Fry onion in butter until soft.
2. Put breadcrumbs in a large bowl, mix in sage and

fried onion, adding tablespoons of milk to moisten *Or* prepare packet of sage and onion stuffing as indicated on packet and allow to cool.
3. Stir in cheese, ham, egg-yolks, some freshly-ground black pepper and the mustard powder. Mix well.
4. Beat egg-whites until stiff and fold them in lightly with a metal spoon.
5. Turn mixture into a greased oven-proof dish.
6. Bake in a moderately hot oven, Gas 5, 375°F, 190°C, for 35 minutes.

Serve with a lightly cooked green vegetable or a green salad.

QUICK PIZZA

No need for an oven.

Serves 3 or 4 but easy to make less

BASE
125 g/4 oz self-raising flour
$\frac{1}{4}$ teaspoon salt
3 tablespoons oil
A little cold water

FILLING
25 g/1 oz butter
1 small onion, finely-chopped
225 g/8 oz tinned or fresh tomatoes skinned (*see page 139*) and chopped
1 teaspoon mixed herbs

TO FINISH
125 g/4 oz grated cheese
2 or 3 rashers of streaky bacon cut in strips, or anchovies soaked for 10 minutes in a little milk to remove excess salt, or olives

1. Mix together flour and salt. Stir in 1 tablespoon of the oil and enough water to make a fairly stiff but pliable dough.
2. Using a floured board, roll out to fit a frying pan about 18 cm/7 inches in diameter.
3. Heat rest of oil in the pan and cook dough over moderate heat for about 5 to 6 minutes.
4. Turn it over and cook 4 to 5 minutes on the other side.
5. Meanwhile make filling. Melt butter and fry onion until beginning to soften but not to colour.
6. Add tomatoes and herbs and cook for 1 minute. Drain off excess liquid.

7. Spread tomato mixture on top of cooked base in pan.

8. Sprinkle with cheese.

9. If using *bacon*, arrange the strips on top of cheese and put under a moderate grill for a few minutes. If using *anchovies*, pat dry, arrange on top of cheese and grill. If using *olives*, use them to decorate after cheese has melted under grill.

ONION TART

Serves 4, but easy to make a smaller tart

CASE
12 to 13 cream crackers (175 g/6 oz)
50 g/2 oz melted butter or margarine

FILLING
2 medium-sized onions
25 g/1 oz butter or margarine
2 lightly-beaten eggs
200 ml/7 fl oz milk
1 teaspoon Salt and Pepper Mix (*see page 17*)
50 g/2 oz grated cheese
A sprinkle of paprika

1. Crush crackers to fine crumbs. Mix in melted butter or margarine and press into bottom and sides of a shallow, 20 cm/8 inch pie plate or quiche dish.

2. Peel and quarter onions and cut into thin slices.

3. Cook in butter or margarine until soft but not brown. Put in tart case.

4. Combine eggs, milk, salt and pepper. Pour over onions.

5. Sprinkle grated cheese on top.

6. Bake near top of a moderate oven, Gas 4, 350°F, 180°C, for about 35 minutes, or until set.

7. Sprinkle paprika on top.

Nice hot or cold.

HAM AND LEEKS WITH CHEESE SAUCE

No need for the oven. The quantity can be varied to suit your household, but there will be *enough sauce for 4 people.*

FOR EACH PERSON
1 leek, not too large
1 slice cooked ham

SAUCE
40 g/1½ oz butter or margarine
40 g/1½ oz white or wholewheat flour
Salt and Pepper Mix (*see page 17*)
150 ml/¼ pint cooking liquid from leeks
A bare 300 ml/½ pint milk
A grating of nutmeg
50 g/2 oz grated cheese

TO FINISH
50 g/2 oz grated cheese and 2 tablespoons fresh wholewheat breadcrumbs (*see page 52*)

1. Trim and wash leeks and cook them in a little boiling water until just barely tender, about 10 minutes. Save the liquid as you drain them.

2. Wrap a slice of ham around each leek and place in a shallow, greased oven dish.

3. Melt butter or margarine, add flour and let it sizzle for 1 minute.

4. Add liquid gradually, stirring as it thickens. Add nutmeg. Bring to the boil and cook for 2 minutes.

5. Add cheese, stir to dissolve and heat but do not boil.

6. Pour sauce over leeks and ham.

7. For the top, mix the second 50 g/2 oz cheese with the breadcrumbs and sprinkle over the sauce.

8. Place dish under a moderately hot grill to heat through and brown a little.

KIDNEY SCRAMBLE

A snack for 4, but easy to make for any number.

4 lamb's kidneys
25 g/1 oz butter
$\frac{1}{4}$ teaspoon Worcestershire sauce
1 level teaspoon tomato ketchup
$\frac{1}{4}$ level teaspoon mustard
Salt and black pepper
4 large eggs
4 tablespoons single cream or top of the milk
4 slices buttered toast

1. Skin kidneys and cut out the core. Chop flesh finely.
2. Fry kidneys in half of the butter, turning them until lightly browned.
3. Stir in sauces and mustard. Season with salt and pepper.
4. Cook over moderate heat for a further 2 minutes, then keep warm.
5. Lightly beat eggs and cream together and season a little.
6. Melt remaining butter in a clean pan, and pour in the eggs. Cook over a low heat, stirring occasionally until just beginning to set.
7. Spoon egg on to toast and top with kidneys.

Serve at once with a crisp salad.

Mrs T. Birch
Weston Zoyland, Somerset

KIDNEY TOAST

Serves 2

3 lamb's kidneys
25 g/1 oz butter
$\frac{1}{2}$ teaspoon chutney
$\frac{1}{2}$ teaspoon curry paste
1 tablespoon Worcestershire sauce
1 teaspoon grated lemon rind
Pinch of salt
Hot-buttered toast

1. Skin kidneys and remove core. Cut each kidney into about 8 pieces.
2. Melt butter in a pan, add chutney, curry paste, Worcestershire sauce and lemon rind and stir together over low heat.
3. When hot, stir in kidneys. Stir over low heat until

kidneys are cooked and lightly browned—about 5 to 8 minutes.
4. Prepare toast.
5. Spread kidney mixture on hot toast and serve without delay as hot as possible.

Mrs Iris Tassell
Bexhill-on-Sea, Sussex

WELSH RAREBIT

25 g/1 oz butter
1 teaspoon made mustard
$\frac{1}{2}$ teaspoon Salt and Pepper Mix (see page 17)
2 tablespoons fresh white or wholemeal bread-
    crumbs
1 egg-yolk
125 g/4 oz strong Cheddar cheese, grated
3 tablespoons beer

TO SERVE
3 slices hot buttered toast

NOTE
This mixture must *never* boil or it will go stringy.
1. Melt butter in saucepan.
2. Add mustard, Salt and Pepper Mix and bread-crumbs. Stir over gentle heat.
3. Add egg-yolk, mix in, then cheese and stir to melt.
4. Add beer, mix in, and reheat.
5. Spread on to hot buttered toast. Can also be browned under the grill if preferred.

MOCK GOOSE

Serves 3 to 4

450 g/1 lb sausage meat
1 beaten egg
1 teaspoon Salt and Pepper Mix (see page 17)
1 teaspoon made mustard
25 to 50 g/1 to 2 oz fresh breadcrumbs, whole-
    meal or white (see page 52)
2 tablespoons dried breadcrumbs (see page 52)

STUFFING
25 g/1 oz dripping
2 large sliced onions
1 teaspoon Salt and Pepper Mix
1 teaspoon sage
25 to 50 g/1 to 2 oz fresh breadcrumbs

1. Mix together sausage meat, egg, Salt and Pepper Mix and mustard using enough fresh breadcrumbs to make a firm mixture.
2. *Stuffing.* Melt dripping and fry the onions to soften a little. Mix in seasonings and sufficient of the fresh breadcrumbs to bind, but do not make too dry.
3. Grease a 450 g/1 lb loaf tin, coat generously with dried breadcrumbs.
4. Spread half of the sausage meat mixture in tin, then stuffing mixture and the rest of the sausage meat on top.
5. Cover with foil.
6. Cook for 1 hour in a moderately hot oven, Gas 5, 375°F, 190°C.

Serve with salads. Can be served hot with apple sauce.

SAVOURY PEANUT LOAF

Serves 2 to 3

175 g/6 oz peanuts, finely-chopped or ground
125 g/4 oz carrot, grated
125 g/ 4 oz celery, finely-chopped
75 g/3 oz fresh wholewheat breadcrumbs
2 beaten eggs
2 tablespoons milk
2 teaspoons tomato purée*
2 teaspoons mixed herbs
Pepper and salt

TO FINISH
50 g/2 oz butter

**To keep tomato purée fresh, see page 84.*

1. Pre-heat oven to moderate, Gas 4, 350°F, 180°C.
2. Mix ingredients, adding pepper and salt to taste.
3. Line the bottom of a greased ½ kg/1 lb loaf tin with greaseproof paper.
4. Spoon mixture into tin and press it down lightly. Dot with butter.
5. Bake near top of oven for 30 to 35 minutes.
6. Leave to cool for 5 minutes before turning out of tin.

Nice hot or cold. If hot, serve with a well-flavoured tomato sauce (*see Cannelloni, page 180 or Meat Balls in Tangy Tomato Sauce, see page 99*). Good for picnics and packed lunches.

Janet Horsley
Headingley, Yorkshire

SANDWICH SPREADS

(*i*) *Beef and pickle*
Put a few slices of cold, cooked beef in the liquidiser with 2 chopped pickled onions and 2 teaspoons horseradish sauce. Blend till smooth.

(*ii*) *Cheese and chutney*
Mix grated, hard cheese with chutney.

Stella Boldy
Sykehouse, N. Humberside

(*iii*) *Cheese and egg*
3 eggs
125 g/4 oz cheese
Salt and pepper
1 to 2 tablespoons salad cream

1. Boil eggs for 5 to 6 minutes and allow to cool.
2. Grate cheese.
3. Shell eggs and put them in a bowl. Mash them up with a fork and mix in grated cheese.
4. Add salt, pepper and salad cream to taste. Mix well together.

Miss Jill-Anne Dudgeon

(*iv*) *Cottage cheese with herbs*
1.2 litres/2 pints milk
1 teaspoon rennet
Salt and freshly-milled black pepper, to taste
1 teaspoon chopped fresh thyme
1 teaspoon chopped chives
2 teaspoons chopped parsley
Half a clove of garlic, crushed (*see page 139*) **or**
 a little chopped onion if preferred
2 to 3 tablespoons double cream (optional) or
 creamy milk

1. Pour the milk into a pan and heat gently to blood temperature.
2. Stir in the rennet, pour the mixture into a jug and leave it for about four hours at room temperature. The milk will set like junket.
3. Place a double layer of muslin over a colander in a bowl.
4. Turn set milk on to the muslin. Tie up the corners with string and hang up to drain overnight.
5. The next day place the cheese (still in the muslin) into a sieve with a weight on top so that the remaining moisture can be squeezed out—about two hours.
6. Take the cheese out of the muslin and put it in a bowl. Mix in the remaining ingredients adding the cream if liked or even a little 'top of the milk'.

7. Leave the mixture for a few hours so that the herbs can flavour the cheese.

8. This cheese will keep five days in the refrigerator.

(v) Curried egg

25 g/1 oz butter, softened
1 level teaspoon curry powder
A little salt
2 hard-boiled eggs

Soften butter without melting it and beat in curry powder and salt. Mix well with finely-chopped eggs.

(vi) Liver spread

125 to 175 g/4 to 6 oz lightly-cooked lamb's liver
1 large spring onion, chopped
25 to 50 g/1 to 2 oz melted butter
Pepper and salt

Put all ingredients in a liquidiser and blend for 2 or 3 minutes.

(vii) Peanut butter, carrot and cress

2 slices wholemeal bread
Peanut butter
Grated carrot
Mustard and cress

Spread peanut butter thinly on both sides of wholemeal bread. Fill with carrot and cress.

(viii) Roe paste

225 g/8 oz cooked cod's roe
50 g/2 oz melted butter
Pepper and salt
A dash of vinegar

1. Skin the roe and mash it.
2. Add melted butter and pepper, salt and vinegar to taste.
3. Beat well or use a liquidiser to blend.

(ix) Sardine

Sardines
Dash of vinegar
Dash of Worcestershire sauce
Pepper

Mash sardines in a saucer, adding the other ingredients to taste.

(x) Tomato paste

Spread on toast or in sandwiches. Will keep for several weeks in the refrigerator.

8 medium-sized tomatoes
1 small onion
125 g/4 oz margarine
1 beaten egg
50 g/2 oz grated cheese
125 g/4 oz brown or white breadcrumbs
Pepper and salt

1. Skin tomatoes (see page 139).
2. Cut up tomatoes quite small.
3. Peel and finely chop onion.
4. Melt margarine in a pan, add tomato and onion and cook gently until tender.
5. Mash, sieve or liquidise the mixture until smooth.
6. Put tomato mixture in pan, add beaten egg and stir over a low heat until mixture thickens. Do not let it boil.
7. Stir in cheese and breadcrumbs, and pot at once.

Mrs M. Skipworth
Louth, Lincolnshire

(xi) Tuna and walnut

A 100 g/3½ oz tin of tuna, drained and chopped
25 g/1 oz walnuts, chopped
A 5 cm/2 inch piece of cucumber, chopped small
2 dessertspoons salad cream
2 dessertspoons chutney
1 level teaspoon dry mustard
Pepper and salt

Combine all ingredients and season to taste. If too thick to spread add a little more salad cream or chutney.

(xii) Watercress and cream cheese

25 g/1 oz butter, softened
50 g/2 oz cream cheese
2 tablespoons chopped watercress
Salt
Black pepper

Soften butter without melting it. Beat it into cream cheese and beat in watercress. Season to taste.

7

PIES
AND
PASTRIES

PASTRY

A few tips

Resting
All pastry is less likely to shrink during cooking if it is allowed to rest in a cool place or refrigerator for 10 to 15 minutes before rolling out, and again immediately before baking. Cover it with greaseproof paper, polythene or cling-film.

Quantities
When recipes indicate a certain quantity of home-baked pastry is required it means that you make up pastry using that quantity of flour—e.g., for 225 g/ 8 oz short-crust you make up pastry based on 225 g/ 8 oz flour.

For Flans
Quantity of pastry required for different-sized flans. It is usually rolled out to 7 mm/¼ inch thick:

15 cm/6 inch ⎫
18 cm/7 inch ⎬ 125 g/4 oz flour
20 cm/8 inch ⎫
23 cm/9 inch ⎬ 175 g/6 oz flour
25 cm/10 inch   225 g/8 oz flour

To Bake a Flan Case Blind
'Blind' means that the flan case is cooked or partly cooked before the filling is added.

1. Put flan ring or flan tin on a baking sheet.
2. Using floured board, roll out pastry to a round, 5 cm/2 inches wider than diameter of your flan ring or tin.
3. Cut a circle of greaseproof paper the same diameter as pastry and grease it.
4. Fit pastry into flan ring. Press in firmly and roll off surplus pastry with rolling pin.

5. Prick base of pastry all over.
6. Crumple up paper to make it easier to fit. Open it out and fit it, greased-side down, into flan.
7. Put in a layer of dried peas or haricot beans, about 1.5 cm/½ inch deep. (Save your baked peas and beans in a jar for the next flan you make—they cannot be eaten.)

To bake a flan case with hard-to-handle, rich short-crust pastry. Lay pastry on the *outside* of an upturned flan or cake tin. Prick base and bake as usual.

Oven Temperatures and Times
White shortcrust: hot oven, Gas 7, 425°F, 220°C, 10 to 12 minutes. Remove beans, foil, reduce temperature to moderate, Gas 4, 350°F, 180°C, and bake for a further 7 to 8 minutes.

Cheese pastry, either white or wholewheat, also wholewheat shortcrust and sweet wholewheat: moderately hot, Gas 6, 400°F, 200°C, for 15 minutes. Remove beans and foil and return to oven for 10 minutes more.

Rich sweet shortcrust: moderately hot, Gas 5, 375°F, 190°C, for 10 minutes. Remove beans and foil and return to oven for a further 10 to 15 minutes. If you have your pastry on the outside of the tin, allow it 20 to 25 minutes complete baking time.

To Avoid a Soggy Bottom in a Flan which has a Moist Filling
1. If flan case is ready-baked, paint inside with beaten egg and allow to dry before putting in filling.
2. If flan case is uncooked, pre-heat a baking sheet at the highest possible oven temperature. Put flan into oven on to this, then turn heat down immediately to the baking temperature required.

Half-cooked Flan Cases

Useful when a flan filling needs lower heat than temperature required to seal pastry. Prepare as if baking blind and bake near top of a moderately hot oven, Gas 6, 400°F, 200°C, for 10 to 12 minutes. Remove from oven, cool, then fill and bake to suit filling.

To Bake Small Pastry Cases

See Mince Meringue Tarts, *page 230.*

Freezing

Flan cases freeze well before or after baking.

SHORTCRUST PASTRY

White or wholewheat
225 g/8 oz plain white or wholewheat flour or a
    mixture
½ level teaspoon salt
50 g/2 oz hard margarine (add an extra 25 g/
    1 oz for wholewheat pastry)
50 g/2 oz lard or hard vegetable fat
2 tablespoons cold water (3 for wholewheat)
    use a measure

Sieve or mix flour and salt in a bowl. Cut fats into small pieces, put them into bowl and rub between fingers until mixture is like fine breadcrumbs. Add water and, using a round-ended knife, stir until mixture begins to bind. Then use your hand to knead lightly and quickly until dough is formed.

SARAH BROWN'S WHOLEWHEAT PASTRY

An unorthodox approach to pastry-making but one that answers complaints that wholewheat pastry is unmanageable and hard. It is meant to be wet as you make it. This way it will roll out easily and thinly. Keeps a week in refrigerator if well-wrapped.

75 g/3 oz mixed hard fats, solid vegetable fat
    and butter are suitable
225 g/ 8 oz wholemeal flour
15 g/½ oz soft brown sugar
A pinch of salt
A pinch of baking powder
125 ml/4 fl oz water
1 teaspoon oil

1. Rub fats into flour.
2. Mix in sugar, salt and baking powder.
3. Add water and oil and mix to a dough, which should be fairly wet. If it seems too wet leave it for a few minutes for flour to absorb some of moisture. Otherwise simply squeeze out excess water.
4. Roll out as required on a floured board.

RICH SWEET SHORTCRUST

Ideal for rich dessert flans and tartlet cases. Almost as rich as shortbread and needs careful handling. 'To bake a flan case blind', *see page 202* for a tip.

225 g/8 oz plain white flour*
A pinch of salt
150 g/5 oz butter or margarine, softened
25 g/1 oz sugar
1 egg-yolk
A squeeze of lemon juice
2 or 3 tablespoons cold water

*There is no benefit in making this with wholewheat flour. The previous previous recipe is rich enough especially if some of the fat is replaced with butter and 1 teaspoon sugar is added.

Sieve flour and salt into a bowl. Rub in butter or margarine as lightly as possible. Add sugar. Mix together egg-yolk, lemon juice and 2 tablespoons water. Stir it into flour with a round-ended knife. Then use your hand to knead lightly to a firm dough, adding 1 or 2 teaspoons more water only if necessary.

SWEET WHOLEWHEAT SHORTCRUST

225 g/8 oz wholewheat flour
Pinch of salt
1 teaspoon dark brown Barbados sugar
75 g/3 oz margarine
50 g/2 oz lard
3 tablespoons water (use a measure)

1. Mix together flour, salt and sugar.
2. Rub in fats.
3. Mix to a firm dough with the water. Knead lightly until smooth and basin comes clean.

CHEESE PASTRY

Delicious for savoury flans, meat pies, sausage rolls, etc.

225 g/8 oz plain white or wholewheat flour
½ level teaspoon salt
½ level teaspoon dry mustard
A pinch of cayenne pepper
75 g/3 oz hard margarine or vegetable fat
75 g/3 oz well-flavoured cheese, finely-grated
1 egg-yolk
2 tablespoons water (3 for wholewheat pastry) use a measure

Sieve or mix flour, salt, mustard and cayenne pepper. Rub in margarine with fingertips until mixture is like breadcrumbs. Mix in cheese. Mix egg-yolk with water and stir it with a round-ended knife. Then knead lightly until smooth and a firm dough is formed.

HOT WATER CRUST

This quantity is enough for a pie 15 cm/6 inches in diameter and 8 cm/3 inches deep including the lid.

125 ml/4 fl oz water
125 g/4 oz lard
275 g/10 oz strong plain flour
½ level teaspoon salt
1 small beaten egg

Boil the water and lard together and pour on to flour and salt. Mix with a knife (it will be hot). Then knead with hands until quite smooth. Allow to cool a little before rolling out. Use beaten egg to seal lid on pie and to brush over the top before baking.

POTATO PASTRY

175 g/6 oz self-raising flour
½ teaspoon salt
125 g/4 oz lard
175 g/6 oz cold, dry, mashed potato

1. Mix flour and salt. Rub in lard.
2. Work in potato using a strong fork or hands. Do not add any water.
3. Knead lightly, roll out on floured board.

RICH PIE PASTRY

For savoury pies. Can be used where a more difficult hot water crust is normally used. The following ingredients make enough pastry to line and cover a ½ kg/1 lb loaf tin.

275 g/10 oz plain flour, or half white and half wholewheat
1 teaspoon salt
140 g/4½ oz lard
1 beaten egg
About 65 ml/2½ fl oz water

1. Sieve or mix flour and salt in a bowl. Rub in lard.
2. Keep 1 teaspoon of the beaten egg for glazing. Mix the rest with water and use it to bind flour and lard into a soft elastic dough. If using wholewheat flour it may take a bit more water.
3. Leave dough to rest for at least 1 hour before rolling out.

Anne Wallace
Stewarton, Ayrshire

SWEET POTATO PASTRY

Easy to cut down for smaller households.

450 g/1 lb potatoes
25 g/1 oz butter or margarine
1 level teaspoon dark brown sugar (Barbados)
125 g/4 oz wholewheat or plain flour

1. Peel potatoes and cut into even-sized pieces. Simmer in a little, lightly-salted water until tender. Drain and dry over a low heat.
2. Mash with a potato masher or fork. Mix in, a little at a time, butter or margarine, sugar and flour. Beat well after each addition.
3. Turn out pastry on to a floured board and knead until smooth.

For Suet Pastry see Baked Savoury Rolls, page 208, Huffed Chicken, page 57, Sussex Bacon Roly Poly, page 130.

FLAKY PASTRY

Cook pastry in a hot oven, Gas 7, 425°F, 220°C. Reduce heat to moderately hot, Gas 5, 375°F, 190°C, if filling is not cooked.

225 g/8 oz plain flour (preferably strong plain flour)
Pinch of salt
75 g/3 oz butter or firm margarine
75 g/3 oz lard
½ teaspoon lemon juice
Approximately 150 ml/¼ pint cold water

1. Sift flour and salt into a bowl.
2. Cut up butter or margarine and lard and mix together well. Chill briefly and divide into quarters.
3. Rub one of the quarters into flour and salt and mix to a pliable but not sticky dough with lemon juice and water. Cover and allow to rest 10 to 15 minutes in a cool place.
4. Using a floured board, roll out pastry 3 times as long as wide—about 7 mm/¼ inch thick.
5. Using a second quarter of fat, place in dabs over the top two-thirds of pastry.
6. Fold bottom third up, and top third down. Seal edges lightly with rolling pin. Turn, leaving pressed edges at top and bottom and at right-hand side. Wrap in greaseproof paper and put it to rest in the refrigerator or in a cold place for 10 minutes.
7. Repeat rollings with third and then fourth quarter of fat, then wrap and leave in a cold place for 1 hour, or overnight. If leaving it overnight, wrap a damp cloth round greaseproof covering to make quite sure it is still soft and has no crust when you need to use it.
8. Roll out and use as required, rolling out quite thinly unless recipe states otherwise.

GROUND ALMOND FLAKY PASTRY

This pastry will keep in refrigerator for 2 or 3 days. Freezes well.

275 g/10 oz plain flour
125 g/4 oz ground almonds
50 g/2 oz ground rice
Pinch of salt
325 g/12 oz butter
1 tablespoon lemon juice
6 tablespoons iced water

1. Sift flour, ground almonds, ground rice and salt into a bowl.
2. Rub one quarter of the butter into flour mixture and mix to a pliable but not sticky dough with lemon juice and iced water as required.
3. Cover and put aside in a cool place to rest for 10 to 15 minutes.
4. Soften remaining butter with a knife and divide into thirds.
5. Using a floured board, roll out pastry 3 times as long as wide, about 7 mm/¼ inch thick.
6. Using one third of the butter, place in dabs over the top two-thirds of pastry.
7. Fold bottom third up, and top third down. Seal edges lightly with rolling pin. Turn, leaving pressed edges at top and bottom and at right-hand side. Wrap in greaseproof paper and put to rest in the refrigerator or in a cold place for 10 minutes.
8. Repeat rollings with second and then third portions of butter. Then wrap and leave in a cold place for 1 hour, or overnight. If leaving it overnight, wrap a damp cloth around greaseproof covering to make quite sure it is still soft and has no crust when you need to use it.

Mrs Angela Mottram
Axbridge, Somerset

ROUGH PUFF PASTRY

As the name implies, an economical and a quickly-made puff pastry. Excellent for Christmas mince pies, sausage rolls and used also in Cheese Strudel Slices (*see page 24*).

225 g/8 oz strong plain flour
A pinch of salt
75 g/3 oz firm margarine
75 g/3 oz firm lard
½ teaspoon lemon juice
About 150 ml/¼ pint water

1. Sieve flour and salt into a basin.
2. Cut fats into 1 cm/½ inch cubes. Mix lightly into flour, but do not break up.
3. Mix to a dough with lemon juice and water. It usually takes the full amount. Form dough into a brick-shape and chill for 10 minutes.
4. On a well-floured board, lightly roll out pastry 7 mm/¼ inch thick, 3 times as long as wide. Fold bottom third up and top third down. Press edges lightly with rolling pin to seal. Wrap in greaseproof paper, polythene or cling-film and chill for 10 minutes.
5. Put pastry on board, folded edges to right and left. Repeat rolling, folding, sealing and chilling 3 times more.

Chill for 30 minutes before using. Freezes well at this stage.

PUFF PASTRY

Usually bought ready made, frozen. This is nevertheless satisfying to make but a long, slow job with frequent use of the refrigerator to chill the pastry at various stages. It is used for very special pastries like vol-au-vents. *See page 186* for a variety of fillings.

225 g/8 oz plain white flour
A pinch of salt
225 g/8 oz unsalted butter
A squeeze of lemon juice
Cold water to mix

1. Sift flour and salt into a bowl and rub in 50 g/2 oz of the butter.
2. Add lemon juice and a little water to make a stiffish dough.
3. Place on a wooden board and knead until smooth.

4. Allow the butter to soften until it is pliable enough to form into a neat brick about 2 cm/¾ inch thick.
5. Roll out dough into a rectangle 30 by 15 cm/12 by 6 inches. Place butter on one half and fold the rest over to enclose it completely. Seal edges. Wrap in a polythene bag and chill for 10 minutes.
6. Put pastry on board with the fold to the left. Roll it out lightly to a long strip about 45 by 15 cm/18 by 6 inches. Fold into 3. Seal edges by pressing lightly with rolling pin. Replace in polythene bag and chill for 10 minutes.
7. Repeat rolling, folding, sealing and chilling so that this process has been done about 7 times in all. For the final chill in refrigerator allow 30 minutes. Pastry is then ready for use. Or it can be frozen.
8. Roll out 7 mm/¼ inch thick for use. When shaped, chill again for 30 minutes before baking.

VOL-AU-VENTS

LARGE
225 g/8 oz puff pastry
Beaten egg

1. Using a floured board, roll out pastry, 2 cm/¾ inch thick into an oval or a round.
2. Put pastry on to a baking sheet. Using a sharp knife or cutter and keeping at least 1 cm/½ inch in from edge of pastry, cut another oval or round, but cut only half-way through the pastry. This inner piece will form the lid of the vol-au-vent.
3. Brush top with beaten egg and leave to rest for 30 minutes.
4. Bake above middle of a hot oven, Gas 7, 425°F, 220°C, for 8 to 10 minutes until well-risen and golden brown. Then reduce heat to moderately hot, Gas 6, 400°F, 200°C, and cook for a further 25 to 30 minutes.
5. Remove from oven on to a wire cooling rack. Lift off the lid and press down the pastry beneath so that there is room for the filling.

Small vol-au-vents are rolled out 1 cm/½ inch thick. Cut and glaze as above. Bake at above temperatures, reducing heat after 8 minutes and continuing at the lower temperature for a further 8 to 10 minutes.

Vol-au-vents can be served hot or cold with a wide variety of fillings. Some suggested savoury fillings are on page 186.

CHEESE PASTRY—FOR CHEESE STRAWS

175 g/6 oz plain flour
$\frac{1}{4}$ teaspoon salt
$\frac{1}{4}$ teaspoon dry mustard
A pinch of cayenne pepper
75 g/3 oz firm margarine
75 g/3 oz finely-grated strong Cheddar cheese
1 egg-yolk
3 teaspoons water

1. Sieve dry ingredients.
2. Rub in margarine.
3. Stir in cheese.
4. Mix to a firm dough with egg-yolk and water. Leave to rest about 15 minutes.
5. Roll out approximately 1 cm/$\frac{1}{2}$ inch thick on a floured board. Cut into fingers 1 by 8 cm/$\frac{1}{2}$ inch by 3 inches. Place on lightly greased baking tray.
6. Bake in a hot oven, Gas 7, 425°F, 220°C, about 12 to 15 minutes until crisp and lightly golden.
7. Turn on to rack to cool. When cold, ends can be lightly dipped in paprika pepper as garnish.

CHEESE PASTRY SAVOURIES

They are delicious.

175 g/6 oz plain flour
$\frac{1}{4}$ teaspoon salt
$\frac{1}{4}$ teaspoon dry mustard
A pinch of cayenne pepper
75 g/3 oz firm margarine
75 g/3 oz finely-grated strong Cheddar cheese
1 egg-yolk
3 teaspoons water

FILLING
A good teaspoon salad cream or mayonnaise
125 g/4 oz cream cheese
Seasoned salt
Garlic salt
Pepper

GARNISH
Stuffed olives, gherkins, shrimps, etc.

1. Sieve dry ingredients.
2. Rub in margarine.
3. Stir in cheese.
4. Mix to a firm dough with egg-yolk and water. Leave to rest about 15 minutes.
5. Roll out approximately 7 mm/$\frac{1}{4}$ inch thick on floured board. Using a 2.5 to 4 cm/1 inch to 1$\frac{1}{2}$ inch cutter, cut into rounds. Cut half of the rounds into halves.
6. Place on lightly greased baking tray and prick each biscuit with a fork.
7. Bake in a hot oven, Gas 7, 425°F, 220°C, for 10 minutes until crisp and lightly golden.
8. Turn on to rack to cool.
9. Meanwhile, for the filling, mix salad cream or mayonnaise into cheese adding seasonings to taste.
10. Pipe with small star nozzle on to whole biscuits. Place two halves like wings on top.
11. Pipe a little more cheese mixture down centre.
13. Garnish with half stuffed olive, pieces of gherkin or a shrimp.

CHOUX PASTRY

This pastry is made in an unusual way. It is almost always associated with éclairs and profiteroles, but it also makes an excellent container for savoury fillings which can be served hot or cold (*see page 186 for some fillings for pancakes or vol-au-vents*).

65 g/2$\frac{1}{2}$ oz flour
A pinch of salt
50 g/2 oz butter
125 ml/4 fl oz water
2 well-beaten eggs

1. Sift the flour and salt on to a piece of paper (this is a help when adding the flour to the hot water and butter).
2. Cut up butter into small pieces and put this with the water into a saucepan. Bring this mixture to the boil. When the butter has melted shoot in the flour and remove pan from heat. Beat well with a wooden spoon until there are no lumps left.
3. Now beat in half of the beaten egg with care and when well mixed add the second egg a bit at a time.
4. At this point the mixture should be slack enough to pipe easily, but firm enough to retain its shape. Put lid on pan and let it cool a little.
5. Put mixture into a forcing bag with a 1 cm/$\frac{1}{2}$ inch plain nozzle. Pipe either small rounds or sausage shapes on a well-greased tin or on a baking sheet lined with non-stick paper.
6. Bake in a moderately hot oven, Gas 6, 400°F,

200°C, for 20 to 25 minutes or until crisp, golden and puffy.

7. As soon as pastries are out of oven, split them down the side to allow steam to escape.

8. Cool on a wire rack. They are now ready to be filled.

Eclairs and Choux Rings

These are usually filled with whipped cream from a piping bag. Ice with chocolate or coffee glacé icing.

Profiteroles

Fill with cream, arrange in pyramid on serving dish, dribble chocolate sauce lightly over top.

CHOCOLATE SAUCE

Melt together 125 g/4 oz plain cooking chocolate, 15 g/½ oz butter and 1 tablespoon of water in a basin over hot water—do not over-heat. Mix in a good teaspoon of cream.

See also Savoury Puffs, page 39 and Soup Nuts, page 20.

BAKED SAVOURY ROLLS

Enough for 3 to 4 helpings (*very filling*)

First, choose a filling.

MINCED MEAT

1 small onion
25 g/1 oz dripping or lard
225 g/8 oz minced meat, cooked or uncooked
Salt and pepper
A little water
1 small carrot
1 small potato

1. Peel and chop onion finely.
2. Melt fat, add onion and meat and fry till browning.
3. Season and, if necessary, add a little water to make a moist paste.
4. Grate carrot and potato and mix them into the meat. Leave it to cool.

BACON AND MUSHROOM

2 to 3 rashers bacon
1 onion
50 g/2 oz mushrooms
3 to 4 tomatoes
A little dripping
Salt and pepper

1. Remove rinds and cut up bacon.
2. Peel and chop up onion.
3. Slice mushrooms.
4. Skin and chop tomatoes. (To skin *see page 139*).
5. Fry bacon and onion for 2 or 3 minutes, adding a little dripping if necessary.
6. Add mushrooms and tomatoes and cook 2 or 3 minutes more. Season to taste. Allow to cool.

CHEESE AND ONION

175 g/6 oz grated cheese
1 grated onion
Salt and pepper

Mix cheese and onion and season lightly.

PASTRY

125 g/4 oz self-raising flour
¼ teaspoon salt
50 g/2 oz shredded suet
3 to 4 tablespoons cold water.

1. Sift flour and salt into a bowl and mix in suet.
2. Add enough water to mix to a pliable dough.
3. Using a floured board, shape pastry into a rectangle. It will be easier then to roll out to about 20 × 25 cm/8 × 10 inches.
4. Brush edges with water, 1 cm/½ inch is enough.
5. Spread on the filling, up to the damped edges.
6. Roll it up lightly like a Swiss roll. Press edges to seal.
7. Put roll on to a greased baking sheet.
8. Bake in middle of a moderately hot oven, Gas 5, 375°F, 190°C, for about 30 minutes until crisp and brown.

Margaret Heywood
Todmorden, Yorkshire

CELERY AND CHEESE FLAN

Serves 4

175 g/6 oz wholewheat cheese pastry (*see page 204) or a ready-baked 20 cm/8 inch flan case

FILLING AND SAUCE

1 head celery
1 onion
25 g/1 oz margarine
25 g/1 oz plain flour
Salt and pepper
150 ml/¼ pint milk
50 g/2 oz grated cheese

1. Roll out pastry, line a 20 cm/8 inch flan ring and bake 'blind' (*see page 202*).
2. Clean celery and slice it into 5 cm/2 inch lengths.
3. Peel and slice onion.
4. Cook celery and onion gently till tender in a little water in a pan with close-fitting lid. Drain and reserve the liquor.
5. Melt margarine in a pan. Stir in flour, salt and pepper. Cook 2 minutes.
6. Gradually stir in milk and 150 ml/$\frac{1}{4}$ pint of celery liquor. Boil for 2 minutes.
7. Add celery, onion and half of grated cheese.
8. Spread filling in flan case. Sprinkle on remaining cheese.
9. Heat through in a moderately hot oven, Gas 6, 400°F, 200°C, for 15 minutes until golden brown on top.

CHEESE AND EGG PIE

Serves 4

125 g/4 oz shortcrust pastry, either white or wholewheat (*see page 203*)
225 g/8 oz Cheddar cheese
4 eggs
Salt and pepper
25 g/1 oz fresh brown breadcrumbs
A very little butter
2 tablespoons milk

1. Line an 18 cm/7 inch flan ring or tin with the pastry.
2. Bake it 'blind' but not brown (*see page 202*). Let it cool for 5 minutes or so.
3. Place half the cheese in the flan case and make 4 small hollows. Break an egg into each.
4. Season with salt and pepper.
5. Cover with rest of cheese and then the breadcrumbs.
6. Dot with a little butter and moisten all over with the milk.
7. Bake in a moderate oven, Gas 4, 350°F, 180°C, for $\frac{1}{2}$ to $\frac{3}{4}$ hour until nicely brown and set.

This is delicious served with sliced tomatoes, either grilled or fresh.

Judith Adshead
Mottram St Andrew, Cheshire

CHEESE AND ONION PIE

A simple-to-make pie which can be made with either wholewheat or white shortcrust pastry (*see page 203*). The strong flavoured Canadian Cheddar gives the filling a bite. Can be frozen either before baking, in which case do not glaze, or after cooking when quite cold.

Serves 4 or 5

325 g/12 oz shortcrust pastry

FILLING
2 large onions, minced or finely-chopped
225 g/8 oz Canadian Cheddar cheese, grated
Pepper
2 tablespoons milk
25 g/1 oz butter

1. Line a 25 cm/10 inch pie tin or flan ring on a baking sheet with two thirds of the pastry. Roll out the rest for the lid.
2. Mix onions and cheese, season to taste and add a little milk to keep pie moist.
3. Put filling into pastry base, dot top with small pieces of butter.
4. Brush edges of pie with water, fit on lid, press to seal. Brush top with milk to glaze. Make two or three slits to let out steam.
5. Bake in centre of a hot oven, Gas 7, 425°F, 220°C, for 30 to 35 minutes. If using wholewheat pastry, bake just above middle of a moderately hot oven, Gas 6, 400°F, 200°C.

Best served just warm or cold.

Mrs Iris Dargavel
Llanellen, Gwent

CHESHIRE ONION PIE

Serves 4

SHORTCRUST PASTRY
175 g/6 oz plain white or wholewheat flour, or
    a mixture of both
¼ teaspoon salt
40 g/1½ oz lard
40 g/1½ oz margarine
3 to 4 dessertspoons water

FILLING
50 g/2 oz butter
450 to 550 g/1 to 1¼ lb peeled and sliced onions
25 g/1 oz plain flour (very bare weight)
1 level teaspoon salt
A qood quantity of black pepper
Grated nutmeg
150 ml/¼ pint top of the milk or cream
1 large egg

1. Place flour and salt in mixing bowl, rub in fats,
mix to a firm dough with the water.
2. Roll out on floured board.
3. Line a 20 cm/8 inch flan ring on a baking tray.
Leave to rest while preparing filling.
4. Melt butter in saucepan, add onions, cook gently
until soft, about 15 minutes. Do not brown.
5. Add flour, let it sizzle then add salt and pepper
and a little nutmeg.
6. Stir in milk, bring to boil and cook 2 minutes.
Remove from heat.
7. Beat egg lightly, spoon into it a little mixture from
pan and stir in, then return to pan and mix in. Taste
for seasoning.
8. Spoon into flan case, level top and grate on a little
more nutmeg.
9. Bake in a moderately hot oven, Gas 6, 400°F,
200°C, for 45 to 50 minutes. After about 30 minutes,
when pastry is set, remove flan ring to allow crust to
brown. Cool on wire tray.

Mrs Sybil Norcott
Irlam, Nr Manchester

CREAMY ONION PIE

Serves 4

Cheese pastry made up as on *page 204* but not
    baked
225 ml/8 fl oz milk
1 small bay leaf
6 to 8 peppercorns
40 g/1½ oz butter
2 large thinly-sliced onions
65 g/2½ oz fresh white or wholewheat bread-
    crumbs (*see page 52*)
2 beaten eggs
1 teaspoon Salt and Pepper Mix (*see page 17*)
1 teaspoon Worcestershire sauce
2 tablespoons double cream
A little grated cheese, optional

1. Make up the pastry as on page 204 and line a
20 cm/8 inch flan ring placed on a baking tray.
2. Place milk, bay leaf and peppercorns in a pan,
heat to nearly boiling. Remove from heat and leave
5 minutes to infuse.
3. Meanwhile, melt butter in pan and add onions.
Cook for a few minutes so that they soften and
become lightly-golden.
4. Have breadcrumbs in a large basin, strain the
milk and pour it over.
5. Add onions and butter from pan, eggs, Salt and
Pepper Mix and Worcestershire sauce. Stir in the
cream.
6. Taste for seasoning, adding extra if necessary.
7. Pour into pastry case and bake in a moderately
hot oven, Gas 6, 400°F, 200°C, for about 25 minutes
until the pastry is golden and the filling is set.
8. Place under medium grill to finish if a little pale
on top. 1 to 2 minutes is enough. If using grated
cheese sprinkle it on top before grilling.

Can be eaten hot or cold. To reheat replace flan ring
and cover with foil, put in a moderately hot oven,
Gas 5, 375°F, 190°C, for 12 to 15 minutes.

*See Chicken and Sweetcorn Flan (page 215) for a way
to make savoury biscuits with surplus pastry.*

WHOLEWHEAT CHEESE AND ONION FLAN

You will need a 20 cm/8 inch flan ring on a baking sheet or flan tin with loose bottom.

Serves 2 or 3

175 g/6 oz wholewheat pastry (*see page 203*)

FILLING
25 g/1 oz butter
1 tablespoon vegetable oil
450 g/1 lb onions
2 eggs
2 tablespoons cream or top of the milk
Salt and pepper
Grating of nutmeg
75 g/3 oz grated cheese

1. First make the pastry, line the flan tin and bake 'blind' for 20 minutes (*see page 202*). Remove from oven, take out baking beans and paper but leave flan in ring. Lower oven temperature to moderate, Gas 4, 350°F, 180°C.
2. Meanwhile, start the filling. Melt butter with oil in a large frying pan and fry onions gently until soft but not brown. They will need turning over with a spoon.
3. In a bowl, beat eggs, cream (or milk top), a little salt, pepper and nutmeg and mix in 50 g/2 oz of the cheese. Add onions.
4. Pour filling into flan case. Sprinkle with the rest of cheese.
5. Put it in moderate oven, Gas 4, 350°F, 180°C, for 30 minutes.

COURGETTE TART

For this you need a 20 or 23 cm/8 or 9 inch pastry case baked blind. Choose a pastry on page 203 and follow instructions given for baking 'blind' (*see page 202*).

Serves 4

325 g/12 oz courgettes
15 g/½ oz butter
1 small onion, chopped
1 teaspoon chopped fresh tarragon or ½ teaspoon dried
2 large eggs
150 ml/¼ pint soured cream
3 heaped tablespoons grated Parmesan cheese
Salt and pepper

1. Wash courgettes and trim off stalks, but do not peel. Cube them. Do not slice.
2. Melt butter, add courgettes, onion and tarragon. Put on lid and cook over a low heat, shaking pan occasionally, until courgettes are barely done. Leave to cool.
3. Beat together eggs and cream. Stir in grated Parmesan cheese.
4. Fold this sauce into courgettes. Add pepper and a little salt to taste.
5. Pour into pastry case.
6. Bake above middle of a moderate oven, Gas 4, 350°F, 180°C, for 30 to 40 minutes.

LEEK FLAN

Tarten Gennin in Wales.

An excellent, rich and well-flavoured flan. Easy to make half the given quantity.

Serves 6

PASTRY
A 25 cm/10 inch ready-baked flan case, of either wholewheat or white shortcrust pastry (*see page 203*)
Or, **two 15 cm/6 inches in diameter**

FILLING
6 large leeks
25 g/1 oz butter
150 g/5 oz bacon, chopped
4 well-beaten eggs
300 ml/½ pint milk or cream
Pepper and salt
75 g/3 oz grated cheese, optional

1. Wash leeks and cut both the white and green into 2.5 cm/1 inch pieces.
2. Heat butter in a saucepan and cook leeks over very low heat with lid on pan until they are soft.
3. Spread leeks in pastry case, and arrange bacon on top.
4. Beat eggs with milk or cream, adding pepper and a little salt. Pour into flan case.
5. Sprinkle cheese over and put at once in the middle or lower part of a moderate oven, Gas 4, 350°F, 180°C, for 35 minutes. If making 15 cm/6 inch flans bake for 25 to 30 minutes.

Serve hot or cold.

Mrs Eileen Trumper
Llanvair Kilgeddin, Gwent

MUSHROOM PIE

Serves 4

**225 g/8 oz shortcrust pastry, wholewheat flour
or a mixture** (*see page 203*)

FILLING
**2 rashers bacon
225 g/8 oz mushrooms
Salt, pepper and a little dried sage
2 eggs, beaten**

1. Grease a 20 cm/8 inch pie dish and line with pastry.
2. Cut bacon into small pieces and cover the bottom of pie.
3. Fill up with sliced seasoned mushrooms and sage.
4. Pour the beaten eggs over the filling (reserving a little to brush pie top).
5. Cover with pastry lid and decorate. Brush top with beaten egg.
6. Bake in moderately hot oven, Gas 6, 400°F, 200°C, about 1 hour, reducing heat to moderate, Gas 3, 325°F, 160°C, after first half hour if pastry is browning too much before the bacon is cooked.

Mrs Sybil Norcott
Irlam, Nr Manchester

EGG AND BACON PIE

Serves 4

SHORTCRUST PASTRY
**175 g/6 oz plain white or wholewheat flour or a
  mixture
¼ teaspoon salt
40 g/1½ oz lard
40 g/1½ oz margarine
3 to 4 dessertspoons water**

FILLING
**175 g/6 oz bacon (pieces can be used but should
  be fairly lean)
2 large eggs
A good shake of pepper
300 ml/½ pint less 2 tablespoons creamy milk**

1. Place flour and salt in bowl, rub in fats and bind to a firm dough with the water. Leave to rest 5 to 10 minutes.
2. Roll out a good 25 cm/10 inches in diameter on floured board, fit into a 20 cm/8 inch flan ring placed on a baking tray. Roll off surplus pastry with rolling pin.
3. Now make the filling. Cut bacon into 2.5 cm/ 1 inch squares, fry lightly for 5 minutes over gentle heat, do not crisp. Drain from the fat.
4. Place eggs in a basin, add a good shake of pepper. Add the milk and whisk gently together without getting it frothy. This ensures a smooth texture.
5. Cover base of flan with bacon and strain on egg and milk mixture.
6. Bake in a moderately hot oven, Gas 6, 400°F, 200°C, for 20 minutes. Reduce heat to moderate, Gas 4, 350°F, 180°C, for a further 10 to 12 minutes until filling is set.

HAM, EGG AND ONION FLAN

Serves 4

**150 g/5 oz wholewheat or white shortcrust pas-
try** (*see page 203*)

FILLING
**25 g/1 oz ham fat or lard
1 small onion, finely-chopped
125 g/4 oz cooked ham
2 beaten eggs
300 ml/½ pint milk
Pepper and a little salt
50 g/2 oz grated Cheddar cheese**

1. Using a floured board, roll out pastry to fit a 20 cm/8 inch flan tin, or a ring set on a baking tray, or a flan dish.
2. *For the filling.* Heat fat and fry onion gently to soften.
3. Put onion and ham in flan.
4. Mix eggs, milk and seasoning and strain into flan.
5. Sprinkle cheese on top.
6. Bake near top of a moderately hot oven.Gas 6, 400°F, 200°C, for 20 minutes. Then reduce heat to moderate, Gas 4, 350°F, 180°C, for another 10 minutes until cooked.

COLD SAVOURY FLAN

For this you need a 20 cm/8 inch flan case baked blind. Cheese or wholewheat pastry is nice for this filling (*see pages 203–4*).

Serves 4

3 eggs
25 g/1 oz butter
2 tablespoons single cream or top-of-the-milk
75 to 125 g/3 to 4 oz lean cooked ham or bacon, chopped small
2 tablespoons mayonnaise
125 g/4 oz frozen mixed vegetables, cooked and cooled
Black pepper and a little salt

TO GARNISH
Tomato or cucumber slices

1. Scramble eggs with butter and cream.
2. Add chopped ham, mayonnaise, vegetables and seasoning.
3. Fill flan case and decorate with slices of tomato and/or cucumber.

SALMON AND CUCUMBER FLAN

Shrimps or prawns may be used instead of salmon.

Serves 4

Shortcrust pastry made up with 125 g/4 oz flour (*see page 203*). *Or,* use a ready-baked 18 cm/7 inch flan case

FILLING
25 g/1 oz margarine
25 g/1 oz plain flour
1 level teaspoon mustard
1 level teaspoon sugar
Good pinch salt
A good sprinkle of pepper
175 ml/6 fl oz milk
1 beaten egg
1 tablespoon white or cider vinegar
125 g/4 oz salmon
Chopped parsley to taste (optional)
Slices of cucumber

1. Set oven at moderately hot, Gas 6, 400°F, 200°C.
2. Use a plain 18 cm/7 inch flan ring on a baking sheet.
3. Roll out pastry on a floured board to a round. The pastry should measure about 5 cm/2 inches more than diameter of the flan ring.
4. Follow instructions for baking 'blind' (*see page 202*, paragraphs 1 to 7).
5. Bake for about 20 minutes until golden brown on the edges. Remove beans and paper and put back in oven for 5 minutes more to 'dry off' centre of the flan.
6. Slide flan off baking sheet on to a cooling wire. Lift off flan ring and leave flan case to cool. If eating it hot, keep flan-case warm.

FOR THE FILLING
1. Melt margarine in a saucepan.
2. Add flour and cook for about 2 minutes.
3. In a small basin, blend mustard, sugar, salt and pepper with a little of the milk.
4. Add blended mustard mixture to remaining milk.
5. Gradually stir into pan.
6. Heat, stirring all the time, until mixture thickens.
7. Remove from heat, cool slightly and beat in the egg. Heat again but do not allow mixture to boil or egg will curdle.

8. Lastly, add vinegar, flaked salmon and chopped parsley.

9. Pour into flan case and garnish with slices of cucumber.

Stella Boldy
Sykehouse, N. Humberside

KIPPER SAVOURY

Serves 4

2 large kippers
50 g/2 oz butter
1 tablespoon chopped chives
½ clove of garlic crushed with a few grains of salt

FOR THE PASTRY
225 g/8 oz plain white or wholewheat flour, or a mixture of both
75 g/3 oz lard
75 g/3 oz peeled and grated raw potato
About 1 tablespoon cold water

TO FINISH
A little melted butter

1. Steam kippers between 2 plates over a pan of simmering water for about 20 minutes. Remove flesh, discard bones and skin.
2. Soften butter in a basin, but do not let it melt to oil.
3. Add flaked kipper-flesh, chives and garlic. Mix well.
4. Rub lard into flour, add potato and mix to a firm dough with water.
5. Roll out half the dough and line a pie plate 18 to 20 cm/7 to 8 inches in diameter.
6. Spread on filling to within 1 cm/a half inch of edge, dampen edge with cold water.
7. Roll out remaining dough to cover, press edges to seal, trim and flute.
8. With a sharp knife, using tip only, make a criss-cross pattern on top of pie cutting through lid to filling.
9. Brush with melted butter.
10. Bake in a moderately hot oven, Gas 6, 400°F, 200°C, for about 35 minutes.

Good served with parsley sauce (*see page 33*). Can also be served in slices for a buffet.

Mrs Joan Ireland
West Suffolk

SMOKED HADDOCK AND COTTAGE CHEESE FLAN

You need a 20 cm/8 inch flan ring on a baking sheet or a flan tin with removable base.

Serves 4

PASTRY
175 g/6 oz wholewheat flour
¼ level teaspoon salt
125 g/4 oz margarine
2 tablespoons cold water (use a measure)

FILLING
175 g/6 oz smoked fillet of haddock or other smoked fish
Water or milk and water to cook fish
1 small onion
50 g/2 oz mushrooms
25 g/1 oz butter
2 eggs
3 tablespoons milk
125 g/4 oz cottage cheese
Freshly-ground black pepper
Juice of ½ lemon
Salt
Chopped parsley

1. Put flour and salt in a bowl, rub in margarine and mix to a firm dough with water. Leave it to rest for 5 to 10 minutes.
2. Roll it out on a floured board to a round about 25 cm/10 inches across. Cut a circle of greaseproof paper about 25 cm/10 inches across and grease it lightly on one side. Fit pastry into flan ring. Roll off surplus pastry with a rolling pin.
3. Bake it 'blind'—i.e., the flan case is partly cooked before filling goes in (*see page 202*).
4. Bake in centre of hot oven. Gas 7, 425°F, 220°C, for 10 minutes. Remove beans and paper and bake another 10 minutes. If pastry is browning too quickly, reduce heat to Gas 5, 375°F, 190°C.
5. Remove from oven but leave pastry in flan ring on baking sheet. Lower oven temperature to Gas 2, 300°F, 150°C.
6. *The filling:* put fish in a shallow pan with water, or milk and water, just to cover. Bring to boil, cover pan and simmer 8 minutes or until cooked.
7. Peel and finely chop onion. Slice mushrooms.
8. Melt butter and fry onion gently till soft. Add mushrooms and cook for 1 or 2 minutes.
9. Drain fish when cooked and flake it.

10. Combine fish, onion and mushrooms and spread over base of flan.

11. Beat together eggs and milk, then beat in cottage cheese, pepper and lemon juice. A little salt may be added, but remember the fish is salty.

12. Pour this mixture over fish and put flan straight into cool oven, Gas 2, 300°F, 150°C, and cook for 40 minutes until filling is set and golden on top.

Serve hot or cold, sprinkled with chopped parsley.

TUNA PLAIT

Serves 4

225 g/8 oz plain flour
Pinch of salt
50 g/2 oz lard
50 g/2 oz margarine
75 g/3 oz grated cheese
2 tablespoons cold water
190 g/7 oz tuna fish
1 small onion, chopped finely
Squeeze of lemon juice
A little beaten egg

1. Sift flour and salt into a bowl.
2. Rub fat into flour until mixture is like fine bread-crumbs.
3. Add 25 g/1 oz of the grated cheese and mix pastry to a stiff dough with cold water.
4. Mix together tuna, chopped onion, grated cheese and lemon juice.
5. Roll out pastry into a rectangle about 20 cm/8 inches wide and 30 cm/12 inches long. Dampen edges.
6. Pile filling down centre of pastry. Make slits on either side of filling at 2.5 cm/1 inch intervals and cross these alternately over filling to form plait. Seal top and bottom.
7. Brush with beaten egg. Bake in a hot oven, Gas 7, 425°F, 220°C, for 25 minutes.

Janet Town
Pudsey, Yorkshire

CHICKEN AND SWEETCORN FLAN

Serves 4

Cheese pastry made up as on *page 204*. There will be enough for a 20 cm/8 inch flan case and a batch of 12 small biscuits
1 small onion, finely-chopped
25 g/1 oz butter
25 g/1 oz flour
½ teaspoon dry mustard
½ teaspoon Salt and Pepper Mix (*see page 17*)
150 ml/¼ pint milk
A 190 g/7 oz can of sweetcorn with peppers
125 g/4 oz diced cooked chicken
2 tablespoons cream
25 to 50 g/1 to 2 oz grated cheese

1. Bake the flan case 'blind' for 20 minutes only. See instructions on *page 202*.
2. Meanwhile, fry onion in butter until soft but not coloured.
3. Stir in flour, mustard, Salt and Pepper Mix and cook for one minute.
4. Drain corn, add liquid to milk. Stir this into onion mixture in pan, bring to boil and cook for 2 minutes.
5. Remove from heat, mix in corn and chicken, cream and extra seasoning to taste.
6. Pour into partly cooked, hot flan case, cover top with cheese.
7. Return to moderately hot oven, Gas 6, 400°F, 200°C, and cook 12 to 15 minutes until cheese is melted and turning golden.

Can be eaten hot or cold. To reheat, replace flan ring, cover with foil and put in a moderately hot oven, Gas 5, 375°F, 190°C, for 12 to 15 minutes.

TO MAKE SAVOURY BISCUITS FROM THE SURPLUS PASTRY
1. Roll out thinly, 5 mm/less than a quarter of an inch thick, on floured board. Prick all over with a fork. Cut into desired shapes.
2. Place on lightly-greased baking tray.
3. Bake in a moderately hot oven, Gas 6, 400°F, 200°C, for 8 to 10 minutes until crisp and lightly golden.
4. Turn on to rack to cool.

Serve with butter or cream cheese. Decorate with sliced, stuffed olives, gherkin, shrimps etc. Can also be used for savoury dips.

See also Chicken and Ham Pie, page 58.

CHESHIRE FIDGET PIE

Serves 4

150 g/5 oz shortcrust pastry (*see page 203*) or wholewheat pastry (*see page 203*)
450 g/1 lb cooking apples, peeled, cored and sliced
225 g/8 oz onions, sliced
325 g/12 oz streaky bacon, chopped
Seasoning
100 ml/3 to 4 fl oz stock or water

1. Make layers in a pie-dish of apple, onion and bacon until all is used. Season between layers with pepper and a very little salt.
2. Pour the stock or water over the layers.
3. Roll out pastry on floured board.
4. Cover pie-dish with pastry.
5. Trim edges.
6. Re-roll trimmings and cut leaves to decorate pie.
7. Bake in a moderate oven, Gas 4, 350°F, 180°C, for 2 hours.

Sybil Norcott
Irlam, Nr Manchester

MINCED BACON AND PORK PIE

Makes about 6 portions

275 g/10 oz rich pie pastry (*see page 204*)

FILLING
175 g/6 oz cheapest bacon
175 g/6 oz minced pork luncheon meat
Pepper and salt
2 eggs
65 ml/2½ oz milk

This quantity is enough for a loaf shape or round pie with a lid.

1. Roll out two thirds of the pastry and line a ½ kg/ 1 lb loaf tin, an 18 cm/7 inch pie plate or flan ring set on a baking sheet.
2. Mince bacon, mix it with pork and season with pepper if necessary.
3. Put it into pastry-lined tin.
4. Beat eggs, adding milk and a little salt, and pour over meat, saving 1 or 2 teaspoons to glaze the pie.

5. Roll out the pastry lid, damp edges, plate it over filling and seal all round.
6. Use trimmings to decorate, and brush the top with remaining egg and milk to glaze. Do not make holes in top yet or filling may boil over and spoil top.
7. Bake near top of a moderately hot oven, Gas 6, 400°F, 200°C, for 1 hour, moving pie down to middle when it has begun to brown.
8. Remove pie from oven and pierce lid in one or two places to let out steam.

Serve hot or cold.

Anne Wallace
Stewarton, Ayrshire

PORK PIE

Freezes satisfactorily but not longer than one month.

HOT WATER CRUST
125 ml/4 fl oz water
125 g/4 oz lard
275 g/10 oz strong plain flour
½ level teaspoon salt
1 small beaten egg

FILLING
450 g/1 lb pork, from the shoulder which should give roughly 325 g/¾ lb lean and 125 g/¼ lb fat
2 level teaspoons Salt and Pepper Mix (*see page 17*)
¼ level teaspoon powdered mace if available

JELLY
1 pig's trotter
1 bay leaf
6 peppercorns

1. Prepare jelly a day in advance. Boil trotter with bay leaf and peppercorns in 600 ml/1 pint of water until quite soft and leaving the bone (about 3 hours).
2. Strain liquid into basin, 150 ml/¼ pint is enough for 1 pie, and leave overnight.
3. Remove any fat from top. If jelly has not set, simmer gently to reduce amount. Discard trotter.
4. Now make the pastry. Boil water and lard, pour on to flour and salt. Mix with a knife (it will be hot) then knead with hands until quite smooth. Allow to cool a little before rolling out.
5. Now mix the filling. Trim gristle from pork which will reduce it to 400 to 425 g/14 to 15 oz. Cut it into very small pieces and mix in the seasonings. Or,

using coarse cutters, put the pork and seasonings through mincer.

6. Roll out $\frac{3}{4}$ of the pastry to fit a loose-bottomed tin, 15 cm/6 inches across and 8 cm/3 inches deep, pressing pastry round sides to make an even thickness.

7. Pack filling in loosely.

8. Roll out lid to fit, brushing edges with beaten egg. Seal firmly. Cut away surplus pastry.

9. Roll this out thinly and cut into leaves. Brush these with beaten egg and arrange on top.

10. Flute edges of pie and brush all over top of pie with beaten egg.

11. Make a hole in the centre with skewer.

12. Bake in a moderately hot oven, Gas 6, 400°F, 200°C, for 30 minutes. Reduce the heat if browning too quickly to Gas 5, 375°F, 190°C, and bake for a further 1 hour.

13. Remove from tin on to wire rack.

14. Boil up jelly.

15. Allow pie and jelly to cool 15 minutes. Using a small funnel, gently pour jelly through hole in centre, as much as it will hold. When jelly has settled into meat, add a little more for extra moistness.

For best flavour leave it 24 hours before eating.

BUCKINGHAMSHIRE LITTLE MUTTON PIES

To make about 8 to 12 pies.

225 g/8 oz shortcrust pastry (*see page 203*)
225 g/8 oz cold cooked mutton or lamb
125 g/4 oz cold potatoes
1 small onion
1 tablespoon chopped parsley
Sage or rosemary, to flavour, (or mixed herbs)
Salt and pepper
Gravy or stock, to moisten
Beaten egg, to glaze

1. Cut up meat and potatoes into small squares. Chop the onion finely.

2. Mix together meat, potato, onion, herbs and seasoning adding gravy or stock to moisten.

3. Roll out pastry thinly. Cut rounds to fit patty tins.

4. Spoon in meat mixture. Dampen edges and cover with pastry tops, pressing to seal. Brush with beaten egg.

5. Bake in a hot oven, Gas 7, 425°F, 220°C, for 15 to 20 minutes.

CORNISH PASTY

We sampled this pasty with members of the Women's Institute in Truro and it was excellent— but the variations are as many in Cornwall as elsewhere.

Serves 1 or 2

125 g/4 oz shortcrust pastry using the flour of your choice (*see page 203*)

FILLING
125 g/4 oz skirt of beef
1 potato
1 small onion
A small piece of swede
Salt and pepper
A little milk
A small piece of butter

1. Make up pastry and leave it in a cool place to rest.

2. Cut meat into strips and then slice finely (but do not mince).

3. Slice vegetables finely and mix together.

4. Roll out pastry into a round, about 23 cm/9 inches in diameter.

5. Place mixed vegetables on one half of pastry and season to taste. Put meat on top of vegetables and season again.

6. Damp edges of pastry with milk and fold it over into a pasty. Seal edges.

7. Crimp the sealed edges. Brush pastry with milk. Cut two slits in top of pasty.

8. Bake in a hot oven, Gas 7, 425°F, 220°C, for 20 minutes or until pastry starts to brown. Then reduce heat to moderately hot, Gas 5, 375°F, 190°C, and bake for a further 30 minutes.

About 10 minutes before cooking time is completed, remove pasty from the oven and put butter in the slits in pastry. Replace in oven to finish cooking.

Mrs Jean Wootton
Cornwall Women's Institute

YORKSHIRE CORNISH PASTIES

Serves 2 to 3

225 g/8 oz shortcrust pastry (*see page 203*)
225 g/8 oz roughly minced beef
Chopped onion, diced potato and carrot to
    weigh about 225 g/8 oz
1 teaspoon Salt and Pepper Mix (*see page 17*)

1. Combine filling ingredients.
2. Roll out pastry and cut into 15 to 18 cm/6 to 8
inch rounds. A saucepan lid can be a good cutter.
3. Place filling down centre of the pastry, damp
edges with water and bring sides to centre. Join on
top.
4. Seal, fluting edges with fingers and thumb.
5. Brush with beaten egg.
6. Place on lightly greased baking tray and bake in
a moderately hot oven, Gas 6, 400°F, 200°C, for 40
minutes, lowering heat if browning too much.

DEVONSHIRE PORK PASTIES

Especially good made with wholewheat pastry and
eaten cold with salad.

Makes about 6 or 7 pasties

350 g/12 oz white or wholewheat shortcrust
    pastry (*see page 203*)
350 g/12 oz cooked pork
1 small onion or 1 stick of celery
1 teaspoon Worcestershire sauce
Salt and pepper

1. Make up pastry and leave it to rest in a cool place
while preparing filling.
2. Cut up pork into 1 cm/½ inch cubes.
3. Grate onion or chop celery very finely.
4. Mix pork and onion with Worcestershire sauce,
adding salt and pepper to taste.
5. Using a floured board, roll out pastry about 7
mm/¼ inch thick and cut rounds about 15 cm/6
inches across, saucer size.
6. Place equal amounts of filling in centre of each
pastry round.
7. Damp edges of pastry and bring edges together to
make a join across top. Press lightly to seal and flute
edges with fingers and thumb. Make 2 slits alongside
the join.

8. Bake above middle of a moderately hot oven, Gas
6, 400°F, 200°C, for 30 minutes until firm and just
golden.

Mrs Becky Blackmore
Exeter, Devon

SUSSEX CHURDLES

Delicious pasties with a crisp cheese topping.

Makes 6

225 g/8 oz shortcrust pastry (*see page 203*)

FILLING
125 g/4 oz lamb's liver
125 g/4 oz bacon
1 medium-sized onion
25 g/1 oz lard
50 g/2 oz mushrooms*
½ dessertspoon chopped fresh parsley
½ teaspoon dried rosemary (optional)
Salt and pepper

TOPPING
1 tablespoon grated cheese
1 tablespoon wholewheat breadcrumbs
Beaten egg to glaze

*Mushrooms can be replaced with tomatoes or apple if pre-
ferred.*

1. Skin liver and cut up small. Cut up bacon and
chop onion finely.
2. Fry these together in the lard for 5 minutes.
3. Add mushrooms, herbs and seasoning and cook
2 or 3 minutes more.
4. Using a floured board, roll out pastry about 7
mm/¼ inch thick. Cut rounds about 15 cm/6 inches
in diameter.
5. Divide filling between rounds of pastry.
6. Damp edges of pastry.
7. Make pasties leaving the centre open.
8. Mix cheese and breadcrumbs and put a little
topping in each pasty.
9. Brush pastry with beaten egg.
10. Bake on a greased baking sheet in a moderately
hot oven, Gas 5, 375°F, 180°C, for 30 minutes.

Serve hot with vegetables. Delicious with redcurrant
jelly.

Mrs Janice Langley
Shoreham-by-Sea, West Sussex

DEEP-FRIED PASTIES

Makes 4 or 5

175 g/6 oz white shortcrust pastry (*see page 203*)
Fat for deep-frying

FILLING
225 g/8 oz cooked meat, beef, chicken, bacon or
    ham, minced
2 teaspoons Worcestershire sauce
1 teaspoon Salt and Pepper Mix (*see page 17*)

1. Using a floured board, roll out pastry, 7 mm/¼ inch thick. Cut 10 cm/4 inch rounds.
2. Mix together minced meat, sauce, salt and pepper.
3. Place a dessertspoon of this mixture on each round of pastry. Damp edges, fold into pasties and seal edges.
4. Heat fat, 340°F, 170°C, is the correct temperature. Otherwise you can test heat by dropping in a 1 cm/½ inch cube of bread. The bread should turn golden in 30 seconds. If it turns brown the fat is too hot, allow to cool a little. If fat is not hot enough the bread will not colour.
5. Cook for 4 to 5 minutes until golden. Drain on brown paper or kitchen paper. Eat piping hot.

Fillings can be varied: add 50 g/2 oz chopped mushrooms if you don't have sufficient meat. Also try minced pork with a little onion, a small apple and 2 to 3 teaspoons sage and onion stuffing or a pinch of dried sage.

RABBIT PIE

Serves 4

1 rabbit or 675 g/1½ rabbit portions
325 g/12 oz belly pork
2 onions
Salt and pepper
25 g/1 oz flour
A little sage
1 teaspoon chopped parsley
150 ml/¼ pint stock from the rabbit bones
225 g/8 oz rough puff or flaky pastry (*see page 206*)

FIRST PREPARE THE RABBIT
1. Skin, draw and wash the rabbit well. (*See page 78*).
2. Bone it and cut into portions.

3. Soak the portions in water for 1 hour.
4. Meanwhile, put into a pan the bones and any bony trimmings from the pork, one of the onions roughly-chopped, and the salt and pepper. Add water just to cover, bring to boil and simmer for at least one hour.
5. Drain water from the rabbit portions and wipe them on a cloth.

THE PIE
1. Put the rabbit into a pie dish, sprinkle with salt and pepper and dredge with flour and sage.
2. Cut the pork into pieces and place them over the rabbit.
3. Sprinkle with parsley and the remaining onion, chopped fine.
4. Add enough stock from the bones to come three quarters up the dish.
5. Cover with pastry. Decorate in the usual manner and make a small hole in the centre.
6. Cook in a fairly quick, that is a moderately hot oven, Gas 5, 375°F, 190°C, for half an hour until pastry is nicely browned then reduce to moderate, Gas 3, 325°F, 160°C, for a further hour.
7. Remove from oven. If liquor has evaporated, add a little more heated bone stock, taking care that it does not touch the pie crust.

This pie is excellent and usually eaten cold, the bone stock making a good jelly.

Mrs M. Pettitt
Ousden, Suffolk

STAFFORDSHIRE RABBIT PIE

Serves 4

225 g/8 oz shortcrust pastry (*see page 203*)
1 rabbit
Water
Salt
Pepper
Seasoning—such as bay leaf, mace, parsley and peppercorns made into a bouquet garni

FORCEMEAT BALLS
175 g/6 oz fresh breadcrumbs (*see page 52*)
75 g/3 oz butter or grated suet
Thyme
Parsley
Salt and pepper
Juice of 1 lemon
A lightly beaten egg

1. Joint the rabbit and leave the pieces to soak for about half an hour in cold, salted water.

2. Put them in a pan with 600 ml/1 pint of water, salt, pepper and other seasoning at pleasure. Cover and simmer for 1 hour.

3. Meanwhile make forcemeat balls by mixing the breadcrumbs with the butter or grated suet. Add thyme, parsley and seasoning and mix well together. Make it into a paste by adding the lemon juice and lightly beaten egg. Form into balls.

4. Drop these into pan in which rabbit is cooking. Simmer very gently for half an hour.

5. When cooked, place rabbit in a pie dish with forcemeat balls on top and pour in 200 to 300 ml/$\frac{1}{3}$ to $\frac{1}{2}$ pint of the liquid.

6. Cover with pastry and bake the pie for 30 minutes in a moderately hot oven, Gas 6, 400°F, 200°C.

Miss P. M. Cherry
Penkridge

See also Somerset Rabbit, page 81, and Steak and Kidney Pie, page 223.

THATCHED HOUSE PIE

Serves 3 to 4

75 g/3 oz butter or margarine
50 g/2 oz vermicelli
325 g/12 oz puff pastry (made up weight) (*see page 206***)**
1 dressed wood pigeon
Pepper and salt

1. Take an oven-to-table dish, deep enough to hold a whole pigeon, pastry etc. A 13 cm/5 inch soufflé dish is ideal, depending on size of pigeon. Rub the inside of the dish with 25 g/1 oz of the butter or margarine.

2. Spread vermicelli on base of the dish.

3. Roll out a piece of pastry and line the base and sides of dish.

4. Fill the pigeon with remaining butter. Season with pepper and salt. Lay the pigeon breast side down in the pastry-lined dish.

5. Cover with a pastry lid, sealing the joins.

6. Bake in a moderately hot oven, Gas 5, 375°F, 190°C, until the pigeon is cooked, about 1$\frac{1}{2}$ hours. When pastry has risen, heat may be reduced to cool, Gas 2, 300°F, 150°C, if pastry is browning too much.

7. Take a hot serving dish and turn out the pie. The vermicelli will appear like thatch—hence the name of the recipe.

Mrs Sybil Norcott
Irlam, Nr Manchester

SAUSAGE PLAIT

Serves 4

Half the quantity of puff pastry given on page 206, roughly 225 g/8 oz made up weight
A little beaten egg

FILLING
225 g/8 oz sausagemeat
A pinch of mixed herbs
Shake of salt and pepper
2 skinned and chopped tomatoes (*see page 139***)**
Mix all together

1. Roll out pastry about 25 by 20 cm/10 by 8 inches. Cut all edges cleanly and brush with beaten egg.

2. Place filling down centre third of pastry leaving 1 cm/$\frac{1}{2}$ inch at top and bottom.

3. Slash sides diagonally at 2.5 cm/1 inch intervals and bring to centre alternately, sealing top and bottom. Leave in cool place for half an hour if possible.

4. Brush with beaten egg.

5. Bake on an ungreased baking tray in a hot oven, Gas 8, 450°F, 230°C, for 15 minutes, reduce heat to moderately hot, Gas 6, 400°F, 200°C, for a further 25 to 30 minutes.

SAUSAGE PIE

Good for a picnic.

Serves 4

225 g/8 oz shortcrust, made with white or wholewheat flour, or a mixture of each (*see page 203***)**

FILLING
225 g/8 oz sausagemeat
2 tablespoons chutney
2 large tomatoes, skinned and thickly-sliced (*see page 139***)**
2 hard-boiled eggs, sliced
A pinch of mixed herbs
Salt and pepper

TO FINISH PIE
A little beaten egg or a teaspoon of top of the milk

1. Cut pastry into 2 portions, one slightly larger than the other. Use larger piece to line a 23 cm/9 inch pie plate. Roll remainder plus trimmings for the lid.
2. Mix together sausagemeat and chutney. Divide into 2 equal portions and spread one portion over pastry in plate.
3. Arrange tomatoes and egg on top, sprinkle on herbs, salt and pepper, and spread remaining sausagemeat on top.
4. Damp edges of pastry, place on lid, press to seal. Trim off surplus pastry and use it for pastry leaves.
5. Flute edges of pie and make 8 small slits in top. Brush with a little beaten egg, if available, or use a teaspoon of top of the milk.
6. Arrange pastry leaves on top between slits and brush with egg or top of milk.
7. Bake in a hot oven, Gas 7, 425°F, 220°C, for 15 minutes, 10 to 12 if wholewheat flour is used. Reduce heat to moderate, Gas 4, 350°F, 180°C, for a further 45 minutes. Cover top with foil towards end of cooking if browning too quickly.

1. Using a floured board, roll out 225 g/8 oz of the pastry to fit two 15 cm/6 inch flan rings or dishes, saving the rest for the lids.
2. *Now for the filling*. Mash up sausagemeat in a large bowl.
3. Mince bacon or pork.
4. Grate the apple.
5. Mix all filling ingredients together, except hard-boiled egg, seasoning with pepper and a little salt if necessary. Save a dessertspoon of beaten egg to glaze pie tops.
6. Divide filling between the two flans. Arrange a quartered hard-boiled egg in each if desired, covering them carefully with sausage mixture.
7. Roll out lids. Moisten edges, secure them in place and pinch edges to seal. Use trimmings to decorate.
8. Prick tops in several places with a fork. Mix a dessertspoon of milk with remaining beaten egg and brush tops of pies to glaze.
9. Bake for 45 minutes in all at top of a moderately hot oven, Gas 5, 375°F, 190°C, for 30 minutes, then if browning too quickly reduce heat to moderate, Gas 4, 350°F, 180°C, for the last 15 minutes.

Mrs Olive Odell
Hartlebury, Worcestershire

SAVOURY SAUSAGE PIE

Mrs Odell had this recipe given her many years ago by a 90-year-old Worcester woman who remembered the filling being minced up pork pieces left after the pig was killed. It was known as 'Bits and Pieces'.

Freezes well.

Quantities given make two 15 cm/6 inch pies, so it is easy to make just one.

350 g/12 oz shortcrust pastry, white or wholewheat or a mixture (*see page 203*)

FILLING
450 g/1 lb pork sausagemeat
125 g/4 oz bacon bits, fat pork or streaky bacon
1 medium-sized cooking apple
1 tablespoon chopped fresh parsley
2 beaten eggs
Pepper and salt

AN OPTIONAL ADDITION
1 hard-boiled egg for each pie, but if you are going to freeze pies it is best to leave this out

SAVOURY SAUSAGE FLAN

Freezes well.

Serves 5 to 6, but easy to make smaller quantities.

225 g/8 oz made-up shortcrust pastry (*see page 203*)

FILLING
450 g/1 lb potatoes
25 g/1 oz margarine
1 medium-sized onion or 1 teaspoon mixed herbs
225 g/8 oz sausagemeat
1 level teaspoon Salt and Pepper Mix (*see page 17*)

1. Cook potatoes in a little salted water. Drain and mash well with margarine.
2. Using a floured board, roll pastry out 7 mm/$\frac{1}{4}$ inch thick. Line a 20 cm/8 inch pie-plate or flan dish.
3. Peel and finely chop or grate onion and add it, or mixed herbs, to sausagemeat with salt and pepper. Mix well.

4. Spread sausagemeat in uncooked pastry case.

5. Pipe potato to cover the sausage. Or spread it over, forking the top.

6. Bake in a hot oven, Gas 7, 425°F, 220°C, for 20 minutes. Reduce temperature to moderately hot, Gas 5, 375°F, 190°C, for 20 minutes more.

Delicious eaten hot or cold. Can also be made as individual tartlets.

Pat Dixon
Holmfirth, W. Yorkshire

SAUSAGE AND APPLE TURNOVERS

Makes 6 turnovers

275 g/10 oz wholewheat pastry (*see page 203*)

FOR THE FILLING
450 g/1 lb sausagemeat
2 lamb's kidneys (optional)
1 medium-sized onion
225 g/8 oz cooking apples
Salt and pepper
A little milk, to glaze

1. First make the pastry.

2. *The filling:* put sausagemeat in the mixing bowl. Remove skin from kidneys. Cut them in half along the round edge. Take out the white core. Cut up kidneys into 1 cm/½-inch pieces. Add them to sausagemeat.

3. Peel and grate onion. Grate apple without peeling it.

4. Mix onion and apple into sausagemeat with a little salt and pepper.

5. Prepare a large space, lightly floured, for rolling out pastry. Divide dough into two pieces. Work each piece lightly into a brick-shaped lump. This will make it easier to roll out as required.

6. Roll out each piece into a rectangle 15 cm × 46 cm/6 inches × 18 inches.

7. Divide each piece into 3 equal portions. Each portion will be 15 cm/6 inches square, and there will be six portions.

8. Place even quantities of filling on to each square.

9. Brush edges of pastry with water. Fold them corner to corner to make triangles. Press edges together to seal well.

10. Brush each turnover with milk and make 3 cuts in the top of each one to let out the steam.

11. Lift them on to a large baking sheet. Bake on centre shelf of a moderately hot oven. Gas 6, 400°F, 200°C, for 45 minutes when they will be golden brown and cooked.

Serve either hot or cold.

CHEESE SAUSAGE ROLLS

Makes about 8 small rolls

CHEESE PASTRY
125 g/4 oz plain flour
Pinch of dry mustard
Salt
Pepper
A few grains cayenne pepper
50 g/2 oz butter
50 g/2 oz grated hard cheese
1 egg-yolk
2 teaspoons cold water
A little milk

FILLING
225 g/8 oz sausagemeat

1. Sieve flour, mustard, salt, pepper and cayenne pepper into a bowl.

2. Rub butter or margarine into flour mixture.

3. Mix in grated cheese.

4. Bind together with the beaten egg-yolk mixed with 2 teaspoons of cold water.

5. Using a floured board, roll pastry out into a long strip about 6–8 cm/2½–3 inches wide.

6. Place sausagemeat in a long roll down the centre.

7. Damp one edge of pastry and roll up sausagemeat, pressing lightly to seal the join. Cut sausage rolls into desired lengths.

8. Place on a baking sheet. Brush a little milk round the basin used for egg-yolk and use this to glaze sausage rolls.

9. Bake in a moderately hot oven, Gas 6, 400°F, 200°C, for about 15 minutes until golden brown.

Stella Boldy
Sykehouse, N. Humberside

STEAK AND KIDNEY PIE

With Potato Pastry Crust—use quantity given on *page 204*

Serves 4

25 g/1 oz beef dripping
125 g/4 oz chopped onion
450 g/1 lb lean, pie beef, cut into 2.5 cm/1 inch cubes
125 g/4 oz kidney, trimmed and cut slightly smaller than the beef
1 level tablespoon flour seasoned with 1 teaspoon Salt and Pepper Mix (*see page 17*)
450 ml/¾ pint water
2 teaspoons Worcestershire sauce
125 g/4 oz mushrooms

Note. Use a pressure cooker (trivet removed) for this if you have one. It saves 1½ hours' cooking time.

1. Melt dripping in pan, add onion and cook 1 minute.
2. Mix beef and kidney into seasoned flour, coating well. Add to pan and stir over heat to seal—it will change colour.
3. Add water and Worcestershire sauce, stir until boiling.
4. Cover and simmer for about 2½ hours until meat is tender, stirring occasionally.
If using a pressure cooker, pressure cook for 40 minutes. Allow to cool at room temperature before removing lid.
5. Place meat in a 750 ml/1¼ pint pie dish with about 4 tablespoons of the gravy and set aside to cool. Keep remaining gravy to serve with pie.
6. When meat is cold cover with sliced mushrooms.
7. Brush edges of pie dish with water, lift pastry on top and press firmly in place. Flute edges, brush top with milk.
8. Bake in a hot oven, Gas 7, 425°F, 220°C, for about 20 minutes until turning golden. Reduce heat to moderately hot, Gas 5, 375°F, 190°C, for a further 15 minutes.
9. Heat reserved gravy and serve with pie.

SAUSAGE CARTWHEEL FLAN

Serves 4

175 g/6 oz cheese pastry (*see page 204*)

FILLING
1 medium-sized onion
15 g/½ oz margarine
225 g/8 oz skinless sausages
1 large egg
150 ml/¼ pint milk
Salt and pepper
50 g/2 oz grated cheese

1. Roll out pastry. Line a 20 cm/8 inch flan ring.
2. Peel and chop onion.
3. Melt margarine and fry onion gently until soft. Lift onion out of pan into flan case.
4. Lightly fry sausages in pan.
5. Cut 6 of the cooked sausages to fit in flan, like the spokes of a wheel. Put aside on a plate for a moment.
6. Cut up remaining sausages and trimmed ends and put these on top of onion.
7. Beat egg, milk and seasonings. Pour into flan.
8. Arrange the 6 sausages like a cartwheel in flan. Sprinkle cheese between the spokes.
9. Bake in a moderately hot to hot oven, Gas 6 to 7, 400° to 425°F, 200° to 220°C, for about 35 minutes.

ALMOND TART I

Serves 4

125 g/4 oz shortcrust pastry (*see page 203*)

FILLING
50 g/2 oz butter or margarine
50 g/2 oz granulated sugar
50 g/2 oz semolina
1 teaspoon almond essence
1 beaten egg
½ teaspoon baking powder
2 tablespoons jam, apricot goes well with this

You can use a small or large sandwich tin, an 18 cm/ 7 inch pieplate or flan ring. You can make it up as tartlets, or you can use a small square tin and serve it in slices.

1. Make up pastry and line the tin.
2. *For the filling:* melt margarine and sugar in a saucepan.
3. Stir in semolina and cook for a few minutes, stirring all the time.
4. Remove from heat, add almond essence and stir well to cool mixture a little.
5. Add beaten egg and baking powder. Mix well.
6. Spread jam over pastry.
7. Pour mixture from saucepan into pastry case and spread evenly.
8. Bake in a moderately hot oven, Gas 6, 400°F, 200°C, until it is nicely brown, about 30 minutes. Tartlets take about 15 minutes.

Mrs Evelyn Taylor
Flixton, Manchester

ALMOND TART II

Makes one 18 cm/7 inch round flan

Shortcrust pastry made up with 125 g/4 oz flour (*see page 203*)

FILLING
75 g/3 oz butter or soft margarine
75 g/3 oz sugar
1 beaten egg
50 g/2 oz cake crumbs
25 g/1 oz ground almonds
A few drops almond essence
Raspberry jam
A few split almonds

1. Roll out pastry on a floured board and fit it into an 18 cm/7 inch flan ring.
2. Now mix the filling. Cream butter and sugar together and then beat in the egg.
3. Fold in cake crumbs and ground almonds and add the almond essence.
4. Spread jam inside flan case then fill it with mixture. Make sure filling spreads nicely to sides of flan case.
5. Scatter split almonds over the top.
6. Bake in a moderately hot oven, Gas 5, 375°F, 190°C, for 30 to 40 minutes. Look in oven after 20 minutes and reduce heat to Gas 4, 350°F, 180°C, if browning too quickly.

APPLE DAPPY

More than enough for 6. Make half the quantities for 3 or 4.

225 g/8 oz self-raising flour
1 teaspoon baking powder
Pinch of salt
50 g/2 oz margarine
150 ml/¼ pint milk
450 g/1 lb cooking apples
1 tablespoon demerara sugar
½ level teaspoon cinnamon, nutmeg, ground cloves or mixed spice

SYRUP
1 lemon or a little lemon essence
1 tablespoon golden syrup
15 g/½ oz margarine
125 g/4 oz sugar
200 ml/7 fl oz water

1. Make syrup first. Peel a fine strip of lemon rind and squeeze lemon. Put rind, juice and all other ingredients in a pan and stir over a gentle heat until sugar is dissolved. Remove from heat and leave in the pan until needed.
2. Sift flour, baking powder and salt into a bowl.
3. Rub in margarine.
4. Mix to a dough with the milk.
5. Roll out on a floured board to a rectangle about 20 × 13 cm/8 × 5 inches, and 7 mm/¼ inch thick.
6. Peel, core and chop apples.
7. Spread them on pastry.
8. Mix sugar and spice together and sprinkle over apple.

9. Roll up pastry and apple like a Swiss roll. Then cut into slices about 2.5 cm/1 inch thick.
10. Grease an ovenproof dish and lay slices flat in it.
11. Remove lemon rind from syrup and pour over the apple slices.
12. Bake in a moderately hot oven, Gas 6, 375°F, 190°C, for about 30 minutes.

Serve with cream or custard.

Joan Guy
Tavistock, Devon

DUTCH APPLE PIE

A much travelled recipe. It reached our contributor from Canada.

Serves 4

For this you need 225 g/8 oz unbaked pastry (*see page 203*) **rolled out to fit a 25 cm/10 inch flan dish, tin or ring set on a baking tray.**

FILLING
225 g/8 oz cooking apples, peeled and cored
2 tablespoons plain flour
½ teaspoon salt
175 g/6 oz sugar
1 beaten egg
A 150 ml/¼ pint carton natural yoghurt
¼ teaspoon nutmeg
1 or 2 drops vanilla essence

SPICY TOPPING
65 g/2½ oz flour
40 g/1½ oz butter
50 g/2 oz sugar
1 teaspoon cinnamon

1. Dice apple.
2. Mix other filling ingredients well.
3. Stir in apple and fill flan.
4. Bake near top of a moderately hot oven, Gas 6, 400°F, 200°C, for 15 minutes. Then reduce heat to moderate, Gas 4, 350°F, 180°C, for about 30 minutes more until filling is firm and golden.
5. Meanwhile, prepare topping. Rub butter into flour, and mix in sugar and cinnamon.
6. Sprinkle topping on pie and bake 10 minutes more until crisp and golden. Serve hot or cold with cream.

June Lambton
Goole, N. Humberside

APPLE MERINGUE FLAN

Makes one 18 cm/7 inch flan

1 baked 18 cm/7 inch rich shortcrust flan case (*see page 203*)

FILLING
450 g/1 lb cooking apples
15 g/½ oz butter
Sugar to taste
Rind of ½ a lemon
1 egg-yolk
A little apricot or raspberry jam or orange marmalade

MERINGUE
2 egg-whites (1 will be left from flan case)
125 g/4 oz caster sugar plus a little more

1. Peel and finely slice the apples.
2. Cook in butter until quite soft.
3. Sieve or liquidise.
4. Add the lemon rind, egg-yolk and sugar to taste.
5. Whisk the egg-whites stiffly, then whisk in 50 g/2 oz of the sugar until shiny. Fold in 50 g/2 oz sugar.
6. Spread base of flan case with jam or marmalade.
7. Place apple in case.
8. Spread meringue on top, being sure that this touches edges of pastry. Sift on a little caster sugar— not too much.
9. Place in cool oven, Gas 2, 300°F, 150°C, for about 20 minutes to set a little.

POTATO APPLE CAKE

Serves 4

Potato pastry as on page 204
450 g/1 lb cooking apples
2 dessertspoons dark brown sugar (Barbados)
25 g/1 oz butter
A little demerara sugar

1. Cut pastry into 2 pieces, one slightly larger than the other.
2. Roll out each piece to a round: one about 19 cm/7½ inches across, the other about 23 cm/9 inches across.
3. Place smaller round on a greased baking sheet.

4. Peel and thinly slice apples. Arrange sliced apples on pastry base, leaving a border about 1 cm/½ inch wide round edge. Sprinkle apples with 1 dessert-spoon of sugar.

5. Brush border of pastry with water and place larger circle of pastry over apples. Seal edges together. Make a small slit in centre of pastry to enable steam to escape.

6. Bake in centre of a moderately hot oven, Gas 5, 375°F, 190°C, for 35 to 40 minutes until cake is lightly-browned.

7. Remove from oven and, using a sharp and pointed knife, carefully cut out a circle from top of cake about 8 cm/3 inches across. Place butter and re-maining dessertspoon of sugar inside cake.

8. Replace 'lid' and return to oven for 5 minutes to allow butter to melt.

9. Lift cake on to a serving plate and sprinkle with demerara sugar.

Serve immediately with fresh cream. Tends to go 'sad' if allowed to go cold.

SUSSEX TARTLETS

Makes 18 tartlets

125 g/4 oz shortcrust pastry, white or whole-wheat (*see page 203*)

FILLING
1 large or 2 small cooking apples, peeled and cored
2 lightly-beaten eggs
Grated rind and juice of 1 lemon
50 g/2 oz caster sugar
A pinch of cinnamon

1. Using a floured board, roll out pastry 7 mm/¼ inch thick and line 18 tartlet tins.

2. Grate apple and put it in a bowl.

3. Mix in eggs, lemon, sugar and cinnamon.

4. Spoon filling into pastry cases.

5. Bake near top of a moderately hot oven, Gas 5, 375°F, 190°C, for 15 to 20 minutes.

6. Allow to cool in tins for 10 minutes and then remove on to a wire rack.

Mrs Ruth Brooke and Mrs Sheila Powell
Hove and Portslade, Sussex

FRUIT PIE

Serves 4

SHORTCRUST PASTRY
175 g/6 oz white or wholewheat flour, or a mix-ture of both
¼ teaspoon salt
40 g/1½ oz lard
40 g/1½ oz butter or margarine
1½ tablespoons water

FILLING
675 g/1½ lb fruit—plums (stoned), gooseberries, rhubarb, apples, or half apples and half blackberries
2 tablespoons sugar
1 tablespoon cornflour

TO FINISH
A little caster sugar

A pie plate, 18 cm/7 inch diameter and about 3 cm/1¼ inches deep, or a pie dish, 750 ml to 1 litre/1¼ to 1½ pint size, is suitable for this quantity.

1. Mix flour and salt, rub in fats, and mix to a firm dough with the water. Allow to rest for 15 minutes. This will prevent shrinkage during cooking.

2. Arrange half the fruit in the pie dish or plate. Mix sugar and cornflour, sprinkle over the fruit, and cover with rest of fruit.

3. Using a floured board, roll out pastry 1 cm/½ inch larger than top of pie dish.

4. Cut a circular 1 cm/½ inch strip from the pastry, damp edges of pie dish with water and press this pastry strip on firmly.

5. Damp the strip, place pastry lid on top, press to seal and trim level.

6. Flute edges, make 4 small slits on top, brush lightly with water and sprinkle with caster sugar.

7. Bake in a moderately hot oven, Gas 6, 400°F, 200°C, for 30 minutes, reduce heat to moderate, Gas 4, 350°F, 180°C, and bake a little longer until fruit is cooked. To test fruit, put a skewer through slit in pastry.

FRUIT FLAN

Fresh or tinned fruit can be attractively presented in a rich shortcrust flan case and nicely glazed on top.

Serves 4 or 5

An 18 cm/7 inch baked, rich shortcrust flan case, (*see page 203*). 'Pastry, a few tips', *page 202* for baking flan cases, and *page 203* for rich shortcrust pastry.

1. Spread a little sieved apricot jam on base of the flan case. This prevents any moisture soaking in.
2. Fill with pieces of fruit arranged in pattern. If using tinned fruit drain off juice and save it for the glaze.

TO GLAZE A FRUIT FLAN
Using fresh fruits:
2 tablespoons sugar
150 ml/¼ pint water
2 squares from a jelly tablet

1. Dissolve sugar in water.
2. Boil 2 to 3 minutes.
3. Add jelly, allow to dissolve.
4. When cool, spoon over fruit in flan.

Using tinned fruit:
1 teaspoon arrowroot
2 squares from a jelly tablet

1. Mix arrowroot into 150 ml/¼ pint of the fruit juice.
2. Boil until clear.
3. Add jelly, allow to dissolve.
4. When cool spoon over fruit in flan.

BAKEWELL PUDDING

Made this way for generations.

Serves 6

SHORTCRUST PASTRY
125 g/4 oz self-raising flour
Pinch of salt
50 g/2 oz butter or margarine
1 brimming tablespoon water

FILLING
50 g/2 oz butter or margarine
50 g/2 oz caster sugar
2 beaten eggs
A few drops almond essence
25 g/1 oz ground almonds (optional)
Strawberry jam

1. Sift flour and salt into a bowl.
2. Rub in butter or margarine.
3. Mix to a firm dough with water.
4. Using a floured board, roll out and line a 20 cm/ 8 inch flan tin.
5. *For the filling:* beat butter and sugar together until creamy.
6. Beat in eggs gradually.
7. Add essence and ground almonds, beat well.
8. Spread a little strawberry jam over pastry case.
9. Pour in egg mixture, making sure it runs to the edges otherwise jam may escape.
10. Bake in a moderately hot oven, Gas 5, 375°F, 190°C, for 25 to 30 minutes or until filling is set.

Eat hot with ice-cream, or cold with or without cream.

Jan Wilson
Youlgrave, Derbyshire

BAKEWELL PUDDING II

Serves 6

350 g/13 oz puff pastry, weighed after making up

FILLING
4 egg-yolks
2 egg-whites
125 g/4 oz melted butter
125 g/4 oz caster sugar
5 drops almond essence
4 tablespoons strawberry jam

1. Well butter a 20 cm/8 inch pie plate or flan tin, then line with pastry and prick base.
2. Blend together egg-yolks and whites until well mixed.
3. Add butter, sugar and essence.
4. Spread base of pricked pastry with strawberry jam.
5. Pour in the egg mixture.
6. Bake in a moderately hot oven, Gas 6, 400°F, 200°C, for about 30 minutes until pastry is pale brown round edges and filling is set.

CUSTARD TART

For this you need a pie tin or dish about 18 cm/7 inches in diameter and 4 cm/1½ inches deep. A custard tart should be deep, so an ordinary flan ring is not the best choice.

Serves 4

PASTRY
175 g/6 oz plain flour
½ teaspoon salt
50 g/2 oz firm margarine
25 g/1 oz lard
3 to 4 dessertspoons cold water

FILLING
225 ml/8 fl oz milk
1 rounded tablespoon sugar
2 large eggs
Nutmeg

1. Mix flour and salt in a bowl.
2. Rub in fats.
3. Mix to a firm dough with 3 or 4 dessertspoons of cold water. Leave to rest while preparing filling.

4. Warm milk, dissolve sugar in it then let it cool. Dissolving the sugar stops it falling to bottom of custard mixture in pastry case. A layer of sugar on pastry base tends to make it go rubbery.
5. Beat eggs lightly but not to a froth. Add to milk mixture.
6. Using a floured board, roll out pastry a good 25 cm/10 inches in diameter. Fit it into pie tin. Roll off surplus pastry with rolling pin.
7. Strain custard mixture into pastry case. Grate a little nutmeg on top.
8. Bake in a hot oven, Gas 7, 425°F, 220°C, for 15 minutes to set pastry. Reduce heat, if pastry is browning too quickly, to moderately hot, Gas 6, 400°F, 200°C, and cook for 25 minutes more or until filling is set.
9. Leave tart in tin for 5 minutes. Drop it gently out on to a clean cloth in your hand. Then immediately place cooling wire against base and turn tart right way up again.

DATE PASTY

Crisp, short pastry with a thick filling.

Serves 4

300 g/11 oz dates, chopped
300 ml/½ pint water

PASTRY
125 g/4 oz fine wholewheat flour
125 g/4 oz wholewheat semolina
150 g/5 oz butter
5 to 6 teaspoons cold water

TO GLAZE
Beaten egg or milk

1. Simmer dates in the water for 10 to 15 minutes until soft. Leave to cool.
2. Pre-heat a moderately hot oven, Gas 5, 375°F, 190°C.
3. To make the pastry, mix dry ingredients in a bowl and rub in butter.
4. Add enough water to make a soft dough.
5. Cut dough into 2 pieces and, using a board well dusted with semolina, roll out each piece to a 23 cm/9 inch square.
6. Lift one piece of pastry on to a lightly-oiled baking tray. Spread cooked dates to within 1 cm/½ inch of the edges.

7. Moisten edges with a little water, put on top piece of pastry, pressing edges to seal. Trim off any surplus pastry.

8. Brush with beaten egg or milk. Prick through top layer of pastry several times with a fork.

9. Bake near top of oven for 20 to 25 minutes.

10. Leave pastry on baking tray for 15 to 20 minutes to cool. Then cut into squares and lift them on to a cooling wire to go quite cold.

Janet Horsley
Headingley, Yorkshire

KENTISH PUDDING

A very old Kentish recipe.

Serves 6

For this you need a ready-baked 18 cm/7 inch shortcrust or sweet shortcrust flan case (*see page 203*).

FILLING
25 g/1 oz ground rice
300 ml/½ pint milk and 1 or 2 tablespoons extra
25 g/1 oz caster sugar
Pinch of salt
15 g/½ oz butter
1 well-beaten egg
A grating of nutmeg
Grated zest of 1 lemon
1 tablespoon currants

1. Put ground rice in a basin and slake it with 2 tablespoons of the cold milk—i.e. mix it to a smooth cream.

2. Put rest of milk, the sugar and salt into a saucepan and bring to the boil.

3. Pour boiling milk on to ground rice, stirring all the time.

4. Pour mixture back into saucepan and simmer for 5 minutes, stirring occasionally.

5. Take pan off heat and let mixture cool for 2 or 3 minutes. Stir in butter, well-beaten egg, nutmeg and finely grated lemon zest. Blend well.

6. Stand pastry case on a baking sheet and fill it with the mixture. Strew the currants over the top.

7. Bake it in a moderate oven, Gas 4, 350°F, 180°C, for 20 minutes when filling will be set and slightly risen.

Mrs W. White, Mrs Sue Marshall,
St Michaels, Tenterden, Kent

FUDGE TART

First published in a book of family recipes 'In a Bisley Kitchen', collected over 100 years.

Serves 3 to 4

For this you need a ready-baked shallow 15 cm/6 inch pastry case (*see page 203*).

FILLING
50 g/2 oz butter
50 g/2 oz light soft brown sugar
200 ml/7 fl oz sweetened condensed milk
25 g/1 oz roughly-chopped walnuts
25 g/1 oz seedless raisins
25 g/1 oz glacé cherries, chopped

1. Melt butter in pan. Add sugar and condensed milk. Stir over low heat until sugar is dissolved and mixture boils. Boil for 5 minutes stirring all the time.

2. Take pan off heat. Stir in walnuts, raisins and cherries.

3. Pour mixture into pastry case and leave to cool.

Mrs A. Bucknell
Bisley, Gloucestershire

TOFFEE CREAM TART

Makes one 18 cm/7 inch round tart

First make an 18 cm/7 inch shortcrust flan case and bake it blind (*see page 202*)

FILLING
150 ml/¼ pint milk
65 g/2½ oz margarine or butter
40 g/1½ oz white or soft brown sugar
25 g/1 oz plain flour
75 g/3 oz golden syrup

1. Heat the milk but do not boil it.

2. Melt margarine and sugar in a small pan and stir in flour.

3. Whisk in the hot milk. Stir as it thickens and reaches boiling point. Cook for 2 or 3 minutes, stirring.

4. Remove from heat, add syrup and whisk again.

5. Spread filling in flan case. For special occasions decorate with grated chocolate and whipped cream.

Mrs A. E. Phillips
Selsey, Sussex

LEMON MERINGUE PIE

Serves 4 to 6

175 g/6 oz shortcrust pastry *(see page 203)*

FILLING
40 g/1½ oz cornflour
125 g/4 oz sugar
2 lemons
Water
15 g/½ oz butter
2 egg-yolks

TOP
2 egg-whites
125 g/4 oz caster sugar
½ teaspoon cornflour
A little extra caster sugar

1. Line a 20 cm/8 inch flan ring with pastry and bake 'blind' *(see page 202)*.
2. *For the filling:* in a pan combine cornflour, sugar, grated lemon rind and lemon juice made up to 300 ml/½ pint with water.
3. Bring to the boil, stirring. Cook for 2 minutes.
4. Remove from heat, beat in butter and then the egg-yolks.
5. Pour into hot or cold flan case.
6. *For the top:* whisk egg-whites stiffly. Whisk in 50 g/2 oz of the caster sugar until firm and shiny.
7. Sift remaining 50 g/2 oz caster sugar with the cornflour and fold into egg-whites.
8. Spread meringue on top of flan, making sure it reaches pastry all round and seals in the lemon filling.
9. Sift on a little caster sugar.
10. Bake in a slow oven, Gas 1 to 2, 275° to 300°F, 140° to 150°C, for 25 to 30 minutes, until set and just golden.

MINCE MERINGUE TARTS

The pastry cases freeze very well and can be made a few weeks in advance. They will keep for 1 week in an air-tight tin.

Makes 8 tarts

SHORTCRUST PASTRY CASES
225 g/8 oz soft plain flour
½ level teaspoon salt
50 g/2 oz firm margarine or butter
50 g/2 oz lard
2 full tablespoons water

1. Rub fats into flour and salt.
2. Mix to a firm dough with water. Allow to rest 15 to 20 minutes.
3. Roll out thinly.
4. Line patty tins with pastry and prick base with a fork.
5. Stand a grease-proof paper bun case with a tablespoon of baking beans in each. (*See page 202*, To bake a flan case blind, paragraph 7.)
6. Bake in a hot oven, Gas 7, 425°F, 220°C, for 15 minutes until set and just golden. Remove from patty tins on to rack to cool.

FILLING
Mincemeat *(see page 371)*

MERINGUE
1 egg-white
50 g/2 oz caster sugar

1. Place 1 to 2 teaspoons mincemeat in cases.
2. Whisk egg-white very stiffly, fold in caster sugar.
3. Using large star nozzle, pipe this meringue around edge of tarts.
4. Place on a baking sheet in a cool oven, Gas 2, 300°F, 150°C, for about 12 to 15 minutes until meringue is set.

LINCOLNSHIRE POTATO CHEESECAKE

First put the potatoes on, for the filling, and while they are cooking make the pastry.

Serves 4 to 6

SHORTCRUST PASTRY
175 g/6 oz soft plain flour
40 g/1½ oz butter or margarine
40 g/1½ oz lard
Salt
3 brimming dessertspoons water

1. Rub fats into flour and salt until like fine bread-crumbs.
2. Mix to a firm dough with the water. Do not be tempted to add more water.
3. Knead lightly until smooth and basin becomes clean.
4. Roll out on floured board.
5. Line a 20 cm/8 inch flan ring on a baking tray. Prick base of flan. Leave to rest while mixing the filling.

FILLING
225 g/8 oz hot, cooked potatoes (steamed or pressure-cooked are best)
Salt
Pinch of nutmeg, optional
125 g/4 oz softened butter
125 g/4 oz caster sugar
2 eggs, well-beaten
Grated rind and juice of 1 medium-sized lemon

1. Sieve hot potatoes with salt and nutmeg if used.
2. Add butter, sugar, eggs, grated rind and lemon juice. Beat thoroughly together.
3. Fill flan case almost to top.
4. Bake on middle shelf of a moderately hot oven, Gas 6, 400°F, 200°C, for 15 minutes. Remove flan ring and bake 10 more minutes until filling is set and browning on top.

Served at Harvest Home suppers.

Mrs Hilda Newland
Louth

DELUXE MINCEMEAT PUFFS

For this you need ground almond flaky pastry—make up quantity given on *page 205*.

Makes about 16 individual puffs

FILLING
225 g/8 oz chopped eating apple, weighed after peeling and coring
225 g/8 oz currants
225 g/8 oz seedless raisins
150 g/5 oz chopped candied orange peel, mixed peel will do but orange is nicer
275 g/10 oz flaked or chopped blanched almonds
Half a nutmeg, grated
4 to 6 tablespoons brandy

Mix all filling ingredients together and leave to soak and infuse for at least 1 hour.

TO MAKE THE MINCEMEAT PUFFS
1 beaten egg
Demerara sugar

1. Roll out cold pastry to about 3.5 mm/⅛ inch thick. Cut into 10 cm/4 inch squares.
2. Place 1 tablespoon of filling on each square.
3. Fold over diagonally, sealing join with beaten egg.
4. Brush top with egg, sprinkle with demerara sugar and place on baking trays.
5. Bake above middle of a hot oven, Gas 7, 425°F, 220°C, for 12 to 15 minutes until risen, golden brown and firm. Puffs at centre of tray may need another 2 to 3 minutes if pastry is still pale underneath.

Instead of individual puffs, a large roly-poly can be made. Roll out pastry as above, spread over it all the filling and roll up, sealing edges with beaten egg. Brush with beaten egg and sprinkle with demerara sugar. Bake for 30 minutes as above, then reduce temperature to moderately hot, Gas 5, 375°F, 190°C, for a further 15 minutes until well-risen, brown and set. Centre of roly-poly will remain quite soft inside.

Delicious served with Rich Brandy Butter (*see page 251*) or a simple Brandy Sauce (*see page 251*).

Mrs Angela Mottram
Axbridge, Somerset

MINCEMEAT AND ALMOND DELIGHT

Serves 6

PASTRY
150 g/5 oz self-raising flour—if using plain wholewheat flour add ½ level teaspoon baking powder
50 g/2 oz butter
25 g/1 oz lard
1 egg-yolk
½ teaspoon lemon juice

FILLING
50 g/2 oz butter
50 g/2 oz caster or soft brown sugar
2 lightly-beaten eggs
50 g/2 oz ground almonds
A few drops of almond essence
4 heaped tablespoons mincemeat
2 bananas, thinly sliced

1. Put flour in a bowl (with baking powder if wholewheat flour is used). Rub in butter and lard.
2. Add egg-yolk and lemon juice and mix to a firm dough.
3. Roll out pastry on a floured board to fit a 20 cm/8 inch flan tin or pie plate.
4. *Filling.* Cream butter and sugar.
5. Stir in eggs, ground almonds and essence and mix well.
6. Fill pastry case with alternate layers of mincemeat and bananas. Then spread almond mixture on top, taking care that it covers fruit right to pastry edge.
7. Bake in middle of a hot oven, Gas 7, 425°F, 220°C, for half an hour, when it will be firm on top and nicely browned. If using wholewheat pastry, reduce heat after 15 minutes to moderately hot, Gas 5, 375°F, 190°C, and cook for another 15 to 20 minutes.

Mrs Becky Blackmore
Exeter, Devon

BANBURY CAKES

Makes 12 cakes

225 g/8 oz flaky pastry (*see page 205*)

FILLING
125 g/4 oz currants
25 g/1 oz butter
50 g/2 oz sugar
½ a beaten egg
Pinch of cinnamon
A little grated lemon rind
25 g/1 oz cake crumbs

TO FINISH
Egg-white
Caster sugar

1. Remove any stalks, etc. from the currants. Clean them either by washing in cold water and patting dry in a tea-towel, or by rubbing them in flour and sifting flour out.
2. Cream butter and sugar.
3. Add beaten egg and mix well.
4. Add cleaned fruit, cinnamon and grated lemon rind, and finally the cake crumbs, and mix well.
5. Roll out pastry on a floured board and cut into twelve 10 cm/3-4 inch rounds.
6. Place a good teaspoon of the filling in centre of each round.
7. Damp round the edges, then join edges together in shape of a Cornish pasty.
8. Turn over with joined edges underneath and flatten gently with rolling pin.
9. Make 3 diagonal cuts across top of each one. Place on a baking sheet.
10. Brush with lightly-beaten egg-white and dredge caster sugar over them.
11. Bake in moderately hot oven, Gas 6, 400°F, 200°C, for about 20 minutes until risen and golden brown.
12. Remove from baking sheet on to a wire rack to cool.

Stella Boldy
Sykehouse, N. Humberside

GODS KITCHEL CAKE

Makes a 25 cm/10 inch square cake

Flaky pastry, made up as on page 205
125 g/4 oz margarine
225 g/8 oz currants
25 g/1 oz sultanas
50 g/2 oz candied peel
75 g/3 oz sugar
50 g/2 oz ground almonds
2 teaspoons powdered cinnamon
1 teaspoon grated nutmeg

1. Melt margarine. Add fruit, peel, sugar, ground almonds and spices. Mix well.
2. Halve the pastry and roll one piece into a square about 30 cm/12 inches across. Place it on a baking sheet. Quantity and size of pastry depend on your baking sheet but rolled out pastry should be quite thin. Moisten edges with milk or water.
3. Spread filling on this square stopping 1 cm/½ inch short of edges.
4. Cover with the second piece of pastry rolled out to fit. Seal the edges, pressing lightly together.
5. Carefully mark the top in 7 cm/2½ inch squares without cutting through.
6. Bake near top of a hot oven, Gas 7, 425°F, 220°C, for about half an hour until it is a nice golden brown.
7. Leave it on baking sheet when it comes out of the oven and sprinkle with caster sugar. Let it cool a little then divide into sections and cool on wire rack.

Mrs Margaret Pettitt
Ousden, Suffolk

HOW D'YOU DO CAKE

For this you need 325 g/12 oz shortcrust pastry (*see page 203*), made up with self-raising flour.

FILLING
325 g/12 oz currants
50 g/2 oz mixed peel
1 tablespoon golden syrup
1 tablespoon demerara or soft brown sugar
1 level teaspoon nutmeg or cinnamon
A pinch of ground cloves. *Or,* **instead of these**
   spices, 1 level teaspoon mixed spice

TO GLAZE
1 dessertspoon golden syrup warmed with 1
   dessertspoon sugar

1. Divide pastry into 2 pieces, one to line tin, the other for top. Shape these into rectangular blocks. Put in a cool place or refrigerator to rest for 20 minutes.
2. Using a floured board, roll out pastry about 7 mm/¼ inch thick and line a Swiss roll tin, about 28 by 18 cm/11 by 7 inches.
3. Warm filling ingredients together in a pan so that they mix easily. Spread filling over pastry in tin.
4. Damp edges of pastry and cover filling with second piece, pressing to seal.
5. Brush with the glaze. Prick top all over with a fork.
6. Bake in a hot oven, Gas 7, 425°F, 220°C, for 25 minutes when it will be shining and golden.
7. Allow to cool in tin and then cut into slices.

Mrs Jill Marshall
Hythe, Kent

KIDDERMINSTER PLUM CAKES

Makes 12 cakes

For this you need a 375g/13 oz packet of puff pastry, just thawed. Or make up your own using recipe *on page 206*. There will be some pastry over if you use home-made.

FILLING
4 glacé cherries
225 g/8 oz mixed dried fruit
50 g/2 oz plain flour
50 g/2 oz soft brown sugar
50 g/2 oz soft margarine
1 egg
½ level teaspoon mixed spice

TO FINISH
Water, granulated sugar

1. Start with filling. Roughly chop cherries and put them in a bowl.
2. Add remaining filling ingredients and beat with a wooden spoon for about 3 minutes to mix thoroughly.
3. Roll out pastry on a lightly-floured board to 3.5 mm/⅛ inch thick.
4. Cut twelve rounds 10 cm/4 inches across; a saucer may be useful to cut round.
5. Place 2 teaspoons of filling in centre of each round. Brush edges with water.

6. Gather pastry together over filling and seal well.
7. Turn each plum cake over and roll out lightly to form a round about 7.5 cm/3 inches across.
8. To finish, brush tops of cakes with water and invert on to a saucer of granulated sugar to give a thick sugary coating on top.
9. Put cakes on a baking sheet and, using a sharp knife, make 3 cuts on top of each.
10. Bake on shelf just above centre of a moderately hot oven, Gas 6, 400°F, 200°C, for 20 minutes when cake will be golden brown.
11. Remove from oven and slide cakes on to a wire rack to cool.

Mrs Cynthia Cooksey
Cofton Hackett, Worcestershire

RICHMOND MAIDS OF HONOUR

Makes 18

600 ml/1 pint milk
1 teaspoon rennet
50 g/2 oz butter
50 g/2 oz caster sugar
1 egg
25 g/1 oz very finely-chopped almonds
2 teaspoons brandy, optional
1 level teaspoon grated lemon rind
¼ level teaspoon cinnamon
Pinch of salt
1 small packet (212 g/7½ oz) puff pastry or make up a similar quantity (*see page 206*)

1. Warm milk to blood heat, add rennet.
2. Pour into a dish and leave in a warm place to set. The resulting mixture is called junket.
3. When set, roughly cut up the junket and place in a nylon sieve over a bowl. Cover and leave in refrigerator overnight.
4. Discard whey (the watery liquid) and place curds in a bowl.
5. Cream butter and sugar together until light.
6. Beat in curds, egg, almonds, brandy (if using), lemon rind, cinnamon and salt.
7. Roll out pastry thinly and line 18 tartlet tins.
8. Divide curd mixture between tins and bake in a hot oven, Gas 7, 425°F, 220°C, for 15 to 20 minutes until pale golden brown.
9. Carefully lift on to a wire rack and leave to cool.

Ruth Morgan
Surrey

SUSSEX PLUM HEAVIES

Adapted from an old recipe in 'Sussex Cooking'. The original called for 3 lb flour. These freeze well.

Makes one 20 cm/8 inch round cake

225 g/8 oz self-raising flour
A pinch of salt
175 g/6 oz butter or butter and margarine mixed
75 g/3 oz currants
1 tablespoon caster sugar
About 2 tablespoons cold water
A little milk

1. Put flour and salt into a bowl.
2. Divide fat into 3 even amounts. Rub one third into flour.
3. Add currants and sugar and mix to a firm dough with water.
4. Using a floured board, roll out to an oblong three times as long as it is wide.
5. Using second lot of fat, put little pieces on to the top two thirds of pastry. Fold up bottom third and fold down top third. Turn pastry so that folds are at sides.
6. Roll out again, use remaining fat and fold as before. If pastry has got hot and sticky leave in a cool place or refrigerator for 15 minutes to firm up.
7. Roll into a 20 cm/8 inch round cake, score top and brush with milk. Place on a greased baking sheet.
8. Bake in middle of a moderately hot oven, Gas 6, 400°F, 200°C, for 30 minutes.
9. Slide off on to a wire rack to cool.

Mrs Janice Langley
Shoreham-by-Sea, West Sussex

PARADISE BARS

Makes 20 pieces

175 g/6 oz white or wholewheat shortcrust pastry (*see page 203*)

FILLING
75 g/3 oz margarine
75 g/3 oz caster sugar
1 beaten egg
75 g/3 oz currants, washed and dried
50 g/2 oz chopped glacé cherries
65 g/2½ oz ground rice
50 g/2 oz ground almonds
3 drops of vanilla essence

1. Using a floured board, roll out pastry 7 mm/ $\frac{1}{4}$ inch thick and line bottom and sides of a Swiss roll tin, 28 by 18 cm/11 by 7 inches.
2. Cream margarine and sugar. Mix in egg and other ingredients gradually.
3. Smooth filling over pastry base.
4. Bake above middle of a moderate oven, Gas 4, 350°F, 180°C, for about 40 minutes.
5. Leave to cool in tin.
6. Then turn out, cut into four and then into bars.

RAISIN CIDER PIE

Makes one 20 cm/8 inch round pie

225 g/8 oz shortcrust pastry made with white or wholewheat flour (or a mixture of both) (*see page 203 for recipes and page 202 for a note about quantities***).**

FILLING
225 g/8 oz seedless raisins
150 ml/$\frac{1}{4}$ pint cider
Grated rind and juice of 1 lemon
50 g/2 oz caster sugar, plus a little more
1 tablespoon cornflour
50 g/2 oz chopped walnuts

1. Soak raisins, cider and lemon rind for a few hours, or overnight.
2. Place in pan. Mix 50 g/2 oz sugar and cornflour with lemon juice and stir in. Bring to the boil, and stir until mixture thickens. Add chopped walnuts. Leave to become quite cold.
3. Use half the above pastry to line a 20 cm/8 inch pie plate. Place filling to within 1 cm/$\frac{1}{2}$ inch of edge. Damp edges of pastry with water.
4. Cover with remainder of pastry rolled to size. Take care not to stretch it when laying it on.
5. Seal, fluting edges with fingers and thumbs, make slits in top and decorate.
6. Brush top lightly with water and sprinkle with caster sugar or demerara.
7. Bake in a hot oven, Gas 7, 425°F, 220°C, for 15 minutes (10 if using wholewheat flour). Then reduce heat to moderately hot, Gas 5, 375°F, 190°C, for a further 15 to 20 minutes.

Serve warm with cream.

PECAN AND RAISIN FLAN

A rich pudding.

Makes one 20 cm/8 inch round flan

PASTRY
225 g/8 oz rich sweet shortcrust pastry (*see page 203***)**

FILLING
125 g/4 oz seedless raisins
150 ml/$\frac{1}{4}$ pint water
1 tablespoon cornflour
Grated rind and juice of 1 orange
Grated rind and juice of $\frac{1}{2}$ lemon
50 g/2 oz soft brown sugar
50 g/2 oz pecans or walnuts, chopped to size of raisins

TO DECORATE
A 150 ml/$\frac{1}{4}$ pint carton of double cream
1 tablespoon rum

1. Using a floured board, roll out pastry 7 mm/$\frac{1}{4}$ inch thick and line a 20 cm/8 inch flan dish or a flan ring on a baking sheet. Prick base with a fork. Chill it for 10 minutes.
2. Cut a piece of foil big enough to line base and sides of flan case. Fill with baking beans.
3. Bake near top of a moderately hot oven, Gas 5, 375°F, 190°C, for 10 to 15 minutes. Remove beans and foil at 10 minutes and return flan to oven to crisp up base. If pastry is already very brown, reduce temperature to warm, Gas 3, 325°F, 160°C, for final few minutes. (Save beans and foil for another occasion.)
4. Take flan out of oven, remove from dish or ring on to a wire rack to cool. (Return it to dish or ring for support while filling.)
5. Put raisins in water and simmer for 10 minutes.
6. Mix cornflour to a paste with 1 tablespoon of the juice and add sugar.
7. Stir cornflour mixture and rind into raisin mix and cook until thick. If too thick add more juice, but consistency should be like jam. Allow to cool.
8. To this cooled mixture add chopped pecans. Pour into cold flan case.
9. Whip cream and add rum. Whip again.
10. Fill a piping bag and, using a star nozzle, decorate surface of flan.

RHUBARB PLATE TART

Other fruits may be used. This pastry is quite satisfactory with a moist filling.

Makes one 25 cm/10 inch round tart

575 g/1¼ lb cooked rhubarb

PASTRY
250 g/9 oz plain flour
75 g/3 oz self-raising flour
Pinch of salt
10 ml/2 level teaspoons caster sugar
125 g/4 oz hard margarine
50 g/2 oz hard vegetable fat
3 tablespoons milk (use 15 ml size or a measuring spoon)

1. Sieve together dry ingredients.
2. Rub in fats until texture is like fine breadcrumbs.
3. Bind to a firm dough with milk.
4. Using a floured board, roll out half of the pastry thinly to line a 25 cm/10 inch pie-plate.
5. Roll out second half of pastry for lid.
6. Place a generous layer of drained rhubarb to within 1 cm/½ inch of edge of pastry.
7. Damp edge with water and put on pastry lid. Seal firmly round edge.
8. Brush top with milk. Cut 2 slits in the top to let steam out during cooking and prevent pastry from becoming soggy.
9. Bake in a moderately hot oven, Gas 5, 375°F, 190°C, for 35 to 40 minutes.

Anne Wallace
Dunlop, Scotland

SHERRY CHIFFON PIE

Makes one 18 cm/7 inch round pie

For this you need an 18 cm/7 inch case of short or sweet shortcrust pastry, baked blind. (See recipes on page 203 and instructions for baking a flan case blind on page 202.)

FILLING
2 tablespoons sherry
1 dessertspoon gelatine
1 large egg, separated
75 g/3 oz caster sugar
225 ml/8 fl oz hot milk
¼ teaspoon almond essence
Nutmeg

1. Measure 1 tablespoon sherry into a cup, sprinkle on gelatine, and stir once to combine. Leave to soften.
2. Beat egg-yolk and 50 g/2 oz of the caster sugar in a large basin. Stir in the hot milk, strain back into milk pan. Cook over gentle heat, stirring gently, until mixture clings to spoon—do not boil.
3. Remove from heat, stir in the gelatine mixture and almond essence. Beat to dissolve gelatine. Add the remaining tablespoon of sherry. Cool until thickening.
4. Whisk egg-white stiffly, then whisk in remaining 25 g/1 oz caster sugar. Fold into the mixture.
5. Pour into cold baked flan case, grate a little nutmeg on top. Leave to set in a cool place.

YORKSHIRE CHEESE TARTS

A recipe using cottage cheese instead of curds.

Makes 24

225 g/8 oz shortcrust pastry (*see page 203*)
50 g/2 oz butter
225 g/8 oz cottage cheese
Pinch of salt
150 g/5 oz sugar
25 g/1 oz cake crumbs
50 g/2 oz currants
Grated rind of ½ lemon
3 egg-yolks*

1. Line 24 tartlet tins with the pastry.
2. Put butter in a warm place to soften, and then cream it.
3. Sieve cottage cheese into a large basin.
4. Add salt, sugar, cake-crumbs, currants and lemon rind and mix well. Add the creamed butter.
5. Beat the egg-yolks and mix well into cheese mixture.
6. Spoon mixture into pastry cases.
7. Bake in a moderately hot oven, Gas 6, 400°F, 200°C, for 20 minutes until golden brown.

**Uses for spare egg-white*

Pavlova (page 273)
Royal icing (page 329)
Macaroons (page 349)
Meringues (page 348)
Or, 1 egg-white whisked and folded into 300 ml/½ pint cream will make it go further.

Stella Boldy
Sykehouse, N. Humberside

STAFFORDSHIRE YEOMANRY PUDDING

SWEET SHORTCRUST PASTRY
1 egg-yolk
25 g/1 oz caster sugar
3 teaspoons water
225 g/8 oz soft plain flour
½ level teaspoon salt
150 g/5 oz firm margarine

FILLING
125 g/4 oz butter
125 g/4 oz caster sugar
¼ teaspoon almond essence
25 g/1 oz ground almonds
2 eggs (using 2 yolks and 1 white)
2 tablespoons raspberry jam

1. For the pastry, mix together egg-yolk, sugar and water.
2. Place flour and salt in a bowl, and rub in margarine.
3. Mix to a firm dough with egg, sugar and water mixture. Leave in a cool place for 15 minutes.
4. Meanwhile, make the filling. Cream butter and sugar, mix in essence and ground almonds.
5. Beat egg-yolks and egg-white together, beat into rest of mixture.
6. Roll out two thirds of pastry just 5 mm/less than ¼ inch thick, and line a shallow pie dish. Trim off surplus pastry and damp edge with water.
7. Spread on jam, then filling.
8. Roll out remaining pastry and trimmings, fit on top. Trim, seal and flute edges, and make 4 or 6 small cuts in top with point of knife.
9. Bake in a moderate oven, Gas 4, 350°F, 180°C, for 40 minutes covering with foil for last 10 minutes as this pastry browns quickly.

Nice eaten while just warm but not too hot. Also very good cold.

Miss P. M. Cherry
Penkridge

TREACLE TART

Makes one 18 cm/7 inch round tart

175 g/6 oz shortcrust pastry (*see page 203*)

FILLING
175 g/6 oz golden syrup (6 level tablespoons, or use a measure)
1 tablespoon lemon juice
50 g/2 oz fresh white or wholemeal bread-crumbs (*see page 52*)

1. Using ¾ of the pastry, line an 18 cm/7 inch pie plate.
2. Add lemon juice to golden syrup and mix in breadcrumbs.
3. Pour filling on to pastry. Lightly damp edge of pastry.
4. Roll out remaining pastry to an oblong 18 cm/7 inches long, cut into 5 mm/¼ inch strips – you should get 10. Twist and place, lattice-fashion, without stretching, across tart, strips on to dampened edge. Flute edges of tart to neaten.
5. Bake in a moderately hot oven, Gas 6, 400°F, 200°C, for approximately 30 minutes.

YORKSHIRE CHEESECAKE OR CURD TART

Makes one 18 cm/7 inch round cake

175 g/6 oz shortcrust white or wholewheat pastry (*see page 203*).

FILLING
225 g/8 oz curd
25 g/1 oz softened butter
1 large beaten egg
1 tablespoon caster sugar
1 tablespoon golden syrup
25 g/1 oz currants
15 g/½ oz candied peel
1 tablespoon rum

1. Roll out the pastry and line an 18 cm/7 inch flan ring placed on a baking sheet.
2. Combine the filling ingredients. Spoon into pastry case.
3. Bake above centre of a moderately hot oven, Gas 6, 400°F, 200°C, for about 30 minutes until pastry is cooked and filling is just firm and golden.

Best eaten while just warm.

COTTAGE CHEESE CAKE

Makes one 18 cm/7 inch round cake

FLAN CASE
125 g/4 oz plain flour
Bare ¼ teaspoon salt
50 g/2 oz softened butter
1 egg-yolk
25 g/1 oz caster sugar
1 teaspoon water (no more)

FILLING
50 g/2 oz sultanas
125 g/4 oz cottage cheese
1 egg (separated)
50 g/2 oz caster sugar
1 level tablespoon cornflour
Grated rind and juice of 1 small lemon
3 tablespoons double cream (or evaporated milk)

1. Start with the flan case. Place flour and salt in a bowl and make a well in the centre.
2. Add butter, egg-yolk, sugar and water.
3. Work these together with a fork, drawing in the flour gradually. Finish combining these ingredients with finger tips. Leave 15 minutes for dough to rest.
4. Roll out on floured board to 23 cm/9 inches diameter.
5. Fit into an ungreased 18 cm/7 inch flan ring placed on a lightly greased tray. Roll off surplus pastry with rolling pin.
6. Prick base well with a fork. Cut a round of grease-proof paper approximately 23 cm/9 inches in diameter, grease lightly, fit into case, greased side down, and weight with dried peas or beans.
7. Bake in a moderately hot oven, Gas 6, 400°F, 200°C, for 15 minutes until set, but only very lightly baked. Remove from oven and remove beans and paper. Reduce oven temperature to moderate, Gas 3, 325°F, 160°C.
8. For the filling. Sprinkle sultanas on base of hot flan.
9. Mix together cheese, egg-yolk, sugar, cornflour, lemon rind and juice and cream.
10. Whisk egg-white until firm but not dry, and fold in.
11. Pour mixture into flan case.
12. Bake on centre shelf of oven (moderate Gas 3, 325°F, 160°C), for about 40 to 45 minutes until set. It should not be allowed to get too brown.
13. Turn off oven. If electric open door just a little. Leave flan in oven a further 15 minutes.
14. Cool on wire tray, removing ring.

Serve cold, first sifting on a little icing sugar.

YORKSHIRE CURD TART

Sometimes called Cheesecake, but not quite the same. This recipe uses home-produced curd. Channel Islands milk is best, pasteurised milk is satisfactory, but skimmed, homogenised, sterilised and "long-life" milks are not suitable.

TO MAKE CURD
1.2 litres/2 pints milk
1 teaspoon Epsom salts

1. Bring milk to boiling point. Remove from heat and add Epsom salts.
2. Leave for a few minutes for curds to form. Stir well and strain.

This makes enough curd for two 15 to 18 cm/6 to 7 inch flans. Will keep in refrigerator for a week.

TO MAKE TART
175 g/6 oz shortcrust pastry (*see page 203*)
225 g/8 oz curd
25 g/1 oz butter or margarine
25 g/1 oz washed currants
1 large beaten egg
1 tablespoon caster sugar
1 tablespoon golden syrup
1 tablespoon rum

1. Roll out pastry and line an 18 cm/7 inch flan ring placed on a greased baking sheet.
2. Combine all other ingredients and fill the pastry case.
3. Bake above middle of a moderately hot oven, Gas 6, 400°F, 200°C, for 30 minutes, until pastry is cooked and the filling firm and golden.

8

PUDDINGS
HOT AND
COLD

ALMOND STUFFED PEACHES

Serves 6

6 large fresh peaches, or 12 halves from a can
   of peaches
2 sponge buns
75 g/3 oz caster sugar
40 g/1½ oz ground almonds
Grated rind of ½ large lemon
2 tablespoons sherry
1 heaped tablespoon demerara sugar
1½ sherry glasses of brandy

1. Skin and halve peaches and remove stones.
2. Remove a little flesh from each peach to make the hollow larger.
3. Crumble sponge buns into a bowl and mix in peach flesh, caster sugar, ground almonds, lemon rind and sherry.
4. Place peach halves in a flat, oven-proof dish and spoon the mixture into each.
5. Sprinkle with demerara sugar.
6. Bake in a moderate oven, Gas 4, 350°F, 180°C, for 15 to 20 minutes until sugar is crisp.
7. Heat a soup ladle over a gas flame, spirit lamp or candle flame. Pour brandy into the hot ladle, allow it to heat and ignite. Pour flaming brandy quickly over all the peaches and bring dish straight to the table while flames are still flickering over it. For maximum effect, turn off the lights.

Serve hot, with or without cream.

Shelagh Robinson
Leeds

APPLE CRUNCH

Serves 4

450 g/1 lb cooking apples
25 g/1 oz butter
2 level tablespoons granulated sugar
Grated rind of 1 lemon

TOPPING
3 slices brown or white bread from small loaf
50 g/2 oz butter
4 level tablespoons desiccated coconut
5 level tablespoons demerara sugar

1. Peel, core and slice apples.
2. Melt 25 g/1 oz butter in a saucepan. Add apples

and granulated sugar. Cover and cook over a low heat, stirring occasionally, until soft and thick.
3. Remove from heat and stir in the lemon rind.
4. Spread apple in a shallow, oven-proof dish and keep warm. Rinse out the saucepan.
5. Remove rack from grill pan and heat grill to moderately hot.
6. Cut bread into 7 mm/¼ inch cubes.
7. Melt 50 g/2 oz butter in the saucepan. Add bread cubes, coconut and demerara sugar and mix well.
8. Pile on top of apple mixture. Place dish in grill pan and grill until golden brown.

Serve immediately.

APPLE AND FIG CRUMBLE

Serves 3 or 4

CRUMBLE
50 g/2 oz wholewheat flour
40 g/1½ oz porridge oats
15 g/½ oz desiccated coconut
50 g/2 oz melted butter, or 2 tablespoons vegetable oil
Several drops of vanilla essence

FILLING
125 g/4 oz figs, chopped
150 ml/¼ pint water
225 g/8 oz cooking apples, peeled, cored and sliced

1. Pre-heat oven to moderately hot, Gas 5, 375°F, 190°C.
2. Mix crumble ingredients well together.
3. Put figs in a pan with water and simmer for 5 minutes.
4. Mix apple and figs in an oven dish and pour over remaining fig juice.
5. Sprinkle crumble on top and bake near top of oven for 25 to 30 minutes.

Janet Horsley
Headingley, Yorkshire

APPLE AND ORANGE PUDDING

Serves 4

325 g/12 oz apples
65 g/2½ oz butter
Sugar to sweeten
175 g/6 oz stale cake-crumbs
Rind and juice of 1 orange

1. Peel, core and slice the apples.
2. Melt 25 g/1 oz of the butter in a pan and add the apple. Cook until soft but not mushy, stirring a little. Remove from the heat and stir in sugar to taste.
3. Melt remaining butter in another pan, stir in crumbs, half of the orange rind and all the orange juice.
4. Grease an 18 cm/7 inch sandwich cake tin, put in half the crumbs and spread them over base. Cover with apple to within 1 cm/½ inch of the sides of tin. Cover with rest of crumbs.
5. Bake in a moderately hot oven, Gas 5, 375°F, 190°C, for 15 minutes.
6. Invert on to warm plate without removing tin. Leave 5 minutes.
7. Lift off tin and sprinkle on the rest of the orange rind.

Serve with custard or cream. It is nicer hot but can be eaten cold.

APPLE OR PINEAPPLE FRITTERS

BATTER
125 g/4 oz plain flour
Pinch of salt
1 tablespoon cooking or salad oil
150 ml/¼ pint tepid water
1 egg-white

1. Sieve flour and salt into a basin. Make a well in the centre and add the oil and half the water.
2. Beat well, then gradually beat in rest of water. Allow to stand 1 hour.
3. Fold in firmly-whisked egg-white just before using.

THE FRITTERS
Cooking apples
Caster sugar
Cinnamon
Or
Tinned pineapple rings
Caster sugar
Oil or fat for deep frying

1. Peel and core required number of cooking apples. Cut into rings about 1 cm/½ inch thick. Each apple should cut into 4 rings. Sprinkle on a little sugar. *Or* thoroughly drain pineapple rings.
2. Dip fruit rings in batter, using a skewer, and deep-fry for 3 to 4 minutes until crisp and golden.
3. Drain on paper. Dust with caster sugar. For the apple fritters mix a little cinnamon with the sugar.

See also Banana Fritters, page 244

APPLE WINE OMELETTE

Serves 2

OMELETTE
3 eggs
1 tablespoon water
1½ dessertspoons vanilla sugar; see below
20 g/¾ oz butter

FILLING
1 cooking apple
20 g/¾ oz butter
1 desertspoon vanilla sugar
1½ tablespoons double cream
1 dessertspoon apple wine

1. Make the filling first. Peel, core and slice the apple thinly and cook gently in the butter. Add sugar, cream and wine and keep warm.
2. Separate the egg-yolks from the whites and remove cords.
3. Add water and sugar to yolks, blend together.
4. Put butter on to melt in omelette or heavy frying pan.
5. Whisk egg-whites until stiff and fold into yolks.
6. Pour into omelette pan and smooth out. Cook the omelette slowly until golden brown.
7. Put under the grill to cook the top.
8. When the omelette is golden brown put on to a serving plate, place the filling on top, fold over.

9. Dust with icing sugar, mark with hot skewers.

Serve at once with thick cream.

See also Jamaican Omelette, page 245

Vanilla Sugar
Break up 1 vanilla pod and put it in a screw-top jar with 450 g/1 lb caster sugar. Replenish sugar and vanilla pod as necessary but vanilla will retain its aroma for some time.

If you cannot make your own vanilla sugar, most recipes can be made using caster sugar and a few drops of vanilla essence.

APPLE AND RAISIN CRISP

Makes one 22 cm/8½ inch round pie

75 g/3 oz butter or margarine
40 g/1½ oz moist brown sugar
40 g/1½ oz demerara sugar
150 g/5 oz rolled oats
2 large cooking apples
50 g/2 oz seedless raisins

1. Grease a deep 22 cm/8½ inch pie plate.
2. Cream butter and sugar together and work in the rolled oats.
3. Peel and core apples, slice into plate and add raisins.
4. Spread mixture over apples.
5. Bake in a moderate oven, Gas 4, 350°F, 180°C, for 45 minutes until crisp and golden brown.

Serve hot or cold with cream or custard.

DORSET APPLE CAKE

Serves 6

225 g/8 oz self-raising flour
A pinch of salt
125 g/4 oz margarine, butter, lard or dripping
  or a mixture of these fats
325 g/12 oz sour cooking apples
125 g/4 oz sugar
1½ to 2½ tablespoons milk
Demerara sugar for sprinkling

1. Sift flour and salt into a bowl and rub in fat.
2. Peel, core and roughly chop up apples.

3. Mix in apple and sugar, adding enough milk to form a soft but not sticky dough.
4. Dust with flour, shape into an oval about 20 by 15 cm/8 by 6 inches and place on a greased baking sheet.
5. Bake in centre of a moderate oven, Gas 4, 350°F, 180°C, for about 50 minutes until the cake is lightly browned and slightly firm when pressed in centre. Cake will spread during baking.
6. Eat hot, straight from oven, sprinkled with demerara sugar.

Very nice buttered or with Lancashire cheese. Also nice cold.

Miss Betty Butt
Woodsford, Dorset

FRIAR'S OMELETTE

Serves 6

6 medium cooking apples
2 tablespoons cold water
75 g/3 oz butter
50 g/2 oz caster sugar
Grated rind of 1 lemon
Pinch of nutmeg or cloves
125 g/4 oz fresh breadcrumbs
4 egg-yolks
Extra butter

1. Score skin around top of apples and put them in a casserole dish with 2 tablespoons water.
2. Put them to bake in a moderately hot oven, Gas 6, 400°F, 200°C, until tender, about ¾ hour.
3. Scrape out pulp and mash.
4. Cream butter and sugar and add rind and pulp with nutmeg or clove.
5. Grease a large pie dish and sprinkle base and sides with about half of the breadcrumbs.
6. Beat egg-yolks and stir into apple mixture and pour into dish.
7. Cover with rest of crumbs and dot with butter.
8. Bake at a slightly lower temperature, Gas 5, 375°F, 190°C, until firm and set.

Eat hot with cream or custard sauce.

Kate Easlea
Hampshire

GOLDEN APPLE BETTY

Serves 4, but easy to make for 1 or more

175 g/6 oz wholewheat or white bread
125 g/4 oz butter
1 level teaspoon cinnamon
125 g/4 oz plus 1 tablespoon light soft brown sugar
450 g/1 lb cooking apples

1. Use a little of the butter to grease a 1.2 litre/2 pint shallow oven dish.
2. Slice bread thickly, remove crusts and cut each piece into 4 triangles.
3. Put remaining butter in a large frying pan and melt over a low heat. Stir in cinnamon and 125 g/4 oz of the sugar. Add bread and turn the pieces over carefully until melted butter and sugar are absorbed.
4. Place one-third of bread mixture in base of dish.
5. Peel and core apples and cut into thick slices. Arrange these in dish. Sprinkle over remaining tablespoon of sugar.
6. Cover with remaining bread mixture.
7. Place dish on a baking sheet in centre of a warm oven, Gas 3, 325°F, 160°C, and bake for 1 to 1¼ hours until bread is crisp on top.

Serve hot with custard or cream.

MALVERN APPLE PUDDING

Malvern is apple-growing country. Although this dish is made with Russet apples, small sweet eating apples can be used. Freezes well.

Serves 6, but it is easy to make half the quantity

125 g/4 oz butter
125 g/4 oz sugar
2 beaten eggs
125 g/4 oz plain or self-raising flour
A pinch of salt
2 smallish Russet apples (about 225 g/8 oz, peeled and cored)
Grated rind of 1 lemon
50 g/2 oz currants
2 to 3 tablespoons brandy*

* It is nearly as nice with sherry, or ½ teaspoon brandy flavouring with 2 tablespoons milk, or even with apple juice.

1. Cream butter and sugar.
2. Add beaten eggs.
3. Fold in flour and salt.

4. Peel, core and chop apples and mix with lemon rind, currants and brandy.
5. Grease a 1.2 litre/2 pint pudding basin. If making half quantity a 450 ml/¾ pint basin suits. Put a small square of greased, greaseproof paper to cover bottom of basin to help when pudding is turned out.
6. Put mixture in basin and cover with greaseproof paper and foil, or tie a double layer of greaseproof paper firmly in place with string.
7. Steam pudding for 1½ to 2 hours. If making half quantity 1 hour will be enough.
If you haven't a steamer, stand basin on a trivet or upturned saucer in a saucepan with a lid. Pour in boiling water to come halfway up sides of basin. Cover pan and boil, replenishing with more boiling water if necessary.
8. Turn pudding out on to a warmed dish and serve it with custard or brandy or sherry sauce (*see page 251*).

If freezing, do so as soon as pudding is cold, covering with fresh paper and foil. To reheat, thaw first, then steam or boil in basin for ½ hour.

Mrs Cynthia Cooksey
Cofton Hackett, Worcestershire

NOTTINGHAM PUDDING

The Bramley cooking apple originates from Southwell, Nottinghamshire. The original tree is still flourishing in a garden in the Minster town.

Serves 6

6 even-sized Bramley apples
75 g/3 oz butter
75 g/3 oz caster sugar
Nutmeg
Cinnamon
6 tablespoons flour
Water
3 eggs
Salt
Milk

1. Peel and core apples.
2. Cream butter and sugar, add pinch of nutmeg and cinnamon.
3. Fill the centre of each apple with this mixture.
4. Place in a well-buttered oven-proof dish.
5. Blend flour with a little cold water and add the well-beaten eggs to it. Add a pinch of salt and sufficient milk to make a thick creamy batter.
6. Pour over the apples and bake in a moderately hot oven, Gas 6, 400°F, 200°C, for 50 minutes.

SPICY APPLE BARS

Makes 6 pieces

175 g/6 oz plain flour
½ level teaspoon salt
75 g/3 oz margarine
75 g/3 oz light soft brown sugar

TOPPING
1 tablespoon soft brown sugar
1 level teaspoon cinnamon
2 small or 1 large cooking apple
25 g/1 oz butter

1. Sift flour and salt and rub in margarine until mixture is like breadcrumbs.
2. Stir in soft brown sugar.
3. Spread this mixture loosely in a greased shallow baking tin, about 18 cm/7 inches square.
4. Now start the topping. Mix together sugar and cinnamon.
5. Peel, core and slice the apples into neat pieces. Lightly press them into the mixture in tin.
6. Sprinkle the sugar and cinnamon on top. Dot with butter.
7. Bake in a moderately hot oven, Gas 6, 400°F, 200°C, for 35 to 40 minutes.
8. Cut into 6 bars and serve hot or cold with cream, ice-cream or custard.

Freezes and re-heats well.

Mrs M.K. Smith
Dartford, Kent

APRICOT AND HAZELNUT PUDDING

Serves 3 to 4

50 g/2 oz dried apricots
50 g/2 oz soft margarine or butter
50 g/2 oz caster sugar
25 g/1 oz hazelnuts
1 large egg, separated
50 g/2 oz plain cake crumbs
Icing sugar

1. Cover apricots with cold water, leave overnight to soften. Dry thoroughly on kitchen paper.
2. Cream margarine or butter and sugar together until fluffy.

3. Grind nuts or chop finely, add to creamed mixture.
4. Chop apricots fairly small.
5. Add egg-yolk with apricots to the mixture. Beat well in.
6. Fold in cake crumbs.
7. Whisk egg-white until stiff and fold into mixture.
8. Pour into an oiled, oven-proof dish and level the surface.
9. Cook on centre shelf of oven at Gas 4, 350°F, 180°C, for 40 minutes until risen a little and fairly firm when pressed with the fingertips.
10. Sprinkle with icing sugar.

Serve hot or cold.

See also Apricot and Orange, page 21

BANANA FRITTERS

Serves 6

50 g/2 oz plain flour
A pinch of salt
2 teaspoons icing sugar
4 tablespoons lukewarm water
2 teaspoons melted butter
White of 1 egg
3 or 4 bananas
Oil for deep frying

1. Sift flour and salt into a bowl.
2. Add sugar and mix with water and butter to a thick, smooth batter.
3. Whisk egg-white until stiff.
4. Fold into batter.
5. Quarter the bananas, cutting each lengthways and then across.
6. Heat the oil until it is nearly smoking hot. Test by dropping in a small piece of bread. It it rises bubbling to surface and turns golden in 30 seconds the oil is ready to cook fritters.
7. Dip each piece of banana in the batter and fry until golden brown.
8. Drain on kitchen paper and serve hot with a jam sauce.

Pineapple Fritters
Same as for Banana Fritters except use pineapple rings in place of banana quarters.

Priya Wickramasinghe
Cardiff

BAKED BANANAS

Serves 4

4 bananas
Lemon juice
50 g/2 oz desiccated coconut
50 g/2 oz demerara sugar
Pat of butter
A little rum (optional)

1. Lay the peeled bananas in a buttered, shallow, fireproof dish.
2. Sprinkle with lemon juice.
3. Mix the coconut and sugar together and sprinkle this over the bananas.
4. Add shavings of butter and a sprinkling of rum if you wish.
5. Bake in a moderate oven, Gas 4, 350°F, 180°C, for about 15 minutes.

Serve with custard or cream.

TO KEEP BANANAS FROM GOING BROWN

Put unpeeled bananas in cold water for 5 to 10 minutes. They may then be peeled, sliced and left for some time without going brown.

Miss M. Owen
Elworth, Cheshire

In our test, with firm bananas, there was only slight discoloration after 4 hours. It was 8 hours before they went brown and soft. Very ripe bananas and a warm kitchen could give less good results.

Ed.

JAMAICAN OMELETTE

Serves 3

3 eggs, separated
50 g/2 oz demerara sugar
Grated rind and juice of 1 lemon
A pinch of salt
1 dessertspoon apricot jam
1 banana
3 tablespoons rum
40 g/1½ oz butter

1. Put egg-yolks, 15 g/½ oz of the sugar and 1 teaspoon lemon rind in a basin. Whisk lightly.
2. In another bowl whisk egg-whites and salt.
3. *For the filling.* Warm the jam. Mash banana and mix with jam. Add rest of the lemon rind and 1 tablespoon of the rum and heat gently.
4. *For the sauce.* Melt 25 g/1 oz of the butter and the remaining sugar in a small pan and let it cook for a few seconds.
5. Stir in 1 teaspoon lemon juice and the last 2 tablespoons of rum.
6. *Now to complete the omelette.* Melt remaining 15 g/½ oz butter in omelette pan.
7. Fold egg mixtures together and pour into hot butter in pan. Cook until golden underneath.
8. Place under a low grill for a minute to firm top and toast it until slightly golden.
9. Lift omelette out on to a warmed dish. Place on it the banana mixture and fold it over.
10. Pour the hot sauce over and serve at once.

BREAD AND BUTTER PUDDING

Serves 3 to 4

150 g/5 oz stale bread (without crusts)
Butter
50 g/2 oz sultanas
A little candied peel
2 tablespoons demerara or plain white sugar
1 large egg
300 ml/½ pint milk
Nutmeg

This is delicious made from stale Hot Cross Buns, Bun Loaf, or Sally Lunn. Where fruit is already incorporated in loaf or buns extra sultanas and candied peel are not needed, nor is it necessary to remove crusts.

1. Butter a pie dish of approximately 1 litre/1½ pint capacity.
2. Slice the bread, butter it and cut into small pieces.
3. Place half the bread in pie dish, sprinkle on the fruit and half the sugar. Cover with remaining bread.
4. Beat the egg and milk, pour over the bread and leave 30 minutes to soak.
5. Sprinkle top with remaining sugar and grate on a little nutmeg.
6. Bake in a moderate oven, Gas 4, 350°F, 180°C, for about 1 hour.

CHICHESTER PUDDING

A very light bread pudding, almost like a soufflé.

Serves 4

4 slices of white bread, preferably real bread
15 g/½ oz butter
2 eggs, separated
2 tablespoons caster sugar
250 ml/9 fl oz milk
Grated rind and juice of 1 large lemon

1. Preheat oven to moderate, Gas 4, 350°F, 180°C.
2. Cut crusts off bread and make it into coarse crumbs. Use the grater.
3. Use butter to grease a 600 ml/1 pint soufflé or oven dish.

4. Beat egg-yolks with sugar and milk.
5. Add crumbs, lemon juice and rind.
6. Whisk egg-whites quite stiff and fold them in.
7. Turn mixture into prepared dish and put straight into pre-heated oven, near top. Bake 35 to 40 minutes until pudding is set, well-risen and golden.

Serve at once or, like a soufflé, it will fall.

Mrs Sheila Powell
Portslade, Sussex

WHITE LADIES PUDDING

This recipe is named after a village near Worcester called White Ladies Aston where a convent of Cistercian nuns lived in the 12th century. They wore white habits.

Can be baked in oven or steamed on top of stove.

Serves 6, but easy to reduce to one third or two thirds for 2 or 4

6 medium-thick slices of white bread
75 g/3 oz butter
125 g/4 oz desiccated coconut
600 ml/1 pint milk
A pinch of salt
Vanilla essence
3 eggs
75 g/3 oz sugar

1. Remove crusts from bread. Butter the slices thickly and cut into squares or triangles.
2. Use remaining butter to grease a 1.5 litre/2½ pint pie dish. Sprinkle it with the coconut. Then arrange bread in dish.
3. Heat milk till it feels comfortably hot when tested with little finger. Add salt and a few drops of vanilla essence.
4. Beat eggs with sugar. Pour in milk, stirring to dissolve sugar, and strain into pie dish. Leave to soak for 30 minutes.
5. Stand dish in a roasting tin and pour hot water around it to come halfway up.
6. Bake in middle of a warm oven, Gas 3, 325°F, 160°C, for about 1½ hours until pudding is set.
Or the pudding can be steamed if you prefer not to use oven.
7. Turn pudding out on to a warmed dish. Delicious hot or cold.

TO COOK ON TOP OF STOVE

Using ingredients scaled down to 2 eggs, pudding will fit a 1.2 litre/2 pint pudding basin. Cover top with greaseproof paper and foil. Steam for 1½ hours. If you do not have a steamer, stand basin on a trivet in a large saucepan. Pour in boiling water to come halfway up sides of basin. Cover pan and boil for 1½ hours, replenishing with more boiling water if necessary.

Mrs Jeanne Round
Cookley, Worcestershire

See also Plum Caramel Pudding, page 258

CARLINS

Many centuries ago the Scots lay siege to Newcastle and it is said that the people were only saved from starvation when a French ship with a load of grey peas crept up the River Tyne. It was Passion Sunday, two Sundays before Easter, when the peas were distributed and on this day each year, now known as Carlin Sunday, it has been the custom, particularly in public houses to serve carlins free.

'Carlins' is a Geordie name for the peas. They are properly named Maple Peas. Outside the North East of England they are stocked by corn merchants and some pet stores for sale as pigeon feed. They are quite rich in protein, about 25%.

225 g/8 oz carlins (maple peas)
Water
Pinch of salt
25 g/1 oz butter
50 g/2 oz soft brown sugar
Dash of rum

1. Soak carlins overnight in water.
2. Drain and place in a saucepan of boiling water with a pinch of salt. Boil for approximately 20 minutes or until cooked but not overdone.
3. Melt butter in a frying pan, add drained carlins and fry for 2 to 3 minutes.
4. Remove from heat, stir in brown sugar and dash of rum.

Serve hot. They are delicious.

Miss P. Howey
Northumberland

CARROT SWEET

Serves 5 or 6

450 g/1 lb carrots, finely-grated
50 g/2 oz whole cashew nuts or blanched almonds, whole or chopped a little
150 g/5 oz sugar
750 ml/1¼ pints milk
75 g/3 oz butter or ghee (*see page 62*)
6 cardamoms

1. Put carrots, nuts, sugar and milk in a pan. Stir over low heat to dissolve sugar. Then cook very gently, stirring occasionally, until carrot has absorbed all the liquid.
2. In another pan melt butter. Stir in the carrot mixture and cook for a few minutes.
3. Crush seeds from cardamom pods and mix in.
4. Pile mixture into a nice dish and serve at room temperature.

Priya Wickramasinghe
Cardiff

CHOCOLATE UP AND OVER PUDDING

A sponge top over a thick fudge sauce.

Serves 4 to 5

PUDDING
75 g/3 oz self-raising flour
25 g/1 oz chocolate powder or 1 rounded tablespoon cocoa
125 g/4 oz margarine, soft
125 g/4 oz granulated sugar
2 eggs

TOPPING AND SAUCE
1 rounded tablespoon cocoa
40 g/1½ oz chopped nuts, walnuts or flaked almonds
125 g/4 oz demerara sugar
300 ml/½ pint hot, strong black coffee (if using instant coffee, pour water on to 3 teaspoons of this)

1. Grease a deep, oven-proof, pudding dish, 1.2 litre/ 2 pint capacity.
2. Sieve flour and chocolate powder into a bowl with other pudding ingredients. This pudding is mixed by the 'all-in' method.

3. Mix up and beat well for 2 minutes with a wooden spoon to make a smooth mixture. Or use an electric mixer for ½ minute.

4. Tip mixture into greased dish and level the top.

5. *For the topping and sauce:* mix cocoa, nuts and 50 g/2 oz of the demerara sugar together and sprinkle this over the pudding.

6. Sweeten the hot coffee with remaining 50 g/2 oz demerara and pour over the pudding.

7. Bake in a moderate oven, Gas 4, 350°F, 180°C, for 50 minutes to 1 hour. During cooking, the sponge rises up and over and the coffee mixture makes a thick fudge sauce underneath.

Serve hot with cream or ice-cream.

Pat Dixon
Holmfirth, W. Yorkshire

DOROTHY SLEIGHTHOLME'S CHRISTMAS PUDDING

Serves 10

175 g/6 oz plain wholewheat or white flour
½ teaspoon salt
1 teaspoon mixed spice
½ teaspoon powdered cinnamon
¼ teaspoon grated nutmeg
125 g/4 oz fresh wholemeal or white breadcrumbs
125 g/4 oz shredded suet
75 g/3 oz demerara sugar
125 g/4 oz raisins
225 g/8 oz currants
225 g/8 oz sultanas
50 g/2 oz chopped candied peel
1 medium-sized apple, grated
1 medium-sized carrot, grated
Juice and grated rind of 1 lemon and 1 orange
1 level tablespoon dark treacle
2 beaten eggs
200 ml/⅓ pint stout*

* *See page 428 for home brewed stout recipe.*

For cooking the pudding you will need one 1.2 litre/ 2 pint basin *or* two 600 ml/1 pint basins *or* four 300 ml/½ pint basins.

1. Remove any stalks or stones from the fruit.
2. Sieve into a large bowl the flour, salt and spices.

3. Add crumbs, suet, sugar and fruit and mix well together.

4. Add grated apple, carrot, rind and juice of lemon and orange, treacle, eggs and stout. Mix very well together.

5. Leave several hours, or overnight. Stir again. Place in greased basin(s), leaving 2.5 cm/1 inch at top. Cover securely with two layers of greased greaseproof paper and one layer of foil, tucking each layer neatly under rim of basin.

6. Stand on a trivet or upturned saucer in a pan with boiling water half way up basin. (Or, use a steamer which will give you a lighter pudding.) Steam as follows:

1.2 litre/2 pint basin—8 hours
600 ml/1 pint basins—6 hours
300 ml/½ pint basins—4 hours

Keep water on the boil, replenishing with boiling water when necessary.

OR

Pressure cook following instructions in your pressure cooker handbook. Cooking time will be reduced considerably.

7. When required, steam 3 hours for 1.2 litre/2 pint pudding, 2 hours for smaller puddings, *or* pressure cook 1 hour for 1.2 litre/2 pint pudding ¾ hour for smaller puddings.

CHRISTMAS PUDDING

Grace Mulligan's excellent pudding, full of fruit. Can be made just a few weeks before Christmas but keeps for 6 months.

A pudding made in a 1.2 litre/2 pint basin will provide 10 to 12 helpings

There is enough mixture for a 1.2 litre/2 pint basin plus a 300 ml/½ pint basin, *or* a 1 litre/1½ pint basin and a 600 ml/1 pint basin. Smaller puddings can be cooked with larger ones and removed from steamer slightly sooner.

225 g/8 oz raisins ⎫ washed
225 g/8 oz sultanas ⎬ and
225 g/8 oz currants ⎭ dried
225 g/8 oz fresh breadcrumbs, wholewheat or white
50 g/2 oz almonds, blanched and finely-chopped
1 apple
Grated rind and juice of 1 lemon
4 small beaten eggs
250 g/9 oz moist brown sugar, try muscovado
225 g/8 oz shredded suet
50 g/2 oz cut mixed peel
50 g/2 oz plain flour, wholewheat or white
1 rounded teaspoon mixed spice
3 tablespoons sherry or brandy

1. Grease basins and place a circle of greaseproof paper or foil in the bottom of each. This will make sure puddings are turned out easily.
2. In a very large bowl, mix all ingredients thoroughly. Make sure you get some help with the stirring.
3. Fill basins to 1 cm/½ inch below the rim. Do not pack the mixture in too tightly.
4. Cover basins with a piece of greaseproof paper, pleated along middle, and then with a piece of pleated foil. Tuck foil securely under rim of basin.
5. Steam the puddings 4 hours for 1.2 litre/2 pint basins and 2 hours for 600 ml/1 pint basins. The longer the steaming, the darker the pudding. If you do not have a steamer, stand basins on a trivet in a large pan of boiling water, put on the lid and boil. Do not let water go off the boil and remember to replenish with more boiling water from time to time. A pressure cooker will reduce cooking time considerably. Follow instructions in the handbook.
6. Remove puddings from steamer, take off paper and foil covers and leave to cool under a clean towel. When quite cold re-cover with fresh greaseproof paper and foil and store in a cool cupboard until required.
7. On Christmas Day, steam puddings 2 hours for a 1.2 litre/2 pint basin and 1 hour for a 600 ml/1 pint basin. Or pressure cook to save time and fuel.

Serve with Rum Sauce or Rich Brandy Butter (*see page 251*).

MOTHER'S EXCELLENT RECIPE FOR A CHRISTMAS PUDDING

Makes 4 puddings weighing approx. 575 g/1¼ lb each, but larger puddings can be made. Or, by reducing quantities of ingredients carefully, just 1 or 2 puddings can be made.

Always made in October to allow time to mature. Keep well for at least a year.

225 g/8 oz butter
275 g/10 oz stale wholemeal or white breadcrumbs
125 g/4 oz plain flour
½ teaspoon ground mace
1 teaspoon ground ginger
1 teaspoon ground nutmeg
225 g/8 oz demerara sugar
125 g/4 oz chopped candied orange peel
50 g/2 oz chopped candied lemon peel
25 g/1 oz chopped candied citron peel
125 g/4 oz chopped glacé cherries
225 g/8 oz currants
450 g/1 lb chopped raisins
75 g/3 oz blanched almonds, chopped
1 grated carrot
6 beaten eggs
2 tablespoons golden syrup or black treacle
300 ml/½ pint ale

1. Grease four 600 ml/1 pint pudding basins, or two 1.2 litre/2 pint basins.
2. Put butter in warm place to melt.
3. Place breadcrumbs in a very large mixing bowl or crock.
4. Sift in the flour and spices.
5. Mix in sugar.
6. Add chopped peels and cherries.
7. Add currants and raisins and mix well.

8. Add almonds and carrot to the mixture and mix well.

9. Stir in beaten eggs and golden syrup or black treacle. Mix well.

10. Add to the mixture the melted butter and ale and stir in well.

11. Divide mixture equally between the basins.

12. Cover tightly with a layer of greased, greaseproof paper and then foil.

13. Place in a steamer, two-thirds full of boiling water or in saucepan of boiling water. Water should come half-way up sides of the basin. A pressure cooker may be used instead of a steamer. Use as directed in the instruction booklet.

14. Steam 3½ to 4 hours. Water should not go off the boil. When it needs replenishing, use boiling water. If making 2 larger puddings steam for 7 to 8 hours.

15. Remove puddings from saucepan and take off the foil and paper. Allow to cool.

16. When puddings are quite cold, cover with fresh greased, greaseproof paper and foil. Store in a cool place.

17. Steam again for 1½ to 2 hours before serving.

Serve with Brandy Sauce (*see page 251*)

Stella Boldy
Sykehouse, N. Humberside

ECONOMICAL CHRISTMAS PUDDING

Serves 5 or 6

50 g/2 oz fresh wholemeal or white bread-crumbs
1 beaten egg
50 g/2 oz self-raising wholewheat or white flour
1 level teaspoon mixed spice
225 g/8 oz mincemeat (up to 325 g/12 oz can be used)
1 tablespoon milk
1 level tablespoon dark treacle

Recipe for mincemeat is given on page 371.

1. Add crumbs to egg in bowl.

2. Sieve the flour and spice and add the mincemeat, milk and treacle. Mix well.

3. Spoon into a greased 600 ml/1 pint basin, cover with greased greaseproof paper and a layer of foil, tucking edges round rim of basin.

4. Place on trivet or upturned saucer in pan with boiling water half way up basin. (Or, use a steamer,

which will give you a lighter pudding). Steam for 4 hours. Keep water on boil, replenishing with boiling water when necessary. Or, pressure cook following instructions given in your pressure cooker hand-book.

The pudding can be eaten now or kept a week or so. If it is to be kept until another day steam it then for 1 hour.

A 600 ml/1 pint basin will take a pudding mixture using 325 g/12 oz mincemeat if you prefer a richer pudding.

VEGETABLE PLUM PUDDING

Serves 4

50 g/2 oz plain wholewheat flour
Pinch of salt
50 g/2 oz grated carrot
50 g/2 oz grated potato
50 g/2 oz Barbados sugar
50 g/2 oz shredded suet
25 g/1 oz raisins
25 g/1 oz currants
1 egg
1 to 2 tablespoons milk

This pudding can be made with white flour and sugar but it looked and tasted even better as above— Ed.

1. Mix all ingredients thoroughly.

2. Grease a 600 ml/1 pint pudding basin and put in the mixture.

3. Cover basin with a sheet of greased, greaseproof paper, pleated across the middle. Cover that loosely with foil, securing it well under rim of basin.

4. Steam for 3 hours. If you do not have a steamer, stand basin on a trivet or upturned saucer in a saucepan. Pour in enough boiling water to come half-way up sides of basin. Keep it boiling for 3 hours. If water boils low replenish with more boiling water.

Or use a pressure cooker. Steam without pressure valve for 15 minutes. Then bring to pressure (lowest pressure) and pressure-cook for 40 minutes.

Mrs M.E. Houslay
Shiptonthorpe, York

FEAST PLUM PUDDING

Serves 6

325 g/12 oz stale wholemeal or white bread, without crusts
125 g/4 oz raisins, or chopped dates
125 g/4 oz currants
25 g/1 oz mixed peel
50 g/2 oz sugar
1 egg
125 g/4 oz grated suet
$\frac{1}{4}$ level teaspoon grated nutmeg

1. Cut bread into cubes. Soak these in water for about 10 minutes, squeeze out moisture and mix with other ingredients.
2. Put into a well-greased, deep, oven-proof dish and cover with foil.
3. Cook in a moderate oven, Gas 4, 350°F, 180°C, for half an hour. Then reduce heat to cool, Gas 1, 275°F, 140°C, for a further two hours. It can then be left in the oven with the heat off. May be reheated or more usually eaten cold.
It was originally cooked in the baker's oven after the day's baking and was left in all night.

Mrs M.D. Dickens
Northamptonshire

RICH BRANDY BUTTER

The mixture can be frozen well in advance or refrigerated for up to four days beforehand.

50 g /2 oz butter
125 g/4 oz icing sugar
1 egg
50 g/2 oz ground almonds
1 dessertspoon brandy
150 ml/$\frac{1}{4}$ pint double cream

1. Use soft but not melted butter.
2. Cream butter with icing sugar.
3. Beat in the egg and ground almonds.
4. Whip cream until it holds soft peaks, then beat in brandy. Fold into the creamed mixture.
5. Refrigerate for at least an hour before use, but preferably overnight.

Serve to accompany the Christmas pudding.

BRANDY BUTTER

75 g/3 oz unsalted butter
75 g/3 oz fine caster sugar
2 to 3 tablespoons brandy

1. Cream butter until white.
2. Beat in sugar gradually.
3. Add brandy 1 teaspoon at a time, beating in thoroughly. If the mixture shows any signs of curdling, do not use all the brandy.
4. The sauce should be white and foamy. Pile into small serving dish and allow to become firm in a cool place or refrigerator. Use with Plum Pudding or mince-pies.

BRANDY SAUCE

To serve with Christmas Pudding.

300 ml/$\frac{1}{2}$ pint double cream
1 tablespoon brandy
25 g/1 oz soft brown sugar
1 egg-white

1. Whisk cream until it is starting to thicken.
2. Add brandy and sugar and whisk until thick.
3. Whisk egg-white with a clean whisk in a clean basin until stiff but not dry.
4. Using a metal spoon, fold egg-white into the cream mixture.
5. Turn into a serving dish.

Stella Boldy
Sykehouse, N. Humberside

RUM SAUCE

For Christmas Pudding.

40 g/1½ oz cornflour
600 ml/1 pint milk
40 gl/1½ oz sugar
2 tablespoons rum, or more if desired

1. Blend cornflour with 2 or 3 tablespoons of the cold milk.
2. Heat rest of milk and, when near boiling point, pour a little over cornflour mixture. Stir and return it all again to the pan. Sweeten with sugar.
3. Bring to the boil and simmer for a few minutes, stirring all the time.
4. Add rum and keep sauce hot in a jug.

Brandy or sherry sauce can be made in exactly the same way.

CUMBERLAND RUM BUTTER

Traditionally served at Christenings—afterwards the empty rum butter bowl is filled with silver coins and given to the baby.

USING THE MELTED METHOD
210 g/7½ oz soft brown sugar
½ wine glass (1½ tablespoons) rum
125 g/4 oz slightly salted butter

1. Crush or sieve brown sugar to ensure there are no lumps.
2. Place sugar into bowl and add rum. Stir until smooth.
3. Put butter into a heat-proof basin and allow to soften near cooker—it should not boil or become oily.
4. Pour butter gradually on to the sugar and rum, stirring with a wooden spoon until well-blended and starting to set.
5. Pour into an old fashioned china bowl and allow to set.

Serve spread on scones or plain biscuits.
Mrs Sadie Wilson
Caldbeck Wigton

BAKED CUSTARD

Serves 4

3 eggs and 1 egg-yolk
1 heaped dessertspoon honey
450 ml/¾ pint milk
A grating of nutmeg

1. Lightly beat eggs and egg-yolk with the honey.
2. Pour the milk into this mixture.
3. Strain into an oven-proof dish. Grate on fresh nutmeg.
4. Stand dish in a small roasting tin. Pour in enough cold water to come half-way up sides of dish.
5. Put in a moderate oven, Gas 3, 325°F, 160°C, for about 1 hour until firm. To test, slip a knife in diagonally. If it comes out clean, custard is cooked.

Serve hot or cold.

POURING CUSTARD

Makes 300 ml/½ pint

300 ml/½ pint milk
1 dessertspoon vanilla sugar (*see page 242*)
2 eggs

1. Heat the milk and vanilla sugar, but do not boil.
2. Pour on to the lightly-beaten eggs.
3. Strain into a heat-proof basin.
4. Stand this over a pan of simmering water, not touching the water. Stir from time to time with a wooden spoon. It is cooked when there is a thin coating of custard on spoon—about 10 minutes.

Serve hot or cold with pies, puddings, etc.

See also Caramel Custard, page 263

STEAMED PUDDINGS

THE BASIC RECIPE

Serves 4

125 g/4 oz margarine
125 g/4 oz caster sugar
175 g/6 oz self-raising flour
Pinch of salt
2 beaten eggs
2 tablespoons milk

1. Grease a 1.2 litre/2 pint heat-proof basin.
2. Beat margarine until soft and creamy and then beat in sugar.
3. Mix flour and salt and add it a little at a time alternately with the beaten egg.
4. Fold in milk.
5. Spoon into greased basin, smooth top.
6. Cover with greased, greaseproof paper and foil, tucking edges securely round rim.
7. Steam the pudding in a steamer. *Or*, stand basin on a trivet or upturned saucer in a saucepan with enough boiling water to come halfway up the basin. Steam for $1\frac{1}{2}$ hours. Keep the water boiling, replenishing with boiling water as necessary.
If you have a pressure cooker, cook at pressure for 30 minutes. Reduce pressure quickly.

Serve with custard or chocolate sauce (*see page 280*) or with warmed golden syrup or a jam sauce.

Try also the following variations based on the Steamed Puddings recipe:

Marble Pudding
When pudding is mixed:
1. Divide mixture into 3 portions.
2. Colour one portion pink with a few drops of red colouring.
3. Mix 2 teaspoons of cocoa with 2 teaspoons of hot water. Fold this into another portion.
4. Spoon into the greased pudding basin alternate spoonfuls of the plain, pink and chocolate mixtures. Smooth top.
Continue from paragraph 6 of the basic recipe.

Serve with custard or chocolate sauce (*see page 280*).

Sultana Pudding
Follow the basic recipe adding 75 to 125 g/3 to 4 oz. sultanas to the flour (paragraph 3).

Chocolate Pudding
Omit 25 g/1 oz flour from the basic recipe and replace it with 25 g/1 oz cocoa. Sieve this with the flour and add as instructed in paragraph 3 of basic recipe.

Coffee Pudding
Dissolve 2 level teaspoons instant coffee into 2 teaspoons boiling water. Mix this with the milk and fold in as instructed in paragraph 4 of basic recipe.

Orange or Lemon Pudding
Omit the milk from the basic recipe and add the rind and juice of 1 orange or 1 lemon.

Jam, Marmalade or Lemon Curd may be used as a topping for the pudding. Follow the basic recipe but put 2 tablespoons of jam, marmalade or curd into the greased pudding basin before spooning in the pudding mixture.

CHOCOLATE SAUCE
1 level dessertspoon cornflour
50 g/2 oz sugar
15 g/$\frac{1}{2}$ oz cocoa
300 ml/$\frac{1}{2}$ pint milk
15 g/$\frac{1}{2}$ oz margarine
$\frac{1}{2}$ teaspoon vanilla essence

1. Blend cornflour, sugar and cocoa with a little of the milk.
2. Bring the rest of the milk to the boil and pour it over the cornflour mixture, stirring to combine.
3. Return mixture to pan and simmer for 2 minutes.
4. Remove from heat and stir in margarine and essence.

CHILTERN HILLS PUDDING

Serves 4 to 5

4 level tablespoons seed tapioca
210 ml/$\frac{3}{8}$ pint (or $7\frac{1}{2}$ fl oz) milk
125 g/4 oz raisins
25 g/1 oz shredded suet
125 g/4 oz sugar
125 g/4 oz fresh white breadcrumbs
1 level teaspoon bicarbonate of soda

1. Place tapioca in a mixing bowl, pour the milk over it and leave to soak for 2 hours.
2. Strain off the milk and reserve it.
3. Add raisins, suet, sugar and crumbs to tapioca.

4. Dissolve bicarbonate of soda in strained milk, add to other ingredients and mix all well together.

5. Pack into a lightly-greased basin. A 1 litre/1½ pint basin is just large enough but a 1.2 litre/2 pint basin is safer as the mixture rises. Cover with lightly-greased foil, sealing well round edges.

6. Steam for 3 hours, keeping water always boiling. Replenish as necessary with more boiling water. If you do not have a steamer stand the pudding on an upturned saucer in a saucepan of boiling water. This should come half-way up the sides of the pudding basin.

Mrs M.E. Smith
Buckinghamshire

FIG DUMPLING

Serves 5 to 6

175 g/6 oz dried figs
225 ml/8 fl oz milk
150 g/5 oz self-raising flour
1 rounded teaspoon baking powder
175 g/6 oz sugar
125 g/4 oz shredded suet
50 g/2 oz fresh white or wholemeal bread-crumbs
1 beaten egg

1. Discard stalks and cut figs into small pieces.
2. Stew them gently in milk for 5 minutes.
3. Sift flour and baking powder into a mixing bowl.
4. Mix in other dry ingredients.
5. Make a well in the centre, pour in stewed figs and milk and beat well to combine thoroughly.
6. Mix in beaten egg.
7. Grease a 1.5 litre/2½ pint, heat-proof pudding basin and put in the mixture.
8. Cover basin with a piece of greased, greaseproof paper and cover that with foil, tucking edges securely round rim.*
9. Place pudding in a saucepan and pour in enough boiling water to come half-way up sides of basin.
10. Steam for 2 hours. Keep water boiling constantly and replenish if necessary with more boiling water.

Mrs Margaret Boyd
Kirkintilloch, Glasgow

* To make it easier to remove the pudding basin from the saucepan, tie some string around the basin to form a handle. The basin can then be lifted out by slipping a wooden spoon under the string.

GINGER MARMALADE PUDDING

Serves 4 to 5 but easy to make less or more

10 small slices or 5 large slices of wholemeal or white bread
Butter or margarine
50 g/2 oz sultanas or raisins
50 g/2 oz demerara sugar
Ginger marmalade
1 large egg
300 ml/½ pint milk
A grating of nutmeg (optional)

1. Grease a small pie dish.
2. Butter the bread.
3. Line bottom and sides of dish with bread, buttered side up.
4. Sprinkle on a few sultanas and some of the sugar.
5. Spread next layer of bread with marmalade.
6. Make as many layers as you can, alternating fruit with marmalade between layers. Save a little sugar for the top.
7. Beat egg and milk together, strain it over the pudding and leave it for 15 minutes to soak.
8. Sprinkle top with sugar and grate on a little nutmeg.
9. Bake in a moderate oven, Gas 4, 350°F, 180°C, for 40 to 50 minutes.

Mrs Wynne Ashby
Gosport, Hampshire

GRANDMA'S 1234 BUNS

Makes a delicious pudding served hot with a fruit sauce (*see below*). Keep the remaining buns for tea.

Makes 12 shallow or 9 deep buns

1 egg
50 g/2 oz margarine
75 g/3 oz caster sugar
125 g/4 oz self-raising flour
A little milk

1. Beat the egg.
2. Cream margarine and sugar until fluffy.
3. Add half the egg, half the flour and mix well. Add remaining egg, flour and 1 tablespoon of milk.
4. Place in greased bun tins. This quantity will make 12 of the shallow type or 9 deeper buns.
5. Bake in a moderately hot oven, Gas 6, 400°F, 200°C, for 15 to 16 minutes until firm.

Miss K.A. Butterworth
Leeds

LEMON DAINTY

Serves 4

175 g/6 oz sugar
40 g/1½ oz soft plain flour
25 g/1 oz butter
Grated rind and juice of 1 large lemon
2 eggs separated
175 ml/6 fl oz (9 brimming tablespoons) milk

1. Mix together in a bowl the sugar, flour, butter shredded in tiny pieces, lemon rind and juice and egg-yolks. Beat well to combine thoroughly.
2. Add milk gradually, beating well.
3. Fold in firmly-whisked egg-whites.
4. Butter a pie dish or a soufflé dish holding about 1.2 litres/2 pints and pour in the mixture.
5. Pour 5 cm/2 inches of hot water into a small roasting tin and stand dish of pudding mixture in it.
6. Bake in a moderate oven, Gas 4, 350°F, 180°C, for 40 to 45 minutes until golden and firm on top.
7. Allow to stand for 5 to 10 minutes before serving.

A FRUIT SAUCE

To serve with hot sponge puddings, pancakes etc. Also delicious served cold with ice-cream. Freezes well.

4 tablespoons jam
4 tablespoons water
Squeeze of lemon juice
1 teaspoon cornflour mixed with 2 teaspoons water

Any variety of jam can be used for this sauce, even a mixture of jams, jelly or marmalade left in jars.
1. Heat jam, water and lemon juice—no need to boil. Sieve.
2. Blend cornflour and 2 teaspoons water. Pour on the jam mixture. Return to pan, bring to boil, stirring all the time.

ORANGE SEMOLINA

Serves 4

600 ml/1 pint milk
Rind 1 orange
40 g/1½ oz (or 2 level tablespoons) semolina
40 g/1½ oz caster sugar
Pinch of salt
25 g/1 oz butter
1 egg, separated

1. Heat the milk with thinly peeled strips of orange rind, bring slowly to boil. Leave 5 minutes to infuse.
2. Remove the orange rind and sprinkle semolina into milk. Stir over a gentle heat until mixture thickens.
3. Remove from heat. Add 25 g/1 oz of the sugar, salt, 15 g/½ oz of the butter, and the egg-yolk. Mix, cool a little, then fold in the stiffly-whisked egg-white.
4. Turn into a buttered 1 to 1.2 litre/1½ to 2 pint dish. Dot with rest of butter, and sprinkle on remaining sugar. Bake in a moderate oven, Gas 4, 350°F, 180°C, for 35 minutes.

PANCAKES

This quantity of batter will make about 14 pancakes 15 cm/6 inches in diameter.

125 g/4 oz plain flour
½ teaspoon salt
1 large egg
300 ml/½ pint milk
Lard

Use a small frying pan.

1. Place flour and salt in basin. Make a well in centre.
2. Drop in egg and begin to mix, gradually adding 150 ml/¼ pint of the milk as the flour is drawn in.
3. Beat well until bubbles are visible.
4. Gradually beat in remaining milk.
5. Put into a jug for easier pouring into the pan.
6. Heat pan and add a piece of lard (size of hazel nut). Allow to spread over pan and become fairly hot.
7. Pour in a little batter, tilting pan to cover. When nicely golden, toss or turn over to cook the other side. Repeat to use batter.

To serve traditionally: sprinkle with lemon juice and sugar and roll up—but there are many other ways.

To freeze: lay pancakes as they are cooked on a clean cloth placed on a large cooling wire. When cool, pack flat, with greaseproof paper or polythene film in between, into a bag and seal. To use: allow to thaw and reheat with a stuffing or in a sauce.

See also Wholewheat Pancakes, page 183, Lager Pancakes, page 183 and Suet Pancakes, page 184.

ORANGE PANCAKES

Pancakes from recipe above.

ORANGE SAUCE
50 g/2 oz butter
Grated rind and juice of 1 large orange
50 g/2 oz caster sugar
4 tablespoons sherry or sweet white wine.

1. Lay pancakes, as they are cooked, on a clean cloth placed on a large cake wire.
2. Fold in quarters.

3. For the sauce. Melt butter in a large frying pan, add orange rind and juice, then sugar, and allow it to dissolve. Add 3 tablespoons of the sherry.
4. Place folded pancakes in sauce and heat through.
5. Pile on to hot serving dish, and pour sauce over them.
6. Add the remaining tablespoon of sherry to pan, swirl round, pour over pancakes, and serve.

To freeze: put pancakes and sauce in a rigid container, allow to become quite cold, cover. To use: heat through, still frozen if necessary, in frying pan. Takes about 15 minutes.

JAM SANDWICHES IN BATTER

An old recipe.

BATTER
50 g/2 oz plain flour
Pinch of salt
2 teaspoons salad oil or melted butter
4 tablespoons luke-warm water
1 egg-white

THE SANDWICHES
Thin slices of bread
Margarine or butter
Raspberry jam, or your own favourite
Oil or fat for frying
Caster sugar

1. Sift flour and salt into a basin. Make a well in the centre and add oil or butter and half of the water.
2. Beat well, then gradually beat in rest of water.
3. Make the sandwiches and cut them into triangles, removing crusts.
4. Whisk egg-white until stiff. Fold it into batter mixture.
5. Dip sandwiches in batter and fry in hot oil until nicely brown.
6. Remove from frying pan on to paper to drain and sprinkle with caster sugar.

Mr A.J. Rayner
Bordesley Green East, Birmingham

PINEAPPLE PUDDING

An oven is not required for this pudding. It is cooked on top of stove and under grill. Can be made with stewed rhubarb or plums.

Serves 5 to 6

50 g/2 oz margarine
125 g/4 oz plain white flour
425 ml/$\frac{3}{4}$ pint milk
50 g/2 oz sugar
A 450 g/1 lb tin of pineapple pieces
2 egg-yolks

MERINGUE
2 egg-whites
75 g/3 oz caster sugar

1. Heat grill to just warm and place a deep 1.2 litre/ 2 pint dish under it.
2. Melt margarine in a large pan. Remove from heat and stir in flour. Cook for 2 minutes, stirring all the time.
3. Remove pan from heat and stir in the milk gradually. Now heat gently until it thickens, stirring all the time. Simmer for 3 minutes.
4. Mix in sugar and 150 ml/$\frac{1}{4}$ pint of juice drained from pineapple.
5. Mix in egg-yolks and cook, stirring for 2 or 3 minutes more. It should bubble but not boil.
6. Lastly, mix in pineapple pieces and pour into the warmed dish. Put it back under grill to keep warm.
7. Whisk egg-whites until they stand up in peaks. Add sugar and whisk again.
8. Spread this meringue over pudding and put dish back under grill. Keep heat low. Grill for 15 minutes until top is a lovely golden brown.

This meringue is not crisp, but soft like marshmallow.

Mrs Patricia Chantry
Hook, Nr Goole, N. Humberside

PINEAPPLE UPSIDE-DOWN PUDDING

Serves 4

BASE
25 g/1 oz butter
50 g/2 oz demerara sugar
4 pineapple rings
6 glacé cherries

PUDDING
50 g/2 oz soft margarine
50 g/2 oz caster sugar
1 large egg
65 g/2$\frac{1}{2}$ oz self-raising flour
15 g/$\frac{1}{2}$ oz semolina
1 to 2 tablespoons milk

GLAZE
1 teaspoon arrowroot or cornflour
150 ml/$\frac{1}{4}$ pint from tin of pineapple (if not sufficient make up with water)

1. Butter an 18 cm/7 inch sandwich tin with the 25 g/1 oz butter, spreading it lightly round sides thicker at the bottom. Sprinkle with the demerara sugar.
2. Arrange pineapple rings and cherries in a pattern over base.
3. Place all pudding ingredients except the milk in a mixing bowl and beat until smooth, adding enough of the milk to make a soft dropping consistency.
4. Spread carefully into the tin on top of fruit and smooth the top level.
5. Bake in centre of a moderately hot oven, Gas 5, 375°F, 190°C, for 30 to 35 minutes until top is firm and pudding is shrinking from sides of tin.
6. Remove from oven, leave 2 to 3 minutes then invert on to a warm plate leaving tin in position.
7. Mix arrowroot and juice in small pan, stir over gentle heat until boiling and transparent.
8. Remove tin carefully from pudding, spoon over a little of the glaze, serve remainder as a sauce.

PLUM CRUMBLE

Serves 4

450 g/1 lb plums
2 tablespoons dark brown Barbados sugar

CRUMBLE TOP
125 g/4 oz wholewheat flour, plain or self-raising
Pinch of salt
65 g/2½ oz brown sugar
A grating of nutmeg
50 g/2 oz butter or margarine

1. Wash plums and put them without drying into a small, round, oven-proof dish. Make them lie as level as possible.
2. Sprinkle with 2 tablespoons sugar.
3. *For the crumble:* mix together flour, salt, sugar and nutmeg.
4. Rub in butter or margarine until mixture is like fine breadcrumbs.
5. Cover plums all over with the crumble.
6. Put at once into a moderately hot oven, Gas 6, 400°F, 200°C, for 20 minutes. Then lower heat to moderate, Gas 4, 350°F, 180°C, for 20 minutes more.

PLUM CARAMEL PUDDING

A delicious bread pudding which can be made in any quantity to suit your household.

Plums
Butter or margarine
Brown sugar
Slices of stale bread, wholewheat, brown or white

1. Wash plums and cut in halves, removing stones.
2. Thickly grease sides and bottom of a pie dish and sprinkle all over with sugar.
3. Line dish with pieces of stale bread.
4. Place a layer of plums over bread, cut side uppermost. Sprinkle with sugar. Cover with another layer of bread, and a second layer of plums and sugar.
5. Finish top with slices of buttered bread, butter-side uppermost.

6. Cover with greaseproof paper and bake in middle of a moderate oven, Gas 3 to 4, 325° to 350°F, 160° to 180°C. Remove paper after 30 minutes.
7. Turn pudding out on to a warmed dish.

Serve with cream or custard.

Mrs Cynthia Cooksey
Cofton Hackett, Worcestershire

QUEEN OF PUDDINGS

Serves 3 to 4

450 ml/¾ pint milk
25 g/1 oz butter
Rind of 1 small lemon
125 g/4 oz caster sugar
75 g/3 oz fresh white breadcrumbs
2 eggs, separated
50 g/2 oz (2 tablespoons) jam

1. Heat milk to nearly boiling point, stir in butter, finely-grated rind of lemon and 25 g/1 oz of the caster sugar.
2. Pour this over the crumbs in a bowl and stir in egg-yolks. Leave 15 minutes.
3. Pour into a lightly-greased 1 to 1.2 litre/1½ to 2 pint pie dish and bake in a moderate oven, Gas 4, 350°F, 180°C, for about 20 to 25 minutes or until set.
4. Remove from oven, lower heat to cool, Gas 1, 275°F, 140°C.
5. Spread jam over top of pudding.
6. Whisk egg-whites stiffly, fold in the remaining 75 g/3 oz caster sugar and spread on top. Sift on a little caster sugar.
7. Return to oven, leave until meringue sets and is just tinged with gold, about 20 minutes.

RHUBARB AND ORANGE MERINGUE

Serves 4

450 g/1 lb young rhubarb
1 orange
50 g/2 oz demerara sugar
40 g/1½ oz cornflour
2 eggs, separated
75 g/3 oz caster sugar

1. Wash and trim rhubarb and cut into short lengths. Place in a 1.2 litre/2 pint shallow oven-proof casserole or pie dish.
2. Grate rind and squeeze juice from orange. Place in a measuring jug and make up to 450 ml/¾ pint with water.
3. Place demerara sugar and cornflour in a saucepan and gradually blend in liquid. Bring to boil, stirring, and simmer for 3 minutes. Allow to cool slightly.
4. Stir egg-yolks into orange sauce and pour over rhubarb.
5. Cook in centre of a moderate oven, Gas 3, 325°F, 160°C, for 20 minutes. Lower temperature to cool, Gas 2, 300°F, 150°C.
6. Meanwhile, whisk egg-whites until stiff and dry, whisk in half the caster sugar and whisk until stiff again. Fold in remaining sugar.
7. Spread meringue over mixture in dish and return to oven to cook for a further 20 to 25 minutes until it is golden brown and the rhubarb is tender.

RHUBARB STIRABOUT

Other fruit, such as gooseberries, cherries or plums can be used instead of rhubarb if desired.

Serves 3 to 4

50 g /2 oz margarine
125 g/4 oz plain flour
50 g/2 oz caster sugar
1 egg and 5 tablespoons milk
225 to 325 g/8 to 12 oz rhubarb
Golden syrup

1. Rub fat into flour till mixture is like breadcrumbs.
2. Stir in the sugar.
3. Add beaten egg and milk to make stiff batter.

4. Cut fruit into 2.5 cm/1 inch pieces and stir into the batter.
5. Pour into greased pie dish and bake for about ½ hour in a hot oven, Gas 7, 425°F, 220°C.
6. Cover with syrup while hot and eat at once.

Kate Easlea
Hampshire

ALMOND JELLIES

Chinese sweets to eat on their own or with fruit salad, tinned fruits, coffee, etc.

10 g/¼ oz agar agar*
1.5 litres/2½ pints cold water
450 ml/¾ pint milk
325 g/12 oz sugar
2½ teaspoons concentrated almond essence

* Agar agar is a type of seaweed and unlike gelatine has setting properties that do not need refrigeration. It is colourless and flavourless and sets to a superb solid texture which can be easily cut into cubes. It is available from Chinese supermarkets and some wholefood and health food shops.

1. Using a pair of scissors, snip the strips of agar agar into 2.5 cm/1 inch pieces.
2. Leave the pieces to soak in the water in a large bowl for about 8 hours.
3. In a pan, bring agar agar and water to the boil. Simmer until dissolved.
4. Add rest of ingredients, stirring to dissolve sugar, then boil for a further 10 minutes.
5. Remove from heat and pour into shallow oiled dishes or baking tins to a depth of about 2.5 cm/1 inch.
6. When set, cut into cubes and pile on to individual serving dishes.

Eat while fresh.

Priya Wickramasinghe
Cardiff

APPLE TRIFLE FOR TWO

2 small buns or pieces of plain cake
2 teaspoons raspberry jam
1 orange
Approximately 225 g/8 oz cooking apples
15 g/½ oz butter
A squeeze of lemon juice
1 to 2 teaspoons sugar
4 tablespoons double cream

1. Cut across buns, sandwich together with jam and place in small serving dish or 2 sundae glasses.
2. Grate rind finely from orange on to a saucer and cover tightly with foil to prevent discoloration.
3. Squeeze the juice from orange and pour over cake.
4. Peel and slice apples wafer thin.
5. Melt butter in small pan, add lemon juice and apples. Stir over gentle heat until soft, but not mushy. Sweeten to taste.
6. Spread apple mixture over cake, leave until cold.
7. Whip cream to spreading consistency and cover apples. Sprinkle on the orange rind and serve.

FARMHOUSE CRUMBLE

Serves 4 to 5

675 g/1½ lb cooking apples
75 g/3 oz butter
Water
Squeeze of lemon juice
1 to 2 tablespoons white sugar
225 g/8 oz fresh white breadcrumbs
75 g/3 oz light brown sugar
150 ml/¼ pint whipping cream
Grated chocolate

1. Peel, core and slice apples.
2. Cook gently in 25 g/1 oz of the butter, and 1 tablespoon water, until soft. Some apples may need a little more water, but keep it to a minimum.
3. Sieve or liquidise, adding a squeeze of lemon juice, and the white sugar to taste. As the dish is quite rich, keep the apple slightly tart. Cool.
4. Mix together crumbs and brown sugar.
5. Heat remaining butter and fry crumbs until crisp and butter is absorbed. Watch carefully to prevent excess browning. Cool.
6. Use a deep, rather than shallow dish, holding approximately 1.5 litres/2½ pints. Place a layer of crumbs, then apples, then crumbs, and so on until

used, leaving crumbs for top. Leave at least 12 hours as this will improve the flavour.
7. Whip cream lightly, pile on top.
8. Decorate with grated chocolate.

Nicer if chilled for about 2 hours before serving.

APRICOT AND RHUBARB REFRESHER

Serves 4

40 g/1½ oz dried apricots
150 ml/¼ pint water
675 g/1½ lb red rhubarb
125 g/4 oz demerara or white sugar
Grated rind and juice of 1 orange
15 g/½ oz (1 envelope) gelatine
3 tablespoons single or whipping cream

TO DECORATE
Angelica
Tiny pieces of rhubarb
Fine slices of dried apricot
4 tablespoons whipped cream (optional)

1. Soak apricots in water overnight.
2. Stew them gently in a pan with a lid until tender.
3. Meanwhile, wash and trim rhubarb, slice it and put it in a casserole dish with the sugar but no water. Cover with lid and cook gently in a moderate oven, Gas 3, 325°F, 170°C, for 15 minutes. This will draw out the juice and cook the rhubarb without breaking it up.
4. Strain juice from rhubarb into a measuring jug. There should be about 450 ml/¾ pint. Allow to cool.
5. Drain apricots. Put juice with the orange juice in a small bowl and sprinkle on the gelatine. Stand bowl over a pan of hot water to melt.
6. Mix gelatine liquid with the rhubarb juice. Pour off ½ cup to use in a moment. Pour the rest equally into 4 serving glasses. Put these in fridge, or a cold place, to set.
7. Meanwhile, rub apricots through a sieve or liquidise them. Add finely-grated orange rind, cream and reserved jelly liquid to the purée.
8. When first layer of jelly is set, top with the creamy one.
9. When this has set, decorate with delicate strips of angelica and fine slices of dried apricot.

The rhubarb may be used in a tart (*see page 236*).

Anne Wallace
Dunlop, Scotland

BLACKBERRY MOUSSE

Raspberries can be used as an alternative.

Serves 4 to 5

450 g/1 lb blackberries
3 level tablespoons sifted icing sugar
15 g/$\frac{1}{2}$ oz gelatine
2 tablespoons water
150 ml/$\frac{1}{4}$ pint whipping cream
2 egg-whites

1. Cook blackberries until soft. This is best done without water in a casserole with a lid in a slow oven (certainly no higher than moderate, Gas 4, 350°F, 180°C). If cooked in a saucepan, 2 to 3 teaspoons water may be required if fruit is dry, but liquid should be kept to a minimum.
2. Sieve the fruit and add icing sugar.
3. Measure purée, there should be 300 ml/$\frac{1}{2}$ pint. Pour into a bowl.
4. Measure water into a small basin, trickle in the powdered gelatine. Stand this in hot water to dissolve gelatine, stirring once to combine.
5. Pour this very gently into fruit, stirring continuously. Allow to become quite cold, and slightly thick.
6. Whip cream until holding its shape. Fold in.
7. Whisk egg-whites until firm but not dry. Fold in.
8. Spoon into a large bowl, or 4 to 5 sundae glasses.

BLACKBERRY AND APPLE FOOL

Serves 6

450 g/1 lb blackberries
450 g/1 lb cooking apples
2 tablespoons honey or Barbados sugar
150 ml/$\frac{1}{4}$ pint double or whipping cream

1. Wash blackberries and place in a saucepan or casserole dish with lid.
2. Wash and slice apples and add to blackberries.
3. Either simmer in pan till fruit is soft or put lid on casserole and put in a slow oven, Gas 2, 300°F, 150°C, and leave till fruit is soft.
4. Sieve fruit and sweeten to taste with honey or sugar. Leave to cool.
5. Whip cream until same thickness as purée.
6. When purée is cold fold together with cream and put in a pretty dish.

COLD FRUIT SOUFFLÉ

Can be made with blackberries, blackcurrants, cranberries, plums, raspberries or strawberries.

Serves 10, but it is easy to make a smaller quantity scaling ingredients down to 1 or 2 eggs

900 g/2 lb fruit, fresh or frozen
Water
About 50 g/2 oz sugar
40 g/1$\frac{1}{2}$ oz gelatine (3 sachets)
3 large egg-whites

TO DECORATE
Chopped nuts, whipped cream for piping (optional)

This can be served in a 1.75 litre/3 pint glass dish or in a specially prepared 1.2 litre/2 pint straight-sided dish. This measures 15 cm/6 inches across and 7.5 cm/3 inches deep.

To prepare a traditional soufflé dish with a paper collar.

1. Cut from a roll of greaseproof paper a single piece measuring 55 cm/22 inches long and 38 cm/15 inches wide.
2. Now fold this lengthways so that you have three thicknesses, 55 cm/22 inches long and 13 cm/5 inches wide.
3. Wind this strip around the outside of the dish and fix it as tightly as you can. Elastic bands are best to hold it in place. It needs to fit very well especially at rim edge.

Now for the soufflé
1. Wash fruit and put it in a saucepan with water barely to cover. Simmer until soft. If using frozen fruit take care to defrost it and add very little water.
2. Push cooked fruit through a nylon sieve, scraping purée from underneath as you do it.
3. Measure purée and, if necessary, top up with water to 1.35 litres/2$\frac{1}{4}$ pints. Return purée to pan.
4. Add sugar according to taste. Stir until it is dissolved. Pour into a large bowl.
5. Put 3 tablespoons water into a cup and sprinkle on the gelatine. Place cup in a small pan of warm water. Heat gently. Stir until gelatine has dissolved, about 2 or 3 minutes.
6. Now strain gelatine mixture into fruit purée, stir well and leave to set in a cool place, or refrigerator.
7. When fruit is set but still wobbly, take a fork and mix it all up again.

8. In a clean, grease-free bowl, whisk egg-whites until stiff. Fold them into fruit.

9. Pour into prepared dish. If you have used a soufflé dish with paper collar, the soufflé will be about 3 cm/ 1¼ inches above top of dish. Put it carefully in refrigerator to set, allowing 2 or 3 hours.

To serve, peel paper gently away using the blunt edge of a knife, and decorate risen edge by gently pressing on chopped nuts. Top can be decorated with a border of chopped nuts or piped rosettes of whipped cream. Otherwise, serve with a jug of pouring cream.

POACHING FRUIT

Poaching fruit as opposed to stewing gives a much better end result both to eat and to look at, particularly as, with a little care, it is possible to keep the fruits whole and unbroken.

The syrup is made first and the fruit very gently simmered in it. For a special occasion a little wine, brandy or liqueur may be added. Soft fruits containing a lot of juice, such as plums, cherries and apricots, require a heavy syrup but only a little of it. Hard fruits such as pears, apples and gooseberries, require a lighter syrup but a greater quantity.
For sweet shortcrust pastry flan cases, *see page 203*.

HEAVY SYRUP
125 g/4 oz sugar to 300 ml/½ pint water

LIGHT SYRUP
75 g/3 oz sugar to 300 ml/½ pint water

1. Place water and sugar in a wide, preferably shallow, pan. Stir over a gentle heat to dissolve sugar and simmer with lid on pan for 2 to 3 minutes.
2. Wash any fruit not to be peeled.
3. If peeling fruit use a stainless steel knife, peeling just the quantity to be poached at one time. Fruit which discolours easily—pears, apples etc.—keep a better colour if a teaspoon of lemon juice is added to syrup.
4. Place prepared fruit into syrup in one layer and simmer very gently with lid on pan until tender. Time will vary according to ripeness of fruit.
5. Lift carefully into serving bowl and repeat process until required quantity of fruit is cooked.
6. If several batches are to be cooked, syrup may require replenishing. If only a small amount of fruit is poached and too much syrup is left, boil it rapidly with lid off pan to reduce a little and to thicken slightly.

7. Add the odd teaspoon of wine, brandy or liqueur to syrup and pour over fruit.

Serve when cold.

RAW FRUIT PURÉE

A refreshing and sustaining dessert.
Made in the liquidiser.

Serves 4

50 g/2 oz dried apricots or prunes
50 g/2 oz raisins
4 dessert apples
½ lemon

TO DECORATE AND SERVE
1 tablespoon freshly-ground nuts
1 tablespoon desiccated coconut
Whipped cream or yoghurt

1. Put apricots or prunes and raisins in a bowl of water. Allow to soak and plump up overnight. Remove stones from prunes.
2. Quarter, core and slice apples, but do not skin them.
3. Pour into liquidiser ½ cup of water in which fruit has soaked. Add apples and blend until smooth.
4. Add apricots, raisins and lemon juice and blend until smooth, adding more of the fruit water if necessary.
5. Pour purée into nice glass bowls.
6. Sprinkle with nuts and coconut and top each glass with a spoonful of whipped cream or yoghurt.
Elizabeth Shears
author of 'Why Do We Eat'

SIMPLE FRUIT SALAD

Quick to make.

Serves 2 or 3

1 large orange
¼ lemon
1 tablespoon raisins
1 large, green eating apple
1 large banana*
5 or 6 hazelnuts

* See To Keep Bananas from going Brown, page 245.

Try also this unusual but delicious ingredient:
A teaspoon of wheatgerm

TO SERVE
4 tablespoons double or whipping cream
1 dessertspoon honey

1. Cut top off orange about a quarter of the way down. Squeeze juice from this small piece into a bowl.
2. Squeeze juice from lemon quarter into bowl.
3. Put raisins into juice.
4. Peel rest of orange and cut it into small pieces.
5. Quarter and core unpeeled apple. Cut it into small pieces.
6. Peel and slice banana.
7. Put fruit in with raisins and juice and toss well to coat with the juice.
8. Slice hazelnuts into thin slivers and sprinkle them on top.
9. Toss in sprouted seed and germinated wheat grains, if using.
10. Whip up cream with honey and serve it in a separate bowl. This cream is very sweet so do not add sugar to fruit salad.

CARAMEL CUSTARD

Serves 4

CARAMEL
75 g/3 oz granulated sugar
1 tablespoon of hot water

1. Dissolve sugar in water in a small heavy pan and then boil, without stirring, until golden.
2. Have ready heated an ungreased, 15 cm/6 inch, heatproof soufflé dish or similar, or a 15 cm/6 inch cake tin. Pour in the caramel, tilting to coat the bottom.
3. Allow to cool and set.

CUSTARD
3 eggs and 1 egg-yolk*
1 tablespoon vanilla sugar (*see page 242*)
450 ml/¾ pint milk

* *Keep the spare egg-white for your Yorkshire Puddings.*

1. Beat eggs and sugar together lightly, but not frothy.
2. Pour on the milk.
3. Strain into caramel dish.

4. Place the dish inside a small dripping tin or container with enough cold water to come halfway up sides of dish.
5. Cook in a moderate oven, Gas 3, 325°F, 160°C, for about 1 hour until firm. To test, slip knife in diagonally, taking care not to touch the caramel. Knife will come out clean if custard is cooked. If not, replace in oven for few more minutes before testing again.
6. Leave until cold. Turn on to a plate to serve.

CHOCOLATE CREAM

Serves 5 to 6

2 tablespoons water
15 g/½ oz (small envelope) gelatine
450 ml/¾ pint milk
3 egg-yolks
75 g/3 oz caster sugar
½ teaspoon vanilla essence, or use vanilla sugar*
125 g/4 oz plain chocolate, coarsely chopped
150 ml/¼ pint whipping cream or 1 small can of evaporated milk plus a good squeeze of lemon juice.

* *For Vanilla Sugar recipe, see page 242.*

TO DECORATE
Chocolate vermicelli

1. Measure water into a cup, sprinkle on gelatine. Stir a little, just to mix. Leave to soften.
2. Heat milk in saucepan *but do not boil*.
3. Cream egg-yolks and sugar in a bowl, pour on the hot milk, stir together and strain back into pan.
4. Stir with a wooden spoon over gentle heat until mixture clings to spoon, *but do not boil*.
5. Pour mixture back into bowl, and stir in vanilla essence if used, the chocolate and the gelatine. Beat until both are dissolved.
6. Leave mixture until quite cold and beginning to thicken slightly, 20 to 30 minutes. Stir occasionally.
7. Whip cream until holding shape, or whisk evaporated milk and lemon juice until thickening, and fold in.
8. Pour into a large serving dish, or 5 to 6 small ones. Sprinkle top of Chocolate Cream with chocolate vermicelli.

CHOCOLATE CREAM PIE

Serves at least 6

BASE
75 g/3 oz butter
75 g/3 oz crushed cornflakes
50 g/2 oz soft brown sugar
25 g/1 oz crushed All Bran

FILLING
90 g/3½ oz plain cooking chocolate
1 tablespoon water
5 ml/1 teaspoon gelatine
1 egg
25 g/1 oz sugar
150 ml/¼ pint double or whipping cream

1. *Start with base.* Melt butter, mix it with cornflakes, sugar and All Bran.
2. Press mixture into a 20 cm/8 inch pie plate.
3. Bake above middle of a moderately hot oven, Gas 5, 375°F, 190°C, for 10 minutes. Remove from oven and leave to cool.
4. *Now the filling.* Grate 15 g/½ oz of the chocolate and keep it for decorating. Break up the rest of it into a small bowl and stand it over a pan of simmering water to melt.
5. Put water in a cup, sprinkle in gelatine and stand cup in a pan of hot water until dissolved.
6. Beat egg and sugar. Add melted chocolate and then gelatine.
7. Whip cream till it will stand in soft peaks. Put 2 tablespoonfuls in a piping bag with fluted nozzle and keep in refrigerator till required. If you haven't a piping bag you can still save 2 tablespoons cream for decorating in a different way.
8. Fold rest of cream into chocolate mixture and pour into cooled case. Put pie in a cool place or refrigerator to set.
9. When set, sprinkle with grated chocolate and decorate with rosettes of piped cream. If you haven't a piping bag, carefully spread cream over surface of pie, fork it and sprinkle with grated chocolate.

Anne Wallace
Stewarton, Ayrshire

CHOCOLATE MOUSSE

Serves at least 4

125 g/4 oz good plain cooking chocolate
3 to 4 eggs, separated
15 g/½ oz butter
1 teaspoon hot water
1 tablespoon brandy*

TO DECORATE
Glacé cherries
Small carton of double or whipping cream

Dry sherry can be used instead of brandy, but brandy is better.

1. Break up chocolate and melt in a basin over a pan of simmering water. Do not let basin touch water.
2. Meanwhile, separate eggs into different bowls. Cut up butter into small pieces.
3. Remove pan and bowl of chocolate from heat. Keep bowl on pan.
4. Beat the egg-yolks and then beat spoonfuls of it into chocolate. Beat well after each spoonful is added until mixture is soft and creamy.
5. Add pieces of butter one at a time and beat in to dissolve them.
6. Beat in hot water.
7. Beat in brandy and leave to cool.
8. Meanwhile, beat egg-whites until stiff.
9. Use a metal spoon and fold egg-whites into chocolate mixture until all white disappears.
10. Pour into glass bowl or individual dishes, and decorate with cherries or cream.

Mrs M. Lucie-Smith
London

CHOCOLATE ORANGE MOUSSE

Makes 6 individual helpings

175 g/6 oz plain cooking chocolate
1 orange
15 g/½ oz butter
3 eggs, separated
150 ml/¼ pint whipped cream (optional)
1 teaspoon caster sugar
Chopped walnuts to decorate

1. Break up chocolate into quite a large basin. Set it to melt over a pan of simmering water. Do not let water touch bowl.

2. Grate zest from orange. Squeeze out juice.
3. Remove bowl of chocolate from pan and stir in butter, orange zest and juice. Mix well.
4. Beat in egg-yolks one at a time.
5. Mix in whipped cream.
6. Whisk egg-whites firmly and then whisk in sugar.
7. Fold egg-whites into chocolate mixture.
8. Serve in small sundae glasses.

Decorate with a sprinkling of chopped walnuts when cool.

CHOCOLATE SUPRÊME

Freezes well up to 3 months.

Very rich. Best made the day before it is needed so that flavour matures.

Serves 6 but you can make half quantity

125 g/4 oz best quality plain eating chocolate
4 eggs, separated
90 g/3½ oz butter, cut in small pieces
1 tablespoon brandy or very dry sherry
2 level dessertspoons icing sugar, sieved
3 tablespoons double cream

TO DECORATE
Toasted flaked almonds, or piped double cream

1. Break up chocolate into a bowl. Stand bowl over a pan of simmering water. Do not let water boil and do not let bowl touch water. Chocolate must melt without getting too hot.
2. Add egg-yolks to melted chocolate and mix gently. Do not beat at any stage in this recipe.
3. Remove bowl from pan. Add the small pieces of butter and stir gently until dissolved.
4. Now add brandy or sherry and sieved icing sugar. Stir until dissolved.
5. Lastly, add cream and stir again.
6. In another bowl, whisk egg-whites until thick and fluffy and fold into chocolate mixture.
7. Pour into tiny glasses, cover with foil or cling film and keep in refrigerator until needed.
8. Just before serving, decorate with a sprinkling of toasted almonds or a whirl of double cream.

CHOCOLATE CHESTNUT DESSERT

Serves 6

175 g/6 oz dark cooking chocolate
75 g/3 oz butter
75 g/3 oz caster sugar
425 g/15 oz can of chestnut purée
3 tablespoons rum or brandy
300 ml/½ pint thick cream

1. Put chocolate in pieces into a small bowl and stand over a pan of simmering water to melt.
2. Cream butter and sugar together. Add chestnut purée, mix thoroughly.
3. Add melted chocolate, then rum or brandy, and lastly the unwhipped cream. Pour into a pretty dish.
4. Leave in fridge to set.

This is very rich and does not require any additional cream for decoration. A sprinkling of grated chocolate looks attractive.

Judith Adshead
Mottram St Andrew, Cheshire

GRACE'S CHOCOLATE FANCY

Can be frozen.

Serves 6

For this you need 1 chocolate fatless sponge, about 20 cm/8 inches across and about 7.5 cm/3 inches deep (*see page 316*).

A 125 g/4 oz jar of maraschino cherries in syrup
125 ml/4 fl oz sherry
125 ml/4 fl oz water
300 ml/½ pint double cream, whipped
2 tablespoons of chocolate mousse, or one 105 ml/3.7 fl oz carton of bought mousse

CHOCOLATE CURLS DECORATION
50 g/2 oz top-quality plain eating chocolate
2 teaspoons salad oil

1. First start preparing chocolate for decorating. Heat a small empty bowl in a moderate oven, Gas 4, 350°F, 180°C. Take it out and put into it the chocolate broken into small pieces.
2. Add oil and stir gently until dissolved.

3. Spread this mixture very thinly over a hard surface and leave to set in a cool place. Ideally a marble slab should be used but you can use a formica surface, such as a large formica chopping board.

4. Now drain syrup from cherries and mix it with sherry and water.

5. Cut each cherry in two.

6. Slice sponge into 3 layers. Place bottom layer on a large serving plate.

7. Use one third of sherry mixture to pour over bottom layer of sponge. Spread with 2 tablespoons of the whipped cream and 1 tablespoon chocolate mousse. Top this with half of the cherries.

8. Put middle slice of sponge in position and repeat the above process with sherry mixture, cream, mousse and cherries.

9. Put on top layer of sponge. Pour over remaining sherry mixture. Press sponge down gently.

10. Now cover sides and top with rest of cream. Set gâteau aside to firm up in a cool place or refrigerator.

11. Make chocolate curls. Draw a sharp knife, held at an angle, across the board making curls of chocolate. Drop curls and broken bits of chocolate all over the gâteau. Chill and serve.

COCOA COFFEE MOUSSE

Serves 4 to 6

2 eggs
75 g/3 oz caster sugar
1 teaspoon vanilla essence
4 level teaspoons cocoa
1 level teaspoon instant coffee
300 ml/½ pint milk
3 tablespoons hot water
15 g/½ oz gelatine, 1 sachet
150 ml/¼ pint double cream
Flaked almonds

1. Separate eggs. Put whites in a clean grease-free basin.

2. In another bowl put yolks, caster sugar and vanilla essence. Beat until light and creamy.

3. In a saucepan, blend cocoa and coffee with a little of the measured milk. Add remaining milk and bring to boil. Remove from heat and let it cool for a minute.

4. Stir into egg-yolk mixture and pour back into pan.

5. Return to heat, bring to the boil and boil for 1 minute, stirring. Remove from heat and pour back into the bowl.

6. Measure 3 tablespoons of hot water into a small bowl, sprinkle on gelatine. Stir a little just to mix. Leave for 5 minutes to soften.

7. Stir gelatine into chocolate mixture. Leave in a cool place until just on setting point.

8. Whip cream until just thick. Keep 2 tablespoons aside until later for decoration.

9. Whisk egg-whites until stiff but not dry.

10. Using a metal spoon, carefully fold cream and egg-whites into chocolate mixture. Pour into a fluted mould or a nice serving dish. Put in refrigerator to set, allowing at least 30 minutes.

11. If using a mould, dip it into a bowl of hand-hot water and turn mousse out on to a serving plate.

12. Put remaining whipped cream in a piping bag with a star nozzle. Pipe on stars to decorate and arrange flaked almonds to look pretty.

Chill until ready to serve.

COFFEE MOUSSE WITH CRUNCHY TOPPING

This dish can be made up to 48 hours before serving if kept in refrigerator.

Serves 6

1 large can evaporated milk
½ cup hot water
15 g/½ oz gelatine, 1 sachet
4 heaped teaspoons instant coffee grains
175 g/6 oz granulated sugar
75 g/3 oz crisp peanut toffee

1. Put evaporated milk to chill in refrigerator for at least 1 hour.

2. Sprinkle gelatine on to the ½ cup of hot water and stir to dissolve it. Stir in coffee until smooth. Allow to cool slightly but stir frequently so that it does not set.

3. Beat evaporated milk until very thick and creamy. Gradually beat in the sugar.

4. Add gelatine mixture slowly, beating continuously. Pour mixture into a large serving bowl.

5. Chop peanut toffee into small bits. It tends to fly everywhere—try using the bread saw on it with a lever action.

6. When mousse has partly set, sprinkle with peanut toffee. Put dish to chill in fridge.

Serve with cream.

Shelagh Robinson
Leeds

CHRISTMAS JELLY

Made in a pudding basin so that the jelly looks like a Christmas pudding.

Serves 4 to 6

450 g/1 lb black grapes
1½ packets of dark jelly (blackcurrant or black-berry)
150 ml/¼ pint port or sherry
Water
50 g/2 oz raisins
50 g/2 oz chopped blanched almonds*

* To blanch almonds: put them in a basin, pour over boiling water to cover. Leave until cool enough to handle when almonds will squeeze easily out of their skins.

1. Cut each grape in half and remove seeds.
2. Make up the jelly according to packet instructions but using the 150 ml/¼ pint of port or sherry so that in all you have 1 litre/1½ pints of liquid jelly.
3. Wet a 1.75 litre/3 pint pudding basin with cold water. Pour the liquid jelly into wet basin.
4. Add to this the grapes, raisins and nuts. Stir occasionally until set.
5. Turn out and decorate with a sprig of holly.

Serve with single cream.

DEVONSHIRE JUNKET

This can be made from pasteurised or farm-bottled milk, but homogenised, sterilised and UHT milk are not suitable. Delicious made with Channel Island milk.

Serves 4

600 ml/1 pint milk
1 tablespoon sugar
2 teaspoons brandy or rum
1 teaspoon essence of rennet
Cinnamon
Grated nutmeg

1. Put milk in a pan with sugar and warm gently till only blood heat, 98°F, 30°C. Stir to dissolve sugar.
2. Remove pan from heat, stir in brandy or rum and pour into a serving dish. Without delay, stir in rennet and put dish aside to set at room temperature. It takes about 1½ to 2 hours.

3. When junket is set, sprinkle cinnamon and nutmeg on top. It can then be chilled.

Serve with sugar to taste and Devonshire cream if you can (*see below*).

Mrs Elizabeth Selby
Exeter, Devon

DEVONSHIRE CREAM

It takes 1 gallon of rich, creamy milk to produce 325 to 450 g/¾ to 1 lb of clotted cream, but the result is delicious. Channel Island milk gives the best result.

1. Put fresh milk in a shallow bowl and leave it at room temperature (55°F, 12°C) for 12 to 24 hours until cream rises to the top.
2. Stand bowl over a pan of boiling water till a crust forms on top of milk. Do not let water touch bowl. This will take about 1 hour.
3. Leave bowl in a cool place till next day.
4. Carefully skim off thick creamy top. Underneath is scalded milk suitable for sauces, soups and puddings.

Mrs Elizabeth Selby
Westleigh, Tiverton, Devon

EGG FLIP

Serves 1 to 2

1 egg, separated
1 or 2 teaspoons honey
300 ml/½ pint milk
Cinnamon or nutmeg

1. Put egg-yolk, honey and half the milk in a bowl and whisk until blended.
2. Whisk in rest of milk.
3. Whisk egg-white separately until stiff. Fold it in.
4. Pour into glasses and sprinkle with a pinch of cinnamon or a fine grating of nutmeg.

FLOATING ISLANDS

Serves 4

600 ml/1 pint milk
2 eggs, separated
50 g/2 oz caster sugar plus 2 level teaspoons
1 level tablespoon cornflour
Vanilla essence
A very little water

TO DECORATE
Grated chocolate or chocolate vermicelli

1. Pour milk into a saucepan, heat to simmering point.
2. Whisk 1 egg-white until stiff, add 25 g/1 oz of the sugar. Whisk again until stiff. Fold in another 25 g/1 oz sugar.
3. Divide egg-white into 4 and spoon each portion on to milk. Poach until set, about 4 to 5 minutes. Lift on to greaseproof paper with a draining spoon.
4. Blend cornflour, egg-yolks, 2 teaspoons sugar and a few drops of vanilla essence with just enough water to slake cornflour.
5. Slowly stir in the milk in which meringue was poached. Return to pan, stir as it thickens but do not let it quite boil.
6. Cool a little. Pour into 4 glass dishes and place 1 egg island on top of each.
7. Sprinkle on a little grated chocolate or vermicelli.

FRESH FRUIT WITH ORANGE CREAM

Serves 4

1 small punnet raspberries or strawberries, or
** 2 large bananas***
A 150 ml/¼ pint carton of double cream
1 dessertspoon caster sugar
1 large orange
½ lemon

* *See To Keep Bananas from going Brown, page 245.*

1. Divide raspberries or strawberries between 4 small bowls or sundae glasses. If using bananas, follow instructions to keep them from going brown, then slice and divide between 4 bowls.
2. Beat cream and sugar until thick.

3. Grate just the zest from orange and half lemon. Squeeze juice from half lemon.
4. Peel orange and roughly chop flesh, catching the juice.
5. Fold orange, juices and zest into the cream.
6. Spoon cream mixture on top of the fruit in the bowls.
7. Chill before serving.

Elizabeth Mickery
Pudsey, West Yorkshire

GOOSEBERRY FOOL

Serves 4

450 g/1 lb gooseberries
2 tablespoons sugar, or more to taste
150 ml/¼ pint whipping or double cream

1. Cook gooseberries until soft. This is best done without water in a casserole with lid in a slow oven (no higher than Gas 4, 350°F, 180°C). If cooked in a saucepan add 1 tablespoon water, put on a very low heat and then strain away liquid when berries are cooked.
2. Sieve and then sweeten to taste. The purée should not be too thin.
3. Whip cream lightly, but not too stiff. Best results are obtained if purée and cream are the same consistency.
4. When purée is cold, carefully fold together with the cream. A few drops of green colouring can be added during folding to enhance the colour.

HAZELNUT MERINGUE GÂTEAU

Serves 4

3 large egg-whites
A pinch of salt
175 g/6 oz granulated sugar
75 g/3 oz ground hazelnuts
40 g/1½ oz fine semolina

TO FILL AND DECORATE
150 to 200 ml/5 to 7 fl oz double or whipping
  cream
50 g/2 oz chopped hazelnuts
A few whole hazelnuts
15 g/½ oz plain cooking chocolate

Try your own fillings, such as fresh raspberries or
pears.

1. Line base of two 18 cm/7 inch sandwich tins with
rounds of Bakewell paper or greased, greaseproof
paper.
2. Beat egg-whites with salt till firm.
3. Add 75 g/3 oz of the sugar and beat again.
4. In another bowl, mix remaining sugar with
ground hazelnuts and semolina. Fold this mixture
into egg-whites.
5. Divide mixture between tins, spread it evenly and
smooth the tops.
6. Bake in a moderate oven, Gas 4, 350°F, 180°C,
for 25 to 30 minutes until crisp and golden.
7. Turn meringues out of tins to cool on a wire rack.
8. When quite cold, sandwich with whipped cream.
9. Spread cream round the sides.
10. Roll sides in chopped hazelnuts.
11. Pipe cream roses on top and decorate with whole
hazelnuts.
12. Finish with decorations of grated chocolate.

The gâteau bases keep well in an air-tight tin before
filling and decorating. Also, when filled and decorated they may be frozen successfully. Will thaw
quite quickly.

Anne Wallace
Dunlop, Scotland

LEMON DELIGHT

Another recipe from the West Sussex Federation of
Women's Institutes' book 'Come Cooking Again'.
A truly delightful sweet, set off by the egg-custard
which accompanies it.

Serves 4

450 ml/¾ pint water
25 g/1 oz cornflour
150 g/5 oz sugar
Grated rind and strained juice of 2 lemons
2 egg-whites

CUSTARD
2 egg-yolks
1 tablespoon sugar
300 ml/½ pint milk

1. Bring to the boil all but 2 tablespoons of the water.
Remove from heat.
2. Mix cornflour with remaining water, stir it into
boiled water and return to the heat. Stir as it thickens
and boil for 1 minute.
3. Stir in sugar until dissolved. Allow to cool a little
and add lemon rind and juice.
4. Whisk egg-whites until really firm. Fold into
mixture. Pour into a dish, and leave to set in a cool
place or refrigerator.
5. Make custard by mixing egg-yolks, sugar and
milk. Pour into a saucepan and heat gently, stirring
as it thickens. Do not let it boil.

Mrs Janice Langley
Shoreham-by-Sea, West Sussex

LEMON FLUFF

Serves 4

450 ml/¾ pint plus 3 tablespoons water
1 good-sized lemon
1 heaped tablespoon cornflour
125 g/4 oz sugar
2 eggs, separated

TO DECORATE
Chopped walnuts or toasted coconut

1. Put 450 ml/¾ pint of the water in a saucepan with
the finely-pared rind of the lemon. Simmer gently
for 5 minutes.

2. Mix cornflour and sugar in a large basin and blend with the 3 tablespoons of water.

3. Remove pan from heat, add juice of the lemon and strain on to cornflour mixture.

4. Return the mixture to the pan, bring to the boil, stirring, and cook for 2 minutes.

5. Put egg-yolks in the basin and egg-whites into another clean basin.

6. Pour lemon mixture on to egg-yolks and beat well together. Set aside until quite cold and thickening slightly.

7. Whisk egg-whites until firm but not dry.

8. Using a metal spoon, fold egg-whites gently into lemon mixture.

9. Pour into 1 large or 4 small dishes, sprinkle top with chopped walnuts or toasted coconut.

LEMON SOLID

An old family recipe.

Serves 4

Rind and juice of 2 lemons
175 g/6 oz caster sugar
600 ml/1 pint milk
15 g/$\frac{1}{2}$ oz gelatine

1. Finely grate rind from the lemons and squeeze the juice.

2. Put lemon rind into a basin with sugar and half of the milk.

3. Heat remaining milk with the gelatine, stirring continuously until gelatine is dissolved. Be very careful not to boil it.

4. Mix heated milk with cold milk mixture, stirring to dissolve sugar.

5. Add lemon juice. Don't be alarmed if milk appears to curdle.

6. Pour into a wet jelly mould and leave to set in a cold larder for about 12 hours or 5 hours in refrigerator.

7. Turn pudding out of mould. It should have separated with a clear jelly at top and 'curds' at bottom.

Mrs Marion Wightman
Piddletrenthide, Dorset

LEMON AND BANANA SOUFFLÉ

Serves 4

3 large eggs
75 g/3 oz caster sugar
2 lemons
3 bananas
15 g/$\frac{1}{2}$ oz (1 envelope) gelatine
3 tablespoons very hot water
1 small carton double cream

1. Separate egg-yolks from whites, put yolks and whites in separate large bowls.

2. Add sugar to the yolks.

3. Wipe lemons, finely grate the rind and add to egg-yolks with juice of 1 lemon.

4. Place bowl over a saucepan of hot water and whisk until mixture becomes rather thick and fluffy.

5. Remove from heat and leave to cool, whisking occasionally.

6. Keep aside $\frac{1}{2}$ banana in its skin and $\frac{1}{2}$ lemon for decoration later.

7. Squeeze out juice from remaining lemons and pour into goblet of an electric blender. Peel other $2\frac{1}{2}$ bananas, cut up and add. Switch on and blend until creamy and smooth. (If preferred, the bananas may be thoroughly mashed with a fork and then worked into the lemon juice.)

8. Whisk banana mixture into the egg-yolks.

9. Put hot water into a small bowl and sprinkle with gelatine. Stand bowl in hot water to dissolve gelatine, stirring once to combine.

10. Cool gelatine slightly and whisk into the banana mixture.

11. Leave until cold and on the point of setting.

12. Whisk egg-whites until stiff.

13. Place cream in a small bowl and whisk until thick but soft.

14. Using a metal spoon, fold cream into the nearly-set banana mixture and lightly fold in egg-whites.

15. Turn into a glass serving dish and leave in a cold place to set.

16. Before serving, squeeze juice from remaining $\frac{1}{2}$ lemon, peel and slice $\frac{1}{2}$ banana and toss in the juice. Arrange round top of dish.

MANGO MOUSSE

Serves 6

2 tablespoons water
2 heaped teaspoons gelatine
325 ml/12 fl oz tinned evaporated milk, chilled
    in refrigerator
2 tablespoons sugar
A 450 g/16 oz tin of mango pulp*

* Can be bought from oriental food shops.

1. Measure water into a cup. Sprinkle in gelatine. Stand cup in hot water to dissolve gelatine, stirring once to combine.
2. Whisk the chilled evaporated milk. Gradually add sugar. Whisk in the gelatine.
3. Fold in the mango pulp and set in a covered mould in refrigerator for 3 hours.

This dish may be decorated with whipped cream and mango slices.

Priya Wickramasinghe
Cardiff

COMPÔTE OF FRESH ORANGES

Serves 4

3 large or 4 smaller oranges
Water
125 g/4 oz sugar

1. Scrub oranges and score the skin into 4 sections. Cover with boiling water and leave 5 minutes. Peel.
2. Reserve 4 to 5 sections of peel, cut away white pith and discard. Cut the remaining rind into very fine strips.
3. Place strips of rind in small pan of water, bring to boil, drain, and half-fill pan with fresh water. (This is to remove any bitterness.) Simmer about 30 minutes, until the rind is really tender. Drain, discard water.
4. Place sugar and 150 ml/¼ pint fresh water in pan. Dissolve sugar over a low heat then bring to boil and simmer for 3 to 4 minutes until looking syrupy.
5. Add shredded peel and simmer 2 to 3 minutes.
6. Peel away any white pith from oranges, cut into thin slices, removing pips.

7. Place orange slices in serving dish, pour over syrup and shredded peel when quite cold. Chill a little before serving.
2 Tablespoons of sherry or even a tablespoon of Grand Marnier, Orange Curaçao or Brandy can be used to cool syrup, and adds a very special flavour.

FLUFFY ORANGE MOUSSE

Serves 3 to 4

2 large oranges
½ lemon
4 tablespoons water
15 g/½ oz (1 envelope) gelatine
3 eggs, separated
75 g/3 oz caster sugar
2 tablespoons very hot water
25 g/1 oz blanched almonds

1. Finely-grate rind from one orange. Squeeze out juice from both oranges and ½ lemon.
2. Place 4 tablespoons water in a small bowl and sprinkle with gelatine. Stand bowl in hot water to dissolve gelatine, stirring once to combine.
3. Set aside to cool slightly but do not let it set.
4. Carefully separate egg-yolks from whites and place them in separate bowls.
5. Add 50 g/2 oz sugar and the very hot water to yolks and whisk at least 5 minutes until mixture is thick and pale in colour. The mixture should be stiff enough to hold the trail of the whisk when lifted.
6. Strain in fruit juices, add orange rind and whisk to mix.
7. Pour in gelatine, stirring really vigorously.
8. Put bowl aside, but whisk occasionally until mixture is cold and beginning to thicken.
9. Beat egg-whites with a clean whisk until very stiff and dry.
10. Add remaining 25 g/1 oz of sugar to egg-whites and whisk again until stiff and glossy.
11. Lightly fold egg-whites into orange mixture until evenly-mixed.
12. Pour immediately into a serving dish and leave in a cold place to set.
13. Heat grill to moderately hot.
14. Finely shred almonds and grill until evenly-coloured, shaking occasionally.
15. Leave to cool. Sprinkle almonds round edge of mousse to decorate.

ORANGE CHEESECAKE

Needs no baking.

Makes 8 reasonable portions

BASE
125 g/4 oz digestive biscuits
2 level tablespoons golden syrup
1 level tablespoon cocoa
25 g/1 oz butter

FILLING
2 tablespoons hot water
15 g/½ oz (1 envelope) gelatine
2 small oranges
1 small lemon
4 level tablespoons caster sugar
450 g/1 lb cottage cheese
2 to 3 tablespoons double cream
1 tablespoon milk

DECORATION
3 thin round slices from an orange, including
   skin
25 g/1 oz grated plain chocolate

1. *To make base:* put biscuits between 2 sheets of greaseproof paper or in a polythene bag. Crush to fine crumbs with rolling pin. Or use electric grinder to make crumbs.
2. Measure golden syrup carefully into a saucepan, levelling off spoon with a knife and making sure there is none on back of spoon.
3. Add cocoa and butter to pan. Heat gently, stirring occasionally, until butter has melted.
4. Remove pan from heat and stir in biscuit crumbs.
5. Spread biscuit mixture in bottom of a round 20 cm/8 inch, loose-based cake tin. Level top and press down lightly. Leave tin in a cool place so that mixture hardens.
6. *To make filling:* measure 2 tablespoons hot water into a small basin and sprinkle in gelatine. Stir until gelatine has dissolved.
7. Scrub oranges and lemon. Grate rind into a bowl.
8. Squeeze juice and pour into a measuring jug.
9. Stir gelatine into juices and make up to ¼ pint with cold water. Add sugar and stir until dissolved.
10. Rub cheese through a sieve on to grated rind. Add fruit syrup mixture and mix well. *Or*, put cheese with grated rind and fruit syrup mixture into liquidiser and switch on to blend until smooth, then return it to bowl.
11. Put cream and milk into a basin and whisk until just thick. Stir into cheese mixture in bowl.

12. Pour cheese mixture over biscuit base in tin. Leave in a cool place to set.
13. *To decorate when cheesecake is set:* cut each slice of orange into 6 triangular pieces.
14. An easy way to remove cheesecake from tin: stand it on top of a large can of fruit or vegetables, or similar. Gently pull cake tin down from cheesecake. Ease cheesecake off base on to a plate with a palette knife.
15. Arrange grated chocolate in a pile in centre and orange triangles, pointing inwards, around edge of top.

Serve in slices. Will keep 2 to 3 days in refrigerator.

ORANGE CREAM CHEESECAKE

For this you need a loose-bottomed 20 cm/8 inch flan tin or a ring set on a baking sheet.

Serves 4 to 6

FLAN CASE
125 g/4 oz digestive biscuits
50 g/2 oz butter

FILLING
65 g/2½ oz sugar
75 ml/3 fl oz concentrated orange juice, the
   frozen variety gives a good strong flavour
275 g/10 oz cream cheese

TO DECORATE
finely-grated orange rind

1. Start with the flan case. Crush the biscuits. To do this lay biscuits flat in a single layer inside a large polythene bag and press with a rolling pin.
2. Melt butter gently. Add crushed biscuits and mix thoroughly until well integrated with butter.
3. Now the filling. Stir sugar and orange juice together until dissolved.
4. Mix in cream cheese very gradually until it is all incorporated.
5. Pour this mixture over the biscuit base and press down gently. Level and smooth the top.
6. Return to refrigerator to set.
7. When needed, sit the flan case on an upturned basin. The ring will drop away leaving you to slide the cheesecake on to a flat plate. Or, if using a flan ring, carefully slide cheesecake and ring on to a flat plate, then lift off ring.

Serve with a jug of single cream.

PLANT POT CHEESECAKE

Serves 6

For this you need a clay plant pot, 12.5 cm/5 inches diameter at top. If you are starting with a new plant pot, bake it in a moderate oven, Gas 4, 350°F, 180°C, for 15 minutes. It can then be used for this pudding or for baking bread.

50 g/2 oz maraschino cherries
50 g/2 oz mixed peel
50 g/2 oz blanched almonds
50 g/2 oz seedless raisins
Finely-grated rind ½ lemon
Finely-grated rind ½ orange
1 tablespoon dry sherry
325 g/12 oz cottage cheese
125 g/4 oz cream cheese
125 g/4 oz caster sugar
125 ml/4 fl oz double cream
1½ tablespoons orange juice
1½ tablespoons lemon juice
2 level teaspoons powdered gelatine

TO DECORATE
125 ml/4 fl oz carton double cream
A few maraschino cherries
A few orange and lemon slices

1. Finely chop cherries, mixed peel, almonds and raisins (liquidiser can be used) and transfer to a small basin.
2. Stir in grated lemon and orange rind, cover with sherry and leave until sherry is absorbed.
3. In another bowl, mix cottage cheese and cream cheese together and beat in the sugar.
4. Beat cream until thick and fold into cheese with the fruit and nut mixture.
5. Put orange and lemon juice in a small heat-proof bowl and sprinkle the gelatine over it. Leave until gelatine is spongy. Place bowl in a pan of hot water and stir over low heat until gelatine has dissolved. Remove from heat and leave to cool slightly, about 20 minutes. Fold into cheese mixture.
6. Line a 12.5 cm/5 inch clay plant pot with a large piece of muslin or a clean tea towel, spoon in cheese mixture and fold cloth over the top.
7. Cover with a saucer which will just fit inside top of pot, place weights on top (1.5 kg/3 lb is enough). Stand pot in a dish and chill in a refrigerator overnight.
8. The next day, remove weights and saucer and unfold the cloth. Place a serving dish over the pot and turn cheesecake out. Remove the cloth.
9. Whip cream for decoration and pipe over the cheesecake. Decorate with halved maraschino cherries and orange and lemon slices.

Stella Boldy
Sykehouse, N. Humberside

PAVLOVA

This recipe first originated in Australia and was named after the Russian ballerina Anna Pavlova.

Serves 6

4 egg-whites
225 g/8 oz caster sugar
1 level teaspoon cornflour
1 teaspoon vinegar
1 teaspoon vanilla essence

FILLING
300 ml/½ pint double or whipping cream
Fruits, such as strawberries, raspberries, bananas, fresh peaches
Juice 1 lemon
Passion fruit pulp (optional)

1. Grease thoroughly a large, flat, round or oval heat-proof dish or tart-plate.
2. Beat egg-whites until stiff, but take care not to overbeat them as the meringue will be dry and crumbly.
3. Gradually beat in sugar.
4. Mix cornflour, vinegar and vanilla and fold in.
5. Spread mixture 2.5 cm/1 inch thick on prepared plate, forming a raised edge that will contain the filling.
6. Bake in a very slow oven, Gas ½, 250°F, 120°C, for 1 hour. Switch off heat and leave pavlova in oven overnight to dry out.
7. Fill with whipped cream.
8. Top with fresh fruits well sprinkled with lemon juice to prevent discolouration. If you can get passion fruit, mix it with the lemon juice.

Mrs Rita McEachern
Adelaide, South Australia

MERINGUES

Makes about 14 halves

4 egg-whites
225 g/8 oz caster sugar
An extra 25 g/1 oz caster sugar for sprinkling

1. Prepare a baking sheet. Cover it with 2 sheets of very lightly-oiled greaseproof paper.
2. Whisk egg-whites until stiff. If the bowl is inverted quickly the whites should not fall out.
3. Add 4 teaspoons of the caster sugar and continue whisking until the whites are stiff again.
4. Fold in remaining sugar with a tablespoon or palette knife.
5. Spoon or pipe on to prepared baking sheet.
6. Sprinkle meringues with the 25 g/1 oz of caster sugar.
7. Put on low shelf in the oven at lowest setting, Gas $\frac{1}{4}$, 200°F, 90°C, and leave for about 2 hours until dry. To test, lightly tap with finger nail. If meringues feel crisp and sound hollow they are done. If any difficulty is experienced in getting meringues to dry out they may be removed from oven after $1\frac{1}{2}$ hours and turned upside down. Using a skewer make a hole in the bottom and return to the oven to dry. Test again before removing from oven.

FRESH PEACHES (OR PEARS) IN A FUDGE SAUCE

Tinned fruit can be used but the contrast of fresh fruit and fudge sauce is particularly delicious.

Serves 4 but easy to make less

4 ripe peaches or pears
A little butter

SAUCE
225 g/8 oz light soft brown sugar
15 g/$\frac{1}{2}$ oz butter
2 tablespoons milk

1. Start with sauce. Put sugar, butter and milk in a heavy pan. Stir over low heat to dissolve sugar.
2. Bring to boil and boil to soft ball stage, 235°F, 114°C. This stage is reached when dribbles of sauce dropped in some cold water set to a soft ball, not crisp. Stir frequently.
3. Peel, stone and halve the peaches. For pears, use soft ripe fruit, peel, quarter and core.

4. Place fruit cut side down in a buttered heat-proof dish.
5. Pour hot sauce over the fruit. Cool and serve really chilled.

PEANUT BRITTLE GÂTEAU

Serves 6

For this you need 1 fatless sponge, about 20 cm/ 8 inches across and 5 to 8 cm/$2\frac{1}{2}$ to 3 inches deep (*see page 316*)

125 g/4 oz peanut brittle
A 150 ml/5 fl oz carton double cream
125 ml/4 fl oz rum
125 ml/4 fl oz water

1. Crush peanut brittle. The best way to do this is to put it inside 2 polythene bags and knock it with a hammer. Do not crush it too fine because the beauty of this gâteau is the crunchy texture of the brittle with the soft rum and cream centre.
2. Whip cream until thick.
3. Mix rum and water.
4. Cut sponge into 2 layers. Lay bottom half on a serving plate, pour about half of the rum and water mix over the sponge. Then spread about half of the whipped cream over this.
5. Lay top half of sponge over the cream and drench this with the rest of the rum and water.
6. Cover top and sides with cream.
7. Sprinkle and pat the crushed peanut brittle over the top and sides of the gâteau. Chill and serve.

PORT AND PRUNES

A party dessert. Can be made with less expensive wine than port.

Remember to start the day before, or even sooner, as it improves with keeping. A liquidiser is useful.

Serves 15 people but easy to make less

450 g/1 lb dried prunes
175 to 225 ml/6 to 8 fl oz ruby port, sweet sherry
  or mature home-made dessert wine
300 ml/$\frac{1}{2}$ pint double cream
50 g/2 oz caster sugar

1. The day before, soak prunes in water to cover.
2. Next day simmer prunes gently until very soft. Leave to cool. Drain.

3. Remove stones and liquidise prunes with 175 ml/ 6 fl oz port to produce a very thick purée. Add more port if necessary.

4. Whisk cream with sugar until it is as thick as purée.

5. Fold purée into cream and spoon into tiny glasses.

Serve with crisp biscuits such as *Shortcake Biscuits* (*see page 343*) or *Shortbread Biscuits* (*see page 343*).

RASPBERRY MOUSSE

This can be frozen and is delicious to eat frozen or just chilled.

Serves 4

A 175 g/6 oz can of evaporated milk
A 375 g/13 oz can of raspberries, or equal
   quantity of frozen raspberries
1 raspberry jelly

TO DECORATE (OPTIONAL)
150 ml/$\frac{1}{4}$ pint whipped cream

1. Put evaporated milk into the refrigerator for about 1 hour so that it is thoroughly chilled when needed.

2. Drain liquid from can of raspberries into a measuring jug and make up with water to 300 ml/$\frac{1}{2}$ pint. Bring to the boil.

3. Make jelly with this hot liquid. If using frozen raspberries just use water for the jelly. Leave till cool and just beginning to set.

4. Whisk evaporated milk until thick.

5. Whisk jelly, add the milk and continue to whisk. It should double its bulk.

6. Fold in raspberries.

7. Leave to set. It will set almost immediately with frozen raspberries.

8. Decorate by piping with whipped cream.

Sybil Norcott
Irlam, Nr Manchester

RHUBARB WITH ORANGE

Serves 4

450 g/1 lb rhubarb
The zest of half an orange, or peel, thinly-
   sliced from half an orange
Brown sugar to taste, either demerara or soft
   brown will do

1. Cut, wash and drain the rhubarb. Put it in a casserole dish. Sprinkle with sugar and orange peel and set aside for 24 hours.

2. Next day cover the casserole and put it in a cool oven, Gas 2, 300°F, 150°C, for about half an hour. The rhubarb should be neither hard nor too soft but exact cooking time depends on the age of the fruit. Serve with whipped cream.

This method produces a lot of delicious juice without the addition of water.

Mrs Marie Holton
Godmanchester, Huntingdonshire

STONE CREAM

A very old Buckinghamshire recipe. Try also using cherry jam or fresh strawberries, raspberries or cherries. Adjust the amount of sugar to taste.

Serves 8

4 tablespoons cold water
15 g/$\frac{1}{2}$ oz gelatine
Strawberry jam
Whites of 2 eggs
300 ml/$\frac{1}{2}$ pint cream, whipping or double
1 dessertspoon vanilla sugar (*see page 242*)
300 ml/$\frac{1}{2}$ pint milk

1. Put water in small basin, sprinkle in gelatine. Place bowl over pan of hot, not boiling, water and stir gently until it becomes clear. Remove from pan and allow to cool a little—take care that it does not go cold or it will set.

2. Put jam in bottom of dish or in small glass sundae dishes.

3. Whisk egg-whites until they hold the impression of the whisk.

4. Whip the cream to the same consistency as the egg. Stir in the sugar.

5. Add the gelatine to the milk and mix this into the cream.

6. When mixture is beginning to thicken fold in egg-whites.

7. Pour quickly into dish or glasses on top of jam.

Serve chilled.

Mrs M.E. Smith
Stoke Mandeville

SYLLABUB

An old English sweet.

Serves 2

150 ml/¼ pint double cream
1 small teaspoon lemon juice
½ teaspoon finely grated lemon rind
1 to 2 teaspoons sugar to taste
Approx. 3 tablespoons sherry or more depending on taste
Chopped almonds

1. Whip the cream until quite thick.
2. Add the other ingredients slowly and whip until thick again.
3. Serve in small glasses, sprinkled with chopped nuts.

If you add a lot more sherry the liquid may separate from the cream, but it is still delicious.

A SYLLABUB FROM KENT

Serves 4

2 egg-whites
50 to 75 g/2 to 3 oz caster sugar
Juice of ½ large lemon
150 ml/¼ pint white wine
150 ml/¼ pint double cream, whipped till thick

1. Beat egg-whites until stiff and frothy.
2. Beat in sugar.
3. Add lemon juice and wine.
4. Beat in the thickly-whipped cream.
5. Pour the thick curdy mixture into little glass dishes and put in a cool place or refrigerator for 4 to 5 hours so that flavours blend.

Mrs Jill Marshall
Hythe, Kent

TIPSY CAKE

Serves 4

FATLESS SPONGE BASE
2 large eggs*
75 g/3 oz vanilla sugar or caster sugar
75 g/3 oz soft plain flour (sometimes called super-sifted)

* *The eggs should be at room temperature, not straight from the fridge.*

TO FINISH THE TIPSY CAKE
150 ml/5 fl oz carton double cream
2 tablespoons top of the milk
300 ml/½ pint white wine (home-made wine is ideal)
3 tablespoons strawberry jam
A little grated chocolate

1. Grease a 1 litre/1½ pint pudding basin which is suitable for the oven. Preheat oven to moderately hot, Gas 5, 375°F, 190°C.
2. Using a mixing bowl, whisk eggs and sugar together until pale in colour and creamy in texture, holding the impression of the whisk. The whisking can be done in an electric mixer, first warming the bowl. If using a rotary whisk, place the bowl over a saucepan of hot water. Do not let the bowl touch the water.
3. Carefully fold in sifted flour.
4. Pour mixture into greased pudding basin and level the top.
5. Put straight into oven and bake for 25 to 35 minutes, until shrinking from sides of bowl and feeling firm.
6. Turn cake out of basin on to a cooling wire and wait until cold.
7. Whip cream until stiff and smooth, adding top of the milk.
8. Slice cake across into three round layers of even depth.
9. Place bottom largest layer on plate from which cake is to be served.
10. Pour a little of the wine over.
11. Spread on a layer of jam and place middle layer on top.
12. Pour wine over middle layer of cake. Spread with jam. Put on top layer of cake and pour wine over this.
13. Spread cream all over and round the cake.
14. Sprinkle a little grated chocolate over top to decorate, or invent your own decoration.

Leave cake to stand in a cool place for about an hour before it is to be served.

HOME-MADE YOGHURT

Yoghurt is a soured milk product thought to have originated among the nomadic tribes of Eastern Europe. It was traditionally a drink, made by allowing the natural milk flora to ferment the milk sugar—lactose—to lactic acid. It has very high food value.

The easiest way to make yoghurt is to buy a kit, which is basically a temperature-controlled or insulated flask and thermometer. However, by trial and error you can make it without special equipment, especially if you have a warm place in which to set or thicken it such as an airing cupboard or gas oven with pilot light. So many factors affect yoghurt in the making that everybody has to experiment.

600 ml/1 pint milk
1 tablespoon dried skimmed milk (optional)
1 tablespoon natural yoghurt, bought or home-made

You can use untreated milk, pasteurised, homogenised or U.H.T., and sterilised milk. However, the flavour and thickness will vary—e.g., U.H.T. and sterilised milk give a thinner yoghurt.
The dried skimmed milk helps to make yoghurt thicker and creamier.
1. Bring milk to boiling point. If using U.H.T. milk heat it only to blood temperature and proceed straight to paragraph 4.
2. Allow to cool to 120°F, 48°C.
3. Stir in dried skimmed milk, if used.
4. Add yoghurt and whisk well.
5. Pour mixture into a clean, warm bowl, or small bowls, wide-necked jars or cartons. Cover with a plate, saucers or lids.
If you have a wide-necked Thermos flask, pre-heat it by rinsing out with boiling water, and pour in the mixture. Put on lid.
6. Containers must be put at once into a slightly warmer place, preferably 110°F, 43°C, and where temperature will remain constant for 4 to 6 hours. During this time (if you are lucky) it will turn to curd. You can wrap container in a warmed blanket or make a box for it out of polystyrene. Any device to keep temperature of yoghurt constant at not less than 110°F, 43°C, is worth trying.
7. As soon as it is set, place it in the fridge. If you leave it in the warmth it will go on working and the acid flavour will become stronger, although it will also become thicker.

Save a tablespoon of your yoghurt to make the next batch. It is best to spoon it out of the middle of the container where the activity of the yoghurt-making bacteria is greater. After 3 batches of yoghurt have been made from your own culture it is advisable to buy another carton of commercially-made yoghurt to use as the next starter. Choose a brand which has as few additives as possible as this will more easily make a good new yoghurt.

YOGHURT AND FRUIT

Serves 1 or 2

Made in the liquidiser.

150 ml/¼ pint natural yoghurt
A handful of blackberries, black- or redcurrants, loganberries, raspberries or strawberries
1 tablespoon runny honey
A little milk
1 or 2 teaspoons wheat germ (optional)

1. Put yoghurt, fruit and honey in liquidiser and blend till mixture is consistency you like. Thin with a little milk if necessary.
2. Pour into glasses or bowls and sprinkle with wheat germ.

Can be made into a drink by blending until smooth, and thinning with milk.

ICE-CREAM

Serves 3 to 4

2 eggs, separated
Few drops vanilla essence
150 ml/¼ pint double cream
50 g/2 oz icing sugar

Fresh fruit may be used to flavour ice-cream instead of vanilla essence. First make a purée of the fruit. A cupful is enough for the above quantity of ice-cream.

1. Beat egg-yolks and vanilla. (If using fruit purée it is added later; leave out vanilla.)
2. Whip the cream.
3. Beat egg-whites and sugar.
4. Combine all three mixtures and beat again.
5. If using fruit purée fold it in now.
6. Pour mixture into a 900 g/2 lb margarine carton or a freezer tray with lid and freeze.

Anne Wallace
Dunlop, Scotland

Try the following delicious sauces to serve with the ice-cream; the recipes are all on *page 280:*
Caramel
Quick Chocolate
Fudge
Melba

ICE-CREAM

A delicious variation on Anne Wallace's recipe (*see previous page*), giving a subtle caramel flavour and a creamy appearance.

Serves 4

2 eggs, separated
50 g/2 oz light soft brown sugar
150 ml/¼ pint double cream

1. Whisk egg-whites until stiff, add sugar and whisk again.
2. Whip cream till stiff.
3. Whisk egg-yolks.
4. Combine all three and whisk together.
5. Pour straight into a plastic food box or margarine carton, put on lid and freeze.

Ice-cream Snowball

Serves 6

2 tablespoons sultanas
1 tablespoon currants
1 tablespoon rum, sherry or orange juice
1 litre/1½ pints firm vanilla ice-cream, not the whipped or 'soft' variety
125 g/4 oz glacé cherries, cut small
1 tablespoon chopped walnuts

TO DECORATE
1 teaspoon of the chopped cherries, angelica, marzipan, *or*, whipped double cream for piping

1. Soak sultanas and currants in rum, sherry or orange juice for 2 hours. Then drain.
2. Allow ice-cream to soften slightly.
3. Reserve 1 teaspoon of the chopped cherries for decorating. Then mix all ingredients together.
4. Pack this mixture into two round pudding basins. (Heat-proof pyrex basins are ideal.) Make sure mixture comes to the very brim of the basins. Any that is left can be frozen separately.
5. Press the two bowls together to form a ball, and freeze until solid.
6. Prepare decorations, cherries and angelica. Or marzipan to look like holly. Or whipped cream in a piping bag.
7. Just before serving, carefully remove basins with the aid of hot damp cloths or a bowl of warm water. Set the snowball on a chilled dish and decorate with the 'holly', or pipe rosettes of cream all over.

Once decorated, the snowball could be returned to freezer, but remember to take it out about 10 minutes before serving so that cream is not too icy.

Ice-cream Surprises
For this you need 10 small washed yoghurt cartons.

1 litre/1½ pints firm vanilla or strawberry ice-cream, not whipped or 'soft' variety
About 1 dozen small meringues
1 dozen grapes
225 g/8 oz toasted* desiccated coconut

* To toast coconut: spread it in grill pan and toast under moderate heat, stirring often until it is evenly-golden. Take care, it burns easily.

1. Allow ice-cream to soften a little. Then fill each carton about ¾ full. Return to freezer.
2. Meanwhile, crumble the meringues and remove pips from grapes.
3. When cartons of ice-cream have frozen hard, take them out one at a time. Scoop out a cavity in the middle of each and fill with one grape and crumbled meringue. Seal up again with a dollop of ice-cream and return to freezer.
4. When frozen again, remove ice-cream from cartons and roll each one in toasted coconut, shaping a rough ball at same time. Either wrap each ball in foil and return to freezer, or open-freeze on a tray and pack in a polythene bag until required.

ICE-CREAM

Serves 4

3 eggs
25 g/1 oz caster sugar
300 ml/½ pint milk
Small tin condensed milk

1. Separate whites from yolks of eggs.
2. Whisk yolks and sugar together until lighter in colour.
3. Bring milk almost to the boil, pour a little on to the egg-yolks whisking all the time.
4. Return mixture to pan and heat, without boiling, until the mixture coats the back of a wooden spoon.
5. Pour mixture into bowl, add condensed milk and mix well. Leave mixture to cool.
6. Pour into a shallow rectangular polythene container (or the refrigerator ice tray with divisions removed) and place in freezing compartment of refri-

gerator or in freezer. Leave it there until ice forms round edge of mixture.

7. Then stir the mixture and put it back in refrigerator or freezer while the egg-whites are whisked.

8. Whisk egg-whites until stiff and fold into ice-cream.

9. Place back in refrigerator or freezer until the ice-cream sets hard.

Try also these flavourings:

Apricot Ice-Cream

1. Drain juice from a 425 g/15 oz tin of apricot halves. Sieve the fruit or liquidise until a purée.

2. Stir in 2 tablespoons of the apricot juice.

3. After folding egg-whites into the ice-cream fold in the apricot purée and freeze.

Brown Bread Ice-Cream

After folding the stiffly-whisked egg-whites into the ice-cream, fold in 50 g/2 oz fresh brown breadcrumbs and freeze.

1 teaspoon of rum can also be added with the breadcrumbs.

Chocolate Ice-Cream

1. Melt 125 g/4 oz plain chocolate in a bowl over hot water.

2. Add 1 dessertspoon golden syrup, mix well and add with the condensed milk at paragraph 5 of the basic recipe.

Sue Nichols
British Sugar Bureau

ICE-CREAM MADE WITH YOGHURT

Switch freezer or refrigerator to lowest setting about 1 hour before starting.

Serves 4

3 eggs, free-range if possible
2 heaped tablespoons honey
300 ml/½ pint warm milk
150 ml/¼ pint yoghurt
150 ml/¼ pint fresh double cream
½ teaspoon vanilla essence

1. Separate one of the eggs.

2. Whisk 2 whole eggs with egg-yolk and honey.

3. Pour on the warmed milk.

4. Stand bowl of egg and milk over a pan of sim-

mering water. Stir this custard mixture until it is thick and creamy. Remove from heat and allow to cool.

5. Lightly whip yoghurt and cream.

6. Stiffly whip remaining egg-white.

7. Fold in yoghurt and cream, egg-white and vanilla.

8. Pour mixture into a shallow, square freezer box or refrigerator tray (18 cm/7 inch square is ideal).

9. Put in to freeze for 1 hour or until mixture has frozen round edges. Chill a mixing bowl at the same time.

10. Turn ice-cream into chilled bowl and whisk for 5 minutes.

11. Return mixture to freezer box for 2 hours more to freeze completely.

Fresh fruit may be added at stage 10. Raspberries, strawberries, pineapple, blackberries, blackcurrants or loganberries. Do not use vanilla if you intend to add fruit.

In winter, use soaked dried fruits—225 g/8 oz soaked dried apricots puréed in the blender and added at stage 10 with 50 g/2 oz chopped almonds. Leave out vanilla.

Try also replacing vanilla at stage 7 with 2 level tablespoons Carob powder. Add 50 g/2 oz chopped walnuts at stage 10.

Elizabeth Shears
author of 'Why Do We Eat'

THREE IDEAS FOR BOUGHT ICE-CREAM

Baked Alaska

Serves 4

This delicious pudding is made of ice-cream on a sponge base with a thick coating of meringue mixture which is baked or 'flashed' in the oven for a few minutes before it is served. Some preparation can be done in advance but it does take about 10 minutes for the assembly and baking. It must then be eaten at once and is well worth waiting for.

FOR THE BASE
2 eggs
65 g/2½ oz vanilla sugar (*see page 242*) **(If no vanilla sugar, use caster sugar, but in this case do not add vanilla essence.)**
65 g/2½ oz soft plain flour

1. Grease a shallow tin 27 cm/11 inches by 18 cm/ 7 inches. A Swiss roll tin is ideal. Line with greased greaseproof paper.

2. Put eggs and sugar in a bowl. Place the bowl over a pan of hot water and whisk until the mixture is thick and pale.

3. Remove bowl from pan and whisk until beaters leave a trail in the mixture.

4. Sift flour on top and fold in with a spatula or metal spoon.

5. Spread mixture evenly in the tin.

6. Bake in a moderate oven, Gas 4, 350°F, 180°C, near top of oven for 20 to 23 minutes until firm and shrinking slightly from sides of tin.

7. Cool on a wire rack and remove paper.

TO ASSEMBLE

2 tablespoons sherry or fruit juice
1 family-sized block of ice-cream, approximately 450 ml/¾ pint
3 egg-whites
140 g/4½ oz caster sugar

1. Trim the sponge so that when the ice-cream is placed on it there is at least 1 cm/½ inch of cake all round the edge. Save the rest of the cake for tea.

2. Place sponge on a heat-proof dish, sprinkle on sherry or fruit juice. Arrange ice-cream on top.

3. Whisk egg-whites until very stiff. Fold in the sugar.

4. Spread over top and sides of cake, sealing completely.

5. Bake near top of a hot oven, Gas 7, 425°F, 220°C, for about 4 minutes, until tinged with gold.

Serve within a few minutes on cold plates.

CARAMEL SAUCE

A sauce to serve either hot or cold with ice-cream.

Serves 4

2 tablespoons golden syrup
25 g/1 oz butter
2 tablespoons water

1. Measure the golden syrup with a warm tablespoon and place in a saucepan.

2. Bring to the boil and continue boiling for about 1 minute until just turning brown.

3. Remove from heat and add the butter, stir well.

4. Add the water and mix well.

When served hot this sauce is very runny. As it cools it becomes thicker. When cold it is fudge-like.

Sue Nichols
British Sugar Bureau

QUICK CHOCOLATE SAUCE

Serves 4

50 g/2 oz sugar
65 m/2½ fl oz water
50 g/2 oz dark cooking chocolate
A small nut of butter

1. Dissolve sugar in water over low heat. Then boil for 3 minutes.

2. Add chocolate broken in pieces, stir until it is melted and simmer sauce for 1 minute.

3. Stir in butter.

Serve hot or cold.

Anne Wallace
Stewarton, Ayrshire

FUDGE SAUCE

For plain ice-cream.

Serves 4

50 g/2 oz butter
50 g/2 oz granulated sugar
75 g/3 oz soft brown sugar
150 g/5 oz golden syrup

Combine ingredients in a pan and stir over low heat until all the sugar grains have dissolved.

MELBA SAUCE

For puddings or ice-cream.

This sauce freezes well.

Raspberries, fresh or frozen
Icing sugar

1. Sieve uncooked raspberries to make a purée.

2. Sift icing sugar and beat it into purée, one teaspoon at a time, until sauce is sufficiently sweet.

Anne Wallace
Stewarton, Ayrshire

To make a quick Peach Melba place peach halves on vanilla ice-cream, cover with Melba Sauce and decorate with whipped cream and split almonds.

MINT PARFAIT

Serves 4

150 g/5 oz caster sugar
150 ml/¼ pint water
2 egg-whites
A pinch of salt
45 ml/3 tablespoons Crème de Menthe
300 ml/½ pint double cream, whipped to soft peaks

TOPPINGS
Grated chocolate or sugared mint leaves (*see below*) **or Quick Chocolate Sauce** (*see page 280*)

1. Dissolve sugar in water over a low heat. Do not let it boil until sugar is dissolved. Then, using a sugar thermometer if you have one, boil to 238°F, 110°C. If you have not got a thermometer, the syrup is boiled when a little forms a very soft ball when tested in a cup of cold water.
2. Whisk egg-whites with salt until stiff but not dry. While still whisking, pour on boiling syrup in a steady stream and keep on whisking until it has cooled.
3. Mix in Crème de Menthe, then fold in cream.
4. Put into a covered plastic box and freeze.

Serve scoops of the parfait sprinkled with grated plain chocolate, or a topping of your choice.

Sugared mint leaves
Paint fresh mint leaves with lightly-beaten egg-white. Coat well with caster sugar. Allow to dry in a warm room.

Anne Wallace
Stewarton, Ayrshire

ORANGE AND LEMON ICE

Serves 4

A generous 150 ml/¼ pint water
200 g/7 oz granulated sugar
Grated rind of 1 lemon
Strained juice of 2 oranges and 2 lemons

1. Put water in a pan and bring to the boil. Reduce heat. Add sugar and stir to dissolve.
2. Bring to boil. Add lemon rind and leave to cool and infuse for 2 hours.

3. Add fruit juice. Stir well.
4. Pour into a shallow container and put into freezer or freezing compartment of refrigerator.
5. When almost frozen—i.e., soft in middle and hard around edges—turn it out into a bowl and whisk very well. It will whisk up into almost a froth of snow.
6. Rinse and dry the container and pour in the mixture. Cover lightly with a lid or foil and freeze until required.

To serve, scoop into glass dishes or fill hollowed out orange or lemon shells.

HOME-MADE MUESLI I

This can be a nourishing and satisfying meal in itself when eaten with plenty of fresh fruits and some yoghurt.

Serves 1

1 dessertspoon crushed or rolled oats
1 dessertspoon barley kernels or barley flakes
1 dessertspoon raisins or sultanas
A sprinkling of sunflower seeds and unroasted buckwheat
1 large eating apple
1 carrot
1 tablespoon lemon juice
1 tablespoon mixed nuts, freshly ground
2 to 4 tablespoons fresh plain yoghurt
1 teaspoon honey
1 tablespoon wheatgerm
A sprinkling of wheatgerm, optional

1. Soak oats, barley and raisins or sultanas in a little water overnight.
2. Soak sunflower seeds and buckwheat separately in a cup.
3. Next morning, wash apple and scrub carrot, leaving skins on, and grate coarsely on to soaked grains. Pour lemon juice over.
4. Mix well, adding nuts, yoghurt, honey and wheatgerm.
5. Sprinkle with soaked sunflower seeds, buckwheat and wheatgerm.

If you like this, experiment with the wide variety of ingredients available: cereals, seeds, nuts, dried apricots, figs, prunes, coconut and sprouts such as alfalfa.

Fresh fruits can be varied according to the season. Fresh fruit and/or vegetables should ideally form over half of each helping of muesli if you want to make a balanced meal of it. If you get seeds and cereals whole, soak them until they begin to germinate.

Elizabeth Shears
author of 'Why Do We Eat'

HOME-MADE MUESLI II

Enough for several days.

25 to 50 g/1 to 2 oz dried apricots
15 g/$\frac{1}{2}$ oz hazelnuts, walnuts or both
50 to 75 g/2 to 3 oz soft brown sugar (optional)
75 g/3 oz sultanas
75 g/3 oz raisins
325 g/12 oz good quality porridge oats or rolled oats

25 to 50 g/1 to 2 oz each of porridge wheatmeal, wheat, rye or barley flakes*
15 to 25 g/$\frac{1}{2}$ to 1 oz bran or millet*

Optional, but try at least one of them

Note: It is worth visiting a high class grocer or health food shop or a shop dealing in whole or natural foods for the oats, etc. There is a wide selection of interesting ingredients available.

1. Cut the apricots into small pieces and chop the nuts roughly.
2. Mix all ingredients together adjusting the fruit, nut and sugar content to suit the quantity of cereal ingredients. Don't be mean with the fruit.
3. Keep in a large covered bowl or tin to use when required.

TO SERVE
The night before, place the quantity required in a bowl and pour on just enough milk. Next morning, add a little top of the milk. It is good to eat like this but even better with grated fresh apple, sliced banana or stewed fruits.

9

YEAST COOKERY
TEA BREADS
SCONES
GIRDLE BAKING
AND SAVOURY
BISCUITS

WHITE BREAD DOUGH

And a number of different ways to shape, bake and vary it.

900 g/2 lb strong plain flour
3 teaspoons salt
75 g/3 oz margarine
3 level teaspoons dried yeast, or 40 g/1½ oz fresh yeast
1 teaspoon sugar
300 ml/½ pint tepid water
300 ml/½ pint tepid milk

This quantity makes approximately 1.4 kg/3¼ lb of risen dough.
Note: Different brands of flour require differing quantities of water to produce a good elastic dough. The quantity of water listed gives a general indication but may be modified slightly as required.

1. Mix together the flour and salt and rub in the margarine.
2. Mix the dried yeast and the sugar into the water. Leave it in a warm place until quite dissolved and beginning to froth.
If using fresh yeast mix it and the sugar into the water stirring to dissolve the yeast. It is now ready for use. Unlike dried yeast it is not necessary to wait until the mixture froths up.
3. Add the yeast mixture with milk to the flour mixture.
4. Mix to a pliable dough and turn on to a floured board.
5. Knead well until the dough is no longer sticky, and is smooth and shiny. If the dough is a little soft, extra flour may be added whilst kneading (up to 50 g/2 oz), but it is difficult to add water if too firm.
6. Lightly grease the bowl and place dough in it. Cover, or place inside a large polythene bag, keep away from draughts, and leave to rise (or 'prove') until doubled in size.
7. Turn on to a floured board and knead lightly to let out air and to make dough pliable again.
The dough at this stage is referred to as 'risen dough'. Cut off quantity required for any of the following:

Standard 450 g/1 lb loaf
Approximately 450 g/1 lb risen dough

1. Grease a 450 g/1 lb loaf tin with a little lard.
2. Lightly shape dough to fit into the tin, cover with muslin or light cloth, or place in polythene bag and leave to rise to the top of the tin.
3. Bake in a hot oven, Gas 7, 425°F, 220°C, for 40 minutes. Redue heat to moderately hot, Gas 6, 400°F, 200°C if it browns too quickly.

Cottage Loaf
325 g/12 oz risen dough

1. Divide into 2 portions of about 225 g/8 oz and 125 g/4 oz each. Pat each piece out until 2.5 cm/1 inch thick, placing smaller piece on top.
2. Make a hole down centre with finger. Put loaf on to a greased baking tray. Cover with muslin or light cloth, or place in polythene bag, and allow to rise until puffy.
3. Bake in a hot oven, Gas 7, 425°F, 220°C, for 35 minutes.

Muffins
1. Roll out 325 g/12 oz of risen dough into a square, 1 cm/½ inch thick. Cut into 8 cm/3 inch rounds (will make 4).
2. Place on greased and floured baking tray. Cover. Allow to rise until quite puffy.
3. Heat a thick frying pan or girdle until moderately hot; grease with a piece of suet.
4. Transfer muffins with a spatula, and cook 6 minutes each side until golden brown on both sides.

Bread Sticks
225 g/8 oz risen dough will make at least 12

1. Break off small pieces, roll out with floured hands until finger thickness. Place on greased baking tray.
2. Cover and leave to rise until puffy.
3. Bake in a hot oven, Gas 7, 425°F, 220°C, until crisp, about 12 to 14 minutes.

Bread Buns, Swiss Buns, Devonshire Splits
325 g/12 oz risen dough will make 8 of any of these

1. Shape, place on greased baking tray, cover and leave to rise until puffy.
2. Bake in a hot oven, Gas 7, 425°F, 220°C, for 10 to 12 minutes.
Bread Buns for dinner rolls, should be glazed with beaten eggs before rising.
Swiss Buns. When cold, ice tops with pink icing.
Devonshire Splits. When cold, fill with whipped cream and strawberry jam, dust with icing sugar.

Sultana loaf

1. Take 325 g/12 oz risen dough. Work in 50 g/2 oz sultanas and 25 g/1 oz vanilla sugar*.
2. Place in greased 450 g/1 lb loaf tin, cover, allow to rise until doubled in size.
3. Bake in a moderately hot oven, Gas 6, 400°F, 200°C, for about 40 minutes.

Apricot and Walnut Twist

1. Take 325 g/12 oz risen dough. Add 50 g/2 oz dried apricots, cut up finely, and scalded (by placing in sieve and pouring over boiling water), 25 g/1 oz chopped walnuts, and 25 g/1 oz of vanilla sugar*.
2. Work together and make into a twist or finish as for Sultana Loaf. Cover and rise until double the size.
3. Bake in a moderately hot oven, Gas 6, 400°F, 200°C, for about 40 minutes.

Ice when cold.

Tea Cakes

1. Take 325 g/12 oz risen dough, work in 50 g/2 oz currants, 25 g/1 oz vanilla sugar*.
2. Divide into 4 portions. Roll out with rolling pin, until 1 cm/½ inch thick. Cover and leave to rise until puffy.
3. Bake in a hot oven, Gas 7, 425°F, 220°C, for 12 to 15 minutes.

*See page 242.

Lardy Cake

325 g/12 oz risen white, bread dough
50 g/2 oz lard
50 g/2 oz caster sugar
50 g/2 oz currants
A little honey

1. Roll out dough to an oblong about 13 by 30 cm/5 by 12 inches.
2. Spread on lard and sprinkle on sugar and currants.
3. Roll up like a Swiss Roll.
4. Roll this out into a square and place in a greased, shallow, 18 cm/7 inch square baking tin. Make light diagonal cuts in top to give a diamond pattern.
5. Cover and leave to rise to the top of the tin.
6. Brush lightly with honey and bake in a moderately hot oven, Gas 5, 375°F, 190°C, for about 35 minutes.

Serve hot with butter.

Oatcakes

225 g/8 oz risen dough
225 g/8 oz rolled oats (packet porridge oats will do)
75 g/3 oz melted lard
25 g/1 oz caster sugar
1 level teaspoon of salt

Work all ingredients together and roll out quite thinly on floured board. Cut into squares or triangles with a sharp knife, and place on greased baking tray. Do not leave to rise. Bake in a moderately hot oven, Gas 6, 400°F, 200°C, for about 10 minutes until just golden.

Mary Berry's Savoury Tart

325 g/12 oz risen, white, bread dough
1 large onion, sliced
A little butter
A 400 g/14 oz can of tomatoes
325 g/12 oz Cheddar cheese, sliced or grated
Salt and pepper
A little chopped fresh thyme
8 slices short back bacon

1. Roll out dough on a large, floured baking sheet into a 30 cm/12 inch circle. If you do not have a large baking sheet make two small tarts.
2. Fry the onion in the butter until soft.
3. Spread onion over the dough. Cover with the tomatoes including most of the juice. Cover tomatoes with the cheese. Sprinkle with salt, pepper and thyme. Arrange the bacon over the top.
4. Cover and put in a warm place to rise for 15 minutes.
5. Cook in a hot oven, Gas 7, 425°F, 220°C, for 15 to 20 minutes until the edges are golden.

Serve at once.

JANET'S QUICK WHOLEMEAL BREAD

675 g/1½ lb wholemeal flour
1 dessertspoon salt
1 tablespoon dried yeast or 25 g/1 oz fresh yeast
1 teaspoon soft brown or white sugar
450 ml/¾ pint milk
150 ml/¼ pint water

The quantity of dough made with these ingredients is enough for a 900 g/2 lb and a 450 g/1 lb loaf tin, or three 450 g/1 lb loaf-tins. Of course, other shapes may be made, such as bloomers, bread rolls etc. using a baking sheet.

Note: Different brands of flour require differing quantities of water to produce a good elastic dough. The quantity of water listed gives a general indication but may be modified slightly as required.

1. Put the flour and salt into a bowl and stand it in a warm place.
2. Warm the milk to blood heat and put half of it into a small bowl. Mix in the dried yeast and sugar. Leave it in a warm place until yeast is quite dissolved and beginning to froth.
If using fresh yeast, warm the milk to blood heat and put half of it into a small bowl. Add the yeast and sugar to the small bowl of milk stirring to dissolve the yeast. It may now be used. Unlike dried yeast it is not necessary to wait until the mixture froths up.
3. Grease tins or baking sheet.
4. Make a well in the centre of the flour. Pour in yeast mixture and mix it into the flour gradually adding the remaining milk and most of the water, enough to make a soft pliable dough.
5. Turn dough out on to a floured board. Knead only lightly making sure your hands are warm. It will only take a few minutes as this dough does not require heavy kneading like white bread dough.
6. Divide dough into 2, 3 or more pieces. Shape them lightly but do not overhandle. Put into tins or on to baking sheet and cover with a clean cloth or a piece of polythene. Stand in a warm, draught-free place and leave to rise. Do not put it near direct heat.
Depending on the warmth of your kitchen it could take about 1 to 1½ hours for dough to rise until doubled in size. Slow rising makes better bread.
If you leave it too long and dough begins to drop down again do not attempt to bake it. Knock it back, re-shape and put to rise again.

7. Try to get all loaves on same shelf and bake above centre of a moderately hot oven, Gas 6 to 7, 400°F, to 425°F; 200° to 220°C. 900 g/2 lb loaf-tins about 45 minutes. Look in the oven after 30 minutes and reduce heat a little if getting too brown. 450 g/1 lb loaf-tins, about 30 to 35 minutes.
Loaves or rolls cooked on baking sheet vary according to size. Small bloomer, about 15 to 20 minutes. Bread rolls, about 12 to 15 minutes.
To test: If it is done it will feel firm and sound hollow when tapped on the bottom.
8. Turn out of tins etc. at once on to a cooling rack and leave in a warm place until cooled.

Provided it is not overbaked this bread keeps moist and good to eat for 4 or 5 days.

WHOLEMEAL ONION, TOMATO AND ANCHOVY FLAN

Freezes well.

Serves 4 for a main course

BASE
125 g/4 oz wholemeal flour
½ level teaspoon salt
25 g/1 oz butter
7 g/¼ oz fresh yeast, or 1 level teaspoon dried yeast with ½ level teaspoon sugar
3 tablespoons tepid water
1 small egg or ½ large egg

FILLING
450 g/1 lb onions
3 tomatoes
1 clove garlic
3 tablespoons cooking oil
Seasoning

GARNISH
1 can of anchovy fillets
A few black olives

1. Mix flour and salt in bowl and rub in butter.
2. Cream fresh yeast in 1 tablespoon of the tepid water. If using dried yeast, put all the water into a small basin. Stir in dried yeast and sugar, place basin in a container of warm water and leave to stand for about 15 minutes until starting to froth.
3. Lightly beat egg.

4. Make a well in centre of flour, add yeast mixture, beat in egg and, if using fresh yeast, remaining 2 tablespoons of tepid water. Mix to a soft dough.

5. Knead dough on a floured board for 5 minutes. Put in a bowl, cover and leave in a warm place to rise until doubled in size.

6. *For the filling:* peel and slice onions finely.

7. Skin and chop tomatoes (*see page 139*). Crush garlic (*see page 139*).

8. Heat oil in a frying pan and slowly cook onions until soft but not brown.

9. Add tomatoes, garlic and seasoning.

10. Continue to cook gently until any liquid from tomatoes has evaporated. Leave to cool.

11. When dough has risen, knock it back—i.e., knead the air out of it. Then knead into a round ball.

12. Put a greased 20 cm/8 inch flan ring on to a greased baking sheet. Put ball of dough in centre of flan ring and press it out over base and up sides of ring.

13. Fill with onion mixture.

14. Drain and dry anchovy fillets and cut into narrow strips. Remove stones from olives.

15. Make a trellis pattern on top of onions with the anchovies and decorate with pieces of olive.

16. Leave to rise for 10 minutes.

17. Bake in centre of moderately hot oven, Gas 6, 400°F, 200°C, for 20 minutes. Reduce heat to moderate, Gas 4, 350°F, 180°C, for 15 to 20 minutes more.

Excellent served with green salad.

Jean Welshman
Malton, E. Yorkshire

QUICK BROWN BREAD

Sufficient for a 900 g/2 lb loaf tin or a 450 g/1 lb loaf, twist, bread rolls.

450 g/1 lb wholewheat flour
125 g/4 oz strong plain white flour
2 teaspoons salt
300 ml plus 4 tablespoons tepid water
25 g/1 oz fresh yeast
15 g/½ oz lard
1 dessertspoon dark treacle

Note: Some wholemeal flours absorb more liquid than others. An extra tablespoon of water may be required to produce a good elastic dough.

1. Mix together in a large bowl the flours and salt.

2. Using a small bowl whisk yeast into half of the water.

3. Using another small bowl dissolve lard and treacle in the remainder of the water.

4. Pour the two liquid mixtures on to the dry ingredients and make into a softish dough.

5. Turn on to a floured board and knead well until smooth and elastic.

6. The dough can now be shaped as required for baking.

7. After shaping put into greased tins or on greased baking sheets. Keep covered and away from draughts and allow to rise until doubled in size.

8. Bake the loaves in a hot oven, Gas 7, 425°F, 220°C, reducing to moderately hot, Gas 5, 375°F, 190°C, after 15 minutes.

A 900 g/2 lb loaf will take one hour.

450 g/1 lb loaves: 40 minutes.

A twist (depending on size): 25 minutes.

Tap the loaves which will sound hollow when ready. Small bread rolls take 12 to 15 minutes in a hot oven, Gas 7, 425°F, 220°C.

SHORT TIME BREAD

WHITE
15 g/½ oz fresh yeast or 7g/¼ oz dried
A 25 mg Vitamin C tablet (buy from chemist, also called ascorbic acid)
½ teaspoon sugar
About 150 ml/¼ pint warm water
225 g/8 oz strong plain flour
½ teaspoon salt
15 g/½ oz margarine

WHOLEWHEAT OR BROWN
Use 225 g/8 oz wholewheat flour, or half wholewheat and half white

1. Blend together the yeast, crushed Vitamin C tablet and half of the water. If using dried yeast, add sugar also and wait until it froths up before using.

2. Sieve flour and salt, rub in margarine.

3. Pour yeast liquid into dry ingredients and mix well.

4. Add sufficient warm water to make a soft, beatable dough.

5. Beat dough until the bowl is clean.

6. Turn out on to a lightly-floured board and knead until smooth, 10 minutes.

7. Rest dough for five minutes, covered lightly.

8. Shape into bread buns or cottage loaf, twist or plait and put on a greased baking tray. Cover with a damp cloth or greased polythene, and leave in a warm place to rise until doubled in size.

9. Bake near top of a hot oven, Gas 7, 425°F, 220°C. Bread buns take 10 to 12 minutes. Loaves take 25 to 30 minutes.

Pizza

The above quantity of dough will make 4 pizza bases 18 to 20 cm/7 to 8 inches in diameter.

For 1 pizza, serves 2

FILLING
$\frac{1}{2}$ to 1 tin anchovy fillets
50 g/2 oz chopped bacon
1 teaspoon oil or melted butter
25 g/1 oz grated cheese
25 g/1 oz sliced mushrooms
2 sliced tomatoes
A large pinch of basil
Black olives (optional) or pickled prunes

TO GARNISH
Chopped parsley

1. If you find the flavour of anchovies rather too strong, drain them and soak in milk for about half an hour.

2. Fry bacon lightly.

3. Roll out a piece of dough to 7 mm/$\frac{1}{4}$ inch thick and 18 to 20 cm/7 to 8 inches in diameter.

4. Place it on a well-greased tin, and brush all over with oil or butter.

5. Sprinkle top of dough with cheese, mushrooms and bacon. Finish with tomatoes and basil.

6. Arrange drained anchovies in a lattice design on top. Place olives in the spaces.

7. Cover lightly and leave aside to rise, or until the pizza dough has doubled in size or puffed up well.

8. Bake near top of a hot oven, Gas 7, 425°F, 220°C, for 20 to 30 minutes, reducing heat to moderately hot, Gas 5, 375°F, 190°C, after 15 minutes if browning too quickly.

9. Garnish with chopped parsley.

Pizzas freeze well. When cooked, allow to cool thoroughly. Put each pizza on a foil plate, place in a polythene bag, seal tightly and freeze. Thaw for 2 hours, then reheat in a hot oven for 10–15 minutes.

Wholewheat Tomato Pizza

Serves 4

25 g/1 oz margarine or 1 tablespoon oil
450 g/1 lb onions, chopped
2 cloves of garlic, crushed
Two 400 g/14 oz tins of tomatoes
$\frac{1}{2}$ teaspoon oregano
Salt and freshly-ground black pepper
A pinch of sugar
75 g/3 oz finely-grated cheese

TO GARNISH
2 or 3 mushrooms, or fine slices of green and
    red pepper

1. Heat margarine or oil and fry onion and garlic until softening.

2. Add tomatoes, oregano, salt, pepper and sugar and cook gently for about 20 minutes until thick.

3. Meanwhile, roll out enough dough to fit a greased Swiss roll tin. Prick all over with a fork. Cover with a cloth and let it rise until puffy.

4. Bake the pizza base near top of a hot oven, Gas 7, 425°F, 220°C, for 5 minutes. Then remove from oven and reduce heat to moderate, Gas 4, 350°F, 180°C.

5. Spread tomato mixture over the hot pizza base. Sprinkle cheese on top and decorate with mushroom slices or rings of pepper.

6. Return to oven near top and bake for 20 minutes until cheese is melted and browning.

Sweet Pears and Cheese Pizza
Eaten hot or cold.

Serves 3 or 4

3 dessert pears
Rind and juice of $\frac{1}{2}$ lemon
50 g/2 oz Lancashire, Cheshire or Mozzarella
    cheese, grated
25 g/1 oz plain cooking chocolate, grated
50 g/2 oz chopped walnuts
25 g/1 oz butter

1. Peel and core pears and cut into slices, about 3 slices to each quarter. Dip into lemon juice to prevent browning.

2. Roll out dough about 7 mm/$\frac{1}{4}$ inch thick and 18 to 20 cm/7 to 8 inches in diameter.

3. Arrange slices of pear on the dough leaving a 1 cm/$\frac{1}{2}$ inch border all round.

4. Scatter on the lemon rind. Cover pears with

cheese, sprinkle on chocolate and chopped walnuts. Dot with butter.

5. Cover lightly and leave aside in a warm place to rise.

6. Bake near top of a very hot oven for 5 minutes, Gas 8, 450°F, 230°C, then lower temperature to moderately hot, Gas 7, 425°F, 220°C, and bake for about 15 minutes more, or until pizza dough is brown.

RICH BREAD DOUGH

This quantity, if divided into 3 even-sized portions, will make 8 dinner buns and 2 small loaves.

7 g/¼ oz (2 level teaspoons) dried yeast *or* 15 g/½ oz fresh yeast
225 ml/8 fl oz warm milk
1 teaspoon sugar
25 g/1 oz butter
450 g/1 lb strong plain flour
1 teaspoon salt
1 egg

Note: Different brands of flour require differing quantities of liquid to produce a good elastic dough. The quantity of milk listed gives a general indication but may be modified slightly as required.

1. If using *dried yeast*, prepare first:
(a) Add half the warmed milk to the yeast and sugar in a small basin.
(b) Put remaining milk in another small basin and add butter.
(c) Place basins in a container of warm water so that contents will be at blood heat when ready to use. Leave like this until yeast is frothy, stirring occasionally to soften yeast granules. This can take from 12 to 15 minutes.

1. If using *fresh yeast:*
(a) Mix in a small bowl the sugar and half the warm milk with the yeast.
(b) Put the butter with warm milk remaining in the pan.
(c) You can proceed with the recipe as soon as yeast is liquified. It is not necessary to wait for it to froth.

2. Mix flour and salt in a large warm bowl.

3. Add liquids and beaten egg and knead firmly until dough is smooth and elastic.

4. Place to rise in a large, greased, warm bowl inside a large polythene bag. Leave until doubled in size and when you can push a finger into the dough and the impression will remain.

5. Turn on to floured board, knead lightly and shape.

6. This mixture is not suitable for baking in loaf tins. Place on greased tray, cover and allow to rise until doubled in size. It should be puffy when lightly touched.

7. Bake in a moderately hot oven, Gas 6, 400°F, 200°C. Dinner buns require approximately 12 minutes. Loaves: 25 to 30 minutes depending on size. The base should sound hollow when tapped with knuckles.

KENTISH HUFFKINS

These are plain, white, flat yeast cakes, traditionally baked with a dimple in the middle.

Makes 10

15 g/½ oz fresh yeast or 1½ teaspoons dried yeast
1 teaspoon caster sugar
300 ml/½ pint warm milk and water mixed
450 g/1 lb strong plain white flour
½ teaspoon salt
25 g/1 oz lard

1. Mix yeast and sugar into warmed milk and water. If using dried yeast, whisk it in with a fork so that granules dissolve without clogging together. Leave in a warm place for 5 minutes until yeast is active and frothy.

2. Mix flour and salt in a bowl. Rub in lard.

3. Add yeast mixture. Mix to a pliable dough and turn out on to a floured board.

4. Knead well until dough is no longer sticky and is smooth and shiny, about 10 minutes.

5. Lightly grease bowl and put in the dough. Cover with a cloth or greased polythene. Keep in a warm place, away from draughts, so that dough will rise (or 'prove') until doubled in size.

6. Turn on to a floured board. Knead lightly to let out air and to make dough pliable again.

7. Divide this dough into 10 equal pieces.

8. Shape into flat oval cakes about 1 cm/½ inch thick. It is best to do this by forming a roll first and then flattening to an oval with rolling pin.

9. Place well apart on greased baking trays and press a floured finger into the centre of each cake. Cover trays and leave to 'prove' until doubled in size.

10. Bake near top of a very hot oven, Gas 8, 450°F, 230°C, for 15 to 20 minutes.

11. Transfer to a wire rack.

Eat hot or cold, split and buttered.

Mrs Jill Marshall
Hythe, Kent

MRS ZACHAROVA'S METHOD OF MAKING BREAD

The essential difference between this and other methods is that the yeast is mixed with the liquid, and the flour is added to the liquid until the desired consistency is achieved. Consequently, it requires less physical effort to get the dough right.

The second feature of Mrs Zacharova's bread-making is that it fits into her daily routine. Sometimes she lets the bread rise for 1 hour in a warm place, and sometimes all day in a cool place, or all night. The main principle is that it should at least double, if not treble, in size during the first rising.

Finally, after the first rising, the loaves are shaped and put straight out of the way into a cold oven and left for 20 to 30 minutes. The oven is then switched on and baking proceeds. So, if you have a gas or electric cooker, why not try it?

White Bread

It is better for newcomers to this method to start with white bread: with white flour it is easier to handle and learn the feel of the dough than it is with brown flours.

Makes two 900 g/2 lb loaf tins

20 g/⅔ oz fresh yeast, or 10 g/2½ teaspoons dried yeast
2 teaspoons sugar
450 ml/¾ pint luke-warm water
About 675 g/1½ lb strong plain white flour
2 teaspoons salt

1. Mix yeast, sugar, 125 ml/4 fl oz of the warm water and 2 to 3 tablespoons of the flour to a cream. Leave in a warm place for 15 minutes until yeast is working actively and mixture is frothing. If using dried yeast, make doubly sure it is completely dissolved and frothing well.
2. Put yeast mixture, salt, and rest of water in a big mixing bowl and start mixing in the flour. Mix with dough hook on electric mixer, a big wooden spoon or clean hands.
3. Continue to add flour and mix thoroughly. This develops the gluten into stretchy, rubbery strands which will hold the gas made by the yeast.
After a while dough will become difficult to mix in the bowl, so transfer it to a well-floured board.
4. Knead, adding more flour as necessary, until dough retains its shape and no longer sticks to the board. At this point you should be able to feel the rubbery strands between your fingers and the dough

should resist when you push against it. Once you recognise the feel of the dough you will know when it is kneaded enough.
5. Put dough into a large bowl, or plastic container, and cover closely with a plate, lid or sheet of polythene. Leave in a warm place, at room temperature or in the cool (depending on when you can complete the next stage) and allow it at least to double in size. It is better to let it rise to three times its original volume than not to let it rise enough. It can be pushed down in the bowl and kneaded a little (but this is not necessary) during this rising period.
6. When dough has risen sufficiently, flour your fingers and scrape and push it back into a small lump.
7. If dough has been allowed to rise for a long period in a cool place it is best to warm it up a little before it is kneaded the second time. Stand covered bowl in the sink or a basin of warm water until dough no longer feels cold. Turn it out on to a floured board. Knead a little, just enough to break down the large air bubbles.
8. Cut into two pieces, shape each piece and place in 2 greased 900 g/2 lb loaf tins.
9. Stand tins out of your way in a cold oven on the top shelf. Leave enough headroom for rising. In 30 minutes the top of the loaf should just about reach the top of the tin. If your oven has a pilot light, look at loaves after 20 minutes.
10. Now switch on oven and set temperature moderately hot, Gas 6, 400°F, 200°C. Set timer for 40 minutes. The loaves go on rising until oven is hot enough to kill the yeast. Loaves on lower shelves may need 10 minutes longer to bake.
11. Drop each loaf out of tin and knock its bottom. If it is ready it will sound hollow. If not ready, return to oven in or out of tins for another 5 or 10 minutes.
12. Turn loaves out of tins on to a wire rack to cool.

Brown Bread

You can buy wholemeal flour for bread-making and 100% extraction wholewheat. Wholemeal flour is easier to work and feels more like a white dough. 100% extraction wholewheat is coarser. The rough bits in the flour make it more difficult to form the gluten into rubbery, stretchy strands.

20 g/⅔ oz fresh yeast, or 10 g/2½ teaspoons dried yeast
2 teaspoons Barbados or demerara sugar
600 ml/1 pint luke-warm water
About 675 g/1½ lb wholemeal or wholewheat flour
2½ teaspoons salt

Follow method for White Bread (*see page 284*), but note 3 points:

1. Dough will be stickier and it will be hard to feel the rubbery strands of gluten. It will end up feeling firmer.
2. Loaves cannot rise as much as white ones or they would be impossibly crumbly. However, dough should be allowed to double or treble in size during first rising.
3. Loaves may take 5 minutes longer to bake.

Spicy Fruit Loaf
20 g/⅔ oz fresh yeast, or 10 g/2½ teaspoons dried yeast
50 g/2 oz demerara or Barbados sugar
450 ml/¾ pint luke-warm water
About 675 g/1½ lb strong plain white flour
2 teaspoons salt
50 to 75 g/2 to 3 oz medium oatmeal, or rolled oats
1 rounded teaspoon mixed spice
75 g/3 oz mixed dried fruit and chopped peel

Follow method for white bread (*see page 284*) but note 3 points:

1. Add oatmeal or the rolled oats and spice at paragraph 2.
2. Add fruit just before turning dough out on to board. Fruit will make dough a bit more difficult to handle.
3. Dough should be allowed to double or treble in size during first rising but, because of oatmeal and fruit, it will be more like brown dough both to handle and in the way it rises in the tins.

Malt Bread
20 g/⅔ oz fresh yeast or 10 g/2½ oz teaspoons dried yeast
450 ml/¾ pint luke-warm milk, milk and water, or reconstituted dried milk
2 teaspoons sugar
About 675 g/1½ lb strong plain white flour, or white and wholewheat flour
½ tablespoon molasses or black treacle
1 tablespoon malt extract
½ tablespoon golden syrup
75 g/3 oz soya flour
2 teaspoons salt
125 g/4 oz mixed dried fruits and peel
A little melted butter

1. Mix yeast, sugar, 125 ml/4 fl oz of the warm milk and 2 to 3 tablespoons of the flour to a cream. Leave in a warm place for 15 minutes until yeast is working

actively and mixture is frothing. If using dried yeast, make doubly sure it is completely dissolved and frothing well.
2. Mix remainder of liquid, molasses, malt and syrup, warming a little if necessary.
3. Put yeast liquid and malt mixture in a large bowl and mix in soya flour and 225 g/8 oz of white flour.
4. Cover bowl closely and leave it in a warm place for 4 or 5 hours.
5. Add salt and start mixing in rest of flour. Mix with dough hook on electric mixer, a wooden spoon or clean hands.
6. Mix in fruit and continue to work in flour. After a while dough will become too difficult to mix in the bowl, so transfer it to a well-floured board.
7. Follow method for White Bread, stages 5 to 7 (*see page 284*, noting dough should be rather tight).
8. Cut it into 3 even-sized pieces, shape and put into tins.
9. Stand tins out of your way in a cold oven on the top shelf. Leave enough headroom for rising. In 30 minutes the top of the loaf should just about reach the top of the tin. If your oven has a pilot light, look at loaves after 20 minutes.
10. Now switch on oven and set temperature at moderately hot, Gas 6, 400°F, 200°C. Set timer for 40 minutes. The loaves go on rising until oven is hot enough to kill the yeast. Loaves on lower shelves may need 10 minutes longer to bake.
11. Turn loaves out of tins on to a wire rack to cool. Brush tops immediately with melted butter to make them shine.

Sour Rye Bread
Start to prepare this bread 48 hours before you want to bake it.
450 ml/¾ pint luke-warm water
325 g/12 oz rye flour

Mix these two ingredients together, cover closely with a lid, plate or sheet of polythene and leave in a warm place (such as on top of central heating boiler, or in airing cupboard) for 48 hours. The mixture must 'sour'. It will develop a strong aroma.

150 ml/¼ pint luke-warm water
20 g/⅔ oz fresh yeast or 10 g/2½ teaspoons dried yeast
1 tablespoon caraway seeds (optional)
2 teaspoons sugar
About 450 g/1 lb strong plain white flour, or wholewheat flour, or a mixture of both. Up to 125 g/4 oz rye flour could be included to make a total of 450 g/1 lb flour
2½ teaspoons salt

Follow method for White Bread (*see page 284*) but note 3 points:

1. Soured rye flour mixture is put in large mixing bowl at paragraph 2, then yeast mixture salt, rest of water and carraway seeds are added.
2. It will seem difficult to work because there is no gluten in rye flour.
3. When oven is switched on, set timer for 50 minutes.

Halla
A Continental bread made from a rich dough and shaped in a twist or plait.

20 g/⅔ oz fresh yeast or 10 g/2½ teaspoons dried yeast
2 teaspoons sugar (more if you like a sweet loaf)
250 ml/9 fl oz warm milk, milk and water, or reconstituted dried milk
About 675 g/1½ lb strong plain white flour
2 teaspoons salt
125 g/4 oz melted margarine, butter or half of each
2 beaten egg

1. Mix yeast, sugar, 125 ml/4 fl oz of the warm milk and 2 to 3 tablespoons of the flour to a cream. Leave in a warm place for 15 minutes until yeast is working actively and mixture is frothing. If using dried yeast, make doubly sure it is completely dissolved and frothing well.
2. Put yeast mixture, salt, rest of milk and a little flour in a big mixing bowl. Mix together. Add melted fat, some more flour and then the eggs. Eggs mix in better if there is already some flour in dough.
3. Continue to add flour and mix very thoroughly at each addition. It is important to develop all the gluten in order to make a really light, well-risen loaf. At some stage it will be too difficult to mix dough in a bowl, so transfer it to a well-floured board.
4. Knead, adding more flour as necessary, until dough retains its shape and no longer sticks to the board. Mix in plenty of flour to make a firm dough. These loaves are baked without the support of a tin, and a soft dough would spread sideways.

5. Put dough into an especially large bowl, or plastic container, and cover closely with a plate, lid or sheet of polythene. Dough that has been well-worked rises very high. It can be punched back if it grows too high. Leave bowl in a warm place, at room temperature or in the cool (depending on when you can complete the next stage) and allow it at least to double in size. It is better to let it rise to three times its original volume than not to let it rise enough. It can be pushed down in the bowl and kneaded a little (but this is not necessary) during this rising period.
6. When dough has risen sufficiently, flour your fingers and scrape and push it back into a small lump.
7. If dough has been allowed to rise for a long period in a cool place it is best to warm it up a little before it is kneaded the second time. Stand covered bowl in the sink or a basin of warm water until dough no longer feels cold. Turn it out on to a floured board. Knead a little, just enough to break down the large air bubbles.
8. Cut into 2 even-sized pieces. Work each piece into a long roll, cut into 2 or 3 strands and plait them. Place on a greased baking sheet, well apart.
9. Place baking sheet in a cold oven and leave to rise. It is not easy to judge when these loaves are ready for baking. Sometimes, if over-risen, they will collapse during baking but if you have worked hard at the mixing and kneading to develop the gluten this will help keep the air in. Look at loaves in 20 to 30 minutes. They should have begun to rise nicely before oven is switched on.
10. Just before switching on oven, gently brush tops of loaves with milk or egg-yolk and milk. This will give them a nice colour.
11. Now switch on oven and set temperature at moderately hot, Gas 6, 400°F, 200°C. Set timer for 40 minutes. The loaves go on rising until oven is hot enough to kill the yeast. Loaves on lower shelves may need 10 minutes longer to bake.
12. Take each loaf off baking sheet and tap its bottom. If it is ready it will sound hollow. If not ready, return to oven for another 5 or 10 minutes.
13. Turn loaves on to a wire rack to cool.
14. Handle gently when baked.

Jeannie Zacharova
London

CHEESE LOAF

Freezes well.

Makes one 900 g/2 lb loaf or two 450 g/1 lb loaves.

400 g/14 oz strong plain flour
1 teaspoon salt
1 teaspoon dry mustard
Bare ¼ teaspoon cayenne pepper
125 g/4 oz finely-grated Cheddar cheese
2 teaspoons dried yeast or 15 g/½ oz fresh yeast
1 teaspoon sugar
Bare 300 ml/½ pint tepid water

1. Sieve flour and seasonings into a large bowl, mix in the cheese.
2. Prepare the dried yeast as indicated in manufacturer's instructions. It is important with dried yeast that it is frothing up well when used.
If using fresh yeast, cream it with the sugar, pour in half of the water, mix and use.
3. Pour yeast mixture into dry ingredients, using rest of water as necessary to make a soft pliable dough.
4. Knead well until quite smooth and elastic.
5. Place in a large, lightly-greased, warm bowl. Cover, keep away from draughts and leave to prove until doubled in size.
6. Turn out on to floured board, and knead until smooth again.
7. Divide into 2 portions. Shape and place in two greased 450 g/1 lb loaf tins, or use one 900 g/2 lb tin.
8. Cover and leave to rise to nearly the top of tin.
9. Bake in the centre of a moderately hot oven, Gas 5, 375°F, 190°C, for 45 to 50 minutes until golden brown. To test, slip loaf out of tin into a clean cloth and tap the bottom. It will sound hollow when loaf is done.

Serve sliced and buttered. Also good toasted.

EGG FINGERS

Particularly good when made with fingers from a Cheese Loaf, see preceding recipe.

1 egg
1 tablespoon milk
Salt and pepper
Fingers of white or brown bread
Bacon fat or a little margarine

1. Beat the egg and milk with a little salt and pepper.
2. Dip bread fingers into the egg mixture.
3. Fry till golden on both sides. This is best done in the fat after cooking bacon, but add a little margarine if necessary.

Serve with bacon. Eat at once or they go like leather.

PITTA BREAD

Freezes well. Reheat from frozen under grill.

Makes 6 or 7 pieces

2 teaspoons dried yeast
A pinch of sugar
300 ml/½ pint warm water
1 teaspoon salt
1½ tablespoons oil
400 g/14 oz strong plain flour, sifted

1. In a large mixing bowl, dissolve yeast and sugar in 3 tablespoons of the warm water. Let it stand for 10 minutes in a warm place until frothy on top.
2. Add rest of water, salt and oil.
3. Stir 125 g/4 oz flour at a time into yeast mixture, forming a sticky dough. If it is too sticky to work when all flour is used, add a little more flour.
4. Transfer dough to lightly-floured board and knead until smooth, about 10 minutes.
5. Shape dough into a ball and coat lightly with oil. Return it to bowl. Cover and let it rise in a warm place until doubled in bulk, about 1½ hours.
6. Punch dough down and form 6 or 7 balls. On a lightly-floured board, roll or press out the dough with the hands into 15 cm/6 inch circles that are 7 mm/¼ inch thick. Dust lightly with flour.
7. Put on to lightly-oiled baking sheets, cover and allow to rise again for 15 minutes.
8. Preheat oven to very hot, Gas 8, 450°F, 230°C.
9. Bake for 8 to 10 minutes. Wrap the bread in foil immediately after removing from oven to preserve moistness.

Serve hot or reheated under grill.

Elizabeth Mickery
Pudsey, Yorkshire

ABERDEEN BUTTERIES

These freeze well.

Makes 8 or 10

225 ml/8 oz tepid milk and water, mixed
1 teaspoon sugar
1½ measured teaspoons dried yeast, or 15 g/½ oz
   fresh yeast
½ teaspoon salt
275 g/10 oz strong, plain white flour
25 g/1 oz butter or margarine
50 g/2 oz lard
50 g/2 oz hard margarine

1. Take out 1 tablespoon of the tepid milk and water mixture and keep aside for use later.
2. Stir sugar into the remaining bulk of liquid. Sprinkle on dried yeast and leave 5 to 10 minutes to start working. It is ready for use when frothing up well.
If using fresh yeast, stir sugar into the liquid, take out half a cupful and mix the fresh yeast into this to liquify it. Mix both liquids together and proceed with recipe. There is no need to wait as with dried yeast.
3. Add salt to flour and roughly rub in the 25 g/1 oz butter or margarine.
4. Add the yeast liquid and mix to a soft elastic dough, adding the extra tablespoon of liquid if required.
5. Knead firmly for about 5 minutes.
6. Return dough to bowl and put bowl into a polythene bag. Leave in a warm place to rise until doubled in size, about 45 minutes.
7. Work together lard with the 50 g/2 oz margarine and divide equally into 3 portions.
8. Knock back risen dough by kneading on a floured board. Roll out to a strip 1 cm/½ inch thick and 3 times as long as it is wide.
9. Spread one portion of mixed fats over bottom two-thirds of dough. Fold top third down and then bottom third up. Turn dough so that fold is at left hand side.
10. Roll out, spread fat, fold and turn twice more. Lay dough aside in a cool place for at least 10 minutes.
11. Roll out again to just over 1 cm/half an inch thick and cut or pull into 8 or 10 pieces. Place on a baking sheet and put baking sheet into polythene bag. Leave in a warm place to rise again, about 15 to 20 minutes.

12. Brush with a little melted butter and bake in a hot oven, Gas 8, 450°F, 230°C, for 15 to 20 minutes until golden brown and flaky.

Mrs Anne Wallace
Dunlop, Scotland

STAFFORDSHIRE OATCAKES

These will keep for several days in a polythene bag in refrigerator. Freeze well. Put paper or polythene tissue between each oatcake. May be taken straight from freezer into frying pan.

Makes approximately 12 oatcakes

225 g/8 oz fine oatmeal
225 g/8 oz plain wholewheat or white flour
1 teaspoon salt
15 g/½ oz fresh yeast
1 litre/1½ pints warm milk and water mixed
1 teaspoon sugar

1. Add salt to flour and oatmeal and stir.
2. Dissolve yeast with a little of the warm liquid and add sugar. Set aside in warm place until yeast begins to work (i.e. bubbles appear on surface).
3. Mix dry ingredients with yeast and rest of warm liquid to make a nice batter.
4. Cover with clean cloth and leave in warm place for about 1 hour.
5. Then bake on well-greased bakestone, girdle, griddle or thick-based frying pan. Turn each oatcake after 2 to 3 minutes, when upperside appears dry and underside will be golden brown, and bake for a further 2 to 3 minutes.

To serve: Fry with bacon and eggs for breakfast or tea, or grill and eat hot with butter.

Miss P. M. Cherry
Penkridge

BUN LOAF AND HOT CROSS BUNS

These freeze very well after they are baked, but do not glaze before freezing.

Makes one 450 g/1 lb loaf and 8 hot cross buns

25 g/1 oz fresh or 15 g/½ oz dried yeast
50 g/2 oz caster sugar
150 ml/¼ pint tepid water
450 g/1 lb strong plain white flour
1 level teaspoon salt
½ teaspoon ground cinammon
1 teaspoon mixed spice
A grate of nutmeg
50 g/2 oz margarine
75 g/3 oz mixed currants, sultanas and peel
Warm milk and 1 beaten egg to make 150 ml/
 ¼ pint bare measure

GLAZE
2 tablespoons milk boiled with 1 tablespoon
 sugar

1. Cream the fresh yeast with 1 teaspoon of the sugar and dissolve in water. If using dried yeast follow instructions on packet.
2. Sift into a large bowl the flour, salt and spices.
3. Rub in margarine.
4. Mix in the rest of the sugar and the prepared fruit.
5. Mix to a pliable dough with liquids.
6. Knead until smooth and elastic in texture.
7. Cover with polythene or clean tea-towel and place to rise in greased bowl away from draughts. It should double in size and take about 1 hour.
8. Turn on to a floured board and knead smooth again.
9. *For Bun Loaf:*
Weigh off 450 g/1 lb dough, shape into a loaf and put into a greased 450 g/1 lb loaf tin, or round tin of similar capacity. Place to rise, covered, and away from draughts.
10. *For Hot Cross Buns:*
Divide remaining dough (approx. 450 g/1 lb) into 8 even pieces. Shape into buns, round or oval. Roll lightly, make a cross on top with knife.
11. Place on greased baking tray, cover, and rise until puffy.

FOR RISING
A slightly warm atmosphere (above the stove, or even the airing cupboard) is an advantage as this type of dough rises more slowly than plain bread.
12. Bake buns for about 15 minutes in a moderately hot oven, Gas 6, 400°F, 200°C, until nicely browned. Remove from oven and turn out on to cooling rack. Brush with glaze while hot.
13. Bake loaf in a moderately hot oven, Gas 6, 400°F, 200°C, for 10 to 15 minutes, reduce heat to moderate, Gas 4, 350°F, 180°C, for a further 25 to 30 minutes until firm. Turn out on to wire rack to cool. Glaze as for buns as desired.

WHOLEWHEAT BUN LOAF AND HOT CROSS BUNS

These freeze very well after they are baked, but do not glaze before freezing.

Makes one 450 g/1 lb bun loaf and 8 hot cross buns

25 g/1 oz fresh yeast or 15 g/½ oz dried yeast
40 g/1½ oz dark brown Barbados sugar
150 ml/¼ pint tepid water
450 g/1 lb plain wholewheat flour
1 level teaspoon sea salt
1 teaspoon mixed spice
½ teaspoon cinnamon
A grating of nutmeg
50 g/2 oz margarine
125 g/4 oz mixed currants, sultanas and peel
Warm milk and 1 beaten egg to make 150 ml/
 ¼ pint bare measure

GLAZE
1 tablespoon demerara sugar dissolved over
 low heat in 2 tablespoons water and boiled
 until syrupy

1. Mix fresh yeast with 1 teaspoon of the sugar and stir it into the tepid water.
If using dried yeast, mix 1 teaspoon of sugar into the tepid water, sprinkle in yeast, whisking with a fork to disperse the grains. Let it stand in a warm place for 10 to 15 minutes when it should be frothing well and ready to use.
2. Mix together in a large bowl flour, salt and spices.
3. Rub in margarine.
4. Mix in rest of sugar and fruit.
5. Mix to a pliable dough with yeast liquid and egg and milk mixture.
6. Knead thoroughly.
7. Place to rise in a greased bowl away from draughts. Cover with polythene or a clean tea-towel. Let it rise for about 1 hour until doubled in size.

8. Turn on to a floured board and knead well.

9. *For bun loaf:* weigh off 450 g/1 lb dough, shape into a loaf and put into a greased 450 g/1 lb loaf tin, or round tin of similar capacity. Cover and leave to rise, away from draughts.

10. *For Hot Cross Buns:* divide remaining dough into 8 even pieces. Shape into buns, round or oval. Roll lightly and make a cross on top with knife.

11. Place on greased baking tray, cover, and allow to rise until puffy.

For rising: a slightly warm atmosphere (e.g., above the stove, or the airing cupboard) is an advantage as this type of dough rises more slowly than plain bread.

12. Bake buns for approximately 15 minutes in a moderately hot oven, Gas 6, 400°F, 200°C, until nicely browned. Remove from oven and turn on to cooling rack. Brush with glaze while hot.

13. Bake loaf in a moderately hot oven, Gas 6, 400°F, 200°C, for 15 minutes. Reduce heat to moderate, Gas 4, 350°F, 180°C, for a further 25 to 30 minutes until firm. Turn out on to wire rack to cool. Glaze as for buns as desired.

MY GRANDMOTHER'S YULE BREAD

This bread improves with keeping, and should be left for 3 weeks before using. Therefore make it at the beginning of December, for Christmas.

Makes one 900 g/2 lb loaf or two 450 g/1 lb loaves

450 g/1 lb strong plain flour
Pinch of salt
15 g/½ oz fresh yeast, or 2 teaspoons dried yeast
300 ml/½ pint luke-warm water
225 g/8 oz butter
225 g/8 oz sugar
Half a grated nutmeg
325 g/12 oz currants
125 g/4 oz candied peel
2 beaten eggs

1. Put flour with a pinch of salt in a warm basin.

2. Dissolve fresh yeast in the luke-warm water. If using dried yeast, add 1 teaspoon of the sugar to the water, sprinkle yeast on top and leave it to froth up.

3. Stir yeast liquid into flour. Cover basin and let it stand 1 hour in a warm place.

4. Meanwhile, cream the butter.

5. Add butter, sugar, nutmeg, currants, candied peel and beaten eggs to flour and yeast. Mix well.

6. Pour into a 900 g/2 lb greased loaf tin, or two 450 g/1 lb loaf tins. Cover tins and leave to rise, about ½ hour, until mixture just reaches top of tins.

7. Bake in a moderate oven, Gas 4, 350°F, 180°C. Large tin takes about 2 hours. Small tins take 1 hour. Should be brown and firm when done.

8. Turn out of tins on to wire rack to cool.

This loaf is particularly nice buttered.

Stella Boldy
Sykehouse, N. Humberside

OXFORD LARDY CAKE

DOUGH
15 g/½ oz fresh yeast
½ teaspoon sugar
150 ml/¼ pint water
225 g/8 oz strong plain flour
1 level teaspoon salt
½ tablespoon lard

FILLING
75 g/3 oz lard
75 to 125 g/3 to 4 oz brown sugar
75 g/3 oz currants

TO FINISH
A little cooking oil
Caster sugar

Note: It was usual to make a large lardy cake using:

900 g/2 lb risen white bread dough
175 g/6 oz lard
225 g/8 oz brown sugar
175 g/6 oz currants

and some think this turns out better than the small one. For this, having prepared your bread dough follow instructions from paragraphs 6 to 13 using a larger, but shallow, roasting tin and baking for 40 to 50 minutes.

1. Cream yeast and sugar in a small basin, pour on the warm water and stir to dissolve.

2. Add the salt to the flour, and rub in the lard.

3. Mix to a pliable dough with the yeast mixture.

4. Knead until smooth and elastic.

5. Place in warm greased bowl. Cover and rise until doubled in size.

6. Turn on to a floured board, and knead a little.

7. Roll out dough 7 mm/¼ inch thick and three times as long as wide.

8. Spread one third of the lard on.

9. Fold in three, and roll out to oblong again.

10. Repeat twice more using sugar, lard and currants.

11. Fold up finally to form a cushion 4 cm/1½ inches thick.

12. Place in a small, greased, roasting tin. Brush top with oil and shake caster sugar over. Leave covered until doubled in size.

13. Uncover and score across with a knife.

14. Bake in a moderately hot oven, Gas 6, 400°F, 200°C, for 30 to 40 minutes. Baste with the fat which escapes during cooling.

Freezes well. Thaw first and then reheat in a moderate oven, Gas 3, 325°F, 160°C.

CHELSEA BUNS AND SALLY LUNN

These freeze very well, unglazed.

Makes one 13 to 15 cm/5 to 6 inch Sally Lunn and 9 Chelsea buns

25 g/1 oz fresh yeast or 15 g/½ oz dried yeast
150 ml/¼ pint tepid milk and water mixed
1 teaspoon salt
450 g/1 lb strong plain flour
75 g/3 oz margarine
75 g/3 oz caster sugar
2 eggs
50 g/2 oz currants

GLAZE
2 tablespoons milk boiled with 1 tablespoon sugar

1. Mix the yeast with 1 teaspoon of the sugar and dissolve in the milk and water. If using dried yeast follow instructions on packet.

2. Mix salt into flour.

3. Rub in 50 g/2 oz of the margarine.

4. Add 50 g/2 oz of the caster sugar.

5. Whisk eggs.

6. Mix eggs and liquids into flour and knead until smooth. If eggs are small an extra 1 or 2 tablespoons of warm water may be required, as the mixture must not be too stiff.

7. Cover with polythene or clean tea-towel and place to rise in greased bowl away from draughts. It should double in size and take about 1 hour.

8. Knead down on a floured board. Divide dough into 2 portions.

9. *For the Sally Lunn:*

Shape 1 portion in a round and put in a deep 13 to 15 cm/5 to 6 inch cake-tin. Cover and place to rise until doubled in size.

10. *For the Chelsea Buns:*

(a) Roll out second piece of dough, approximately 25 by 20 cm/10 by 8 inches.

(b) Spread with the remaining 25 g/1 oz margarine, softened but not melted.

(c) Sprinkle on the remaining caster sugar and the currants.

(d) Roll up lengthways, to make a roll 25 cm/10 inches long.

(e) Cut into 9 even slices, place—cut sides down—in an 18 cm/7 inch square, greased, shallow tin.

(f) Cover, rise until puffy.

11. When Sally Lunn has doubled in size bake in centre of a moderately hot oven, Gas 5, 375°F, 190°C, for about 45 minutes. Turn out of tin while hot on to cooling wire.

12. Bake Chelsea Buns on top shelf of a moderately hot oven, Gas 5, 375°F, 190°C, for about 30 minutes. As this is a rich mixture the buns may need to be covered with foil towards end of cooking time or they may brown too much. Cool on wire rack.

13. Brush with glaze while still hot.

CURRANT LOAF

Freezes well.

Makes a 900 g/2 lb loaf

15 g/½ oz fresh yeast or 7 g/¼ oz dried
300 ml/½ pint warm milk
25 g/1 oz caster sugar
450 g/1 lb strong plain white flour
1 teaspoon salt
1 level teaspoon cinnamon
25 g/1 oz margarine
125 g/4 oz washed and dried currants
Beaten egg

1. Blend the yeast into the warm milk. If using dried yeast, add 1 teaspoon of the sugar and wait until it froths up before using.

2. Sift together flour, salt and cinnamon.

3. Add sugar and rub in fat.

4. Stir in yeast and milk and mix to a soft dough.

5. Turn on to a floured board and knead until smooth.

6. Cover and leave to rise until doubled in size, about 1 hour.

7. Work the currants into the risen dough until evenly distributed.

8. Form into loaf shape and place in a greased 900 g/2 lb loaf tin.

9. Brush the loaf with beaten egg. Cover and leave to 'prove' again, about 1 hour, until well-risen and puffy.

10. Bake near top of a moderately hot oven, Gas 6, 400°F, 200°C, until golden brown, about 50 minutes.

11. Cool on a wire rack.

DOUGHNUTS

Makes 10 to 12

15 g/½ oz fresh yeast*
½ teaspoon sugar
90 to 125 ml/3 to 4 fl oz milk, warmed
225 g/8 oz strong plain flour
½ teaspoon salt
25 g/1 oz margarine
1 small beaten egg
75 to 125 g/3 to 4 oz caster sugar
Powdered cinnamon
Oil or lard for frying

*If using dried yeast, use 7 g/¼ oz and follow manufacturer's instructions.

1. Cream yeast and sugar in a basin, stir in most of the milk and mix well to dissolve yeast.

2. In a large bowl, mix flour and salt, rub in margarine.

3. Make a well in centre, add yeast mixture and beaten egg. Mix to a pliable dough, adding remaining milk if necessary. The mixture should be softish but firm enough to knead.

4. Turn out on to a floured board, knead until smooth and elastic, using a little flour if necessary.

5. Grease the bowl, place mixture in and cover. A good idea is to place bowl in a large polythene bag.

6. Prove (which means leave to rise) until doubled in size, preferably in a warm place away from draughts or direct heat.

7. Turn on to floured board and knead smooth.

8. Roll out about 1 cm/½ inch thick, cut into 8 cm/3-inch rounds with a plain cutter. Cut out centres with a 4 cm/1½ inch cutter and put these with the trimmings to roll out again.

9. Place doughnuts on a greased and floured baking tray spacing them carefully. Cover with muslin and leave to rise until just about doubled in size and quite puffy.

10. Heat a pan of oil or good clarified dripping or lard which should be 7 to 8 cm/2½ to 3 inches deep. It is hot enough when a 2.5 cm/1 inch cube of bread will sizzle at once and gradually turn golden.

11. Using a spatula or broad knife carefully lift doughnuts into fat, a few at a time, leaving room to turn them over. Fry for 3 minutes, turning 2 or 3 times.

12. Lift on to kitchen paper and then toss in caster sugar sifted with a little cinnamon.

LOAF CAKE

Teisen Dorth
A Glamorgan recipe for a rich fruit loaf. Can be made with white or wholewheat flour or a mixture of wholewheat and white. With wholewheat flour the loaf will not be as light as with white. Freezes well.

15 g/½ oz fresh yeast, or 2 teaspoons dried yeast
300 ml/½ pint lukewarm milk
450 g/1 lb plain flour
A pinch of salt
¼ teaspoon mixed spice
65 g/2½ oz butter or lard
65 g/2½ oz soft brown sugar
150 g/5 oz sultanas
150 g/5 oz currants
65 g/2½ oz raisins
25 g/1 oz candied peel
1 beaten egg

1. Mix yeast with a little of the warm milk and leave in a warm place for 5 minutes. If using dried yeast, add a teaspoon of the sugar also, wait until it is active and frothy before using.

2. Put flour, salt and spice into a bowl and rub in fat.

3. Mix in rest of dry ingredients.

4. Make a well in centre, add yeast mixture, well-beaten egg and enough warm milk to make a soft dough. Mix and then knead in basin for 5 minutes.

5. Grease the mixing bowl. Put dough in it, cover with greased polythene or a damp cloth and leave it in a really warm place to rise for about 1½ hours, until it has doubled in size.

6. Knead dough again to knock out the bubbles.

7. Shape and place in a well-greased 900 g/2 lb loaf

tin. Cover again and leave 20 minutes in a really warm place to rise again. Dough should rise well above top of tin.

8. Bake just above middle of a hot oven, Gas 7, 425°F, 220°C, for 20 minutes. Then reduce heat to warm, Gas 3, 325°F, 160°C, for 45 minutes more.

9. Turn loaf out on to a wire rack immediately to cool.

Mrs Doreen Owen
Llanwenarth Citra W.I., Gwent

SAVARIN AND RHUM BABA

Baking moulds for these dishes are available in 2 sizes. Quantities of ingredients are given for both.

SMALL MOULD
7 g/$\frac{1}{4}$ oz fresh yeast or 1 level teaspoon dried yeast
$\frac{1}{2}$ teaspoon sugar
75 ml/2 fl oz tepid milk
50 g/2 oz butter
125 g/4 oz plain white flour
$\frac{1}{4}$ teaspoon salt
1 large beaten egg

FOR RHUM BABA
25 g/1 oz currants

LARGE MOULD
Bare 15 g/$\frac{1}{2}$ oz fresh yeast or 2 level teaspoons dried yeast
1 level teaspoon sugar
75 ml/2 fl oz tepid milk
75 g/3 oz butter
175 g/6 oz plain white flour
$\frac{1}{4}$ teaspoon salt
2 small eggs

1. Grease and flour mould.
2. Mix yeast and sugar in the milk. If using dried yeast leave mixture in a warm place until it begins to froth up.
3. Rub butter into flour and salt.
4. Mix in yeast mixture and beaten egg, adding 25 g/1 oz currants if making Rhum Baba. Beat well until bubbles appear in batter.
5. Pour into tin. Cover and rise until tin is three-quarters full.
6. Bake in centre of a moderately hot oven, Gas 6, 400°F, 200°C, for 20 to 25 minutes, until springy, golden brown, and will come away from the sides of the tin. If browning too quickly, reduce heat after 15 minutes to moderate, Gas 4, 350°F, 180°C.

TO FINISH
Rhum Baba. Place on wire rack over a deep plate, prick all over with skewer, and soak with warm syrup.

Syrup: dissolve 50 g/2 oz sugar in 150 ml/$\frac{1}{4}$ pint hot water. Simmer a few minutes until glossy. Add rum to taste. Pleasant if served slightly warm.

Savarin. As above, soaking in warm syrup flavoured with sherry if liked.

Allow to cool and decorate with fruit and whipped cream. If using tinned fruits the syrup from the tin may be used.

SWEDISH TEA RING

Serves 4

225 g/8 oz plain flour
$\frac{1}{4}$ teaspoon salt
50 g/2 oz margarine
40 g/1$\frac{1}{2}$ oz sugar
15 g/$\frac{1}{2}$ oz fresh yeast or 7 g/$\frac{1}{4}$ oz dried
150 ml/$\frac{1}{4}$ pint warm milk and water mixed
1 beaten egg

MARZIPAN FILLING
40 g/1$\frac{1}{2}$ oz ground almonds
40 g/1$\frac{1}{2}$ oz caster sugar
Beaten egg

DECORATION
A little glacé icing
4 glacé cherries, chopped
Angelica, chopped
25 g/1 oz chopped walnuts

1. Sieve flour and salt, rub in margarine, add sugar, except for one level teaspoon.
2. In a small jug work together the yeast and the level teaspoon of sugar until it is liquid. Add a little of the warm milk and water mixture to the jug. If using dried yeast, combine yeast, sugar and enough liquid to dissolve and leave jug in a warm place to froth up.
3. Make a well in the centre of the flour and pour in the yeast liquid. If using fresh yeast, leave it to become frothy, about 10 to 15 minutes. If using dried yeast, it is better to wait until you are certain it is active before adding to flour.
4. Add beaten egg and more milk if required to make a soft dough.

5. Turn out and knead well until the dough is smooth and elastic, about 10 minutes. Leave aside in a warm place to rise for about 1 hour until doubled in size.

6. Roll out dough to a rectangle 30 by 10 cm/12 by 4 inches.

7. Make up almond paste by mixing ground almonds and caster sugar with just enough egg to bind. Form it into a roll about 30 cm/12 inches long.

8. Lay the roll of paste on the dough and roll up.

9. Form it into a ring on a greased baking tray and leave aside, covered lightly, to rise again until doubled in size.

10. Bake above middle of a hot oven, Gas 7, 425°F, 220°C, for 20 to 25 minutes.

11. Remove it on to a wire rack to cool.

12. When cold, spread with a little glacé icing and scatter chopped cherries, angelica and nuts on top while icing is wet.

IRISH SODA BREADS

The mixing of soda bread is done lightly and quickly, like scones. This ensures light fluffy results. Freezes well, up to 6 months.

(i) Brown
275 g/10 oz wholewheat flour
175 g/6 oz strong plain white flour
2 teaspoons sugar (optional but not traditional)
1 teaspoon bicarbonate of soda
1 teaspoon salt
1 teaspoon cream of tartar*
About 300 ml/½ pint milk*

It is usually made with sour milk which makes its own contribution to the rising. If fresh milk is used then add cream of tartar, but not otherwise.

1. Put wholewheat flour in a large bowl and sieve in all the other dry ingredients.

2. Mix to a soft dough with the milk, adding extra if required. The dough should be slack but not wet.

3. With floured hands knead until smooth, then flatten the dough into a circle about 3.5 cm/1½ inches thick. Put on a greased baking tin, score a large cross over the top.

4. Bake in a moderately hot oven, Gas 5, 375°F, 190°C, for about 40 minutes. The bread should feel light when fully cooked.

Eat fresh.

Mrs June Hodgson
Loch Corrib, Ireland

(ii) Wholewheat
250 g/9 oz self-raising wholewheat flour
½ level teaspoon salt
½ level teaspoon Barbados sugar
10 g/¼ oz butter or margarine
150 ml/¼ pint buttermilk or sour milk

1. Mix flour, salt and sugar in a large bowl.

2. Rub in butter or margarine.

3. Mix in the milk to form a soft dough.

4. Turn on to a floured surface and knead lightly to form a smooth dough. Shape into a small, round, flat loaf.

5. Place on a lightly-floured baking sheet and brush top with a little milk.

6. With a sharp knife slash a cross on the top.

7. Bake on centre shelf of a moderately hot oven, Gas 6, 400°F, 200°C, for 30 minutes. Cool on a wire rack.

Eat the same day. Easily made with double quantities, in which case bake for 40 minutes.

(iii) Using Granary Flour
450 g/1 lb granary flour
225 g/8 oz strong plain white flour, or 175 g/
   6 oz of this plus 50 g/2 oz bran
1 teaspoon bicarbonate of soda
1 teaspoon cream of tartar
1 teaspoon salt
2 teaspoons sugar
Just under 600 ml/1 pint milk or milk and
   water mixed

1. Put granary flour in a large bowl. Sieve in white flour, bicarbonate of soda, cream of tartar and salt. Add bran, if used.

2. Now gradually mix with milk until dough is soft but not wet.

3. Turn out on to a floured board and knead fairly quickly until smooth.

4. Flatten the dough into a large circle about 3.5 cm/ 1½ inches thick. Place it on a greased baking tin. Score over the top a large cross (this ensures even distribution of heat).

5. Bake in a moderately hot oven, Gas 5, 375°F, 190°C, for about 50 to 60 minutes. Test with a skewer to check that it is fully cooked. The skewer will come out clean if the bread is ready.

CHEESE AND WALNUT LOAF

225 g/8 oz self-raising flour
1 level tablespoon dry mustard, bare measure
A good pinch of salt
A shake of pepper
125 g/4 oz margarine
125 g/4 oz grated Cheddar cheese
25 g/1 oz chopped walnuts
2 beaten eggs
150 ml/$\frac{1}{4}$ pint milk

1. Sieve together into a bowl the flour, mustard, salt
and pepper.
2. Rub in margarine.
3. Mix in cheese and walnuts.
4. Add eggs and milk and mix well.
5. Grease a 450 g/1 lb loaf tin and line base with
greased, greaseproof paper. Tip mixture in.
6. Bake just below middle of a moderately hot oven,
Gas 5, 375°F, 190°C, for 1$\frac{1}{2}$ hours. Leave to cool for
a few minutes before turning out on to wire cooling
rack.

Eat cold with butter.

Mrs M. Owen
Elworth, Cheshire

APPLE CAKE

Serves 4

175 g/6 oz self-raising white flour
75 g/3 oz margarine, lard or good dripping
175 g/6 oz apples, weight when peeled and
    cored
75 g/3 oz sugar
Milk

1. Rub fat into flour.
2. Add the diced apple.
3. Cover well with the sugar and mix together with
a little milk into a very firm dough.
4. Roll out if it will or, if a bit sticky, press out to a
round about 18 to 20 cm/7 or 8 inches across. Mark
into sections.
5. Put on a greased baking sheet and bake in a
moderately hot oven, Gas 5, 375°F, 190°C, for 20
minutes. Then reduce heat to moderate, Gas 3,
325°F, 160°C, for a further 20 to 25 minutes until
the apples are cooked.

Split open, butter well and eat hot. Good as a pudding eaten hot with custard or thin cream.

Mrs Joan Ireland
West Suffolk

WALNUT AND APPLE TEABREAD

All-in-one mix.

1 large apple
50 g/2 oz chopped walnuts
125 g/4 oz soft brown sugar
125 g/4 oz soft margarine
125 g/4 oz sultanas or raisins
2 large eggs
1 tablespoon honey
175 g/6 oz self-raising flour
50 g/2 oz wholemeal flour
1 teaspoon mixed spice
Pinch of salt

1. Grease a 900 g/2 lb loaf tin or two 450 g/1 lb loaf
tins and line with greased, greaseproof paper.
2. Peel, core and chop apple.
3. Place all ingredients in a large bowl and beat well
for 2 minutes.
4. Put mixture into the prepared tins.
5. Bake in a moderate oven, Gas 4, 350°F, 180°C,
for 1 hour. Reduce heat to Gas 3, 325°F, 160°C, for
a further 15 to 20 minutes.
6. Turn out on to a wire rack to cool.

Serve sliced with butter.

Sybil Norcott
Irlam, Nr Manchester

BANANA LOAF

A good use for over-ripe bananas.

Freezes well packed in a polythene bag with all air
excluded.

2 ripe bananas
50 g/2 oz margarine
150 g/5 oz caster sugar
2 eggs
225 g/8 oz self-raising flour*
A pinch of salt

**If you prefer wholewheat flour, this works with half whole-
wheat and half white. If you cannot buy self-raising wholewheat, add $\frac{1}{2}$ teaspoon baking powder.*

1. Mash bananas.
2. Cream margarine and sugar.
3. Beat in eggs.
4. Add flour, salt and banana and mix well.

5. Put in a greased and floured 675 g/1½ lb loaf tin, or slightly larger.

6. Bake in middle of a moderately hot oven, Gas 5, 375°F, 190°C, for about 1 hour, until loaf is golden brown, springy to touch and shrinking slightly from sides of tin.

7. Turn loaf out on to a wire rack to cool.

Serve sliced and thinly-buttered, this is delicious.

Anne Wallace
Stewarton, Ayrshire

BUN LOAF

225 g/8 oz mixed dried fruit
175 ml/6 fl oz cold strained tea
225 g/8 oz self-raising white flour
Pinch of salt
125 g/4 oz soft brown sugar
1 beaten egg

1. Soak fruit in tea overnight.
2. Place flour, salt and sugar in bowl.
3. Drain the fruit, reserving liquid.
4. Mix fruit and beaten egg into flour using a little liquid to make a firm dropping consistency. Depending on size of egg, about 1 to 2 tablespoons of liquid will be required.
5. Grease a 450 g/1 lb loaf tin and line base with greased, greaseproof paper. Tin ought to be at least 1 litre/1½ pints capacity.
6. Bake in a moderate oven, Gas 4, 350°F, 180°C, for about 1 hour, until firm.
7. Leave in tin about 5 minutes. Then turn on to wire rack to cool.

Mrs V. Nation
Lambeth, London

CANADIAN MALT BREAD

375 g/13 oz sultanas
50 g/2 oz butter
325 ml/12 fl oz hot water
375 g/13 oz self-raising flour
½ teaspoon bicarbonate of soda
250 g/9 oz sugar
2 beaten eggs

1. Put sultanas, butter and water in a pan, bring to the boil and simmer for 4 minutes. Allow to cool a little.

2. Mix together flour, bicarbonate of soda and sugar.
3. Mix warm fruit mixture into flour mixture.
4. Mix in the beaten eggs.
5. Grease two 450 g/1 lb loaf tins and put in the mixture. Level the tops.
6. Bake in a moderately hot oven, Gas 5, 375°F, 190°C, for 1 hour.

Mrs J. Barsby
Kirkby in Ashfield, Notts

DATE BREAD

225 g/8 oz dates
½ teaspoon bicarbonate of soda
150 ml/¼ pint milk and water mixed
40 g/1½ oz butter or margarine
225 g/8 oz self-raising flour
125 g/4 oz sugar

1. Chop dates and put in a bowl with bicarbonate of soda.
2. Heat milk and water to boiling point and pour over the dates. Leave to cool.
3. Rub butter or margarine into flour.
4. Add sugar.
5. Drain dates, saving liquid, and mix them in with enough liquid to form a fairly soft mixture.
6. Grease a 450 g/1 lb loaf tin and line it with greased, greaseproof paper.
7. Put mixture in tin.
8. Bake just below middle of a moderate oven, Gas 3, 325°F, 170°C, for 1 hour, until well-risen, brown and firm on top.

Mrs M. Naylor
Manston, Leeds

DATE AND WALNUT LOAF

225 g/8 oz chopped dates
125 g/4 oz caster sugar or vanilla sugar* (preferable)
A pinch of salt
1 level teaspoon bicarbonate of soda
50 g/2 oz margarine
175 ml/6 fl oz water
1 beaten egg
50 g/2 oz chopped walnuts
225 g/8 oz self-raising flour

*1 teaspoon vanilla essence (if vanilla sugar is not used)

1. Place dates, sugar, salt, soda and margarine (cut into small pieces) in a mixing bowl.

2. Boil water, pour over, and mix well to melt margarine. Cool a little.

3. Add beaten egg, walnuts and flour, and vanilla essence if used, and mix to a smooth, batter-type consistency.

4. Grease a 900 g/2 lb loaf tin and line base with greaseproof paper. Pour mixture in.

5. Bake in centre of a moderate oven, Gas 3, 325°F, 160°C, for approximately $1\frac{1}{4}$ hours until firm. Cool in tin 10 to 15 minutes, then turn out on to a wire rack.

Eat cold sliced and buttered. Ideal for picnics or packed lunches as well as teatime. Keeps well.

GIPSY BREAD

275 g/10 oz self-raising flour
Pinch of salt
Pinch of mixed spice
$\frac{1}{2}$ teaspoon ground ginger
125 g/4 oz soft brown sugar
175 g/6 oz sultanas
25 to 50 g/1 to 2 oz chopped peel
175 g/6 oz black treacle
1 tablespoon milk and a little extra
1 egg
$\frac{1}{4}$ teaspoon bicarbonate of soda

1. Grease a 900 g/2 lb loaf tin well.
2. Mix together in a bowl flour, salt, mixed spice, ginger, sugar, sultanas and peel.
3. In a pan, warm treacle with 1 tablespoon milk. Do not boil. Remove from heat, add egg and whisk.
4. Dissolve bicarbonate of soda in a little milk and add with treacle mixture to ingredients in bowl.
5. Mix well and pour into loaf tin.
6. Bake in a moderate oven, Gas 4, 350°F, 180°C, for three quarters of an hour. Then reduce heat to Gas 3, 325°F, 160°C, for a further half hour.
7. Cool in tin for 10 minutes. Turn out on to wire cooling rack.

Eat sliced and spread with butter.

Kate Easlea
Hampshire

GRANDMA BASTON'S FRUIT BREAD

This keeps well, and will also freeze well.

This quantity makes 3 large loaves but easy to make one third or two thirds of this quantity.

325 g/12 oz currants
325 g/12 oz raisins
225 g/8 oz sultanas
900 g/2 lb plain white flour
1 dessertspoon baking powder
A pinch of salt
325 g/12 oz butter or margarine
450 g/1 lb moist brown sugar
3 beaten eggs
About 150 ml/$\frac{1}{4}$ pint milk
$\frac{1}{2}$ teaspoon bicarbonate of soda
50 g/2 oz mixed peel, grated or fine-chopped
50 g/2 oz glacé cherries, chopped

1. The day before baking put currants, raisins and sultanas in a basin of hot water to cover. Leave to steep for 2 or 3 hours.
2. Then squeeze out excess moisture and spread fruit in a large baking tin. Put it to dry in a warm place, stirring the fruit from time to time.
3. Sieve flour, baking powder and salt into a large bowl.
4. Rub in fat and add sugar.
5. Mix in eggs and enough milk to achieve a fairly stiff mixture. Continue mixing until consistency is smooth.
6. Mix bicarbonate of soda with 1 tablespoon milk and add to the mixture.
7. Lastly, add fruit, peel and cherries. Stir well.
8. Grease three 900 g/2 lb loaf tins and line the bottoms with greaseproof paper. Divide the mixture between them.
9. Bake below middle of a moderate oven, Gas 4, 350°F, 180°C, for $2\frac{1}{2}$ to 3 hours until well-risen and firm to the touch.

Mrs Patricia Chantry
Hook, Goole, N. Humberside

HONEY RAISIN LOAF

175 g/6 oz wholewheat flour
175 g/6 oz self-raising flour
½ teaspoon salt
40 g/1½ oz soft brown sugar
275 g/10 oz seedless raisins
50 g/2 oz chopped walnuts (optional)
40 g/1½ oz butter or margarine
10 tablespoons honey
1 beaten egg
Grated rind of 1 orange
¼ teaspoon bicarbonate of soda
150 ml/¼ pint milk

1. Mix together flours, salt and sugar in a large bowl.
2. Mix in raisins and walnuts.
3. Melt butter or margarine with honey until runny. Do not overheat. Add to bowl and mix in.
4. Add beaten egg and orange rind.
5. Mix bicarbonate of soda into a little of the milk and add with the rest of the milk.
6. Mix well together.
7. Grease and flour, or line with greased, greaseproof paper, a 900 g/2 lb loaf tin.
8. Pour in the mixture.
9. Bake in centre of a moderate oven, Gas 3, 325°F, 160°C, for 1½ hours.

This cake improves with keeping. Try and keep it a week, or at least 2 to 3 days, before cutting.

Renée Rouston
Kippax, W. Yorkshire

MARY BERRY'S HONEY AND ALMOND LOAF

175 g/6 oz butter
75 g/3 oz caster sugar
3 tablespoons clear honey
3 eggs, beaten
225 g/8 oz self-raising white flour, sifted
150 g/5 oz glacé cherries, quartered
3 tablespoons milk

TOPPING
2 level tablespoons clear honey
25 g/1 oz blanched split almonds, toasted
25 g/1 oz glacé cherries, quartered

1. Well grease and line a 900 g/2 lb loaf tin (about 20 by 12 by 8 cm/8 by 4½ by 3 inches deep).

2. Cream together butter, sugar and honey until it is light and creamy.
3. Beat in the egg a little at a time, beating well after each addition. Add a tablespoon of the flour with the last amount of egg.
4. Blend cherries with flour and fold in with milk.
5. Turn mixture into the prepared loaf tin and bake in a moderate oven, Gas 4, 350°F, 180°C, for 55 to 60 minutes. Turn loaf out to cool on a wire rack.
6. Heat honey for topping in a pan until warm. Add prepared almonds and cherries, then spoon over top of loaf.

Note. The topping is delicious but if you prefer you can leave it plain and serve sliced with butter instead.

LAGER LOAF

This loaf smells delicious whilst cooking and is even more delicious sliced and buttered for tea. It will keep well as it does not go dry quickly.

75 g/3 oz butter
1 tablespoon golden syrup or treacle
75 g/3 oz soft brown sugar
2 eggs
275 g/10 oz self-raising flour
¼ teaspoon bicarbonate of soda
½ teaspoon cream of tartar
Pinch salt
150 ml/¼ pint lager
2 bananas, peeled and mashed
125 g/4 oz dates, chopped
50 g/2 oz walnuts, chopped

1. Well grease a 900 g/2 lb loaf tin or two 450 g/1 lb loaf tins.
2. Gently heat the butter, syrup and sugar in a saucepan until melted. Remove from heat and whisk the eggs into the mixture.
3. Sift flour, bicarbonate of soda, cream of tartar and salt into a bowl.
4. With a wooden spoon briskly mix in the syrup mixture and add the lager. Mix to a smooth batter then quickly add the mashed bananas, chopped dates and walnuts. Pour the mixture into the prepared loaf tin.
5. Bake in the centre of a moderate oven, Gas 4, 350°F, 180°C, for 1½ hours. Turn out on to a cake-rack and cool.

Serve sliced and buttered.

MALTED WHOLEWHEAT TEABREAD

350 g/12 oz wholewheat flour
2 level teaspoons baking powder
$\frac{1}{2}$ level teaspoon salt
50 g/2 oz muscovado sugar
50 g/2 oz sultanas
50 g/2 oz dates
2 rounded tablespoons malt extract
50 g/2 oz butter or margarine
150 ml/$\frac{1}{4}$ pint plus 1 tablespoon milk
2 beaten eggs

1. Mix flour, baking powder and salt in a large bowl.
2. Add sugar and sultanas.
3. Chop the dates and mix in.
4. Gently heat malt and butter or margarine together until fat has just melted.
5. Add milk to beaten eggs.
6. Combine malt mixture with egg and milk mixture and stir into dry ingredients.
7. Mix together to form a soft dough.
8. Turn mixture into a greased 900 g/2 lb loaf tin, or into two greased 450 g/1 lb tins. Level the surface of the mixture.
9. Bake in a warm oven, Gas 3, 325°F, 160°C, for 1 hour. Then turn out to cool on a wire rack.

Wrap in foil and keep one day before eating and the bread will be nice and moist. Freezes well.

Serve sliced and buttered.

NUTTY TREACLE BREAD

50 g/2 oz soft margarine
75 g/3 oz sugar
175 g/6 oz (6 level teaspoons) dark treacle
225 ml/8 fl oz milk
75 g/3 oz plain flour
3 teaspoons baking powder
1 small teaspoon salt
225 g/8 oz wholewheat flour
75 g/3 oz chopped walnuts

1. Grease a 900 g/2 lb loaf tin and line base with greased, greaseproof paper.
2. Beat together margarine, sugar and treacle and beat in milk.

3. Sift together plain flour, baking powder and salt. Add with wholemeal flour and walnuts to milk mixture. Mix to a dough.
4. Spoon into tin and level the top.
5. Bake in a moderate oven, Gas 3, 325°F, 160°C, for about $1\frac{1}{4}$ hours until firm to the touch and shrinking slightly from sides of tin.

OLD-FASHIONED SPICE BREAD

2 level teaspoons dried yeast, or 15 g/$\frac{1}{2}$ oz fresh yeast
$\frac{1}{2}$ teaspoon sugar
150 ml/$\frac{1}{4}$ pint tepid milk
325 g/12 oz plain flour
$\frac{1}{2}$ teaspoon salt
$\frac{1}{2}$ teaspoon mixed spice
$\frac{1}{2}$ teaspoon powdered cinnamon
$\frac{1}{2}$ teaspoon bicarbonate of soda
50 g/2 oz margarine
50 g/2 oz lard
175 g/6 oz soft brown sugar
125 g/4 oz currants
125 g/4 oz sultanas
50 g/2 oz chopped candied peel
1 beaten egg
1 dessertspoon dark treacle
A little more milk, as required

1. Grease a 900 g/2 lb loaf tin and line base with greased, greaseproof paper.
2. Add dried yeast and sugar to milk, stir and leave until frothy (note manufacturer's directions on packet).
Or, if using fresh yeast, stir into milk with sugar to dissolve. This mixture can be used at once.
3. Sieve together flour, salt, spices and bicarbonate of soda.
4. Rub in fats, add soft brown sugar and fruit.
5. Add yeast mixture, egg and treacle. Mix together adding a little more milk, about 2 to 3 tablespoons, if necessary, to make a dropping consistency.
6. Spoon into tin and level the top.
7. Bake in a cool oven, Gas 2, 300°F, 150°C, for $1\frac{1}{2}$ hours, until firm on top and leaving sides of tin.
8. Leave in tin about 10 minutes, then remove and cool on a wire rack.

Serve sliced and buttered. It is particularly good with Wensleydale cheese. Keeps well.

BASIC SCONE MIXTURE

225 g/8 oz self-raising white flour
$\frac{1}{4}$ teaspoon salt
50 g/2 oz margarine
5 to 6 tablespoons milk

1. Sift flour and salt into a bowl, and rub in the margarine.
2. Mix to a soft, but not sticky, dough with milk.
3. Turn out on to a floured board, knead very lightly, and roll out just over 1 cm/half an inch thick.
4. Cut into 5 cm/2 inch rounds, re-rolling and cutting the trimmings, and place on a lightly greased baking tray.
5. Bake in a hot oven, Gas 7, 425°F, 220°C, for 12 to 14 minutes until lightly golden and firm to the touch.

Serve with a savoury filling such as:—
50 g/2 oz softened margarine or butter, 50 g/2 oz finely-grated cheese, $\frac{1}{2}$ level teaspoon mixed mustard beaten together.
Or, beat together 50 g/2 oz softened butter or margarine and 1 good teaspoon chopped, fresh parsley with salt and pepper to taste.

Try also the following:

Herb Scones
1. After rubbing in the margarine, add a shake of pepper and 1 level teaspoon of mixed dried herbs, then mix to a soft, but not sticky, dough with the milk.
2. Turn out on to a floured board, knead very lightly, and roll out just over 1 cm/$\frac{1}{2}$ an inch thick.
3. Cut into about 10 fingers, place them on a lightly-greased baking tray and brush with milk.
4. Bake in a hot oven, Gas 7, 425°F, 220°C, for 12 to 14 minutes as for basic scone recipe.

Cheese Scones
After rubbing margarine into flour and salt, add $\frac{1}{2}$ teaspoon dry mustard, a pinch of cayenne pepper, 75 g/3 oz finely-grated cheese. Finish according to basic recipe.

Sweet Scones
After rubbing margarine into flour and salt, add 25 g/1 oz caster sugar and 50 g/2 oz sultanas. Finish according to basic recipe.

WHOLEMEAL SCONES

Makes about 10
125 g/4 oz plain white flour
$\frac{1}{2}$ level teaspoon salt
$\frac{1}{2}$ teaspoon bicarbonate of soda
1 teaspoon cream of tartar
125 g/4 oz wholemeal flour
25 g/1 oz caster sugar
40 g/1$\frac{1}{2}$ oz lard
Bare 150 ml/$\frac{1}{4}$ pint milk

1. Sieve together the plain flour, salt, soda and cream of tartar into a bowl.
2. Add wholemeal flour and sugar.
3. Rub in the lard.
4. Mix to a soft, but not sticky, dough with as much milk as necessary. It could leave a tablespoon of milk. Knead lightly until smooth.
5. Roll out just over 1 cm/$\frac{1}{2}$ inch thick and cut into 6 cm/2$\frac{1}{2}$ inch rounds.
6. Bake on greased tray above centre of a hot oven, Gas 7, 425°F, 220°C, for about 12 minutes.

WHOLEWHEAT SCONES

Makes 10
175 g/6 oz wholewheat flour
50 g/2 oz plain flour
1 teaspoon cream of tartar
$\frac{1}{2}$ teaspoon bicarbonate of soda
$\frac{1}{4}$ teaspoon salt
50 g/2 oz dark brown sugar, try muscovado
1$\frac{1}{2}$ tablespoons safflower or sunflower oil
1 egg
75 to 125 ml/3 to 4 fl oz milk

1. Mix dry ingredients, sifting cream of tartar and bicarbonate of soda with plain flour and salt.
2. Beat oil, egg and milk together.
3. Mix this into the dry ingredients adding a little more milk if necessary, sufficient to make a soft elastic dough.
4. Turn dough on to a floured board and knead it lightly.
5. Roll out just over 2 cm/1 inch thick. Cut into rounds. Place the scones on lightly-greased baking sheets.

6. Bake in a very hot oven, Gas 8, 450°F, 230°C, for 10 to 12 minutes, when scones will be browned and nicely risen.

Note: wholemeal scones tend not to rise as much as plain white ones.

7. Slide scones on to a wire rack to cool.

Anne Wallace
Stewarton, Ayrshire

YOGHURT WHOLEMEAL SCONES

Makes 8

225 g/8 oz wholewheat flour
½ teaspoon salt
1½ teaspoons baking powder
25 g/1 oz margarine
150 ml/¼ pint yoghurt

1. Mix together flour, salt and baking powder.
2. Rub in margarine.
3. Form into a stiff dough with the yoghurt.
4. Turn on to a floured board and shape with the hands until 2 cm/¾ inch thick.
5. Cut into rounds with a pastry cutter.
6. Place on a lightly-greased baking tray and bake in a moderately hot oven, Gas 6, 400°F, 200°C, for 10 to 12 minutes.

Serve hot with butter.

Sybil Norcott
Irlam, Nr Manchester

CHEESE OATMEAL SCONES

Makes 6 to 8

125 g/4 oz plain flour
½ teaspoon bicarbonate of soda
1 teaspoon cream of tartar
½ teaspoon salt
25 g/1 oz margarine or lard
125 g/4 oz oatmeal
50 g/2 oz grated cheese
A little milk

1. Sift together into a bowl the flour, bicarbonate of soda, cream of tartar and salt.
2. Rub in fat. Mix in oatmeal and cheese.
3. Add enough milk to form a stiffish dough.

4. Turn dough on to a floured board, knead lightly, roll out quite thick and cut into rounds.
5. Put scones on a greased baking sheet.
6. Bake in a hot oven, Gas 8, 450°F, 230°C, for 12 minutes.

Mrs Margaret Hussey
Leeds

CORN MUFFINS

Makes 12

175 g/6 oz wholewheat flour
125 g/4 oz cornflour
3 teaspoons baking powder
½ teaspoon salt
1 egg
2 tablespoons honey
300 ml/½ pint milk
2 tablespoons oil
Half a 190 g/7 oz tin of sweetcorn
75 g/3 oz grated cheese

1. Mix flours, baking powder and salt.
2. In another bowl mix egg, honey and milk. Then mix this thoroughly into flours.
3. Stir in oil, sweetcorn and cheese.
4. Grease a tray of 12 deep bun tins, and spoon in the mixture.
5. Bake near top of a hot oven, Gas 7, 425°F, 220°C, for 10 to 12 minutes.

Delicious served piping hot with cheese or soups, or with New England Casserole (*see page 168*).

Sarah Brown
Scarborough, Yorkshire

CHEESE AND POTATO SCONES

Makes 6 or 8

225 g/8 oz cold, cooked potato, mashed
50 g/2 oz margarine
50 g/2 oz plain flour
Salt and pepper
75 g/3 oz grated cheese
Oil, pork or bacon dripping, to fry

1. Prepare the potato.
2. Warm margarine to soften but do not melt.

3. Mix margarine into potato with flour, a little salt and pepper and the cheese.

4. Form into rounds about 1 cm/½ inch thick on a floured board.

5. Put in fridge to stiffen up.

6. Heat 2 teaspoons of oil in a frying pan and fry scones until golden brown, 3 minutes on each side. Drain on kitchen paper.

FRIED INDIAN WHOLEWHEAT FLOUR BREAD

These are known as puris. They are usually eaten with vegetables, or at the start of a meal, and are a great favourite among children and adults alike.

They go well with Cauliflower Bhaji (*see page 150*), Curried Bhindi (*see page 149*) and Onion Salad (*see page 144*).

This quantity makes 12 or 13

175 g/6 oz wholewheat flour
175 g/6 oz plain white flour
1½ teaspoons salt
2 teaspoons oil
150 to 175 ml/5 to 6 fl oz tepid water
Oil for deep frying

1. In a bowl mix flours, salt, 2 teaspoons oil and sufficient water to form a soft pliable dough.

2. Knead the dough thoroughly and leave covered at room temperature for about 1 hour.

3. Roll out one third of the dough at a time into a large pancake, less than 7 mm/¼ inch thick. Cut circles about 6 to 8 cm/2½ to 3 inches in diameter, using a pastry cutter or wine glass.

4. The success of a puri is in its cooking. The oil should be heated until it begins to smoke, and the puris should be carefully immersed one at a time.

5. After about 6 seconds in the hot oil the puri will begin to surface. Using a frying spoon, gently pat it down to keep it submerged in the hot oil until it puffs up.

6. Turn it over and allow it to cook for a couple of seconds more. This whole frying process should take about 15 to 20 seconds per puri.

Priya Wickramasinghe
Cardiff

FRUIT SCONES

Makes 8

225 g/8 oz plain flour
½ level teaspoon salt
½ teaspoon bicarbonate of soda
1 teaspoon cream of tartar
40 g/1½ oz margarine
25 g/1 oz caster sugar
25 to 40 g/1 to 1½ oz sultanas or currants
Bare 150 ml/¼ pint milk

1. Sieve together the flour, salt, soda and cream of tartar into a bowl.

2. Rub in the margarine.

3. Add sugar, sultanas (or currants).

4. Mix to a soft, but not sticky, dough with as much milk as necessary. It could leave a tablespoon of milk. Knead lightly until smooth.

5. Roll out just over 1 cm/½ inch thick and cut into 6 cm/2½ inch rounds.

6. Bake on greased tray above centre of a hot oven, Gas 7, 425°F, 220°C, for about 12 minutes.

LEMON SCONES

Makes 12 to 14

225 g/8 oz plain or wholewheat flour
Pinch of salt
1 rounded teaspoon cream of tartar
1 level teaspoon bicarbonate of soda
50 g/2 oz margarine
35 g/1¼ oz Barbados sugar
Grated rind 1 lemon
150 ml/¼ pint milk

1. Set oven at hot, Gas 7, 425°F, 220°C.

2. Grease a baking sheet.

3. Sieve together or mix well the flour, salt, cream of tartar and bicarbonate of soda. Rub in the margarine.

4. Add the sugar and lemon rind and mix well.

5. Mix to a soft dough with the milk.

6. Roll out lightly and quite thick on a floured board.

7. Cut into rounds with a 5 cm/2 inch cutter. You should get 12 to 14 scones.

8. Place on greased baking sheet.

9. Brush tops with a little milk.

10. Bake for 10 to 12 minutes until nicely-risen and golden brown.
11. Cool on a wire rack.
12. Cut scones across and spread with lemon curd.
13. Pipe fresh whipped cream on the top.

Stella Boldy
Sykehouse, N. Humberside

OLD HANNAH'S POTATO CAKES

Ideal for freezing uncooked. Left-over cooked ones can be reheated but have a crispy surface.

Makes 10

225 g/8 oz self-raising flour, either white or a mixture of white and wholewheat*
½ teaspoon salt
50 g/2 oz butter or margarine
225 g/8 oz left-over mashed or creamed potatoes
1 beaten egg
A little milk if required

Use ½ teaspoon baking powder if you cannot buy self-raising wholewheat flour.

1. Place flour and salt (plus baking powder if needed) in a bowl with the fat.
2. Rub the fat into the flour.
3. Rub or fork in the potatoes.
4. Make a well in centre of the bowl and drop in the beaten egg.
5. Fork egg into mixture using a little milk if necessary to give a soft pliable dough. Finish by kneading until the dough is smooth.
6. Place dough on a floured board and roll out to just over 1 cm/½ inch thickness. Cut into rounds about 5 to 8 cm/2 to 3 inches in diameter. If no large cutter is available use the top of a glass or cup.
7. Space out on baking sheet and bake for 30 minutes in a moderately hot oven, Gas 5, 375°F, 190°C.
8. Take out of oven and wrap in a clean tea-towel to keep them soft and warm.
9. Split and butter or fill with jam or syrup. Eat while hot.

Mrs Sybil Norcott
Irlam, Nr Manchester

SCONE DROPS

Makes 12 to 15

190 g/7 oz self-raising flour
25 g/1 oz porridge oats
125 g/4 oz margarine
75 g/3 oz sugar
50 g/2 oz mixed dried fruit
6 glacé cherries, chopped
1 large beaten egg
A little milk

1. Mix flour and oats in a bowl.
2. Rub in margarine.
3. Add sugar, dried fruit and cherries.
4. Mix in the beaten egg, using a fork. Add a dessertspoon of milk if too stiff to mix.
5. Put rough heaps on a greased baking sheet.
6. Bake near top of a moderately hot oven, Gas 5, 375°F, 190°C, for 10 to 15 minutes.

Nice hot or cold. Freeze and reheat well.

Margaret Heywood
Todmorden, Yorkshire

SUSSEX HEAVIES

Not a bit heavy, just simple nicely-flavoured fruit scones.

Makes 10

225 g/8 oz self-raising white flour, or half white and half wholewheat*
A pinch of salt
25 g/1 oz caster sugar
50 g/2 oz lard
50 g/2 oz mixed currants and raisins
175 ml/6 fl oz sour milk, or fresh milk 'soured' with juice of half a lemon

Use ½ teaspoon baking powder if you cannot buy self-raising wholewheat flour.

1. Mix flour, salt and sugar (plus baking powder if needed).
2. Rub in lard and add dried fruit.
3. Mix to a soft dough with most of the liquid.
4. Using a floured board, roll out and cut into 5 cm/2 inch rounds. Brush with remaining sour milk. Place on greased baking sheets.
5. Bake near top of a hot oven, Gas 7, 425°F, 220°C, until golden brown, about 10 minutes.

Mrs Gaye Goodall
Steyning, West Sussex

SCOTTISH CRUMPETS

Makes 10 to 12

1 large egg
1 tablespoon caster sugar
150 ml/¼ pint milk plus 1 extra tablespoon
125 g/4 oz plain white flour
1 good level teaspoon cream of tartar
1 scant level teaspoon bicarbonate of soda
Pinch of salt

1. Beat egg and sugar to a thick cream.
2. Mix in the 150 ml/¼ pint of milk, then the sieved flour.
3. Dissolve cream of tartar, bicarbonate of soda and salt in 1 tablespoon milk and stir gently into mixture.
4. Pour large tablespoons of the mixture on to a heated, ungreased girdle or heavy frying pan, cook till brown, flick over and brown the other side.
5. Cool in a cloth and serve with butter and jam.

Mrs Anne Wallace
Dunlop, Scotland

SCOTCH PANCAKES OR DROP SCONES

Makes 12 to 14

175 g/6 oz plain white flour
A pinch of salt
½ level teaspoon bicarbonate of soda
1 level teaspoon cream of tartar
1 tablespoon caster sugar
1 beaten egg
1 teaspoon golden syrup
150 ml/¼ pint plus about 3 tablespoons milk
A piece of beef suet or lard for greasing

1. Sieve dry ingredients. Add egg, syrup and enough milk to make a pouring batter, but this must not be thin.
2. Heat a heavy frying pan or hot-plate and grease it with the suet or lard. Pour batter on 1 tablespoon at a time, not too close together. When bubbles appear on top of the scone and just start to burst, turn scone over and cook about 1 minute until golden. It is a good idea to test one scone before doing a batch. If the pan is too hot it will brown too quickly before bubbles burst. If too cool bubbles will burst but scone will not be brown.

WHOLEMEAL DROPPED SCONES

These freeze well.

Makes about 15

225 g/8 oz wholemeal flour
1 teaspoon cream of tartar
½ teaspoon bicarbonate of soda
Pinch of salt
50 g/2 oz dark brown Barbados sugar
25 g/1 oz (1 dessertspoon) black treacle
1 egg
200 ml/7 fl oz milk

1. Mix together dry ingredients very thoroughly.
2. Beat together treacle, egg and milk and mix into dry ingredients to make a smooth batter.
3. Heat a girdle or heavy frying pan. (If it is cast aluminium there is no need to grease it.)
4. Drop dessertspoons of mixture on to hot girdle. When scones are full of bubbles and brown, turn them over and bake until brown on other side and cooked through.
5. Place on a cooling rack covered with a clean cloth.

Anne Wallace
Dunlop, Scotland

SAVOURY DROP SCONES OR PANCAKES

Can be made on a girdle, griddle, bakestone or hot-plate—whatever name you give it—or in a heavy frying pan. They freeze well.

Makes about 15

225 g/8 oz plain white or wholewheat flour
1 teaspoon cream of tartar
½ teaspoon bicarbonate of soda
A pinch of salt
1 dessertspoon finely-chopped onion
1 egg
About 150 ml/¼ pint milk

TO GREASE GIRDLE

A knob of beef suet or a very little lard or
    margarine

1. Put flour in a bowl. Sieve in cream of tartar, bicarbonate of soda and salt. Mix in chopped onion.

2. Mix to a thick pouring batter with egg and milk.

3. Heat girdle and grease it if necessary.

4. Drop spoonfuls of batter on girdle. When bubbles appear, turn over and cook other side.

5. Cool scones in a towel. This stops them drying out.

MUFFINS

Made on a girdle or griddle or in a heavy frying pan. Freeze well.

Makes 4

125 g/4 oz plain white flour or half wholewheat and half white
$\frac{1}{2}$ teaspoon cream of tartar
$\frac{1}{4}$ teaspoon bicarbonate of soda
15 g/$\frac{1}{2}$ oz sugar
20 g/$\frac{3}{4}$ oz melted butter or margarine
2 teaspoons of beaten egg
About 4 tablespoons milk
A knob of suet to grease girdle, or a *very* little lard

1. Mix dry ingredients, sifting in cream of tartar and bicarbonate of soda.

2. Mix in butter, egg and enough milk to make a soft dough.

3. Using a floured board, roll out to 1 cm/$\frac{1}{2}$ inch thick. Cut rounds.

4. Heat girdle, grease lightly and cook muffins for 3 to 4 minutes each side until nicely golden brown.

Good to eat hot or cold.

OATMEAL SCONES

Makes 6 to 8

50 g/2 oz medium oatmeal
50 g/2 oz plain wholewheat or white flour
A pinch of salt
1 teaspoon soft brown sugar (or more, to taste)
$\frac{1}{2}$ teaspoon cream of tartar
$\frac{1}{4}$ teaspoon bicarbonate of soda
15 g/$\frac{1}{2}$ oz dripping or bacon fat
About 3 tablespoons milk, to mix

1. Put oatmeal, wholewheat flour, salt and sugar in a bowl.

2. Sift in cream of tartar and bicarbonate of soda to be sure there are no lumps.

3. Rub in fat.

4. Mix to a soft dough with milk.

5. Using a floured board, roll out about 7 mm/$\frac{1}{4}$ inch thick and cut rounds.

6. Cook on a hot, lightly-greased girdle or heavy frying pan for about 4 minutes each side. Cool in a towel.

TREACLE GIRDLE SCONE

225 g/8 oz plain white flour
A pinch of salt
1 teaspoon cream of tartar
1 level teaspoon bicarbonate of soda
$\frac{1}{4}$ teaspoon ground cinnamon
$\frac{1}{4}$ teaspoon ginger
$\frac{1}{4}$ teaspoon mixed spice
1 large tablespoon black treacle
Approximately 150 ml/$\frac{1}{4}$ pint milk

1. Sieve dry ingredients together and make a well in the centre.

2. Pour in slightly-warmed black treacle.

3. Pour milk on top of treacle and gradually draw in flour to make a fairly soft dough.

4. Turn on to a floured board and knead very lightly till smooth and free from cracks.

5. Roll out to a round 1 cm/barely $\frac{1}{2}$ inch thick.

6. Place on a hot, ungreased girdle or in a heavy frying pan. When browned turn over and continue baking till cooked through, about 4 to 5 minutes.

7. Cool in a cloth on a wire tray.

Mrs Anne Wallace
Dunlop, Scotland

POTATO SCONES

Cooked on a girdle or griddle or heavy frying pan. They freeze well.

Serves 4

15 g/$\frac{1}{2}$ oz melted butter or margarine
A pinch of salt
225 g/8 oz cold mashed potato (no lumps)
About 50 g/2 oz plain flour, white or wholewheat
A knob of beef suet, or a little lard to grease girdle

1. Add melted butter or margarine and salt to mashed potatoes.

2. Mix in flour gradually until a working dough is produced.

3. Roll out very thinly. Cut rounds and prick well with a fork.

4. Use a knob of beef suet to grease the girdle lightly.

5. Cook scones on hot girdle for about 3 minutes each side.

6. Cool in a towel.

Eat fresh with butter. Excellent with bacon. Fry in bacon fat with the bacon.

SINGING HINNIE

A real Singing Hinnie would never be cut before it was baked. In order to turn it on the girdle without breaking it into pieces a pair of wooden 'hands' is required.

Serves 3 to 4

125 g/4 oz plain flour
½ teaspoon baking powder
¼ teaspoon salt
25 g/1 oz butter
25 g/1 oz lard
15 g/½ oz currants
Milk and sour cream to mix (sour milk alone
**   can be used)**

1. Sieve together the flour, baking powder and salt.
2. Rub in the fats.
3. Add currants.
4. Mix to a soft dough with a little milk and sour cream (or sour milk).
5. Roll out on floured board a round 18 to 20 cm/7 to 8 inches across. Cut in half or quarters.
6. Heat a girdle or heavy frying pan and grease it— a piece of suet is ideal.
7. Bake about 3 minutes each side until pale golden and firm.

Best eaten hot.

Miss Peggy Howey
Northumberland

WELSH CAKES

These are cooked on a bakestone, as it is known in Wales, or a girdle, as used in Scotland. A heavy-based frying pan gives best results if you have neither of these.

Makes 40 to 50, but they freeze well. Or you can make half quantity, using 1 small egg and very little milk.

450 g/1 lb self-raising flour
A pinch of salt
125 g/4 oz lard
125 g/4 oz margarine
175 g/6 oz granulated sugar
50 g/2 oz currants
1 beaten egg
About 3 tablespoons milk
A little extra lard to grease pan

1. Sift flour and salt into a basin.
2. Rub in lard and margarine.
3. Add sugar and currants.
4. Mix to the consistency of pastry dough with beaten egg and milk.
5. Roll out on a floured board to approximately 7 mm/¼ inch thick. Cut with a 6.5 cm/2½ inch plain scone cutter.
6. Heat bakestone, girdle or heavy frying pan and grease it lightly with lard. It is wise to test heat by cooking one cake on its own. If it is too hot, cakes burn before inside is cooked. Cook cakes on both sides until just golden. Grease pan very lightly between batches.
7. Put on wire rack to cool. Store in a tin or plastic box.

Traditionally eaten cold, but they are hard to resist straight from the pan, especially when children are about. They are never buttered.

Mrs Beryl Hawkins
Little Mill W.I., Gwent

SCOTTISH OATCAKES

Makes about 8

1 tablespoon bacon fat
125 g/4 oz fine to medium oatmeal
A generous pinch of salt
A generous pinch of bicarbonate of soda
Tepid water to mix

1. Melt fat and add to dry ingredients.
2. Bind to a softish dough with water.
3. Sprinkle a little oatmeal on to a board. Turn dough on to it and knead to remove cracks. Roll out thinly into a round.
4. Cut into three 'farls' or even-sized 3-sided pieces. True Scottish oatcakes are always shaped this way.
5. Bake on a hot, ungreased girdle or in a heavy frying pan till edges start to curl.
6. Toast second side under the grill till crisp but not brown.

Mrs Anne Wallace
Dunlop, Scotland

NORFOLK RUSKS

175 g/6 oz self-raising flour
A good pinch of salt
65 g/2½ oz margarine
1 beaten egg

1. Sift flour and salt into a bowl.
2. Rub in margarine.
3. Mix to a firm dough with the egg.
4. Roll out on a floured board to 7 mm/¼ inch thick, cut into rounds and place on a baking sheet.
5. Bake in moderately hot oven, Gas 6, 400°F, 200°C, for 15 to 20 minutes until golden.
6. Remove from oven and, when cool enough to handle, split in half with a sharp knife.
7. Return rusks to oven, cut side up, for 5 minutes longer to dry and colour a little.
8. Turn on to a cooling wire.

Delicious spread with butter, and served with cheese. Keep in an air-tight tin.

Mrs E. M. Bettell
Bedford

OATEN BISCUITS

Makes about 32

125 g/4 oz self-raising white flour
125 g/4 oz medium oatmeal or porridge oats
¼ teaspoon salt
75 g/3 oz firm margarine
2 teaspoons sugar
1 beaten egg

1. Mix together flour, oatmeal and salt.
2. Rub in margarine, add sugar and bind to a firm dough with the beaten egg.
3. Divide mixture into 2 portions for easier rolling and roll out quite thinly on a floured board.
4. Cut into rounds with a plain cutter about 6 cm/2½ inch diameter. Re-roll and cut the trimmings.
5. Place on a lightly-greased baking sheet.
6. Bake in a moderate oven, Gas 4, 350°F, 180°C, for 10 to 12 minutes until firm but not coloured. Do not overbake.

CHEESE CRACKERS

Makes about 20

225 g/8 oz self-raising flour
½ teaspoon salt
75 g/3 oz margarine
Approx. 5 tablespoons water
75 g/3 oz finely-grated cheese

1. Place flour and salt in a bowl and rub in margarine.
2. Mix to a pliable dough with water. Leave to rest for 5 minutes.
3. Roll out on a floured board to an oblong three times as long as wide.
4. Sprinkle 25 g/1 oz of the cheese on bottom two-thirds of pastry, fold top third down, then fold down again. Turn once to the left.
5. Roll out, sprinkle on 25 g/1 oz of cheese as before, fold and turn twice more. Pastry may need to rest before final rolling.
6. Divide dough into 2 pieces. Using a floured board, roll out thinly, 6 mm/less than ¼ inch thick is best. Prick well all over with a fork.
7. Cut into squares about 6 cm/2½ inches across.
8. Place on very lightly-greased baking tray. Bake in a moderately hot oven, Gas 5, 375°F, 190°C, for about 15 minutes.

HONEY BISCUITS

These are like exceptionally good digestive biscuits and are particularly nice with cheese.

Makes about 24

225 g/8 oz wholewheat flour
½ level teaspoon salt
125 g/4 oz margarine or butter
2 tablespoons clear honey

1. Mix flour and salt in a bowl.
2. Rub in margarine or butter.
3. Mix with honey.
4. Using a floured board, roll out thinly and cut into rounds with a 5 cm/2 inch cutter.
5. Bake in a cool oven, Gas 2, 300°F, 150°C, for 20 minutes.

OATCAKES

Makes 20 oatcakes 6.5 cm/2½ inches in diameter

125 g/4 oz vegetable margarine
50 g/2 oz soft brown sugar
125 g/4 oz wholewheat flour
125 g/4 oz porridge oats
A little milk

1. Cream margarine and sugar.
2. Mix in flour and oats and work into a paste. Moisten if necessary with a teaspoon of milk.
3. Using a floured board, roll out about 7 mm/¼ inch thick and cut into rounds. Put on a greased baking tray.
4. Bake just above middle of a moderately hot oven, Gas 5, 375°F, 190°C, for 20 minutes, until pale brown.
5. Take straight off baking tin on to a wire rack to cool.

Sarah Brown
Scarborough, Yorkshire

10

CAKES
BUNS
COOKIES
AND
BISCUITS

FATLESS SPONGE

The mixture can also be used for a sponge flan, sponge drops and sponge fingers.

This quantity is sufficient for one 20 cm/8 inch tin 7.5 cm/3 inches deep. Or for two 15 cm/6 inch sandwich tins.

3 eggs
75 g/3 oz caster sugar
75 g/3 oz plain flour

1. Grease tin and put a circle of greaseproof paper in the bottom.
2. Using an electric mixer or a hand whisk, whip eggs and caster sugar together until very, very thick. It takes at least 5 minutes in an electric mixer-less time in a food processor.
3. Using a sieve, sprinkle about one third of the flour over surface of egg mixture. Fold this in carefully with a spatula using a figure of eight movement. Do this twice more, taking care to cut through the mixture only with sharp edge of spatula in order to keep mixture as fluffy as possible.
4. When flour has been incorporated, pour mixture into tin(s).
5. Bake a 20 cm/8 inch cake in centre of a warm oven, Gas 3, 325°F, 160°C, for about 40 minutes until cake is well-risen, golden, firm to touch and just shrinking from sides of tin.
In 15 cm/6 inch sandwich tins bake for about 30 minutes.

Chocolate Fatless Sponge
When flour has been weighed out, remove 2 teaspoons and replace this with 2 teaspoons sifted cocoa (not drinking chocolate). Proceed as before.

Sponge drops
Using a dessertspoon, drop blobs on a baking tray lined with non-stick paper. Bake at the above temperature for about 12 minutes or until golden. Do not overbake.

Sponge fingers
Using a piping bag with 7 mm/¼ inch plain nozzle, pipe 7.5 cm/3 inch strips on to a baking tin lined with non-stick paper. Use a knife to make a clean cut through the sponge mixture. Bake at the above temperature for about 12 minutes or until golden. Take care not to overbake.

VICTORIA SPONGE

125 g/4 oz margarine
125 g/4 oz caster sugar
2 large eggs
125 g/4 oz self-raising white flour

TO FINISH
2 tablespoons raspberry jam
2 teaspoons caster sugar

1. Grease two 17 to 18 cm/6½ to 7 inch sandwich tins and line their bases with greased grease-proof paper.
2. Beat margarine and sugar until creamy.
3. Add eggs one at a time, beating and adding 2 teaspoons of the flour to prevent curdling.
4. Fold in rest of flour. Pour into tins.
5. Bake in a moderately hot oven, Gas 5, 375°F, 190°C, 20 to 25 minutes until firm on top and shrinking slightly from edges of tins.
6. Remove to wire to cool.
7. When cold, peel off paper and spread raspberry jam on base of one cake. Place the other cake on top so that both bases are together.
8. Sprinkle caster sugar lightly on top.

See also Victoria Sandwich for Small Iced Cakes, page 337, and Mandarin Gâteau, page 323.

4-5-6 SPONGE CAKE

This mixture will make an 18 cm/7 inch sandwich, or one small cake and 4 or 5 Madeleines

125 g/4 oz soft margarine
150 g/5 oz caster sugar
175 g/6 oz self-raising flour
2 large eggs
1 or 2 drops vanilla essence
1 tablespoon boiling water

1. Cream margarine and sugar until light and fluffy.
2. Sieve flour into another bowl.
3. Add eggs one at a time, beating with a spring whisk or an electric whisk between each egg.
4. Fold in flour as lightly as possible, and lastly the vanilla essence and boiling water. With the last of the flour, the consistency should be not quite dropping from the spoon.
5. Grease two 18 cm/7 inch sandwich tins and line bases with a circle of greaseproof paper.

6. Bake for about 15 to 20 minutes in a moderately hot oven, Gas 6, 400°F, 200°C. When done, the cakes should be golden, firm on top and springy.

7. Turn out immediately on to a wire rack.

8. When cool, sandwich together with jam or lemon curd (*see page 370*). Sprinkle caster sugar on top.

Mrs Joan Gould
Hook, Goole, N. Humberside

Madeleines
4-5-6 sponge mixture
2 tablespoons raspberry jam
Desiccated coconut
4 or 5 glacé cherries

1. Grease 4 or 5 dariole moulds or castle pudding tins and stand them on a baking tray.

2. Three quarters fill with above mixture.

3. Bake for 15 minutes as above or until risen and golden brown.

4. Turn out of tins to cool on a wire rack.

5. Coat with melted raspberry jam all over and cover with coconut. Set a cherry on top.

Mrs Joan Gould
Hook, Goole, N. Humberside

SWISS ROLL

65 g/2½ oz soft plain flour
2 eggs
65 g/2½ oz vanilla sugar*
1 dessertspoon warm water
A little extra caster sugar
2 tablespoons jam or lemon curd

*See page 242.

1. Grease a shallow (Swiss Roll) tin approximately 27 by 18 cm/11 by 7 inches and line with greased greaseproof paper.

2. Sift the flour on to a piece of paper and place in the warming drawer of oven so that chill is taken off it.

3. Place eggs and vanilla sugar in a bowl. Place the bowl over a pan of hot water and whisk until thick and pale.

4. Remove bowl from pan and whisk until beaters leave a trail in the mixture.

5. Carefully fold in the warmed flour and warm water.

6. Spread evenly in tin.

7. Bake above centre of a hot oven, Gas 7, 425°F, 220°C, for 7 to 8 minutes until lightly golden and springy to the touch.

8. While cake is baking, place a damp (not wet) tea-towel on table, then a piece of greaseproof paper 5 cm/2 inches all round larger than Swiss roll. Dust this with a little flour and dredge with caster sugar.

9. Prepare jam. If it is a little stiff, warm just sufficiently to spread.

10. As soon as Swiss roll is out of oven turn it out upside-down on to paper, trim off edges quickly, spread with jam and roll up.

For other recipes and gâteaux using the fatless sponge see:
Chocolate Log Cake, page 320.
Grace's Chocolate Fancy, page 265.
Peanut Brittle Gâteau, page 274.
Tipsy Cake, page 276.

CHOCOLATE BUTTER CREAM

125 g/4 oz plain cooking chocolate
125 g/4 oz butter or table margarine
175 g/6 oz icing sugar

1. Break up chocolate in a bowl and put it to melt over a small pan of simmering water. Do not let water touch bowl.

2. Cream butter or margarine and icing sugar.

3. When light, add melted chocolate and beat again.

This filling is worth making in this quantity as it keeps in a cool place or refrigerator for quite some time and can be used as required to fill or top cakes or biscuits. If too firm to spread beat up with a very little boiling water when using.

Anne Wallace
Stewarton, Ayrshire

SIMPLE LEMON CRUNCH TOPPING FOR A PLAIN SPONGE

Juice of 1 whole lemon (about 2 tablespoons)
125 g/4 oz granulated sugar

Allow the sponge to cool slightly on a wire tray.

Then mix the lemon juice very swiftly with the sugar and before it dissolves the sugar spread evenly over the sponge. The lemon sugar should stay on top of the sponge and the juice should sink into the cake. This gives a lovely crunchy lemon topping with little effort, but it must be done swiftly.

RASPBERRY AND COCONUT TOPPING FOR A PLAIN SPONGE

For a 20 cm/8 inch sponge use:

2 level tablespoons raspberry jam
25 g/1 oz desiccated coconut

Spread jam over top of cooled sponge and sprinkle coconut evenly over the surface.

OAT CRISP

For decorating cakes. An economical replacement for chopped nuts.

40 g/1½ oz margarine
125 g/4 oz porridge oats
50 g/2 oz brown sugar

1. Melt fat in large pan over very gentle heat.
2. Add oats and sugar. Mix well.
3. Spread mixture loosely on a baking tray. Do not press down.
4. Toast in a moderate oven, Gas 4, 350°F, 180°C, for 15 to 20 minutes or until golden brown. Stir with a fork several times during cooking.
5. Cool and stir again.
6. When cold, store in an air-tight container. Will keep several months.

Sybil Norcott
Irlam, Nr Manchester

BATTENBERG CAKE

CAKE
125 g/4 oz margarine
125 g/4 oz caster sugar
2 beaten eggs
125 g/4 oz self-raising white flour
A few drops of pink colouring
1 tablespoon raspberry jam
2 tablespoons apricot jam (or use all raspberry jam throughout)

ALMOND PASTE
75 g/3 oz ground almonds
25 g/1 oz semolina
75 g/3 oz caster sugar
75 g/3 oz sifted icing sugar
A few drops of almond essence
Beaten egg to bind

TO FINISH
A little caster sugar

1. Grease two 450 g/1 lb loaf tins and line the base of each with a piece of greased greaseproof paper.
2. Cream margarine and sugar, beat in eggs, fold in flour.
3. Divide mixture exactly into 2 portions and colour one pink.
4. Place a portion of mixture in each tin.
5. Bake in the centre of moderate oven, Gas 4, 350°F, 180°C, for about 25 minutes until firm and beginning to leave the sides of the tins.
6. Remove from tins and cool.
7. Remove paper, trim sides and level tops.
8. Cut each cake exactly in half lengthways. All the pieces must be the same size.
9. Using raspberry jam, sandwich the four portions together, arranging pink and white squares alternately.
10. *For the paste.* Combine ingredients using enough egg to make a firm paste.
11. Use a piece of waxed paper, sprinkle well with caster sugar and on it roll out paste to fit around the sides of cake.
12. Spread the paste with sieved apricot or raspberry jam, place cake on at one end. Carefully wrap paste round cake, pressing so that it adheres. Press edges together to seal.
13. Trim ends of cake, flute along the two top edges, make a diamond pattern on top with back of knife. Dredge lightly with caster sugar.

APPLE CAKE

Looks and tastes superb.

190 g/7 oz self-raising flour
A pinch of salt
150 g/5 oz butter, or half margarine half butter
75 g/3 oz caster sugar
1 egg
325 g/12 oz cooking apples
A squeeze of lemon juice
2 tablespoons apricot jam
2 tablespoons granulated or demerara sugar
A little icing sugar

1. Grease and line a 20 cm/8 inch cake tin, which should be at least 4 cm/1½ inches deep.
2. Sieve flour and salt.
3. Cream butter and caster sugar until light and fluffy.
4. Beat in the egg.
5. Fold in flour and salt.
6. Using a lightly-floured board, gently pat or roll out three-quarters of the mixture and fit it into prepared tin.
7. Peel, core and slice apples and squeeze lemon juice over to keep their colour. Arrange overlapping slices on the cake mixture.
8. Heat jam and brush it over apples. Sprinkle with the 2 tablespoons of sugar.
9. Take small pieces of the remaining mixture, roll into strips with floured hands and arrange a lattice pattern over the apples.
10. Bake above middle of a warm oven, Gas 3, 325°F, 160°C, for 1 hour.
11. Take cake out of tin on to a wire rack to cool.
12. Dust with icing sugar and serve cool or cold.

Mrs Aileen Houghton
Kemsing, Nr Sevenoaks, Kent

CHOCOLATE SPONGE SANDWICH

Made all in one bowl.

175 g/6 oz self-raising white flour
175 g/6 oz caster sugar
175 g/6 oz margarine, softened
1 level tablespoon cocoa
1½ level teaspoons baking powder
3 eggs
2 tablespoons warm water

1. Grease two round 20 cm/8 inch sandwich tins and line the base of each with a circle of greaseproof paper.
2. Put all the ingredients together in a warm bowl, sifting in the cocoa and baking powder. Mix well until smooth. Beating is not required.
3. Divide mixture between tins, and level tops.
4. Bake above middle of a warm oven, Gas 3, 325°F, 160°C, for 30 minutes until cakes are risen and firm to the touch.
5. Turn cakes straight out of tins on to a wire rack to cool.

SANDWICH FILLING
50 g/2 oz soft margarine
125 to 175 g/4 to 6 oz icing sugar
1 large teaspoon cocoa
1 teaspoon hot water
1 teaspoon sherry or liqueur (optional)

1. Beat margarine in a bowl.
2. Sieve in 125 g/4 oz of the icing sugar and the cocoa.
3. Add other ingredients, including 1 extra teaspoon hot water if sherry is not used.
4. Beat until smooth, sieving in extra icing sugar if necessary.
5. Fill sponge with about half of this quantity.
6. Use the rest to spread on top, saving a little to pipe decorations around edge. Nuts or flaked chocolate can also be used to decorate.

CHOCOLATE LOG CAKE

50 g/2 oz soft plain white flour
15 g/½ oz cocoa
2 eggs
65 g/2½ oz vanilla sugar*
1 dessertspoon warm water

CHOCOLATE BUTTER CREAM
125 g/4 oz plain chocolate
125 g/4 oz butter or margarine
175 g/6 oz icing sugar

See page 242.

1. Grease a shallow (Swiss roll) tin approximately 27 by 18 cm/11 by 7 inches and line with greased, greaseproof paper.
2. Sieve together flour and cocoa on to a piece of paper and put in warming drawer of oven so that chill is taken off it.
3. Place eggs and sugar in bowl. Place the bowl over a pan of hot water and whisk until thick and pale.
4. Remove bowl from pan and whisk until beaters leave a trail in the mixture.
5. Carefully fold in warmed flour, sifted cocoa and the warm water.
6. Spread evenly in tin.
7. Bake above centre of a hot oven, Gas 7, 425°F, 220°C, for 7 to 8 minutes until lightly golden and springy to the touch.
8. While cake is baking, place a damp (not wet) tea-towel on table, then a piece of greaseproof paper 5 cm/2 inches all round larger than Swiss roll. Dust this with a little flour and dredge with caster sugar.
9. As soon as cake is out of oven turn out upside-down on to paper, trim edges, place a clean piece of greaseproof paper over it and roll cake up lightly with paper inside. Leave to cool.
10. Meanwhile, melt chocolate gently in basin over hot water.
11. Beat together butter (or margarine) and sifted icing sugar.
12. Beat in chocolate.
13. Unroll cake. Spread with a layer of butter cream and roll up. Place on cake board or serving dish.
14. Spread the remaining butter cream on cake and then mark it with a fork to resemble bark of tree, or pipe with fine nozzle.

To freeze. Place on cake-board and freeze uncovered overnight. When hard, slide into polythene bag, seal and freeze until required. Take out of bag while still hard—the icing may be damaged if allowed to thaw in bag.

DECORATED CHOCOLATE CAKE

50 g/2 oz plain cooking chocolate
65 g/2½ oz soft margarine
65 g/2½ oz vanilla sugar*
1 level tablespoon golden syrup
½ level teaspoon bicarbonate of soda
75 ml/2½ fl oz milk, warmed to blood heat
150 g/5 oz self-raising white flour
1 large beaten egg

See page 242.

1. Grease two 15 to 16 cm/6 to 6½ inch sandwich cake tins, and line base with a circle of greased, greaseproof paper.
2. Place chocolate to melt in a basin over hot water.
3. Thoroughly beat margarine and sugar until creamy.
4. Beat in syrup and melted chocolate.
5. Dissolve bicarbonate of soda in milk.
6. Fold flour, egg and milk alternately into creamed mixture. Mix but do not beat.
7. Divide mixture evenly between the two tins.
8. Bake second shelf down in a moderate oven, Gas 4, 350°F, 180°C, for 20 to 25 minutes. Remove to wire tray to cool.
9. When cold, remove papers. Sandwich with butter icing, and decorate top if desired.

BUTTER ICING
125 g/4 oz soft margarine or butter, or a mixture
A few drops vanilla essence
225 g/8 oz sifted icing sugar

Beat together until creamy. This will make filling and also enough to decorate top. Either, sprinkle on grated chocolate. Or, make half this quantity of butter icing, for filling only, and decorate as follows:—

GLACE ICING
175 g/6 oz icing sugar
5 teaspoons warm water
1 level teaspoon cocoa

1. Mix the icing sugar and water. The mixture should coat the back of a spoon, a ½ teaspoon more water may be needed.
2. Remove 2 heaped teaspoons of the mixed icing to a separate basin. Add to it the sieved cocoa and 2 to

3 drops warm water. This is the piping mixture and should be a bit firmer than the white icing.

3. Spread the white icing on the cake, using a wet palette knife to obtain a smooth finish.

4. Take a 25 cm/10 inch square of greaseproof paper, fold to make a triangle, make into a cone, leaving a tiny hole at the point.

5. Spoon the chocolate icing into cone. Pipe parallel lines approximately 2.5 cm/1 inch apart across cake.

6. *For feather icing:* draw the point of a knife or a skewer in alternate directions across the piped lines.

7. To make a spider's web: pipe a spiral from the centre out to the edge leaving approximately 2.5 cm/1 inch between lines.

8. Starting in centre, draw a knife across the lines, to the edge of the cake in alternate directions, making 8 sections.

GREAT AUNT ANNIE'S CHOCOLATE COCONUT CAKE

125 g/4 oz soft margarine
125 g/4 oz caster sugar
2 large eggs
125 g/4 oz self-raising flour
1 tablespoon cocoa
$\frac{1}{4}$ level teaspoon baking powder
25 g/1 oz coconut
25 g/1 oz ground almonds
A little milk, if necessary

1. Grease and flour an 18 cm/7 inch square tin.

2. Cream together in a mixing bowl margarine and sugar until light and fluffy.

3. Beat eggs well in a small basin.

4. Sieve flour, cocoa and baking powder together into another basin.

5. Mix coconut and ground almonds into flour mixture.

6. Add a little of the beaten egg and a little of the flour mixture to creamed fat and sugar. Add a little of each alternately, folding in until all ingredients are mixed.

7. Add a little milk, if necessary, to make a soft, dropping consistency.

8. Put mixture into prepared tin.

9. Bake in a moderate oven, Gas 4, 350°F, 180°C, for about 40 minutes, until it is shrinking from sides of tin and feels firm to the touch.

10. Cool on a wire rack.

This cake may be decorated with chocolate glacé icing, melted chocolate and walnuts or chocolate drops. No filling is necessary. The cake can be used to make a Chocolate Easter Cake by decorating with yellow, fluffy chickens and tiny Easter eggs.

CHOCOLATE GLACÉ ICING
(for top and sides of cake)
325 g/12 oz sieved icing sugar
3 to 4 tablespoons hot, not boiling, water
3 tablespoons cocoa

Never use boiling water for glacé icing or the finished icing will be dull.

1. Sieve icing sugar into a bowl.

2. Blend cocoa into hot water and beat into the icing sugar. Beat well with a wooden spoon. The icing should just coat the back of the spoon.

3. Use immediately, putting spoonfuls on top of the cake. Using a palette knife with a round blade, spread icing over top of cake and let it run down the sides. Spread evenly round sides. Dip knife in hot water if icing does not run very well. The icing should be smooth and shining.

Stella Boldy
Sykehouse, N. Humberside

WALNUT AND CHOCOLATE GÂTEAU

Freezes well—thaw for 2 hours.

BASE
125 g/4 oz margarine
225 g/8 oz crushed digestive biscuits
50 g/2 oz chopped walnuts

CAKE
225 g/8 oz caster sugar
125 g/4 oz margarine
125 g/4 oz plain chocolate
2 eggs
190 g/7 oz self-raising flour
$\frac{1}{2}$ teaspoon cinnamon
$\frac{1}{4}$ teaspoon salt
150 ml/$\frac{1}{4}$ pint soured or single cream, or top of milk
150 ml/$\frac{1}{4}$ pint strong, black coffee

DECORATION
150 ml/$\frac{1}{4}$ pint double cream
150 ml/$\frac{1}{4}$ pint single cream
50 g/2 oz walnuts

START WITH THE BASE

1. Melt margarine in pan, add biscuits and chopped walnuts. Press into a greased 20 cm/8 inch loose-bottomed cake tin.

FOR THE CAKE

2. Beat margarine and caster sugar together.

3. Melt chocolate in a small basin over a pan of simmering water. Add to the creamed mixture.

4. Beat eggs into the mixture.

5. Sift together flour, cinnamon and salt.

6. Mix together cream and coffee.

7. Fold flour, and the cream and coffee alternately into egg mixture.

8. Pour cake mixture on to base.

9. Bake in a moderate oven, Gas 4, 350°F, 180°C, for 1¼ hours.

10. Leave cake in tin until cold, then turn out carefully.

TO DECORATE

11. Whip single and double cream together until thick. Coat top and sides of cake. Decorate with walnuts.

Janet Town
Pudsey, Yorkshire

LEMON CUSTARD CAKE

CUSTARD FILLING
25 g/1 oz cornflour
300 ml/½ pint milk
2 egg-yolks
2 dessertspoons sugar
Rind and juice of ½ lemon
3 dessertspoons lemon curd

CAKE
225 g/8 oz self-raising flour
125 g/4 oz margarine
75 g/3 oz sugar
1 beaten egg
¼ teaspoon vanilla or almond essence
A little milk
A little egg-white

MAKE THE FILLING FIRST

1. Blend cornflour in a cup with a little of the milk.

2. Mix egg-yolks and sugar with a fork. Add blended cornflour and gradually mix in rest of the milk.

3. Put in a pan over a low heat and, stirring continuously, bring to the boil. If mixture goes lumpy whisk vigorously.

4. Remove from heat, beat in lemon rind, juice and lemon curd. Leave this custard to cool.

FOR THE CAKE

5. Put flour in a bowl and rub in margarine.

6. Mix in sugar, beaten egg, vanilla or almond essence. Add a little milk, a tablespoon at a time, and mix to a stiff, scone-like consistency.

7. Grease a 20 cm/8 inch cake tin with removable base. Line base with greased, greaseproof paper.

8. Roll out just over half the mixture to a round about 27 cm/10½ inches across.

9. Fit this into the tin and fill with cooled custard mixture.

10. Brush top edges of cake base with a little egg-white.

11. Roll out remaining cake mixture and fit on top, pressing lightly round edges to seal it in place. Brush top with egg-white.

12. Bake in centre of a moderate oven, Gas 4, 350°F, 180°C, for about 30 minutes until quite firm and golden on top.

13. Lift out of tin on removable base and slide off base on to a cooling wire.

Serve warm or cooled as a sweet course or at tea-time. When cool, serve with a little cream.

Mrs Carol Goldsmith
Beccles, Suffolk

TANGY LEMON CAKE

125 g/4 oz butter
175 g/6 oz caster sugar
Grated rind and juice 2 lemons
2 beaten eggs
175 g/6 oz self-raising flour
A little milk
50 g/2 oz granulated sugar

1. Cream butter, caster sugar and lemon rind until fluffy.

2. Gradually beat in eggs.

3. Mix in flour and add about 4 tablespoons milk to soften mixture. It should be soft enough to drop off end of spoon when shaken gently.

4. Grease a 1 kg/2 lb loaf tin.

5. Bake in a moderate oven, Gas 4, 350°F, 180°C, for 45 to 50 minutes until risen and golden, firm on top and shrinking from sides of tin.

6. Just before cake is ready to come out of oven,

prepare the lemon syrup. Heat lemon juice and granulated sugar gently until sugar is dissolved.

7. As soon as cake is out of oven, while still in tin, pierce top all over with a skewer. Pour over the lemon syrup. Leave cake in tin until cold.

Mrs Judith Perry
Sutton St Nicholas, Hereford

MANDARIN GÂTEAU

CAKE MIXTURE
125 g/4 oz margarine
125 g/4 oz caster sugar
2 eggs
125 g/4 oz self-raising white flour

ORANGE BUTTER CREAM
175 g/6 oz butter or margarine
Grated rind of 1 orange
325 g/12 oz icing sugar
1 tablespoon orange juice

DECORATION
50 to 75 g/2 to 3 oz toasted coconut*
1 tin mandarin oranges
Cherries and angelica

GLAZE
1 teaspoon arrowroot
4 tablespoons mandarin juice

Toasted coconut: Put in shallow tin in low oven turning occasionally so that it becomes golden evenly.

1. Grease a shallow tin approximately 27 by 18 cm, 11 by 7 inches and line with greased, greaseproof paper.
2. Beat margarine and sugar until creamy.
3. Add eggs, one at a time, beating, adding 2 teaspoons of the flour to prevent curdling.
4. Fold in rest of flour.
5. Bake in a moderately hot oven, Gas 5, 375°F, 190°C, for about 20 minutes.
6. Remove to wire to cool.
7. Remove paper, cut away edges and cut cake in half lengthways.
8. Beat orange cream ingredients together. Keep some aside for piping, and use some to sandwich two pieces of cake together. Spread some more round sides and cover with toasted coconut. Cover top with a thin layer of butter cream. (The cake can be frozen at this stage to finish when required.)
9. Drain mandarin oranges. Arrange two lines lengthways down the cake, leaving 7 mm/¼ inch around edge.
10. Mix arrowroot and juice for glaze in small pan. Bring to boil and cook until clear. Cool. Brush oranges lightly.
11. Place rest of butter cream in piping bag, using a star nozzle. Pipe a line down centre and then round edges of cake.
12. Decorate with pieces of cherry and angelica.

YORKSHIRE PARKIN

250 g/9 oz plain wholewheat or white flour
190 g/7 oz brown or white sugar
100 g/3½ oz porridge oats
2 heaped teaspoons powdered ginger
75 g/3 oz soft margarine
50 g/2 oz lard
190 g/7 oz golden syrup
75 g/3 oz black treacle*
1 slightly rounded teaspoon bicarbonate of soda
A few drops (about 1 dessertspoon) vinegar
150 ml/¼ pint milk

If you have no treacle use 275 g/10 oz golden syrup. Add 1 or 2 drops of gravy browning when you stir the mixture at Paragraph 5, to get the true dark Parkin colour.

1. Mix the flour, sugar, oats and ginger together in a bowl and make a well in centre.
2. Melt the fats in a pan. Before they get too hot, add the syrup and treacle and let it melt a little. Do not overheat, certainly do not boil.
3. Pour this mixture into dry ingredients in bowl. Drop bicarbonate of soda into centre, sprinkle the vinegar on the soda and watch it fizz.
4. Put the milk into the syrup pan, warm it a little to clean the syrup from the pan and then add to the bowl.
5. Now stir it all up well. When mixed it should pour like a batter mixture. Pour it into large greased and floured roasting tin.
6. Bake slightly above the middle of a moderate oven, between Gas 3 and 4, 335°F, 170°C, for 1 hour. Look at it after 15 to 20 minutes to see if middle has lifted. If so, shake it to let it sink again, turn tin round and allow to continue cooking.
7. Allow to cool in tin. Cut into quarters. Best if stored 3 days before eating. Keeps well if stored in an air-tight container.

CHESHIRE PARKIN

Keeps well—freezes well.

225 g/8 oz coarse oatmeal
75 g/3 oz wholewheat or white flour
50 g/2 oz demerara sugar
1 teaspoon ground ginger
A bare $\frac{1}{2}$ teaspoon bicarbonate of soda
A pinch of salt
225 g/8 oz syrup or treacle
125 g/4 oz margarine
70 ml/2$\frac{1}{2}$ fl oz milk

1. Mix the dry ingredients together.
2. Melt the syrup and fat in a pan and add to dry ingredients.
3. Stir in milk to make a soft consistency.
4. Grease a 20 cm/8 inch round sandwich tin, or an 18 cm/7 inch square tin and line it with greased, greaseproof paper. Put in the mixture.
5. Bake in the middle of a moderate oven, Gas 4, 350°F, 180°C, for 1$\frac{1}{4}$ hours when parkin will be firm to the touch.
6. Leave in tin to cool.

Best kept 2 days before eating.

Judith Adshead
Mottram St Andrew, Cheshire

SOFT GINGERBREAD

This cake will bake in a 23 cm/9 inch square tin, a 19 by 29 cm/7$\frac{1}{2}$ by 11$\frac{1}{2}$ inch dripping tin, or in two 900 g/2 lb loaf tins.

125 g/4 oz butter
125 g/4 oz golden syrup
150 g/5 oz dark treacle
125 g/4 oz granulated sugar
275 g/10 oz plain flour
$\frac{1}{2}$ teaspoon salt
2 teaspoons ground ginger
1 teaspoon cinnamon
1 level teaspoon bicarbonate of soda
1 beaten egg
225 ml/7 to 8 fl oz sour milk

1. Grease tin and line with greased, greaseproof paper.

2. Melt butter, syrup, treacle and sugar gently in a pan. Allow to cool.
3. Sieve together flour, salt, ginger, cinnamon and bicarbonate of soda.
4. Pour contents of pan into flour.
5. Beat in egg and milk.
6. Pour into prepared tin(s).
7. Bake in a moderate oven, Gas 3, 325°F, 160°C, for about 1 hour. Could take 15 minutes longer in the loaf tins.
8. Turn out of tin on to wire rack to cool.

WHOLEWHEAT GINGERBREAD

125 g/4 oz plain white flour
$\frac{1}{4}$ teaspoon salt
$\frac{1}{2}$ level teaspoon ground cinnamon
3 level teaspoons ground ginger
1 level teaspoon bicarbonate of soda
125 g/4 oz wholewheat flour
40 g/1$\frac{1}{2}$ oz demerara sugar
40 g/1$\frac{1}{2}$ oz sultanas
40 g/1$\frac{1}{2}$ oz candied peel
125 g/4 oz butter
125 g/4 oz golden syrup
125 g/4 oz dark treacle
1 large egg
150 ml/$\frac{1}{4}$ pint milk
15 g/$\frac{1}{2}$ oz flaked almonds

1. Sieve into a bowl, the plain flour, salt, cinnamon, ginger and bicarbonate of soda.
2. Add the wholewheat flour, demerara sugar, sultanas, candied peel.
3. Warm in pan the butter, golden syrup and dark treacle.
4. Beat the egg and to it add the milk.
5. Mix liquids into dry ingredients.
6. Pour into a greased tin lined with greased, greaseproof paper. This is best baked in a tin 18 cm/7 inches square and about 6.5 cm/2$\frac{1}{2}$ inches deep, or a small dripping tin 23 by 14 cm/9 by 5$\frac{1}{2}$ inches. Sprinkle on the flaked almonds.
7. Bake in the centre of a cool oven, Gas 2, 300°F, 150°C, for about 1 hour until just firm and slightly springy to touch.
8. Store for a few days. Cut into squares to serve.

NOTTINGHAM GINGERBREAD

225 g/8 oz plain white or wholewheat flour, or half of each
3 to 4 level teaspoons ground ginger
1 level teaspoon bicarbonate of soda
125 g/4 oz butter or margarine
125 g/4 oz brown sugar
225 g/8 oz golden syrup or black treacle (or half of each)
150 ml/¼ pint milk
1 egg

1. Grease an 18 cm/7 inch square cake tin and line with greased, greaseproof paper.
2. Sieve the flour, ginger and bicarbonate of soda together into a mixing bowl.
3. Melt the fat with the sugar, syrup and milk over a low heat, stirring all the time. Cool a little.
4. Beat the egg.
5. Add the liquid mixture with the egg to the dry ingredients. Mix well then beat for five minutes.
6. Pour into prepared tin. Spread evenly.
7. Cook in a cool oven, Gas 2, 300°F, 150°C, for about 1 hour until it is springy and leaving the sides of the tin.
8. When cooked turn out carefully, remove the paper and store in an airtight tin for a few days to let it become sticky.

SHEARING CAKE

Cacen Gneifo—a seed cake traditionally baked in Wales at sheep-shearing time. Keeps quite well in a tin for over a week.

Easy to make half this quantity.

450 g/1 lb plain white flour, or half wholewheat, half white
1 teaspoon grated nutmeg
1 rounded teaspoon baking powder
A pinch of salt
225 g/8 oz butter or margarine
325 g/12 oz soft brown sugar
1 tablespoon caraway seeds
Grated rind and juice of 1 lemon
300 ml/½ pint milk
2 beaten eggs

1. Sift together white flour, nutmeg, baking powder and salt. Mix in wholewheat flour if used.
2. Rub in butter or margarine.
3. Add sugar, caraway seeds, lemon rind and juice.
4. Pour in milk slowly, mixing well all the time. Finally, mix in well-beaten eggs.
5. Grease a 23 cm/9 inch round cake tin and line base and sides with greased greaseproof paper. If making half quantity an 18 cm/7 inch round tin is suitable, or a 450 g/1 lb loaf tin.
6. Pour in cake mixture.
7. Bake in middle of a moderate oven, Gas 4, 350°F, 180°C, for 30 minutes, then reduce temperature to cool, Gas 2, 300°F, 150°C, for another 1½ hours when it will be golden brown and firm to the touch. If making half quantity, bake as above but it will need only 1 hour when temperature has been reduced.
8. Leave cake in tin till slightly cooled. Then turn it out on to a wire rack.

Mrs Eileen Trumper
Llanvair Kilgeddin, Gwent

SOMERSET CIDER CAKE

A moist cake. Keeps well in an airtight tin.

125 g/4 oz butter
125 g/4 oz soft brown sugar
2 beaten eggs (must be at room temperature)
225 g/8 oz wholewheat flour
1 teaspoon bicarbonate of soda, use a measure
Half a nutmeg, grated
About 225 ml/8 fl oz dry cider

1. Cream butter and sugar until really light and fluffy.
2. Beat in eggs a little at a time.
3. Sift together flour, bicarbonate of soda and nutmeg. Fold it in.
4. Add cider slowly to form a soft dropping consistency.
5. Grease an 18 cm/7 inch round tin and line bottom with greased greaseproof paper.
6. Put mixture into tin and bake near top of a moderately hot oven, Gas 5, 375°F, 190°C, for 1 to 1¼ hours or until brown on top, shrinking from sides of tin and springy to the touch.

Mrs Angela Mottram
Axbridge, Somerset

4 DIFFERENT CAKES: SAME METHOD

METHOD
1. Grease 18 cm/7 inch square tin or 20 cm/8 inch round tin and line with greased, greaseproof paper.
2. Beat together fat, sugar and any zest or rind.
3. Beat in eggs, one at a time.
4. Sift flours, salt, baking powder (if used) and mix with other dry ingredients such as fruit, nuts, etc.
5. Fold dry ingredients into egg mixture.
6. Lightly mix in any other liquid.

Cherry Cake
175 g/6 oz margarine, soft type
175 g/6 oz caster sugar
3 eggs
125 g/4 oz self-raising flour
75 g/3 oz plain flour
50 g/2 oz ground almonds
175 g/6 oz glacé cherries, washed, dried and cut in halves and quarters

Moderate oven, Gas 3, 325°F, 160°C, for 1¼ hours or until firm and shrinking slightly from sides of tin.

Madeira Cake
150 g/5 oz margarine, soft type
150 g/5 oz caster sugar
Zest of 1 lemon
3 eggs
175 g/6 oz plain flour
Pinch of salt
2 teaspoons cornflour
1½ level teaspoons baking powder

Moderate oven, Gas 4, 350°F, 180°C, for 1¼ hours or until firm on top and shrinking slightly from sides of tin.

Rice Cake
225 g/8 oz margarine, soft type
225 g/8 oz caster sugar
Zest of 1 lemon
3 large eggs
175 g/6 oz ground rice
150 g/5 oz self-raising flour
3 dessertspoons lemon juice

Moderate oven, Gas 3, 325°F, 160°C, for 1¼ hours or until firm and shrinking slightly from sides of tin.

Walnut Cake with Fudge Icing
175 g/6 oz margarine, soft type
175 g/6 oz caster sugar
3 eggs
225 g/8 oz plain flour
1½ level teaspoons baking powder
75 g/3 oz chopped walnuts
2 tablespoons milk

Moderate oven, Gas 3, 325°F, 160°C, for 1¼ hours or until firm on top and shrinking slightly from sides of tin.

Fudge Icing
75 g/3 oz margarine
3 dessertspoons milk
1 dessertspoon water
1 dessertspoon instant coffee
325 g/12 oz icing sugar

1. Warm together margarine, milk, water and coffee. Allow to cool.
2. Beat in icing sugar.
3. Swirl over cake when cool.

WHOLEMEAL CARROT CAKE

2 slightly-rounded teaspoons baking powder
Pinch of salt
1 level teaspoon cinnamon (optional)
175 g/6 oz wholemeal flour
125 g/4 oz grated carrot
125 g/4 oz margarine
125 g/4 oz soft, dark brown sugar
Grated zest of ½ orange
2 large eggs
About 1 tablespoon milk

1. Sift baking powder, salt and cinnamon into the flour and mix well.
2. Mix in grated carrot.
3. Cream margarine and sugar until light and fluffy. Add orange zest.
4. Add eggs one at a time, beating well, and spoon in a little of the flour mixture to prevent curdling.
5. Gradually mix in flour. Add milk a little at a time until consistency is soft but not runny.
6. Grease a 15 cm/6 inch round cake tin and line base with greased, greaseproof paper. Tip in the mixture.
7. Bake in a moderate oven, Gas 3, 325°F, 160°C, for ¾ to 1 hour.

For a special occasion, ice with orange glacé icing and decorate with pieces of walnut.

ORANGE GLACÉ ICING
125 g/4 oz sifted icing sugar
Zest of ½ orange and 4 teaspoons orange juice

1. Mix the orange juice and zest with the icing sugar. The mixture should evenly coat the back of a spoon.
2. Spread icing over cake, using a wet palette knife to obtain a smooth finish. Decorate with walnut halves before icing sets.

Mrs H.D. Harvey
Sherfield-on-Loddon, Hants

ALMOND PASTE

To cover top of 19 to 20 cm/7½ to 8 inch Christmas Cake:

FOR THE PASTE
225 g/8 oz ground almonds
175 g/6 oz caster sugar
175 g/6 oz sifted icing sugar
1 teaspoon lemon juice
Few drops almond essence
1 or 2 beaten eggs
1 to 2 teaspoons sherry, optional
Also: **1 tablespoon sieved apricot jam**

1. Mix almonds, caster sugar, icing sugar, lemon juice, almond essence and 1 beaten egg. If very stiff and will not bind, add 1 to 2 teaspoons of sherry or a little more beaten egg. If soft add more almonds and/or sugar. It should roll without cracking.
2. Roll out almond paste to fit top of cake.
3. Spread sieved apricot jam over top of cake.
4. Press paste firmly on top.
5. Colour any trimmings: a little red to make berries and a little green for leaves. Arrange on top of cake, painting undersides with beaten egg if they will not stick.

See also Marzipan Sweets, page 397.

DOROTHY SLEIGHTHOLME'S CHRISTMAS CAKE

225 g/8 oz butter
225 g/8 oz soft brown sugar
1 tablespoon dark treacle
Grated rind and juice of 1 lemon
250 g/9 oz plain white flour
1 level teaspoon baking powder
1 level teaspoon mixed spice
A little grated nutmeg
A pinch of salt
225 g/8 oz currants
225 g/8 oz sultanas
225 g/8 oz raisins
125 g/4 oz cherries
125 g/4 oz candied peel
50 g/2 oz chopped whole almonds
50 g/2 oz ground almonds
5 eggs

1. Line a 20 cm/8 inch square or 23 cm/9 inch diameter round cake tin with a layer of foil and a layer of greaseproof paper lightly greased both sides. Allow both foil and greaseproof paper to extend above sides of tin about 4 cm/1½ inches. Tie a double thickness of brown paper around outside of tin.
2. Cream together butter, sugar, treacle and lemon rind.
3. Sift flour, baking powder, spice, nutmeg and salt. Add fruit and both chopped and ground almonds.
4. Beat eggs until frothy.
5. Add half of the beaten egg and 4 tablespoons flour and fruit mixture to butter and sugar, beat in.
6. Add remaining egg and rest of dry ingredients, gradually mixing in strained lemon juice. Do not beat, but mix thoroughly.
7. Spoon into tin.
8. Have oven heated to moderate, Gas 3, 325°F, 160°C. Place cake in centre. Turn heat control down immediately to cool, Gas 2, 300°F, 150°C, and bake for 1½ hours. Over next half hour reduce heat by degrees to quite cool, Gas 1, 275°F, 140°C, if at this stage, cake is browning too quickly, cover loosely with foil. Total time, 4¼ to 4½ hours until firm. Leave in tin to cool.
9. Next day wrap in foil and store. This cake will keep several months.

CHRISTMAS CAKE WITH ALMOND PASTE AND ROYAL ICING

Bake this cake in September or October as it improves with keeping.

125 g/4 oz raisins
125 g/4 oz glacé cherries
125 g/4 oz mixed peel
450 g/1 lb currants
125 g/4 oz sultanas
2 tablespoons brandy, sherry or rum
4 eggs
225 g/8 oz butter
225 g/8 oz soft brown sugar
225 g/8 oz plain white flour
1 teaspoon mixed spice
125 g/4 oz ground almonds

1. Chop raisins, cherries and mixed peel.
2. Put them in a bowl with currants and sultanas, pour over the brandy, sherry or rum and leave overnight.
3. Line a 20 cm/8 inch diameter round cake tin or an 18 cm/7 inch square tin, with greased, grease-proof paper.
4. Prepare a cool oven, Gas 2, 300°F, 150°C.
5. Beat eggs.
6. Cream butter and sugar in a large bowl.
7. Sift flour and mixed spice into a separate bowl and add soaked fruit and ground almonds. Mix well together.
8. Add spoonfuls of egg then flour mixture to bowl of creamed ingredients. Mix well at each addition until all has been mixed thoroughly.
9. Put mixture into prepared tin.
10. Wrap a double thickness of brown paper or newspaper round outside of tin. Let it stand up a good 5 cm/2 inches above tin. Tie it on with string. This will protect cake from browning on the outside before middle is cooked.
11. Bake cake for 3 to 4 hours, until firm and fruit stops 'singing' and 'sissing'.
12. Remove cake from tin on to a cooling wire.
13. When cold, store in an air-tight tin and let it mature as long as possible (at least 3 months). It will keep for a year.

ALMOND PASTE
Makes enough to cover top and sides of a 20 cm/8 inch diameter round cake or an 18 cm/7 inch square cake.

325 g/12 oz ground almonds
175 g/6 oz sieved icing sugar
175 g/6 oz caster sugar
1 large egg and 1 egg-white
Juice of $\frac{1}{2}$ lemon
A few drops ratafia essence
A few drops almond flavouring
A few drops vanilla flavouring
1 teaspoon orange flower water (buy it from a chemist)
2 teaspoons brandy, rum or sherry

1. Mix ground almonds and sugars together.
2. Beat whole egg and add lemon juice, ratafia, flavourings, orange flower water and brandy, rum or sherry.
3. Using a wooden spoon, mix liquid carefully into almond and sugar. Do not add it all at once because if mixture becomes too soft it will be difficult to roll out. Work it into a firm, but manageable paste, kneading a little with hands.
4. Brush top and sides of cake with a little beaten egg-white. This gives a tacky surface to help the paste stick to the cake.
5. Dredge a board with sifted icing sugar and have more icing sugar ready for the rolling pin.
6. Take off two-thirds of the almond paste for the sides of the cake.
7. Measure the circumference of your cake—a piece of string will do—and measure the height of the sides. Your measurements will give a long, narrow rectangle.
8. Roll out the larger piece of paste just longer than this measurement and it will fit nicely round sides of cake. Press lightly with rolling pin at join.
9. For the top of the cake, shape remaining piece of paste into a round or a square and roll it out slightly larger than top of cake. Using the piece of string, check size of paste against size of cake top. Do not lift paste on to cake.
10. Turn cake upside-down on to the paste and trim neatly. Turn cake right side up again with paste in position. By doing it this way you get a nice flat surface to the paste.
11. Brush almond paste all over with egg-white and leave to dry.

ROYAL ICING

To cover the cake only, not for decoration.
Mix icing the day before you mean to ice the cake.

450 g/1 lb icing sugar
2 egg-whites
2 teaspoons glycerine (buy at a chemist)
2 teaspoons lemon juice, strained

1. Sieve icing sugar three times. This is necessary because the icing must not have any lumps in it—even tiny ones.
2. Put egg-whites into a bowl and beat, but only lightly.
3. Add icing sugar to egg-whites, a tablespoon at a time. Beat each spoonful in quickly with a round-bladed knife.
4. Add glycerine and strained lemon juice and mix in well. Glycerine is used to stop icing going hard.
5. Put a damp cloth over bowl of icing. Put bowl into a polythene bag and leave it overnight.
6. Next day, put cake on a board that is at least 8 cm/3 inches wider than the cake.
7. Put a first coat of icing on the sides. Use a plastic scraper, a hot knife or metal ruler. Dip it in a jug of boiling water, but wipe it dry before use. Never use a wet knife with this type of icing as it makes icing too soft and it may start to run.
8. Allow icing on the sides to dry overnight, then put a first coat on the top. It is better to use a hot knife or metal ruler for top, not a plastic scraper.
9. Allow time for icing to dry on top, then give the sides a second coat. Two coats of icing give a better finish. Finally, finish icing the top.

TO DECORATE CAKE

225 g/8 oz icing sugar
1 egg-white
1 teaspoon strained lemon juice
Vegetable colouring

1. Prick the design on the cake-top with a darning needle or hat pin.
2. Sieve icing sugar three times to ensure there are no tiny lumps.
3. Put egg-whites into a bowl and beat, but only lightly.
4. Add icing sugar to egg-whites, a tablespoon at a time. Beat each spoonful in quickly with a round-bladed knife.
5. Add strained lemon juice and mix in well. Consistency should be very firm: it should form peaks in the bowl when you lift up the spoon.
6. Be very careful in colouring the icing. Add colour by dipping a skewer into the bottle and shaking it into icing.
7. Use a greaseproof paper or parchment bag with icing nozzles.

TO MAKE A PAPER ICING BAG

1. Take a piece of greaseproof paper, 25 cm/10 inches square. Fold along the line A—B.
2. Twist in point A to meet point C and hold it firmly in place. Then twist point B towards point C to complete the cone.

Fold the points over firmly to secure the cone. Then snip off the tip so that piping nozzle will project through hole.

Mrs Stella Boldy
Sykehouse, N. Humberside

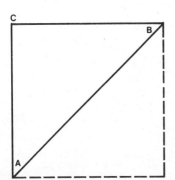
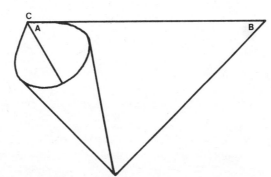

MRS ROBIN'S FRUIT CAKE

It is hard to make a mistake with this reliable recipe. It produces a good everyday cake and is perfectly suitable as a simple Christmas cake, especially if iced with sherry icing, *see below*.

125 g/4 oz margarine
175 g/6 oz sugar, dark brown, light or white
175 g/6 oz currants
175 g/6 oz sultanas
50 g/2 oz candied peel
225 ml/8 fl oz water
1 level teaspoon bicarbonate of soda
1 heaped teaspoon of mixed spice
2 beaten eggs
125 g/4 oz plain flour, wholewheat or white
125 g/4 oz self raising flour wholewheat or white
Pinch of salt

1. Place margarine, sugar, currants, sultanas, peel, water, bicarbonate of soda and mixed spice in a pan, bring to boil and simmer 1 minute. Pour into large mixing bowl. Allow to cool.
2. Line an 18 cm/7 inch square or 20 cm/8 inch round tin, or use loaf tins if preferred, with greased, greaseproof paper.
3. Add eggs, flours and salt to cooled mixture, mix well, pour into tin.
4. Bake in the centre of a moderate oven, Gas 4, 350°F, 180°C, for 1¼ hours.

SHERRY BUTTER ICING

For a fruit cake or a Christmas cake.

125 g/4 oz butter or margarine or 50 g/2 oz of each
225 g/8 oz sifted icing sugar
2 tablespoons sherry

1. Beat butter or margarine until soft.
2. Work in icing sugar and sherry.
3. Spread over cake, fork top and put in a cool place to set.

A TIP
If it is to be kept for some time, cake may cause discoloration of icing. To prevent this:
1. Lightly beat white of an egg until runny but not fluffy.

2. Brush egg-white over top and sides of cake. Leave to dry before icing. To be doubly sure, give cake a second coat of egg-white and allow to dry before icing.

MINCEMEAT CAKE

This cake keeps well.

75 g/3 oz margarine
25 g/1 oz lard
125 g/4 oz soft brown sugar
2 large eggs
325 g/12 oz mincemeat
190 g/7 oz self-raising white flour
A little milk, if necessary

1. Grease an 18 cm/7 inch round cake tin and line with greased, greaseproof paper.
2. Cream fat and sugar and beat in eggs.
3. Stir in mincemeat and fold in flour. Mixture should be moist (this depends on how runny mincemeat is). If necessary, add a little milk.
4. Bake in a moderate oven, Gas 3, 325°F, 160°C, for 10 minutes. Reduce heat to cool, Gas 2, 300°F, 150°C, for about 1¼ hours until the top is firm and cake is shrinking slightly from edge of tin.

Mrs Ward
Warwickshire

APPLE FRUIT CAKE

450 g/1 lb cooking apples
Water
225 g/8 oz plain flour
1 level teaspoon bicarbonate of soda
1 level teaspoon powdered cinnamon
½ level teaspoon mixed spice
½ level teaspoon ground ginger
175 g/6 oz sultanas
50 g/2 oz candied peel
50 g/2 oz seedless raisins
50 g/2 oz chopped walnuts
50 g/2 oz chopped glacé ginger
150 g/5 oz butter
175 g/6 oz soft brown sugar
Rind of 1 lemon, finely grated
2 eggs
Caster sugar

1. Cook apples until quite soft, using a minimum of water, 1 to 2 tablespoons.
2. Sieve or liquidise.
3. Measure 225 ml/8 fl oz of this sauce.
4. Grease and line base of a 20 cm/8 inch round or 18 cm/7 inch square cake tin.
5. Sieve together flour, bicarbonate of soda, cinnamon, mixed spice and ginger.
6. Add sultanas, peel, seedless raisins, walnuts and glacé ginger, and mix.
7. Cream together in another bowl the butter, soft brown sugar and finely grated lemon rind. Beat in eggs.
8. Fold in dry ingredients alternately with the apple sauce.
9. Place in tin. Dredge top with caster sugar. Bake in centre of a moderate oven, Gas 3, 325°F, 150°C, for 1¼ hours.

SOMERSET APPLE CAKE

75 g/3 oz butter
175 g/6 oz caster sugar
1 orange rind, grated
225 g/8 oz self-raising flour
450 g/1 lb Bramley apples, peeled, cored and cubed.
2 eggs, beaten
2 tablespoons milk
25 g/1 oz candied peel, chopped
About 1 tablespoon granulated sugar

1. Grease and flour a 23 cm/9 inch cake tin.
2. Cream butter, sugar and orange rind, and beat until light and creamy.
3. Mix 1 tablespoon of the flour with apples in a dish.
4. Put eggs and milk in bowl with the creamed butter.
5. Add remaining flour, peel and apples to the creamed mixture and blend well with a metal spoon.
6. Turn into prepared tin, sprinkle with granulated sugar.
7. Bake in a moderate oven, Gas 4, 350°F, 180°C, for 40 to 50 minutes until golden brown.

Serve cold as a cake or hot as a pudding with cream.

WHOLEWHEAT MINCEMEAT CAKE

Keeps well for several weeks.

125 g/4 oz butter
125 g/4 oz Barbados sugar
3 large eggs
325 g/12 oz mincemeat
190 g/7 oz self-raising wholewheat flour
About 4 tablespoons milk

1. Grease an 18 to 20 cm/7 to 8 inch round cake tin and line bottom with greased, greaseproof paper.
2. Cream butter and sugar well.
3. Beat in eggs, one at a time. If it begins to curdle add a little of the flour.
4. Stir in mincemeat and fold in flour, adding milk to obtain a moist mixture.
5. Bake in a moderate oven, Gas 3, 325°F, 160°C, for 10 minutes. Lower heat to slow, Gas 2, 300°F, 150°C, for about 1¼ hours, until cake is firm on top and shrinking slightly from edge of tin.

Stella Boldy
Sykehouse, N. Humberside

CHINCHILLA CAKE

Will keep for about 4 weeks.

190 g/7 oz butter or margarine
225 g/8 oz caster sugar
4 eggs
50 g/2 oz ground rice
125 g/4 oz ground almonds
50 g/2 oz chopped walnuts
50 g/2 oz split or whole blanched almonds
50 g/2 oz red glacé cherries
50 g/2 oz green glacé cherries
25 g/1 oz angelica, cut small
125 g/4 oz self-raising flour
1 teaspoon vanilla essence

1. Grease a 20 cm/8 inch round cake tin or an 18 cm/7 inch square tin and line with greased, greaseproof paper.
2. Prepare moderate oven, Gas 4, 350°F, 180°C.
3. Cream butter or margarine and sugar until light and fluffy.
4. Beat eggs.
5. Chop almonds and cherries.
6. Mix ground rice, ground almonds, chopped walnuts, almonds, cherries, angelica and flour.
7. Add half of the beaten egg and about 4 tablespoons of the fruit and flour mixture to the creamed butter and sugar, and beat in.
8. Add remaining egg, rest of dry ingredients and vanilla. Mix thoroughly.
9. Put mixture into prepared tin.
10. Bake for about 1¼ hours until firm to the touch.
11. Remove from oven and leave for 2 minutes. Carefully turn out of tin on to a cooling wire.

Mrs Grace Wilson
Pudsey, W. Yorkshire

CIDER CAKE

225 g/8 oz mixed sultanas, raisins and currants
4 tablespoons sweet cider
175 g/6 oz butter or margarine
175 g/6 oz soft brown sugar
3 eggs
225 g/8 oz self-raising flour
1 teaspoon mixed spice (optional)

1. Soak mixed fruits in the cider overnight.
2. Cream butter or margarine and add sugar. Cream until fluffy.

3. Lightly beat eggs and gradually beat them into the mixture.
4. Mix in fruit and cider.
5. Sift flour and spice together.
6. Fold in half of the flour, mix well. Mix in rest of flour.
7. Grease a 20 cm/8 inch round or 18 cm/7 inch square tin and line bottom with greased, greaseproof paper.
8. Bake in a moderate oven, Gas 4, 350°F, 180°C, for 1 hour and 10 minutes.

Mrs Peggy Hughes
Skewen, Glamorgan

DEVONSHIRE BLOCK CAKE

This recipe is easily reduced to make a smaller cake. It also freezes well so that the whole quantity can be made and the cake cut in 3 or 4 pieces to freeze. Very good flavour; improves with keeping.

175 g/6 oz butter or margarine
175 g/6 oz sugar
125 g/4 oz black treacle
3 large eggs
1 tablespoon milk
450 g/1 lb currants or sultanas, or a mixture of both
125 g/4 oz mixed peel
325 g/12 oz plain flour

1. Work butter or margarine to a cream.
2. Beat in sugar and treacle.
3. Add eggs one at a time, beating well.
4. Add milk.
5. Mix in currants, sultanas, peel and lastly the flour.
6. Use a greased tin 18 cm/7 inch square or two 900 g/2 lb loaf tins and line with greased, greaseproof paper.
7. Put mixture into tin and bake in middle of a cool oven, Gas 2, 300°F, 150°C, for 2½ hours, when cake will be a rich brown and firm to the touch. Look in oven after 1½ hours and, if cake is already very brown, reduce heat to Gas 1, 275°F, 140°C, and lay a doubled sheet of greaseproof paper over top.

Mrs Becky Blackmore
Exeter, Devon

DUNDEE CAKE

Keeps very well.

175 g/6 oz soft margarine
175 g/6 oz light soft brown sugar
½ teaspoon almond essence
190 g/7 oz plain flour
1 level teaspoon baking powder
175 g/6 oz sultanas
175 g/6 oz currants
50 g/2 oz chopped cherries
25 g/1 oz ground almonds
3 large eggs
Whole blanched almonds

1. Grease an 18 cm/7 inch square tin or a 20 cm/
8 inch round tin and line it with greased, greaseproof
paper.
2. Cream together margarine, sugar and almond
essence.
3. Into another bowl sift flour and baking powder.
Into this mix prepared fruit and ground almonds.
4. In a third bowl beat the eggs.
5. Fold egg a little at a time, and fruit likewise, into
the creamed mixture. Do not beat.
6. Turn into tin. Level the top.
7. Bake in a warm oven, Gas 3, 325°F, 160°C, for
about 1¾ hours, when cake will be brown and firm
to the touch. During baking whole almonds are
carefully placed on cake. Do this while top of cake
is still just moist but not too soon or they will either
sink into the mixture or burn before cake is cooked.
8. Leave in tin to cool.

FRUIT LOAF

225 g/8 oz self-raising flour
A pinch of salt
125 g/4 oz firm margarine
Grated rind of 1 lemon
125 g/4 oz caster sugar*
50 g/2 oz currants
50 g/2 oz sultanas
50 g/2 oz quartered cherries
1 large egg
4 to 5 tablespoons milk

*Try also using 125 g/4 oz vanilla sugar (see page 242)
instead of the caster sugar in which case omit the lemon rind.

1. Grease a 900 g/2 lb loaf tin or a 15 cm/6 inch
square cake tin, and line base with greased, greaseproof paper.
2. Put flour and salt in a bowl and rub in margarine.
3. Add lemon rind and sugar and mix together.
4. Add fruit. Mix to a firm dropping consistency
with beaten egg and 4 tablespoons milk, adding extra
milk if mixture will not fall from spoon with a flick
of the wrist.
5. Place in tin, smooth top with the back of a spoon.
6. Bake in centre of a moderate oven, Gas 4, 350°F,
180°C, for 1 to 1½ hours until firm and leaving sides
of tin.
7. Cool on a wire rack.

HEAVY CAKE

In Cornwall this was made in the fishing villages
south of Truro. When the seine net was being hauled
in and the men shouting 'heave' with every pull, the
wives would know the men would soon be in for tea
and would make this quick flat cake to be eaten
warm or cold.

225 g/8 oz flour*
¼ teaspoon salt
50 g/2 oz lard
75 g/3 oz sugar
175 g/6 oz currants
2 to 3 tablespoons milk
50 g/2 oz butter

*If you prefer wholewheat flour it is best made with two
thirds wholewheat and one third white flour, otherwise too
heavy!

1. Mix flour and salt in a bowl and rub in lard.
2. Add sugar and currants. Mix to a soft dough with
milk.
3. Using a floured board, roll out to a long strip
about 15 cm/6 inches wide and 3 times as long,
about 45 cm/18 inches.
4. Dot half of the butter over the top two-thirds of
the pastry. Fold the bottom third, without fat, upwards. Then fold the top third down over it.
5. Give the pastry a half-turn so that folds are at
sides.
6. Roll out again into a thin strip and spread the rest
of the butter as before, repeating the folding in the
same way.

7. Roll out finally into a square about 1 cm/$\frac{1}{2}$ inch thick. Criss-cross the top with a knife, like a net. Brush with a little milk.

8. Bake above middle of a moderately hot oven, Gas 6, 400°F, 200°C, for 25 to 30 minutes. Remove on to a wire rack to cool.

Eat fresh.

Mrs Jean Daybell
Cornwall Women's Institute

KENTISH HOP-PICKERS CAKE

Moist and spicy. Inclined to sink in middle. Keeps well.

Makes 2 cakes in $\frac{1}{2}$ kg/1 lb loaf tins

275 g/10 oz self-raising flour
1 teaspoon ground ginger
1 teaspoon mixed spice
175 g/6 oz margarine
125 g/4 oz soft brown sugar
125 g/4 oz sultanas
125 g/4 oz currants
50 g/2 oz mixed peel
450 ml/$\frac{3}{4}$ pint milk
1 tablespoon black treacle
1 level teaspoon cream of tartar
$\frac{1}{2}$ level teaspoon bicarbonate of soda

1. Sift flour and spices into a bowl.
2. Rub in margarine.
3. Add sugar and fruit.
4. Warm milk with treacle and dissolve in it the cream of tartar and bicarbonate of soda.
5. Mix liquid into dry ingredients with a wooden spoon. The mixture should drop from the spoon.
6. Grease and line two 450 g/1 lb loaf tins and put in the mixture.
7. Bake in middle of a warm oven, Gas 3, 325°F, 160°C, for about 1$\frac{1}{2}$ hours until cakes are firm to the touch.
8. Leave cakes to cool in tins.

Mrs Zina Barnard
Whitstable, Kent

LINCOLNSHIRE FARMHOUSE DRIPPING CAKE

225 g/8 oz plain flour
$\frac{1}{2}$ level teaspoon salt
175 g/6 oz dripping
50 g/2 oz candied peel
225 g/8 oz raisins
175 g/6 oz sugar
1 tablespoon black treacle
300 ml/$\frac{1}{2}$ pint milk (approx.)
2 eggs, beaten
1 level teaspoon bicarbonate of soda

1. Grease a 20 cm/8 inch square cake tin and line with greased, greaseproof paper.
2. Sift flour with salt, rub in dripping.
3. Add chopped candied peel, stoned raisins and sugar to the flour.
4. Warm the treacle in half of the milk, mix with the eggs and add to ingredients in bowl.
5. Dissolve bicarbonate of soda in 1 tablespoon of the milk and add.
6. Stir all together using remaining milk as necessary to make a consistency that will just drop from the spoon when it is shaken.
7. Put into prepared cake tin. Level the top with back of a spoon.
8. Bake in moderate oven, Gas 4, 350°F, 180°C, for 1$\frac{1}{2}$ to 2 hours. Reduce temperature to moderate, Gas 3, 325°F, 160°C, after 1 hour.

Mrs G. Farrow, Thornton Abbey
Mrs Howard, Welbourn

SULTANA CAKE

A moist cake. Keeps well.

225 g/8 oz sultanas
125 g/4 oz butter, or firm margarine, cut in small pieces
175 g/6 oz sugar
2 small beaten eggs
A little almond essence
175 g/6 oz self-raising flour
Pinch of salt
50 g/2 oz chopped nuts (optional)

Note: If using nuts reduce quantity of sultanas to 175 g/6 oz.

1. Cover sultanas with water and soak overnight. Next day, bring to the boil.
2. Strain sultanas and mix them, while hot, into butter or margarine.
3. Add sugar, eggs and almond essence.
4. Sift in flour and salt.
5. Lastly, add chopped nuts, if desired. Mix well.
6. Grease a 20 cm/8 inch round tin and line bottom with greased, greaseproof paper. Tip cake mixture in and smooth the top.
7. Bake in a moderate oven, Gas 4, 350°F, 180°C, for 30 minutes. Lower heat to cool, Gas 2, 300°F, 150°C, until firm to touch in centre.

Mrs C. M. Armstrong
Canonbie, Dumfriesshire

PORTLAND RICE CAKE

A recipe from 'What's Cooking in Dorset', published by the Dorset Federation of Women's Institutes.

225 g/8 oz self-raising flour
½ teaspoon bicarbonate of soda
½ teaspoon cinnamon
½ teaspoon nutmeg
125 g/4 oz ground rice
75 g/3 oz butter or margarine
175 g/6 oz lard
75 g/3 oz soft brown sugar
450 g/1 lb currants
50 g/2 oz mixed peel
2 beaten eggs
300 ml/½ pint milk
1 teaspoon vinegar

1. Sift together flour, bicarbonate of soda, cinnamon and nutmeg.
2. Stir in ground rice.
3. Rub in butter and lard.
4. Add sugar, currants and peel and mix well.
5. Add eggs, milk and vinegar and beat into mixture.
6. Grease a 23 cm/9 inch square tin and line it with greased, greaseproof paper. Put in the mixture and smooth the surface.
7. Bake in the lower part of a cool oven, Gas 2, 300°F, 150°C, for 1 hour. Then reduce heat to Gas

1, 275°F, 140°C, for a further 30 minutes, when cake will be firm and golden brown in colour.
8. Leave it to cool in the tin.

Mrs S. Patterson
Buckland Newton, Dorset

BLAKENEY FRITTERS

Makes 10

75 g/3 oz plain flour
40 g/1½ oz margarine
25 g/1 oz sugar
1 large egg-yolk
Jam

1. Put flour in a bowl and rub in margarine.
2. Add sugar and egg-yolk and work mixture into a paste.
3. Roll little balls of mixture and put them on a lightly-greased baking sheet.
4. Make a hole in each with the end of a wooden spoon. Brush over with a little white of egg.
5. Bake above middle of a moderate oven, Gas 4, 350°F, 180°C, for 30 minutes until just turning golden.
6. Slide off on to a wire rack to cool. Fill the hole in each biscuit with jam.

Mrs Phyl Drinkwater
for Blakeney W.I., Glos.

BRIGHTON ROCKS

Certainly not rock-like.
They freeze well.

Made small the yield is 35, easy to make half this quantity.

125 g/4 oz butter or margarine
125 g/4 oz caster sugar
2 beaten eggs
50 g/2 oz currants
50 g/2 oz ground almonds
225 g/8 oz plain flour
1 teaspoon rose-water or lemon juice

1. Cream butter and sugar.
2. Save 1 tablespoon of egg for glazing and beat in the rest with rose-water or lemon juice.
3. Work in currants, ground almonds and flour.
4. Form into walnut-sized balls and place on greased baking trays. Brush with a little beaten egg.
5. Bake in middle of a hot oven, Gas 7, 425°F, 220°C, for about 10 minutes until just golden.
6. Cool on a wire rack.

Mrs Ruth Brooke and Mrs Gaye Goodall
Hove and Steyning, West Sussex

COCONUT BUNS

Makes about 16

125 g/4 oz self-raising white or wholewheat flour
125 g/4 oz desiccated coconut
75 g/3 oz sugar, either white or dark brown Barbados
125 g/4 oz margarine
1 beaten egg

Using wholewheat flour and Barbados sugar gives good flavour, but buns are not so light and tend to dry out a bit after 3 or 4 days.

1. Mix flour, coconut and sugar in a bowl.
2. Rub in margarine.
3. Use a fork and mix thoroughly with beaten egg.
4. Fork out rough heaps of the mixture on to a greased baking sheet.
5. Bake towards top of a moderately hot oven, Gas 5, 375°F, 190°C, for 10 to 15 minutes.

Margaret Heywood
Todmorden, Yorkshire

COCONUT DROPS

Makes about 25

225 g/8 oz self-raising flour*
125 g/4 oz margarine
175 g/6 oz caster sugar
50 g/2 oz desiccated coconut
2 medium-sized beaten eggs

*Can be made with half white and half wholewheat flour. If you cannot buy self-raising wholewheat flour, add ½ level teaspoon baking powder. Delicious also with light soft brown sugar.

1. Put flour in a bowl and rub in margarine.
2. Mix in the rest of the ingredients. Mixture will be firm but not stiff.
3. Roll mixture into balls and place, well apart, on a greased baking tray. Press each biscuit lightly with a fork.
4. Bake near top of a moderately hot oven, Gas 5, 375°F, 190°C, for 10 to 12 minutes or until pale brown. For a crisper result leave in oven till a shade darker.

Mrs Elsie Kaye
Saltmarshe, N. Humberside

GOOSNARGH CAKES

225 g/8 oz plain white flour
A pinch of salt
1 large teaspoon coriander powder (optional)
1 small teaspoon caraway seeds (optional)
175 g/6 oz butter (fresh farm butter makes the best Goosnargh cakes)
Caster sugar to coat

Note: The coriander powder and caraway seeds give the Goosnargh cakes a delicate flavour but they are very good without.

1. Mix together flour, salt, coriander powder and caraway seeds.
2. Rub in butter and knead to smooth dough with hands.
3. Roll out on floured board to about 7 mm/¼ inch thick.
4. Cut into 5 cm/2 inch rounds with a plain cutter—a wineglass is ideal.
5. Coat liberally with caster sugar and place on baking sheet.

6. Leave overnight.

7. Bake in a very cool oven, Gas $\frac{1}{2}$, 250°F, 130°C, for 30 to 45 minutes until firm but not golden. They should be pale in colour.

8. While still warm sift on a little more sugar.

When cool put in a tin. They will keep for months.

Mrs J. Seed
Garstang

VICTORIA SANDWICH MIXTURE FOR SMALL ICED CAKES

125 g/4 oz margarine
125 g/4 oz vanilla sugar*
125 g/4 oz self-raising flour
A pinch of salt
1 teaspoon cornflour
2 large beaten eggs

TO ICE AND DECORATE
Butter icing (*see page 320*)
Coconut
Chocolate vermicelli
Nuts, cherries, etc.

*See page 242.

1. Beat margarine until soft.
2. Beat in sugar until fluffy.
3. Sieve flour, salt and cornflour into another bowl.
4. Add egg and flour alternately to creamed mixture.
5. Grease a tin 18 cm/7 inches square and approximately 4 cm/1$\frac{1}{2}$ inches deep, line base. Put in the mixture.
6. Bake in the centre of a moderate oven, Gas 4, 350°F, 180°C, for approximately 40 minutes until firm and springy and shrinking from tin.
7. Next day cut into small rounds or squares, spread butter icing around sides, roll in coconut or chocolate vermicelli and pipe butter icing on top. Decorate with nuts, cherries etc.

These cakes will freeze. Pack into shallow foil containers—1 layer only. Place in freezer overnight. Place in polythene bags next day. Remove from bag before thawing.

ROCK BUNS

These will freeze very well.

Makes 18 to 20 buns.

225 g/8 oz self-raising flour
$\frac{1}{2}$ level teaspoon salt
125 g/4 oz firm margarine
75 g/3 oz vanilla sugar (*see page 242*)
40 g/1$\frac{1}{2}$ oz currants
15 g/$\frac{1}{2}$ oz candied peel
1 beaten egg
2 tablespoons milk
Caster sugar

1. Put flour and salt in a bowl. Rub in margarine. Add sugar and fruit.
2. Mix to a stiff consistency with beaten egg and milk.
3. Grease 2 baking trays. Place mixture on trays using 2 forks dipped in milk. Leave rough. Dredge with caster sugar.
4. Bake in a hot oven, Gas 7, 425°F, 220°C, for about 12 to 15 minutes until firm and slightly golden.
5. Cool on wire rack.

BANANA AND NUT FINGERS

225 g/8 oz porridge oats
225 g/8 oz sugar
225 g/8 oz wholewheat flour
$\frac{1}{2}$ teaspoon bicarbonate of soda
225 g/8 oz butter or margarine
2 beaten eggs
4 bananas
A few chopped nuts (optional)

1. Mix all dry ingredients together.
2. Rub in butter or margarine.
3. Mix to a stiff dough with the beaten eggs.
4. Divide into 2 equal portions.
5. Grease a shallow tin, 23 cm/9 inches square.
6. Line tin with half the mixture.

7. Cover with finely-sliced bananas and chopped nuts.

8. Spread remainder of mixture over and press down firmly.

9. Bake in a moderately hot oven, Gas 5, 375°F, 190°C, for 20 to 25 minutes until golden brown.

10. Cut into fingers while still warm and leave to cool in the tin.

Sybil Norcott
Irlam, Nr Manchester

COCONUT BROWNIES

Rich chewy cakes.

Makes 9 or 12

50 g/2 oz plain cooking chocolate
125 g/4 oz butter or margarine
2 large eggs, lightly-beaten
½ teaspoon vanilla essence
225 g/8 oz sugar
50 g/2 oz self-raising flour
¼ level teaspoon salt
50 g/2 oz desiccated coconut

1. Break chocolate in pieces. Put it with butter in a pan and heat *very* gently until both are melted.

2. Remove from heat and, using a wooden spoon, gradually beat in the eggs. The mixture will thicken.

3. Add vanilla and sugar, then flour, salt and coconut. Mix thoroughly.

4. Grease an 18 cm/7 inch square shallow tin and line base with greased foil. Pour in mixture.

5. Bake above middle of a moderate oven, Gas 4, 350°F, 180°C, for 50 to 60 minutes when the cake will be crisp at the edges and feel firm in the middle.

6. Leave to cool a little, trim the edges and loosen cake from sides of tin with a knife. Leave to go firm then turn out and remove foil.

7. When quite cold cut into 9 or 12 pieces.

Margaret Heywood
Todmorden, Yorkshire

CHOCOLATE BROWNIES

Makes 12

75 g/3 oz margarine
50 g/2 oz plain cooking chocolate
2 beaten eggs
175 g/6 oz caster sugar
1 teaspoon vanilla essence
50 g/2 oz walnuts, chopped
75 g/3 oz plain white flour
½ level teaspoon baking powder

1. Grease an 18 cm/7 inch square, shallow tin and line base with greased, greaseproof paper.

2. Stand a large basin over hot water, put in the margarine and chocolate and allow it to melt. Cool.

3. Stir in eggs, sugar, vanilla essence and walnuts. Mix well. Sift flour and baking powder, and fold into mixture.

4. Pour into tin. Bake in a moderate oven, Gas 4, 350°F, 180°C, for about 40 minutes until firm. Leave in tin to cool. While still just warm sprinkle with caster sugar.

5. Cut into 12 pieces when cold.

CHOCOLATE AND CHERRY COOKIES

Makes about 30

125 g/4 oz margarine
50 g/2 oz soft brown sugar
1 level tablespoon honey
25 g/1 oz glacé cherries, chopped small
25 g/1 oz chocolate chips
125 g/4 oz plain white flour or half wholewheat half white

1. Beat together margarine, sugar and honey until fluffy.

2. Mix in cherries, chocolate chips and flour and work together.

3. Place teaspoons of the mixture well apart on a greased baking tray.

4. Bake in middle of a moderate oven, Gas 4, 350°F, 180°C, for 15 to 18 minutes until golden.

5. Leave on baking tray for 1 minute to firm up. Then lift on to a wire rack to cool.

CHOCOLATE COCONUT SLAB

160 g/5½ oz margarine
175 g/6 oz self-raising flour
1 good dessertspoon cocoa
125 g/4 oz coconut
75 g/3 oz brown sugar
125 g/4 oz cooking chocolate
A walnut of butter

1. Melt margarine in a large pan. Remove from heat.
2. Sift together flour and cocoa and add it, with the coconut and sugar, to the margarine. Mix well.
3. Grease a shallow, flat tin (a Swiss roll tin is suitable).
4. Spread mixture in the tin.
5. Bake in middle of a moderate oven, Gas 4, 350°F, 180°C, for 20 to 25 minutes.
6. Remove from oven and leave in tin to cool.
7. Meanwhile, melt cooking chocolate and butter in a bowl over a pan of simmering water. Do not let bowl touch water.
8. Spread chocolate mixture evenly over top of cooked coconut slab.

Leave until chocolate is set and cake is cold then cut into desired shapes.

J.M. Klüver
Hillingdon, Middlesex

CHOCOLATE PEPPERMINT SQUARES

A recipe from 'What's Cooking In Dorset', published by the Dorset Federation Of Women's Institutes.

Makes 16

125 g/4 oz margarine
50 g/2 oz caster sugar
3 level teaspoons baking powder
125 g/4 oz plain flour
50 g/2 oz desiccated coconut

BUTTER CREAM
50 g/2 oz margarine
75 g/3 oz icing sugar
1 small teaspoon peppermint essence
Drop of green colouring

TOPPING
175 g/6 oz plain cooking chocolate

1. Beat margarine until soft and cream with the caster sugar.
2. Sift in baking powder and flour.
3. Add coconut and mix well.
4. Press mixture into a greased tin approximately 20 cm/8 inches square.
5. Bake in lower part of a warm oven, Gas 3, 325°F, 160°C, for about 30 minutes when cake will be soft but springy to the touch, slightly risen and golden.
6. Allow to cool in tin until firm, crisp and biscuit-like. Then cover with butter cream.

BUTTER CREAM
1. Beat margarine till soft.
2. Sift in icing sugar, adding essence and colouring carefully.
3. Spread over cold cake base.
4. Melt chocolate in a small bowl over a pan of simmering water. Do not let water touch bowl.
5. Spread warm chocolate over butter cream.
6. Cut into squares with a sharp knife when chocolate has almost set. Leave in tin until set.

Mrs Joane Robinson
Cranborne, Dorset

BRIGHTON SANDWICH

225 g/8 oz self-raising flour
25 g/1 oz semolina, optional
125 g/4 oz caster sugar
125 g/4 oz butter
1 egg, well-beaten
2 tablespoons apricot jam
25 g/1 oz almonds, blanched and split

1. Grease a 20 cm/8 inch cake tin and line with greased, greaseproof paper, or use a 20 cm/8 inch flan ring placed on a baking sheet.
2. Put flour, semolina and sugar in a bowl. Rub in butter.
3. Add beaten egg and bind together. Divide mixture in half.
4. Roll out one half of mixture and fit it into tin or flan ring. Spread jam in centre.
5. Roll out second half of mixture and place on top. Cover with split almonds.
6. Bake in centre of a moderate oven, Gas 4, 350°F, 180°C, for 15 minutes, then reduce heat to moderate, Gas 3, 325°F, 160°C, for a further 20 minutes.

Miss V.M. Secker
Bury St Edmunds

DATE BARS

No baking in oven.

Makes 6 to 8

125 g/4 oz margarine
125 g/4 oz sugar
225 g/8 oz chopped dates
225 g/8 oz sweet biscuits, broken into pieces

1. Melt margarine and sugar in pan.
2. Add chopped dates, mix well and cook 2 or 3 minutes.
3. Remove from heat and add broken biscuits. Mix well.
4. Press into a shallow, greased Swiss roll tin. Leave to cool.
5. Cut into bars when cold.

May be iced with melted chocolate before cutting into bars. Or dip the ends into melted chocolate.

Sybil Norcott
Irlam, Nr Manchester

GINGER SHORTCAKE

SHORTCAKE
225 g/8 oz plain flour
1 teaspoon ground ginger
75 g/3 oz sugar
175 g/6 oz margarine or butter

TOPPING
1 tablespoon golden syrup
50 g/2 oz butter or margarine
2 tablespoons icing sugar
1 level teaspoon ginger

1. Sieve flour and ginger into a bowl and stir in the sugar.
2. Rub in the margarine or butter until mixture works into a ball.
3. Press mixture into a Swiss roll tin or a shallow tin measuring about 18 by 28 cm/7 by 11 inches. Level top with a palette knife.
4. Bake in moderate oven, Gas 4, 350°F, 180°C, for 40 minutes. The mixture will still be slightly soft when it comes out of oven.
5. Meanwhile, mix the topping. Melt syrup and butter in a pan and stir in icing sugar and ginger.
6. Pour topping over shortcake while both are still hot.
7. Allow to cool slightly, then cut into fingers.

Pat Dixon
Holmfirth, W. Yorkshire

MATRIMONIAL CAKE

This cake keeps very well. It has a rough, crunchy top, a smooth filling and a firm base. Its old-fashioned name seems entirely suitable: you take the rough with the smooth.

125 g/4 oz porridge oats
75 g/3 oz wholewheat flour
50 g/2 oz Barbados sugar
75 g/3 oz butter

FILLING
225 g/8 oz stoned dates
25 g/1 oz Barbados sugar
125 ml/4 fl oz water

1. *Start with the filling:* chop dates and cook gently with the sugar and water until like a paste, soft but not sloppy. Leave to cool.
2. Mix oats, flour and sugar.
3. Rub in butter until it is like a 'crumble' mixture.
4. Put half this mixture into a greased tin, about 18 cm/7 inches square. Pat down firmly.
5. Spread with the date paste.
6. Cover with rest of crumble mixture and pat down gently.
7. Bake just above middle of a moderately hot oven, Gas 4, 350°F, 180°C, for 15 to 20 minutes until golden brown.
8. Cut into squares while still hot, then leave to cool in tin. Lift slices out when cool.

Margaret Heywood
Todmorden, Yorkshire

SHORTBREAD TOFFEE PIECES

Makes about 16

SHORTBREAD
125 g/4 oz margarine
50 g/2 oz caster sugar
150 g/5 oz self-raising white or brown flour

TOFFEE
125 g/4 oz margarine
125 g/4 oz caster sugar
2 tablespoons golden syrup
Half a 383 g/13.5 oz tin of condensed milk

TOPPING
125 g/4 oz plain cooking chocolate

1. *Shortbread base*. Cream margarine and sugar. Mix in flour. Spread in a greased 28 by 18 cm/11 by 7 inch Swiss roll tin.

2. Bake above centre of a moderate oven, Gas 4, 350°F, 180°C, for 20 minutes. Allow to cool in tin.

3. *Toffee*. Melt margarine, sugar, syrup and condensed milk in a pan and cook gently, stirring, until the mixture leaves the sides of the pan.

4. Pour over the cooled shortbread and leave to cool again.

5. *Topping*. Heat an ovenproof bowl. Break chocolate into it in small pieces and let it melt in the hot bowl. Spread melted chocolate over toffee. Allow to cool.

6. Turn out on to a board and cut into small pieces.

BISCUITS

Using the Viennese Mixture.

175 g/6 oz soft margarine (or butter)
50 g/2 oz vanilla sugar*
175 g/6 oz soft plain flour

TO DECORATE
Plain chocolate
Cherries
Jam or lemon curd
Icing sugar

**See page 242.*

1. Cream butter and sugar until very soft, work in the flour.

2. Use a large forcing bag and fluted nozzle:

Fingers

1. Pipe fingers 6.5 cm/2½ inches long on to a greased baking tray.

2. Bake in a moderate oven, Gas 4, 350°F, 180°C, for about 10 minutes until firm, but only very slightly coloured.

3. Allow to cool.

4. Dip ends in melted chocolate.

Stars

1. Pipe star shapes, place a small piece of cherry in centre.

2. Bake as above.

Tea Cakes

1. Pipe mixture into paper baking cases in a spiral, leaving a small dent in the centre of each.

2. Bake as above, for approximately 20 minutes. Cool, leaving in paper cases.

3. Before serving, place a little jam or lemon curd in centre and sift on a little icing sugar.

PLAIN BISCUITS

Makes about 24

190 g/7 oz plain white flour
¼ teaspoon salt
25 g/1 oz semolina
125 g/4 oz margarine
125 g/4 oz caster sugar
1 beaten egg

1. Mix flour, salt and semolina.

2. Rub in the margarine.

3. Add sugar.

4. Bind with beaten egg to make a firm paste. If a little soft, wrap in greaseproof paper and leave in a cool place for a short while.

5. Roll out thinly on a floured board and cut into shapes. Place on a lightly greased baking tray.

6. Bake near top of a moderately hot oven, Gas 5, 375°F, 190°C, for 12 minutes approximately until pale golden.

7. Leave on tray 1 to 2 minutes to crisp. Remove carefully on to a cooling wire. When quite cold, store in airtight tin.

These can be glacé iced and decorated.

VARIATIONS
Use vanilla sugar (*see page 242*) in place of caster sugar.

Add 1 teaspoon lemon or orange rind with the caster sugar.

Add 25 g/1 oz currants with the caster sugar (an unfluted cutter is easier to use with this mixture). ½ level teaspoon mixed spice or powdered cinnamon can be sieved with the flour if desired.

A TIP
Biscuits should never be stored in a tin containing cakes or pastry. They will lose their crispness.

SUGAR BISCUITS

Makes about 24

125 g/4 oz butter or firm margarine
125 g/4 oz caster sugar
1 teaspoon lemon rind
1 egg (separated)
¼ teaspoon salt
175 g/6 oz plain flour
25 g/1 oz semolina
Extra caster sugar for dredging

1. Lightly cream together butter, sugar and lemon rind.
2. Work in egg-yolk and salt until blended.
3. Add flour and semolina and combine to make a firm paste. If a little soft, wrap in greaseproof paper and leave in a cool place for a short while.
4. Roll out thinly on a floured board and cut into shapes. Place on a lightly greased baking tray.
5. Whisk egg-white lightly to liquify and brush it over the tops of biscuits. Dredge with caster sugar.
6. Bake near top of a moderate oven, Gas 4, 350°F, 180°C, for 12 to 15 minutes until pale golden. They may require checking half way through baking as sugar browns easily.
7. Leave on tray 1 to 2 minutes to crisp. Remove carefully on to a cooling wire. When quite cold, store in airtight tin.

VARIATIONS
Use orange rind instead of lemon. Use vanilla sugar (*see page 242*) in place of plain caster sugar and omit lemon rind.

ABERNETHY BISCUITS

Makes about 30

50 g/2 oz sugar
3 tablespoons milk
225 g/8 oz self-raising flour
A pinch of salt
75 g/3 oz margarine
50 g/2 oz cooking fat

1. Put sugar and milk in a small pan over low heat and stir until dissolved. Allow to cool.
2. Sift flour and salt into a bowl, rub in fats and bind to a dough with the cooled liquid.

3. Using a floured board, roll out dough to 7 mm/¼ inch thick. Cut round biscuits and place them a little apart on baking trays. *Or*, make small balls of the dough, place on baking tray and flatten them with fingertips. Prick each biscuit with a fork.
4. Bake near top of a moderately hot oven, Gas 5, 375°F, 190°C, for 15 minutes when biscuits will be pale golden brown.
5. Slide off baking trays on to a wire rack to cool.

Anne Wallace
Stewarton, Ayrshire

SHORTBREAD

225 g/8 oz butter
125 g/4 oz vanilla sugar*
(If no vanilla sugar, use caster sugar, but in this case do not add vanilla essence)
325 g/12 oz plain white flour

*See page 242.

1. Work the butter until soft in mixing bowl.
2. Mix in the sugar until creaming, but do not beat in any more air than necessary.
3. Mix in the flour using hands if necessary. The mixture should be firm—the consistency of short-crust pastry. Knead lightly until smooth and free from cracks, leave to rest if possible until a little firmer and easy to roll.
4. Using half the quantity, roll out a circle 1 to 1.5 cm/½ to ¾ inch thick, flute the edges, and mark with knife into 8 sections. Prick with skewer to prevent bubbling during baking. Place on lightly greased baking tray.
5. Use second half of the pastry to make shortbread fingers. Roll out 1 cm/½ inch thick, cut into oblongs 2.5 by 5 cm/1 inch by 2 inches. Prick with a fork.
6. Bake in a moderate oven, Gas 4, 350°F, 180°C, until straw-coloured and firm, about 30 minutes.

Shortbread is broken into wedges, not cut.

VARIATIONS
1. Try adding some chopped nuts or chopped candied peel.
2. Add the grated rind of an orange or a lemon with ½ teaspoon of ground ginger or cinnamon. This produces a slightly crisper shortbread.

SHORTBREAD BISCUITS

Try the variations in flavours and finishing given below.

Can be done by hand or with an electric mixer. Freeze well.

225 g/8 oz unsalted or slightly salted butter
125 g/4 oz caster sugar
325 g/12 oz plain white flour, sifted

TO FINISH
Extra caster sugar

1. Use softened butter but do not let it melt and become oily. Put it in a warm bowl.
2. Beat in sugar and flour and work mixture together thoroughly. If using an electric mixer, warm the bowl, put all ingredients in together and beat until mixture looks like damp breadcrumbs.
3. Form into a fat sausage about 4 cm/1½ inches thick. Roll this on a board sprinkled with caster sugar, and put into refrigerator for one hour to firm up.
4. Then, using a sharp knife, cut thin slices from the roll, 7 mm/¼ inch thick or less.
5. Place on greased baking trays, or trays lined with non-stick baking paper.
6. Bake above middle of a cool oven, Gas 2, 300°F, 150°C, for about 30 minutes until golden. Take care not to overbake or the biscuits will develop a bitter taste.
7. Remove from oven and dredge with caster sugar while still hot. Leave on trays to firm up. Then slide on to a wire rack to cool.
8. When cold, store in airtight tins and remove from tins just before serving.

VARIATIONS
1. Delicious made with wholewheat flour, but it is not so easy to make perfectly-shaped biscuits.
2. Unusual fragrance by incorporating ½ teaspoon dried or ¼ teaspoon fresh rosemary, finely chopped. Work it in at paragraph 3.
3. Another unusual flavour using ¼ teaspoon caraway seeds.
4. *Dorset Shortbread*. The 'sausage' is rolled in demerara sugar at paragraph 3 above. Do not dredge with caster sugar at paragraph 7. Although this recipe is different, this method of finishing is typical of traditional Dorset shortbread. This method was contributed by members of Dorset Women's Institute.

SHORTCAKE BISCUIT STARS

Swiftly made with an electric mixer but can also be done by hand.

Makes about 24

225 g/8 oz softened margarine
50 g/2 oz icing sugar
225 g/8 oz plain white flour or half white and half wholewheat

TO DECORATE
Glacé cherries (optional)

1. Cream margarine until soft and fluffy.
2. Sift in icing sugar. Beat again.
3. Add flour and beat until smooth.
4. Using a forcing bag with a large star nozzle, pipe star shapes on to a greased baking tray. Put a tiny piece of cherry on top of each star.
5. Bake in the middle of a cool oven, Gas 2, 300°F, 150°C, for 30 minutes until golden. Do not overbake or biscuits will develop a bitter flavour.

BRANDY SNAPS

Makes about 24

65 g/2½ oz golden syrup (measure carefully)
50 g/2 oz butter
50 g/2 oz caster sugar
50 g/2 oz plain flour
½ level teaspoon ground ginger

FILLING
150 ml/¼ pint double cream
1 teaspoon brandy

1. Warm together in a pan the syrup, butter and sugar, until all are melted, but not too hot. Sieve flour and ginger and mix in.
2. Well grease a large baking sheet and place on it teaspoons of the mixture, well apart to allow for spreading, not more than 4 at a time.
3. Bake in a moderate oven, Gas 3, 325°F, 160°C, for about 8 to 10 minutes until golden.
4. Remove tray on to a damp cloth on table and have ready a large wooden spoon, with the handle greased. Leave for a few seconds for brandy snaps to become firm enough to lift from tray with palette

knife. Roll each one quickly round spoon handle and slide off on to wire rack to cool.

5. Follow same procedure until all mixture is used. Will make about 24.

6. Whip the cream, fold in brandy and pipe a rosette of cream at each end of brandy snap.

DEMERARA BRANDY SNAPS

Makes about 24

50 g/2 oz plain white flour
50 g/2 oz golden syrup
50 g/2 oz demerara sugar
50 g/2 oz butter
1 teaspoon ground ginger
2 teaspoons lemon juice

TO FINISH
Whipped cream
A pinch of sugar
Brandy

1. Put flour to warm in a warm oven, Gas 3, 325°F, 160°C, for 10 minutes.

2. Weigh a saucepan and weigh into it the golden syrup. This is the easiest way to measure syrup without getting sticky.

3. Melt syrup, sugar and butter. Remove from heat.

4. Mix in warmed flour, sift in ginger and add lemon juice. Stir well.

5. Put teaspoons of the mixture on to well-greased baking trays, or trays lined with non-stick baking paper. Keep them 15 cm/6 inches apart because they spread out very thinly while baking.

6. Bake in a warm oven, Gas 3, 325°F, 160°C, for 10 minutes or until nicely golden.

7. Leave for 1 or 2 minutes to firm up a little. Then quickly roll each brandy snap into a tube around the greased handle of a wooden spoon. Leave to cool.

8. Mix sugar and brandy to taste into whipped cream. Using an icing bag with a 1 cm/½ inch star pipe, fill each brandy snap.

Mrs Amy Cannon
Goole, N. Humberside

CHOCOLATE BUTTONS

Makes about 24 single buttons

125 g/4 oz margarine
50 g/2 oz vanilla sugar*
Pinch of salt
125 g/4 oz self-raising flour
25 g/1 oz drinking chocolate powder
Approximately 50 g/2 oz plain chocolate

**See page 242.*

1. Cream margarine and sugar until fluffy.

2. Add salt, work in the flour sieved with chocolate powder.

3. With damp hands roll into balls about the size of a walnut.

4. Place on greased baking tray, leaving room for spreading. Mark tops with a fork dipped in cold water, and flatten slightly.

5. Bake in a moderate oven, Gas 4, 350°F, 180°C, for 8 to 10 minutes. They will rise a little at first, then flatten, and are soon baked when this happens. Do not overbake, it spoils the flavour.

6. Leave on tray for 1 minute to crisp, remove carefully with spatula on to a wire tray. Leave until cold. Sandwich in pairs with melted chocolate.

WARWICKSHIRE CHOCOLATE BISCUITS

Quick to make.

Makes about 20

75 g/3 oz margarine
50 g/2 oz soft brown sugar
2 teaspoons cocoa
Pinch of salt
Vanilla essence
125 g/4 oz self-raising flour
25 g/1 oz cornflakes, crushed

TO DECORATE
Melted chocolate
Almonds, optional

1. Cream together margarine and sugar.

2. Stir in cocoa, salt and vanilla essence. Mix well.

3. Beat in gradually and alternately the self-raising flour and crushed cornflakes.

4. Knead well. Shape into balls about the size of a walnut.

5. Place on a lightly greased baking sheet and flatten a little. Allow space for them to spread.

6. Bake in moderate oven, Gas 3, 325°F, 160°C, for 15 minutes until just firm.

7. When cool ice with melted chocolate. Decorate with almonds if liked.

FLORENTINES

225 g/8 oz plain cooking chocolate
50 g/2 oz margarine
125 g/4 oz soft brown sugar
1 egg
5 heaped tablespoons desiccated coconut
3 heaped tablespoons chopped nuts
2 heaped tablespoons chopped glacé cherries
2 heaped tablespoons mixed peel
2 heaped tablespoons sultanas

1. Melt chocolate in a small bowl over a pan of simmering water.

2. Spread melted chocolate in bottom of a Swiss roll tin. Leave to set.

3. Beat together margarine and sugar.

4. Beat in the egg.

5. Add all other ingredients.

6. Spread mixture over the chocolate.

7. Bake in moderate oven, Gas 3, 325°F, 160°C, for 30 to 40 minutes.

8. Leave to cool. Cut into slices.

9. Remove from tin when quite cold.

10. Store in an air-tight tin in a cool place.

Sybil Norcott
Irlam, Manchester

FLAPJACKS

Makes 15

75 g/3 oz margarine
2 tablespoons golden syrup or black treacle
75 g/3 oz Barbados sugar
150 g/5 oz porridge oats

1. Lightly grease a shallow 18 cm/7 inch square tin.

2. Put margarine and syrup or treacle in a saucepan. Heat gently until margarine has melted. Remove from heat.

3. Stir in sugar and rolled oats. Mix well.

4. Spread mixture evenly into tin.

5. Bake in centre of moderate oven, Gas 4, 350°F, 180°C, for 20 minutes.

6. Remove from oven. Leave to cool in tin for 5 minutes.

7. Cut into 5 strips down tin and into 3 across, to make 15 bars. Leave in tin until cold. Break into bars.

Flapjacks improve with keeping. Store in an air-tight tin for up to 4 weeks.

TRY THESE VARIATIONS

1. Add 2 rounded teaspoons grated orange rind and 50 g/2 oz currants to mixture at stage 3 of recipe.

2. Top flapjack mixture with 125 g/4 oz halved glacé cherries before baking.

3. Replace 25 g/1 oz of the rolled oats with 25 g/1 oz desiccated coconut.

GARIBALDI BISCUITS

Makes 18

125 g/4 oz self-raising white flour
A pinch of salt
25 g/1 oz quick creaming fat (ordinary lard is not as good)
2 tablespoons milk
50 g/2 oz currants
25 g/1 oz caster sugar

1. Combine flour, salt, fat and milk in a bowl, using a fork. Mix to a smooth dough.

2. Cut into 2 even-sized pieces, and roll out one piece on a floured board, no more than 7 mm/¼ inch thick.

3. Lift this on to a lightly-greased baking sheet. (Use a baking sheet without sides.)

4. Chop currants, mix in with 1 teaspoon of the sugar and sprinkle them over the pastry leaving a 1 cm/½ inch edge. Damp edges with water. Scatter remaining sugar over filling.

5. Roll out second piece of pastry to same size, place on top and seal edges.

6. Roll the rolling pin lightly over top until currants are just showing but not quite breaking through the pastry.

7. Mark into 9 squares, then across diagonally to make 18 triangles, brush with water and sprinkle on a little extra sugar.

8. Bake in a moderately hot oven, Gas 5, 375°F, 190°C, for about 15 minutes until firm and crisp.

GINGER BISCUITS

Makes about 40

225 g/8 oz sugar
125 g/4 oz golden syrup
125 g/4 oz margarine
325 g/12 oz self-raising flour
2 teaspoons ginger
¼ teaspoon cinnamon (optional)
1 level teaspoon bicarbonate of soda
1 beaten egg
A little butter (optional)

1. Put sugar, syrup and margarine in a pan and melt over a very low heat.

2. Sift flour, spices and bicarbonate of soda into a bowl.

3. Mix in the melted ingredients and add beaten egg. Mix again well.

4. Roll teaspoons of the mixture into little balls and place them well apart on a buttered* or greased baking sheet.

5. Bake in moderate oven, Gas 4, 350°F, 180°C, for about 20 minutes until they are golden and 'crazed' all over.

6. Leave on baking sheet for 1 to 2 minutes to firm up, then remove on to a wire rack to cool.

Mrs Boyer recommends buttering the baking sheets as the resulting flavour suggests biscuits have been made with butter instead of margarine.

Mrs Ruth Boyer
Cononley, W. Yorkshire

GINGER NUTS

Makes 24 –26 biscuits

125 g/4 oz self-raising flour
2 level teaspoons ground ginger
A pinch of salt
1 level dessertspoon caster sugar
½ level teaspoon bicarbonate of soda
50 g/2 oz margarine
50 g/2 oz golden syrup
A little milk

1. Sieve dry ingredients into a bowl.

2. Melt margarine and syrup over very low heat but do not allow to boil. Cool a little and mix into dry ingredients.

3. Grease a baking sheet. Roll mixture into small balls and place well apart on sheet to allow for spreading.

4. Flatten slightly with pastry brush dipped in milk.

5. Bake on the second shelf of a moderate oven, Gas 4, 350°F, 180°C, for 12 to 14 minutes until firm but not hard.

6. Leave on tray to crisp—1 to 2 minutes. Remove with spatula to cooling wire.

GRANDMA'S GINGER BISCUITS

Makes about 40

125 g/4 oz golden syrup
75 g/3 oz lard
50 g/2 oz sugar
1 teaspoon ginger
½ teaspoon bicarbonate of soda
225 g/8 oz self-raising flour

1. Put all ingredients except flour into a fairly large saucepan and heat gently until lard is melted.

2. Remove from heat and stir in flour, 2 tablespoons at a time.

3. Roll mixture into walnut-sized balls. Put them on a greased baking tray 5 cm/2 inches apart.

4. Bake above middle of a warm oven, Gas 3, 325°F, 160°C, for 10 minutes.

5. Leave on tray for a few minutes to firm up. Then lift on to a wire rack to cool.

Mrs Kathleen Smith
Armley, W. Yorkshire

MRS OADES' GINGER CRISPS

Makes about 325 g/¾ lb biscuits

225 g/8 oz plain flour
25 g/1 oz caster sugar
1 teaspoon ground ginger
1 level teaspoon bicarbonate of soda
125 g/4 oz golden syrup
50 g/2 oz butter or margarine

1. Sift dry ingredients into a bowl.
2. To be precise with golden syrup, put a small pan on to scales, weigh it and then weigh syrup into it.
3. Melt fat and syrup together over low heat.
4. Mix this very thoroughly into dry ingredients.
5. Line a 450 g/1 lb loaf tin with greaseproof paper.
6. Press the soft mixture into tin. Make top level and smooth. Leave for several hours, or overnight, in a cool place or refrigerator.
7. Turn biscuit loaf out of tin and use a sharp knife to cut very thin biscuits, about 7 mm/¼ inch thick or less.
8. Put biscuits on greased baking trays, or use non-stick baking paper to line tin.
9. Bake in middle of a warm oven, Gas 3, 325°F, 160°C, until golden. 3.5 mm/⅛ inch thick biscuits take about 12 minutes.
10. Leave on baking tin for 5 minutes to firm up, then put biscuits on to a wire rack to cool.

GRANTHAM GINGERBREADS

Makes 24 biscuits

125 g/4 oz butter or firm margarine
125 g/4 oz caster sugar
2 level teaspoons ground ginger
125 g/4 oz self-raising flour

1. Cream the fat and sugar lightly together until softening.
2. Add the ginger and then the flour and make into a stiff dough.
3. Roll into balls about half the size of a golf ball.
4. Put these on ungreased baking trays well apart and bake in the lower part of a cool oven, Gas ½, 250°F, 130°C, for three quarters of an hour.

Mrs J. Wilcox
Harlaxton, Lincolnshire

ASHBOURNE GINGERBREAD

225 g/8 oz butter
150 g/5 oz caster sugar
275 g/10 oz plain flour
2 level teaspoons ground ginger
Pinch of salt
Rind of 1 lemon, finely grated or 25 g/1 oz candied peel, finely-chopped

1. Cream together butter and sugar until quite soft.
2. Sift in flour, ginger and salt. Add lemon rind or peel.
3. Knead with the hands until a smooth dough is obtained.
4. Roll out with the hands into a long roll about 2.5 cm/1 inch thick. Cut into lengths 5 cm/2 inches long.
5. Put on lightly greased baking tray and flatten each roll a little with three fingers.
6. Bake for about 20 minutes in moderate oven, Gas 4, 350°F, 180°C.

Derbyshire

GRASMERE GINGERBREAD

175 g/6 oz wholewheat flour
50 g/2 oz porridge oats
½ level teaspoon bicarbonate of soda
1 level teaspoon cream of tartar
2 level teaspoons ginger
175 g/6 oz margarine
175 g/6 oz brown sugar, muscovado gives a nice flavour
50 g/2 oz mixed peel, finely-chopped (optional)

1. Put flour and oats in a bowl and sift in bicarbonate of soda, cream of tartar and ginger. Mix well.
2. Rub in margarine, stir in sugar and mixed peel.
3. Press mixture into a greased Swiss roll tin, 28 by 18 cm/11 by 7 inches. They will be thin biscuits.
4. Bake in a warm oven, Gas 3, 325°F, 160°C, for about 30 minutes until firm and brown.
5. Allow to cool in tin for 5 minutes then cut into fingers.

KRISPIE BISCUITS

Makes about 40

150 g/5 oz margarine
150 g/5 oz caster sugar
50 g/2 oz sultanas
1 beaten egg
175 g/6 oz self-raising flour
50 g/2 oz Rice Krispies

1. Put margarine and sugar in a large pan over low heat.
2. When margarine has melted, remove pan from heat and add sultanas, beaten egg and flour. Mix well. The mixture will be very soft.
3. Put the Rice Krispies in a flat dish and, using a teaspoon, drop in the biscuit mixture. Toss each teaspoon of mixture about so that it is well-covered.
4. Grease baking trays or line with non-stick baking paper. Space biscuits 5 cm/2 inches apart. Press each biscuit down with a fork.
5. Bake in middle of a warm oven, Gas 3, 325°F, 160°C, for 15 to 20 minutes until golden.
6. Leave on baking trays for 10 minutes to firm up. Then slide off on to a wire rack to cool.

CRUNCHY OAT COOKIES

Makes 14

75 g/3 oz porridge oats
50 g/2 oz plain flour
50 g/2 oz margarine
50 g/2 oz granulated sugar
1 level tablespoon golden syrup
½ level teaspoon bicarbonate of soda

1. Mix together porridge oats and flour.
2. Melt margarine in a large pan with sugar and syrup.
3. Stir bicarbonate of soda into mixture in pan.
4. Add flour and oats and mix well.
5. Make walnut-sized balls of mixture and place them, well apart, on well-greased baking sheets.
6. Bake in a moderate oven, Gas 4, 350°F, 180°C, for 11 to 15 minutes.
7. Let cookies cool slightly on baking sheet before removing them to a cooling wire.

Mrs J.M. Bell
Macclesfield, Cheshire

ORANGE CRISPS

Makes about 20

125 g/4 oz butter
50 g/2 oz caster sugar
Grated rind of 1 orange
150 g/5 oz self-raising flour

TO FINISH
Extra caster sugar

1. Rub butter into other ingredients until mixture resembles fine crumbs. Work together into a dough.
2. Roll small balls about 2.5 cm/1 inch in diameter. Put them 5 cm/2 inches apart on greased baking trays. Flatten with a fork dipped in cold water.
3. Bake above middle of a moderate oven, Gas 4, 350°F, 180°C, for 10 to 12 minutes until pale gold in colour.
4. Remove from baking trays on to a wire rack. Sprinkle with caster sugar while still hot.

From Cheshire W.I. 'Cook Book'

MERINGUES

Using an electric whisk.

Notes: Do not use fresh eggs. Be careful to use a grease-free bowl. Store meringues in a tight-lidded tin. Remove from tin at last minute. Sugar attracts moisture and the meringues will go soft if uncovered.

2 large egg-whites
A pinch of salt
A pinch of cream of tartar
125 g/4 oz caster sugar*

*Try also grinding demerara sugar to caster sugar consistency in electric grinder.

1. Whisk the egg-whites. When frothy, add salt and cream of tartar. Continue to whip at high speed until stiff.
2. Now lower the speed and add caster sugar, 2 tablespoons at a time, and continue beating well between each addition until all the sugar is used up and the mixture is thick and peaks easily.
3. Line a baking tray with foil or non-stick baking parchment.
4. Put the meringue mixture into a large icing bag with a 1 cm/½ inch star nozzle. Many different shapes can be made:

Meringue Baskets

Swirl round in a circle about 5 cm/2 inches across. Then pipe round edge to make a small wall. This amount will make about 10 baskets.

Various fillings can be used and should be put in just before serving. For example: whipped cream and fresh raspberries or strawberries; or, blend lemon curd and whipped cream and decorate with grated lemon rind.

Meringue Rounds

For a Pavlova-type cake. Draw three 20 cm/8 inch rounds on the paper or foil. Starting at the centre, pipe round and round until you meet the pencilled edge. This amount will make three rounds.

5. Bake below middle of a very cool oven, Gas $\frac{1}{4}$, 225°F, 110°C, for $1\frac{1}{2}$ hours or until dry and firm.

ALMOND MACAROONS

Makes about 12

Sheets of rice paper
65 to 75 g/$2\frac{1}{2}$ to 3 oz ground almonds
75 g/3 oz caster sugar
1 teaspoon ground rice or rice flour
1 egg-white
A few drops orange flower water

TO FINISH
Another egg-white
Split blanched almonds

1. Prepare a moderate oven, Gas 4, 350°F, 180°C.
2. Place rice paper on a baking sheet.
3. Mix ground almonds, sugar and ground rice or rice flour.
4. Beat one egg-white stiffly and fold into almond mixture.
5. Mix in the orange flower water.
6. Roll mixture into small balls. Place on the prepared baking sheet. Flatten slightly.
7. To finish, brush with lightly-beaten egg-white and put a split almond on top of each.
8. Bake for 15 to 20 minutes until golden brown.
9. Cool on a wire rack.
10. Trim off rice paper neatly round each macaroon while still warm.

Stella Boldy
Sykehouse, N. Humberside

BARBADOS MACAROONS

Makes about 12

50 g/2 oz ground almonds
1 teaspoon ground rice
125 g/4 oz Barbados sugar
Few drops of almond essence
1 egg-white, free-range if possible
Whole almonds, to decorate
Sheets of rice paper

1. Mix ground almonds, ground rice and sugar.
2. Add essence and some of unbeaten egg-white. Mix to a stiff paste, adding more egg-white as necessary. Beat well.
3. Lay sheets of rice paper on baking trays.
4. Take out teaspoons of the mixture, roll into neat balls and place on to prepared baking trays. Press down a little.
5. Brush lightly with water to give a gloss.
6. Put an almond on top of each macaroon.
7. Bake in a moderate oven, Gas 4, 350°F, 180°C, for about 20 minutes.
8. Trim off rice paper and cool before storing in an airtight container.

COCONUT MACAROONS

Makes 18

2 sheets rice paper, optional
2 egg-whites
2 level teaspoons cornflour
125 g/4 oz caster sugar
150 g/5 oz desiccated coconut
9 almonds, blanched and split into halves

1. Place rice paper on baking trays, smooth side downwards. Or, lightly grease the trays.
2. Beat egg-whites until frothy but not firm.
3. Mix cornflour and sugar, fold into egg-whites, then mix in coconut.
4. Place in teaspoons a little apart on the rice paper, smooth tops with a pastry brush dipped in cold water.
5. Place a halved almond on each.
6. Bake in a moderate oven, Gas 4, 350°F, 180°C, for about 20 minutes until firm and golden.
7. Tear away surplus rice paper. Allow to cool and store in airtight tin.

JAPS

Makes about 30

3 egg-whites
A pinch of cream of tartar
160 g/5½ oz caster sugar
125 g/4 oz ground almonds
20 g/¾ oz custard powder
4 drops almond essence
Butter Cream Mousse (*see next recipe*) flavoured
   with coffee or rum

TO FINISH
40 g/1½ oz desiccated coconut, toasted*
25 to 50 g/1 to 2 oz plain cooking chocolate

**To toast coconut, spread it in a baking tin and put under a
moderately hot grill until golden. Stir often. It burns easily.*

1. Whisk egg-whites with cream of tartar until stiff.
Add 125 g/4 oz of the caster sugar and whisk again.
2. Add all at once the ground almonds, remaining
sugar, custard powder and essence. Fold in carefully.
3. Put this mixture in a piping bag with a 1 cm/
½ inch plain pipe.
4. Pipe in small heaps on a well-greased baking tray,
or a baking tray lined with non-stick paper.
5. Bake in middle of a moderate oven, Gas 4, 350°F,
180°C, for about 20 minutes until just coloured.
6. Cool on a wire tray.
7. Sandwich with the butter cream mousse.
8. Coat sides with more butter cream and roll cakes
in toasted coconut.
9. Melt chocolate in a small jug standing in a pan of
simmering water and dribble it over the finished
cakes.

Mrs Joan Hudson
Finsthwaite, Ulverston, Cumbria

BUTTER CREAM MOUSSE

This is much less sweet than ordinary butter cream
and is excellent for filling cakes. The quantity given
here would fill two cakes. Will keep for a week in a
covered container in refrigerator.

50 g/2 oz caster sugar
65 ml/2½ fl oz water
2 egg-yolks
125 g/4 oz unsalted or slightly salted butter
Coffee essence or rum to flavour

1. Dissolve sugar in water and boil until the syrup
is sticky and will pull a thread between finger and
thumb. Cool slightly.
2. Beat egg-yolks, pour syrup over them and whisk
until thick.
3. Cream butter and gradually beat mousse mixture
into it.
4. Flavour with coffee essence or rum.

Mrs Joan Hudson
Finsthwaite, Ulverston, Cumbria

COCONUT KISSES

These keep well after filling, stored in airtight containers.

Makes about 30 double kisses!—easy to make 15

2 egg-whites
150 g/5 oz caster sugar
125 g/4 oz desiccated coconut

BUTTER ICING
25 g/1 oz butter or margarine
50 g/2 oz icing sugar
Almond essence and pink colouring
Or, pistachio essence and green colouring

1. Line baking sheets with oiled, greaseproof paper.
2. Whisk egg-whites till firm. Then add half of the
sugar and whisk again.
3. Fold in coconut and remaining sugar.
4. Put small teaspoons of the mixture on to prepared
baking sheets.
5. Bake on the 2 middle shelves of a cool oven, Gas
2, 300°F, 150°C, for 35 to 40 minutes until golden
brown.

6. Meanwhile, prepare butter icing. Beat butter and sifted icing sugar together, flavouring and colouring.
7. Take coconut kisses off baking sheets to cool on a wire rack. When they are cold, sandwich in pairs with butter icing.

Anne Wallace
Stewarton, Ayrshire

CHOCOLATE CLUSTERS

No cooking.

Makes 20

A 150 g/5.3 oz block of plain cooking chocolate
1 level tablespoon golden syrup
2 teaspoons water
75 g/3 oz raisins
75 g/3 oz salted peanuts*
25 g/1 oz mixed peel, finely-chopped

Can be made with unsalted nuts but rub off brown skins.

1. Place a bowl over a saucepan of boiling water. Do not allow bowl to touch the water. Allow bowl to warm up. Then turn off heat.
2. Break up chocolate and put it in the bowl with the golden syrup and the water. Allow to melt and blend together, stirring occasionally.
3. Stir in raisins, peanuts and mixed peel.
4. Put small teaspoons of the mixture on to a sheet of waxed paper (from a cornflakes packet).
5. Leave to set in a cool place before removing from paper.

SHERRY SLICES

No cooking. Use the same cup to measure all the ingredients.

225 g/8 oz marzipan

FILLING
¾ cup digestive biscuit crumbs
½ cup desiccated coconut
½ cup mixed dried fruit, chopped
¼ cup chopped nuts
½ cup raspberry jam
1 tablespoon icing sugar
1 dessertspoon cocoa
1 to 2 tablespoons sherry

TO FINISH
About 175 g/6 oz plain cooking chocolate

1. You need a tin about 23 cm/9 inches square.
2. Divide marzipan in half. Using a board dusted with icing sugar or cornflour, roll each piece out to 23 cm/9 inches square. Put one piece in tin.
3. Mix all the filling ingredients, spread over marzipan and put on the marzipan top.
4. Break chocolate into a small basin and stand it over a pan of simmering water to melt. Do not let basin touch water.
5. Spread melted chocolate over and leave till cold.
6. Slice into small fingers.

Judith Adshead
Mottram St Andrew, Cheshire

SEMOLINA HALVA

Serves 4

300 g/11 oz coarse semolina
125 g/4 oz butter or ghee (*see page 62*)
600 ml/1 pint milk
275 g/10 oz sugar
50 g/2 oz blanched almonds, coarsely-chopped
A few drops of almond essence
¼ teaspoon saffron powder, dissolved in ¼ teaspoon water

1. Using a heavy-based pan, dry roast semolina over low heat until pale brown, stirring frequently or it will burn.
2. Add the butter, milk and sugar and stir continuously over low heat to prevent semolina sticking to pan.
3. When quite stiff, add almonds, essence and saffron.
4. Mix thoroughly and pat on to a buttered tray to about 7 mm/¼ inch thick.
5. Cut into 2.5 cm/1 inch squares.

Keep in a cool place and eat within a day or two of making.

Priya Wickramasinghe
Cardiff

11
PRESERVES

JAMS AND JELLIES

There are two stages in the making of jams and jellies. *First*, there is the gentle simmer in water which breaks down the fruit and extracts the natural setting agent, pectin. With jellies the fruit needs to be crushed well with a potato masher while it is simmering. The initial simmering also softens the fruit. If the sugar is added too soon it makes tough-skinned fruit chewy. *Second*, after the sugar has been added, comes the fast rolling boil to obtain a set quickly which will give the preserve the best flavour and the brightest colour.

Always use dry, fresh fruit, slightly underripe, and try to make the preserve on the same day as the fruit is picked. The pectin content does decrease even if the fruit is left overnight. Frozen fruit, if it has been frozen in perfect condition, is excellent but will also have lost a little pectin, and to counteract this add a little extra fruit—e.g., in marmalade making add an extra orange to the recipe weight.

Good Pectin Content

Blackcurrants
Cranberries
Damsons
Gooseberries
Some Plums
Quince
Freshly picked Raspberries
Redcurrants
Seville Oranges

Medium Pectin Content

Fresh Apricots
Early Blackberries/Brambles
Greengages
Lemons
Limes
Loganberries
Sweet Oranges

Poor Pectin Content

Late Blackberries
Cherries
Elderberries
Grapefruit
Marrows
Medlars
Pears
Rhubarb
Strawberries
Tangerines
Tomatoes

The Pectin Test

Half-way through the jam making, before the sugar has been added, it is possible to test the pulp for pectin:

1. Take a teaspoon of juice from the pan of simmered fruit, put it in a glass and cool it.
2. Add three teaspoons of methylated spirit. Shake gently.

If plenty of pectin is present, a clear jelly clot will form. If a medium amount of pectin is present several small clots will form. If a poor amount of pectin is present, no real clot will be formed.

If after further cooking no clot is formed, additional pectin should be added:

50 to 125 ml/2 to 4 fl oz per 450 g/1 lb of fruit— e.g., to 1.8 kg/4 lb fruit, add 2 tablespoons lemon juice, or $\frac{1}{2}$ level teaspoon citric or tartaric acid, or 150 ml/$\frac{1}{4}$ pint redcurrant or gooseberry juice.

Testing for a Set

Do this when the sugar has been added and boiling has started:

After 10 minutes if fruit is in the high pectin list.
After 15 minutes if it is in medium pectin list
After 20 minutes if in poor pectin list
There are several ways.

1) *Volume test.* If you know the expected yield of your fruit—e.g., the recipe says you will get, say 2.5 kg/5 lb of jam, then measure out in water that amount. Take a 450 g/1 lb jam jar (not a 325 g/12 oz jar), fill it five times and pour this into your pan. Use a wooden spoon handle, stand it upright in the water and mark this level with a pencil. Keep the spoon handy. Then, when you are testing for a set, draw pan off heat. Wait until bubbling subsides and stand spoon in the jam. When the volume has returned to the level of the pencil mark, the jam is ready to pot.

2) *Cold plate test.* Have some plates cooling in the refrigerator, and take a teaspoon of jam and drop it on the cold plate. Wait a minute and, if it wrinkles when pushed, the jam is ready. If not, go on boiling a little longer.

3) *Flake test.* Dip a clean wooden spoon in boiling jam. Allow the cooling jam to drop from the spoon. If the drops run together and form a flake or curtain it is ready to pot.

4) *Temperature test.* Use a sugar thermometer. It is important to dip the thermometer in hot water immediately before using it in the jam. Submerge the bulb fully in the boiling jam but do not let it touch bottom of pan. When the thermometer registers 220°F or 106°C the jam is ready to pot.

To Pot the Jam

1. Have your jam pots washed, dried and warming on a low heat in the oven. You should be able to hold them by the rim.

2. Draw the pan off heat, stir in a knob of butter. This helps disperse the foam. If it still persists, scoop it off into a bowl and use it in the kitchen—it is just jam with a lot of air in it.

3. Now, with a heatproof glass or metal jug, fill jam pots to the brim and cover either with a metal twist top lid or seal with a waxed tissue. Make sure that no bubbles of air are trapped underneath.

4. Wipe jars when hot.

5. When cold, cover with dampened cellophane jam pot covers, placing them dry side down. Stretch the cellophane and fix with an elastic band.

6. Label with name of preserve, and the date, and store in a cool, dark, airy place.

Strawberry jam and marmalade may be left to stand for a few minutes before potting to prevent fruit rising in the jars.

Jelly is best potted in small jars so that it is eaten up quite quickly. In large jars it tends to 'weep' after opening.

Aluminium or stainless steel pans are best, then they can be used for pickles and chutneys as well.

Always use a roomy pan for jam and jelly making. The preserve rises very high during the final boiling and spits fiercely. Aim to have your pan not more than half full before you start.

Granulated sugar is excellent but proper preserving sugar crystals are said to give a brighter result when making jelly. Caster and brown sugar produce a lot of extra froth. It is best to warm sugar before adding to pan of fruit. It will then dissolve quickly.

Jelly bags can be bought, but a piece of sheeting or even old blanket can be used. In each case scald it before using by pouring boiling water through it and wringing it out. If jelly is to be clear the bag of pulp must not be squeezed. Allow at least 2 hours for juice to drip through.

APPLE OR CRAB APPLE JELLY

1. Choose crab apples or cooking apples with a decided flavour, or add a flavouring such as ginger, cloves or lemon peel. Windfall apples can be used.

2. Wash and cut up the fruit, discarding any bad portions.

3. Put it in a saucepan with ginger, cloves or lemon peel to taste. Add just enough water to cover, 1.2 to 1.75 litres/2 to 3 pints water to 1.8 kg/4 lb fruit, and simmer for about 1 hour.

4. Strain through a scalded jelly bag or several thicknesses of scalded muslin. Do not press. Allow to drip.

5. Make a pectin test (*see page 353*). If result is poor, boil apple liquid to reduce water content and test again until correct. Discard samples.

6. Measure juice. Place in pan, add 450 g/1 lb granulated sugar for each 600 ml/1 pint of juice.

7. Stir gently over low heat until sugar is dissolved.

8. Bring to boil and boil rapidly until setting point is reached (*see page 353*).

9. Pour into small hot sterile jars, and place a waxed paper disc on top of each.

10. Can be covered at once with jam-pot covers or left covered with cloth until quite cold, then covers placed on.

11. Label and store in cool dark place.

See also Apple Butter, page 368.

APRICOT AND ALMOND JAM

Yields 3.3 kg/7½ lb

675 g/1½ lb dried apricots
2.5 litres/4½ pints cold water
2 kg/4½ lb granulated sugar
125 g/4 oz almonds, blanched and halved
Juice of 1 large lemon

1. Snip apricot halves into about 4 pieces, soak 24 hours in the cold water.

2. Bring to boiling point and simmer gently for three quarters of an hour, stirring from time to time until apricot skins are soft and tender.

3. Add sugar, almonds and lemon juice, lower heat and stir until sugar has dissolved.

4. Boil rapidly for about half an hour until setting point is reached (*see page 353*).

5. Cool until almonds are suspended then pot and place waxed paper discs on jam.

6. Cover when cold.

BLACKBERRY JAM

Made from a purée. No pips. Goes well with bread and butter, hot sponge puddings, milk puddings and ice-cream.

Blackberries
Sugar

1. Pick over the blackberries and rinse them in a colander.

2. Tip blackberries into a large pan.

3. Cover pan and put on a low heat. There will be enough moisture from washing fruit, provided heat is kept low. Bring slowly to boil and simmer gently for 15 minutes.

4. Press berries through an ordinary nylon kitchen sieve.

5. Measure the purée and pour into a large pan.

6. For every 600 ml/1 pint of purée allow 450 g/1 lb of sugar. (Or for every 450 ml/$\frac{3}{4}$ pint of purée allow 325 g/$\frac{3}{4}$ lb sugar.)

7. Warm sugar in a very cool oven, Gas $\frac{1}{4}$, 225°F, 110°C.

8. Heat purée to boiling point, remove from heat and add the warm sugar. Stir over low heat until sugar is completely dissolved.

9. Bring jam to the boil and boil rapidly until setting point is reached (*see page 353*).

10. Meanwhile, put clean jam pots in the oven to warm.

11. While jam is hot, fill the pots to the brim. Put on the waxed paper discs, waxed side down. Put jam pot covers on at once or leave till jam is quite cold. Never put covers on while jam is between hot and cold.

12. Label pots with name and date.

13. Store in a cool, dark, dry, well-ventilated cupboard.

Mrs Patricia Sweetland
Milton Keynes

BLACKBERRY AND APPLE JAM

Yields 4.5 kg/10 lb

1.8 kg/4 lb blackberries
300 ml/$\frac{1}{2}$ pint water
675 g/1$\frac{1}{2}$ lb cooking apples, weighed after peeling and coring
2.7 kg/6 lb sugar

This jam is particularly good if fruits are cooked until soft but not mushy.

1. Place the blackberries in a pan over a low heat, adding half the quantity of water and stew until tender.

2. Slice the apples, put in another pan, add the remaining water and cook until quite soft.

3. Combine the two fruits in one pan.

4. Make a pectin test (*see page 353*). If result is poor boil fruit for a few minutes and test again.

5. Add the sugar and stir until dissolved. Then boil rapidly until setting point is reached (*see page 353*). Take care while testing for setting point not to over-boil the rest of the jam.

6. Pour into hot, dry jars. Fill right to the top. Put on waxed discs immediately. Covers may be put on when jam is either hot or cold.

7. Label and store in a cool dark place.

BLACKBERRY AND APPLE JAM

No seeds.

Yields about 2.25 kg/5 lb jam for every 1.3 kg/3 lb sugar used

1.8 kg/4 lb blackberries
300 ml/$\frac{1}{2}$ pint water
675 g/1$\frac{1}{2}$ lb cooking apples, weigh after peeling and coring
Sugar (*see paragraphs 3 and 4 below*)

1. Simmer blackberries very gently in half of the water until tender. Then sieve to remove the seeds.

2. Meanwhile, prepare apples and slice finely. Simmer them in remaining water till soft and pulpy.

3. Combine blackberry purée and apple pulp and weigh it.

4. Weigh out an equal quantity of sugar and put it

in a bowl to warm in a very cool oven, Gas $\frac{1}{4}$, 225°F, 110°C.

5. Boil the pulp until it is thick. Then add the warmed sugar and stir without boiling till it is dissolved.

6. When it is completely dissolved bring to boil and boil rapidly till setting point is reached. It may be only a few minutes (*see notes, page 353*).

7. Fill warmed jars to the brim. Put on at once a well-fitting waxed tissue, waxed side down. This is to seal the jam and protect it from the atmosphere.

8. Wipe the jars and put on outer covers, either while hot or when cold, *never* in between.

9. Label with name and date and store in a cool, dark, dry well-ventilated place.

BLACKBERRY AND APPLE JELLY

Yields about 1.8 kg/4 lb

1.3 kg/3 lb blackberries
1.3 kg/3 lb sound cooking apples
1.2 litres/2 pints water
Sugar

Note: Do not use large jars for jelly as once opened it tends to liquify at the edges.

1. Wash fruit, slice apples thinly but do not peel, core or remove pips.

2. Place in large pan with water and simmer gently until quite soft, approximately $1\frac{1}{2}$ hours.

3. Strain through a jelly bag (several layers of muslin or fine woven cotton cloth will do). Do not press fruit, just allow juice to drip. It is advisable to scald jelly bag with boiling water before use as this speeds up the process of dripping which can take from 1 to 2 hours.

4. Make a pectin test (*see page 353*). If result is poor, boil juice again to drive off more moisture and then test again.

5. Measure juice, weigh out 450 g/1 lb sugar to each 600 ml/1 pint. Put sugar into a warm oven. Put jars in oven to warm at same time.

6. Heat juice in clean pan, stir in warm sugar and dissolve before bringing to boil.

7. Have thermometer in a pan of hot water. Boil jelly rapidly without stirring (as stirring causes bubbles to form in jelly.) Place thermometer in pan of jelly and when it registers 220°F, 106°C, remove pan from heat, skim away any scum and pot at once into

hot jars. Place waxed paper discs on top. *See page 353* for other methods of testing for setting point if you do not have a thermometer.

8. Cool away from draughts. Cover and label when cold.

9. Store in a cool, dark place.

BLACKBERRY, ELDERBERRY AND APPLE JAM

Yields about 2.25 kg/5 lb

450 g/1 lb elderberries
450 g/1 lb blackberries
450 g/1 lb apples
A little water
Juice of 1 lemon
1.3 kg/3 lb sugar

1. Remove elderberries from stalks. To do this, hold them over a large bowl and strip off berries with a table fork. (A large bowl is necessary because berries tend to fly everywhere.)

2. Pick over the blackberries.

3. Peel and core apples and chop them as small as the blackberries.

4. Put less than 1 cm/$\frac{1}{2}$ inch water in a large saucepan and tip in the fruit.

5. Cover pan and gently simmer fruit until it is soft.

6. Meanwhile, put sugar in a very cool oven, Gas $\frac{1}{4}$, 225°F, 110°C.

7. When fruit is soft add lemon juice and sugar and stir over a low heat until it is completely dissolved.

8. Bring jam to the boil and boil rapidly until setting point is reached (*see page 353*).

9. Meanwhile, put clean jam pots to warm in oven.

10. Pot the jam straight away, filling each pot to the brim. Put on the waxed paper discs, waxed side down and leave to cool.

11. When pots of jam are quite cold put on the jam pot covers and label pots with name and date.

12. Store in a cool, dark, dry, well-ventilated cupboard.

Mrs Lynda M. White
Sturton by Stow, Lincoln

See also Blackberry Syrup, page 371 and Blackberry Vinegar, page 387.

BLACKCURRANT JAM

Yields about 6 kg/13 to 14 lb but easy to make half the quantity.

1.8 kg/4 lb blackcurrants
2 litres/3½ pints water
3.2 kg/7 lb sugar

1. Remove stems and wash fruit in plenty of cold water. Strain in a colander.
2. Put fruit in a preserving pan with the water.
3. Bring to the boil and simmer gently until skins are quite tender. Stir from time to time in case fruit begins to stick and burn. Contents of pan will be reduced considerably.
4. Meanwhile put sugar into a bowl and warm it in a very cool oven, Gas ¼, 225°C, 110°C.
5. Prepare clean jars and put them in coolest part of the oven to warm.
6. When fruit is broken down and skins are tender, add the warmed sugar and stir until it is dissolved. Do not let it boil again before sugar is dissolved.
7. Bring to the boil and boil rapidly until setting point is reached. This may take only ¼ hour (*see page 353*).
8. Remove scum from top of jam with a metal spoon.
9. Fill warmed jars to the brim. Put on waxed paper discs straight away, waxed-side down. This seals the jars and protects them from the atmosphere.
10. Wipe the jars. Either put outer covers on while jam is hot or when it is quite cold, *never* in between.
11. Label with name and date and store in a cool, dark, dry, well-ventilated place.

Sybil Norcott
Irlam, Nr Manchester

CRANBERRY AND ORANGE PRESERVE

Delicious with roast turkey. Sets like jelly.

Yields about 900g/2 lb

450 g/1 lb granulated sugar
450 g/1 lb fresh or frozen cranberries
Finely-grated rind and juice of 1 orange
Water

1. Put sugar to warm in very cool oven, Gas ¼, 225°F, 110°C. Put clean 225 g/8 oz jars into oven at same time.
2. Pick over fruit and discard any that is bruised. Put cranberries into a roomy saucepan.
3. Mix orange juice with water to make 300 ml/ ½ pint. Add to pan with rind.
4. Bring to the boil over gentle heat and simmer for 10 minutes, stirring occasionally. Cranberries will cook down to a thick pulp. Draw pan off heat.
5. Push pulp through a nylon sieve to make a purée, scraping as much as possible from under the sieve.
6. Put purée in a clean pan, add sugar and stir over low heat until sugar is dissolved.
7. Now turn up heat and boil for 4 to 5 minutes.
8. Pour hot preserve into prepared jars. Finish as indicated *on page 354.*

DAMSON JAM

Yields 4.5 kg/10 lb but easy to make half the quantity
2.1 kg/4¾ lb damsons
750 ml to 1.2 litres/1¼ to 2 pints water
2.7 kg/6 lb sugar

1. Pick over the fruit, removing stems. Wash if necessary and drain well.
2. Put fruit in preserving pan or very large saucepan and add water. If fruit is ripe use the smaller quantity of water. If it is not very ripe it will need to boil longer to make it tender, so use the larger quantity of water.
3. Simmer fruit gently until quite tender (contents of pan will be reduced considerably). Stir from time to time to make sure it does not stick and burn.
4. Meanwhile, put sugar in a bowl to warm in a very cool oven, Gas ¼, 225°F, 110°C.
5. Prepare clean jars and put them in coolest part of oven to dry and warm.
6. Add warmed sugar and stir until dissolved. Do not let it boil again before sugar is dissolved.
7. Bring to the boil and boil rapidly until setting point is reached. This may take only ¼ hour (*see page 353*). During the boiling the stones will start rising to the surface. Remove as many as you can before potting the jam.
8. Fill warmed jars to the brim. Put on well-fitting waxed tissues immediately, waxed side down. This seals the jam and protects it from the atmosphere.
9. Wipe jars and put on outer covers while jam is hot or cold, but *never* in between.
10. Label with the name and date and store in a cool, dark, dry, well-ventilated place.

See also Suffolk Damson Cheese, page 369 and Pickled Damsons, page 373.

FIG AND LEMON PRESERVE

Yields over 2.25 kg/5 lb

900 g/2 lb dried figs
1.2 litres/2 pints cold water
1.3 kg/3 lb sugar
Rind and juice of 4 lemons

1. Wash the figs, removing stalks, and cut into about 6 pieces.
2. Put them into a basin with the water and leave soaking for 24 hours.
3. Turn into a pan, add sugar and cook slowly until dissolved, then bring to the boil and remove the scum.
4. Wipe lemons and grate rind finely, squeeze out juice and strain it.
5. Add rind and juice to the figs and boil all together until setting point is reached (*see page 353*). Keep it stirred and skimmed as required.
6. Cool, pot and, when cold, tie down.

Miss Peggy Mills
Leicestershire

GOOSEBERRY AND ORANGE JAM

Yields about 2.7 kg/6 lb

1.3 kg/3 lb gooseberries
2 oranges
450 ml/$\frac{3}{4}$ pint water
1.5 kg/3$\frac{1}{2}$ lb sugar

1. Top and tail gooseberries and wash them, if necessary.
2. Wash oranges, cut them in halves and squeeze out juice. Put the peel through mincer.
3. Put gooseberries, minced orange peel, juice and water in preserving pan or large saucepan. Bring to the boil and simmer until fruit is tender.
4. Meanwhile, put sugar in a bowl to warm in a very cool oven, Gas $\frac{1}{4}$, 225°F, 110°C.
5. Prepare clean jars and put them in coolest part of oven to dry and warm.
6. Add warmed sugar to pan and stir until it is dissolved. Do not let it boil again before sugar is dissolved.
7. Bring to the boil and boil rapidly for 8 to 10 minutes or until setting point is reached (*see page 353*).

8. Fill warmed jars to the brim. Put on well-fitting waxed tissues immediately, waxed side down. This seals the jam and protects it from the atmosphere.
9. Wipe jars and put on outer covers either while jam is hot or cold, but *never* in between.
10. Label with name and date and store in a cool, dark, dry, well-ventilated place.

Mrs Doreen Allars
Welbourn, Nr Lincoln

GREEN GOOSEBERRY AND ELDERFLOWER JAM

Has a delicate flavour.

Yields about 3.6 kg/8 lb

1.8 kg/4 lb green gooseberries
$\frac{1}{2}$ to 1 teacup elderflowers
600 ml/1 pint water
2.25 kg/5 lb sugar

Use flowers from the green-leaved elder which has small flower heads. The big heads from the yellow-leaved shrub have a pungent, if not rank, flavour.

1. Top and tail gooseberries and wash them, if necessary.
2. Tie elderflowers into a piece of muslin.
3. Put fruit, flowers and water in a preserving pan or large saucepan and bring to the boil. Simmer for about 20 minutes or until fruit is soft. Contents of pan will be reduced considerably.
4. Meanwhile, put sugar in a bowl to warm in a very cool oven, Gas $\frac{1}{4}$, 225°F, 110°C.
5. Prepare clean jars and place in coolest part of oven to dry and warm.
6. Lift out bag of elderflowers and squeeze juice into pan.
7. Now add the warmed sugar and stir until it is dissolved. Do not let it boil again before sugar is dissolved.
8. Bring to the boil and boil rapidly until setting point is reached. This may take 15 to 20 minutes (*see page 353*).
9. Fill warmed jars to the brim. Put on well-fitting waxed tissues immediately, waxed side down. This seals the jam and protects it from the atmosphere.
10. Wipe jars and put on outer covers, either while jam is hot or cold, but *never* in between.
11. Label with name and date and store in a cool, dark, dry, well-ventilated place.

Sybil Norcott
Irlam, Nr Manchester

See also Mint Jelly made with Gooseberries, page 364.

BUSY WOMAN'S MARMALADE

Yields about 3.6 kg/8 lb

4 Seville oranges
1 large juicy orange
1 juicy lemon
3.6 litres/6 pints water
2.25 kg/5 lb sugar

1. Cut all fruit in halves across. Squeeze out juice and add this to 2.8 litres/5 pints of the water.
2. Put pips in a jug with remaining 600 ml/1 pint cold water and leave till the following day.
3. Cut the halved fruit cases in pieces to fit mincer. Put twice through mincer using finest blades. If you have an electric mincer or like a coarser marmalade you may prefer to put fruit through only once.
4. Put the minced fruit into the juice and water and leave to soak for 24 hours.
5. Then turn soaked fruit, juice and water into a preserving pan, adding the strained water from the pips.
6. Bring to the boil and boil gently until peel is soft when pinched between finger and thumb.
7. Add warmed sugar, stir until dissolved, then bring to the boil again and boil rapidly until setting point is reached (*see page 353*). Do not allow the marmalade to boil rapidly while testing or the setting point may be missed.
8. Allow to cool a little in pan so that fruit will remain suspended and not rise to top of jars, but pot while still warm into clean, dry, warmed jars. Place a waxed paper disc on each jar to cover the surface of the jam completely. Cover jars with a clean cloth and leave till cold.
9. Fasten on jam pot covers, label and store in a cool, dark place.

LEMON MARMALADE

A marmalade following the same method as Busy Woman's in which the fruit is soaked and minced but which may be made at any time of the year.

Yields about 1.8 kg/4 lb

4 lemons
1 sweet orange
(Total weight of fruit should be 575 to 675 g/1$\frac{1}{4}$ to 1$\frac{1}{2}$ lb)
1.75 litres/3 pints water
1.1 kg/2$\frac{1}{2}$ lb sugar

1. Cut all fruit in halves across. Squeeze out juice and add this to 1.5 litres/2$\frac{1}{2}$ pints of the water.
2. Put pips in a jug with remaining 300 ml/$\frac{1}{2}$ pint of cold water and leave till the following day.
3. Cut the halved fruit cases in pieces to fit mincer. Put twice through mincer using finest blades. If you have an electric mincer or like a coarser marmalade you may prefer to put fruit through only once.
4. Put the minced fruit into the juice and water and leave to soak for 24 hours.
5. Then turn soaked fruit, juice and water into a preserving pan adding the strained water from the pips.
6. Bring to the boil and boil gently until peel is soft when pinched between finger and thumb.
7. Add warmed sugar, stir until dissolved, then bring to the boil again and boil rapidly until setting point is reached (*see page 353*). Do not allow the marmalade to boil rapidly when testing or the setting point may be missed.
8. Allow to cool a little in pan so that fruit will remain suspended and not rise to top of jars, but pot while still warm into clean, dry, warmed jars. Place a waxed paper disc on each jar to cover the surface of the jam completely. Cover jars with a clean cloth and leave till cold.
9. Fasten on jam pot covers, label and store in a cool, dark place.

MINCED SEVILLE MARMALADE

Yields about 3.2 kg/7 lb

900 g/2 lb Seville bitter oranges*
1 large lemon
2.25 litres/4 pints water
1.8 kg/4 lb granulated sugar
15 g/½ oz butter

*If using oranges taken from the freezer add one extra orange.

1. Scrub fruit and remove green stalk ends.
2. Cut each orange in two. Squeeze out all pips and put them in a piece of muslin tied with a long string.
3. Cut lemon in two and squeeze out juice.
4. Put water in a large deep pan. Add lemon juice and bag of pips tied to handle of pan.
5. Put orange shells through mincer or a food processor, then into pan. Leave overnight.
6. Next day, simmer this mixture in pan with the lid on for 15 minutes. Then remove lid and simmer uncovered for about 1 hour, to reduce mixture by about half.
7. Meanwhile put sugar to warm in a very cool oven, Gas ¼, 225°F, 110°C, prepare clean jars and put them to warm in oven too.
8. Test marmalade for pectin strength (*see page 353*).
9. Add warmed sugar. Stir well. Do not let it boil before sugar has dissolved. Then turn up heat and bring to a fast rolling boil, lid off pan. Stir occasionally.
10. After 15 to 20 minutes test for a set (*see page 353*).
11. When setting point has been reached, remove pip bag. Remove pan from heat. Add butter to disperse scum. Stir again.
12. Let marmalade stand for about 5 minutes to cool a little, otherwise peel may rise in jars, leaving a gap at the bottom. Then stir again to distribute peel and pour into warmed jars. Fill to brim.
13. Put on a well-fitting waxed tissue immediately to seal surface and complete according to notes *on page 354.*

Very economical marmalade

In place of 900 g/2 lb Seville oranges use:

450 g/1 lb Sevilles
450 g/1 lb peel from sweet oranges and grapefruit

This peel can be frozen at any time of year until enough is collected to make marmalade or until Seville season returns.

Proceed with recipe as before.

SEVILLE ORANGE MARMALADE I

In the pressure cooker.

Yields 2.7 kg/6 lb

900 g/2 lb Seville oranges
2 lemons
Water
1.8 kg/4 lb sugar

1. Scrub the oranges and cut in half.
2. Remove pips and place these in a square of scalded muslin. Tie securely.
3. Shred oranges, place in pressure cooker without trivet. Add bag of pips.
4. Squeeze juice from lemons, make this up to 2 pints with water. Strain through a nylon strainer into pressure cooker.
5. Place lid on pressure cooker, and bring to pressure. Place valve weight on top, and pressure cook for 10 minutes. This ensures that the peel is quite soft.
6. Remove from heat, leave 15 minutes when valve weight will remove easily.
7. Remove bag of pips and squeeze out any liquid. The contents of pressure cooker should measure 1.6 litres/2¾ pints.
8. Make a pectin test (*see page 353*). If result is poor, return pan to heat and boil again for a few minutes without lid and test again.
9. Add the warmed sugar and stir until completely dissolved.
10. Place over heat, bring to a rolling boil, and boil to setting point, 220°F, 106°C. This will only take a short time, usually 10 to 15 minutes at the most. If not using a thermometer, setting point can be determined by the cold plate method (*see page 353*). Take care while conducting the test not to over-boil the rest of the marmalade.
11. Remove from heat, allow to cool a little (15 to 20 minutes) until peel remains suspended when stirred and does not rise to the top.
12. Pour into dry, clean, warmed jars, place waxed discs on top immediately and then leave until quite cold.
13. Cover, label, and store in a cool, dark place.

SEVILLE ORANGE MARMALADE II

Made with whole fruit.

Made in the pressure cooker. The following recipe may be used with fresh or frozen fruit. If you can get a case of Sevilles, or share a case with someone, wash and dry them and pack in large polythene bags in the freezer. Marmalade can then be made in small batches as and when required.

Yields 4.5 kg/10 lb

1.3 kg/3 lb Seville oranges
Juice of 2 lemons, or 1 teaspoon citric or tar-
taric acid
1.2 to 1.7 litres/2 to 3 pints water
2.7 kg/6 lb sugar

1. Put whole fruit in pressure cooker (trivet not required) with lemon juice or acid. Add 1.2 litres/2 pints or more water until pressure cooker pan is not more than half full of liquid.
2. Put lid on pressure cooker, keeping vent open. Heat gently until steam comes out of vent. Close vent and bring to 15 lb or high pressure. Keep at pressure for 20 minutes, then remove from heat and cool in the air for 10 minutes. Open vent and remove lid from pressure cooker.
3. Lift out fruit on to a large plate and allow to cool for a few minutes.
4. Divide sugar, putting 1.3 kg/3 lb each into two separate containers. Put in oven on lowest heat to warm through, Gas $\frac{1}{4}$, 225°F, 110°C. Put clean jars in oven also, to dry and warm.
5. Cut fruit in half and, using a teaspoon, take out pips and return them to liquid in the pressure cooker pan.
6. Boil pips in open pressure cooker for 5 minutes. Strain liquid into a measuring jug and discard pips.
7. Meanwhile, divide oranges into 2 equal portions. Cut them up, small or chunky, as preferred. Fruit, sugar and liquid are divided because pressure cooker pan is not large enough to boil up full quantity.
8. As soon as you have cut up one portion of fruit, put it with half of liquid in measuring jug back into the pressure cooker pan and bring to boil.
The rest may be boiled up simultaneously in a separate large pan to save time.
9. Lower heat and add 1.3 kg/3 lb sugar. Stir with wooden spoon over very low heat until sugar is completely dissolved.

10. Bring up to the boil and boil rapidly until setting point is reached. This may take only a few minutes because pressure cooker method requires much less water than conventional methods.
11. Test for setting point (*see page 353*). Test frequently.
12. When it is ready, remove scum from surface with a metal spoon.
13. Allow pan of marmalade to cool for a while. This prevents peel rising to top of jars.
14. Pour into warmed jars and cover with waxed paper discs while still hot.
15. Cover with jam-pot covers when quite cold.
16. Label with name and date and store in a dry, dark, cool, ventilated cupboard.

ORANGE AND CIDER MARMALADE

Yields about 2.25 kg/5 lb

675 g/1$\frac{1}{2}$ lb Seville oranges
Juice of 2 lemons
1.2 litres/2 pints dry cider
600 ml/1 pint water
1.3 kg/3 lb sugar

1. Wash oranges and cut them in half.
2. Squeeze out juice and pips and cut peel into thin strips.
3. Squeeze lemon.
4. Put orange peel, orange and lemon juice into a large pan with the cider and water.
5. Tie pips in a muslin bag and put in pan.
6. Cook gently for 1$\frac{1}{2}$ hours or until peel is soft.
7. Meanwhile, put sugar in a bowl to warm in a very cool oven, Gas $\frac{1}{4}$, 225°F, 110°C. Prepare clean jars and put them to dry and warm in coolest part of oven.
8. Lift out bag of pips and squeeze juice out by pressing it against side of pan with a wooden spoon.
9. Add warmed sugar and stir without boiling until completely dissolved.
10. Bring to the boil and boil rapidly until setting point is reached (*see page 353*).
11. Remove scum with a metal spoon.
12. Allow marmalade to cool for $\frac{1}{2}$ hour. This will prevent the peel rising in the jars.

13. Fill warmed jars to the brim. Immediately put on well-fitting waxed discs, waxed side down. This seals the jam and protects it from the atmosphere.
14. Wipe jars and put on outer covers, either while jam is hot or cold, but *never* in between.
15. Label with name and date and store in a cool, dark, dry, well-ventilated place.

Mrs Doreen Allars
Welbourn, Nr Lincoln

GRAPEFRUIT MARMALADE

Yields 2.25 kg/5½ lb

2 large grapefruit (approximately 900 g/2 lb)
450 g/1 lb lemons
2.25 litres/4 pints water
1.3 kg/3 lb sugar

1. Wash fruit, peel thinly (a potato peeler helps) and cut peel finely with scissors.
2. Remove pith from fruit, cut up roughly.
3. Cut up flesh, reserving pips. This is best done on a deep plate to prevent loss of juice.
4. Tie pips and pith in scalded muslin and place in pan with the water, peel, flesh and juice.
5. Simmer for two hours or until peel is very soft. The contents of the pan should be reduced by half.
6. Remove muslin bag on to a plate, cool, squeeze well to extract juice and add juice to pan. Test for pectin (*see page 353*).
7. Add warmed sugar and stir until dissolved. Then boil until set is obtained, 220°F, 106°C is setting point. Or else use the cold plate test (*see page 353*).
8. Skim off any scum, then allow to stand for 15 to 20 minutes to stabilise peel as this rises to top of jars if potted at once.
9. Fill warmed jars to brim and put on waxed paper discs. Cover with a clean cloth and leave until quite cold. Fasten on jam pot covers, label and store in a cool, dry, well-ventilated place.

JELLY MARMALADE

Yields 2.25 kg/5 lb

Grapefruit
2 grapefruit ⎫ combined weight
3 lemons   ⎭ 900 g/2 lb
2.6 litres/4½ pints water
1.3 kg/3 lb sugar

Orange
900 g/2 lb Seville oranges
2.6 litres/4½ pints water
Juice of 2 lemons or 1 teaspoon citric or tartaric acid
1.3 kg/3 lb sugar

1. Score the fruit in quarters then scald. To do this, pour boiling water over and leave for 5 minutes. Then drain.
2. Remove peel and cut white pith away from rind. Shred the rind finely.
3. Cut pith and fruit coarsely, put in a saucepan with 1.5 litres/2½ pints of the water (plus lemon juice or acid for Orange Jelly). Put on lid, bring to boil and simmer for 2 hours.
4. Meanwhile, put shredded rind in another pan with 600 ml/1 pint water, put on lid and simmer 1½ hours or until tender.
5. Drain liquid from shreds into pan of pulp.
6. Set up jelly bag (*see notes on page 354*).
7. Empty pan of pulp into jelly bag and allow to drip for 10 to 15 minutes.
8. Return pulp to pan with remaining 600 ml/1 pint of water. Cover pan and simmer for 20 minutes more.
9. Pour this into jelly bag and let it drip without squeezing bag for at least 2 hours.
10. Meanwhile, put sugar to warm in a very cool oven, Gas ¼, 225°F, 110°C, and put small clean jars to warm at same time.
11. Put juice into a roomy pan, bring to the boil, turn down heat and add sugar. Stir until it is dissolved.
12. Then add shredded rind and boil rapidly until setting point is reached (*see notes on page 353*).
13. Quickly skim off froth, then allow jelly to cool until a skin forms, 5 to 10 minutes.
14. Stir gently and pot following the notes *on page 354.*

GRAPEFRUIT JELLY

Yields about 2.25 kg/5 lb

2 grapefruit, 2 lemons, 1 orange (combined weight 900 g/2 lb)
2.6 litres/4½ pints water
1.3 kg/3 lb sugar

1. Score skins of grapefruit into 4 segments. Put them in a bowl and scald by pouring boiling water over them. Leave them for 10 minutes.
2. Remove peel, cut away the thick pith and shred the yellow part finely. Keep shreds until later.
3. Cut up coarsely the pith and rest of the fruit, including lemons and orange.
4. Put pith and fruit in a pan with a lid, add 1.5 litres/2½ pints of the water, cover pan and simmer for 2 hours.
5. In a separate pan with a lid, simmer shreds in 600 ml/1 pint water for 1½ hours or until tender.
6. Drain off liquid from shreds, add it to the pulp and tip it all into a scalded jelly bag. Let it drip into a bowl for 10 to 15 minutes.
7. Return pulp to preserving pan, add remaining 600 ml/1 pint water, simmer for a further 20 minutes, and strain through jelly bag again. Let it strain without squeezing the bag.
8. Meanwhile, put sugar in a bowl to warm in a very cool oven, Gas ¼, 225°F, 110°C. Put clean jars to warm in coolest part of oven.
9. Combine 2 extracts of juice and take a pectin test (*see page 353*). If pectin quality is poor, simmer juice again without the lid for about 10 minutes to drive off some of the excess water, then test again.
10. Add warmed sugar. Stir without boiling until sugar is dissolved.
11. When sugar is completely dissolved, add shreds of grapefruit rind, bring to the boil and boil rapidly until setting point is reached (*see page 353*).
12. Skim off scum quickly with a metal spoon.
13. Leave jelly to cool slightly, for 10 to 15 minutes. This ensures that shreds will be suspended evenly in the jelly when potted. If it is potted hot, shreds tend to rise to surface.
14. Fill warm jars to the brim and immediately put on well-fitting waxed discs, waxed side down. This seals the surface of the jelly and protects it from the atmosphere.
15. With jelly it is easier to put outer covers on jars when it is set, but wait until it is quite cold.
16. Label with name and date and store in a cool, dark, dry, well-ventilated place.

MEDLAR JELLY

Yields about 1.1 kg/2½ lb

1.8 kg/4 lb medlars
1 large lemon or 2 teaspoons citric acid
About 1.75 litres/3 pints water
Sugar

It is a good idea to use small jars for jelly because when it has been opened for a little time it begins to go runny.

1. Wash and cut up medlars and put into a preserving pan or large saucepan with enough water to cover. Simmer slowly, until fruit is reduced to a pulp.
2. Strain through a scalded jelly bag. To be sure of getting a clear jelly it is best not to squeeze the bag.
3. Measure the juice and return it to the pan. To every 600 ml/1 pint juice weigh out 325 g/12 oz sugar.
4. Put sugar in a bowl to warm in a very cool oven, Gas ¼, 225°F, 110°C. Prepare clean, small jars and put them to dry and warm in coolest part of oven.
5. Add citric acid (if lemon has not been used) and bring pan of juice to the boil. Add warmed sugar. Stir without letting it boil until sugar is dissolved.
6. Boil rapidly until setting point is reached (*see page 353*). It usually takes about 25 minutes.
7. Skim off the scum with a metal spoon. Then fill the jars without delay before jelly starts to set.
8. Put on at once well-fitting, waxed tissues, waxed side down. This is to seal the jelly and protect it from the atmosphere.
9. With jelly it is easier to put outer cover on jars when it is set, but wait until it is quite cold.
10. Label with name and date and store in cool, dark, dry, well-ventilated place.

Mrs Doreen Allars
Welbourn, Nr Lincoln

PEAR AND GINGER JAM

This makes use of every bit of the fruit, so don't throw away peel and cores.

Yields about 4.5 kg/9 to 10 lb

3.2 kg/7 lb pears
1.2 litres/2 pints water
3 lemons
1 piece fresh root ginger, approx. 2.5 cm/1 inch
is enough
2.25 kg/5 lb sugar

1. Peel, quarter and core pears. Slice them and put them in a preserving pan with the water.
2. Thinly peel yellow rind from lemons. Squeeze the juice.
3. Peel ginger and bruise it. To do this, put it on a chopping board and bang it with the rolling pin.
4. Tie pear peelings and cores with lemon rinds and ginger in a large piece of muslin and put in preserving pan.
5. Bring to the boil and simmer pears for 30 minutes or until soft.
6. Meanwhile, put the sugar in a bowl to warm in a very cool oven, Gas ¼, 225°F, 110°C, and prepare clean jam jars. Put them to dry and warm in coolest part of oven.
7. Lift out the bag and with the back of a wooden spoon press it against side of pan and squeeze out as much juice as possible.
8. Add the warmed sugar and stir without boiling until dissolved.
9. Add the lemon juice.
10. Increase heat and bring jam to the boil. Boil for 15 minutes or until setting point is reached (*see page 353*).
11. Skim off scum and let jam stand for 5 minutes. This will prevent pieces of pear rising in the jars.
12. Fill warmed jars to the brim. Immediately put on well-fitting waxed tissue, waxed side down. This seals the jam and protects it from the atmosphere.
13. Wipe jars and put on outer covers either while jam is hot or cold, but *never* in between.
14. Label with name and date and store in a cool, dry, dark, well-ventilated place.

Mrs Doreen Allars
Welbourn, Nr Lincoln

MINT JELLY

Made from gooseberries.

Often made with apples. However the combination of mint and gooseberries is lovely, especially with lamb.

Not a clear jelly.

Yields about 450 g/1 lb

450 g/1 lb small green gooseberries
Water
Sugar
A bunch of fresh mint, about 10 to 12 fresh
stalks, tied together
1 or 2 drops of green food colouring (optional)

1. There is no need to top and tail gooseberries. Just wash and put them into a pan.
2. Just cover with water and cook gently until very mushy.
3. Strain through a nylon sieve, pressing gently but not pushing the pulp through.
4. Measure this juice and for every 600 ml/1 pint add 450 g/1 lb sugar.
5. Put sugar to warm in a very cool oven, Gas ¼, 225°F, 110°C. Put small clean jars to warm also.
6. Put juice, sugar and mint in a pan. Heat gently, stirring until sugar is dissolved.
7. Bring to the boil and boil rapidly, stirring occasionally until setting point is reached (*see notes on page 353*).
8. Remove mint and add green food colouring, if used.
9. Pour carefully in warm jars and finish according to notes *on page 354*.

PLUM, ORANGE AND WALNUT JAM

Any plums may be used, including greengages.

Yields about 1.5 kg/3½ lb

1.3 kg/3 lb plums
2 oranges
1 small cupful of water
1.1 kg/2½ lb sugar
225 g/8 oz shelled walnuts

1. Wash plums in case they have been sprayed. Stone them and tie stones in a piece of muslin.
2. Wash oranges, cut them in halves and squeeze out juice. Put peel through mincer.
3. Put plums, stones, minced orange peel, juice and water in preserving pan or large saucepan. Bring to the boil and simmer until fruit is soft (about 1 hour). Stir occasionally to see that it is not sticking and add a little more water if necessary. Remove muslin bag.
4. Meanwhile, put sugar in a bowl to warm in a very cool oven, Gas ¼, 225°F, 110°C.
5. Prepare clean jars and place in coolest part of oven to dry and warm.
6. Roughly chop walnuts.
7. Add warmed sugar to pan and stir until dissolved.
8. When sugar is completely dissolved, bring to the boil and add walnuts.
9. Boil jam rapidly until setting point is reached (*see page 353*).
10. Fill warmed jars to the brim. Put on well-fitting waxed tissues immediately, waxed side down. This seals the jam and protects it from the atmosphere.
11. Wipe jars and put on outer covers, either while jam is hot or cold, but *never* in between.
12. Label with name and date and store in a cool, dark, dry, well-ventilated place.

Mrs Doreen Allars
Welbourn, Nr Lincoln

GREEN EGG PLUM JAM

Look out for these plums in mid-August and buy green ones if you can. This is important as it produces a nice tangy jam with a good green colour.

Yields about 2.25 kg/5 lb

1.3 kg/3 lb plums
300 ml/½ pint water
1.3 kg/3 lb sugar

1. Wash plums and remove stalks.
2. Simmer them in the water in a large pan until skins are really tender. Skim off stones as they rise to the surface.
If liked a few plum kernels may be cracked out of the stones and added to the jam at this stage.
3. Meanwhile, put sugar in a dish in a very cool oven, Gas ¼, 225°F, 110°C, for about 20 minutes to warm. Put clean jars in oven to warm at same time.
4. Add warmed sugar to pan of fruit, stir until dissolved without letting it boil.
5. Then boil rapidly, stirring occasionally, until setting point is reached (*see page 353*). Begin testing after 6 minutes.
6. Pot, seal, cover and store as directed on *page 354*.

Mrs Olive Odell
Hartlebury, Worcestershire

POTTED RASPBERRY JAM

Keeps for only 5 to 6 months. This preserve does not set like ordinary jam. The fruit rises and there is a layer of jelly at the bottom. However, its flavour is superb and it is good for sponges, tarts, etc. Give it a stir in jar before using.

Loganberries can also be used but always pick slightly under-ripe, dry fruit.

Yields 3.6 kg/8 lb—easy to make less

1.8 kg/4 lb raspberries, in perfect condition
1.8 kg/4 lb caster sugar, dissolves more easily than granulated

1. Do not wash raspberries. They must be perfectly dry. Put sugar in another bowl. Put both bowls in the oven. Put clean jars to warm in oven at same time.
2. Set oven to cool, Gas 2, 300°F, 150°C, for about 25 minutes or until the juice starts to run. Switch off heat.
3. Now mix the sugar and raspberries and stir until sugar has dissolved.
4. Pot into warm jars, put on a waxed tissue and leave till cold before covering jars (*see notes on page 354*).
5. Label the jars with name and date, and store in a cool, dark, dry, well-ventilated place.

RAW RASPBERRY JAM

A very old Scottish recipe. Tastes delicious and has a lovely bright-red colour.

Yields 675 g/1½ lb

450 g/1 lb raspberries
450 g/1 lb caster sugar

1. Crush fruit slightly.
2. Put sugar to warm in a very cool oven, Gas ¼, 225°F, 110°C. Put clean jars to warm in oven also.
3. Put fruit in a saucepan over very low heat. Stir continuously until just boiling.
4. Take pan off heat and stir in warm sugar.
5. Return pan to low heat and stir until sugar is completely dissolved. Stir until jam reaches boiling point.
6. If there are some whole fruits in the jam allow it to stand in the pan for a short time until a thin skin forms. Stir skin in gently and pour jam into pots, filling each one to the brim. This method ensures that the larger pieces of fruit remain suspended in the jam instead of floating to the top.
7. Put waxed paper discs on at once, waxed side down. Put on the jam pot covers immediately, or wait until jam is quite cold. Never put the top covers on when jam is half-way between hot and cold. Condensation can form and this can lead to mouldy jam.
8. Label jam pots with the name and date, and store in a cool, dry, dark, well-ventilated cupboard.

> Mrs W. White and Mrs S. Marshall
> St Michaels, Kent

See also Raspberry Vinegar, page 387.

REDCURRANT JELLY

A mixture of red and white currants may be used. If you cannot make this jelly when fruit is ripe, put fruit in polythene bags and freeze it. No preparation of fruit is needed. Small stems, etc., will be disposed of in the jelly bag.
This recipe may also be used for blackcurrant jelly.

Yields about 1.8 kg/4 lb

2.7 kg/6 lb red and/or white currants
1.75 litres/3 pints water
Sugar

1. Wash fruit and put in preserving pan.
2. Add 1.2 litres/2 pints of water and simmer until fruit is tender.

3. Mash fruit down, then tip it into a scalded jelly bag and let it drain for 10 to 15 minutes into a bowl.
4. Now remove pulp from jelly bag, return it to the pan, add the remaining 600 ml/1 pint of water and simmer again for about ½ hour.
5. Tip all this into a jelly bag and let it drain into another bowl. Do not squeeze the bag or the jelly may not be clear.
6. Mix together the two extracts of juice. Then make a pectin test to ascertain the setting quality of the jelly. This test will also tell you how much sugar to use (*see page 353*).
If pectin test shows very poor setting quality, it is advisable to return juice, or both juice and pulp, to the pan and simmer again to drive off some of the excess water content. Then test again.
7. Measure juice and, according to the result of pectin test, weigh out the sugar.
8. Put sugar in a bowl to warm in a very cool oven, Gas ¼, 225°F, 110°C. Put clean small jars to warm in coolest part of oven.
9. Bring juice to the boil, add warmed sugar and stir, without boiling, until dissolved.
10. When sugar is completely dissolved bring to the boil and boil rapidly until setting point is reached (*see page 353*).
11. Skim off scum with a metal spoon. Fill jars without delay before jelly starts to set.
12. Put on well-fitting waxed tissues immediately, waxed side down. This seals the jelly and protects it from the atmosphere.
13. With jelly it is easier to put outer covers on jars when it is set, but wait until it is quite cold.
14. Label with name and date and store in a cool, dark, dry, well-ventilated place.

RHUBARB AND ORANGE JAM

Good as a filling for a plate-pie.

Yields about 3.4 kg/7½ lb

1.8 kg/4 lb rhubarb
2.25 kg/5 lb sugar
2 oranges
1 lemon
450 g/1 lb seedless raisins*

**As an economy raisins may be replaced by 450 g/1 lb bananas. Slice them just before they are added at paragraph 4 below.*

1. Wash and trim rhubarb. Cut it into 2.5 cm/1 inch lengths. Put into preserving pan or large saucepan and sprinkle over the sugar.

2. Grate rind from oranges and lemon. Squeeze juice.

3. Add raisins, juice and rind. If using bananas, do not put them in at this stage. Mix with a wooden spoon and allow to stand for 1 hour.

4. Bring to the boil, stirring to ensure there is no undissolved sugar. If using bananas add them now, thinly-sliced. Cook slowly for about 45 minutes, stirring occasionally until liquid evaporates from the fruit and jam is thick. Do not boil this jam hard or rhubarb goes to a mush.

5. Meanwhile, prepare clean jam jars. Put them to dry and warm in a very cool oven, Gas $\frac{1}{4}$, 225°F, 110°C. Although this jam is not boiled hard to reach setting point it still keeps well as long as it is potted in the usual way, as follows.

6. Fill warmed jars to the brim with the hot jam. Immediately put on well-fitting waxed tissues, waxed side down. This seals the jam and protects it from the atmosphere.

7. Wipe jars and put on outer covers, either while jam is hot or cold, but *never* in between.

8. Label with name and date and store in a cool, dark, dry, well-ventilated place.

Mrs Doreen Allars
Welbourn, Nr Lincoln

1 pint of juice weigh out 450 g/1 lb sugar. Put sugar in a bowl to warm in a very cool oven, Gas $\frac{1}{4}$, 225°F, 110°C.

7. Put clean small jars to warm in coolest part of oven.

8. Put sugar and juice in pan, place over low heat and stir until sugar is dissolved.

9. When sugar is completely dissolved bring to the boil and boil rapidly until setting point is reached (*see page 353*).

10. Skim off scum with a metal spoon.

11. Stir in a few drops of colouring, just enough to give it a delicate tint. Do not stir too hard or you may get bubbles in the jelly.

12. Fill warmed jars without delay before jelly starts to set.

13. Put on well-fitting, waxed tissues immediately, waxed side down. This seals the jelly in the jam and protects it from the atmosphere.

14. With jelly it is easier to put outer covers on jars when it is set, but wait until it is quite cold.

15. Label with name and date and store in a cool, dark, dry, well-ventilated place.

Mrs Doreen Allars
Welbourn, Nr Lincoln

ROSEMARY JELLY

Use with lamb instead of mint sauce. Made with fresh, not dried, rosemary.

Yields about 3.2 kg/7 lb

2.25 kg/5 lb cooking apples
600 ml/1 pint water
4 tablespoons fresh rosemary leaves
225 ml/8 fl oz cider vinegar or malt vinegar
Sugar
Green vegetable colouring (optional)

1. Wash apples. Cut them up but do not peel or core.

2. Put apple in preserving pan with water and rosemary.

3. Bring to the boil and simmer for 40 minutes or until soft.

4. Add vinegar and boil for 5 minutes.

5. Tip all into a scalded jelly bag and allow to drip. To ensure jelly is clear do not squeeze the bag. It will take about 12 hours to drip through.

6. Meanwhile, measure the juice. For each 600 ml/

STRAWBERRY JAM I

This recipe does not make a firm jam but flavour is excellent.

Yields 1.3 kg/3 lb

900 g/2 lb small firm strawberries
900 g/2 lb granulated sugar
Juice of 1 large lemon

1. Hull strawberries, place with sugar, in layers, in a bowl. Pour over juice. Cover and leave for 24 hours.

2. Drain away juice into a large pan (a large sieve is a help). Scrape in any undissolved sugar but keep strawberries aside.

3. Heat gently to dissolve sugar, bring to a brisk boil and boil to 220°F, 106°C.

4. Add strawberries and any more drained-away juice. Boil again to 220°F, 106°C, stirring as little as possible.

5. Pour carefully into a cold bowl and stir once or twice so that fruit mingles in syrup and stops rising to the surface.

6. When cool, pour into sterile jars. Place on waxed paper discs, waxed side down, to cover surface of jam completely. Cover with a clean cloth and leave until quite cold.

7. Fasten on jam pot covers, label and store in cool, dark place.

STRAWBERRY JAM II

A recipe particularly suitable for frozen fruit which does not set easily. Fresh fruit can be used.

Yields 3.6 kg/8 lb

1.8 kg/4 lb strawberries
2.25 kg/5 lb sugar
10 ml/2 teaspoons alum, can be bought at chemists

1. Allow fruit to thaw a little. Then put it in a large saucepan with the sugar and bring to the boil, stirring all the time until sugar has dissolved.
2. Boil briskly for 10 minutes.
3. Meanwhile, put clean jars to warm in a very cool oven, Gas $\frac{1}{4}$, 225°F, 110°C.
4. Take pan off heat and allow bubbling to stop.
5. Stir in alum, then return pan to heat and bring to the boil again. Remove from the heat.
6. Allow jam to cool for 10 minutes so that fruit will remain evenly suspended when potted.
7. Pot jam following notes *on page 354.*

Anne Wallace
Stewarton, Ayrshire

GREEN TOMATO JAM

Yields about 4.5 kg/10 lb

2.7 kg/6 lb green tomatoes
2 lemons
1 teaspoon citric acid
2.7 kg/6 lb sugar

1. Remove skins from tomatoes (*see page 139*).
2. Slice tomatoes and put them in a large pan.
3. Squeeze juice from lemons and add with citric acid to pan.
4. Tie pips and peel of lemons in a piece of muslin and put this in pan.
5. Simmer until fruit is well broken down.
6. Meanwhile, put sugar to warm in a very cool oven, Gas $\frac{1}{4}$, 225°F, 110°C.

7. Put clean jam jars to dry and warm in oven.
8. Add warmed sugar to pan, stir over gentle heat until dissolved. Bring to the boil.
9. Boil rapidly until setting point is reached (*see page 353*).
10. Pour into warm jars. Place waxed paper tissue on at once.
11. Cover with jam pot covers at once, or leave until quite cold—*never* in between. Label with name and date.
12. Store in a cool, dark, dry, well-ventilated place.

Sybil Norcott
Irlam, Nr Manchester

APPLE BUTTER

This unusual preserve can be served with rice pudding or porridge.

Yields about 1.8 kg/4 lb

1.3 kg/3 lb apples, crab apples or windfalls can be used
600 ml/1 pint cider or apple wine, or, if you don't use cider or wine: 300 ml/$\frac{1}{2}$ pint water will be sufficient
Granulated sugar
Powdered cinnamon
Ground cloves

1. Wash apples. Remove damaged parts if any, but do not peel or core. Cut into small pieces.
2. Place in pan with liquid. Cover and simmer until soft.
3. Sieve and weigh pulp. (If very fluid, simmer in clean pan to thicken a little.) Add 325 g/12 oz granulated sugar for each 450 g/1 lb of weighed pulp, and $\frac{1}{2}$ a level teaspoon of powdered cinnamon plus $\frac{1}{2}$ teaspoon of ground cloves.
4. Simmer gently until a spoon drawn across the mixture leaves its own impression.
5. Pot at once into sterile, hot jam jars. Place on waxed disc to cover surface completely. Cover with a clean cloth and leave until quite cold.
6. Fasten on jam pot covers, label and store in cool, dark place.

PLUM BUTTER

Any plums, including greengages and damsons, may be used.
This will not keep for more than a few weeks.

Plums
A little water
Honey
Ground allspice
Ground nutmeg

1. Put plums in a pan with a very little water, barely 1 cm/½ inch deep.
2. Cover pan with a well-fitting lid and allow plums to simmer until they are tender.
3. Put plums through a sieve to make a purée.
4. Measure purée in a measuring jug and put it back in pan.
5. Now measure out honey to exactly half the quantity of purée. Add this to the pan with just enough of the spices to flavour it gently.
6. Cook slowly, stirring often, until it is thick and creamy with no loose liquid.
7. Meanwhile, prepare clean jars with air-tight lids and put jars to dry and warm in a very cool oven, Gas ¼, 225°F, 110°C.
8. Pour hot, plum butter into warmed jars. Put on air-tight lids at once.
9. Label with name and date.

GRAPEFRUIT AND GINGER CHEESE

An interesting way to use the pulp remaining after making Grapefruit Jelly Marmalade (*see page 362*). It may be sliced and eaten as a dessert with whipped cream or a few chopped nuts, or with plain biscuits or wholemeal scones and butter.
It is best potted in straight-sided jars, moulds or even old mugs, so that when served it can be turned out on to a plate.

Can be eaten a week after making. Best used within 6 months.

Pulp from 2 grapefruit and 3 lemons used for Grapefruit Jelly Marmalade
Sugar
About 1 level teaspoon ground ginger

FOR POTTING
A little glycerine

1. Sieve the pulp.
2. Weigh the purée. It will probably be 325 g/12 oz.
3. Put the same weight of sugar in a dish into a very cool oven, Gas ¼, 225°F, 110°C, for 20 minutes to warm. Put clean, straight-sided jars or moulds into oven to warm at same time.
4. Heat purée in a pan. Remove from heat and add sugar, stirring until it is completely dissolved.
5. Add up to 1 level teaspoon ginger, according to taste. Bring to the boil then simmer, stirring occasionally, for about 10 minutes until mixture coats back of spoon thickly.
6. Smear glycerine inside warmed jars. This helps release cheese from jars when it is turned out.
7. Pour hot cheese into jars, press waxed tissues, waxed-side down, on to the hot surface to seal it. Cover and store as directed for jams (*see page 354*).

Mrs R. Punt
Wychbury W.I., Worcestershire

SUFFOLK DAMSON CHEESE

Fruit cheese is very rich and should be potted in small quantities. Use small moulds or jars, even old cups, from which it can be turned out whole and served on a plate. The moulds should be warm and preferably smeared with glycerine on the inside so that the cheese will turn out easily.

1. Wash damsons well. Cover with water and stew well.
2. Rub flesh through sieve leaving stones and skins behind.
3. Measure pulp. Allow 450 g/1 lb sugar to 450 g/1 lb pulp.
4. Put pulp and sugar in pan and stir over low heat until sugar is dissolved.
5. Bring to boil and simmer gently until a spoon drawn across the bottom of the pan will leave a clean line.
6. Meanwhile, prepare the moulds or jars.
7. Pour the cheese into moulds. Cover immediately with waxed paper discs. Cover with a clean cloth until cool and then put on jam pot covers.

Store at least a year before eating—if you can wait that long.

Turn out to serve. Decorate with blanched almonds to make a hedgehog. Serve whipped cream if desired.

It is also eaten with cold meats.

Mrs Nancy Leeson
Horringer

GOOSEBERRY CURD

Delicious as a filling for tartlets and sponges. Also in meringue baskets, but fill them, of course, at the very last minute. Can be eaten straight away. Keeps for 6 weeks. Best kept in a refrigerator.

Yields 900 g/2 lb

675 g/1½ lb young green gooseberries*
300 ml/½ pint water
125 g/4 oz butter
325 g/12 oz sugar
3 eggs

If you cannot get young gooseberries, 1 or 2 drops of green food colouring can be used.

1. There is no need to top and tail gooseberries. Put them in with the water in a pan, bring to boil and simmer until pulpy.
2. Meanwhile, put clean jars to warm in a very cool oven, Gas ¼, 225°F, 110°C.
3. Push gooseberries through a nylon sieve, taking care to scrape purée from underside of sieve.
4. Put butter and sugar into a double saucepan or into a basin standing in a pan of simmering water. Stir to dissolve sugar. Add gooseberry purée.
5. In another bowl, beat eggs but do not whisk. Stir in hot gooseberry mixture, then return to double cooker.
6. Cook, stirring all the time until mixture thickens.
7. Pour into warmed jars. Put a waxed tissue on top.
8. When quite cold, put on jam pot covers.

LEMON CURD

Yields 450 g/1 lb

125 g/4 oz butter
175 to 225 g/6 to 8 oz caster sugar*
2 large lemons, rind and juice
2 large eggs, beaten

Use 175 g/6 oz sugar for a sharp taste, 225 g/8 oz sugar for a sweeter curd.

1. Put butter, sugar, lemon rind and half of the strained lemon juice in the top part of a double saucepan with boiling water in the lower part (or use a basin fitting well over a pan of water).
2. Stir well until butter has melted and sugar has dissolved.

3. Add remainder of strained lemon juice and beaten eggs.
4. Continue cooking over pan of simmering water, stirring frequently until mixture has thickened enough to coat the back of a spoon.
5. Pour into small hot jam jars—glass baby-food jars are ideal. Cover surface immediately with waxed paper disc. Cover with a clean cloth until quite cold and then fasten on jam pot covers.

Store in refrigerator if possible and use within 6 weeks.

LEMON OR ORANGE CURD

For an interesting change use the orange curd to make Orange Meringue Pie. Also delicious in Meringue Baskets (*see page 349*).

Yields about 450 g/1 lb

2 lemons or oranges
75 to 125 g/3 to 4 oz butter
225 g/8 oz granulated sugar
2 eggs and one extra yolk

1. Scrub fruit and grate it, removing only the zest. *Or*, peel fruit very finely with potato peeler. Squeeze juice.
2. Put rind and juice with butter and sugar into an earthenware jar or basin. Stand this in a pan of simmering water. A double saucepan is ideal. Take care that water in outside pan never splashes into mixture. Keep water simmering and stir until sugar dissolves.
3. Meanwhile, put clean jars to warm in a very cool oven, Gas ¼, 225°F, 110°C.
4. In another basin beat the eggs with a fork, removing the germ. Do not whisk.
5. Pour fruit mixture over eggs, through a strainer if whole pieces of rind were used, and return to the double cooker.
6. Cook until curd thickens, stirring in one direction. It may take 30 to 45 minutes before it is really thick. Stir every 4 or 5 minutes. Curd thickens a little more in jars as it cools.
7. Pour into warmed jars. Put a waxed tissue on top.
8. When quite cold put on jam pot covers.

Keeps for 6 weeks. Best kept in a refrigerator.

DOROTHY SLEIGHTHOLME'S MINCEMEAT

Cooking the apple helps mincemeat to keep longer. With raw apple it can ferment after a few weeks.

A cheaper version can be made—substituting chopped dates for raisins and omitting rum.

Yields nearly 2 kg/4½ lb

450 g/1 lb apples
15 g/½ oz butter
225 g/8 oz currants
225 g/8 oz raisins
225 g/8 oz sultanas
125 g/4 oz candied peel
125 g/4 oz dates, chopped small
225 g/8 oz soft brown sugar
175 g/6 oz grated suet
Grated rind and juice of 1 lemon
1 teaspoon cinnamon
½ teaspoon grated nutmeg
4 tablespoons rum

1. Peel, core and finely chop apples.
2. Melt butter in pan, add apple and cook gently to soften. Allow to become cold.
3. Add rest of ingredients and mix all well together.
4. Leave in bowl, covered, stirring occasionally during next 24 hours.
5. Put in cold but sterile jars, do not fill quite to top. Place waxed paper discs on top of the jam and cover with jam-pot covers. Label.
6. Store in cool, dry, dark place.

GRACE MULLIGAN'S MINCEMEAT

As mincemeat is liable to ferment, it is best if potted in a large jar and kept in refrigerator.

Yields about 900 g/2 lb

225 g/8 oz seedless raisins
125 g/4 oz sultanas
125 g/4 oz eating apples, peeled
125 g/4 oz mixed peel
50 g/2 oz grated suet
225 g/8 oz currants
Grated rind and juice of 1 lemon

125 g/4 oz soft brown sugar
1 tablespoon golden syrup
1 teaspoon mixed spice
1 teaspoon cinnamon
¼ teaspoon grated nutmeg
4 tablespoons brandy or whisky

1. Mince the raisins, sultanas, apple, peel and suet using the coarse mincing plates. Leave the currants whole.
2. Put all ingredients together and mix well.
3. Pot as suggested in previous recipe with a good lid, and keep in refrigerator.

BLACKBERRY SYRUP

1. Fruits should be sound but fully ripe.
2. The best method of extracting the juice is to place fruit in a casserole, adding 150 ml/¼ pint water to 1.3 kg/3 lb fruit. Cover and leave in very slow oven for several hours. *OR*, fruit can be placed in a large bowl over a pan of simmering water for 2 to 3 hours.
3. Strain through 3 to 4 thicknesses of muslin. It will require 1 to 2 hours. The fruit can be gently pressed until all liquid is released.
4. Measure juice, allow 325 g/12 oz sugar to each 600 ml/1 pint and place in large pan. For flavouring, a few cloves or a piece of cinnamon stick tied in muslin can be added.
5. Heat to dissolve sugar. Do not boil.
6. Pour into sterile bottles to within 4 cm/1½ inches of top. Place on screw tops, not too tightly.
7. To sterilise. Place a wire rack or false bottom in a deep vessel. Place the bottles on this and fill with cold water up to neck of bottle. Bring to simmering, 180°F, 82°C, in one hour and maintain for 20 minutes.
8. Remove, screw down tops, label and store in dark, cool place.

See also Blackcurrant Syrup and other cordials in chapter 13, pages 430–2.

PICKLES, CHUTNEYS AND SAUCES

Vinegar. Use a good quality malt vinegar, with a 5% acetic acid content for a good flavour and keeping quality.

Fruits for pickling need to be firm and sound but not of the finest quality. Vegetables should be young, fresh and crisp. Cheaper fruit, provided it is firm, usually forms the basis for chutney.

Aluminium and stainless steel pans are best. Use only wooden spoons, a nylon sieve and stainless steel knives.

Fruit and vegetables for chutney are chopped or minced and cooked to soften in a covered pan with very little water. A pressure cooker is ideal. Vinegar is not usually added at first as it can have a hardening effect and so prolong cooking, thus making the product less economical.

Once all ingredients are combined, chutney is cooked gently until thick, stirring often so that it does not stick. When a spoon drawn through the mixture leaves its trail, and does not at once fill with excess liquid, the chutney is ready to pot.

Pot into clean, dry, warm jars, filling to the brim.

Covers for jars need to be vinegar-resistant—e.g., metal twist top with plastic inner coating, soft plastic snap-on type, or hard plastic screw-on type. Cellophane jam pot covers are not suitable because vinegar will evaporate. Plain metal tops will corrode and rust and impart a metallic taste.

Labels should always be used, stating type of chutney, date and whether mild, sweet or hot.

Allow chutneys to mature for 1 or 2 months before using.

Spiced vinegar for pickles can now be bought, but there are 2 methods for home-made:

SPICED VINEGAR FOR PICKLES

Either brown or white vinegar can be used, depending on type of pickle. White vinegar is more expensive, but looks better with onions and cauliflower.

1.2 litres/2 pints best vinegar (use bottles for your finished product)
¼ oz cinnamon bark
¼ oz whole cloves
12 peppercorns
¼ oz whole mace
¼ oz whole allspice
1 or 2 bay leaves

Tie spices in a small piece of muslin and put them with the vinegar into a wide-necked jar. Cover jar with a vinegar-proof lid, or a saucer, and let the spices steep in the vinegar for 1 to 2 months for a good flavour.

QUICK METHOD

Place vinegar and spices in a glass or china bowl (not metal or polythene) standing on a pan of water. Cover bowl, bring water slowly to boil. Remove from heat. Allow to get quite cold—at least 2 hours. Spiced vinegar need not be used at once. Remove bag of spices or strain vinegar and put back into original bottles.

Spiced vinegar is used for most pickles. Those to be kept crisp should be covered with cold vinegar, softer types with hot vinegar.

PICKLED ONIONS

For best flavour keep about 3 months before eating.

1. Select small, even-sized onions. Place without peeling in a brine made from 450 g/1 lb salt to 4.5 litres/1 gallon water. Place a plate on top to keep onions submerged.
2. Leave 12 hours, peel and place in fresh brine for 24 hours.
3. Drain thoroughly, pack into screw-top jars, and cover with cold, spiced vinegar (*see above*) which should be 1 cm/½ inch above onions. Cover securely with vinegar-resistant tops.

PICKLED BABY BEETS

TO COOK THE BEETROOT
Baby beetroot
Vinegar
Salt
Water

FOR THE PICKLE
Spiced vinegar (*see this page*)
Sugar

1. Wash young beetroots carefully. Do not break the skins.
2. Put them in a saucepan. Measure water into the pan and for every 1.2 litres/2 pints of water add 1 dessertspoon vinegar and 1 teaspoon salt.
3. Boil the beets for 30 minutes or until tender.
4. Prepare clean, dry, wide-necked jars with vinegar-proof lids.
5. Dip cooked beets in cold water. It will make them easier to handle. Rub off the skin and grade them into sizes.

6. Pack into jars.

7. Now mix sugar into the spiced vinegar. Allow 6 teaspoons sugar per pint of vinegar.

8. Bring spiced vinegar to the boil, stirring to dissolve the sugar.

9. Pour the hot, sweet, spiced vinegar into the jars to cover beetroot.

10. Put lids on at once and screw up tightly.

Mrs Doreen Allars
Welbourn, Nr Lincoln

See also Beetroot in Jelly, page 376.

PICKLED CAULIFLOWER

1. Select sound, firm, white cauliflowers, break heads into small pieces.

2. Place in brine (as for onions) leave 24 hours.

3. Drain well, pack into jars, cover with cold, spiced vinegar (*see page 372*). Cover securely with vinegar-proof tops as for pickled onions.

PICKLED RED CABBAGE

Suitable for eating after 1 week, but will lose its crispness after 3 months.

1. Choose a firm cabbage of a good colour. Remove any discoloured outer leaves, cut cabbage into 4 portions, remove any very large white pieces. Shred finely.

2. Place on a large dish, layered with a good sprinkling of salt, using approximately 50 g/2 oz coarse salt to each 450 g/1 lb cabbage. Leave for 24 hours.

3. Drain well, rinsing away any surplus salt. Pack loosely into jars, cover with cold spiced vinegar (*see page 372*). Screw tops down securely. (Kilner jars are good for storage, but make sure lids are vinegar-proof.)

PICKLED DAMSONS

3.6 kg/8 lb damsons
1.8 kg/4 lb sugar
1.2 litres/2 pints vinegar
15 g/½ oz whole cloves
15 g/½ oz allspice
7 g/¼ oz root ginger
7 g/¼ oz stick cinnamon
Rind of ½ lemon

1. Wash and stalk the damsons, prick all over with a needle and place in a bowl.

2. Dissolve the sugar in the vinegar.

3. Crush the spices and tie them with the lemon rind loosely in a piece of muslin.

4. Put this into vinegar syrup and bring to the boil.

5. Pour the hot spiced vinegar over the damsons. Cover and leave 5 to 7 days.

6. Drain vinegar off the damsons, reboil it and pour back over the damsons. Cover and leave 5 to 7 days.

7. Once more drain the vinegar off the damsons, reboil and pour back over the damsons. Cover and leave 5 to 7 days.

8. Drain the vinegar off the damsons, reboil—allowing it to reduce and thicken slightly.

9. Pack the damsons into clean dry jars, pour the syrup over the fruit.

10. Cover immediately with vinegar-proof lids.

This method ensures damsons remain whole and undamaged in the finished pickle.

This fruit can also be pickled in unsweetened spiced vinegar—the ingredients and method of pickling are as above omitting the sugar.

QUICKER METHOD

Note: With this method the damsons tend to burst and the result is not as good as the first method.

1. Wash and stalk the damsons.

2. Make the spiced vinegar as above.

3. Simmer the fruit in the spiced sweetened vinegar until tender, then drain the liquid from the fruit and pack the damsons neatly into jars.

4. Boil the vinegar gently until slightly thick and fill each jar with enough hot vinegar syrup to cover the fruit.

5. Cover with vinegar-proof lids.

SWEET PICKLED PRUNES

These can be eaten immediately, do not need to mature but will keep for a year. Good with cold meat and a good alternative to black olives on pizza.

225 g/8 oz dried prunes
225 g/8 oz soft brown sugar
300 ml/½ pint malt vinegar
150 ml/¼ pint water
A 5 cm/2 inch piece of cinnamon

1. Put prunes in a basin, add sugar, vinegar, water and cinnamon. Cover and leave overnight.

2. Next day, turn everything into a saucepan. Sim-

mer until the prunes are tender, about 10 minutes.
Leave to cool.

3. Lift out the prunes, split and remove the stones.

4. Pack prunes into jars.

5. Return the pan of syrup to the heat. Simmer for one minute and pour over the prunes to cover.

6. Put on vinegar-proof lids, label and store.

PICKLED ORANGES

4 oranges
450 ml/¾ pint water
Pinch of bicarbonate of soda
300 ml/½ pint white malt vinegar
225 g/8 oz granulated sugar
1 teaspoon ground cloves
⅓ inch stick of cinnamon bark
A few whole cloves (optional)

1. Wash the oranges and place in pan with water and soda. Cover and simmer approximately 20 minutes, but watch for signs of peel cracking.

2. Remove to plate and allow to cool. Reserve the water.

3. Cut into 8 wedges or 6 rings.

4. Make a syrup as follows: measure 300 ml/½ pint of the orange water, add vinegar, sugar, ground cloves and cinnamon. Stir over gentle heat to dissolve sugar, then bring to the boil.

5. Add orange, a few pieces at a time, simmer until turning transparent, about 10 minutes.

6. Lift out and allow to drain on to a plate. Simmer remaining oranges and drain.

7. Pack into preserving or honey jars with screw tops (jam jars not recommended) and pour over hot syrup. Cover at once.

Whole cloves may be placed in jars to give added flavour.

PICKLED RUNNER BEANS

A sweet pickle—delicious served with cold beef or cheese.

675 g/1½ lb runner beans
Salt
600 ml/1 pint good malt vinegar
675 g/1½ lb granulated sugar
1 level teaspoon ground allspice
Pepper

1. String and slice beans.

2. Cook in boiling, slightly-salted water for 8 to 10 minutes until tender.

3. Meanwhile, put vinegar, sugar, allspice and pepper into a pan over a low heat. Stir until sugar dissolves. Bring to the boil.

4. Drain beans, add them to the spiced vinegar and simmer for 5 minutes. Pour off vinegar into a jug.

5. Pack beans into clean jars and pour over the vinegar to completely cover them.

6. Put on vinegar-proof lids immediately.

7. Store in a cool, dark, dry place for a fortnight to mature before eating.

Mrs Susan Crawford
Thorpe Bay, Nr Southend-on-Sea

PICKLED EGGS

For this you will need a wide-mouthed jar with a well-fitting vinegar-proof lid.

6 eggs
600 ml/1 pint white vinegar, preferably wine or cider vinegar
25 g/1 oz pickling spice
Small piece of bay leaf

1. Put eggs into pan of cold water, bring to boil and boil 10 to 11 minutes according to size of eggs. Plunge them into cold water.

2. When cool remove shells and pack eggs loosely into jar.

3. Boil vinegar, spice and bay leaf for 10 minutes. Strain and allow to cool.

4. Pour over eggs in jar.

5. Cover with well-fitting vinegar-proof lid.

6. Leave 3 to 4 weeks before eating. Save the vinegar. It can be used for 2 or 3 batches of pickled eggs before going cloudy.

TO PICKLE NASTURTIUM SEEDS

These are a substitute for capers. Useful for sauces including Sauce Tartare.

1. Pick the green seeds when tiny, about the size of dried peas.

2. Soak for three days in salted water, changing the water daily.

3. Drain and pat dry.

4. Use jars with vinegar-proof lids. Coffee jars with plastic lids can be used.

5. Pack seeds into jars with a little finely-chopped onion if liked.

6. Cover with cold spiced vinegar (*see page 372*) and leave for one week to mature.

PICCALILLI

Keep 2 or 3 months before eating to allow to mature.

Yields about 4.5 kg/10 lb

2.7 kg/6 lb prepared vegetables (a mixture of diced cucumber, marrow, beans, small onions, cauliflower florets and, if liked, green tomatoes)
450 g/1 lb cooking salt
4.5 litres/1 gallon water (optional)

Note: (a) When preparing vegetables make sure they are cut to even sizes.
(b) Copper, brass or iron pans should not be used.

1. *Either* spread the prepared vegetables on a large dish and strew with salt between layers and on top. *Or* dissolve the salt in the water and place the prepared vegetables in this brine. Keep the vegetables submerged by a weighted plate or board.

2. After 24 hours, drain and rinse the vegetables and finish by one of the following methods:

FOR SHARP HOT PICCALILLI
25 to 40 g/1 to $1\frac{1}{2}$ oz dry mustard
25 to 40 g/1 to $1\frac{1}{2}$ oz ground ginger
175 g/6 oz white sugar
1.2 litres/2 pints vinegar, preferably white
20 g/$\frac{3}{4}$ oz flour or cornflour
15 g/$\frac{1}{2}$ oz turmeric

FOR SWEET MILD PICCALILLI
20 g/$\frac{3}{4}$ oz dry mustard
$1\frac{1}{2}$ teaspoons ground ginger
250 g/9 oz white sugar
1.75 litres/3 pints vinegar, preferably white
40 g/$1\frac{1}{2}$ oz flour or cornflour
15 g/$\frac{1}{2}$ oz turmeric

3. Stir mustard, ginger and sugar into most of the vinegar.

4. Add the prepared vegetables and simmer until texture is as liked, either crisp or tender, but not hard or mashed.

5. Blend the flour and turmeric with the rest of the vinegar and then add to the other ingredients in the pan. Bring to the boil, stirring carefully, and boil for 2 to 3 minutes.

6. Pour into hot, dry screw-top jars, taking care that the lids are vinegar-proof. While still hot, place waxed paper discs on top of each.

7. Cover jars with a clean cloth until quite cold. Screw on lids, label and store in a cool dark place.

If preferred, the vegetables can be strained out of the vinegar before the thickening is added. They are then packed into the jars, the liquid drained off and the piccalilli sauce added. It is difficult to avoid air pockets with this method but it allows more careful packing.

APPLE, ONION AND MINT PICKLE

Yields about 900 g/2 lb

This preserve will keep for up to 3 months.

225 g/8 oz onions
450 g/1 lb hard cooking apples
2 teaspoons lemon juice
3 to 4 tablespoons finely-chopped, fresh mint leaves
75 g/3 oz caster sugar
2 teaspoons mustard
$\frac{1}{2}$ level teaspoon ground ginger
2 level teaspoons salt
200 ml/$\frac{1}{3}$ pint white vinegar or cider vinegar

1. Mince onions and apples. Add lemon juice.

2. Mix mint thoroughly with apples and onions.

3. Dissolve sugar, mustard, ground ginger and salt in a little of the vinegar. Simmer for 10 minutes.

4. Bring rest of vinegar to boil and pour over sugar mixture.

5. Allow vinegar mixture to get cold and mix it into the mint, apple and onions.

6. Put into clean jars with vinegar-proof lids. Coffee jars with plastic lids are ideal.

7. Store for 1 month before using to allow pickle to mature and flavour to mellow.

Stella Boldy
Sykehouse, N. Humberside

APPLE AND SAGE PRESERVE

Not a long keeping preserve. Should be used within 8 to 10 weeks.

Can be made at any time of year if apples are cheap. Good with pork, duck or sausages, particularly spread over a sausage pie.

Yields about 1.3 kg/3 lb

1 onion
1.8 kg/4 lb cooking apples
150 ml/¼ pint water
225 g/8 oz caster sugar
50 g/2 oz butter
2 teaspoons salt
1 teaspoon pepper
3 teaspoons dried sage
1 teaspoon Worcestershire sauce
3 tablespoons vinegar

1. Peel and chop up onion.
2. Wash apples. Do not peel or core but remove damaged parts and cut fruit roughly into quarters.
3. Put onion, apple and water into a pan, put lid on and simmer gently until soft.
4. Rub mixture through a nylon sieve to make a purée.
5. Return purée to the pan and cook without the lid until it is a thick pulp. Stir from time to time.
6. Stir in all remaining ingredients and continue to cook gently, stirring often, until no excess liquid remains.
7. Meanwhile, prepare clean jars with vinegar-proof lids. Coffee jars with plastic lids are ideal. Paper covers are not satisfactory because vinegar can evaporate through them and preserve will dry out. Plain metal lids should not be used because vinegar corrodes the metal.
Put clean jars into a very cool oven to dry and warm, Gas ¼, 225°F, 110°C.
8. Fill warm jars nearly to the brim with hot mixture. Put lids on at once.
9. Label and date jars. Store in a cool, dark place.

Mrs Doreen Allars
Welbourn, Nr Lincoln

BEETROOT IN JELLY

900 g/2 lb beetroot
300 ml/½ pint white vinegar
6 cloves
6 peppercorns
A small bay leaf
Half a packet of raspberry jelly

1. Wash beetroot, trim stalks leaving 1 inch. Do not cut away root as beetroot 'bleeds' when cooking if skin is pierced.
2. Pressure cook 20 to 25 minutes or boil for 1½ to 2 hours. Exact time depends on size of beetroots.
3. Allow to cool, rub away skin and trim ends. Cut into half inch dice. Pack into jars.
4. Place vinegar and spices in a pan and cover. Bring to boil and simmer for 10 minutes, strain, discarding spices.
5. Pour on to jelly and dissolve it completely. Cool but do not allow to set.
6. Pour over beetroot, covering completely. When set, put on waxed paper disc, screw on top (preferably non-metallic). If lids are not available pour over 2 to 3 teaspoons of melted paraffin wax and cover with jam-pot covers.

SWEET CUCUMBER PICKLE

Yields about 1.5 kg/3½ lb

900 g/2 lb cucumbers
2 large onions
1 large green pepper
25 g/1 oz salt
600 ml/1 pint cider vinegar
450 g/1 lb soft brown sugar
½ level teaspoon ground turmeric
¼ level teaspoon ground cloves
1 level teaspoon mustard seed
½ level teaspoon celery seed

1. Wash and dice cucumber but do not peel.
2. Peel onions and slice them finely.
3. Cut core out of green pepper, knock out seeds and shred flesh.
4. Put cucumber, onion and green pepper into a large mixing bowl with the salt. Mix well, cover the bowl with a plate and leave for 2 hours.
5. Rinse vegetables thoroughly under cold running water. Drain well and put in a large pan.

6. Add vinegar and bring to the boil.

7. Simmer gently for 20 minutes or until vegetables are soft.

8. Add sugar and spices and stir over a low heat to dissolve sugar. Bring to the boil and remove pan from heat.

9. Tip it all into a large mixing bowl and set it aside until cold.

10. Meanwhile, prepare clean, dry jars with vinegar-proof, screw-top lids. Coffee jars with plastic lids are ideal.

11. Pour into jars and put on the tops.

Mrs Doreen Allars
Welbourn, Nr Lincoln

SWEET MIXED PICKLE

Use pears, peaches, apricots, damsons. Very good with curry or cold meats.

Yields about 2.25 kg/5 lb

1.8 kg/4 lb fruit
900 g/2 lb sugar
600 ml/1 pint spiced vinegar (*see page 372*)
1 teaspoon coriander seeds
1 teaspoon lemon juice

1. Prepare the fruit.
Pears: Peel, core and cut in quarters or eighths.
Peaches: Skin, halve, or quarter and remove stones.
Apricots: Skin, halve and remove stones.
Damsons: Wash, and remove stalks.

2. Prepare, clean, wide-necked jars with vinegar-proof lids. Put jars to dry and warm in a very cool oven, Gas $\frac{1}{4}$, 225°F, 110°C.

3. Dissolve sugar in vinegar, add coriander seeds, lemon juice and fruit.

4. Simmer very carefully until fruit is tender. Do not allow to boil hard or fruit may go ragged at edges and damsons may burst, which would spoil the appearance of the finished product.

5. Strain fruit, returning liquid to the pan.

6. Pack fruit into warmed jars and keep hot while you finish the vinegar syrup.

7. Re-boil vinegar liquid in pan until it is thick and syrupy.

8. Pour over the fruit and while it is hot put vinegar-proof lids on jars.

9. Label jars with name and date and store for 3 months before use. Store in a cool, dark, dry place.

Mrs Doreen Allars
Welbourn, Nr Lincoln

GREEN TOMATO PICKLE

Yields about 900 g/2 lb

1.3 kg/3 lb green tomatoes
2 tablespoons salt
1.2 litres/2 pints vinegar
4 tablespoons black treacle
1 tablespoon made mustard
1 dessertspoon curry powder
$\frac{1}{2}$ teaspoon mixed spice
450 g/1 lb onions
$\frac{1}{2}$ teaspoon cayenne pepper

1. Wash tomatoes, slice thinly and layer in a bowl with salt. Allow to stand 24 hours.

2. In a large saucepan place vinegar, treacle, mustard, curry powder and spice. Bring to boiling point.

3. Drain tomatoes and add to pan with thinly-sliced onions and cayenne pepper. Bring to boil again and simmer for 10 minutes.

4. Pack into screw-top jars, preferably with plastic lids. If metal lids are used, place a vinegar-proof disc inside.

See also 2 recipes for Green Tomato Chutney, page 383 and Green Tomato Jam, page 368.

UNCOOKED CHUTNEY

This chutney is ready to eat as soon as it is made. Good fill-in between seasons. Best eaten within 6 weeks.

Yields nearly 1.3 kg/3 lb

225 g/8 oz each of dates, sultanas, apple, onion
225 g/8 oz soft brown sugar, try muscovado
300 ml/$\frac{1}{2}$ pint spiced vinegar (*see page 372*)
5 g/1 teaspoon salt
A pinch each of pepper, mustard and cayenne
pepper

1. Using coarse plates of mincer, mince the dates, sultanas, apple and onion.

2. Mix well with all other ingredients.

3. Use clean dry jars with vinegar-proof lids. Fill jars, cover and store in a cool dry, well-ventilated place.

Anne Wallace
Stewarton, Ayrshire

APPLE AND RAISIN CHUTNEY

An excellent chutney, particularly good with cheese dishes.

Does not keep as long as other chutneys because of low vinegar content.

Yields about 2.7 kg/6 lb—possible to make half the quantity but, if you do, keep to the 100 ml/4 fl oz of vinegar.

2.25 kg/5 lb apples
Juice and finely-chopped rind of 2 oranges
125 g/4 oz chopped walnuts or almonds
900 g/2 lb granulated sugar
275 g/10 oz raisins
⅓ teaspoon ground cloves
100 ml/4 fl oz distilled vinegar

1. Peel and core apples and cut into small pieces.
2. Prepare oranges and nuts.
3. Put all ingredients into a pan, stir well and simmer with lid on until tender.
4. Remove lid and simmer, stirring often until chutney is thick. It is thick enough when a spoon drawn through it leaves its mark without at once filling with excess liquid.
5. Meanwhile, choose jars with vinegar-proof lids. Coffee jars with plastic lids are ideal. Paper covers are not satisfactory because vinegar can evaporate through them and chutney will dry out. Plain metal lids should not be used because vinegar corrodes the metal. Put clean jars into a very cool oven to dry and warm, Gas ¼, 225°F, 110°C.
6. Fill warm jars nearly to the brim with hot chutney. Put lids on at once.
7. Label and date the chutney. Store in a cool, dark place. Can be eaten at once.

Mrs Doreen Allars
Welbourn, Nr Lincoln

KENTISH APPLE CHUTNEY

Traditionally made late in winter with stored apples. A mild, sweet, firm chutney, quick to make. Allow to mature 6 weeks before eating.

Yields about 1.8 kg/4 lb

900 g/2 lb apples
600 ml/1 pint spiced pickling vinegar (*see page 372*)
450 g/1 lb sugar
1½ teaspoons salt
1 teaspoon ground allspice
125 g/4 oz preserved ginger
325 g/12 oz sultanas

1. Peel, core and chop apples into small pieces.
2. Put vinegar, sugar, salt and allspice into a large saucepan and bring to the boil, stirring to dissolve sugar. Add apples. Simmer for 10 minutes.
3. Meanwhile, wash syrup from ginger, dry and chop into very small pieces. Add to pan with sultanas.
4. Simmer until chutney thickens, stirring occasionally so that it does not burn. It is thick enough when a spoon drawn through the mixture leaves its trail and does not at once fill with liquid.
5. Meanwhile, choose jars with vinegar-proof lids. Coffee jars with plastic lids are ideal. Put clean jars to warm in a very cool oven, Gas ¼, 225°F, 110°C.
6. Allow chutney to cool slightly before putting it into jars. Put on waxed paper discs and, when chutney is quite cold, put on vinegar-proof lids.
7. Label with name and date and store in a cool, dry, well-ventilated cupboard.

Mrs Jill Marshall
Hythe, Kent

SHROPSHIRE APPLE CHUTNEY

An excellent chutney from Mary Berry's collection.

Leave to mature 3 months before using.

Yields 2.2 to 2.7 kg/5 to 6 lb

2 kg/4½ lb apples, peeled and cored
900 g/2 lb soft brown sugar
675 g/1½ lb onions, chopped
1.2 litres/2 pints malt vinegar
675 g/1½ lb sultanas or raisins
25 g/1 oz ground ginger
15 g/½ oz garlic, crushed
25 g/1 oz mustard seed
7 g/¼ oz cayenne pepper

1. Cut apples in small pieces and put in a large pan with sugar, onions and vinegar.
2. Bring to boiling point and simmer until pulpy.
3. Add all other ingredients and simmer 10 minutes or until thick.
4. Bottle and cover with a waxed paper disc. Leave till cold.
5. Cover with vinegar-proof lids. Label and store in cool dark place.

DATE CHUTNEY

This chutney is made in small quantities to be eaten as soon as it is made. Keeps well.

Yields about 450 g/1 lb

225 g/8 oz dates
325 ml/12 fl oz malt vinegar
6 tablespoons demerara or muscovado sugar
4 cloves of garlic, finely-chopped
1 teaspoon fresh ginger, finely-chopped
50 g/2 oz sultanas
2 teaspoons paprika
1 teaspoon salt

1. Chop dates quite small.
2. Put vinegar and sugar in a pan, stir over low heat to dissolve sugar, then bring rapidly to the boil.
3. Reduce heat and add dates, garlic and ginger.
4. Cook on a low heat for 5 minutes, stirring all the time.

5. Add the sultanas, paprika and salt and cook for a further 5 minutes. Do not overcook or it will turn to caramel.
6. Pot in the usual way.

Priya Wickramasinghe
Cardiff

DATE AND BANANA CHUTNEY

Can be made at any time of year. Good with curry. Leave to mature for at least 3 months before eating.

Yields 1.3 kg/3 lb but easy to make double quantity

450 g/1 lb onions
225 g/8 oz dates
125 g/4 oz crystallised ginger
2 level teaspoons salt
300 ml/½ pint vinegar
6 bananas
225 g/8 oz treacle
1 teaspoon curry powder

1. Peel and chop onions finely.
2. Chop up dates and crystallised ginger.
3. Put these in a saucepan with salt and half the vinegar. Cover pan and simmer until soft.
4. Peel and chop up bananas and add them to the pan with the treacle, curry powder and rest of vinegar.
5. Simmer until all is soft and consistency is thick. When you draw the spoon through it the trail should remain and not at once fill with excess liquid.
6. Meanwhile, choose jars with vinegar-proof lids. Coffee jars with plastic lids are ideal. Paper covers are not satisfactory because vinegar can evaporate through them and chutney will dry out. Plain metal lids should not be used because vinegar corrodes the metal.
Put clean jars into a very cool oven to dry and warm, Gas ¼, 225°F, 110°C.
7. Fill warm jars nearly to the brim with hot chutney. Put lids on immediately.
8. Label and date chutney. Store in a cool, dark place.

Sybil Norcott
Irlam, Nr Manchester

ELDERBERRY CHUTNEY I

A sharp chutney.
Let chutney mature for 3 months before eating. It will keep for years if correctly covered and stored.

Yields about 675 g/1½ lb

1.2 litres/2 pints elderberries
125 g/4 oz seedless raisins
125 g/4 oz demerara sugar
50 g/2 oz onions
15 g/½ oz salt
Pinch cayenne pepper
Pinch allspice
600 ml/1 pint cider vinegar or good malt vinegar

1. Wash elderberries if necessary. Remove them from stalks by running a fork down the stems.
2. Put all ingredients into a large saucepan and stir over low heat until sugar is dissolved.
3. Cook until ingredients are soft, stirring from time to time. Continue cooking until consistency is thick. When you draw a spoon through it the mark should remain without filling at once with liquid.
4. Meanwhile, choose small jars with vinegar-proof lids. Jars with plastic lids are ideal. Paper covers are not satisfactory because vinegar can evaporate through them and chutney will dry out. Plain metal lids should not be used because vinegar corrodes the metal.
Put clean jars into a very cool oven to dry and warm, Gas ¼, 225°F, 110°C.
5. Fill warmed jars nearly to the brim with hot chutney. Put lids on at once.
6. Label and date jars. Store in a cool, dark place.

Mrs Doreen Allars
Welbourn, Nr Lincoln

ELDERBERRY CHUTNEY II

Yields about 1.8 kg/4 lb

450 g/1 lb elderberries
450 g/1 lb onions
450 g/1 lb cooking apples or windfalls—weigh them after peeling and coring
125 g/4 oz dried fruit—raisins, sultanas or both
1 teaspoon mixed spice
1 teaspoon ginger
1 teaspoon salt
¼ teaspoon cayenne pepper
300 ml/½ pint malt vinegar
325 g/12 oz sugar

1. Remove elderberries from stalks. To do this, hold them over a large basin and strip off berries with a table fork. (A large basin is necessary because berries tend to fly everywhere.)
2. Peel and finely chop onions. Chop apples finely. Put in a large pan.
3. Add dried fruit, spices, salt, pepper and half the vinegar.
4. Bring to the boil and simmer until ingredients are soft.
5. Add sugar and remaining vinegar. Stir over low heat until sugar is dissolved.
6. Then simmer until chutney is thick. It is thick enough when you can draw a wooden spoon through the mixture and the trail of the spoon remains without filling with excess liquid. Stir frequently to prevent sticking.
7. Meanwhile, prepare clean jars with vinegar-proof lids. Coffer jars with plastic lids are ideal. Warm the jars in a very cool oven—Gas ¼, 225°F, 110°C.
8. Fill jars to the brim with hot chutney and put on waxed paper discs, waxed-side down. Leave to cool.
9. When quite cold, put on the vinegar-proof lids. Label jars with the name and date.
10. Store in a cool, dark, dry, well-ventilated cupboard.

Mrs Lynda M. White
Wroot, Nr Doncaster

MARROW AND RED TOMATO CHUTNEY

Let it mature before eating.

Makes about 1.8 kg/4 lb

450 g/1 lb marrow (weighed after peeling and
    removing seeds)
450 g/1 lb tomatoes
225 g/8 oz onions
1 clove garlic
1 tablespoon pickling spice
1 teaspoon ground ginger
225 g/8 oz sultanas
175 g/6 oz white sugar
175 g/6 oz brown sugar
2 teaspoons salt
300 ml/$\frac{1}{2}$ pint malt vinegar

1. Peel marrow, remove seeds and cut flesh into small cubes.
2. Skin the tomatoes (*see page 139*). Cut them up roughly.
3. Peel and chop onion small.
4. Crush garlic (*see page 139*).
5. Tie pickling spice in a piece of muslin.
6. Put all ingredients in a saucepan and stir over low heat until sugar is dissolved.
7. Allow to simmer, stirring occasionally until mixture is thick (about 1 hour). Chutney is thick enough when a spoon drawn through it leaves a trail which does not at once fill with excess liquid.
8. Meanwhile, prepare clean jars with vinegar-proof lids. Put jars to dry and warm in a cool oven. Gas $\frac{1}{4}$, 225°F, 110°C.
9. Pour hot chutney into warmed jars, put on waxed tissues immediately, waxed side down. This seals surface of chutney and protects it.
10. When cold, put on vinegar-proof lids.
11. Label with name and date and store for a few weeks in a cool, dark, dry place.

Mrs A. E. Phillips
Selsey, W. Sussex

ORANGE CHUTNEY

Delicious with cold pork or hot sausages.

Yields 2.25 to 2.7 kg/5 to 6 lb

450 g/1 lb onions, peeled and sliced
Water
900 g/2 lb apples, peeled, cored and sliced
2.25 litres/4 pints good malt vinegar
1.8 kg/4 lb sweet oranges
450 g/1 lb sultanas or raisins
15 to 20 fresh green or red chillis, deseeded, or
    8 dried red chillis*, deseeded and tied in a
    muslin bag
2 dessertspoons cooking salt
2 teaspoons ground ginger
900 g/2 lb white sugar

Fresh chillis are quite mild. It is the dried chillis which are peppery and 4 would be enough if you don't like chutney too hot.

1. Cook onions until tender, in water just to cover. Strain (saving liquid for soup).
2. Add apple and about a cup of the vinegar and continue cooking gently until mushy. Remove from heat.
3. Meanwhile, scrub oranges and peel them. Remove white pith from outer skin and discard. Reserve the peel.
4. Put peel and orange flesh through mincer, removing as many pips as possible.
5. Mince sultanas or raisins and the chillis, if fresh ones are used.
6. Put dried chillis and other ingredients, except sugar, into the pan with about half the remaining vinegar. Simmer until thick, stirring occasionally.
7. Add sugar and rest of vinegar. Stir to dissolve sugar and simmer again until thick. Stir occasionally or it will stick and burn.
8. Remove muslin bag if dried chillis are used. Finish, pot and store as indicated *on page 372.*
9. Allow to mature for 6 weeks before using.

PRUNE CHUTNEY

Yields 1.3 to 1.8 kg/3 to 4 lb

900 g/2 lb prunes
450 g/1 lb onions, sliced
25 g/1 oz salt
1 teaspoon ground ginger
1 teaspoon cayenne pepper
50 g/2 oz mustard seed
25 g/1 oz mixed pickling spice
600 ml/1 pint vinegar
450 g/1 lb soft brown sugar

1. Soak prunes for 48 hours in just enough water to cover.
2. Drain off water and remove stones.
3. Put prunes and onions through mincer into pan.
4. Add salt, ginger and cayenne pepper, also mustard seeds and pickling spices tied in muslin.
5. Add half the vinegar, bring to boil and simmer until mixture is thick.
6. Add sugar, stir to dissolve.
7. Add remaining vinegar.
8. Simmer until thick again. Chutney is ready if no liquid is visible when a wooden spoon is drawn through the mixture.
9. Pot at once into hot, sterile jars and place waxed discs on top of each. Leave until cold.
10. Cover with vinegar-proof lids or melted wax. Label and store in a cool dark place.

PLUM CHUTNEY

Can be made with all types of plums but dark-skinned varieties give it the best colour.

Yields 1.8 kg/4 lb

1.1 kg/2½ lb plums
450 g/1 lb onions, finely-chopped
Water
900 g/2 lb cooking apples
600 ml/1 pint cider vinegar
A piece of root ginger
1 dessertspoon each of whole cloves, whole allspice and peppercorns
450 g/1 lb soft brown sugar
3 level teaspoons salt

1. Wipe, halve and stone the plums.
2. Put onions in a saucepan, cover with water and boil for 5 minutes to soften them. Drain (saving liquid for soup, etc.).
3. Peel, core and chop apples. Put these in a large pan with half of the vinegar. Bring to the boil and cook for 20 minutes to a soft pulp.
4. Meanwhile, bruise the ginger by hitting it with a hammer. Then tie it with the other spices in a piece of muslin.
5. Put spice bag with vinegar and sugar into another pan. Bring to the boil and simmer for 5 minutes, stirring all the time. Draw pan off heat and let the vinegar infuse for 30 minutes. Remove spice bag.
6. Add with onions, plums and salt to apples. Bring to the boil and simmer for about 2 hours until chutney is thick and pulpy. Stir frequently to avoid burning.
7. Finish, pot and store as indicated *on page 372.*
8. Allow to mature for 4 weeks before using.

RHUBARB AND DATE CHUTNEY

Yields 2.2 to 2.7 kg/5 to 6 lb

1.8 kg/4 lb rhubarb
450 g/1 lb dates
450 g/1 lb onions
15 g/½ oz ground ginger
50 g/2 oz mixed spice
7 g/¼ oz curry powder
15 g/½ oz salt
900 g/2 lb sugar (brown or white)
1 litre/1½ pints malt vinegar

1. Cut up rhubarb, chop dates finely, mince or finely chop onions.
2. Place in pan and add spices, salt and sugar with 300 ml/½ pint of the vinegar.
3. Simmer gently for at least 2 hours until tender, adding a little more vinegar if necessary to prevent mixture sticking to pan. Stir from time to time.
4. Add most of the vinegar, simmer until mixture is thick and leaves no loose liquid when a spoon is drawn through. Rhubarb may be fairly moist and therefore up to 150 ml/¼ pint vinegar may not be required. Reserve this amount until a final test is made.
5. Pot at once into hot, sterilised, screw-top jars, cover with waxed paper discs.
6. When cold cover with vinegar-proof lids. Label and store in cool, dark place.

RHUBARB AND ORANGE CHUTNEY

Let it mature for 3 months before eating.

Yields about 1.8 kg/4 lb

900 g/2 lb rhubarb (weighed after trimming)
3 onions
2 oranges
450 g/1 lb raisins
900 g/2 lb demerara sugar
1 litre/1½ pints good malt vinegar
1 tablespoon mustard seed
1 tablespoon white peppercorns
1 level teaspoon powdered allspice

1. Wash and wipe rhubarb, cut it into short pieces and put in preserving pan or large saucepan.
2. Peel and chop onions and add to pan.
3. Finely shred yellow rind from the oranges, squeeze out juice and discard pith. Add to pan.
4. Add raisins, sugar and vinegar.
5. Tie up the 3 spices in a piece of muslin and put this into the pan.
6. Bring to the boil and simmer gently until thick. It is thick enough when a spoon drawn through the chutney leaves its mark and does not immediately fill with excess liquid.
7. Meanwhile, choose jars with vinegar-proof lids. Coffee jars with plastic lids are ideal. Paper covers are not satisfactory because vinegar can evaporate through them and chutney will dry out. Plain metal lids should not be used because vinegar corrodes the metal.
Put clean jars to dry and warm in a very cool oven, Gas ¼, 225°F, 110°C.
8. Remove muslin bag from chutney.
9. Fill warmed jars nearly to the brim with hot chutney. Put lids on at once.
10. Label and date chutney. Store in a cool, dark place.

Mrs Doreen Allars
Welbourn, Nr Lincoln

TOMATO RELISH

Yields about 1.8 kg/4 lb

1.5 kg/3½ lb firm ripe tomatoes, skinned (*see page 139*) or use two 675 g/1½ lb tins of tomatoes
900 g/2 lb onions, finely-chopped
1 teaspoon salt
900 g/2 lb sugar
90 g/3½ oz demerara sugar
25 g/1 oz fresh ginger, finely-chopped
7 g/¼ oz chilli powder
600 ml/1 pint malt vinegar

1. Chop tomatoes and place all ingredients, except vinegar, in a pan. Stir over low heat until sugar is dissolved. Cook gently for about 1 hour to a thick consistency, stirring occasionally.
2. Add vinegar and cook for another 10 minutes.
3. Pour the mixture while hot into warmed, clean, dry jars with vinegar-proof lids.
4. Put on the lids when relish is cold. Label and store in a cool, dry place.

Priya Wickramasinghe
Cardiff

GREEN TOMATO CHUTNEY I

Yields 2.7 to 3.2 kg/6 to 7 lb

1.3 kg/3 lb green tomatoes
450 g/1 lb apples
450 g/1 lb marrow
450 g/1 lb onions
125 g/4 oz dates
225 g/8 oz raisins or sultanas
900 g/2 lb soft brown sugar
15 g/½ oz salt
¼ teaspoon cayenne pepper
25 g/1 oz root ginger
25 g/1 oz mustard seeds
1 litre/1½ pints malt vinegar

1. Wipe tomatoes and cut into small pieces.
2. Peel, core and chop apples.
3. Peel marrow, remove seeds and cut flesh into 1 cm/½ inch cubes.
4. Peel and chop onions finely (or mince).
5. Chop dates finely.

6. Place prepared fruit and vegetables in pan with raisins or sultanas, sugar, salt and pepper.
7. Bruise the ginger, tie in a piece of muslin with mustard seeds and put into pan.
8. Add 600 ml/1 pint of the vinegar.
9. Stir over gentle heat to dissolve sugar. Bring to boil, cover and simmer gently for approximately 2 hours, stirring occasionally. Add more vinegar if mixture thickens before contents are quite soft.
10. To test, draw a wooden spoon across mixture, there will be a mark which should disappear slowly. If mixture is too thick add a little more vinegar and bring to boil. Chutney thickens a little on cooling.
11. Remove muslin bag and press out juices. Mustard seeds can be added to mixture if you like them.
12. Pour into hot, sterile jars. Cover with waxed paper disc and leave until cold, covered with a cloth.
13. Use vinegar-proof lids. If these are not obtainable, pour on 1 to 2 teaspoons of melted paraffin wax, allow to set, then cover with jam-pot covers. If chutney is not sealed, it will shrink during storage. Plain metal tops should not be used, as vinegar will corrode them.
14. Label and then store in a cool, dark place for at least 2 months before eating.

GREEN TOMATO CHUTNEY II

Yields 2.2 to 2.7 kg/5 to 6 lb

1.8 kg/4 lb green tomatoes
450 g/1 lb apples
575 g/1¼ lb shallots, or onions
225 g/8 oz stoned (or seedless) raisins
15 g/½ oz dried whole ginger
12 red chillies
450 g/1 lb brown sugar
15 g/½ oz salt
600 ml/1 pint vinegar

Note: Copper, brass or iron pans should not be used.
1. Cut up the tomatoes, peel and cut up the apples and shallots or onions and chop the raisins.
2. Bruise the ginger and chillies and tie in muslin bag.
3. Place all ingredients in pan. Bring to boil and simmer until all the vinegar has been absorbed, that is, when a spoon drawn across the mixture leaves its impression. Simmering may take 2 or more hours.

4. Remove the bag of spices and pour chutney into hot dry screw-top jars, taking care that the lids are vinegar-proof. While still hot place waxed discs on top of each one.
5. Cover jars with a clean cloth until quite cold. Screw on lids, label and store in a cool dark place.

SAUCES

A TIP
These can be made from chutney, which is sieved and thinned down with a little vinegar at the rate of 600 ml/1 pint of chutney to 300 ml/½ pint vinegar. Spiced vinegar (*see page 372*) can be used instead of plain to give a more piquant flavour. The sauce is then boiled and poured through a funnel, into hot sterilised jars. Put in a well-fitting cork boiled in readiness and dipped in molten paraffin wax to give a good seal. Alternatively, vinegar-resistant screw-tops can be used. The Rhubarb and Date Chutney (*see page 382*) makes a pleasant brown sauce following this method.

PLUM SAUCE

This sauce keeps well and does not need sterilising.

Yields about 1 litre/nearly 2 pints

1.8 kg/4 lb damsons
125 g/4 oz currants
225 g/8 oz onions
25 g/1 oz mixed pickling spice
¼ teaspoon mustard
600 ml/1 pint vinegar
450 g/1 lb sugar
25 g/1 oz salt

1. Cut up plums and finely chop onions. Put them in a large pan with the currants and spices and half the vinegar.
2. Cover pan and allow contents to simmer for half an hour.
3. Rub it all through a nylon sieve, returning the purée to the pan.
4. Add sugar and remaining vinegar, stir until sugar is dissolved and allow to simmer without a lid for about 1 hour, or until consistency is like thick cream. Stir often to stop it sticking.

5. Meanwhile, prepare clean bottles or jars with vinegar-proof lids. Put bottles to dry and warm in a very cool oven, Gas $\frac{1}{4}$, 225°F, 110°C.

6. Fill bottles almost to the brim with the hot sauce and put on lids immediately.

7. When bottles have cooled, label them with name and date and store in a cool, dark, dry place. Let sauce mature for 2 months.

Sybil Norcott
Irlam, Nr Manchester

BROWN PLUM SAUCE

A simple recipe. Keeps very well.

Yields about 1.75 litres/3 pints

1.1 kg/2$\frac{1}{2}$ lb red plums
3 medium-sized onions, sliced
125 g/4 oz sultanas
15 g/$\frac{1}{2}$ oz root ginger
25 g/1 oz pickling spice
1.2 litres/2 pints malt or white vinegar
225 g/8 oz granulated sugar
50 g/2 oz salt
25 g/1 oz dry mustard
1 teaspoon ground nutmeg
1 level teaspoon turmeric

1. Wipe and stone plums and put them in a large pan. Don't worry if stones are firmly anchored— pick them out later.

2. Add onions and sultanas.

3. Bruise the ginger by hitting it with a hammer. Tie it with pickling spice in a piece of muslin. Put it in pan.

4. Add half of the vinegar and boil for 30 minutes.

5. Meanwhile put sugar to warm in a very cool oven, Gas $\frac{1}{4}$, 225°F, 110°C. Put clean bottles into oven to warm at same time. (Choose bottles with vinegar-proof lids.)

6. Remove spice bag and stir in all the other ingredients. Stir to dissolve sugar and bring to boiling point.

7. Simmer for 40 to 60 minutes, stirring occasionally, then leave to cool.

8. When cool, push contents of pan through a nylon sieve. Remember to scrape all the purée off underside of sieve.

9. If the sauce is too thin, simmer and reduce the volume by evaporation until it is thicker but still of pouring consistency.

10. Pour into warmed bottles, right to the brim and put on clean lids immediately. Label and store.

11. Leave for 4 weeks to mature.

RIPE TOMATO SAUCE

Choose really red, ripe tomatoes.

As this sauce has to be sterilised to ensure it keeps, you need bottles of roughly the same height with vinegar-proof tops or new corks, and a pan or a tin deep enough to contain water up to the necks of the bottles.

Yields about 2.25 kg/5 lb

2.7 kg/6 lb tomatoes
20 g/$\frac{3}{4}$ oz salt
A small pinch of cayenne
4 g/$\frac{1}{8}$ oz paprika
$\frac{1}{2}$ teaspoon ground ginger
225 g/8 oz sugar
300 ml/$\frac{1}{2}$ pint spiced vinegar (*see page 372*)

1. Wash and cut up tomatoes. Place in a pan over gentle heat. Cook until skins are free and they have softened.

2. Rub tomato pulp through a sieve and return purée to the pan.

3. Add salt, cayenne, paprika and ginger and cook gently until it begins to thicken.

4. Add sugar and spiced vinegar and cook gently until the consistency of thick cream. Stir from time to time.

5. Meanwhile, prepare clean bottles with vinegar-proof, screw caps or new corks and put them to dry and warm in a very cool oven, Gas $\frac{1}{4}$, 225°F, 110°C. Put caps or corks to sterilise for 15 minutes in a small pan of boiling water.

6. Pour hot sauce into warmed bottles. Leave 5 cm/ 2 inches between sauce and top of bottle. Put in the sterilised corks and tie them down with string. If using screw tops, screw them on but not too tightly.

7. Stand bottles on a trivet or a folded cloth in the pan or tin. Support them with folds of newspaper. Pour in water to just under the lower level of corks. Heat water just to simmering point and keep it, just simmering, for 25 minutes.

8. Lift bottles out of pan. Tighten screw tops and push corks right in as soon as sauce has cooled enough to allow this. Re-tie the strings to ensure corks stay right in.

9. When bottles have cooled and corks are dry, dip tops in melted paraffin wax to make an air-tight seal. Screw caps do not need dipping in wax.

10. Label bottles with name and date and store in a cool, dark, dry place. Let sauce mature for 1 to 2 months.

Sybil Norcott
Irlam, Nr Manchester

LONG-KEEPING HORSERADISH SAUCE

This will keep 12 months or more.

Horseradish

FOR THE SYRUP
300 ml/½ pint white vinegar to 225 g/8 oz white sugar and a little salt

1. Dig horseradish root in mid-summer.
2. Wash well and peel under water, (to avoid severe eye-watering).
3. Cut the root up roughly and put through finest cutters of mincer.
4. In meantime make syrup by dissolving the sugar and salt in the vinegar over a low heat. Allow to go cold.
5. Use a wide-necked jar with vinegar-proof lid. Pack in a little horseradish then add a little syrup and fill the jar in this manner. Make sure it is tightly packed and no air spaces are left.

TO SERVE
To a tablespoon of horseradish add same quantity of thick cream and extra vinegar to taste.

Use with roast beef or beef dishes. Also very good with cold ham.

LONG-KEEPING MINT SAUCE

This will keep 12 months or more.

Mint leaves

FOR THE SYRUP
300 ml/½ pint white vinegar to 225 g/8 oz white sugar and a little green colouring

1. Gather a good quantity of mint, when about 45 cm/18 inches high.
2. Wash and shake as dry as possible.
3. Remove leaves from the stems and pass them through a liquidiser, a herb mill or fine plate of mincing machine.
4. Heat the vinegar, sugar and colouring to dissolve sugar and make the syrup.
5. Use a wide-necked jar with a vinegar-proof lid. Pack in a little mint then add a little syrup, which can be either hot or cold, and fill the jar in this manner. Cover. Make sure jar is tightly packed. If it is not packed tightly enough the mint may rise in the jar. Check the next day and top up with more mint if necessary.

Use as required adding extra vinegar to taste.

TO MAKE HERB VINEGARS

Tarragon, thyme, mint, garlic or any mixture of your choice.

1. Take a good handful of your chosen herb, bruise it well and then put it into a wide-necked glass jar (a bottling jar is suitable).
2. Cover with white vinegar. Put on a vinegar-proof lid.
3. Allow this to stand in full sunlight in a warm room for at least two weeks.
4. Then strain into vinegar bottles and label.

A fresh sprig of the herb inserted into the bottle looks attractive.

BLACKBERRY OR RASPBERRY VINEGAR

An old-fashioned remedy for sore throats. Good to eat with a plain steamed pudding. Sometimes served in the North poured over hot Yorkshire Puddings and eaten as a sweet course.

450 g/1 lb fruit
600 ml/1 pint best cider vinegar or malt vinegar (keep bottle for finished product)
450 g/1 lb granulated sugar (optional)

1. Put fruit and vinegar into a glass or china bowl. Cover with a cloth and allow to stand for 3 to 5 days, stirring occasionally.
2. Strain off liquid into a saucepan. Set it over a low heat and add sugar, if used. Stir until dissolved.
3. Boil mixture for 10 minutes, then pour it into the bottle.

If you prefer not to sweeten the vinegar at paragraph 2, then sugar may be added to taste when vinegar is used.

DRYING HERBS

Most herbs should be gathered for drying just before they flower.

1. Gather in fairly large bunches, wash in clear water and swing to dry.
2. For large-leafed herbs like sage and mint take the leaves off the stem. Small leaved herbs like thyme and winter savory can be left on stem. Put leaves into a large piece of butter muslin.
3. Have ready a large pan of fast boiling water. Holding the four corners of the butter muslin plunge the leaves into water for about 10 seconds.
4. Lift out and lay cloth on cake cooling racks. Spread herbs out evenly.
5. Put racks into a very cool oven, leaving the door ajar, for 2 to 3 hours. They should be brittle when cold.
6. Rub large-leafed varieties through a fine mesh sieve and crush small-leafed varieties between your hands discarding the stems. Sieve if necessary. If there is any leatheriness, return to oven or leave in airing cupboard overnight.
Always store dried herbs away from light, preferably in dark bottles with tight lids.

TO DRY PARSLEY

This method preserves Vitamin C and good green colour.
1. Blanch without thick stems and then put into a baking tin, (without muslin).
2. Dry in a hot oven, Gas 7, 425°F, 220°C, for about 7 to 10 minutes. Keep turning to prevent burning at the edges.

TO DRY FENNEL STEMS

Cut stems in autumn into short lengths and leave in airing cupboard for about 48 hours.
These are used to infuse in milk when making fennel sauce to accompany fish.

BOTTLING

To achieve good results, it is essential to observe the recommended processing times.

THE JARS

Only proper bottling jars should be used and the discs must be in perfect condition to ensure correct sealing.
Sterilise jars and sealing discs beforehand. Rub the inside of metal rings with a little cooking oil.

FRUIT PREPARATION

All fruit should be in prime condition.
Most fruits bottle well and should be clean and cut into even-sized pieces. For example: rhubarb, about 2.5 cm/1 inch long. Pears, apricots and peaches skinned and halved. Plums can be bottled whole where small, but larger fruit, like Victoria plums, can be halved and stoned. Tomatoes are classified as fruit for the purpose of preservation and should always be skinned (*see page 139*). Large tomatoes are better halved.

THE SYRUP

Fruit can be packed in water but a syrup gives a better flavour and colour. A very heavy syrup may cause fruit to rise in jars. The maximum strength syrup is made with 225 g/8 oz sugar to 600 ml/1 pint water, first dissolving the sugar over a low heat, then bringing to boiling point. Less sugar can be used according to taste. Syrup is used boiling when bottling by the Pressure Cooker Method but cold for the Slow Water Bath Method.

PACKING THE JARS

Pack fruit firmly but without damaging into sterile bottling jars. Pour on the syrup or brine. Be sure that the fruit is covered and top of jar is clear from particles of fruit, seeds especially, before placing on sealing disc.

Screw metal ring on to jar. Give the ring a slight turn backwards to allow for expansion and prevent jars bursting during processing.

SOLID PACK

Tomatoes are best packed into jars with a sprinkling of salt and a very little sugar between each layer.

Apples, particularly windfalls, may also be bottled solid pack and are then ready for use in pies, etc. Peel and core apples and remove all damaged parts. Cut into even-sized slices. Pack into jars, sprinkling sugar between each layer, 3 teaspoons of sugar for the small bottling jars is sufficient.

PRESSURE COOKER METHOD

Pressure cooker must be deep enough when rack is in bottom to allow a space between bottling jars and lid.

Pour in about 4 cm/1½ inches in depth of water and 1 tablespoon vinegar to prevent discolouration of pan. If more than one jar is to be processed at a time, place pieces of firm cardboard between them to prevent them touching each other and cracking. Place lid on pan, without pressure control, over medium heat, and allow between 5 and 10 minutes for steam to escape through vent. Then put on 2.25 kg/5 lb valve weight, raise heat, bring to pressure and leave for recommended time. If your pressure cooker does not have a variable valve weight, check manufacturer's handbook for procedure.

All soft fruits, gooseberries, rhubarb and small plums require 1 minute at pressure.

Peaches, large plums, apricots and solid pack apples require 3 to 4 minutes depending on size.

Pears and whole tomatoes, 5 minutes.

Solid pack tomatoes, 15 minutes. After this time, remove pan carefully from heat, leave 15 minutes before removing valve weight.

Lift jars from pan and screw down tightly.

Do not touch the jars during the next ½ to 1 hour. The seal is not complete until the sealing disc goes pop and appears concave. Leave overnight before removing ring and testing seal.

Label jars indicating contents, date of processing and method used.

SLOW WATER BATH METHOD

This method is perhaps better than the pressure cooker for preserving the colour and shape of the fruit or tomatoes, but is NOT to be used for vegetables as it does not kill the bacteria present in these. Use a vessel deep enough to allow bottling jars to be immersed in water. A fish kettle is ideal, but any vessel, providing a rack is fitted in bottom, can be used.

Place jars in pan, cover completely with cold water. Insert thermometer, if used.

Raise from cold to required temperature in 90 minutes.

Soft fruits to 165°F, 74°C, or until the odd bubble breaks on top of the water, maintain for 10 minutes. Gooseberries, rhubarb, plums, apples, peaches, apricots: raise temperature to 180°F, 82°C; maintain 15 minutes.

Pears and whole tomatoes: raise to 190°F, 88°C, maintain 30 minutes.

Solid pack tomatoes: raise to 190°F, 88°C, maintain 40 minutes. After this time, remove jars, screw down, leave to seal.

Do not touch the jars during the next ½ to 1 hour. The seal is not complete until the sealing disc goes pop and appears concave. Leave overnight before removing ring and testing seal.

Label jars indicating contents, date of processing and method used.

BOTTLING FRENCH OR RUNNER BEANS

Note: Read general instructions on bottling (*see page 387*) before proceeding.

1. Wash, slice and blanch beans.
2. Pack tightly into jars.
3. Make a brine by dissolving 15 g/½ oz salt in 1.2 litres/2 pints boiling water. Pour the boiling brine over the beans.
4. Be sure that the beans are covered and that the top of the jar is clean from particles or seeds before placing on sealing disc.
5. Screw metal ring on to jar. Give a slight turn backwards to prevent jars bursting during processing.
6. Process in pressure cooker using 4.5 kg/10 lb valve weight following instructions above. Recommended time 35 minutes. If your pressure cooker does not have a variable valve weight, check manufacturer's handbook for procedure.

Recommended book on all methods of preservation: 'Home Preservation of Fruit and Vegetables', Bulletin 21, produced by Ministry of Agriculture, Fisheries and Food. Obtainable from H.M. Stationery Offices, or their agents.

The essentials in
DOROTHY SLEIGHTHOLME'S STORECUPBOARD

Plain flour
Self-raising flour
Strong plain flour
Soft plain flour
Wholemeal flour

Baking powder
Bicarbonate of soda
Cream of Tartar

Cornflour
Arrowroot

Granulated sugar
Caster sugar
Vanilla sugar
Soft brown sugar
Demerara sugar
Icing sugar
Golden syrup

Currants
Raisins
Sultanas
Candied peel
Glacé cherries
Dates
Dried fruit salad

Mixed spice
Powdered cinnamon
Cloves
Ground ginger
Whole nutmeg
Plain cooking chocolate

Cooking salt
Savoury salt
Pepper
Peppercorns
Mustard

Curry powder
Mixed herbs
Bay leaves
Sage
Garlic
Stock cubes
Tomato purée

Cooking/salad oil
Vinegars
Plastic lemon
Salad cream
Worcestershire sauce

Tea

Coffee
Cocoa

Macaroni
Spaghetti
Rice
Semolina

Gelatine
Jelly squares

Oatmeal
Porridge oats

Dried milk powder
Evaporated milk
Cream

Dried peas
Lentils

Shredded suet

Parmesan cheese

Condensed soup
Sardines
Ham
Sweetcorn
Tomatoes

Vegetables

Mandarin oranges
Pineapple rings
Grapefruit segments
Orange juice

Butter
Margarines
Lard
Yeast
Cheese
Eggs
Bacon

Home-made essentials:
Jams
Jellies
Pickles
Chutneys

Dried breadcrumbs

Dripping

Stock*
Fresh breadcrumbs*

*kept in freezer

12
HOME-MADE
SWEETS

EQUIPMENT FOR SIMPLE SWEET-MAKING

You may have most of the following in the kitchen already:

Large strong saucepan with thickish base
Wooden spoon
Metal spatula (a clean paint scraper is ideal)
Tins for setting toffee, etc. (roasting, dripping, or Swiss roll tins will do)
Large crockery meat platter or marble slab

SUGAR THERMOMETER

It is helpful to have a sugar thermometer. When using one, have it beside the pan in a saucepan of very hot water. Do not put it cold into a pan of hot mixture. While using thermometer, always replace in very hot water. Never cool it too quickly or allow even a few grains to adhere to it after use as they might spoil future batches of sweets.

GUIDE to stages in boiling sweets mixtures for those without a thermometer: to test, drop a teaspoon of mixture in a cup of cold water. Always remove pan of mixture from heat when conducting the test:

Soft ball (240°F, 116°C): when you remove from water and feel it between fingers and thumb it is like a soft ball.

Hard ball (265°F, 130°C): when you remove from water and feel it between fingers and thumb it is a hard ball, but still chewy.

Soft crack (280° to 285°F, 140° to 142°C): when you remove from water and feel it between fingers and thumb it is hard but not brittle.

Hard crack (300°F, 150°C): when you remove from water and feel it between fingers and thumb it is brittle.

Caramel (310° to 320°F, 155° to 160°C): *this is not tested in water*. If you test for hard crack you will know when it has reached 300°F, 150°C. Then you must watch mixture closely, taking care it does not burn. It will turn a deep brown colour.

Anne Wallace
Stewarton, Ayrshire

COCONUT ICE

Makes about 35 pieces

325 g/12 oz sugar
150 ml/¼ pint milk
125 g/4 oz desiccated coconut
1 or 2 drops of vanilla essence

The same ingredients are used again for a second batch, which is coloured pink.

1. Put sugar and milk in a saucepan and stir over low heat until sugar is dissolved. Then boil for 5 minutes.
2. Pour into a basin and add coconut and vanilla. Beat until mixture becomes thick.
3. Spread in a buttered dish or tin.
4. Make the second batch, using a few drops of red food colouring. Spread it on top of white.

Nathalie Jowett
Yea, Victoria, Australia

FONDANT

For this it is helpful to have a sugar thermometer (*see this page*).

Makes about 450 g/1 lb

450 g/1 lb granulated sugar
150 ml/¼ pint water
25 g/1 oz powdered glucose (buy from a chemist)

1. Dissolve sugar completely in water, stirring over a low heat. Do not let it boil until every grain of sugar is dissolved.
2. Boil to soft ball stage (*see this page*).
3. Add glucose and boil until it is dissolved.
4. Dampen a meat platter slightly with water and pour on to it the transparent fondant mixture. Allow to cool until a skin has formed (about 5 minutes).
5. Beat with a metal scraper or spatula, or palette knife, until a white mass forms. Leave it until cold.
6. When cold, work it by hand, like kneading, until smooth. Press into a jar with a good lid.
7. Store in the store-cupboard and use as required. It will keep for many months.

USES OF FONDANT

1. Colour and flavour to make centres for chocolates. Shape by hand, or roll out and cut pretty shapes

with tiny cutters. Dip in melted chocolate and put on waxed paper to set.

2. Flavour with instant coffee dissolved in a very little hot water. Work in chopped walnuts. Roll in finely-chopped walnuts.

3. Knead in some fine coconut: 1 part coconut to 4 parts fondant. Make into log shapes and roll them in coconut.

4. A simple way to make coconut ice: knead in 50 g/2 oz coconut to 190 g/7 oz fondant. Colour half of it pink. Roll both colours out to even thickness. Press the two colours together, then cut into bars.

5. Melt down, flavour, colour and pour into fancy moulds. Or roll out, cut into pretty shapes and leave on waxed paper to dry off. (Paper from a cornflakes packet is useful.)

6. Work in a nut of butter to a small quantity of fondant and use as a filling for small biscuits.

7. Try, also, recipe for Chocolate Fudge, using fondant, *page 393*.

Anne Wallace
Stewarton, Ayrshire

FRUIT JELLIES

Blackcurrant, gooseberry and raspberry jellies can be made from the fresh fruit.

Fruit of your choice
Sugar
Lemon juice

1. Make a purée of the fruit by simmering it in the minimum of water to soften. Then rub through a sieve to remove skins and pips.

2. Measure the purée. To every 300 ml/½ pint allow 175 g/6 oz sugar and the juice of half a lemon.

3. Put purée, sugar and lemon juice in a pan. Heat gently, stirring to dissolve sugar before it boils.

4. Boil carefully, stirring most of the time to prevent burning. Test every minute or two after it gets thick by putting a little into a cup of cold water. When this forms a firm ball in the water it is ready.

5. Pour mixture into a wetted baking tin.

6. When the jelly is set, turn it out on to greaseproof paper covered in sugar and leave till completely cold.

7. Cut into suitable shapes. Toss in sugar.

Anne Wallace
Stewarton, Ayrshire

APRICOTINES

This sweet is delicious and really enhances a box of assorted sweets.

Makes about 300 g/11 oz

A 450 g/1 lb can apricots
175 g/6 oz granulated sugar
A squeeze of lemon juice
Granulated sugar, to coat

1. Sieve or liquidise fruit with about one-third of the syrup.

2. Put pulp, sugar and lemon juice in a pan. Bring to the boil.

3. Stand pan on an asbestos mat, if you have one. Boil apricot mixture very carefully, stirring most of the time so that it does not burn. Because this mixture is so thick a thermometer cannot be used. Boil until a little, tested in a cup of cold water, forms a really firm ball. This sweet is rather like overboiled jam.

4. Pour mixture into a wetted, round tin, 13 cm/5 inches diameter. Allow to set.

5. When set, cut into rounds and crescents and toss in granulated sugar.

Anne Wallace
Stewarton, Ayrshire

SPANISH QUINCE PASTE

Can be eaten as a dessert with cream cheese.

1.8 kg/4 lb quinces
300 ml/½ pint water
Sugar

TO FINISH
Caster sugar

1. Wash the quinces. Cut them in quarters and put them in a saucepan with the water.

2. Simmer until soft, then put them through a sieve.

3. Weigh the pulp and put it in a large, clean pan.

4. Weigh an equal quantity of sugar and mix it in.

5. Stir over low heat until sugar dissolves. Continue cooking until mixture becomes very thick. Stir continuously.

6. Pour into shallow tins lined with sheets of greaseproof paper.

7. Leave it in a warm place, such as an airing cupboard, for 3 or 4 days. It will dry out a little and be easy to handle.

8. Peel off the paper and cut the paste into pieces. Roll them in caster sugar and store between layers of greaseproof paper in an airtight tin or plastic box.

Miss Elisabeth Gruber
Winchester

See also Almond Jellies, page 259.

FUDGE

Makes about 1.3 kg/3 lb

225 g/8 oz butter
900 g/2 lb granulated sugar
1 large can (411g/14½ lb) evaporated milk
Half the milk tin of water

1. Place all ingredients in a large, heavy saucepan.
2. Stir gently over a low heat until the sugar is quite melted.
3. Bring to boil and boil steadily, stirring occasionally, until thermometer reaches 238° to 240°F, 116°C, or 'soft ball' stage (*see page 391*).
4. Remove from heat, dip base of pan in cold water to check cooking. Leave five minutes. Beat with a wooden spoon until the mixture loses its gloss, looks 'grainy', thickens a little and will just pour from pan.
5. Pour into a buttered or oiled shallow tin; 30 by 20 cm/12 by 8 inches is suitable. Leave until cool and nearly set. Cut into squares.

CHOCOLATE FUDGE

Makes about 675 g/1½ lb

50 g/2 oz butter
125 g/4 oz granulated sugar
50 g/2 oz dark cooking chocolate
1 large can condensed milk
2 tablespoons golden syrup
75 g/3 oz fondant (*see page 391*)

1. Put butter, sugar, chocolate, condensed milk and syrup in a large saucepan and melt gently over a low heat, stirring until sugar is dissolved and all is well mixed.
2. Bring to the boil and boil gently, stirring constantly, until it reaches soft ball stage (*see page 391*), 240°F, 116°C. Remove pan from heat.
3. Mix in fondant, and stir gently until melted.
4. Pour into a greased 18 cm/7 inch square tin.
5. Cut into cubes when cold.

Anne Wallace
Stewarton, Ayrshire

NOUGAT

For this it is advisable to have a sugar thermometer (*see page 391*).

Makes about 600 g/1¼ lb

50 g/2 oz blanched almonds
25 g/1 oz glacé cherries
25 g/1 oz angelica
50 g/2 oz powdered glucose (buy at a chemist)
325 g/12 oz granulated sugar
125 g/4 oz honey
150 ml/¼ pint water
1 egg-white

You need 2 sheets of rice paper and some waxed paper or cling film for wrapping sweets.

1. Butter an 18 cm/7 inch square tin and line it with rice paper.
2. Chop almonds, cherries and angelica.
3. Put glucose, sugar, honey and water in a large pan and stir over gentle heat until sugar is completely dissolved.
4. Boil carefully to 290°F, 145°C. It burns readily towards end of boiling time and tends to froth up. If you do not have a thermometer, put a teaspoon of mixture in a cup of cold water. If it is ready it will go into brittle threads.
5. Meanwhile, beat egg-white in a heat-proof bowl until it is stiff and stands up in peaks.
6. When contents of pan reach the correct temperature, pour it slowly over the beaten egg-white, beating all the time.
7. When mixture thickens as you beat it, beat in the fruit and nuts.
8. Pour into prepared tin and place a piece of rice paper on top. Texture is improved if a weight is placed on top for a few hours.
9. Leave it to set overnight. Cut into bars and wrap in waxed paper or cling film wrap.

Anne Wallace
Stewarton, Ayrshire

SWISS MILK TABLET

For this it is helpful but not essential, to have a sugar thermometer (*see page 391*).

Makes about 1.3 kg/3 lb

900 g/2 lb granulated sugar
200 ml/7½ fluid oz fresh milk
50 g/2 oz butter
1 small can condensed milk (190 g/7 oz)
¼ teaspoon vanilla essence

1. Put sugar, fresh milk and butter in a large pan over a low heat and stir until sugar is completely dissolved.
2. Bring to the boil and add condensed milk.
3. Boil carefully (i.e., stir occasionally so that it does not catch or burn) to soft ball stage (*see page 391*), 240°F, 116°C.
4. Remove from heat and when bubbles subside add vanilla essence.
5. Beat thoroughly until mixture begins to sugar on pan bottom.
6. Pour into an oiled Swiss roll tin, a shallow tin about 18 by 28 cm/7 by 11 inches.
7. When it is set, mark into squares. When cold it should break apart neatly.

Anne Wallace
Stewarton, Ayrshire

See also Uncooked Raisin Fudge, page 397.

SALTED ALMONDS

125 g/4 oz whole almonds
15 g/½ oz butter
Salt

1. Blanch almonds as follows: Place in small basin, cover with boiling water. Leave 5 to 8 minutes, drain and press away the skin between finger and thumb. Pat the almonds dry.
2. Heat butter in small frying pan until just frothing.
3. Tip in almonds, stir over gentle heat until golden.
4. Drain on kitchen paper and sprinkle liberally with salt.

When cold, store in an airtight container.

TOFFEE

Without a thermometer.

Makes about 225g/8 oz

125 g/4 oz butter
225 g/8 oz granulated sugar
2 tablespoons vinegar
2 level tablespoons golden syrup

Use a heavy pan, not too small, as the mixture froths a little.

1. Place butter in pan over heat to begin melting. Add rest of ingredients and stir until sugar is melted.
2. Bring to boil and boil briskly, stirring very occasionally, until mixture turns golden brown.
3. Pour into a greased, shallow tin; 18 cm/7 inches square is a suitable size.
4. Mark into squares before quite set. It will then break more easily.

TOFFEE HUMBUGS

Fun to make because of pulling and shaping required.
For this it is helpful, but not essential, to have a sugar thermometer (*see page 391*)

Makes about 600 g/1¼ lb

450 g/1 lb soft, dark brown Barbados sugar
50 g/2 oz butter
150 ml/¼ pint water
1 tablespoon golden syrup
¼ teaspoon cream of tartar
2 drops of oil of peppermint or clove oil

You need some butter to oil tin, and a scraper and scissors. Humbugs are usually wrapped in cellophane paper to stop them sticking to each other in the tin, but it is not essential if your tin is absolutely air-tight.

1. Put sugar, butter, water and syrup into a large pan over a low heat. Stir until sugar is dissolved. Do not let it boil before sugar is completely dissolved.
2. Bring to the boil, add cream of tartar and boil to soft crack stage (*see page 391*), 280° to 285°F, 140° to 142°C.
3. Pour into oiled tin or on to oiled marble slab. Add essence.

4. Leave until it forms a skin, then start turning edges to centre with an oiled, metal spatula or scraper.

5. When cool enough to handle, start pulling and folding until it begins to harden and has a good sheen.

6. Quickly pull into a rope about 2 cm/¾ inch thick. It will pull out to 1 metre/1 yard in length, so make 2 ropes.

7. Cut with oiled scissors, half-turning the rope each time so that there is a twist in each sweet.

8. When they are quite cold, wrap each sweet in cellophane paper and store in an air-tight tin.

Anne Wallace
Stewarton, Ayrshire

RUSSIAN TOFFEE

For this it is helpful, but not essential, to have a sugar thermometer.

Makes about 600 g/1¼ lb

50 g/2 oz butter
125 g/4 oz sugar
125 g/4 oz golden syrup
400 g/1 large tin condensed milk
25 g/1 oz redcurrant jelly
A few drops of vanilla essence

1. Put butter, sugar and syrup in a large saucepan over a low heat, and stir until sugar is completely dissolved.

2. Bring to boiling point and add condensed milk and redcurrant jelly.

3. Continue to boil to 265°F, 130°C, hard ball stage (*see page 391*), stirring all the time.

If using a thermometer, be sure to have it by the pan in a container of very hot water, so that it is hot before it enters the toffee. Hard ball stage can be tested without a thermometer by dropping a teaspoon of the mixture into a cup of cold water. When you feel it between thumb and fingers it is a hard ball but still chewy.

4. Add vanilla and pour into a greased 18 cm/7 inch square tin.

5. When set, mark into squares. When cold, cut and wrap in waxed paper.

6. Store in an airtight container.

Anne Wallace
Stewarton, Ayrshire

CREAM TOFFEE

A toffee with a soft texture.

Makes about 450/1 lb

175 g/6 oz butter
325 g/12 oz demerara sugar
2 tablespoons golden syrup
A 400 g/14 oz tin of condensed milk

1. Melt butter, sugar and golden syrup. Stir over low heat to dissolve sugar.

2. Add condensed milk.

3. Stirring often, boil for about 10 minutes until the soft ball stage—that is, when a few drops are put into a jug of iced water and the mixture forms a soft ball between the fingers. If it dissolves immediately continue to boil for a further 3 or 4 minutes.

4. Pour into a greased Swiss roll tin 28 by 18 cm/11 by 7 inches.

5. When cold, cut into squares and wrap each one in waxed paper. Because of the soft texture of this toffee it must be wrapped or all the pieces will stick together.

CHOCOLATE COCONUT BALLS

Makes 775 g/1¾ lb

225 g/8 oz desiccated coconut
125 g/4 oz icing sugar
1 small can condensed milk (190 g/7 oz)
A 250 g/9 oz block of plain or milk cooking chocolate, for coating

You need some waxed paper on which to set finished sweets. (Paper from a cornflakes packet is ideal.)

1. Mix coconut and sugar into milk. If coconut is very dry use less than the quantity given, otherwise sweets may go hard.

2. Make small balls from the mixture.

3. Melt chocolate in a small basin over a pan of simmering water.

4. To coat the balls, drop them into the melted chocolate, lift each one out with a fork and tap it on the edge of the bowl to allow excess chocolate to drop off.

5. Put the balls on waxed paper to set.

Anne Wallace
Stewarton, Ayrshire

TREACLE TOFFEE

For this it is helpful, but not essential, to have a sugar thermometer (*see page 391*).
For a good variation, substitute half of the treacle with honey.

Makes about 900 g/2 lb

450 g/1 lb Barbados sugar
450 g/1 lb black treacle or molasses
2½ tablespoons cider vinegar
125 g/4 oz butter

1. Put sugar, treacle or molasses and vinegar in a large saucepan and stir over a low heat until sugar is completely dissolved.
2. Bring very slowly to boiling point. Keep it boiling for 10 minutes, stirring occasionally.
3. Carefully and gradually stir in the butter, in thin pieces, piece by piece.
4. Continue to boil to 284°F, 142°C, soft crack stage (*see page 391*).
5. Remove from heat and allow toffee to settle a minute. Pour gently into a well-greased tin. A tin 23 cm/9 inches square gives pieces just over 1 cm/½ inch thick.
6. When cool, mark into squares. When cold, break into pieces.
7. Wrap in waxed paper or store in an air-tight container.

Anne Wallace
Stewarton, Ayrshire

See also Toffee Apples, page 399.

CHOCOLATE TRUFFLES

Makes about 25

125 g/4 oz plain cooking chocolate
15 g/½ oz butter
125 g/4 oz icing sugar
125 g/4 oz sieved cake crumbs, or plain digestive biscuits, crumbled and sieved
1 egg-yolk
2 to 3 tablespoons rum

TO FINISH
Chopped walnuts
Vermicelli or drinking chocolate powder

1. Place broken chocolate and butter to melt in a large basin over a pan of hot, but not boiling, water. Make sure bowl does not touch water.
2. Remove bowl from pan, stir in sifted icing sugar, crumbs and then egg-yolk. Add rum to taste, if mixture is a little soft, leave for 5 to 10 minutes to firm up.
3. Roll into balls the size of a small walnut.
4. To finish, roll the balls in finely chopped nuts or chocolate vermicelli or chocolate powder and leave to harden before placing in sweet papers.

RICH RUM TRUFFLES

No cooking required.

Makes about 12

75 g/3 oz dark cooking chocolate
1 teaspoon cream
1 egg-yolk
15 g/½ oz butter
Rum to taste (1 to 2 teaspoons)
Chocolate vermicelli

1. Break chocolate into a small basin. Stand basin over a pan of simmering water. Do not let water touch basin. Allow chocolate to melt, then remove from heat.
2. Add cream, egg-yolk, butter and rum and beat mixture until thick and like a paste.
3. Form little balls of the mixture and roll them in chocolate vermicelli.

Anne Wallace
Stewarton, Ayrshire

CREAMY CHOCOLATE

Makes about 30

150 g/5 oz plain cooking chocolate
50 g/2 oz butter
A few drops of vanilla essence
175 g/6 oz sweetened condensed milk
125 g/4 oz icing sugar
1 level tablespoon cocoa

1. Break the chocolate into pieces and put in a basin with the butter. Place the basin over a pan containing a little hot water. Heat the water gently to melt chocolate and butter.
2. Remove basin from heat, add vanilla essence and beat in the condensed milk.
3. Add icing sugar sieved with cocoa and beat until creamy.
4. Place a teaspoon each of mixture in paper sweet cases (waxed or foil ones are best) and leave to set.

Margaret Heywood
Todmorden, Yorkshire

UNCOOKED RAISIN FUDGE

Makes 900 g/2 lb

75 g/3 oz butter
125 g/4 oz plain cooking chocolate
1 egg
450 g/1 lb icing sugar
75 g/3 oz chopped walnuts
50 g/2 oz raisins
$2\frac{1}{2}$ tablespoons condensed milk (100 g/$3\frac{1}{2}$ oz)
A few drops vanilla essence

It is useful to have some waxed paper to line the tin.

1. Oil an 18 cm/7 inch square tin, or line it with waxed paper.
2. Put butter and chocolate to melt in a bowl over a pan of simmering water. Do not let water touch the basin.
3. Beat the egg.
4. Remove bowl of chocolate and butter from heat and add to it the beaten egg and all the other ingredients. Beat well together.
5. Smooth mixture into prepared tin and leave to set.
6. Cut it into squares.

Anne Wallace
Stewarton, Ayrshire

MARZIPAN SWEETS

Makes about 300 g/11 oz

1 egg
225 g/8 oz ground almonds
225 g/8 oz icing sugar
A few drops almond essence
$\frac{1}{2}$ teaspoon orange flower water (optional)

TO FINISH
Vegetable colourings
Chocolate powder
Melted chocolate
Cherries
Dates
Walnuts

1. Beat the egg.
2. Mix all the other ingredients together and add enough beaten egg to make a pliable paste.

Marzipan can be used in many ways. Colour green, pink, yellow, orange, etc. Or use a little chocolate powder. Build into striped sweets, make scraps into harlequin balls. Cut out shapes with small cutters to dip in melted chocolate. Use to stuff cherries, dates or walnuts. Make marzipan fruits.

Anne Wallace
Stewarton, Ayrshire

PEANUT BUTTER BON-BONS

Makes about 24

125 g/4 oz seedless raisins, chopped
125 g/4 oz icing sugar, sieved
125 g/4 oz peanut butter
25 g/1 oz melted butter or margarine
50 to 75 g/2 to 3 oz plain cooking chocolate

1. Put raisins in a bowl with sugar and peanut butter. Mix to a paste with melted butter or margarine.
2. Shape into balls about the size of a grape and leave on foil or waxed paper to harden overnight.
3. Put chocolate to melt in a small bowl set over a pan of simmering water.
4. Dip the top of each bon-bon in melted chocolate and, when set, put in paper sweet cases.

Margaret Heywood
Todmorden, Yorkshire

PEPPERMINT CREAMS

Makes about 30

1 egg-white
450 g/1 lb icing sugar
Oil of peppermint or peppermint essence

TO DECORATE
Plain cooking chocolate (optional)

1. Beat the egg-white until frothy but not stiff.
2. Sieve icing sugar, mix with egg-white and add peppermint to taste. The exact amount of icing sugar needed depends upon the size of the egg-white. Mix and knead to a firm paste.
3. Roll out on a board well-dusted with sifted icing sugar. Cut small rounds. Or, make small balls and flatten them with a fork. Place on waxed paper, (use the paper from a cornflakes packet). Leave overnight.
4. The plain round sweets may at this stage be dipped in melted chocolate to give a half coating. Place on waxed paper to allow to set.

TO CANDY FRUIT

Use fruit of a distinct flavour e.g. pineapples, apricots, plums, dessert pears, crab apples, orange and lemon peel. Angelica stems and ginger root may also be candied.

USING CANNED OR BOTTLED FRUIT
1. Take 300 ml/½ pint syrup from the can (or bottle) and put it in a saucepan. To it add 225 g/8 oz sugar and bring to the boil. Great care should be taken all through the process to stir the sugar and dissolve it before boiling point is reached. Pour boiling syrup over the drained fruit in basin. Cover with weight to keep fruit below surface of liquid. As much fruit as possible should be used, but must be submerged in syrup. Leave for 24 hours.
2. Strain syrup from fruit into pan and add 50 g/2 oz sugar. Stir until dissolved, boil and pour over fruit. Cover and leave for 24 hours.
3. Repeat for 2 more days adding 50 g/2 oz sugar in the same manner daily.
4. On fifth day, drain syrup and add 75 g/3 oz sugar, stir to dissolve and boil, then add the fruit to boiling syrup and simmer for 3 or 4 minutes. Return all to basin and leave for 2 days.

5. Then repeat with 75 g/3 oz sugar, dissolve and re-boil again. Leave for 3 or 4 days in heavy syrup.
6. Lift out pieces of fruit and spread separately on a cake cooling rack over a tin to catch drips. Dry in a cool oven (not more than 120°F, 50°C) with door open for 3 hours, or for a longer period in an airing cupboard. Fruit should feel dry on surface when cool.

TO CRYSTALLISE CANDIED FRUIT
Dip each piece in boiling water and shake, then roll in sugar. Re-dry.

TO GLACÉ
Make fresh syrup of 225 g/8 oz sugar to 75 ml/2½ fl oz water. Dissolve sugar then bring to boil and dip each piece of fruit quickly into syrup and spread to dry on cake cooling rack for about 1 hour. This results in a hard coating of sugar on the surface.

FOR FRESH FRUIT
Cook until just tender, but not broken. Take 300 ml/½ pint of water in which fruit was cooked and add 225 g/8 oz sugar. Stir over low heat to dissolve and cook fruit for a minute, then allow to stand for 3 days. Then proceed as for canned fruit starting with 225 g/8 oz sugar in paragraph 1 above.

The left over syrup can be used to stew other fruit in season. Can be used in a cake mixture or as a base for sauce for ice-cream or pudding.

CANDIED GINGER MARROW

1 well-ripened marrow
Water
Sugar
To every 450 g/1 lb marrow allow 15 g/½ oz root
ginger and 1 lemon

CRYSTALLISING SUGAR
450 g/1 lb caster sugar
½ teaspoon bicarbonate of soda
½ teaspoon cream of tartar

1. Peel marrow, cut it in half lengthways and scoop out pips. Cut flesh into even-sized cubes, about 2.5 cm/1 inch.
2. Cover marrow with water and soak for 12 hours. Strain well.
3. Weigh marrow to calculate quantity of sugar, ginger and lemon.
4. Strew marrow with equal weight of sugar. Leave for 12 hours.

5. Tie bruised ginger and finely-pared lemon rind in a piece of muslin.

6. Tip marrow, sugar and liquid it has made into a pan and simmer until sugar is dissolved. Add muslin bag and lemon juice. Simmer until marrow is clear and syrup thickens.

7. Pour into a jar, cover and leave to soak for 1 week.

8. Strain off syrup.

9. Place marrow on greaseproof paper on a cake rack and leave it in a warm place to dry.

10. Mix and sieve caster sugar, bicarbonate of soda and cream of tartar.

11. Roll marrow pieces in sugar mixture to coat it completely.

12. Pack in greaseproof paper in an air-tight box.

Sybil Norcott
Irlam, Nr Manchester

GLACÉ FRUITS

Fresh fruits such as strawberries, orange or mandarin segments, clusters of two grapes, etc., are dipped in caramel, giving them a shiny crisp coating. Canned fruit can also be used, including maraschino cherries, provided the syrup is dried off carefully before they are dipped in the caramel.

Lovely for a party, but cannot be made too far ahead as they go sticky in a day or so, particularly if weather is humid.

The quantity of syrup given is enough to coat about 20 pieces of fruit. You will need tiny crinkled paper sweet cases which can be bought at good stationers. Also, several wooden cocktail sticks for dipping. It is useful, but not essential, to have a sugar thermometer.

SYRUP FOR CARAMEL
125 g/4 oz sugar
60 ml/2½ fl oz hot water
5 ml/1 teaspoon glucose

1. Brush baking trays lightly with oil.

2. Prepare fruit, making sure it is clean and thoroughly dried.

3. Put sugar in the hot water in a pan, stirring over a low heat until dissolved.

4. Bring to boil and add glucose.

5. Boil to 290° to 300°F, 145° to 150°C, or until just before syrup turns brown.

6. Set pan on a wet cloth to stop it boiling.

7. As soon as syrup has stopped bubbling start dipping fruits, holding them by the stems or spearing them with a pair of wooden cocktail sticks.

8. Put each dipped fruit on oiled tray to set. Then place in small paper cases.

Anne Wallace
Stewarton, Ayrshire

TOFFEE APPLES

For this you need a large heavy-based pan, wooden lolly sticks and a large greased baking tin.

12 small eating apples
450 g/1 lb white or brown sugar
50 g/2 oz butter
1 tablespoon golden syrup
2 teaspoons vinegar
150 ml/¼ pint water

1. Wash and dry the apples. Push a stick into each stalk end.

2. Put all remaining ingredients into a large pan. Stir over gentle heat until sugar is dissolved, then boil rapidly for 5 minutes. Stir just a little.

3. The syrup in the pan has to boil until it comes to the hard ball stage (*see page 391*). This means that when a little of the syrup is dropped into a jug of ice-cold water it forms a hard ball and this tells you when your toffee is ready. Go on boiling until this point is reached.

4. Remove pan from heat and, as quickly as possible, dip the apples. Twirl them around in toffee for a few seconds, shake off the surplus and put on to the greased baking tin to set. If the toffee starts to set in the pan, heat it gently again.

13

WINE
BEER
AND OTHER
DRINKS

Sterilisation of Equipment

This is important. If equipment cannot be boiled, wash first with detergent or household bleach but rinse thoroughly, i.e. several times, in cold tap water. Then rinse in a solution of sodium metabisulphite. Finally rinse well in cold tap water.

Alternatively, many home-brewers and wine-makers prefer a chlorine-based sterilising agent, following instructions on the packet.

A NOTE ON HYDROMETERS

An hydrometer is an instrument for measuring the density of water mixtures.

When an hydrometer is put into pure water at 60°F, 15°C it gives a reading of 0. This is sometimes expressed as 1.000 or 1000. Whenever wine or beer is made, sugar is added in some form. When you put the hydrometer into the solution you will find that it does not sink as much as it does in plain water.

The reading is taken where the level of the solution cuts the stem—this first reading is usually called Original Gravity and should be noted down.

When yeast is added to either the 'must' or 'wort' it ferments using the sugar and producing carbon dioxide and alcohol.

If the sugar is added in stages you must always remember to take a reading before adding sugar *and* after the sugar has been stirred in. The first reading is deducted from the second, showing the increase in gravity. For example:

Day 1:	Original Gravity		1035
Day 3:	Gravity:	1028	
	Gravity after adding		
	450 g/1 lb sugar	1063	35
			1070
Day 5:	Gravity	1060	
	Gravity after adding		
	675 g/1½ lb sugar	1112	52
	Total gravity		1122

For wine-making: when wine becomes stable take a final gravity reading. In the example above, subtract final reading, say 1005, from total gravity:
1122 − 1005 = 117
Most hydrometers have two or three scales: gravity, alcohol and sugar-per-gallon. Find 117 on the gravity scale. It equals approximately 15.5% alcohol.

For beer-makers: the hydrometer is essential for your own safety. You measure Original Gravity just the same as in wine-making—e.g. 1042, but this must drop for malt-extract beers to 1005 or less, and for mashed beers (using pale malt) to 1012 or less. If you bottle the beer before it gets down to these gravities the tops may be forced out. At worst, they can explode, possibly causing injury and damage. This is due to the very high pressure that can build up in a bottle if too much sugar is present. So, be warned—buy an hydrometer for your own safety and, most important, use it to produce first-class brews.

YEAST STARTER

175 ml/6 fl oz water
1 dessertspoon malt extract
1 dessertspoon sugar
A pinch citric acid
A pinch yeast nutrient
The yeast, as indicated in recipe

1. Put water in a small pan, stir in malt extract, sugar and citric acid. Bring to the boil, then turn off heat.
2. Cool this solution a little, then pour it into a small pop bottle, 300 ml/½ pint. Plug neck of the bottle with cotton-wool and cool to below 70°F, 21°C.
3. Add yeast. If it is a liquid yeast culture, shake the phial before emptying it into bottle. Replace cotton-wool plug and leave in a warm place.
4. The yeast will ferment vigorously and be ready to use in 2 to 3 days.

FRESH OR DRIED APRICOT WINE

A dry wine. Peach wine may be made in the same way, using fresh or dried peaches.

Makes 4.5 litres/1 gallon

1.8 kg/4 lb fresh apricots or
450 g/1 lb dried apricots
Pectin-destroying enzyme*
Yeast nutrient*
½ teaspoon citric acid
¼ teaspoon tannin
900 g/2 lb sugar
1 Campden tablet
Water to 1 gallon (4.5 litres)

Use quantity recommended by supplier.

YEAST
Hock

Note: Equipment should be sterilised (*see page 401*).

1. 48 hours before you start to make the wine, prepare a yeast starter (*see page 401*) so that yeast is actively working when it is required for the wine.
2. *For the wine:* halve apricots and remove stones (if using fresh fruit). Cut up the fruit and put in a sterilised polythene bucket.
3. Add pectin-destroying enzyme and pour on 2.8 litres/5 pints cold water.
4. Cover bucket and leave for 36 hours, stirring occasionally.
5. Add yeast nutrient, citric acid, tannin and 900 g/ 2 lb sugar. Stir until sugar is dissolved.
6. Make up quantity to 4.5 litres/1 gallon by adding cold water.
7. Add actively-working yeast starter.
8. Stir well, cover bucket and leave to ferment for 48 hours, stirring twice daily.
9. Strain liquid into a sterilised 4.5 litre/1 gallon fermenting jar and insert an air-lock.
10. Leave in a fairly warm place about 75°F, 24°C, to ferment to dryness (about 6 to 8 weeks). Sediment will collect during this fermentation. Rack the wine—i.e., syphon it off the sediment into a sterile jar from time to time, topping up jar with fresh, cold water. It is unwise to leave the wine on the lees (sediment) for any length of time.
11. When all ferment is finished, rack into a sterile jar and add one Campden tablet. This acts as an anti-oxidant. Top up jar with cold water.
12. Set it aside to clear. This could take 2 to 3 months.
13. When wine is brilliantly clear, bottle it and leave it in a cool, dark place to mature for at least 6 months.

Alan Briggs
Batley, W. Yorkshire

BEETROOT AND PARSNIP WINE

A sweet, tawny dessert wine. Improves if allowed to mature for a year or two.

Makes 4.5 litres/1 gallon

1.3 kg/3 lb beetroot
Water
1.3 kg/3 lb parsnips
225 g/8 oz raisins or dates
1.7 kg/3¾ lb sugar
1 teaspoon citric acid

YEAST
Sherry

1. Yeast must be actively working before you start making the wine. 2 or 3 days before you begin the wine, make up the yeast starter (*see page 401*) using the sherry yeast.
2. *For the wine:* wash beetroots and cut into 1 cm/ ½ inch cubes.
3. Cook in 2.3 litres/½ gallon of water until almost tender.
4. Pour off beetroot water into a large polythene bin or bucket, 22.7 litre/5 gallon capacity.
5. Prepare and cook parsnips in exactly the same way, pouring liquid into bin with beetroot water. Leave to cool to 65° to 70°F, 18° to 20°C.
6. Meanwhile, chop up raisins or dates. When temperature of liquid in bin has dropped sufficiently, add them with 450 g/1 lb of the sugar, the citric acid and the actively-working yeast.
7. Cover bin loosely with a cloth or lid. This keeps dust and flies out but lets air in. Leave in a warm place for 21 days. Stir wine carefully every day. It has a tendency to froth excessively when stirred. That is why a large bin is essential or it may froth over the top of the bin.
8. On fifth or sixth day, add another 450 g/1 lb sugar.
9. On tenth or eleventh day, add another 450 g/1 lb sugar.
10. On fifteenth or sixteenth day, add remaining 325 g/12 oz sugar.
11. After another 5 to 6 days, strain through a muslin or nylon cloth laid in a sieve, into a 4.5 litre/1 gallon dark-glass jar. Fill jar to 2.5 cm/1 inch from top. Put any left-over liquid into a small dark-glass bottle. Top jar up with water if necessary.

12. Fit an air-lock, or cover top with a piece of polythene secured with a rubber band. Cover the small bottle in the same way.

13. Keep jar and bottle in a warm place, 60° to 65°F, 16° to 18°C, for 2 to 3 months.

14. After 2 to 3 months, rack off i.e., syphon wine off the sediment into a clean jar. Top up jar with spare wine from bottle or with cold water to 2.5 cm/ 1 inch from top. Re-fit air-lock or cover as before. Be sure to taste wine in small bottle before using in case it has gone off.

15. Rack again every 3 to 4 months.

16. Bottle the wine when a year or more old and when it is stable and clear. Wash thoroughly 6 wine bottles. Syphon wine into the bottles. If you want to keep the wine, cork bottles with straight-sided corks and lay them on their sides. If it is going to be used in a few months, use flanged-type corks, but leave bottles standing upright.

17. It improves outstandingly if kept to mature for a few years.

Dennis Rouston
Kippax, W. Yorkshire

BILBERRY WINE

As a Dry Red Wine makes 4.5 litres/1 gallon

A 1 kg/2 lb 2 oz jar of bilberries in syrup. If using fresh or frozen bilberries 450 g/1 lb is needed. Allow also an extra 150 g/5 oz sugar as a substitute for syrup in jar

If using dried bilberries 125 g/4 oz are needed with an extra 150 g/5 oz sugar as syrup substitute

325 g/12 oz grape concentrate

675 g/1½ lb sugar

1 only 3 mg Vitamin B₁ tablet

Yeast nutrient and pectin-reducing enzyme (follow manufacturer's instructions)

General purpose wine yeast

Campden tablets

Cold boiled water

As a Sweet Dessert Wine makes 4.5 litres/1 gallon

A 1 kg/2 lb 2 oz jar bilberries in syrup. If using fresh, frozen or dried bilberries see under Dry Red Wine ingredients for extra sugar required

675 g/1½ lb grape concentrate

1.1 kg/2 lb 6 oz sugar

3 only 3 mg Vitamin B₁ tablets

Yeast nutrient and pectin-reducing enzyme (follow manufacturer's instructions)

General purpose wine yeast

Campden tablets

Cold boiled water

1. At least 3 to 4 days before you begin to make the wine, prepare yeast starter following directions on *page 401.*

2. Make sure that all the equipment is clean and sterilised. If the fruit is fresh, frozen or dried, wash well in a sulphited solution (3 Campden tablets to 4.5 litres/1 gallon water) to kill wild yeasts and clean the fruit. Rinse several times in fresh cold water.

3. Have on hand about 3.6 litres/6 pints cold boiled water.

4. Put the fruit in syrup and the grape concentrate into a fermenting bucket. Dilute with about 1.2 litres/2 pints of the cold boiled water. (If using fresh, frozen or dried bilberries the additional 150 g/5 oz sugar should be made into syrup with less than 300 ml/½ pint water and added with the fruit). Stir well to mix the concentrate. Then add the Vitamin B₁ tablet, yeast nutrient, pectin-reducing enzyme and yeast starter. Cover closely and leave in a warm place to ferment for about 36 hours.

5. Strain off through fine mesh, sterilised muslin or cloth, to separate fruit, and pour into a 4.5 litre/ 1 gallon fermenting jar.

6. (As a dry red wine)
Meanwhile, make a syrup of the sugar using 1.75 litres/3 pints cold boiled water.

6. (As a sweet dessert wine)
Meanwhile, make a syrup of 675 g/1½ lb of the sugar using 1.75 litres/3 pints of cold boiled water.

7. Mix this syrup into contents of the glass jar, shake well, and then make up to about 4 litres/7 pints with cold boiled water. Fit airlock, stand jar in warm place, and allow to ferment. The fermenting must will form a thick sticky head but, because the jar is not full, this will not percolate through the airlock.

8. (As a dry red wine)
When, after a few days, the frothing head has subsided, add the balance of the cold boiled water, making it up to about 4.5 litres/1 gallon. Leave to ferment right out, which should take some three weeks at the most.

8. (As a sweet dessert wine)
When, after a few days, the frothing head has subsided, gradually make up the contents of the jar to

4.5 litres/1 gallon with syrup made from cold boiled water and the remaining sugar. This syrup must be introduced with care to the fermenting must and a little at a time, because there is usually a lot of frothing which can come over the top if too much is put in at once. Leave in a warm place to ferment right out. It will take about three months.

9. When fermentation finishes, allow to stand for a few days so that the majority of the suspended matter falls to the bottom.

10. The new raw wine is now ready for racking. This means taking the reasonably clear wine off the heavy deposit which is on the bottom of the jar. In doing this, be careful to use tubing, and *never, never* pour it from one jar to the other. Syphon the clear wine off leaving the deposit in the original jar, then top up the new jar with, at worst, cold boiled water, and at best, with wine of a similar nature. Add one Campden tablet, fit airlock, and set aside in a cool dark place to clear.

11. After a few weeks, clarity should have come. You can then rack the wine off again, following exactly the same procedure as before. Don't forget to top the jar up again, cork it and then leave in dark place to mature for as long as you can.

12. When you come to drink the wine carefully syphon the whole lot off into bottles which should be sealed with good fitting corks, and store in a cool dark place.

Dry Red Wine

After 2 months there will be an appreciable increase in quality. Quality will improve up to a year when the wine will be very good. After this further improvement is not likely. Drink before two years.

Sweet Dessert Wine

If in the end the wine is not sweet enough, then add some *invert* sugar just prior to drinking, at the rate of 25 to 125 g/1 to 4 oz per bottle according to taste. Dessert Wine is likely to take 6 months longer maturing than the table wine to reach the same relative quality. It will be very good if you can wait a year before drinking.

BLACKBERRY AND APPLE WINE

Red Table Wine
For 4.5 litres/1 gallon

Burgundy or Bordeaux yeast in starter form (*see page 401*)
2.25 kg/5 lb apples
1.3 kg/3 lb blackberries
450 g/1 lb elderberries
225 g/8 oz sultanas or raisins
125 g/4 oz dried bananas
Water to 4.5 litres/1 gallon
Sugar to adjust to gravity of 1.080
Pectic enzyme, use quantity indicated by manufacturer
1 teaspoon yeast nutrient
$\frac{1}{4}$ teaspoon yeast energiser

1. Wash apples, pulp them and press out juice. Place only the juice in a clean sterile bin.

2. Wash blackberries and elderberries, pulp or squash them and add both pulp and juice to apple juice.

3. Wash and mince sultanas and dried bananas and add to bulk in bin.

4. Make volume in bin up to 4.5 litres/1 gallon with boiling water.

5. When cold, strain out sufficient juice to take specific gravity and adjust bulk with sugar to a specific gravity of 1.080. (*See note on hydrometers, page 401*). A useful tip is that 450 g/1 lb sugar dissolved in 4.5 litres/1 gallon water will raise gravity by 37°.

For example: if the sample of juice reads 1.025 this means that it is desired to raise the gravity by 55° to 1.080, so 675 g/1$\frac{1}{2}$ lb sugar would have to be added.

6. Now stir in all other ingredients including active yeast started and ferment on the pulp for 3 to 4 days.

7. Strain carefully, without squeezing pulp, into a 4.5 litre/1 gallon jar and top up with cold boiled water. Fit airlock and ferment out to dryness. The final gravity should be .990 or below.

8. Rack, avoiding lees, i.e. syphon off leaving the sediment behind, into a sterile jar, add 1 Campden tablet and re-fit airlock.

9. Leave to mature for at least 12 months, racking every 4 months if a deposit forms.

10. The wine should now be bottled and allowed to mature at least a further 6 months in bottle.

Alan Briggs
Batley, West Yorkshire

BLACKBERRY AND ELDERBERRY WINE

A medium-sweet, red wine. The two hedgerow fruits balance each other nicely. However, as blackberries usually ripen 2 or 3 weeks before elderberries, pick both when really ripe, weigh up 900 g/2 lb lots and put them in the freezer. You can then make wine at your leisure.

Makes 4.5 litres/1 gallon

900 g/2 lb blackberries
900 g/2 lb elderberries
Boiling water
225 g/8 oz dates, or 125 g/4 oz red-grape concentrate
15 g/½ oz citric acid
1.3 kg/3 lb sugar

YEAST
Port

1. Yeast must be actively working before you start making the wine. 2 or 3 days before you begin the wine, make up the yeast starter (*see page 401*) using the Port yeast.
2. *For the wine:* thaw the fruit first.
3. Put blackberries into a large basin and pour over them ½ to 1 litre/1 to 2 pints boiling water.
4. Put on rubber gloves and squeeze berries.
5. Strain juice through a piece of muslin or net curtain, laid in a nylon strainer, into a polythene fermenting bin or bucket of at least 13.5 to 22.7 litre/3 to 5 gallon capacity. It is wise to measure the 4.5 litre/1 gallon level and mark it on the side of bin.
6. Pour another ½ to 1 litre/1 to 2 pints of boiling water over blackberries, squeeze again and strain juice into the bin.
7. Do exactly the same with the elderberries. Then throw pulp away on to the compost heap.
8. Make the volume of juice in bin up to 4.5 litres/1 gallon with cold water. Let it cool to 65° to 70°F, 18° to 20°C.
9. Meanwhile, chop dates and, when temperature of juice has dropped sufficiently, add them, or the grape concentrate, with the citric acid, 450 g/1 lb of the sugar and the actively-working yeast starter.
10. Cover bin loosely with cloth or lid. This keeps out dust and flies but allows air in. Keep in a warm place for 7 to 10 days, stirring daily.
11. On third day, add another 450 g/1 lb sugar.
12. On fifth day, add the last 450 g/1 lb sugar.

13. After another 2 or 3 days pour the juice—through a piece of muslin and a strainer if you have used dates—into a 4.5 litre/1 gallon glass jar. Fill jar to 2.5 cm/1 inch from top. Put any left-over juice into a small bottle. Top jar up with cold water if necessary.
14. Fit an air-lock, or cover top with a piece of polythene secured with a rubber band. Cover small bottle in the same way.
15. Leave jar (and bottle) in a warm place for 3 months.
Note: do not put it in airing cupboard. It usually becomes too hot.
16. After about 3 months, rack off into a clean jar—i.e., syphon liquid off the sediment. Top up with spare wine from bottle, or with water, to 2.5 cm/1 inch from top of jar. Be sure to taste wine in small bottle before using in case it has gone off. Re-fit air-lock or cover.
17. After 6 to 8 months rack again.
18. When wine is stable and clear it can be bottled. Thoroughly wash 6 bottles. Syphon wine into the bottles. If you want to keep the wine, cork bottles with straight-sided corks and lay them on their sides. If it is going to be used in a few months, use flanged-type corks, but leave bottles standing upright.
19. This wine is usually ready to drink in about 1 year.

Dennis Rouston
Kippax, W. Yorkshire

DAMSON WINE

Makes a very nice steady sipping wine for a cold winter's evening. Sugar content can be varied to give a dry or sweet wine.

Makes 4.5 litres/1 gallon

1.8 kg/4 lb damsons
4.5 litres/1 gallon boiling water
125 ml/4 fl oz red grape concentrate
1 teaspoon yeast nutrient
1 teaspoon tartaric acid
1 teaspoon pectin-destroying enzyme
1 kg/2 lb sugar, for a dry wine
***Or*, 1.5 kg/3¼ lb sugar, for a sweet wine**

PORT YEAST

1. Make up a yeast starter 3 to 4 days before beginning to make wine. Follow instructions *on page 401*.

2. Then chop up damsons, removing stones and put chopped fruit into a fermentation bin or bucket.

3. Pour over boiling water, stir in 450 g/1 lb of the sugar and allow to cool.

4. Add other ingredients, including yeast starter.

5. Cover loosely with a cloth or lid and let it ferment on the pulp for 4 to 5 days. Stir at least twice daily.

6. Strain, taking care not to squeeze fruit or it may produce a hazy wine. Return liquor to bin.

7. Over the next 4 to 5 days add sugar, about 450 g/ 1 lb at a time, until the required amount has been used. Stir to dissolve.

8. Syphon into a 4.5 litre/1 gallon jar. Fir an airlock or a piece of polythene secured with a rubber band. Leave in a reasonably warm place.

9. Rack (i.e., syphon wine off sediment) at 3 to 4 month intervals until wine is clear and ready to drink.

It may take a year or more to mature before it will be drinkable, but it is well worth waiting for. Once a jar is opened for drinking the rest of the wine should be bottled. Otherwise flavour may be spoilt.

Dennis Rouston
Kippax, W. Yorkshire

DANDELION WINE

This is an inexpensive, easily-made wine with an attractive yellow colour, nice bouquet and a pleasant flavour. Medium sweet. If you pick the dandelions on the traditional day—St George's day (23rd April)—the wine should be ready at Christmas.

Makes 4.5 litres/1 gallon

2.25 litres/4 pints dandelion flowers
4.5 litres/1 gallon boiling water
1 orange
1 lemon
125 g/4 oz dates
1.3 kg/3 lb sugar
1 heaped teaspoon yeast nutrient

YEAST
Sauternes

1. Yeast must be actively working before you start making the wine. 2 or 3 days before you begin the wine, make up the yeast starter (*see page 401*), using the Sauternes yeast.

2. *For the wine:* pick the flowers on a sunny day so that they are open, but not from a busy roadside where they will have been sprayed with mud and dosed with exhaust fumes.

3. Pull off the green calyx from most of the flowers and discard.

4. Put flowers into a polythene fermenting bin or bucket. Pour over the boiling water. Let the flowers soak for 4 days, stirring daily.

5. Strain liquid, discarding the flowers.

6. Slice orange and lemon, chop dates and add them to the liquid with 450 g/1 lb of the sugar, yeast nutrient and the actively-working yeast.

7. Cover bin loosely with cloth or lid. This keeps out dust and flies but lets air in. Leave it in a warm place for 7 days, stirring daily.

8. On third day, add second 450 g/1 lb sugar.

9. On fifth day, add remaining 450 g/1 lb sugar.

10. On seventh day, strain through a muslin or net curtain and a nylon strainer into a 4.5 litre/1 gallon jar. Fill jar to the neck. Put any left-over juice into a small bottle. Top up jar with water if necessary.

11. Fit an air-lock or cover top with a piece of polythene secured with a rubber band. Cover small bottle in the same way.

12. Keep jar (and bottle) in a warm place, 60° to 65°F, 16° to 18°C, for 2 to 3 months.

13. After 2 to 3 months, rack off into a clean jar— i.e., syphon the wine off the sediment. Top up jar with spare wine from the bottle, or with cold water. Re-fit air-lock or cover as before. Be sure to taste wine in small bottle before using in case it has gone off.

14. Rack again after another 2 to 3 months.

15. By Christmas, or approximately 8 months after making wine, it should be ready to drink.

16. When the wine is stable and clear it can be bottled. Thoroughly wash 6 bottles. Syphon wine into the bottles. If you want to keep the wine, cork the bottles with straight-sided corks and lay them down on their sides. If it is going to be used in a few months, use flanged-type corks but leave bottles standing upright.

Dennis Rouston
Kippax, W. Yorkshire

FARMHOUSE KITCHEN 'NOUVEAU'

A nice, light, rosé type of wine, with a fresh, clean taste and a pleasant bouquet, that just asks to be drunk young.

Because the various fruits ripen at different times, pick when ripe and freeze, then make the wine at your leisure.

Makes 4.5 litres/1 gallon

675 g/1½ lb blackberries
225 g/8 oz elderberries
125 g/4 oz blackcurrants
12 raspberries
Boiling water
1 kg/2.2 lb sugar
125 ml/4 fl oz white or rosé grape concentrate
1 teaspoon tartaric acid
1 teaspoon yeast nutrient
1 Campden tablet

Bordeaux or Port yeast

1. Make up yeast starter 3 to 4 days before beginning to make the wine. Follow instructions on *page 401*.
2. Put fruit into a large basin and pour over about 1.2 litres/2 pints of boiling water.
3. Put on rubber gloves and squeeze fruit.
4. Strain juice through muslin into a polythene fermenting bin or bucket.
5. Repeat this process twice—i.e., pour boiling water on to pulp, squeeze and strain. Then throw the pulp away on to the compost heap.
6. Add the sugar and stir to dissolve.
7. Make up the volume of juice to 4.5 litres/1 gallon with cold water. Let it cool to 65° to 70°F, 18° to 20°C.
8. Add the grape concentrate, tartaric acid, yeast nutrient, Campden tablet and the yeast starter.
9. Cover bin loosely with a cloth or lid.
10. Stir daily for 3 to 4 days, then pour into a 4.5 litre/1 gallon jar, top up to 2.5 cm/1 inch from top with cold water.
11. Fit airlock or cover top with a piece of polythene secured with a rubber band.
12. Leave in a warm place, not the airing cupboard, to ferment.
13. After about 3 months, rack off (i.e., syphon wine off sediment) into a clean jar, topping up to 2.5 cm/1 inch from top with water.
14. Rack again once or twice more at 3-month intervals. The wine should be ready to drink in less than a year.
15. Once a jar is opened for drinking, the rest of the wine should be bottled. Otherwise it may oxidise, and flavour and appearance could be spoilt.

Dennis Rouston
Kippax, Yorkshire

HOCK-TYPE GOOSEBERRY WINE

Makes 4.5 litres/1 gallon

Water
2 tablespoons light dried malt extract
900 g/2 lb sugar
7 g/¼ oz tartaric acid
7 g/¼ oz malic acid
7 g/¼ oz citric acid
Yeast energiser or nutrient*
Grape tannin*
Pectin reducing enzyme*

**For quantities, follow manufacturer's instructions.*

900 g/2 lb hard green gooseberries
Hock Champagne or General Purpose yeast.
    Use liquid culture if possible
5 Campden tablets

1. 48 hours before you begin to make the wine prepare a yeast starter using one of the yeasts suggested. See method *page 401*.
2. Bring to boil 3.6 litres/6 pints or so of cold tap water, then remove from heat and allow to cool. When cool, pour into a sterilised plastic bucket and then dissolve into it all the ingredients except the gooseberries, yeast and Campden tablets. Stir well to ensure that everything has thoroughly dissolved. Allow mixture to become cold, that is, room temperature. Now aerate it well by pouring back and forth into another sterilised container, but finishing in the plastic bucket.
3. Meanwhile, wash the gooseberries well, preferably in sulphited water (3 Campden tablets per 4.5 litres/1 gallon) then rinse well to remove any sulphite. Cut the berries in half with a stainless steel knife, and drop into the now cold mixture in the plastic bucket. Finally add the yeast starter preparation. It is important that this is working properly before it is added. Stir well, cover closely and set aside to ferment for 24 to 36 hours.

4. After 24 to 36 hours, strain off the pulp into a sterilised 4.5 litre/1 gallon glass fermenting vessel. A fine cotton muslin or a piece of cotton sheeting is ideal, but do not squeeze the liquid through. Top up with cold boiled water to 4.5 litres/1 gallon, fit air-lock and allow fermentation to proceed to dryness at a fairly constant temperature, ideally 65° to 70°F, 18° to 20°C. This should take from three to four weeks, no longer. The time taken depends upon temperature and care with which the must has been prepared.

5. When fermentation ceases, carefully rack from the lees, i.e., syphon off leaving the sediment, into another sterilised 4.5 litre/1 gallon jar, without introducing air into the wine. Top up jar with similar wine, or if the space is small, with cold boiled water. Add 1 Campden tablet, fit airlock and set aside in cool, dark place to clarify.

6. In 5 to 6 weeks the wine should be quite clear. Rack it off its lees once again, top up jar, add 1 Campden tablet, cork jar well and leave preferably for about a month before drinking. It will improve somewhat with keeping for a few months but no great improvement will occur as the wine will already be fine and good for drinking. Always serve the wine well cooled.

Points to remember

DON'T at any time use hot water

DON'T use more than 900 g/2 lb sugar

DON'T ferment on the pulp for more than 24 to 36 hours

DON'T squeeze the fruit when straining off

DON'T expect the same results if you alter the recipe

DO make sure all equipment and fermenting vessels have been sterilised and rinsed well with cold tap water before use

DO make sure your yeast starter is active before starting wine making

DO be accurate with the quantities, particularly the acid

Arthur Francis
York

SWEET ORANGE WINE

A good recipe for beginners. Can be made all year round.

Makes 4.5 litres/1 gallon

First make a yeast starter at least 48 hours before you make the wine (*see page 401*).

The Wine
1.8 kg/4 lb oranges
450 g/1 lb raisins
1.3 kg/3 lb sugar
1 teaspoon yeast nutrient
$\frac{1}{2}$ teaspoon yeast energiser
Pinch of grape tannin
1 dessertspoon wheat cereal, crushed (optional)
Cold boiled water
1 Campden tablet

1. Wash the oranges, squeeze them and place juice in a sterilised fermenting vessel, a 10 litre/2 gallon plastic bucket is ideal.

2. Take the skins of half the number of oranges used, remove all the white pith, then roast the skins in a moderate oven, Gas 3, 375°F, 160°C, until they are crisp and brown, about 25 to 30 minutes.

3. Meanwhile, wash and mince the raisins.

4. Add the roasted orange skins to the fermenting vessel with the raisins, sugar, yeast nutrient and energiser, tannin, wheat cereal, if used, and the yeast starter, adding cold boiled water until the volume reaches 4.5 litres/1 gallon.

5. Cover the fermenting vessel loosely and ferment on the pulp for 48 hours at room temperature (maximum 75°F, 24°C) stirring twice daily.

6. Strain carefully into a sterilised 4.5 litre/1 gallon jar, fit airlock and leave at room temperature (maximum 75°F, 24°C) to allow fermentation to complete, topping up jar with cold boiled water after 7 days if necessary. Fermentation will take 6 to 8 weeks but this depends on temperature.

7. When all fermentation has finished, rack, i.e., syphon, wine into another sterile jar, avoiding disturbing the lees, which is the dead yeast and debris at bottom of jar.

8. Add 1 crushed Campden tablet and top up jar again with either cold, boiled water or sugar syrup if wine is not sweet enough.

9. Leave until brilliantly clear, racking again within 4 months if a heavy deposit forms.

10. Leave to mature at least 9 months when the wine will be ready for drinking.

Alan Briggs
Batley, West Yorkshire

PEACH WINE

A sweet wine with a pleasant bouquet. Easy-to-make, especially for beginners.

Makes 4.5 litres/1 gallon

800 g/1¾ lb canned peaches
125 g/4 oz dates
1 heaped teaspoon citric acid
900 g/2 lb granulated sugar
450 g/1 lb demerara sugar
4.5 litres/1 gallon cold water

YEAST
Sauternes *or* **1 level tablespoon dried wine-making yeast**

1. The Sauternes yeast starter must be 'working' before you start making the wine. 2 or 3 days before you want to begin the wine, make up the yeast starter (*see page 401*).
2. *For the wine:* empty tinned peaches, with their syrup, into a polythene bucket or bin.
3. Chop dates and put them into bucket with citric acid and 450 g/1 lb of the granulated sugar.
4. Pour over the water.
5. Add the actively-working yeast starter, or the dried yeast.
6. Cover bin loosely with cloth or lid. This keeps out dust and flies but lets air in. Leave in a warm room for 7 days, stirring it up at least twice daily.
7. On third or fourth day, add remaining 450 g/1 lb granulated sugar.
8. On fifth or sixth day, add the 450 g/1 lb demerara sugar.
9. On seventh day, strain liquid through a piece of muslin and a nylon strainer into a 4.5 litre/1 gallon jar. Fill jar to 2.5 cm/1 inch from the top. If there is any left-over liquid put it into a small bottle.
10. Fit an air-lock in jar, or cover top with a piece of polythene secured with a rubber band. This simple cover will also do for the small bottle.
11. Leave jar (and bottle) in a warm place, 65° to 70°F, 18° to 20°C, for 2 or 3 months.
12. Syphon liquid off the sediment into a clean jar every 2 to 3 months. Always top up jar with spare wine or with water. Always taste wine in the topping-up bottle before using in case it has gone off.
13. Ready to drink in 6 to 9 months.
14. When the wine is stable and clear it can be bottled. Thoroughly wash 6 bottles. Syphon wine into the bottles. If you want to keep the wine, cork the bottles with straight-sided corks and lay them down on their sides. If it is going to be used in a few months, use flanged-type corks but leave bottles standing upright.

Dennis Rouston
Kippax, W. Yorkshire

RED TABLE WINE

Makes 4.5 litres/1 gallon

450 g/1 lb runner beans
900 g/2 lb fresh elderberries
1 kg/2.2 lb sugar
1 teaspoon yeast nutrient
Pectin-destroying enzyme (use quantity indicated on packet)
½ teaspoon citric acid
1 Campden tablet

YEAST
Burgundy or Bordeaux

Note: Equipment should be sterilised (*see page 401*).
1. 48 hours before you begin to make the wine, prepare a yeast starter with the Burgundy or Bordeaux yeast (*see page 401*). Wait until it is actively working before going on.
2. *For the wine:* prepare runner beans as for table use. Boil them for 30 minutes, but no salt must be used.
3. Meanwhile, wash elderberries, put them in a sterilised polythene bucket and crush them with hands.
4. Strain off liquid from runner beans and pour into bucket of elderberries. (Eat beans later.)
5. Add sugar, yeast nutrient, pectin-destroying enzyme and citric acid. Stir to dissolve sugar.
6. Add cold water to bucket to make quantity up to 4.5 litres/1 gallon.
7. When wine 'must' is cool add actively-working yeast starter. Cover bucket and allow to ferment on the pulp for 48 hours.
8. Strain into a sterile 4.5 litre/1 gallon jar, fit an air-lock and let wine ferment out. This could take from 6 to 8 weeks.
9. When all ferment has ceased, syphon liquid off sediment into a sterile jar and top up with cold boiled water.
10. Leave wine to clear. This could take about 3 months.
11. Syphon wine into sterile bottles, cork them and leave the wine for 12 months to mature.

Alan Briggs
Batley, W. Yorkshire

RHUBARB WINE

A medium-sweet wine, which is not only good to drink, but also very useful for blending with other wines. With a freezer, it can be made at your leisure.

Makes 4.5 litres/1 gallon

2.7 kg/6 lb rhubarb
125 ml/4 fl oz white grape concentrate
1 teaspoon bentonite
1 Campden tablet
1 teaspoon yeast nutrient
1.3 kg/3 lb sugar

Sauternes yeast

1. Pick the rhubarb as early as possible until the end of June—while it is still pink or red.
2. Trim and wipe clean, cut long sticks in half, put into polythene bags to weigh 450 g/1 lb. Then put into freezer.
3. Make up a yeast starter 3 to 4 days before beginning to make wine. Follow instructions *on page 401.*
4. Put a strainer over your fermentation bin, put a frozen packet of rhubarb into the strainer. Let it thaw.
5. When the rhubarb has thawed squeeze the last few drops out—throw away the pulp (or use it for a pie).
6. Repeat until 2.7 kg/6 lb rhubarb is used.
7. Add to the rhubarb juice the white grape concentrate, bentonite, Campden tablet and yeast nutrient and 450 g/1 lb of the sugar. Stir to dissolve. Then stir in yeast starter.
8. Add water to make up volume to 4.5 litres/1 gallon. Cover the bin loosely with a cloth or lid.
9. Stir daily. On third day add 450 g/1 lb sugar. Stir to dissolve.
10. On the fifth day add the last 450 g/1 lb sugar. Stir to dissolve.
11. Next day syphon into a 4.5 litre/1 gallon jar, top up to within 2.5 cm/1 inch of top. Fit airlock or a piece of polythene secured with a rubber band. Leave to ferment in a reasonably warm place.
12. Syphon wine off sediment at 3 month intervals.

Should be ready to drink in 9 months. After opening a jar to drink, bottle the rest of the wine. Otherwise it may oxidise and flavour as well as appearance could be spoilt.

Dennis Rouston
Kippax, West Yorkshire

DRY SHERRY-TYPE WINE

To be made in early spring.

Makes 4.5 litres/1 gallon

Sherry yeast in starter form (*see page 401*)
4.5 litres/1 gallon birch sap
450 g/1 lb sultanas, washed and cut up or minced
175 g/6 oz dried bananas, washed and cut or minced
1.1 kg/2 lb 10 oz sugar
1 teaspoon tartaric acid
1 level teaspoon grape tannin
1 teaspoon yeast nutrient
¼ teaspoon yeast energiser
Polish spirit or vodka to fortify the wine after fermentation
A few drops per bottle of sherry essence when bottling

Birch sap is collected in early spring when the sap is rising in the trees and the buds have not yet burst into leaf. It is obtained by drilling a small hole inclined upwards into the tree for about 4 cm/1½ inches. It is best to drill the hole about 60 cm/2 feet from ground level. A rubber tube, the same size as the drill used, is then inserted in the tree and the sap is allowed to drip into a 4.5 litre/1 gallon jar. Only mature trees of at least 25 cm/10 inches girth should be tapped and care should be taken to knock a wood plug into the drilled hole after tapping is finished to prevent further bleeding and damage to the tree.

1. When 4.5 litres/1 gallon of birch sap has been collected it should be brought slowly to the boil and simmered for 15 minutes, to ensure sterility.
2. Then pour on to the washed and minced sultanas and bananas in a clean sterile bin. Stir in sugar.
3. When cold add acid, tannin, nutrient, energiser and actively-working yeast.
4. Ferment on the pulp for 4 to 5 days, then carefully strain into a clean sterile 4.5 litre/1 gallon jar and fit airlock.
5. Allow all ferment to complete. Then rack into another jar, avoiding disturbance of the lees, i.e., syphon wine off sediment. Re-fit airlock.
6. After 3 months the wine should be clear. Rack it once again and fortify to taste with Polish spirit and sherry essence.
7. The wine may now be bottled and will mature in bottle for a number of years, but will be fit to drink within 12 months.

Mr Alan Greenwood
Bradford

WHITE DRY TABLE WINE

A handy recipe as the *main ingredients come from the supermarket*. Ready to drink in 3 to 4 months but improves with keeping.

Makes 4.5 litres/1 gallon

Two 675 ml/24 fl oz bottles pure apple juice
One 675 ml/24 fl oz bottle pure grape juice
3 level teaspoons (15 g) tartaric acid
1 teaspoon pectin-destroying enzyme
½ teaspoon yeast nutrient
600 g/1 lb 5 oz granulated sugar

Sauternes yeast

1. Make up a yeast starter 4 to 5 days before you want to make the wine. Follow instructions *on page 401*.
2. Then put all ingredients, including yeast starter, into a fermentation bin or bucket with water to make volume up to 4.5 litres/1 gallon. Stir to dissolve sugar, etc. Cover loosely.
3. Stir daily for 3 to 4 days.
4. Syphon into a 4.5 litre/1 gallon jar and top up to within 2.5 cm/1 inch of top with water. Fit airlock or cover with a piece of polythene held in place with a rubber band.
5. Leave in a reasonably warm place, about 70°F, 20°C, until wine is all but clear.
6. Syphon wine off sediment into a clean jar, topping up with cold water, refitting airlock or polythene cover.
7. After about 3 months the wine will be clear. If there is any sediment on the bottom of the jar, syphon into a clean jar and it should be ready to drink. But it will improve with keeping.
8. Once a jar is opened for drinking, the wine should be bottled, otherwise it will oxidise and the flavour and appearance will be spoilt.

Ted Adcock
Northolt, Middlesex

WHITE DRY TABLE WINE—QUICK

Gives you plenty of drinkable table wine in 6 to 8 weeks, but it does improve with keeping.

Makes 13.5 litres/3 gallons

Three 1 litre/35 fl oz cartons of apple juice
600 ml/1 pint Riesling grape concentrate
2.5 kg/5½ lb granulated sugar
2 teaspoons each tartaric acid, yeast nutrient, pectin-destroying enzyme and bentonite

Chablis or Sauternes yeast

1. Make up a yeast starter, at least 3 to 4 days before you want to make the wine, following instructions *on page 401*.
2. Put all the other ingredients into fermentation bin with water to make volume up to 13.5 litres/3 gallons. Stir well to dissolve.
3. Add the yeast starter. Ferment in the bin for 14 days, stirring occasionally. Keep bin covered loosely.
4. Syphon into 4.5 litre/1 gallon jars. Top up with cold water to within 2.5 cm/1 inch of top, fit airlock or a piece of polythene held in place with a rubber band.
5. After 3 to 4 weeks the wine should be clearing. Rack off (i.e., syphon wine off sediment) into clean jars.
6. Rack off the sediment again when clear and it should be ready to drink.
7. Once a jar is opened for drinking the wine should be bottled otherwise it will oxidise and the flavour and appearance will be spoilt.

Keith Simpson
Hartburn, Darlington

WHITE DESSERT WINE

Can be made at any time of year.

Makes 4.5 litres/1 gallon

**900 g/2 lb wheat
450 g/1 lb raisins
1 orange
1 lemon
1.3 kg/3 lb sugar
Water
½ teaspoon citric acid
1 teaspoon yeast nutrient salts**

YEAST
Sauternes

Note: Equipment should be sterilised (*see page 401*).

1. 48 hours before you begin to make the wine, prepare a yeast starter with the Sauternes yeast (*see page 401*).
2. Wash wheat and put in a sterilised polythene bucket.
3. Wash and mince raisins and put them in bucket.
4. Wash orange and lemon. Slice thinly and add to bucket.
5. Add sugar and enough water to bring contents of bucket up to 4.5 litres/1 gallon. Stir to dissolve sugar.
6. Add citric acid, yeast nutrient salts and actively-working yeast starter. Cover bucket well and allow contents to ferment for 72 hours. (This is called fermenting on the pulp.) Stir, if possible, twice daily.
7. Strain into a sterile 4.5 litre/1 gallon jar, top up with cold boiled water, fit an air-lock and let wine ferment out. This could take 6 to 8 weeks.
8. Rack off the wine—i.e., syphon it off the sediment. Add 1 Campden tablet and replace air-lock.
9. Leave wine to clear. This could take 3 to 4 months.
10. Syphon the wine into sterile bottles, cork them and leave to mature for at least 12 months.

Alan Briggs
Batley, W. Yorkshire

THREE WINES SAME METHOD

Each recipe makes 4.5 litres/1 gallon

**White table wine
Dry or Sweet**
This recipe gives a dry wine in the Muscadet style. If sweetened with white grape concentrate, as suggested in the method, it gives it a Vouvray style.

**900 g/2 lb gooseberries, fresh, frozen or tinned
225 g/8 oz very ripe bananas, peeled
625 g/1 lb 6 oz sugar
225 ml/8 fl oz white grape concentrate
3 level teaspoons tartaric acid
½ teaspoon yeast nutrient**

Sauternes yeast

Red table wine
This recipe gives a dry red wine in the Valpolicella style, but can be blended with the white wine for a Rosé. It can then be sweetened with white grape concentrate for an Anjou-style Rosé.

**570 g/1 lb 4 oz blackberries
150 g/5 oz elderberries
225 g/8 oz very ripe bananas, peeled
650 g/1 lb 7 oz sugar
225 ml/8 fl oz red grape concentrate
2 level teaspoons (10 g) tartaric acid
½ teaspoon yeast nutrient
Bordeaux or Port yeast**

Dessert wine
This wine will become medium-sweet in the Madeira-style. The sweetness can be adjusted with white grape concentrate to give a Malmsey-style.

**200 g/7 oz dried rosehip shells (soak for 1 hour in warm water)
125 g/4 oz dried figs (soak for 1 hour in warm water)
225 g/8 oz very ripe bananas, peeled
1 kg/2.2 lb sugar
10 g/2 level teaspoons tartaric acid
½ teaspoon yeast nutrient**

Madeira yeast

Sugar syrup made up with 900 g/2 lb sugar stirred over low heat to dissolve in 600 ml/1 pint water is added during fermentation. At paragraph 7 in the method begin to take gravity readings. When gravity reaches 1.005 start feeding in 50 ml/2 fl oz syrup once a week until fermentation stops. This could take a month or more.

Method
For this you need a liquidiser.
For each of the above wines you need:

2 Campden tablets
1 teaspoon pectin-destroying enzyme

1. Prepare a yeast starter (*see page 401*) and activate with the suggested yeast 3 to 4 days before it is required for the wine.
2. Liquidise the fruit with the minimum of water.
3. Add 1 crushed Campden tablet and 1 teaspoon pectin-destroying enzyme. Cover with a cloth and leave overnight.
4. Next day dissolve sugar by heating gently in about 1 litre/1½ pints water, stirring. Pour over fruit pulp, add the grape concentrate, tartaric acid and yeast nutrient.
5. Make up volume to about 4.5 litres/1 gallon then add yeast starter.
6. Ferment on the pulp for 3 to 5 days. Stir daily.
7. Strain and put into a 4.5 litre/1 gallon jar. Top up with water to within 2.5 cm/1 inch of top. Fit airlock or a piece of polythene held with a rubber band. If possible keep jar at a controlled temperature of 70°F, 20°C, while fermentation proceeds.
8. When wine has finished fermenting, remove to a cool place, add 1 crushed Campden tablet and leave for 2 to 3 days.
9. Then rack (i.e., syphon it off sediment). If it throws another sediment rack again.
10. Once a jar is opened for drinking, the wine should be bottled. Otherwise it will oxidise and the flavour and appearance will be spoilt.
11. If you require the sweeter version, add white grape concentrate as the bottle is needed.

Ted Adcock
Northolt, Middlesex

SPARKLING WINES

Sparkling wines are produced by starting a secondary fermentation, in the bottle, in a basic wine which has been made for the purpose. The Elderflower, Gooseberry, White Currant and Apple Wines given here, if prepared strictly according to the instructions, can be made into sparkling wine. They will however make good drinking even if you do not make them into sparkling wines.

Four important rules upon which depends success in making sparkling wines:—
1. The basic wine is dry and has finished fermenting.
2. The alcoholic content of the basic wine is not really more than 10% by volume, which is equivalent to a *total* sugar content of about 900 g/2 lb per 4.5 litres/1 gallon including the sugar of the ingredients. A hydrometer is necessary (*see page 401*).
3. The yeast used as a primer in the secondary fermentation is active and will do its job.
4. No more sugar is added to each bottle for the secondary fermentation than is strictly recommended.
Failure to observe the first and fourth rules can bring disastrous consequences due to excess pressure—namely, exploding bottles.
Failure to observe the second and third rules will result in a non-sparkling wine.

Elderflower
Makes 4.5 litres/1 gallon

Champagne yeast culture
Cold boiled water
600 ml/1 pint fresh elderflowers
2 tablespoons light dried malt extract
15 g/½ oz wine acid (a mixture, if possible, of citric, malic, and tartaric) *Or* juice of 2 good lemons
Yeast nutrient, quantity as given by manufacturer
900 g/2 lb sugar
Campden tablets

1. 48 hours before you begin to make the wine prepare a yeast starter using the Champagne yeast culture. The best results in wine making are derived from liquid yeast cultures. Instructions to prepare a starter may come with the culture. (If not, *see page 401*.)
2. Choose if possible white, not cream-coloured flowers.
3. Pick on a dry, fine day. Flowers deteriorate so quickly that this is essential.
4. Lightly dry the flowers in the sun, if possible, to facilitate stripping and shake each head well to remove maximum pollen. (Too much pollen in the wine may make it hazy.)
5. Strip off all the petals into a measuring jug.
The taste of elderflowers is quite powerful, and overdoing things will not help, unless you particularly like the extra flavour.

6. Having previously boiled some water and allowed it to become cold, pour about 3.6 litres/6 pints of it into a plastic bucket, and into this dissolve the malt extract, wine acid (or lemon juice), yeast nutrient and sugar.

7. Add the actively working yeast starter, then the flowers. Stir well.

8. Cover closely and leave for 36 to 48 hours to ferment. Stir at intervals, about 2 or 3 times a day. Do make sure you don't forget any of the ingredients. Flower wines have no yeast foods or nutrients in them, consequently these must be added. Failure to do this might result in the fermentation not being completely successful, which is most important when making sparkling wines.

9. After 36 to 48 hours strain off through a fine cloth, pour into a 4.5 litre/1 gallon glass fermenting vessel, top up with cold boiled water, fit airlock and allow to ferment to dryness. This should be about 3 weeks if the must has been prepared properly and the fermentation temperature is correct at 65° to 70°F, 18° to 20°C.

10. When fermentation has ceased, carefully rack the wine off the lees, into another 4.5 litre/1 gallon jar, without introducing air. That is, with rubber tubing, syphon from one jar to another without splashing the wine, leaving the sediment at the bottom of the jar.

11. Top up the new jar with similar wine, right to the top or, in the absence of similar wine and if the space is small, cold boiled water. Add 1 Campden tablet, and set aside in cool dark place to clarify.

12. In five or six weeks the wine should be quite clear. Rack it off its lees once again, top up the jar, close neck with a cork or well-fitting lid, and set aside.

This wine should now be quite dry to the taste, i.e. without any taste of sweetness, and if tested with a hydrometer, the hydrometer reading should certainly read below 1000.

If the wine does taste sweet, and the hydrometer reading is well above 1000, or if there has been any sign of slackening of the fermentation at an early stage, then do not proceed with the sparkling wine making with this batch.

However, if all is well, and there is no reason why it should not be if the wine has been made properly and allowed to ferment in the proper temperature of some 65° to 70°F, 18° to 20°C, then at this stage the wine is ready for converting into sparkling wine. Turn to page 416 and continue: 'To Make Sparkling Wine from Basic Wine'.

Gooseberry
Makes 4.5 litres/1 gallon

Champagne yeast culture
Cold boiled water
2 tablespoons light dried malt extract
850 g/1 lb 14 oz sugar
15 g/½ oz wine acid (a mixture if possible, of tartaric, malic and citric)
Grape tannin, enough to cover
Yeast nutrient, quantity as given by manufacturer
Pectin-reducing enzyme, quantity as given by manufacturer
900 g/2 lb green hard gooseberries
Campden tablets

1. 48 hours before you begin to make the wine prepare a yeast starter using the Champagne yeast culture. The best results in wine making are derived from liquid yeast cultures. Instructions to prepare a starter may come with the culture. If not (*see page 401*).

2. Bring to boil approximately 3.6 litres/6 pints of cold tap water, then remove from heat and allow to cool. When cool, pour into a sterilised plastic bucket and then dissolve into it all the ingredients except the gooseberries, yeast and Campden tablets. Stir well to ensure that everything has thoroughly dissolved. Allow mixture to become cold, that is, room temperature. Now aerate it well by pouring back and forth into another sterilised container, but finishing in the plastic bucket.

3. Meanwhile, wash the gooseberries well, preferably in sulphited water (3 Campden tablets per 4.5 litres/1 gallon), then rinse well to remove any sulphite. Cut the berries in half with a stainless steel knife, and drop into the now cold mixture in the plastic bucket. Finally, add the yeast starter preparation. It is important that this is working properly before it is added. Stir well, cover closely and set aside to ferment for 24 to 36 hours.

4. After 24 to 36 hours, strain off the pulp into a sterilised 4.5 litre/1 gallon glass fermenting vessel. A fine cotton muslin or a piece of cotton sheeting is ideal, but do not squeeze the liquid through. Top up with cold boiled water to 4.5 litres/1 gallon, fit air-lock and allow fermentation to proceed to dryness at a fairly constant temperature, ideally 65° to 70°F, 18° to 20°C. This should take from three to four weeks, no longer. The time taken depends upon temperature and care with which the must has been prepared.

5. When fermentation ceases, carefully rack from the lees, i.e., syphon wine off sediment, into another sterilised 4.5 litre/1 gallon jar without introducing air into the wine. Top up jar with similar wine or, if the space is small, with cold boiled water. Add 1 Campden tablet, fit airlock and set aside in cool, dark place to clarify.

6. In 5 to 6 weeks the wine should be quite clear. Rack it off its lees once again, top up the jar, close neck with a cork or well-fitting lid. Set aside.

This wine should now be quite dry to the taste, i.e. without any taste of sweetness, and if tested with a hydrometer, the hydrometer reading should certainly be below 1000.

If the wine does taste sweet, and the hydrometer reading is quite above 1000, or if there has been any sign of slackening of the fermentation at an early stage, then do not proceed with the sparkling wine-making with this batch.

However, if all is well, and there is no reason why it should not be if the wine has been made properly and allowed to ferment in the proper temperature of some 65° to 70°F, 18° to 20°C, then at this stage the wine is ready for converting into sparkling wine. Turn to *page 416.*

White Currant
Makes 4.5 litres/1 gallon

Champagne yeast culture
Cold boiled water
675 g/1½ lb sugar
Yeast nutrient ($\frac{3}{4}$ amount recommended by manufacturer for 4.5 litres/1 gallon)
Pectin-reducing enzyme, quantity as given by manufacturer
7 g/¼ oz malic acid, optional (for those who like a high acid finish)
Campden tablets

The method is the same as for Gooseberry but it is necessary only to remove the stalks from the currants after washing and rinsing and then to squeeze the fruit gently in order to burst the berries. Do not pound them to pulp.

Apple
Makes 4.5 litres/1 gallon

The trouble with apple wine is that there are so many varieties of apples, some of which are of general poor quality, particularly 'Seedlings', that you have to be more specific about the recipe. Cookers or eaters on their own tend not to make the best

wine. About two thirds eaters for flavour, and one third cookers for crispness and freshness (acidity) are about right. Alternatively, *cultivated* crab apples, the 'John Downie' variety, are superb on their own, or perhaps other cultivated crab apples, with the same virtues as the John Downie, that is—a good flavour level, neither sweet nor over-sharp, and with some tannin in them. Perhaps this is why John Downies make the finest Crab Apple Jelly. However, we want a mixture of flavours and acidity just as these provide.

Champagne yeast culture
Approximately 3.6 kg/8 lb prepared apples (do not use windfalls, see paragraph 1)
575 g/1¼ lb sugar
Pectin-reducing enzyme, quantity as given by manufacturer
Yeast nutrient, quantity as given by manufacturer
Grape tannin, enough to cover 2 sq cm (not required if crab-apples are used)
Cold boiled water
Campden tablets

Note: The exact quantity of sugar is adjustable according to the sweetness in the apples used. Ideally the hydrometer should read 1080 when the juice and the sugar are added together—however pulp fermentation makes this somewhat difficult so some skill in judgement is required, as all apples contain some sugar. It is better to be on the low side than on the high side.

1. 48 hours before you begin to make the wine prepare a yeast starter using the Champagne yeast culture. (*See page 401.*)

2. Wash the apples well in sulphited water (3 Campden tablets per 4.5 litres/1 gallon), remove all dirt, air pollution, and other foreign substances. Rinse or wash well in clear cold water. Inspect all the apples for badly bruised or torn skins and cut out the affected parts (hence the reason for not using windfalls). Bruised apples with broken skins usually have infections which can lead to poor tasting wine or even vinegar.

3. Put about 2.25 litres/4 pints boiled and now cold water into a sterilised plastic bucket. To this add one crushed Campden tablet.

4. Now crush apples, or chop with a stainless steel knife, and quickly drop crushed or chopped apple into the cold water, submerging completely. This will help prevent the apple from browning and thus retain good colour and taste.

5. When all the apples are in the bucket, stir in pectin enzyme, nutrient and tannin (if used) and the actively working yeast.

6. Then if possible keep the apples submerged continuously with block of wood or similar. A little difficult, but not impossible. This keeps the apples from the air thus continuing their retention of colour and taste.

7. Each day, on two or three occasions, squeeze the apples by hand. After two or three days, they will be quite soft, and are then ready for straining off.

8. Quickly separate the bulk of the apple pulp from the juice by pouring through a plastic or aluminium colander. Then restrain through fine-meshed cloth, sheeting being ideal. Be sure to remove the maximum of solids from the juice.

9. To this add the sugar, already dissolved in about 1.2 litres/2 pints of boiled water to make a syrup. Stir well to mix, pour into a 4.5 litre/1 gallon glass fermenting vessel, top up with cold boiled water, fit an airlock and allow to ferment to dryness at a fairly constant temperature, ideally 65° to 75°F, 18° to 24°C. This should take no longer than 3 weeks. The time taken depends upon temperature and care with which must has been prepared. Proceed now as for Gooseberry wine, from Paragraph 5.

To Make Sparkling Wine From Basic Wine

*Notes:*1. The wine *must* be quite dry, finished working and clear before proceeding.

For maximum safeguard, newcomers might invest in a Sugar Test Kit, obtainable from chemists and some home wine-making stockists. This will indicate the presence of inverted sugar in the finished basic wine, which is a guide additional to the hydrometer and your sense of taste. As this test will not indicate the presence of ordinary white sugar, care should be taken that none has been added to the basic wine after fermentation has finished. This should not normally apply as the sugar is added at the beginning of the fermentation, and this will automatically 'invert' in the course of fermentation.

2. You *must* use proper Champagne-type bottles, in good condition without scratches or defects. All scratches and defects weaken the bottle, as will the scratch of a glass cutter on sheet glass. Thus great care should be taken in removing the label, and other decorations, and plastic tools are recommended for doing this as opposed to any metal scrapers.

Champagne bottles are originally made to withstand about 6 kg per square cm/80 lbs per square inch pressure from within. It is not advisable to go to this pressure with second-hand bottles, or with 'home-made' expertise. Consequently the syrup used in the secondary fermentation process gives some 3 kg per square cm/40 to 43 lbs pressure per square inch and this should not be exceeded.

3. You *must* use the proper form of closing the bottle. Get plastic Champagne-type stoppers and the wires from home wine-making stockists.

4. *Do not* attempt to increase the alcohol strength of the wine. Either it will not 'sparkle' in the bottle, or probably sparkle too much, causing the bottle to explode.

5. Before you start, it is as well to decide where the bottles will be stored for the duration of the secondary fermentation and maturation. If you are prepared to drink the wine without removing the sediment, store the bottles upright for the period of secondary fermentation and maturation. If you prefer the sediment removed obtain a bottle carton in which wine merchants normally receive their bottles and put the filled bottles in upside-down. (*See To drink after removing the sediment, page 417.*) When basic wines requiring long maturation are used for sparkling wine it may be preferable to store the bottles on their sides. This can in fact be done for all wines. When they are ready to drink stand them upright—or upside-down, as described above—but allow time for the sediment to re-settle before opening the bottles.

Makes 4.5 litres/1 gallon

6 Champagne-type bottles
6 plastic Champagne-type stoppers
6 or 7 Champagne-type wires to secure stoppers
4.5 litres/1 gallon suitable wine, already tested for residual sugar and found to be satisfactory
180 ml/6 fl oz sugar syrup made with 40 g/1½ oz sugar dissolved in boiling water and allowed to cool. (Do not boil after sugar is added or it will not dissolve)
180 ml/6 fl oz active yeast starter, using for preference a liquid Champagne yeast culture
Campden tablets

1. 48 hours in advance make the yeast starter. Follow the instructions provided with the culture, or those on page 401, but use only sufficient water to bring total quantity of starter up to 180 ml/6 fl oz.

2. Soak the bottles overnight in a detergent solution, remove all the labels etc. then rinse the inside of the

bottles in a sulphite solution (2 Campden tablets per 4.5 litres/1 gallon). Finally, rinse the bottles very well to remove all traces of sulphite.

3. Now, assemble the six bottles on the floor beneath the 4.5 litre/1 gallon jar of selected wine. Carefully syphon the clear wine into the bottles, filling each to a level not only to leave sufficient room in each for the syrup and yeast (60 ml/2 fl oz) but also to leave about 2.5 cm/1 inch of air space. (A test run with ordinary water beforehand will establish this level quite easily.)

4. Now add to each bottle 30 ml/1 fl oz of the syrup and 30 ml/1 fl oz of the active yeast starter. These measurements must be exact.

5. Drive home the plastic stopper and seal in with the Champagne wires, making sure that the wires engage in the grooves provided in the stoppers. Tighten each wire securely, making sure that it has engaged under the lip of the bottle.

6. Shake the bottle well so as to distribute the syrup uniformly throughout the contents. Now set aside ideally in a temperature of say 65°F, 18°C, either standing upright or upside down in a carton, or lying down. (*See note 5, page 416*). If space at this temperature is not available either one can leave the making of such wine until the warmer weather, or make allowances for the fact that little is likely to happen in the bottle whilst the temperature is much below this. Thus the wine can be bottled, syruped and yeasted during the cooler months, but no fermentation will take place in bottle until milder temperatures prevail which will allow the yeast in the bottle to work.

Having satisfactorily fulfilled these conditions it can be seen that the yeast has done, or is doing, its work from the fact that the wire retaining the stopper has become strained, and the stopper tends to protrude under the force. Also, on carefully lifting the bottle, a deposit, perhaps quite slight, can be seen. Should this be so, then all is proceeding well. It is difficult to say how long this will be, but easier to say that if after 6 months no such developments look as though they have taken place, then a test bottle can be opened to find out. (How to open bottles is described later.) A failure can develop through there being too much alcohol in the basic wine, or the yeast not being properly active.

7. When it can be seen that the progress described above has taken place, the bottles should be transferred to a cooler place for maturation. Long maturation is not necessarily desirable, and the lighter the wine, the quicker it can be drunk, even to the point of no maturation at all. Sparkling wine based on the

Elderflower, Gooseberry, White Currant and Apple recipes given here will be delicious if drunk as soon as the secondary fermentation is complete.

It must be understood that each bottle if well made now has a sparkling interior together with an undesirable sediment, consisting mostly of dead yeast cells. A decision has therefore to be made as to whether you want to drink the wine without first removing the sediment and risk any cloudiness, or whether first to disgorge the sediment and be sure of drinking the wine bright.

It is useful, too, to know that the colder the wine is the less the pressure will be when opening the bottle.

To drink without removing the sediment

The bottles should have been standing in an upright position. Thus all the sediment will have formed around the punt at the base of the bottle.

To get the best from this:

(a) Lift the bottle without tipping into the refrigerator and cool it down to the lowest temperature you can. (Not in a freezer.)

(b) Then, with one hand, carefully tip the bottle to the horizontal position without disturbing the sediment. Point the stopper to the interior of a plastic bucket previously laid in a semi-horizontal position.

(c) Deftly undo or cut the wires. In all probability, the stopper will blow out gently into the bucket, with slight frothing of the contents.

(d) Pour the contents of the bottle into the waiting glasses, taking care not to tip the bottle back, which would disturb the sediment.

If the glasses are also cool there will be little frothing. You should get some 5 to 7 glasses from each bottle.

To drink after removing the sediment

The bottles have stood upside-down. In this way the sediment will have accumulated in the hollow of the stopper.

(a) Without tipping the bottle from its upside-down position, put it in the refrigerator and cool it down to the lowest temperature you can. This can be a little difficult. It will be easier if you have a freezer. Place the inverted bottle in the freezer, propped up in some suitable manner. Leave it there for half an hour. During this time, the sediment in the stopper will freeze up with the liquid in the stopper, and thus facilitate easy removal.

(b) Withdraw the bottle from the freezer (using gloves as the bottle will be very cold), slowly turn it to the horizontal, pointing the stopper to a bucket previously laid in a semi-horizontal position.

(c) Cut or remove the wire cage. The stopper will

blow out, or may be eased out gently, and the sediment with it.

(d) The contents can then be poured without worry one or two glasses at a time.

Always keep sparkling wine in a cool place when it has finished working in the bottle, and always serve it cool.

Red wine can be made sparkling, but it seems less desirable than white or rosé. This is possibly due to the extra tannin content of the wine.

Further reading
Making Sparkling Wines, by Cyril Lucus. Published by Mills and Boon.
How to Make Wines With A Sparkle, by J. Restall & D. Hebbs. Published by Amateur Winemaker.
Arthur Francis
York

CIDER

A nice drink. Also very useful in the kitchen for cooking. A press is required which can be bought or made, or it is possible to hire one. Ready to drink in a month or so.

Makes 4.5 litres/1 gallon

10 kg/20 lb windfall apples, a mixture of eaters and cookers is ideal
Granulated sugar
1 teaspoon tartaric acid

Sauternes yeast

1. Make up a yeast starter 3 to 4 days before starting to make the cider. Follow instructions *on page 401*.
2. Wipe the apples clean. Do not bother to cut out the bruises.
3. Mince them using coarsest mincer blades.
4. Put the minced apples into a coarse-woven bag, hessian is ideal. Then press, collecting the juice in your fermenting bin. Make up volume to 4.5 litres/1 gallon with water.
5. Measure the gravity with an hydrometer and add sugar until the gravity is 1.055 (15 g/½ oz sugar raises the gravity of 4.5 litres/1 gallon by one degree.)
6. Add tartaric acid and the Sauternes yeast starter. Stir to dissolve acid and sugar.
7. After 3 to 4 days syphon into a 4.5 litre/1 gallon jar, fit airlock or a piece of polythene held in place with a rubber band. Ferment to 1.005.
8. Then syphon off sediment into another jar, and if the cider is nice and clear syphon into clean, strong, screw-topped cider or beer bottles. Returnable cider or beer bottles are suitable but the non-returnable are not strong enough. Add 1 level teaspoon sugar per pint. Screw down the top. If it is not clear leave it to settle before bottling.

The cider should be ready to use after a month or so.

CYSER

An old fashioned drink with more of a punch than cider, but a still drink, not sparkling. Matured for a year. As for cider you need a press (*see introduction to previous recipe*).

Makes 4.5 litres/1 gallon

10 kg/20 lb windfall apples, a mixture of eaters and cookers is ideal
900 g/2 lb honey
1 teaspoon tartaric acid
1 teaspoon yeast nutrient

Sauternes yeast

1. Make up a yeast starter 3 to 4 days before starting to make the cyser. Follow instructions *on page 401*.
2. Wipe the apples clean. Do not bother to cut out the bruises.
3. Mince them using coarsest mincer blades.
4. Put the minced apples into a coarse-woven bag, hessian is ideal. Then press as for cider, collecting juice in a fermenting bin.
5. Heat up 1.75 litres/3 pints of the apple juice to 140° to 150°F, 60° to 65°C.
6. Stir honey into hot juice. When dissolved, add to remaining juice. Leave to cool.
7. Add tartaric acid, yeast nutrient and Sauternes yeast starter. Put bin in a warm place.
8. Allow to ferment in the bin for 3 to 4 days.
9. Syphon into a 4.5 litre/1 gallon jar, fit airlock or a piece of polythene held in place with a rubber band. Any liquid over, put into a small bottle and plug neck with cotton wool.
10. Rack at 3 to 4 month intervals (i.e., syphon off the sediment). Top up jar to within 2.5 cm/1 inch of top with liquid from the little bottle. The cyser should be ready to drink in about a year.

Once the jar is opened for drinking the rest should be bottled or it may oxidise and deteriorate in flavour and appearance.

Dennis Rouston
Kippax, W. Yorkshire

LIGHT MEAD

A light type of mead, good to drink with dinner. Serve chilled.
For this mead, use clover honey or similar. Do not use oil seed rape, which looks like lard: it is no good for mead.

Makes 4.5 litres/1 gallon

4.5 litres/1 gallon water
1.1 kg/2½ lb light honey
15 g/½ oz citric acid
2 teaspoons yeast nutrient
1 heaped tablespoon light, dried malt extract
¼ teaspoon grape tannin

YEAST
Sauternes

1. 48 hours before you begin the mead, make up a yeast starter, using the Sauternes yeast, so that it is actively working when required (*see page 401*).
2. Heat the water to 135° to 140°F, 57° to 60°C. Stir in the honey. Keep at this temperature for 5 minutes.
3. Pour honey water into a bin. Cover bin. Let it cool to about 70°F, 30°C.
4. Add other ingredients, including actively-working yeast. Stir well. Cover the bin and leave it in a warm place, about 65° to 70°F, 18° to 20°C, for 4 to 5 days. Stir it daily.
5. After 4 to 5 days, syphon liquid off sediment into a 4.5 litre/1 gallon jar. Fit an air-lock, or cover top with a piece of polythene secured with a rubber band.
6. Keep jar in a warm place. Rack every 2 or 3 months—i.e., syphon mead off the sediment into a clean jar, replacing air-lock or polythene cover until fermentation has ceased completely.
7. When mead is stable and clear it can be bottled. Thoroughly wash 6 bottles. Syphon mead into the bottles. If you want to keep the wine, cork the bottles with straight-sided corks and lay them down on their sides. If it is going to be used in a few months, use a flanged-type cork but leave bottles standing upright.

Should be ready to drink in 9 to 12 months.

Dennis Rouston
Kippax, W. Yorkshire

MEDIUM SWEET MEAD

A medium to sweet mead.

Makes 4.5 litres/1 gallon

4.5 litres/1 gallon water
900 g/2 lb Australian or Tasmanian Leather-wood honey
900 g/2 lb general flower honey, English or clover
15 g/½ oz citric acid
7 g/¼ oz tartaric acid
½ level teaspoon grape tannin
3 teaspoons yeast nutrient
2 tablespoons light, dried malt extract

YEAST
Sauternes

1. 48 hours before you begin the mead, make up a yeast starter, using the Sauternes yeast, so that it is actively working when required (*see page 401*).
2. Heat water to 135° to 140°F, 57° to 60°C. Stir in the honey. Keep at this temperature for 5 minutes.
3. Pour honey water into a bin. Let it cool to about 70°F, 20°C.
4. Add other ingredients, including actively-working yeast. Stir well. Cover bin and leave in a warm place, about 65° to 70°F, 18° to 20°C, for 4 to 5 days. Stir it daily.
5. Follow method for Light Mead, stages 5 to 7 (*see last recipe*).

Should be ready to drink in 9 to 12 months, but if kept it will improve and mature.

Dennis Rouston
Kippax, W. Yorkshire

SWEET MEAD

Makes 4.5 litres/1 gallon

Mead yeast in starter form (*see page 401*)
900 g/2 lb heather honey
450 g/1 lb clover honey
Water to 4.5 litres/1 gallon
1 teaspoon yeast nutrient
¼ teaspoon yeast energiser
1 vitamin B₁ tablet, 3 mg size
15 g/½ oz malic acid
7 g/¼ oz tartaric acid
½ teaspoon grape tannin

FOR SWEETENING AFTER FERMENTATION
225 g/8 oz demerara sugar

1. Dissolve all the honey in about 1.2 litres/2 pints of water and bring up to a temperature of 140°F, 60°C. Hold at this temperature for half an hour to pasteurise the honey.
All honey is high in its content of wild yeasts, bacterias, moulds etc. which must be destroyed before fermentation begins, otherwise strange off-flavours may develop in the mead.
2. After pasteurisation, pour honey into clean sterile bin, making up to 4.5 litres/1 gallon with cold boiled water. Cover the bin with towels or fit lid.
3. When cold add all the other ingredients, except demerara sugar, and ferment in bin for 4 to 5 days.
4. Transfer into 4.5 litre/1 gallon jar, fit airlock and keep at a temperature of about 75°F, 25°C, until all ferment ceases.
5. Then dissolve the demerara sugar in as small a volume of water as possible, best done in a small pan over a low heat, stirring constantly. Then boil for 10 minutes.
6. Cool this sugar-syrup as quickly as possible, pour into a clean, sterile jar and rack, i.e., syphon the mead on to this sugar syrup. Avoid disturbing lees, i.e., sediment, at bottom of jar. If the now-racked mead does not fill the jar, top up with cold boiled water and re-fit airlock.
Further fermentation may take place, but this can only increase the alcoholic strength.
7. The mead should be racked every 4 months if a heavy deposit forms on bottom of jar, then again topped up with cold boiled water. It may take up to 2 years for the mead to become star-bright, but mead should be matured for a long period—up to 4 years when using heather honey.
Other flower honey may be used but it is recommended not to use Australian honey which may be derived from eucalyptus which would impart an unpleasant flavour.

Mr Alfred Francis Buckley
Dewsbury, Yorkshire

MULLED WINE

Excellent on a cold winter's evening.
Pinch of nutmeg
3 tablespoons brown sugar
Juice and rind of 1 lemon or orange
1 stick of cinnamon
3 cloves
300 ml/½ pint hot water
1 bottle of dry red wine—such as elderberry or blackberry, but, if you have to buy a bottle, a cheap, dry, red table wine will do

1. Simmer all the ingredients except wine for 20 minutes, then add wine. Reheat but do not boil.
2. Serve immediately in thick glasses.

Alan Briggs
Batley, W. Yorkshire.

WASSAIL

6 cooking apples
Soft brown sugar
15 g/½ oz ground ginger
Half a grated nutmeg
Pinch of powdered cinnamon
225 g/8 oz demerara sugar
1.75 litres/3 pints ale, mild or brown
½ bottle raisin wine, or ¼ bottle sherry
1 lemon
Lump sugar

1. Core apples but do not peel them. Fill the holes with soft brown sugar and roast in a moderate oven, Gas 3, 325°F, 160°C, for 45 minutes to 1 hour. Take care they do not burst.
2. Mix in a saucepan the ginger, nutmeg, cinnamon and demerara sugar. Add 600 ml/1 pint of the ale and bring to boil.
3. Stir in the rest of the ale, the wine and 10 lumps of sugar that have been rubbed on the rind of the lemon. Heat the mixture but do not allow it to boil this time.
4. Put the roasted apples in a bowl and pour in the hot ale mixture with half the peeled and sliced lemon.

Alan Briggs
Batley, W. Yorkshire

BEER—SOME NOTES

Water treatment

Water can be roughly divided into two types: soft and hard.

Soft is ideal for Brown Ales, Mild Ales and Stouts— i.e., the sweeter types of beer.

Hard is ideal for Bitters, Pale Ales and Light Ales— i.e., the dry, bitter, hop-flavoured beers.

You must therefore use water treatment to adjust your water supply for the type of beer you wish to make.

Soft to hard: add 1 to 2 teaspoons gypsum and ½ teaspoon Epsom salts.

Hard to soft: add 1 teaspoon bicarbonate of soda and 1 teaspoon salt. If very hard, it may be a good idea to boil water first, let it go cold and then syphon off the top three quarters of it, discarding what is left.

Chlorinated water is not suitable for brewing. To correct this it should be pre-boiled.

See also a note on hydrometers, page 401.

Sterilisation is important, see page 401.

BITTER

Makes 18 litres/4 gallons

Water
900 g/2 lb malt extract
325 g/12 oz cracked crystal malt
75 g/3 oz Golding hops
Water treatment (use a proprietary brand) *or*
    1 teaspoon gypsum (*see above*)
½ teaspoon Epsom salts
1.3 kg/3 lb sugar

YEAST
British Ale yeast

FOR PRIMING
Granulated sugar

Original gravity 1.044 (*see page 401, Hydrometers*)

1. 48 hours before you begin the brew make up a starter bottle with the British Ale yeast (*see page 401*) so that yeast will be actively working when it is required.
2. Bring 10 litres/2 gallons water to the boil.

3. Add all ingredients, except yeast and priming sugar. Do not use water treatment if your water is very hard already (*see left*).
4. Boil for 45 minutes.
5. Strain through a nylon sieve into a bin. Before you start, put a mark on bin at 18 litre/4 gallon level.
6. Rinse hops with a kettle of boiling water and strain liquid into bin.
7. Make up to 18 litres/4 gallons with cold water and let it cool to 65° to 70°F, 18° to 20°C.
8. When cool, add yeast.
9. Cover bin and leave in a warm place so that brew can ferment until gravity is 1.005 or less.
10. Syphon liquid off sediment into beer bottles. Be sure to use real beer bottles. Any other type of bottle may burst with build up of gas during secondary fermentation.
11. Prime bottles with ½ teaspoon sugar per 600 ml/ 1 pint and screw in stoppers tightly, or fix new crown corks.
12. Keep in a warm place for 3 to 4 days.
13. Ready to drink 4 weeks after bottling. Will go on improving up to 6 months.

Dennis Rouston
Kippax, W. Yorkshire

TED'S BITTER BEER

A simple recipe.

Makes 22.7 litres/5 gallons

75 g/3 oz dried hops
50 g/2 oz black patent malt
Water
1.3 kg/3 lb dried malt extract
1 kg/2.2 lb bag of sugar
1 pkt beer yeast
Extra sugar, to prime bottles

1. Place hops and black patent malt in muslin bag (these can be obtained at any wine supply shop). Place bag in large pan of water, at least 5.7 litres/10 pints, and bring to boil. Simmer for ½ hour.
2. Meanwhile, place malt extract and sugar in a 22.7 litre/5 gallon bin and pour two kettles of boiling water over it. Stir until dissolved.
3. Add hop liquid and top up with cold water to 22.7 litre/5 gallon level.
4. When it has cooled to luke-warm, sprinkle yeast on top and cover.
5. Leave for 7 days.

6. Have ready 38 clean 600 ml/1 pint beer bottles. Do not use pop bottles or screw cap bottles. Put 1 level teaspoon sugar in each bottle.

7. Syphon beer into bottles leaving about 2.5 cm/1 inch air space.

8. Cap with crown corks.

Ready to drink in 3 weeks and guaranteed to be crystal clear. Be careful, when pouring, to leave sediment in the bottle.

Judith Adshead
Mottram St Andrew, Cheshire

2 BEERS—SAME METHOD

Mild Beer

Makes 18 litres/4 gallons

1.1 kg/2½ lb malt extract
450 g/1 lb dark dried malt extract
225 g/8 oz crystal malt
125 g/4 oz roasted barley or black malt
450 g/1 lb soft brown sugar
50 g/2 oz hops (Fuggles recommended)
Water to 18 litres/4 gallons
Top-fermenting beer yeast
Caster sugar for priming
Original gravity: 1.038

Light Bitter Beer

Makes 18 litres/4 gallons

1.3 kg/3 lb malt extract
450 g/1 lb crystal malt
450 g/1 lb glucose chippings
75 g/3 oz hops: recommended mixture is 50 g/
    2 oz Golding type and 25 g/1 oz Fuggles
Water to 18 litres/4 gallons
Top-fermenting beer yeast
Caster sugar for priming
Original gravity: 1.032

1. Boil all ingredients, except the yeast and priming sugar, in 10 litres/2 gallons water for at least 1 hour. If a 10 litre/2 gallon container is not available use a minimum of 4.5 litres/1 gallon water but take care that the sugar or glucose chips do not stick.

2. Strain into fermenting vessel through fine muslin or similar.

3. Wash the grains and hops by pouring cold water, preferably boiled first, through them until volume in fermenting vessel reaches 18 litres/4 gallons.

4. When cold, below 70°F, 20°C, pitch with top-fermenting beer yeast and cover brew with lid or towels to exclude dust, flies, bacteria, etc.

5. Ferment 4 or 5 days, at room temperature, skimming froth from the surface after first 24 hours.

6. Skim again, then rack (i.e. syphon off leaving sediment behind) into closed container (4.5 litre/1 gallon jars may be used) and fit airlock. Leave for a further 7 days to allow ferment to finish and to allow yeast to settle.

7. Bottle into proper glass beer bottles priming each 600 ml/1 pint with ½ teaspoon caster sugar. Screw stoppers in tightly or fit crown corks to ensure bottles are thoroughly sealed.

8. Leave at room temperature for 7 days, then leave to mature for at least 14 days.

Alan Briggs
Batley, W. Yorkshire

BROWN ALE

Makes about 10 litres/2 gallons

575 g/1¼ lb dried malt extract
125 g/4 oz crushed crystal malt
50 g/2 oz crushed black malt
225 g/8 oz soft brown sugar
225 g/8 oz brewing sugar
20 g/¾ oz hops
Water

YEAST
Top-fermenting beer yeast

FOR PRIMING BOTTLES
Caster sugar
Original gravity 1.036 (*see page 401, A Note on Hydrometers*)

1. Boil all ingredients, except the yeast and priming sugar, in 4.5 litres/1 gallon of water for at least 1 hour, stirring occasionally so that sugars do not stick.
2. Strain into fermenting vessel through fine muslin or similar.
3. Wash grains and hops by pouring pre-boiled cold water over them, until volume in fermenting vessel reaches 10 litres/2 gallons.
4. When cool, below 70°F, 21°C, pitch with a top-fermenting beer yeast and cover brew with lid or towels to exclude dust, flies, bacteria, etc.
5. Ferment 4 or 5 days, at room temperature, skimming froth from surface after first 24 hours.
6. Skim again, then syphon liquid off into closed container (4.5 litre/1 gallon jars may be used). Fit air-lock. Leave further 7 days to allow ferment to finish and until hydrometer reads 1.002. Allow yeast to settle before bottling.
7. Bottle into beer bottles, priming each 600ml/1 pint with ½ teaspoon caster sugar. Screw stoppers in tightly or fit crown corks to ensure bottles are thoroughly sealed.
8. Leave at room temperature for 7 days, then leave to mature for at least 14 days.

Alan Briggs
Batley, W. Yorkshire

LIGHT ALE

Easy to make. An ideal thirst-quencher after a day in the garden.

Makes 18 litres/4 gallons

Water
Water treatment (*see page 421*)
1.8 kg/4 lb crushed pale malt
675 g/1½ lb glucose chippings
70 g/2½ oz Golding hops

YEAST
British Ale

FOR PRIMING BOTTLES
Granulated sugar

Original gravity 1.035 (*see page 401*)
1. 2 or 3 days before you begin the brew make up a small starter bottle using the British Ale yeast (*see page 401*) so that yeast will be actively fermenting when it is required.
2. Heat 12.4 litres/2½ gallons water to 165°F, 74°C.
3. Dissolve in this the water treatment, if used. (Use water treatment for this ale if your water supply is very soft. Hard water makes good light ales.)
4. Add crushed pale malt. Stir in carefully so that no dry lumps form.
5. The temperature should now drop to 150°F, 65.5°C. This should be maintained, as near as possible, for 2 hours, during which time saccharification of the starch takes place.
6. At the end of 2 hours, strain the liquid off the grain, and spray or wash the grain with water at 170°F, 76°C, until volume reaches 18 litres/4 gallons.
7. Return all liquid to boiler or pan and bring to the boil. Throw away the grain.
8. Boil until frothing ceases, then add glucose chippings and hops. Stir to dissolve glucose.
9. Boil for 1½ hours. Then switch off heat. The volume will now be about 13.5 litres/3 gallons.
10. Allow hops to sink to bottom of boiler or pan, then drain off into a polythene fermenting bin or bucket. Pour a kettle of boiling water over hops to wash them. Drain off into bin.
11. Make up volume of 'wort' in fermenting vessel to 18 litres/4 gallons with cold water. Cool as rapidly as possible to 70°F, 21°C.
12. Pitch yeast—i.e., empty bottle of actively-working yeast starter into wort.
13. After 12 hours, skim off any scum, stir, and leave

at room temperature for about 5 days or until an hydrometer reading gives a gravity of 1.010.

14. Then skim off yeast head.

15. Syphon ale off the sediment into proper beer bottles. Other bottles are not strong enough to take the build-up of gas during the secondary fermentation.

16. Prime bottles with ½ teaspoon sugar per 600 ml/ 1 pint and screw in stoppers tightly, or fit new crown corks.

17. Keep in a warm place for 6 to 7 days, then put in a cool place.

18. Ready to drink in 4 to 6 weeks after bottling.

Dennis Rouston
Kippax, W. Yorkshire

MILD ALE

An ale which is halfway between a bitter and a stout, dark in colour, a favourite tipple with many folk.

Makes 22.7 litres/5 gallons

1.8 kg/4 lb malt extract
125 g/4 oz crushed black malt
50 g/2 oz Fuggles hops
325 g/12 oz soft dark brown sugar

YEAST
Top-fermenting, British Ale

Soft water is necessary for this. If you do not live in a soft water area 1 teaspoon bicarbonate soda and 1 teaspoon salt can be added to a 22.7 litre/5 gallon brew. However, it is best to consult a local home-brew shop about the most suitable quantity in your area.

Follow the method given for Pale Ale (*see right*). This ale, however, does not require further maturing after the 3 to 4 weeks in the bottle.

PALE ALE

Makes 22.7 litres/5 gallons

1.3 kg/3 lb dried light malt extract
450 g/1 lb crushed crystal malt
50 g/2 oz Golding hops
40 g/1½ oz Northern Brewer hops
450 g/1 lb soft light brown sugar

YEAST
British Ale

FOR PRIMING BOTTLES
Granulated sugar

1. Make up a yeast starter 3 to 4 days before starting to make the pale ale. Follow instructions *on page 401.*

2. Warm up about 10 litres/2 gallons of water. When hot, stir in the malts and hops and boil for 45 minutes.

3. Strain into fermenting bin.

4. Rinse the hops and malt with 1 or 2 kettles of hot water.

5. Add the sugar and stir to dissolve.

6. Make up volume to 22.7 litres/5 gallons with cold water.

7. When cool, 65° to 70°F, 18° to 20°C, pitch the yeast starter.

8. Cover bin loosely. Leave in a warm place to ferment for about 4 to 5 days.

9. If the bin has an air-tight lid with an air lock, use this. Otherwise, syphon pale ale into containers, such as 4.5 litre/1 gallon jars, or larger vessels if you have them, to which an air-lock can be fitted.

10. Leave containers in a warm place and let pale ale ferment to a gravity of 1.005 or less.

11. Syphon into proper beer bottles. Be sure to use real beer bottles. Other bottles are not strong enough to take the build up of gas during the secondary fermentation.

12. Prime bottles with ½ teaspoon sugar per 600 ml/ 1 pint and screw in stoppers tightly or fit new crown corks.

13. Keep in a warm place for 3 to 4 days to allow priming sugar to ferment and so give the pale ale condition.

14. Ready to drink 3 to 4 weeks after bottling but improves if kept 2 to 4 months.

EXPORT PALE ALE

Makes 18 litres/4 gallons

Water treatment, if required (*see page 421*)
  either proprietory brand, or,
1 teaspoon gypsum
1 teaspoon Epsom Salts
1 teaspoon salt
18 litres/4 gallons water
2.7 kg/6 lb crushed pale malt
125 g/4 oz crushed crystal malt
125 g/4 oz flaked maize
125 g/4 oz wheat flour
65 to 75 g/2½ to 3 oz Golding hops
275 g/9 oz glucose chips
125 g/4 oz soft brown sugar
Carragheen Irish Moss (use quantity indicated
  on packet)
Top-fermenting beer yeast
Caster sugar for priming bottles

1. Heat 11.25 litres/2½ gallons water to 165°F, 74°C.
2. Dissolve in this the water treatment, if used.
3. Add crushed pale malt, crushed crystal malt, flaked maize, and wheat flour. It is best to cream the wheat flour with cold water before adding, to avoid lumps.
4. The temperature will now have dropped to 150°F, 65.5°C, and this temperature should be maintained, as near as possible, for two hours, during which time saccharification of the starch takes place.
5. At the end of two hours strain sweet liquid (wort) off the grain and sparge, i.e., spray, with water at 170°F, 76°C, until volume reaches 18 litres/4 gallons.
6. Return all liquid to boiler or pan and bring to the boil. Boil until frothing ceases and then add the hops, glucose chips and soft brown sugar. Boil for 1½ hours, adding Carragheen Irish Moss 10 minutes from end of boil. Switch off heat. The volume will now be about 13.5 litres/3 gallons.
7. Allow hops to sink to bottom of boiler, or remove bag of hops if they have been boiled in a muslin bag. Cool to about 180°F, 82°C, then drain off into fermenting vessel.
8. Make up volume of wort in fermenting vessel to 18 litres/4 ggllons cold water. Cool as rapidly as possible to 70°F, 20°C.
9. Pitch yeast. Skim after 12 hours. Stir. Leave at room temperature for about 5 days or until an hydrometer reading reaches a gravity of 1.010. (*See page 401 for a note on hydrometers.*) Then skim off

yeast head. Syphon into containers such as 4.5 litre/1 gallon jars fitted with corks and airlocks. Leave seven days, then bottle into proper beer bottles priming with ½ teaspoon caster sugar to each 600 ml/1 pint bottle.
10. Leave in a warm place for seven days. Then store in a cool place for at least six weeks.

Alan Briggs
Batley, W. Yorkshire

STRONG OR OLD ALE

To be drunk in small quantities.

Makes 13.5 litres/3 gallons

Water to 13.5 litres/3 gallons
2.7 kg/6 lb crushed pale malt
175 g/6 oz crushed crystal malt
450 g/1 lb flaked barley
450 g/1 lb barley syrup (or maize or wheat
  syrup)
450 g/1 lb glucose chips
250 g/9 oz soluble dextrin
325 g/12 oz soft brown sugar
25 g/1 oz Kent Golding hops
25 g/1 oz Northern Brewer hops
15 g/½ oz Bullion hops
General purpose yeast

The starting gravity will be 1.076 to 1.080, giving about 9° alcohol so the beer should be sipped rather than quaffed.

FOR PRIMING BOTTLES
Caster sugar

1. Heat 10 litres/2 gallons water to 165°F, 74°C.
2. Stir in pale malt, crystal malt and flaked barley. The temperature will now have dropped to 150°F, 65.5°C, and this temperature should be kept steady for 1½ hours.
3. Now strain out the sweet wort and wash grains with water at 170°F, 76°C, until volume collected is 13.5 litres/3 gallons.
4. Bring this to the boil and boil vigorously for half an hour. Then add all other ingredients, except yeast, and boil vigorously for a further 1 hour.
5. Strain out the hops, make up to 13.5 litres/3 gallons with boiled water and cool as quickly as possible.
6. When below 70°F, 20°C, add yeast and ferment 7 days in fermenting bin which should be kept covered at all times.

7. Then transfer to 4.5 litre/1 gallon jars, fit airlocks, and leave till all fermentation ceases.

8. Then bottle into proper glass beer bottles, adding priming sugar at the rate of ½ teaspoon per 600 ml/ 1 pint bottle.

9. Mature in bottle for at least 3 months before drinking.

Alan Briggs
Batley, W. Yorkshire

BARLEY WINE

Makes 10 litres/2 gallons

1.1 kg/2½ lb malt extract
450 g/1 lb crystal malt
40 g/1½ oz roasted barley or chocolate malt
450 g/1 lb glucose chippings
675 g/1½ lb soft brown sugar
125 g/4 oz soluble dextrin (or glucose polymer)
65 g/2½ oz hops: recommended mixture is 50 g/
    2 oz Fuggles and 15 g/½ oz Northern Brewers
Water to 10 litres/2 gallons
Top-fermenting beer yeast *and* general purpose yeast
Original gravity: 1.085

1. Boil all ingredients, except the yeasts, in 10 litres/ 2 gallons water for at least 1 hour. If a container of this size is not available use a minimum of 4.5 litres/ 1 gallon water but take care that the sugar or glucose chips do not stick.

2. Strain into fermenting vessel through muslin or similar.

3. 'Wash' the grains and hops with cold boiled water until volume reaches 10 litres/2 gallons.

4. When cold, below 70°F, 20°C, take out 2.2 litres/ ½ gallon and pitch with general purpose yeast. Add the top fermenting beer yeast to the other 6.75 litres/ 1½ gallons and cover both brews.

5. Ferment for 5 days, at room temperature. Skim froth from surface after first 24 hours and again after 5 days.

6. Now blend both fermenting brews together, rack into two 4.5 litre/1 gallon jars and fit airlocks. Keep at room temperature, allow ferment to continue until finished. This may take as long as 6 weeks. DO NOT bottle whilst the beer is still fermenting.

7. When all ferment has finished, bottle in 300 ml/ ½ pint or nip bottles adding NO priming sugar.

8. Store for at least 6 months and drink with caution. It is very potent.

Alan Briggs
Batley, W. Yorkshire

BARLEY WINE BEER

Makes about 10 litres/2 gallons

900 g/2 lb light, dried malt extract
225 g/8 oz crystal malt
40 g/1½ oz black malt
450 g/1 lb glucose chips
450 g/1 lb brewing sugar
225 g/8 oz soft brown sugar
125 g/4 oz soluble dextrin
70 g/2½ oz hops
Water

YEAST
General purpose beer yeast

FOR PRIMING BOTTLES
Caster sugar
Original gravity 1.083 (*see page 401, A Note on Hydrometers*)

1. Boil all ingredients, except the yeast and priming sugar, in a minimum of 4.5 litres/1 gallon of water, stirring occasionally so that the glucose chips and sugars do not stick.

2. Strain into fermenting vessel through fine muslin, or similar.

3. Wash grains and hops by pouring on pre-boiled cold water until volume in fermenting vessel reaches 10 litres/2 gallons.

4. When cold, below 70°F, 21°C, pitch with a general-purpose beer yeast and cover brew with lid or towels to exclude dust, flies, bacteria, etc.

5. Ferment 4 or 5 days, at room temperature, skimming froth from surface after first 24 hours.

6. Skim again, then syphon liquid off sediment into closed container (gallon jars may be used). Fit airlock. Leave until fermentation has ceased and hydrometer reads about 1.008. This may take 6 to 8 weeks.

7. Bottle into beer bottles, priming each 600 ml/1 pint with ½ teaspoon caster sugar. Screw stoppers in tightly, or fit crown corks, to ensure bottles are thoroughly sealed.

8. Leave at room temperature for 7 days. Leave to mature for at least 12 months before drinking. Will keep and improve for 2 or 3 years.

Alan Briggs
Batley, W. Yorkshire

ALAN BRIGGS's LAGER

Makes 10 litres/2 gallons

First make a Yeast Starter at least 48 hours before you start the main brew using a lager yeast, either liquid culture, tablets or granules (*see page 401*).

THE MAIN BREW
675 g/1½ lb light dried malt extract
450 g/1 lb brewing sugar or white invert sugar
25 g/1 oz Hallertauer hops
½ teaspoon ground Irish Moss
Lager yeast starter, as above
Water
Campden powder (for sterilisation)
Caster sugar (for priming)

1. Boil malt extract, brewing sugar and hops in 6.75 litres/1½ gallons water for 1 hour. If a 6.75 litre/1½ gallon container is not available use a minimum of 4.5 litres/1 gallon water but take care the sugar and malt used do not stick. Add the Irish Moss for the last 15 minutes of the boil.
2. Strain into a sterile fermenting vessel through muslin or similar.
3. 'Wash' the hops etc. by pouring through them cold water (preferably previously boiled). In this way, bring volume in fermenting vessel up to 10 litres/2 gallons.
4. Allow to cool to below 70°F, 20°C, and then add the active lager yeast and stir. Then cover the brew with a lid or towel to exclude dust, bacterias etc.
5. Ferment in this vessel for 4 or 5 days at room temperature. Skim the froth from the surface after the first 24 hours.
6. After 5 days skim the surface again if necessary, then syphon the brew into two 4.5 litre/1 gallon jars. Fit airlocks. Leave for a further 7 to 10 days to allow ferment to finish and yeast to settle.
7. Bottle into proper glass beer bottles, priming each bottle with half a teaspoon of caster sugar per 600 ml/1 pint bottle. OR: If you can get a 4.5 litre/1 gallon plastic barrel the beer may be stored in bulk.
(a) Dissolve 60 g/2¼ oz caster sugar in a very little water.
(b) Put this priming solution into the barrel.
(c) Syphon in the beer and fix the bung securely.
8. Leave at room temperature for 7 days then remove to a cool place to clear and condition. This will take approximately 4 to 6 weeks.

Lager can be used with good results in cooking. See Lager Loaf on page 304 and Lager Pancakes on page 183.

Alan Briggs
Batley, W. Yorkshire

LAGER

Makes 22.7 litres/5 gallons

Water
1.5 kg/3½ lb liquid light malt extract
900 g/2 lb sugar
225 g/8 oz cracked crystal malt
50 g/2 oz Hallertauer hops
1 level teaspoon salt
1 level teaspoon citric acid

YEAST
Lager

FOR PRIMING BOTTLES
Granulated sugar
Original gravity 1.042 (*see page 401, Hydrometers*)

1. 48 hours before you begin the brew, make up a starter bottle using the Lager yeast (*see page 401*) so that yeast will be actively working when it is required.
2. Heat 10 litres/2 gallons water until warm enough to dissolve malt extract and sugar. Stir well, making sure they dissolve and do not stick on bottom of pan and burn.
3. When they are dissolved, add rest of ingredients, except yeast and priming sugar.
4. Bring to the boil and boil hard for 45 minutes.
5. Strain through a nylon sieve into a bin. Mark bin beforehand at the 22.7 litre/5 gallon level.
6. Make up volume of liquid in bin to 22.7 litres/5 gallons with cold water. Let it cool to about 65° to 70°F, 18° to 20°C.
7. When it is cool, add the actively-fermenting lager yeast starter.
8. Cover bin loosely with a cloth or loose lid. Leave in a warm place and let it ferment for about 36 hours.
9. If the bin has an air-tight lid with an air-lock use this. Otherwise, syphon lager into containers, such as 4.5 litre/1 gallon jars or larger vessels, if you have them, to which an air-lock can be fitted.
10. Leave containers in a warm place and let lager ferment to a gravity of 1.005 or less.
11. Syphon into proper beer bottles. Be sure to use

real beer bottles. Other bottles are not strong enough to take the build up of gas during the secondary fermentation.

12. Prime bottles with $\frac{1}{2}$ teaspoon sugar per 600 ml/1 pint and screw in stoppers tightly or fit new crown corks.

13. Keep in a warm place for 3 to 4 days to allow priming sugar to ferment and so give the lager condition.

14. Ready to drink 3 to 4 weeks after bottling but improves if kept for 4 to 6 months.

Serve chilled.

Dennis Rouston
Kippax, W. Yorkshire

SWEET STOUT

Makes 22.7 litres/5 gallons

1.3 kg/3 lb dried dark malt extract
225 g/8 oz crushed black malt
225 g/8 oz crushed crystal malt
450 g/1 lb soft dark brown sugar
50 g/2 oz Fuggles hops
10 to 15 sweetening tablets

YEAST
Top-fermenting

Soft water is necessary (*see Mild Ale*).
Follow method given for Pale Ale (*see page 424*) adding sweetening tablets when wort is still hot (*paragraph 5*).

Dennis Rouston
Kippax, W. Yorkshire

DRY STOUT

Makes 10 litres/2 gallons

First make a yeast starter at least 48 hours before you start the main brew using Stout yeast (*see page 401*).

THE STOUT
675 g/1$\frac{1}{2}$ lb dried malt extract
225 g/8 oz barley syrup
150 g/5 oz roasted barley
75 g/3 oz soluble dextrin (glucose) polymer
50 g/2 oz Fuggles hops
Water to 10 litres/2 gallons

FOR PRIMING BOTTLES
Caster sugar

1. Boil all stout ingredients in water for at least 1 hour.

2. Strain into sterilised fermenting vessel (11.25 litre/2$\frac{1}{2}$ gallon plastic bucket is ideal) through muslin or similar. (*See page 401 for a note on sterilisation.*)

3. Make up to 10 litres/2 gallons with cold boiled water and allow to cool to below 70°F, 20°C.

4. Then add activated yeast, cover brew loosely to keep out dust and bacteria, and ferment 5 days at room temperature, skimming froth from top as necessary.

6. Rack, or syphon, into sterilised 4.5 litre/1 gallon jars, fit airlocks and allow to ferment out (about 5 to 10 days).

7. Rack or syphon into proper beer bottles, adding $\frac{1}{2}$ teaspoon caster sugar per 600 ml/1 pint bottle.

8. Leave at room temperature for 7 days, then store in a cool place for at least 4 weeks.

This stout can be used for Christmas puddings 2 or 3 weeks before it is ready to drink.

Alan Briggs
Batley, W. Yorkshire

STOUT: IRISH TYPE!

Makes 18 litres/4 gallons

Water
3 kg/6$\frac{1}{2}$ lb crushed pale malt
275 g/10 oz cracked crystal malt
275 g/10 oz cracked black malt
125 g/4 oz wheat flour
125 g/4 oz East Kent Golding hops
15 g/$\frac{1}{2}$ oz Northern Brewer hops
$\frac{1}{2}$ teaspoon citric acid
1 teaspoon salt
Sugar

YEAST
Stout or British Ale yeast

FOR PRIMING BOTTLES
A little caster sugar
Original gravity 1.055/7 (*see page 401*)

1. 2 or 3 days before you start the main brew make up a yeast starter (*see page 401*) so that the yeast is actively working when required in the brew.

2. Heat 11.25 litres/2$\frac{1}{2}$ gallons water to 165°F, 74°C.

3. Add pale malt, crystal malt and black malt. Stir in carefully so that no lumps form.

4. Put wheat flour in a basin and mix with cold water until like a creamy liquid. Then stir it into brew.

If you add wheat flour straight to a hot brew it tends to turn to lumps.

5. The temperature will now have dropped to 150°F, 65.5°C. This temperature should now be maintained, as near as possible, for 2 hours, during which time saccharification of the starch takes place.

6. At the end of 2 hours, strain the liquid, known as 'wort', off the grain and sparge with water at 170°F, 76°C, until volume reaches 18 litres/4 gallons. (To sparge is to spray or wash the grain with water at a given temperature.)

7. Return all liquid to boiler or pan and bring to the boil. Boil until frothing ceases. Add the hops.

8. Boil for 1½ hours. Switch off heat. Volume of brew will now be about 13.5 litres/3 gallons.

9. Allow hops to sink to bottom of boiler. Drain the liquid off into fermenting bin. Pour a kettle of boiling water over hops to wash them. Drain off into bin.

10. Make up volume of wort in fermenting bin to 18 litres/4 gallons with cold water. Cool as rapidly as possible to 60°F, 15°C. Take an hydrometer reading and slowly add sugar, continuously stirring until gravity reaches 1.055 to 1.057.

11. Pitch yeast—i.e., empty bottle of actively-working yeast starter into the wort.

12. After 12 hours, skim off the dark brown scum on the yeast head and stir up contents of bin.

13. Leave it at room temperature, 65° to 70°F, 18° to 21°C, for about 5 days. Stir daily, until hydrometer reading reaches a gravity of approximately 1.020.

14. Syphon into containers, such as 4.5 litre/1 gallon jars, fitted with corks and air-locks. Or cover tops with a piece of polythene secured with a rubber band.

15. Leave jars at room temperature for 7 days, or until gravity reaches 1.012 or less.

16. Bottle the stout into proper beer bottles. *Do not* use non-returnable bottles. These are made of very thin glass and can explode during secondary fermentation in bottle.
Put ½ teaspoon caster sugar into each 600 ml/1 pint bottle. This is known as 'priming'. Screw in the stoppers firmly, or fix crown corks.

17. Leave in a warm place for 7 days. Then store in a cool place for 6 to 8 weeks.

Dennis Rouston
Kippax, W. Yorkshire

HONEY BEER FOR HARVEST

Makes 4.5 litres/1 gallon

15 g/½ oz or 1 cup hops
225 g/8 oz honey (or sugar)
4.5 litres/1 gallon water
1 teaspoon granulated yeast (baker's will do) *or*
1 tablespoon fresh brewer's yeast

1. Boil hops and honey or sugar for 1 hour in a large pan with as much of the water as possible.

2. Strain into a plastic bucket and make up to 4.5 litres/1 gallon with cold water. Allow to cool to 70°F, 20°C.

3. Add granulated yeast, or float a slice of toast spread with brewer's yeast.

4. Cover closely and leave in a warm place for 48 hours.

5. Syphon off, without disturbing yeast deposit, into a 4.5 litre/1 gallon jar or flagons, put in corks.

6. Stand in a cool place for a week, when it will be ready to drink. Tie the corks down if keeping it longer than a week, although this is a quickly-made, thirst-quenching drink and should not be kept for long.

Mrs H. Lawson
West Suffolk

GINGER BEER I

Makes 10 litres/2 gallons

500 g/1 lb 2 oz sugar
2 level teaspoons ground ginger
2 level tablespoons dried baking yeast
Juice of 2 lemons
10 litres/2 gallons water

1. Dissolve (but do not boil) the sugar in a saucepan containing a little of the water.

2. Meanwhile clean a plastic bucket thoroughly, sterilise it with household bleach and rinse thoroughly. Put the rest of the water in the bucket.

3. Add the ginger, yeast, lemon juice and sugar solution and stir.

4. Cover bucket and let it stand in a warm place to ferment for one week.

5. After one week prepare bottles and stoppers (preferably beer, cider or pop bottles with inserted screw stoppers), sterilise with household bleach and rinse well.

6. Bottle the ginger beer with a jug or syphon tubing leaving as much of the scum and sediment behind as possible.

7. Add ½ teaspoon sugar to each 600 ml/1 pint bottle or 1 teaspoon sugar to each 1.2 litre/2 pint bottle.

8. Screw stoppers tightly into bottles and leave for one more week. The ginger beer will then be ready to drink.

GINGER BEER II

Two drinks from a ginger beer plant.

GINGER BEER PLANT
15 g/½ oz general purpose dried yeast
300 ml/½ pint water
Sugar
Ground ginger
Juice of 2 lemons

1. Put yeast into a jar, add water, 2 level teaspoons sugar, 2 level teaspoons ginger and mix together.

2. Cover jar with a sheet of polythene kept in place with a rubber band.

3. Each day, for 7 days, add 1 level teaspoon sugar and 1 level teaspoon ginger.

4. Now strain the mixture through a piece of fine muslin and add the lemon juice to the liquid.

The ginger beer may now be made, either as a sweet, still drink or dry and sparkling. *It is important*, however, to follow the instructions carefully so that there is no risk of bursting bottles and flying glass.

SWEET STILL GINGER BEER
Prepared ginger beer plant
450 g/1 lb sugar
600 ml/1 pint water

1. Put all in a saucepan. Stir until sugar is dissolved.

2. Bring to boil and simmer 5 minutes to ensure that yeast is killed.

3. Make up to 4.5 litres/1 gallon with cold water.

4. Bottle the ginger beer, cork tightly. Keep for a few days before drinking.

DRY SPARKLING GINGER BEER
Prepare ginger beer plant
50 g/2 oz sugar
Water

1. Add sugar to ginger beer plant and make up to 4.5 litres/1 gallon with cold water, stirring to dissolve sugar.

2. Bottle into screw-stoppered cider, beer or pop bottles. Screw in stoppers tightly. Keep for 7 to 10 days when the ginger beer is sparkling and ready for drinking.

Note: Keep the sediment you have left after straining the ginger beer plant. Divide it into 2 jars and give 1 plant away to a friend. To the sediment add 300 ml/½ pint water, 2 level teaspoons sugar, 2 level teaspoons ginger and carry on as before.

BLACKCURRANT SYRUP

The same method can be used for blackberries, loganberries, raspberries and strawberries. Use really ripe, clean, dry fruit.

Blackcurrants
Sugar
Campden tablets

1. Put fruit in an earthenware jar or a tall, straight-sided jug. Crush it with a wooden spoon or pulper.

2. Cover the container with a thin cloth and leave in a warm room to ferment just a little. It will take 3 to 5 days. Other fruits mentioned above may only take 1 day to ferment, so keep an eye on it.

3. When bubbles of gas are forming on the surface, tip fruit into a scalded jelly bag. Allow it to drain overnight.

4. Next day press the bag thoroughly to remove any remaining juice.

5. Measure juice and to every 600 ml/1 pint add 450 g/1 lb sugar. Stir until sugar is dissolved.

6. Strain syrup through jelly bag to make sure it is clear but this step is not essential.

7. For every 600 ml/1 pint of syrup add 1 Campden tablet dissolved in 1 tablespoon warm water.

8. Use really clean bottles. To be sure of this put them in a large pan of water. Bring to the boil, take bottles out and drain. Boil the caps for 15 minutes just before use.

9. Fill bottles to 1 cm/½ inch of the top.

10. Once opened, keep bottles in a cool place or refrigerator.

See also Blackberry Syrup, page 371.

LEMONADE

Makes about 16 glasses

8 large lemons
225 g/8 oz caster sugar
2.25 litres/4 pints boiling water

1. Wash and dry the lemons.
2. Peel off lemon peel very thinly with potato peeler.
3. Squeeze juice from lemons and put in covered plastic container in refrigerator.
4. Put peel in large bowl or jug with sugar.
5. Pour over boiling water, stir briskly, cover and leave overnight in cool place.
6. Next day add reserved lemon juice. Strain into jugs and chill.

LEMON CORDIAL

2 thin-skinned lemons
1.2 litres/2 pints water
450 g/1 lb sugar
1 level teaspoon citric acid

1. Cut lemons into quarters and place in liquidiser with 300 ml/½ pint of the water. Switch to maximum speed for 10 seconds only.
2. Pour into a pan, add remaining water, sugar and citric acid and bring to boil, stirring to dissolve sugar.
3. Remove from heat, allow to cool, strain and bottle. Dilute to taste with water or soda water.

Store in fridge. Will keep for 2 or 3 weeks.

Judith Adshead
Mottram St Andrew, Cheshire

WILLAWONG LEMON CORDIAL

3 to 4 lemons
450 g/1 lb white sugar
1 dessertspoon tartaric acid
600 ml/1 pint boiling water

1. Peel lemons finely to produce rind with no pith.
2. Squeeze lemons.
3. Put rinds, juice, sugar and tartaric acid into a bowl. Pour over boiling water. Stir till dissolved. Leave to cool, preferably overnight.
4. Strain and bottle.
5. Keep in a cool place or refrigerator.
6. Dilute with water to taste.

Nathalie Jowett
Yea, Victoria, Australia

ORANGE CORDIAL

Juice and zest of 2 oranges
900 ml/1½ pints water
325 g/12 oz sugar
1 level teaspoon citric acid
¼ teaspoon orange food colouring

1. Prepare oranges, discarding pith.
2. Dissolve sugar in water and simmer 5 minutes.
3. Add citric acid to zest and juice of oranges. Pour on the hot syrup.
4. Add colouring carefully.
5. Allow to cool slightly, strain and bottle.
6. Store in refrigerator. Dilute with water or soda water to taste.

Will keep up to 3 weeks in fridge.

Judith Adshead
Mottram St Andrew, Cheshire

APRICOT NECTAR

Made in the liquidiser.

125 g/4 oz dried apricots
15 g/½ oz sunflower seeds
1 tablespoon honey
300 ml/½ pint coconut milk
15 g/½ oz desiccated coconut
15 g/½ oz chopped almonds

1. Soak apricots in water overnight.
2. Keep a few of the sunflower seeds aside for decoration. Soak rest with the apricots.
3. Next day, strain apricots and sunflower seeds and put them into liquidiser with honey, coconut milk, coconut and almonds. Blend until smooth, adding apricot liquid or milk if it is too thick.
4. Serve in tall glasses with the unsoaked sunflower seeds sprinkled on top.

Elizabeth Shears
author of 'Why Do We Eat'

COLD MILK DRINKS

Made in the liquidiser.

Banana

Makes 3 glasses

**600 ml/1 pint milk
1 banana
1 level tablespoon clear honey
A grating of whole nutmeg
3 tablespoons whipped cream**

1. Pour milk into liquidiser.
2. Peel and chop banana and add the pieces with the honey and nutmeg.
3. Switch on the machine for about 1 minute, or until banana has blended completely with the milk.

4. Pour into three glasses and top each with a spoon of whipped cream and a fine grating of nutmeg.

Drink at once.

Chocolate

Makes 3 glasses

**600 ml/1 pint milk
2 level tablespoons drinking chocolate
1 tablespoon boiling water
4 tablespoons vanilla ice-cream
A little grated chocolate**

1. Pour milk into liquidiser.
2. Dissolve drinking chocolate in the water and add it to the milk with 2 tablespoons of the ice-cream.
3. Switch machine on for a minute. Pour into the glasses, spoon on top the rest of the ice-cream and sprinkle each with a little grated chocolate.

Drink at once.

INDEX